Gorbachev's Russia
and American Foreign Policy

An East-West Forum Publication

Gorbachev's Russia and American Foreign Policy

EDITED BY
Seweryn Bialer
and Michael Mandelbaum

Westview Press
BOULDER & LONDON

William G. Hyland's Chapter 12, "East-West Relations," is adapted from his book, *Mortal Rivals,* published by Random House in 1987 (© copyright William G. Hyland).

Published in 1988 in the United States of America by Westview Press, Inc.; Frederick A. Praeger, Publisher; 5500 Central Avenue, Boulder, Colorado 80301

Library of Congress Cataloging in Publication Data
Gorbachev's Russia and American foreign policy.
  Includes index.
  1. United States—Foreign relations—Soviet Union.
  2. Soviet Union—Foreign relations—United States.
  3. Soviet Union—Politics and government—1982– .
  4. Gorbachev, Mikhail Sergeevich, 1931– .
  I. Bialer, Seweryn. II. Mandelbaum, Michael.
  E183.8.S65G673 1988   327.73047   88-275
  ISBN 0-8133-0748-1
  ISBN 0-8133-0751-1 (pbk.)

Printed and bound in the United States of America

The paper used in this publication meets the requirements of the American National Standard for Permanence of Paper for Printed Library Materials Z39.48-1984.

10   9   8   7   6   5   4   3   2   1

Contents

Contributors

Part One: Patterns of Change

S. Frederick Starr. President of Oberlin College and a leading authority in U.S.-Soviet relations whose interests include linguistics, music, and art. He is the author of *Melnikov: Solo Architect in a Mass Society* (1978) and, with Hans van Herwarth, edited *Against Two Evils: Memoirs of a Diplomat Soldier During the Third Reich* (1981).

Sheila Fitzpatrick. Oliver H. Radkey Regents' Professor of History at the University of Texas at Austin. Her publications include *Education and Social Mobility in the Soviet Union* (1979) and *The Russian Revolution* (1983). Her specialty is Soviet social history of the 1920s and 1930s.

Part Two: Russia After Stalin

Robert Campbell. Distinguished Professor of Economics at Indiana University. He is the author of *Soviet Energy Technology* (1980) and "The Economy" in Robert Byrnes, ed., *After Brezhnev: Sources of Soviet Conduct in the 1980s* (1983). His current research interests are Soviet telecommunications, energy policy, and military-economic affairs.

Robert Legvold. Director of the W. Averell Harriman Institute for Advanced Study of the Soviet Union, Columbia University. He is the author of *Soviet Policy in West Africa* (1970) and *The Soviet Union and the Other Superpower: Soviet Policy Towards the United States, 1969 to Present* (forthcoming). His special interest is Soviet foreign policy, particularly towards Western Europe, Asia, Africa, and the United States.

Robert Cullen. *Newsweek* Diplomatic Correspondent; Moscow Bureau Chief, 1982–1985. He is the author of "Soviet Jewry," *Foreign Affairs* (Winter 1986-1987).

Part Three: Gorbachev's Russia

Timothy J. Colton. Professor of Political Science; Director, Center for Russian and East European Studies, University of Toronto. He is the author of *The Dilemma of Reform in the Soviet Union,* revised edition (1986) and *Commissars, Commanders, and Civilian Authority* (1979). He is a specialist in Soviet domestic politics.

Thane Gustafson. Associate Professor of Government at Georgetown University. He is the author of *Reform in Soviet Politics* (1981), *Selling the Russians the Rope?* (1981), and *Crisis Amid Plenty* (in press). His special interests are decision-making in Soviet politics and power and authority in the Soviet system.

Seweryn Bialer. Robert and Renee Belfer Professor of International Relations at Columbia University; Director, Research Institute on International Change. He is the author of *The Soviet Paradox: External Expansion and Internal Decline* (1986) and *Stalin's Successors* (1980). His areas of interest are international relations, particularly U.S.-Soviet relations, Soviet domestic and foreign policy, Soviet–East European relations, and Sino-Soviet-Japanese-American relations.

Part Four: Russia and the West

John Gaddis. Distinguished Professor of History at Ohio University. He is the author of *Strategies of Containment* (1982) and *The Long Peace: Essays on the History of the Cold War* (1987). He is a specialist in postwar American foreign and national security policy.

Michael Mandelbaum. Senior Fellow and Director of the Project on East-West Relations, Council on Foreign Relations. He is the author of *The Nuclear Future* (1983) and co-author, with Strobe Talbott, of *Reagan and Gorbachev* (1987). His interests are international politics and national security.

Part Five: Gorbachev and the United States

Joseph S. Nye, Jr. Director, Center for Science and International Affairs, Ford Foundation for International Security, Kennedy School of Government, Harvard University. He is the author of *Nuclear Ethics* (1986) and the editor of *The Making of America's Soviet Policy* (1984). He is a specialist in international security and American foreign policy.

William H. Luers. President of The Metropolitan Museum of Art. He served as the U.S. Ambassador to Czechoslovakia from 1983 to 1986. He is the author of "The U.S. and Eastern Europe," *Foreign Affairs* (Summer 1987).

William G. Hyland. Editor, *Foreign Affairs* (since 1984). He is the author of *Mortal Rivals: Superpower Relations from Nixon to Reagan* (1987) and "Reagan-Gorbachev III," *Foreign Affairs* (Fall 1987). He is a specialist in U.S.-Soviet arms control and has held numerous and high-level positions in government.

Preface

The East-West Forum is a New York–based research and policy analysis organization sponsored by the Samuel Bronfman Foundation. Its goal is to bring together experts and policy leaders from differing perspectives and generations to discuss changing patterns of East-West relations. It attempts to formulate long-term analyses and recommendations.

In preparing the chapters of this book, the authors drew upon the work of a series of workshops initiated by the Forum. Aside from the authors, workshop participants included Jeremy Azrael, Donna Bahry, Joseph Berliner, Archie Brown, Fritz Ermarth, Gregory Grossman, Mark von Hagen, Arthur Hartman, Peter Hauslohner, Grey Hodnett, Stanley Hoffmann, Robert Hormats, Alex Inkeles, Gail Lapidus, I. Mac Destler, Mary McAuley, Alex Motyl, Robert Osgood, William Schneider, Jutta Scherrer, Helmut Sonnenfeldt, Fritz Stern, William Taubman, and Ted Warner.

We would like also to express thanks to Stephen E. Herbits, Executive Vice President, Joseph E. Seagram and Sons, Inc., and William K. Friedman, Trustee of the Samuel Bronfman Foundation, as well as to Thomas Sherlock, our rapporteur, and to Anne Mandelbaum for her editorial work.

David E. Morey
Executive Director,
East-West Forum

Introduction

Winds of change are sweeping the Soviet Union. The General Secretary of the Communist Party writes a book that gains international circulation and is serialized in American newspapers. It tells of his efforts to restructure the Soviet system, and Americans learn a new Russian word—*perestroika*. What does all this mean? What does it *really* mean?

Even before this dramatic development emerged to challenge and redefine U.S.-Soviet relations, a number of scholars and leaders and I established the East-West Forum in the belief that effective management of the total process of superpower relations can flow only from a sophisticated understanding of the Soviet society and the Kremlin's own policy considerations. The East-West Forum aims, without jeopardizing scholarship, to strengthen the bonds between studying Soviet-related policies and formulating them.

When I became President of the World Jewish Congress (WJC) in 1980, I was determined to give highest priority to the issue of human rights for Jews living in the Soviet Union. All four of my grandparents emigrated from Russia to Canada. No wonder then that the fate of more than two million Soviet Jews who weren't so lucky as to have had ancestors who sought a fresh start in the New World should be a natural concern to me. To be sure, the WJC's three goals for Soviet Jewry are not in themselves very complicated: the release of all prisoners of Zion, free emigration for those who want to leave and live in Israel, and cultural and religious freedom for those who want to remain Soviet citizens.

Still, it was clear that achieving these goals would require thorough charting of a great many other paths in the maze of the East-West relationship. One cannot study and develop strategies for managing that relationship in a Jewish-oriented vacuum. A deep appreciation of its dynamics is vital to any effort toward improving it and in turn bettering the condition of Jews in the Soviet Union.

In personal terms, the East-West Forum has enabled me to study with some of the best minds in the field. I shall continue to study the myriad factors that go into any international relationship and the especially fascinating composition of the East-West relationship.

This book, which has grown out of the Forum's deliberations, is intended to examine in depth the question of the changing Soviet Union and U.S. foreign policy. The chapters that follow testify to the scholarship and expertise the East-West Forum is applying to the issues that are implicit in and emanate from the changing superpower relations. They begin with an examination of the meaning of change itself. They note that change in the Soviet Union isn't what it used to be and explore the reasons why. Ensuing chapters expand upon the basic premise that if our policy makers are to understand where we are and where we're going, they had best understand with total clarity how we got here.

The Soviet post-Stalin period is examined in its economic, political, and foreign policy dimensions, stressing the factors that provided the gestation environment for Gorbachev's reforms. There follows an analysis of the nature, sources, and plausible outcomes of Gorbachev's "revolution" and the strategies he is applying to it. A separate part of the book examines the changing goals of past U.S. policies toward the Soviet Union and their effectiveness in influencing Soviet behavior. The final part puts forth suggestions and prescriptions for a U.S. approach to the changes in Soviet economic, security, and foreign policies.

I have said often that the best way to begin a difficult negotiation is for both sides to agree upon that on which they are basically in agreement. This clears the air for discussion of those matters on which, on the surface at least, they don't agree. We have seen that happen. The United States and the USSR are beginning to agree that since there can be no winner in the arms race, the resources of both sides can be put to much better use. Furthermore, both sides see the inherent dangers of escalation. At the December 1987 Summit they agreed on the elimination of short- and intermediate-range missiles. They must next agree on consecutive radical cuts in strategic weapons. Such cuts have to be accompanied by agreements on balanced restructuring and redeployment of the conventional forces in Europe. And while they're at it, it is imperative that both sides recognize that regional instability is dangerous and that, conversely, stability is a crucial goal.

As this is written, there are tortuous discussions going on over the desirability of an international conference on the Middle East. Also some eastern European countries have begun the early stages of renewing relations with Israel, which were broken off in the aftermath of the Six-Day War of 1967. Moscow is anxious to find a solution to its Afghanistan problem, as is Washington with respect to political stability in Central America.

It will of course take time, but there are signs that both sides will learn how to manage the process for non-confrontational, and perhaps in some respects even cooperative, existence. General Secretary Gorbachev is determined that the Soviet Union be a first-class economic power as well as a military superpower. Of all the insults hurled by President Reagan during his incumbency, the one that hurt most was his labeling the USSR "a third world country with a first-class army." When asked whether preventing a widening of the technological gap with the West by the year 2000 would be considered a success of the "*perestroika*," a highly placed Russian answered, "Anything more would be a miracle." Thus in order to modernize Russia, Mr. Gorbachev is trying to change profoundly an entire society.

Reading his programmatic speech on economic reform to the Central Committee of the Communist Party on June 24, 1987, one is struck by two things: the sweeping changes he is already advocating in the face of determined resistance from the *apparat* and the lack of specifics as to how the nation will accomplish what the General Secretary insists is necessary.

Clearly, he will need Western help in his quest for an economic renaissance and technological advance. On several occasions I have listened to Soviet officials brag that every time we refuse to transfer some form of technology we are doing them a favor because we force them to develop it themselves (and, they claimed, better). One doesn't hear that any more.

The leadership is aware that the heart of the new revolution is communication. The USSR is slowly, perhaps reluctantly, entering the computer age. This means, among many other things, that information will be more freely available. This must come as a shock to the old-line conservatives who are much more comfortable in a closed, thoroughly controlled society. But it is inevitable if the Soviet Union is not to fall even farther behind in the technology race.

Thus trade with the West, particularly the United States, becomes a matter that affects, and will become even more important in, U.S.-USSR relations. While the Soviets publicly deny that trade can be linked with human rights, privately they acknowledge that the two are related because the United States insists on it. Both the Jackson-Vanik amendment, denying Most Favored Nation status unless a satisfactory number of Jews are allowed to emigrate, and the Stevenson amendment, more damaging yet by denying credits under the same conditions, are cumbersome clouds hanging over the trade issue.

The human rights issue is a legitimate U.S. concern. While successive administrations have not been totally consistent in their attitudes worldwide, the American people have a deep, almost evangelical, feeling about this issue. Human rights go beyond the number of Jews allowed to leave, but somehow this aspect of the issue has become the litmus test of Soviet behavior. U.S.-USSR trade is insignificant, especially if you remove grain sales from the calculation. There is almost nothing the Soviets can manufacture currently that could find a market here. For any quantum leap in this field, the Soviets will have to entice U.S. business to form joint ventures with Soviet producers. So far this has been very difficult. I serve on the board of directors and on the executive committee of the U.S.-USSR Trade and Economic Council, which was set up in the *detente* period by Donald Kendall, the Chairman of Pepsico (and a good friend to former President Richard Nixon), and his colleagues in the business world anxious to open the Soviet market to U.S. goods. I have watched with curiosity as both sides seem to be talking to themselves.

It becomes obvious that as great technological advances shrink the world, they increase its complexity. It is no accident that the stock markets in differing time zones are computer linked, not to mention computer driven. The world economy is also mutually linked. Thus, sound and comprehensive management of the process of East-West relations becomes more critical. It is not too difficult to forecast a world increasingly troubled and in need of a system of global management that can be secured only in a condition of cooperation between the superpowers.

The Soviet Union is an exciting country to watch. What is happening there will influence the fate of its own 280 million multinational citizens. It will, moreover, shape international relations well into the twenty-first century—whether Mr. Gorbachev succeeds or fails. His determination to modernize Russia is not in question. Yet the bureaucratic resistance to his efforts and the historically indifferent attitudes of the working strata make the implementation of his reforms terribly difficult. Will democratization, *perestroika,* and *glasnost'* survive? Can and should America help the new Soviet leader in his program of change?

These and other questions are addressed in the pages that follow. I hope the reader will profit from them.

Edgar M. Bronfman
President,
East-West Forum

PART ONE

Patterns of Change

1

The Changing Nature of Change in the USSR

S. Frederick Starr

Introduction

The problem of change has preoccupied Russian thinkers for nearly three centuries. Experiencing change around them, they have tried to characterize it and analyze its sources. A Russian's position with respect to the sources and processes of change has always been a key to his world view as a whole and remains so today. Both before and after the brief period on the eve of the 1917 Revolution when political parties were legal, groupings of intellectuals on issues of change represented the main factions within educated society. A "Slavophile" or "Westernizer," Menshevik or Bolshevik, Stalinist or Bukharinite, Gorbachevian or Brezhnevite—each represents a different attitude towards change. Considering the impact of these alignments on Russian and Soviet life, it is clear that differing approaches to change have dramatically altered the very *process* of change in that country.

Foreign observers have been similarly drawn to the problem of change in Russia. Concentrating mainly on political and economic institutions, Western writers from Leibnitz's day to our own have put forward schemes for the improvement of Russia—roadmaps, as it were, for change. Few Western statesmen in the twentieth century have failed to ground their actions *vis à vis* the USSR in some implicit assumptions of how change occurs in the Soviet state and how such change affects Soviet international behavior.

This chapter seeks to identify the sources of change in Russian and Soviet history, the bearers of change, and the opponents of change. It will range freely over several centuries of Russian and Soviet history, and will treat change both as the product of deliberate policies— "innovation" would be a good synonym—and as the consequence of

3

demographic and other more spontaneous processes. It will seek generalizations at the expense of the often-revealing exception or nuance. This will be justified by any perspective it lends to our understanding of contemporary developments and especially to the question of whether fundamental alterations in the very process of change are occurring today in the USSR.

The problem of change in Russia and the USSR assumes great importance in part because so many have felt that genuine change there is at best incomplete and at worst nonexistent. A century and a half ago the Marquis de Custine charged that Russians were barely disguised Tatars, while his contemporary, Baron Haxthausen, revelled in what he considered Russia's "timeless" quality.[1] Following the October Revolution, Nicolas Berdyaev was quick to find Muscovite qualities in the new Soviet regime, just as Arnold Toynbee was eager to trace the sources of Stalinism to Byzantium.[2] More recently, the debates between Alexander Solzhenitsyn and Richard Pipes have addressed the same proposition that however much the USSR may have developed, it has not really changed at all.[3]

I will note the various continuities that pervade the political and economic development of Russia and the USSR but, while recognizing these, I will give due emphasis to the fact that, according to most indices pertinent to the social sciences, the society occupying the present territory of the USSR has changed dramatically over the centuries. Even within the memory of people alive today, the USSR has evolved from a predominantly rural society to an urban one; from agrarian to industrial; from illiterate to literate; from a nation of high birth and high death rates to one of low birth and low death rates; from an economy based on inanimate sources of power to one dependent upon steam, petroleum, and nuclear energy; and from a people whose values were dominated by the culture of the traditional village to one open to stimuli from around the planet and brought to them by modern technologies of communication.

It would be unnecessary to emphasize this point had the USSR not recently passed through a period of great caution, if not outright opposition to deliberately induced change. This has led some observers to infer that the processes of demographic, social, economic, and even political change that have obtained in every other industrial society have somehow been interrupted in the USSR, and can only be restarted through some exceptional act of leadership.[4]

As will be clear from the concluding section of this chapter, I believe this misstates the case. To reach this conclusion, however, I will first examine the present era in the context of the most recent epoch in Russian and Soviet history, namely, the decades between the rise of

Khrushchev and the death of Brezhnev, and see that era in turn against the background of the two main earlier phases of Russian development. I will then identify some of the major forces that have triggered innovation in all three stages of Russian development. Finally, I will discuss the main social bearers and opponents of innovation, not as permanent factors operating steadily throughout the historical evolution of Russia and the USSR, but as forces specific to defined phases, appearing on the scene and then passing from it. This is not to ignore the undeniably important role of ideas in bringing about change in Russia. It merely acknowledges that such ideas are brought to bear through the agency of specific persons and groups in society.

Three Phases of Change

The USSR is among some two dozen organized political communities that have successfully transformed themselves into industrialized, urbanized, and educated societies, and one of even fewer large scale societies to have done so. The process of that transformation can be divided into an almost limitless number of phases.[5] For the sake of simplicity, however, I will reduce that number to three.[6]

The Pre-Industrial Base for Successful Change

First, a pre-industrial phase extended from the formation of the Muscovite state in the fifteenth century to the third quarter of the nineteenth century. By the end of this period, Russia had acquired many attributes essential to its attainment of rapid development later. Thus, it gained a centralized government capable of imposing its decisions on a large and ethnically diverse population. That government, in turn, commanded the loyalty of a large corps of civil servants and an even larger body of service gentry. In comparison with most other traditional societies, this elite was relatively large, constituting nearly four percent of the population.[7] Moreover, the government ruled from a large capital city that maintained contact with the nation's periphery through regular mail service and, by the end of the period, railroads and telegraph lines. Modern knowledge readily entered the country through the Academy of Sciences and a system of universities, and was disseminated among the elite through a unified language capable of expressing the full range of modern ideas. Finally, the government proved itself capable of defending its territory by means of a relatively modern army, and of imposing its will on its principal neighbors by force when necessary.

While this period did not witness the beginning of the drive to industrialize, it provided the base from which that transformation could be launched. Pre-industrial Russian history was " . . . not so much an unmoving line or point as . . . a dynamic continuum in which trends [were] set in motion that greatly affect the modernization drive."[8]

Political and institutional innovations introduced by Peter I, Catherine II, and her successors did not *cause* the rapid economic transformation later, but rather rendered it possible. No act of will by subsequent rulers could have unleashed the rapid development reached in late nineteenth-century Russia had these earlier rulers not so fully paved the way. Anomalies and problems in the subsequent drive for economic and social change may be explained as much by shortcomings in this pre-industrial phase of development as by any tactical errors on the part of the later leadership.

The Period of Transformation

The second and most dynamic phase in Russia's development extended from the late nineteenth century to the 1950s. During that era the state changed, first through reform and then through revolution, into an instrument dedicated above all to the economic and social transformation of the society. The notion of state-guided industrialization recalls the experiences of Prussia, France and other earlier models, not to mention the practice of tsarist Russia itself in the era of Peter I. But the pace in nineteenth and twentieth century Russia was different. Industrialization in Russia after the 1880s occurred at a rate surpassing that of the earlier developing countries of Western Europe and equalled only by that of Japan in the same years.[9]

The old elite was either absorbed into the new system or eliminated, and a much larger new elite created in the 1930s through the mobilization of heretofore marginal social groups. Using quasi-military means—a forced modernization—the Communist government, like that of the tsars, shaped the application of new technologies. Where the imperial government had co-opted the printing press and steam engine, the government of Lenin and Stalin seized control of electricity, the radio and telephones, and channeled the application of the internal combustion engine into the service of state industries rather than private citizens. Parallel to these political and economic innovations, the demographic transition from a rural to an urban population occurred, as did a massive increase in the population itself, as a result of reduced mortality. Thanks to state control, literacy and education were placed in the service of the overall process of industrial development.

This description would be incomplete without noting the sharp differences between the political institutions that fostered rapid change in the USSR and the West, and also the suppression of liberal economic institutions in the USSR. Still more striking are the exceptionally high levels of coercion employed in the USSR, and the great loss of life caused by international and civil wars, as well as by collectivization and the purges of the 1930s.[10] At no period of Russia's history was the link between violence and innovation closer. In acknowledging these grim realities, however, one must also concede that, first, very high rates of mobilization and change were sustained, and, second, that the indices by which such changes were measured in the USSR— industrial productivity, educational and demographic shifts, among others—came to be the same ones by which the advanced industrial societies of Western Europe and North America evaluated themselves. Stated differently, however distinctive the political and social *process* of innovation and change in the Soviet Union during this period, its *contents* were similar in many respects to economic and social transformations elsewhere.

The Period of Advanced Development

The chief characteristic of deliberately induced change in late imperial Russia and the USSR through the 1950s was the *extensive* utilization of resources under the centralized guidance of the state rather than their *intensive* exploitation through decentralized and smaller-scale instruments of control. For example, rather than extracting greater yields from the same acreage through more efficient farming, Soviet leaders increased yields by placing more land under relatively primitive cultivation. The essential difference between the era of transformation— the second phase—and the age of advanced development is the shift from extensive to intensive exploitation, and all its political, organizational, sociological, and psychological concomitants.

This strategic shift did not advance significantly during the period of 1955–1985. The victory of the USSR in World War II not only vindicated Stalin's rule but also strengthened the entire nexus of organizations and practices created during the period of transformation— precisely at the time when they should have been replaced by structural and behavioral arrangements more appropriate to an advanced industrial society. Russians refer to the post-1956 era as a "thaw," especially in the easing of repression and opened channels of expression. But in terms of other fundamental needs of the society no such thaw occurred. The patterns of forced modernization that contributed to effective change between the late nineteenth century and the mid-twentieth, became the chief impediment to further development.[11]

These considerations help to define the problem of change today. The challenge facing the Gorbachev government is not merely "to get the country moving again," but rather, to institute the fundamental innovations that should have been introduced a generation ago.

To understand the depth of the present predicament, it will be helpful to identify the triggers for change in the past and to enumerate the social forces that have served as the bearers of change, as well as those that have thwarted it. Although brief, this summary will indicate the ways in which the processes of change are themselves changing in the USSR today.

The Triggers of Change in Russia

Leaders as Innovators

Change in Russia and the USSR has rarely been as discontinuous as it appears to those who are interested in politics. For example, social and economic change went forward briskly during the years before World War I when the imperial court was moribund, while the period of the New Economic Policy (NEP) was not as stagnant as later Stalinist critics claimed. Indeed, the genuine torpor that set in in the late Brezhnev years represents an unprecedented discontinuity in twentieth-century Russia. Even then, however, demographic processes were proceeding apace, with important implications for the succeeding era.

To the extent that discontinuity is perceived as characteristic of Russian development, it is generally linked with the rise and fall of strong leaders. The role of individual Russian and Soviet leaders in promoting change has been particularly emphasized in the West. According to this view, change in Russia generally occurs "from above." Lacking the diverse sources of initiative characteristic of civil societies in the West, Russia has had to depend on strong leaders to trigger innovations in these spheres. Hence, according to this interpretation, it is quite appropriate to organize Russian and Soviet history by the reigns of rulers. This explains the emphasis on the leaders' personal qualities and rhetoric, which are taken to be prime factors in mobilizing people and redirecting resources in Russia. The fact that some social scientists have stressed the role of charismatic leadership in the evolution of late-developing nations as a group seems to strengthen the case.

Russians themselves emphasize the role of leadership in effecting social and economic change. Alexander Herzen's panegyric to the emancipation of the serfs in 1861 was dedicated to Alexander II and entitled "Galilean, Thou Hast Conquered."[12] The cults of neither Lenin nor

Stalin would have been possible had the role of individual leaders not been widely accepted in the culture. Lenin's own objections to cults of leaders do not alter the fact that Leninism as such was an effort to organize innovation from above.

Today, as Westerners and Soviets once more focus their attention on a single Russian leader, it is important to note the limitations of leadership in provoking changes in society at large. A few examples will suffice. The historian, Vasilii Kliuchevskii, observed that the most enduring legacy of Peter I was an unintended consequence of his actions, while he generally failed at what he deliberately sought to accomplish.[13] Herzen's plaudits notwithstanding, Alexander II's initiative was far less important to the abolition of serfdom than was the economic crisis that followed the Crimean War. During the Civil War, Lenin called for large collective farms to replace the landed estates,[14] but was unable to bring them into being and had to abandon the idea. Stalin boasted of his ability to move labor to wherever it was needed, but was unable to force millions of peasants to return to collective farms (*kolkhozes*) after demobilization occurred in 1946.

The same need to deemphasize the role of leadership extends both to the strong deputies of the Russian head of state and to the formal plans that embodied the will of the tsars and the general secretaries. Sergei Witte, the Minister of Finances under the last tsar, never succeeded in quelling the bureaucratic opposition to his program of economic reforms, any more than Minister of Finances Petr Stolypin was able successfully to mobilize the imperial bureaucracy to implement his pre–World War I land reforms.[15] The failure of War Communism has been noted, but failures in planning in areas as diverse as agriculture and urban development are no less significant. For all its specificity, the first Five Year Plan failed to anticipate the slaughter of livestock and hence the decline in agricultural productivity that continued to the mid-1930s.[16]

Some changes attributed to official measures are more properly traced to spontaneous action. Thus, every regime or leader since 1900 has claimed credit for the expansion of literacy in Russia. Nonetheless, census data indicates that, while almost 90 percent of working age males in major cities were literate by 1914, only a third had been taught by government schools, the remaining two-thirds having studied in parish schools or on their own.[17] General studies of literacy elsewhere suggest that self-education and informal learning might have accounted for a similar percentage of those who became literate after 1917.[18] Conversely, the Russian governments both before and after 1917 have claimed credit for controlling the movement of peasants to the cities, although demographic data suggest that the rate of urbanization under the strict migratory laws based on communal agriculture did not differ appreciably from what it would have been had such laws not existed, or from the rate of other industrializing countries.[19]

Such examples are not intended to deny entirely the role of leadership in effecting change "from above," but rather to emphasize the need to approach the question with caution. At the least, they should prompt us to consider the question of leadership in its historic context rather than as an unchanging continuum of the culture, and to distinguish between the various dimensions of change.

Viewing leadership in Russia against the background of the division into historical eras proposed above brings out certain general features. First, it is clear that immense powers of initiative rested with the tsar during the centuries preceding the abolition of serfdom. Without it, Ivan IV and Peter I could not have succeeded in destroying or containing all previously independent sources of political initiative. Later, the state's large role in the nascent industrial economy and its status as guarantor of the gentry's security on the land undergirded autocratic prerogatives and knit them ever more deeply into the political culture of Russia.

The period 1850–1950 can be viewed as a search for a new principle of rule "from above." In the first or tsarist phase, a combination of a series of weak tsars and the growing complexity of the economy caused the initiative for change to shift from the throne to such leading officials as Witte and Stolypin. However limited their success, these two leaders introduced innovations in agriculture, industry, and Russia's foreign relations that were as great as those championed by Peter I. Lenin, in the second phase of this period, attempted to replace autocratic rule with the rule of a political cadre but at the same time extended the area of control "from above" far beyond what it had been under the autocracy. It remained for Stalin to reconcentrate all the elements of initiative under his own control and to use them to restructure both the economy and the society.

Individual leadership, then, attained an unprecedented importance during the years of radical change under Stalin. Obviously, this has not continued since Stalin's death. The question arises whether the relative weakness of Soviet rulers since Stalin is caused by the fact that potential leaders as resolute as Stalin no longer exist, or because the circumstances of advanced industrialization no longer permit one person to concentrate such power in his own hands.

It is the latter that is the case, because of the diffusion of initiative and responsibility that takes place naturally in developed and integrated societies. Nikita Khrushchev attempted to revive the old party-based command system but was bound to fail, even if he had been less capricious. Brezhnev scarcely made the attempt, and while Gorbachev has tried to engender an atmosphere in which bold initiatives could emerge, his emphasis has been more on unleashing the energies of others than on providing them with detailed guidance.

Assuming for the moment that the power of individual leaders peaked in the era of rapid transformation and waned thereafter, we then face the question of whether, in the phase of high development that began a generation ago, we may expect centralized directives to play as important a role as they did in the era of transition.

Soviet leaders after Stalin have assumed they would. Accordingly, they have continued to invoke plans as the voice of legitimate authority and as a force for motivating the populace. However, a series of unfulfilled plans in the 1970s and early 1980s suggest that comprehensive plans cannot motivate an urban labor force unless they are also reinforced with the promise of ever greater rewards or the threat of more dire punishments.

Defense as a Stimulus to Change

No concept is more deeply rooted in the general literature of economic development than that of "defensive modernization." Many students believe this notion to be particularly relevant to Russia and to the USSR. As Alexander Gerschenkron said of the developmental process, "There is very little doubt that, as often before, Russian industrialization in the Soviet period was a function of the country's foreign and military policies."[20]

Arguments for the centrality of military considerations to Russia's development turn on their impact on the allocation of human and material resources. Examples abound in all three periods of Russian and Soviet development. In the pre-industrial era the creation of a service gentry and the enserfment of the peasantry can be traced to military considerations.[21] In the tsarist phase of the period of transformation, the timing and character of railroad development can be linked to military factors,[22] as can the establishment of free trade and, indirectly, the creation of the largest international debt on earth by 1914.[23] The post-revolutionary policies of War Communism and central planning were also devised in part as responses to the urgent demands of wartime.[24] Similarly, persuasive although not dispositive arguments have been advanced that Stalin's "second revolution" of 1928–1932 occurred as a reaction to a perceived military threat.[25]

So thoroughly has the case been developed for defensive modernization in Russia and the USSR that there is no need to repeat it here. It should, however, be qualified in several ways. First, it is clear that the mere *fear* of foreign assault has been at least as significant a trigger for change in Russia as have been actual invasions. Suffice it to say that war scares in the late 1920s, however baseless, contributed to more actual innovation than did the impending invasion by fascist Germany a decade later. And whenever such fears are present, it becomes impossible to distinguish between defensive and offensive motives in the Russian response.

A second qualification to the notion of "defensive modernization" as a spur to innovation in Russia is that the supposed threat has often come from within the country rather than from abroad. The destruction of local elites by Ivan IV, the curtailment of aristocratic privileges by Peter I, the militarization of local rule under Nicholas I, the suspension of local codes of law under Alexander III, the re-collectivization of agriculture and the mass purges under Stalin, and the establishment of a bureaucratic oligarchy under Brezhnev were all, to a greater or lesser extent, responses to perceived threats from within. The decision to deploy large numbers of Soviet troops in the Warsaw Pact nations may be traced as much to the impulse to defend the regime against foes who are internal to the bloc as against the West.

A third qualification to the notion of national defense as a stimulus to innovation in Russia is that the main champions of such concerns and those bearing responsibility for implementing policies resulting from them have generally been civilian rather than military leaders. In the tsarist period this was because imperial Russia, unlike many Third World states, possessed a strong central government prior to the onset of rapid industrialization and did not have to fall back on the military for leadership. It continued during the Soviet period because neither Lenin nor Stalin was prepared to relinquish to officers of dubious political reliability any powers they considered to be properly their own or their party's. It is revealing of the predominance of civilian power in military decision-making that Khrushchev's decision to invest heavily in rocket defense rather than conventional arms was taken in direct opposition to the views of most military leaders. Although they succeeded in shaping that policy to their own interests, the military leaders were unable to alter it in any fundamental way.

The only period in Russia's entire history in which military leaders came even remotely close to usurping civil authority was in the years of 1760–1825. In this period, officers participated in two successful coups against the rulers (Peter II, and Paul I) and a third unsuccessful coup—the so-called "Decembrist Uprising" of 1825. At no point did military authorities themselves aspire to rule, however. If one excludes the controversial case of the Soviet General Tukhachevskii, who once described himself as a "Red Bonaparte," the only would-be military ruler in Russian history who himself proposed to lead the country was General Kornilov, during the anarchic summer of 1917.[26]

The concept of defensive innovation holds that a country may initiate reforms in order to remove or reduce a threat posed by another country. While the threat may be military in nature, it may also be cultural-ideological, demographic, or economic. Such non-military challenges to Russia and the USSR have increased steadily since the eighteenth century, reaching a peak during the period of transformation that began in the 1860s and ended in the 1950s.

To be sure, such non-military challenges existed earlier. However, when confronted by the ideology of the Reformation, the printing press, or the general expansion of trade in northern Europe, Russians responded first by confining the element of change in order to limit its impact, then by co-opting it, and finally by *adapting* it to Russian circumstances rather than simply *adopting* it outright. This process, which has certain parallels in Japan, limited the impact in Russia of external challenges. Although it was less apparent, it also made it possible for the Russian culture and economy to absorb far more from abroad than a comprehensive policy of cultural and economic autarky or of superficial assimilation would have permitted.

Beginning with the transformation of military technology in the late seventeenth century, Russia had to meet various challenges from abroad. Through the era of NEP, the country became increasingly open to Westernizing influences. Stalin considered some of these to be dangerous, and attempted to squelch them by force. The essence of his response to the challenge from abroad, however, was not simply to oppose it but also to reassert traditional controls over the process of importation, so that the USSR could absorb the foreign influences that were useful, but could filter out their negative aspects. Neither Khrushchev nor Brezhnev changed this policy, but its practical implementation became increasingly difficult. Today, a policy that seeks to manage all foreign influences "from above" has become untenable.

Wars as Stimuli to Innovation

I noted earlier that there have been discontinuities in the process of change in Russia and the USSR. While less deep than is commonly thought, such discontinuities are nonetheless real, the result of the system allowing too few of the small, day-to-day adjustments that moderate the need for more dramatic shifts. Whatever the cause, crises of various types have been among the most important triggers to innovation throughout Russian and Soviet history.

No cliché about Russia and the USSR is more common than that military defeat engenders political and economic change. This impetus surely occurred after the Poles occupied Moscow in the seventeenth century, after the debacle of Peter I at Narva, after the unsuccessful Crimean War of 1852–1855, after the Russo-Japanese war of 1903–1905, and after World War I. The failure of the USSR to gain a swift and clear victory there doubtless gave rise to thoughts on the need for additional changes. Conversely, many of the eras of harshest rule have come on the heels of Russian and Soviet victories, which have had the effect of confirming the existing system in all its particulars. The aftermath of the Napoleonic wars and of World War II are cases in point.

However valid the hypothesis that lost wars trigger innovation while victories thwart it, there are notable exceptions to it. Russia acquitted itself with honor in the Seven Years War of 1755–1761, the nation's first entry into the great power struggles of Europe, but victory was followed by important reforms under Catherine II. Similarly, the Bolshevik victory in the Civil War, with its triumph over foreign intervention, also led to epochal changes in the form of the New Economic Policy. More important, the notion that military defeat triggers change, even if true, is too general to be of particular predictive use. One need only compare the various post-defeat episodes of reform to realize how little they have in common.

Economic Crisis and Change

Why is Gorbachev today contemplating reforms when the war in Afghanistan falls so far short of being "the USSR's Vietnam"? The principal argument of this chapter is that certain changes in the nature of change are taking place in the USSR today. An important secondary argument, relevant to Gorbachev's actions today, is that economic crises have been the main factor provoking innovation in all three phases of Russian and Soviet history. Often related to wars, security issues, and even the fate of leaders, the government's most severe budgetary crises have invariably given rise to changes beyond those traceable directly to defense or the nature of leaders. Of course, the history of Europe as a whole is replete with examples of innovation caused by governmental fiscal crises. Such crises have been especially severe in Russia, however, because of the chronic shortage of capital available to the state. Lacking the resources to carry out its mission, the state has had to turn to the public, which has often led to basic reforms.

To test this hypothesis I shall examine five periods of innovation, three in the tsarist period and two in the Soviet:

1. The 1760s, when members of the service gentry were freed from state service, allowed to return to their estates, and encouraged

to engage in agricultural and proto-industrial development; when a number of state industrial monopolies were turned over to private ownership; and when greater public initiative was permitted in publishing and the dissemination of information. (The term *glasnost'* was widely used in this connection.)

2. The decade of 1856–1866, when privately-owned and state serfs were emancipated; a new system of local government introduced; and when the courts, banks, and military systems were reformed.

3. The years 1905–1907, when a semi-parliamentary system was introduced; political parties legalized; imperial control of non-Russian territories somewhat relaxed; greater private initiative permitted in industry; and, slightly later, individual peasants permitted to hold title to land.

4. The NEP period, when key instruments of War Communism were dismantled; certain industries turned back to their previous owners; private initiative allowed in small-scale economic and cultural activities; and individual peasants once more permitted to function as private farmers under market pricing.

5. The years 1960–1966, in which Khrushchev established his unsuccessful councils of the economy (*sovnarkhozy*) to bring greater Party influence to bear on local economic units; twenty-five ministries were abolished; controls over writers and artists relaxed; controls over internal travel and choice of work reduced; and the Kosygin/Liberman changes in local administration and accounting introduced, if only tentatively.

While these eras of change differ greatly among themselves they have important common features nonetheless. In each case the state found itself financially unable to carry out tasks it had arrogated to itself and therefore resorted to the administrative solution of decentralization or privatization. In each case the state withdrew from functions it had long managed, and placed authority for them upon either local societal (*obshchestvennye*) groups or private forces. Moreover, in each period this process involved strong elements of both administrative decentralization and regional or local self-administration. In no case were public functions abolished, nor did public bodies—whether central or local, public or private—assume responsibility for the execution of functions that had been ignored. Stated differently, these five great periods of change in Russia and the USSR may be characterized as episodes of economically induced administrative reorganization, in which the power of central authorities to make basic decisions was preserved but a greater efficiency in their implementation sought by means of administrative decentralization, devolution, and limited self-adminis-tration.

Why have such policies provided the basis of so many reform movements in Russia and the USSR? While it is accurate to say that they are an inevitable reaction to a dominant tradition of statism and centralization, it also begs the question. To address this issue it is necessary to ask what events triggered each of these eras of change, and what were the goals of those who directed them.

In each of the five episodes of reform, economic erosion assaulted the national budget and impeded the ability of the government to execute the tasks it had claimed for itself. In the first four periods the economic difficulties had been precipitated by wartime expenditures. In the second era, Russia's economic crisis coincided with an inter-national panic, i.e. the world banking crisis of 1857, which caused the collapse of the tsarist state bank. In the third era, the economic crisis coincided with the runaway inflation after World War I. In neither instance—nor, for that matter, in the 1760s or 1960s—did the govern-ment succeed in borrowing funds from abroad sufficient to its needs. Nor was it in a position to assuage the problem simply by printing more money or by extracting it from the populace through taxation. For Catherine II to have done so in the 1760s would have jeopardized the support of officers and gentry who had backed her coup; for Alexander II to have done so would have been to risk the rebellion of the peasants; for either Nicholas II or Lenin to have done so would have renewed the warfare of the peasants against the state and its local representatives. With these various possibilities foreclosed, the government had no choice but to make timely political and admin-istrative concessions.

A 6.6 percent growth rate in industrial production and a 4.9 percent growth in Gross National Product (GNP) for the years 1961–1965 suggests that the crisis was less severe in that period and the potential for forced savings greater than in the earlier periods. However, these figures represent a decline from 8.9 percent and 5.8 percent respectively for the period of 1956–1960, a sharp reversal and cause for deep concern.[27] Moreover, social tranquility and support for the regime had been achieved in the post-Stalin years through commitments to higher wages and improved consumer goods, both of which would have been imperiled by forced savings. However, the fact that the economic crisis was relatively less severe in the 1960s than in the other periods doubtless helps to explain the fact that at that time the reforms were limited.

The stimulus to innovation in each of these reforming eras arose from economic crisis. Whether the result of war or of peacetime difficulties, each time the economic problems were real. Leaders deemed each crisis sufficiently serious that they allowed it to supercede their drive to achieve direct control over every subject or citizen. To be sure, there were periods of economic hardship that did not immediately give rise to change: the impact of the general economic crisis after 1873 and the sharp decline in productivity after 1978 are good examples. In both periods, however, aging leaders were able to resist pressures for decentralizing and devolutionary change, largely because exports (grain for Alexander II and oil for Brezhnev) cushioned the impact of a declining economy on the governmental budget.

A notable feature of four of these five episodes of reform is that they were presided over by leaders newly installed in power, a fact which made it easier for them to repudiate earlier policies. However, the governments of both Nicholas II and Lenin had themselves created the policies which their reforms repudiated, suggesting that a shift in leadership is a useful but not essential factor in the process of managed change. More important by far is the leader's conviction that a failure to make concessions through decentralization and devolution would imperil one's rule, if not the legitimacy of the regime itself. Such are the absolute limits on absolute authority.

Mass Revolt as a Trigger to Change

These episodes of reform raise the question of whether economic crisis was, in fact, the motivating force for innovation. Both the post-1905 reforms and the NEP came on the heels of social breakdown and civil war. Moreover, Soviet historians have maintained that the Great Reforms of the 1860s were preeminently the result of a mass movement,[28] while Western specialists have often noted the manner in which the collectivization and destruction of the class of prosperous farmers (*kulaki*) in 1929–1931 stormed out of control, sweeping beyond the more limited program envisaged in the first Five Year Plan.[29] Other scholars, both Soviet and Western, have emphasized the degree to which the Bolshevik takeover itself was the result of a mass movement, as opposed to a coup by an elite corps in the midst of general collapse.[30]

In spite of the populist sentiments of such writers, it is difficult to trace fundamental changes throughout the sweep of Russian and Soviet history directly to mass agitation. The greatest peasant rebellions of the seventeenth and eighteenth centuries—those of Stenka Razin and Emilion Pugachev—led to greater repression rather than to greater reform. Although Soviet scholars have documented virtually every uprising of the peasants in the early nineteenth century, they have failed to show any causal relationship between those acts and emancipation. Alexander II's warning to the Moscow gentry that it would be better for emancipation to occur from above than from below was good politics but was scarcely an accurate description of the situation.[31] The case for 1905 is far clearer, especially concerning land reform.[32] However, if mass rebellion in the provinces led to the devolution of power onto local officials, it probably discouraged those who would have preferred to shift more functions to self-administration through the local publicly elected councils or *zemstvos.*

Granting, however, that mass violence played a definite role in the reforms of 1905, in the October Revolution, in the events leading up to NEP, and in the pace and extent of collectivization, it is still significant that all four of these episodes were confined to a thirty year period in Russia's history, the same thirty years in which the epochal movement from village to city occurred, and in which the governing structure was itself in turmoil. Both before and after this interval of three decades, either mass uprisings were less potent or the political authorities were better able to contain them.

As Alexander II's statement to the Moscow gentry exemplifies, a desire to forestall or preempt upheaval may be as powerful a force for change as actual rebellion. In the pre-industrial phase of development, however, this consideration was of only minor importance, for the goals of peasant rebellion were limited and the government was willing to use extreme force in subduing them. It was more frequently apparent in the period of transition when, under both tsarist and Communist leaders, preemptive concessions were seen as an alternative to the use of force. Labor legislation under Alexander III, land reform under Stolypin, and both factory and agricultural policies under NEP may all be considered manifestations of such a policy of preemption.

Both the need and the desire to preempt public unrest through concessionary policies grew during the third phase of development, beginning in the 1950s. The traumatic changes of the preceding period had left members of the general populace more concentrated in urban centers and therefore in closer contact with both the government and with one another. Because of this process of integration, not only did governmental actions affect individuals more frequently and directly than before, but the public also had greater opportunities to make known its will to the government. The expression of public sentiment could occur through expanded channels of direct expression, as well as through such negative forms of behavior as absenteeism, low productivity, and alcoholism. By the 1970s, the effort to thwart or preempt these forms of mass "action" had become major stimuli for change in the USSR, and continue to be so today.

The Bearers and Opponents of Innovation in Russia

My focus thus far has been on the people who have initiated change and on the circumstances that have promoted it. Without strong forces to carry them to completion, however, policies of change remain stillborn. It is the nature of innovation to affect negatively some segment of the population. In Russia, lacking regular channels for expressing disagreement, such opposition can readily become intransigent. As Peter I observed in a letter to a colleague, "You know yourself that anything that is new, even though it is good and needful, will not be done by our people without compulsion."[33]

Who, then, have been the chief bearers of innovation in Russia, and what social groups have been its chief opponents? Both of these forces have changed continually over the centuries and both are changing significantly even now.

The role of bearers of change in the pre-industrial era first fell to members of the tsar's immediate retinue and, by the eighteenth century, to elites within the civil and military bureaucracies. To the end of the tsarist regime, reforming bureaucrats were the most consistent agents of deliberate change, often coopting the emperor himself for their purposes.[34] From the late nineteenth century to the early years of Soviet rule, however, powerful agents of change emerged outside the government among leaders of the bourgeoisie and the intelligentsia. The merchant class, especially in Moscow, gained coherence as a political force,[35] and the intelligentsia, in the process of formation for a century, coalesced in such independent professions as law, medicine, and journalism and launched political actions from that base.

By no means have all potential bearers of innovation in Russia succeeded in fulfilling that role. Generational movements, for example, made themselves felt in the 1820s, 1840s, and 1960s, but in each case failed to bring about the fundamental shift in policy that was sought. Similarly, national minorities in both the imperial and Soviet eras have exerted pressure on behalf of cultural autonomy and a looser relationship between center and periphery. These have enjoyed but little success, though, the only partial exception being the Baltic provinces and Finland during the period of 1900–1914. In both cases the social base of the group was too narrow and its members too isolated from the larger Russian society to be effective bearers of change at the national level.

Lenin decried the relative weakness of the industrial class and declared that the intelligentsia, by a process of substitution, must instead provide leadership to the proletariat. The obvious problem was that most members of the intelligentsia lacked access to precisely those levels of government at which change might be initiated. With the two revolutions of 1917 it gained that access, only to lose it again to the reconstituted civil administration in the late 1920s.

For a generation and a half after 1930 the primary bearers of innovation in the USSR were men and women who owed their upward mobility to the revolution, and who lodged themselves in the bureaucracy. These people, known as "those who were pushed ahead" (*vydvizhentsy*), in turn became the preservers of the *status quo* by 1960, at which time young members of a new and fully Soviet intelligentsia, including scientists and cultural leaders, stepped forward as innovators and would-be reformers.[36] The question facing the Soviet leadership today is whether the activist values of that intelligentsia can be grafted on to the Communist Party and imposed as well on the civil bureaucracy and managerial classes.

This dynamic coexists with an older competition between members of the Communist Party and the managerial class over which group will be the bearer of change. Under Lenin, it was clearly the Party, while Stalin shifted the function decisively to the state bureaucracy. Khrushchev attempted to revive the Party's former role by broadening its control over local industry.[37] Brezhnev permitted the ministerial apparatus to regain much of its old hegemony, but the price he extracted was that the bureaucracy was forced to abandon its role as a bearer of change. To date, Gorbachev appears to be trying to reshape the Party through infusions from the intelligentsia of the 1960s and to use the reconstituted Party to batter the ministerial bureaucracies.

Just as differing social groups have functioned as innovators in different periods, so have different groups taken the lead in opposing change. There is a strong tendency among students of Soviet affairs to view the general Russian populace as passive, the inert agent upon which governmental policies act but which does not react in turn.[38] Such a view violates common sense, especially considering the high investments that have been achieved by extracting onerous taxes in labor or kind and through other means of forceable nonconsumption. In reality, opposition to change has significantly shaped the process of change throughout Russian history.

Who have been the principal opponents of innovation in the main phases of Russian and Soviet development? In both the pre-industrial period and the era of transition, by far the most important opponents of change were the peasantry. From the revolt of the Old Believers in the seventeenth and eighteenth centuries through the twentieth century peasantry's bitter hostility to the collectivization of agriculture and its passive resistance to post-war campaigns to raise productivity, peasant opposition has made itself felt against those spearheading innovation. The one period in which the peasantry itself emerged as a bearer of change were the years between the late-1890s and the establishment of NEP, when peasants fought actively for the right to own the land that they cultivated.[39] Except for this brief interlude, the peasantry fought to save itself from incursions from every quarter. As we will see, the disappearance of the traditional peasantry and thus of its voice of protest is one of the primary changes in the nature of change today.

After the peasantry, the main opponent of change in all three phases of Russian and Soviet development has been the civil bureaucracy. As we have seen, leading civil servants figured both as initiators and bearers of change in the pre-industrial era and in the period of economic transformation. However, even when modernizing officials led change, they were impeded by the intractable lower bureaucracy. Stalin's revolution succeeded in good measure because of his ability to reorganize the bureaucracy around his own loyalists, the youthful *vydvizhentsy*, but that group's commitment to basic change did not survive the early middle age of its members.

Examples of bureaucratic opposition to reform abound. When Peter I introduced his new ministries (*kollegii*) from Sweden, he was unable to alter the ingrained habits of the old administrators who manned them.[40] Similarly, Alexander II introduced some local self-governance through his elective local councils (*zemstvos*), but they were hamstrung by the heavy-handed controls imposed by the unreformed local administration.[41] Lenin's system of political commissars and party watchdogs was an effort to bring the civil and military administrations to heel, but fell so far short of expectations that Stalin simply purged the administrative apparatus and installed his own *vydvizhentsy* in its place.

Following the October Revolution, many technical experts, scientists, and professional people came under suspicion on the grounds that they were opposed to change.[42] It is likely that Stalin would have treated them as ruthlessly as he treated recalcitrant bureaucrats had it not been for the fact that they were irreplaceable. Accordingly, he approached them with the carrot of special privileges and the stick of compulsory membership in national unions that functioned under close Party tutelage.

The manner in which the local officialdom thwarted Khrushchev's attempts at reform forced his successors to choose between reform and the good will of the bureaucracy. They opted for the latter, an arrangement which continued to the appointment of Gorbachev as general secretary.

One of the few social groups to have consistently supported innovation is the military. To be sure, the pre-Petrine elite corps led the opposition to Peter's reforms, but it was soon crushed. Thereafter, military officers generally functioned within the framework of national policy, with the partial exception of the period 1760–1825, as discussed above. The high continuity of personnel between the imperial and Red armies reflects this situation.[43] Notwithstanding Stalin's purge of the officer corps in 1937, that group had not become a focus of opposition to Stalin or to the changes that he championed.

There is some basis for the belief that at least part of the armed forces have become opponents of change in the post-Stalin period of high industrialization. Partisans of conventional forces and tank armies have opposed the rise of the navy and of the rocket forces.[44] More recently, military leaders have spoken out against the supposed softening of draft-age youths, their declining sense of discipline, and so forth. Such complaints, even when they come from officers who might otherwise strongly support the adoption of the most modern and technologically advanced weapons, represent a criticism of the kind of society that produces such technologies and an idealization of old peasant virtues.

Several independent groups that have appeared during various periods in Russian history must also be counted as sources of opposition to change. With notable exceptions, regional elective assemblies of the gentry opposed emancipation before 1861. While they could not derail the reform, they at least saw to it that it would tie peasants to the communal land and require them to make payments of redemption for their own freedom. Even more successful were the millions of small-scale enterpreneurs who created the so-called "second economy" during the Brezhnev years. Like the gentry before them, they had an abiding interest in the *status quo* under which they flourished.[45] Unlike the gentry, however, they prevented the state's efforts to wipe out their economic base and forced it instead to co-opt them by legalizing their endeavors through new laws regulating self-employment.

Many observers might consider the final source of opposition to innovation to be the most important: namely, certain of the top leaders of Russia and the USSR. To the contrary, surprisingly few Russian leaders have dug in their heels against social and economic change and against policies fostering it. In the last two hundred years, the only examples have been Nicholas I and Nicholas II, although, to be sure, Alexander I, Stalin, and Brezhnev all came to oppose certain types of change during the late years of their regimes. Even these examples must be qualified, for in each case the opposition was directed not so much at economic innovation as at the social effects of such changes. In each of these cases, too, the leader's opposition was fueled by members of his own retinue whose hostility to change was more intense than that of the leader himself.

Changes in the Nature of Change

Having summarized the main periods of Russian and Soviet development and touched briefly on the changing stimuli, bearers, and opponents of change, we return to the main question: in what ways is the very nature of change in the USSR itself undergoing change today? The issue turns on the manner in which one interprets Soviet history since the death of Stalin. According to the 1960 Soviet census, the fundamental transformation from an agrarian to an industrial society had largely occurred by that year.[46] Because of three-quarters of a century of intense mobilization, the population of the former tsarist empire had shifted from farm to factory, and had acquired the essential skills necessary for life in a large scale urban and integrated society. Even allowing for the important differences between, respectively, the USSR and the earlier developing countries of western Europe, central Europe, and Japan, the overall pattern was nevertheless recognizably the same as in other industrial societies. The fact that the USSR continued to sustain a solid, albeit declining, level of growth into the 1970s gave an appearance of soundness to the enterprise. Since the 1960s, there was ample cause for unease, but few Soviets and few of the more thoughtful Western observers took these as evidence of fundamental breakdown. Somehow the USSR would muddle through. The task of Western analysts should be to understand how the Soviet system works, not why it does not.[47]

Although the harshest aspects of the Stalinist system were toned down, the institutional structure and overall pattern of relationships created in the early 1930s persisted. Stalin himself may have been an aberration, but the essence of the system he built with materials he inherited from Lenin and the tsarist past remained intact and serviceable. Stripped of its excesses, the Stalinist system was an extreme, particularly brutal and, for a time, more or less successful variant of the state-centered path to modernity that many nations were pursuing at the time.

As the decline of the late 1970s and early 1980s deepened, however, its origins in the earlier post-Stalin period became more apparent. Far from being a cyclical *malaise,* the downturn now appeared as evidence that more fundamental change was needed—in Gorbachev's words, "reconstruction," and "a new way of thinking."

Without pausing to consider what Gorbachev meant by this, it is fair to conclude, as I suggested earlier, that the transition from the period of transformation to that of advanced industrial development never really took place in the USSR. In spite of the Twentieth Party Congress, the "Thaw," Khrushchev's reforms, and the limited economic experiments of the 1960s and 1970s, the fundamental transition from extensive to intensive development had not been achieved. The much-touted notion of "developed socialism" turned out to be nothing more than a rhetorical excess, since this basic shift never occurred. Most Soviet theorizing on the "scientific-technical revolution" was flawed for the same reason, although in fairness, it must be acknowledged that at least a few Soviet economists began to focus their attention on the extensive-intensive issue as they debated the concept.

Seen in this light, the entire course of post-Stalinist development must be viewed as having been deeply conservative in the literal sense of that word, fostering only such limited changes as were necessary to preserve the basic system and otherwise suppressing structural reforms. Even Kosygin and Brezhnev's localized experiments to improve economic management were essentially conservative, resembling nothing so much as the many experiments in serf reform that occurred under Nicholas I.[48]

Such thoughts suggest the hypothesis that what is taking place today is the beginning of the move to the third, advanced phase of development that failed to occur in the years after 1953. This shift will require fundamental changes in the organization and relations in the Soviet Union. Should they take place, the Stalin era will indeed appear in retrospect to have been an episodic relapse, a transitory phase in Russia's overall process of change.

Stated differently, the current debate in the USSR turns on the necessity of change in the process of innovation. The shift from extensive to intensive development will require vast new outlays of capital, e.g., a major program of savings and investment. Foreign credit is limited, and simply to print more money would be to stimulate the no longer hidden inflation. As I have noted, Russia's industrial transformation occurred through the imposition of policy of non-consumption and the forced extraction of savings, neither of which is possible today. The combination of gradually advancing wages and inadequate consumer goods have piled up private savings to the level of 70 percent of all annual income.[49] Consumption cannot be further depressed, nor can private savings be extracted without material compensation. To do either, let alone to carry it to excess, would further lower the motivation of laboring men and women, on whose productivity all improvement eventually depends. It is revealing that Gorbachev's opening to private initiative was launched by the Ministry of Finances, as a means of claiming taxes from private enterprises that already exist under the "second economy."

The example of savings and investment reveals the extent to which innovations can no longer be introduced in the old way. Many equally compelling examples also exist. All point to the basic fact that the nature of change has changed in the USSR. This transformation, equal in significance to the process by which the country girded itself to mobilize for industrialization between the 1860s and 1930s, will affect the initiation and the execution of change, as well as the social nature of its opponents.

Leadership will continue to be important in fostering innovation. However, as the example of saving and investment indicates, leaders will not be able to resort to mass compulsion as they could when Russia was being transformed from an agrarian to an industrial society. The use of terror and other forms of force will decline not merely because there will be too few Stalinists to exert it, but also because it will no longer be as efficacious as it was in the past.[50]

More dependent upon the support of the populace at large, Soviet leaders of the future will confront a different task. Rather than impose programs of their own creation, as did Peter I or Lenin, they will more likely become the articulators and advocates of ideas already current in educated society.[51]

The same consideration suggests that the range of policy options open to future leaders of the USSR will become increasingly narrow. Foreign stimuli will play an ever-larger role in the less autarkic Soviet economy but foreign models must be thoroughly reworked and adapted to Soviet conditions if they are to play more than a polemical role in the USSR. Far more than at any time in the past three-quarters of a century, leaders will be constrained by the actual political and social culture of the populace at large.

It will no longer be possible for Soviet leaders to view the labor force as infinitely malleable, an observation which in turn suggests that the leaders will be less able than in the past to implant foreign models in the USSR, however desirable they may seem. The challenge for future Soviet leaders will be to identify leading currents in society, to give them voice, and to open institutional channels for their expression, rather than to blaze utopian trails *ab initio*.

Nor is it likely that defense and military considerations will trigger innovation to the extent they have in the past. While they will continue to stimulate major investments in technology, and to justify changes that produce greater efficiency and intensity in defense industries, the process of change in the military's command economy will have decreasing relevance for the growing demand economy in the civilian sector, although the latter will continue to be influenced by the former.[52] In addition, the importance of the military as an inculcator of basic education, national values, and technical skills is already declining— not absolutely but relatively—as the capabilities of the rest of Soviet society expand. Increasingly, the complex processes of life in a large-scale modernized society themselves become a kind of school, shaping the outlook of those exposed to them.

Economic crises, by contrast, will probably assume ever greater importance as a trigger for innovation. In the more developed Soviet Union of today, economic gains and shortfalls already directly affect a far larger proportion of the inhabitants than in the past. Hence, the leaders will gain their widest public support in times of economic strain by attacking entrenched interests and by promoting organizational change. Conversely, economic well-being appears to weaken the climate for introducing directed change, although it fosters the evolutionary development of society at large, which in turn shapes the parameters in which leadership must operate.

The Emerging Civic Culture and Change

One of the fundamental alterations in the process of change in the USSR today is the decline in the importance of political and bureaucratic elites as the bearers of innovation. As the economy and the society grow more sophisticated and complex, the numbers of persons able to contribute to change increases. More diverse and numerous points of initiative arise, as the number of institutions, organizations, and individuals engaged in modern production and contemporary issues multiplies. For example, the diversion of the Siberian rivers to Central Asia was conceived and planned in government agencies and institutes, but was abandoned as a result of actions initiated by educated persons acting as citizens.[53] Even if the level of activity in governmental offices were to expand, it is unlikely that it could keep pace with the pro-liferation of skilled manpower in other posts. Whatever their official duties, political and bureaucratic elites will necessarily find themselves spending more time coordinating the energies of others rather than initiating change themselves.

By this process the educated classes have acquired a kind of power, not merely as agents of a single and centrally coordinated political will, as occurred under Stalin, but as individuals upon whose support the political structure rests. The most highly skilled segments of the population, whatever their political affirmations, have become the chief bearers of innovation.

The same processes are taking place in Soviet labor, although the sphere of individual action of a common worker is more limited than that of a better educated person. Whatever its pace with specific subgroups of the population and whatever elements of coercion still linger, the inevitable decline of regimentation in Soviet society is transforming subjects into citizens. In the process, it is gradually creating a new and, for Russia, an unprecedented civic culture. This expansion of the civic realm should not be equated with Westernization, even though the first models of civil societies developed in the West and were first described by Western political philosophers. The emerging civic culture of the USSR may differ significantly from the civic environment existing in France, Great Britain, Germany, or even Japan. However it resembles other modern civic cultures in that it is based upon the individuation of citizens, their ability to participate actively and independently in the life of their communities, and to exercise choice not only in personal decisions but in the very direction and character of society.

There is abundant evidence of the expansion of the civic realm in the USSR. Russian jurists have written on this issue since the eighteenth century.[54] Today, however, a civic culture is coming into being not so much as the result of the influence of some abstract theory as through what one observer many years ago predicted would be "freedom by default."[55] Where in the past, the state claimed the power to determine such basic life decisions as the subject's place of residence, line of work, and style of life, such matters are now left to individual choice.[56] Stated differently, where individuals formerly permitted life decisions to be made for them, they have now successfully asserted their right to make such decisions on their own. This development, which began in the realm of private life, inevitably gives rise to the expectation that a similar degree of choice exist in the public or political realm.

Where the Communist Party in the past claimed responsibility for forming the values of "the masses," individual citizens now exercise nearly complete freedom of choice in this area, provided they do not disrupt others. Just as the command economy gradually gives way to a demand economy, so official culture inculcated "from above" gives way to popular culture or "mass culture," a term that has recently gained currency in the USSR. Popular culture chooses its own media, forms, and content. It receives inspiration from domestic and international sources, with which it maintains unmediated contact through channels wholly independent of the state. Having abdicated the function of control, the state must content itself with co-opting popular expression and limiting its most glaring excesses. It is revealing that in most fields of the arts, the people emerging as the new spokesmen all have some degree of contact with the values of popular culture.

Virtually every field of endeavor today provides evidence of growing democratization and the spread of civic culture. To cite but one example, until the early 1980s both films and television programs were produced for a single undifferentiated market. This was compatible with Marxist notions of social evolution but did not fit Soviet reality. Numerous groups, especially youths and the highly educated, found little of interest in the fare offered them and in fact paid little attention to television or their local theaters. Finally, both the film industry and national television authority permitted studios to differentiate production for a more segmented market. Recently, the film industry has gone further, linking the budget of production studios with ticket sales, while viewer response to television programming is also being more closely monitored. Command yielded to demand, and authority to democracy.

The *de facto* democratization of Soviet society places limits on intrusive and comprehensive planning. The planning process might well continue as a means of codifying policy, but the will that it expresses will increasingly be that of the general populace, which will be known through countless formal and informal channels for the expression of public opinion, rather than that of aloof planners. Assuming that the shift from a command to a demand economy will never be complete, it is likely that planning will remain a useful means of establishing the general direction and extent of desired change. However, even in the 1970s Gosplan, the central planning agency of the state, had begun to lose its power as an instrument of control, a process that now appears all but irreversible.

Beyond Gosplan, it is clear that the economic, legal, and political structures of Soviet society will all have to be modified in order to accommodate a more sophisticated and intensive economy and a more differentiated, democratic, and "civic" society. This process began under Brezhnev in such inconspicuous acts as the opening of the trial of Daniel and Siniavsky to the public, the guarded encouragement given to innovating economists, and the extension of the rights to intellectual and artistic property.[57] As the first lawyer to lead the USSR since Lenin, Gorbachev has already shown himself to be attuned to organizational relationships in the economy and to questions of legal rights. Thus, his law on self-employment activity provides a legal basis for widespread individual initiatives heretofore considered outside the law. Proposed reforms affecting judicial procedure and the work of prosecutors, defense attorneys and judges will, if enacted, not only resolve practical anomalies within the courts but also insulate the courts from political interference. At the beginning of 1988, it is too early to judge how far such reforms may go, or how rigorously they will be implemented.[58]

Even limited reform can call forth opposition. Such opposition, however, is likely to come from different quarters than in the past. The peasantry has already disappeared as the principal opponent of change in the USSR, its place having been taken by large segments of the bureaucratic and administrative structure. Gorbachev's strongest speeches have been directed against this quarter. Except for Stalin during the period of mass terror, it is doubtful that any Soviet leader has launched so broad an attack upon the personnel of the government he heads, or has done so in the name of the educated public. The firing of 10,000 police officers in 1987 suggests that the state apparatus itself had become the main object of state coercion under Gorbachev.[59]

Meanwhile, for the first time since the early twentieth century, labor is positioned to emerge as a source of opposition.[60] Having chosen to build his base of support mainly among the educated and taste-making classes of the USSR, Gorbachev now must confront labor. He challenges laborers to work soberly and in a self-disciplined fashion, but holds out the reward of material benefits for those who follow him. Under the new circumstances, if those rewards are not forthcoming, or if they are not commensurate with the amount of work that Gorbachev demands, labor could avail itself of the new two-way communication and signal its discontent to the leader. In this manner a more complex and genuinely political process of change will overtake the old command system.

To a far greater extent than Khrushchev or Brezhnev acknowledged, Soviet labor—the proletariat—had already become a force of opposition in the post-Stalin years. The regime's policy of mollifying labor with increased wages notwithstanding, Soviet factory workers increasingly engaged in passive protest. This led in turn to new rounds of oppression and general alienation. By the 1960s, low productivity, poor work discipline, and what the regime regarded as antisocial forms of individualism such as rock music had all become manifestations of this passive opposition. For the time being, the alienated elements of the Soviet labor force have failed to define their positive goals. If and when they do so, they could move from being a force of mere opposition to a force for change.

A more conspicuous force of opposition in the Khrushchev-Brezhnev period was the intelligentsia, especially scientists, technical experts, and writers, whose relative salary level declined steadily through the 1960s and 1970s.[61] The so-called dissent movement of the late-1960s drew on this opposition, and set forth several agendas of change that were privately debated during the next decade. To some extent Gorbachev seems to have drawn upon the thinking of this privileged group for his own program, a conspicuous example of the manner in which a civic culture is beginning to function. The test of his approach to change and of his rule generally will be whether he is able to listen equally well to the Soviet blue collar worker.

Manifestations of alienation in the two social groups most important for the regime belied the outward tranquility of the Brezhnev years and were the earliest indications that the fundamental reorientation that had been declared after the death of Stalin had not in fact occurred. That change appears to be taking place today. However, it is not enough simply to ask the direction of changes currently under way. It is equally important to inquire into the *process* of change, and particularly into the manner in which the regime deals with opposition. Symbolic gestures toward journalists, artists, and prominent Soviet human rights advocates provide no more than hints of future intentions. More revealing is a recent *Izvestiia* article with the unusual title of "A Ballad of Differing Opinions; Polemical Remarks on the Etiquette of Polemics."[62] According to the author, Soviets have yet to learn how to deal with diversity of views. "This intolerance and refusal to permit another person to have his own opinion," he writes, "is not such an innocent thing. We know the price we paid for this attitude in the past." While the *Izvestiia* writer bemoans the tendency of the common citizen to want to suppress that which he dislikes, his observations could pertain equally to the government itself.

Many views heretofore excluded from public discourse have naturally tended to assume a categorical or extreme form. If legitimized, such views in the future will probably be moderated as they are subjected to public discussion. As part of the same process, the range of opinion on many topics will in all likelihood grow narrower, even though the number of publicly expressed positions on any question might increase.

Meanwhile, the same new conditions will doubtless give encouragement to those expressing views that are hostile to fundamental policies of the day. Champions of nationalism in both non-Russian republics and in the Russian republic itself, of Communist traditionalism, of religion, of genuine opposition to Party programs (whether domestic or foreign), and even of the need to abolish one-party rule, could all seek to articulate their positions publicly. Paradoxically, the very success of the Kremlin's new regime in legitimizing certain forms of opposition *within* the system will exacerbate the problem of dealing with opposition *to* the system. Assuming that the new policy of openness continues, one might expect the more thoroughgoing currents of opposition to grow ever more isolated from the mainstream of legitimate Soviet debate, and, in the process, to become more uncompromising in their demands. This could easily give rise to calls for a return to primitive forms of control in the USSR. In conclusion, it is perhaps worth recalling that modern censorship traces its roots not to the Dark Ages but to the age of Enlightenment, when such progressive leaders as Joseph II of Austria sought to suppress the views of those who would pull their nation back into darkness.

Notes

1. Marquis de Custine, *Russia* (New York, 1954), p. 49, pp. 328–331, 426–427. August von Haxthausen, *Studies on the Interior of Russia*, S. Frederick Starr, ed. (Chicago, University of Chicago Press, 1972), pp. 3–14.

2. Nicolas Berdyaev, *The Origins of Russian Communism* (Ann Arbor, University of Michigan Press, 1960); Arnold Toynbee, *A Study of History*, 10 vols. (London, Oxford University Press, 1954), VIII, p. 143.

3. See Aleksandr Solzhenitsyn, "Misconceptions About Russia Are a Threat to America," *Foreign Affairs*, Spring, 1980, p. 801 ff.

4. This is the thrust of Marshall I. Goldman's interesting *USSR in Crisis: The Failure of an Economic System* (New York and London, Norton Press, 1983).

5. On Soviet debates over periodization in the first four decades of Soviet rule see Leo Yarosh, "The Problem of Periodization," *Rewriting Russian History*, Cyril E. Black, ed. (New York, Vintage Books, 1962), pp. 34–77.

6. This periodization follows that of Cyril E. Black *et al.*, *The Modernization of Japan and Russia* (New York, Free Press, 1975), pp. 10–11.

7. *Ibid.*, p. 55.

8. *Ibid.*, p. 10.

9. *Ibid.*, pp. 161–183.

10. For a comparative view of state terror in the USSR see Alexander Dallin and George W. Breslauer, *Political Terror in Communist Systems* (Stanford, Stanford University Press, 1970), Ch. 4, 5.

11. On Stalinism in the 1960s and 1970s see Roy A. Medvedev, *On Stalin and Stalinism*, Ellen de Kadt, translator (Oxford, Oxford University Press, 1979), Ch. 8. See also Allen Kassof, "The Administered Society: Totalitarianism Without Terror," *World Politics*, XVI, July, 1964, p. 58 ff.

12. *Kolokol*, No. 95, April 1, 1861, p. 797. By June of 1861, however, Herzen had grown critical of the emancipation (*Kolokol*, No. 101, June 15, 1861, p. 845 ff.).

13. V. O. Kliuchevskii, *Sochineniia*, 8 Vols. (Moscow, Akademiia nauk, 1958-1959), IV, pp. 220–222. This view is challenged by Arcadius Kahan, "Continuity in Economic Activity and Policy During the Post-Petrine Period in Russia," *Journal of Economic History*, XXV, 1965, pp. 61–85.

14. Peter Scheibert, *Lenin an der Macht; Das russische Volk in der Revolution 1918-1922* (Weinheim, Acta humaniora, 1984), pp. 160–192.

15. On Witte see Theodore H. Von Laue, *Sergei Witte and the Industrialization of Russia* (New York, Atheneum, 1969), Ch. 7; on Stolypin and the

bureaucrats see George Yaney, *The Urge to Mobilize; Agrarian Reform in Russia 1861-1930* (Urbana, University of Illinois Press, 1982), Ch. 7, 8.

16. Lazar Volin, *A Century of Russian Agriculture; From Alexander II to Khrushchev* (Cambridge, Harvard University Press, 1970), pp. 236-237.

17. Gregory Guroff and S. Frederick Starr, "Zum Abbau des Analphabetismus in den russischen Stadten," *Wirtschaft und Gesellschaft in vorrevolutionaren Russland,* Dietrich Geyer, ed. (Cologne, Kiepenheuer and Witsch, 1975), pp. 340-342.

18. Harvey Leibstein, "Shortages and Surpluses in Education in Underdeveloped Countries, A Theoretical Foray," in *Education and Economic Development,* C. Arnold Anderson, Mary Jean Bowman, eds. (Chicago, University of Chicago Press, 1965), p. 61 ff.

19. See Barbara A. Anderson, *Internal Migration During Modernization in Late Nineteenth Century Russia* (Princeton, Princeton University Press, 1980).

20. Alexander Gershenkron, "Problems and Patterns of Russian Economic Development," *The Structure of Russian History,* Michael Cherniavsky, ed. (New York, Random House, 1970), p. 303.

21. Richard Hellie, *Enserfment and Military Change in Muscovy* (Chicago, University of Chicago Press, 1971).

22. William L. Blackwell, *The Beginnings of Russian Industrialization, 1800-1860* (Princeton, Princeton University Press, 1968), p. 283.

23. See B. V. Ananich, "Finansovyi krizis tsarizma v 1905-1906gg.," *Vnutrenniaia politika tsarizma (seredina XVI-nachalo xx v.),* N. E. Nosov, ed. (Leningrad, Nauka, 1967), pp. 281-320.

24. On the influence of wartime mobilization and the Prussian example on subsequent Soviet planning and labor policies see N. Valentinov (Volskii), *NEP i krizis partii posle smerti Lenina* (Stanford, Hoover Institution, 1971), pp. 101 ff.; and Lenin on the immediate tasks of the Soviet government, *Kommunist,* 1962, No. 14, p. 13.

25. Stalin himself declared in 1931 "Those who fall behind get beaten," J. Stalin, *Works* (Moscow, Gosizdat, 1955), XIII, pp. 39-40.

26. Hans von Herwarth, *Against Two Evils* (New York, Rawon, Wade, 1981), p. 56 ff. On Kornilov see A. S. Lukomskii, *Vospominaniia,* 2 vols. (Berlin, Kirkhner, 1922), from p. 227 ff.; also N. Ia. Ivanov, *Kornilovshchina i ee razgrom* (Leningrad, Izd. leningrad. univers., 1965).

27. Rush v. Greenslade, "The Real Gross National Product of the U.S.S.R., 1950-1975," U.S. Congress, Joint Economic Committee, *Soviet Economy in a New Perspective: A Compendium of Papers* (Washington, U.S. Government Printing Office, 1966), p. 272.

28. *Revoliutsionnaia situatsiia v. Rossii 1859-1961 gg.,* M. V. Nechkina, ed., 4 vols. (Moscow, Akademiia nauk, 1960-1965).

29. R. W. Davies, *The Socialist Offensive. The Collectivization of Soviet Agriculture, 1929-1930* (Cambridge, Harvard University Press, 1980); also Lynne Viola, "The Campaign to Eliminate the Kulak as a Class, Winter 1929-1930: A Reevaluation of the Legislation," *Slavic Review,* Vol. 45, No. 3, Fall 1986, pp. 503-524.

30. Two studies reflecting this view are Alexander Rabinowitch, *The Bolsheviks Come to Power: The Revolution of 1917 in Petrograd* (New York, Norton, 1976), and Ronald G. Suny, *The Baku Commune, 1917-1918* (Princeton, Princeton University Press, 1972).

31. See Terence Emmons, "The Peasant and Emancipation," *The Peasant in Nineteenth Century Russia*, Wayne S. Vucinich, ed. (Stanford, Stanford University Press, 1968), pp. 47-51. Alexander II's statement is in *Materialy dlia istorii uprazdneniia krepostnogo sostoianiia pomeshchichikh krestian v Rossii v tsarstvovanie Imperatora Aleksandra II*, 3 vols. (Berlin, F. Schneider, 1860-1862), I, p. 114.

32. On the peasantry in 1905 see Howard D. Mehlinger and John M. Thompson, *Count Witte and the Tsarist Government in the 1905 Revolution* (Bloomington, Indiana University Press, 1972), pp. 178-208.

33. Quoted in B. H. Sumner, *Peter the Great and the Emergence of Russia* (London, English University Press, 1950), p. 168.

34. "I always give in and in the end am made the fool, without will, and without character." Nicholas II to his uncle, Grand Duke Vladimir, 1896, *Krasnyi arkhiv*, XVII, p. 220; also Von Laue, *Sergei Witte and the Industrialization of Russia*, p. 123.

35. Alfred J. Rieber, *Merchants and Entrepreneurs in Imperial Russia* (Chapel Hill, University of North Carolina Press, 1982).

36. Milovan Djilas, in his *The New Class* (New York, Praeger, 1957, p. 45); stressed the bureaucratic aspect of this group in its early phase. David Lane underscores the technical bias of the ascendent intelligentsia of the 1960s and '70s, *The Socialist Industrial State: Towards a Political Sociology of State Socialism* (Boulder, Westview Press, 1976), p. 92.

37. Barbara Ann Chotiner, *Khrushchev's Party Reform* (Westport, London, Greenwood Press, 1984), Ch. 8.

38. On this view see Robert C. Tucker, *The Soviet Political Mind: Studies in Stalinism and Post-Stalin Change* (New York, London, Pall Mall Press, 1963), pp. 69-90. On the possible basis for such a view in Russian psychology see Margaret Mead, *Soviet Attitudes Towards Authority* (Santa Monica, McGraw-Hill, 1951), pp. 71-88.

39. Lenin acknowledged the peasant as the chief opponent of changes introduced during the Civil War; see Moshe Lewin, *Lenin's Last Struggle* (New York, Vintage Books, 1970), p. 27. On the revolutionary impact of such conservatively motivated rebellions see Eric R. Wolf, *Peasant Wars of the Twentieth Century* (New York, Harper and Row, 1969), p. 291 ff.

40. Kliuchevskii, *Sochineniia*, IV, p. 169 ff.

41. S. Frederick Starr, *Decentralization and Self-Government in Russia, 1830-1870* (Princeton, Princeton University Press, 1972), Ch. 5.

42. For a review of this interaction see Nicholas Lampert, *The Technical Intelligentsia and the Soviet State* (London, Holmes and Meier Publications, 1979), Ch. 1-3.

43. D. Fedotoff White, *The Growth of the Red Army* (Princeton, Princeton University Press, 1944), p. 51.

34   S. Frederick Starr

44. Walter A. McDougall, *The Heavens and the Earth: A Political History of the Space Age* (New York, Basic Books, 1985), Ch. 13.

45. Cf. Gregory Grossman, "The 'Second Economy' of the USSR," *Problems of Communism*, XXVI, September–October 1977, pp. 25–40; and Aaron Katzenelenboigen, "Coloured Markets in the Soviet Union," *Soviet Studies*, XXIX, No. 1, January 1977, p. 62 ff.

46. Whereas in 1939 kolkhoz peasants constituted 49.8 percent of the population, their number by 1971 had sunk to 20 percent of the total, 2 percent less than that of white collar workers. *Vestnik statistiki*, 1972, No. 6, p. 87, table 10.

47. Jerry F. Hough saw "incrementalism" rather than "immobilism," *The Soviet Union and Social Science Theory* (Cambridge, Harvard University Press, 1977), p. 34.

48. A more positive view of such experiments is set forth by Timothy J. Colton, *The Dilemma of Reform in the Soviet Union* (New York, Council on Foreign Relations, 1986), pp. 54–55.

49. Igor Birman, Roger A. Clarke, "Inflation and the Money Supply in the Soviet Union," *Soviet Studies*, XXXVII, October, 1985, p. 494 ff.

50. See Dallin and Breslauer, *Political Terror in Communist Systems*, Ch. 6.

51. This notion was suggested in 1979 by Jerry F. Hough and Merle Fainsod, *How the Soviet Union is Governed* (Cambridge and London, Harvard University Press, 1979), p. 531. Even earlier, Zbigniew Brzezinski and Samuel P. Huntington had acknowledged limits on the freedom of leaders to mould society, *Political Power USA/USSR* (New York, Viking Press, 1964), p. 75.

52. David Holloway, "Soviet Military R&D: Managing the Research-Production Cycle," *Soviet Science and Technology: Domestic and Foreign Perspectives*, John R. Thomas, Ursula M. Kruse-Vaucienne, eds. (Washington, U.S. Government Printing Office, 1977), pp. 190–191.

53. See the polemic on this issue by S. Zalygin and S. Lezhnev, "S kogo spros?" *Izvestiia*, No. 110, April 20, 1987, p. 4.

54. For example, S. E. Desnitskii and M. M. Speranskii, cf. *Iuridicheskie proizvedeniia progressivnykh russkikh myslitelei vtoroi poloviny XVIII veka*, S. A. Pokrovskii, ed. (Moscow, Akademiia nauk, 1959), pp. 56–57; and M. Raeff, "Le climat politique et les projets de reforme dans les premieres annees du regne d'Alexandre Ier," *Cahiers du Monde Russe et Sovietique*, II, No. 4, Oct.–Dec. 1961, pp. 415–432.

55. Allen Kassof in *Prospects for Soviet Society*, Allen Kassof, ed. (New York, Washington, London, published for the Council on Foreign Relations, by Praeger, 1968), p. 501.

56. Colton, *The Dilemma of Reform in the Soviet Union*, p. 50.

57. See Michael A. Newcity, *Copyright Law in the Soviet Union* (New York, London, Praeger, 1978), pt. III. On the rise of legal norms at the workplace see Louise I. Shelley, *Lawyers in Soviet Work Life* (New Brunswick, Rutgers University Press, 1984), p. 142 ff.

58. Early indications give grounds for doubting that their application will be thoroughgoing. On limits of pluralism in industry see Iu. Tikhomirov in

Sotsialisticheskaia industriia, May 13, 1987, p. 2; on bureaucratic impediments to the self-employment law see V. Tolstov in *Izvestiia,* May 16, 1987, p. 2.

59. S. Korepanov, "Militsiia pri obstoiatelstvakh glasnosti," *Sotsialisticheskaia industriia,* May 27, 1987, p. 4.

60. See Alex Pravda, "Spontaneous Workers' Activities in the Soviet Union," *Industrial Labor in the USSR,* Arcadius Kahan, Blair Ruble, eds. (New York, Pergamon Press, 1979), p. 333 ff. Also Seweryn Bialer, *The Soviet Paradox: External Expansion, Internal Decline* (New York, Knopf, 1986), pp. 79–80; and Lane, *The Socialist Industrial State,* p. 97.

61. Bialer, *The Soviet Paradox,* p. 23.

62. Aleksandr Vasinskii, "Ballada o razlichnykh vzgliadakh," *Izvestiia,* October 28, 1986, p. 3.

2

Sources of Change in Soviet History: State, Society, and the Entrepreneurial Tradition

Sheila Fitzpatrick

History is more important to people and politicians in the Soviet Union than it is in the United States. The interpretation and reinterpretation of Soviet history is part of Soviet political discourse, and the political leaders have always used historical references and analogies to make points about their present policies and future intentions. The educated public listens attentively for nuances in Gorbachev's references to key historical periods and figures such as Lenin, the New Economic Policy (NEP) of the 1920s, Stalin, collectivization and the Twentieth Party Congress in 1956. When Gorbachev or any other Soviet leader makes such historical references, he is assumed to be telling the Soviet public something important about his own policies and position.

However, in the current explosion of *glasnost'*,[1] the many reappraisals and discussions of Soviet history to be found in the Soviet press cannot automatically be treated as elaborations of a Gorbachev "line." To be sure, the discussions do in part reflect Gorbachev's thinking, or what the writers think he is thinking. But the point of *glasnost'* is that people should say what *they* think—that the media should send up signals from below, as well as doing the traditional job of disseminating the signals that come from above. Soviet history is a subject on which Soviet intellectuals have strong opinions, many of which they were unable adequately to express in the pre-*glasnost'* years, and which they regard as particularly relevant to the current restructuring (*perestroika*) of public policy. The mass media and the "thick" journals[2] are in the process of publishing those opinions now.

In Gorbachev's view, *glasnost'* and *perestroika* are inextricably linked: reform programs will not work unless there is broad public participation in their formulation and implementation. *Perestroika* "will only spin its wheels unless the main actor—the people—is included in it in a thoroughgoing way—in the sphere of economics, in the social sphere, in the sphere of politics, in the spiritual sphere, in the sphere of management," Gorbachev has said. "In order to make restructuring irreversible and to prevent a repetition of what happened in the past everything must be placed under the control—once again—of the people. There is only one way to accomplish these tasks—through the broad democratization of Soviet society."[3]

The development of societal and individual initiative is a precondition for successful *perestroika*, according to Gorbachev. "We have resolutely embarked on a course aimed at supporting enterprising, thinking and energetic people, who can and want to advance boldly and know how to achieve success. . . . "[4] He praises innovators and administrators who find ways to put innovation into practice, and risk-taking managers who will bend rules if the rules are impeding progress. The desirability of enterprising (perhaps even entrepreneurial?) leadership in industry has become a favorite topic as the Soviet press examines the implications of *perestroika*.[5]

Although Gorbachev is outlining current policy when he speaks in these terms of initiative and participation, his comments also imply a judgement about the past. The view that societal initiative and popular participation have been a missing element in previous efforts at reform is one that is widely held by Soviet intellectuals, including those who are policy advisors to Gorbachev. Tatiana Zaslavskaia, for example, identifies informed public participation and initiative as a key element in the success of Gorbachev's *perestroika*, in contrast to the abortive reforms under Khrushchev.[6] Behind such comments lie memories of the unusual passivity of Soviet society under Stalin, and, more broadly, an interpretation of Russian history since Peter the Great that emphasizes the active interventionist role of the state in the country's modernization and Westernization.[7]

Thus the problem of initiative—what kinds of initiative were absent or inhibited in the past, what kinds were present, in what ways the relationship of state and society has changed and in what ways it *ought* to change, how initiative can be developed to serve the ends of *perestroika*—has been placed on the agenda of historical discussion in the Soviet Union. Already, at least one collective volume by Soviet historians, addressing the problem from 1917 to the present in the light of *perestroika*, is being prepared for speedy publication. These questions are equally relevant for Western scholars now weighing the prospects of success for Gorbachev's reforms.

This essay explores the subject of change in the Soviet Union from an historical and historian's perspective, isolating two major themes. The first is the historical problem of initiative in the Soviet Union, and its significance for *perestroika*. The second is Soviet reassessment of the different stages of Soviet history in the age of *glasnost'*, and the light it sheds on Gorbachev's policy intentions and the attitudes of the educated Soviet public.

Russian Marxism and Modernization

Marxism in late nineteenth- and early twentieth-century Russia was not only an ideology of revolution. It was also, in practice, an ideology of modernization, emphasizing the necessity of overcoming Russia's backwardness and following the Western pattern of industrialization and economic development. All Russian Marxists agreed that the capitalist phase of development was an essential precursor of their short-term goal, proletarian revolution, as well as their ultimate goal, socialism. Initially, they also agreed that proletarian revolution could occur only after capitalism had matured further than it had in early twentieth-century Russia.

But the Bolsheviks, the most impatient and ambitious of Russia's Marxist revolutionaries, were not content to sit through the whole capitalist cycle in Russia with folded arms. They seized power "prematurely" (in orthodox Marxist terms) in October, 1917. Then, mindful that socialism could not be achieved in a society that was still economically under-developed, they set about industrializing and modernizing the country, using the revolutionary state to direct a process that would normally, according to their analysis, be organized spontaneously by a profit-seeking and exploitative capitalist bourgeoisie.

Although the Bolsheviks would scarcely have acknowledged it, this meant that the new Bolshevik regime was following in the footsteps of its Imperial predecessors, beginning with Peter the Great and culminating in the late nineteenth- and early twentieth-century modernizing ministries of Count Witte and Stolypin. Like them, the Bolsheviks were using the state as the sponsor and driving force of Russia's economic modernization—substituting the entrepreneurial initiative of the state, at least in part, for the initiative of private capitalist entrepreneurs that had provided the dynamic for development in Western Europe and the United States.

The role of the Russian state in fostering economic development was not unique, as the comparable example of early twentieth-century Japan aptly demonstrates. Still, it made a considerable impact on Russian and foreign observers in the late nineteenth and early twentieth

centuries. Russian intellectuals, already disposed to emphasize the remarkable historical role of the Russian state, stressed (indeed, perhaps
too much) the weakness of native entrepreneurial talent and initiative.
Radical intellectuals, who formed a significant proportion of the whole
group, became frantic at the thought of the hopeless inertia and passivity of the society they sought to mobilize against the autocratic
regime. In post-1917 retrospect, it may seem that they not only exaggerated the passivity of Russian society but also made an unjustly
low assessment of their own powers of initiative and organization.

What was unique about the role of the Soviet state in sponsoring
industrialization and economic development was that the new leaders
of the state were Marxist. Despite some bold reworking of Marxist
theory, the Bolsheviks retained a Marxist intellectual framework which
convinced them, in the first place, that capitalism was a normal phase
of the historical progression, and, in the second place, that capitalist
impulses were likely to be spontaneously generated by a society at
Russia's level of economic development. In political terms, these beliefs
were very important. They implied that, as the Bolsheviks used the
state to substitute for capitalist forces, they were going against the
grain of history, and could therefore expect that the natural impulses
of Russian society would continually pull in another direction.

Since the Bolsheviks believed that spontaneous societal impulses
were virtually bound to work against them, their reaction to such
impulses in the first decades of Soviet power was one of deep suspicion
and intense hostility. This led them to insist, in a way that was at
odds with the more popular democratic aspects of their tradition, on
the absolute necessity of rigid state control and, where possible, a
monopolization of initiative by the Communist Party and state organs.

A further consequence was that the Bolsheviks developed a strong
distrust of the very groups in society that might have been their natural
allies in Russia's modernization. They suspected the loyalty of the
traditional professional and technical elite, although many members of
that group were basically in sympathy with Bolshevik objectives of
modernizing and nation-building. They distrusted those peasants who
tried to improve their agricultural techniques, because such peasants—
although less backward than their fellow villagers—might become "kulaks," rural peasant capitalists who exploited other peasants. Objec-
tively, according to the Bolsheviks' Marxist logic, these "bourgeois
specialists" and "kulaks" were instinctive enemies, not allies, of the
new regime, because they were the leaders *manqués* of Russia's putative
capitalist development. Thus, their energy and initiative could only be
used in the most cautious way for the Bolsheviks' modernization drive,

with the Bolsheviks maintaining the greatest vigilance against the possibility of betrayal.

The NEP Model of Change

The New Economic Policy (NEP) was introduced by Lenin in 1921 and remained in force for eight years until the beginning of the First Five-Year Plan in 1929. NEP was a response to the failure of the Bolsheviks' Civil War policies of "War Communism," which had maximized centralized state control of the economy. The introduction of NEP signified the re-legalization of the market, a partial denationalization of industry, and the substitution of a tax in kind on the peasantry for requisitioning. Later, NEP came to acquire broader connotations of social conciliation, tolerance and pluralism in culture.

NEP was not immediately perceived as a developmental model. At the time of its introduction, it was seen as an ideological retreat required by the acute economic crisis and social and political discontent. Before his death in 1924, however, Lenin wrote a series of articles that could be seen as creating a NEP model for development in the direction of socialism, based on gradualism, education and the encouragement of peasant cooperatives. Unfortunately, Lenin did not explain how these policies were also to provide for the rapid industrial growth to which the party was strongly committed.

The debates on capital accumulation for the industrialization of the mid-1920's disclosed the existence of a general assumption among the party's economic theorists that rapid industrialization would only be possible if the regime were prepared to "squeeze" the peasantry, a course that was incompatible with the NEP policy of conciliation. Two distinct viewpoints emerged out of these debates. Bukharin's position was that confrontation with the peasantry must be avoided at all costs, even if it meant proceeding with industrialization at "a snail's pace." The other viewpoint, which came to be associated with Stalin's faction by the late 1920s, was that rapid industrialization was essential, even if it meant squeezing the peasantry and risking major confrontations. The issue was finally resolved at the end of the 1920s with a victory for Stalin and the rapid industrializers and the political defeat of Bukharin.

Another aspect of the arguments over industrialization was the debate on whether it was possible or theoretically acceptable to obtain Western loans and credits. The very existence of such a debate would appear to suggest that the "NEP model" could accommodate economic ties with the outside world and reintegration into the world economic system. In fact, however, Lenin had made any such outcome most unlikely by insisting that no settlement on the question of Tsarist debts could be negotiated, and that the state retain a monopoly on foreign trade.[8] During NEP, the economic isolation of the Soviet Union was less extreme than it would become under Stalin, but was nonetheless significant. Limited foreign investment was possible only under special and rare conditions. With Bolshevik memories of foreign military intervention in the Civil War still fresh, the Western powers were perceived as a chain of capitalist enemies encircling and threatening the existence of the new revolutionary state.

It was only in retrospect, after the gruelling experience of Stalinist forced-pace industrialization and postwar industrial rebuilding, that NEP acquired a benign image for Communists and the "Bukharin alternative" gained nostalgic appeal. At the beginning of the 1920s, most Communists saw NEP as, at least, an ideological retreat and a postponement, if not an absolute shattering, of their revolutionary hopes of social and economic transformation. The party's mood was militant in the NEP years, and the official policy of conciliating the peasantry was constantly undercut by the actions of local Communists who saw the "kulak" (a term often applied to any relatively prosperous peasant) as a class enemy to be destroyed.

NEP was a period of demoralization for the party, comparable in some respects to the Brezhnev period of the 1970s. The new Communist official class was suspected of degenerating politically under the influence of material privilege and contact with the NEP bourgeoisie, and the flourishing of the free-market economy seemed corrupt and distasteful to many revolutionary enthusiasts. It was feared that NEP was the "Thermidor" of the Russian revolution. The cry "What did we fight for?" was frequently raised in the Communist youth organization, the Komsomol, and Communist press, and nostalgia for the heroism of the Civil War period was widespread among Party members.

The Communists' distaste for the economic environment they had created was particularly evident in their treatment of Nepmen—the private businessmen, speculators, commercial facilitators and traders, many of whom were former blackmarketeers of the War Communism period, who formed the "new bourgeoisie." Always uneasy about the possibility of a spontaneous resurgence of capitalism, they feared the Nepmen as its avant-garde, barely tolerated their activities as private entrepreneurs even in the first years of NEP, and looked with great dismay at their growing influence in the working of the public sector.[9] In the mid-1920s, only a few years later, the regime began the process of harrassing and taxing them out of existence, a process that came to be known as "squeezing out the Nepmen."

For all its problems of half-suppressed class and revolutionary hostility, NEP was a relief to the population after the rigors of War Communism. Peasants were freed from Civil War requisitioning of grain, and more or less left alone by the state throughout the 1920s. Educated professionals—the so-called bourgeois specialists, the majority of whom were not Communists and were wary, in fact, of the new regime—experienced less harrassment from Communist officials than either before or immediately after, and benefitted from an increasingly high status and greater material rewards. For the urban middle and lower-middle classes, NEP seemed to be a return to comparative normality after the social and economic revolution, war and hunger that had disrupted their lives in previous years.

In culture and in intellectual life, NEP was a period of comparative freedom of association, with private publishing houses and theaters in operation, and writers, artists and scientists permitted to organize their own, often competing, groups and to maintain contact with their counterparts in the West, and during which state censorship was relatively relaxed. The image of NEP tolerance should not, however, be exaggerated. Cultural groups whose members had belonged to political parties other than the Bolsheviks before the revolution were always at risk from the OGPU, the security police of the NEP period, though the harrassment was much less than that from its predecessor, the Cheka, during the Civil War. Groups with religious affiliations led a precarious existence, and some forms of organization, including church schools and Sunday schools, were not permitted at all. Groups that were part of an international movement, such as the Russian Boy Scouts, found it difficult to survive even in the comparatively permissive climate of NEP.

The Stalinist Model of Change

In contrast to the gradualism of NEP, the First Five-Year Plan (1929–32) inaugurated what Stalin described as "revolution from above." In this model, initiative and planning from the top, supported by the mobilization and coercion of the society were designed to achieve the regime's goals of forced-pace economic development. The goals included rapid industrialization within a framework of centrally planned development, the abolition of the urban private sector, the collectivization of peasant agriculture, an attack on "bourgeois hegemony" in culture and a drive to educate and promote a new cohort of proletarian administrators and specialists.

Forced-pace industrialization demanded major sacrifices from the population. Although enthusiasm existed in some quarters—notably the

Communist Party and its youth branch, the Komsomol, and the younger urban generation in general—the state still needed to use large doses of coercion, as well as to justify the sacrifices in terms of a partly fraudulent imminent threat of renewed foreign intervention. In a much-quoted speech, Stalin said the nation had ten years to fight its way out of economic backwardness or succumb to its enemies. This patriotic theme was a basic underpinning of the whole fortress-storming mentality of the period. The sense of danger and isolation was underscored by the decision in the late '20s to end the search for foreign credits and financial support (a largely futile search, given the earlier decision not to recognize Tsarist debts) and go it alone, with "economic autarky" as the Soviet goal.

In contrast to NEP, when the regime had tended to restrain the militant energies of Communists as well as the possibly pro-capitalist energies of other social groups, the First Five-Year Plan put enormous demands for aggressive, enterprising and ruthless leadership and management on party, industrial and agricultural cadres. While "initiative" (as opposed to bureaucratic formalism and legalism) had always been a quality the leaders have recommended to and prized in the cadres, this quality had never been so highly valued as it was during the First Five-Year Plan.

This was not only because the Plan was ambitious, and the workforce difficult to mobilize for new tasks. It was also because planning, as defined during the First Five-Year Plan period, did not imply detailed allocation of resources and setting of realistic production goals in terms of resources. This was politicians' planning, not planners'. The politicians set unrealistically high targets and exhorted industry to "fulfil and over-fulfil" production quotas, without any serious attempt to calculate what amounts of raw materials, parts, equipment and labor would be necessary to meet the production targets.

That, in turn, meant that industrial and party cadres, in particular, had to become risk-taking, problem-solving entrepreneurs on behalf of the state in order to fulfill the Plan. They could not merely take orders from above, because the orders told them only what targets to meet, not how to meet them. In industry, the manager's authority was buttressed by increasing his powers over labor and decreasing those of the trade unions.

While encouraging a new degree of initiative (albeit sometimes under conditions of panic and desperation) on the part of Communist management, the Stalinist regime dealt harshly with other enterprising social groups, especially those whose activities were potentially capitalist. Not only Nepmen but also all smaller private traders and many artisan manufacturers were driven from business as the entire urban private sector was "liquidated"—or, more precisely, once again pushed into blackmarket status, as it had been under War Communism—at the end of the 1920s; and in the process, many former Nepmen were arrested or forced to flee and start life anew in another town under an assumed name. The liquidation of the private sector, together with the extension of centralized state planning over a large part of the economy, was hailed as a great symbolic victory. Capitalism had now been definitively defeated in Russia, the Communists proclaimed, and the economic base for the building of socialism had been firmly established.

In the drive to "eliminate kulaks as a class" that accompanied the campaign for all-out collectivization of peasant agriculture, more than a million "kulaks" and their families were deported, leaving the villages demoralized, leaderless and without their most enterprising and productive members. At the same time, peasant agriculture was collectivized, against the will of the majority of the peasants. This enabled the state to extend its hitherto shaky control over the village, impose fixed low prices for agricultural produce, and set compulsory quotas for delivery.

Another potentially enterprising group that found itself severely harrassed at this time was the educated professional class, especially engineers. Still largely non-Communist and skeptical about what they saw as the regime's over-ambitious timetables and targets, this group was nevertheless not unsympathetic to the First Five-Year Plan. However, this did not prevent the regime from arresting a significant number of engineering specialists and senior experts in the industrial ministries as "wreckers" and "saboteurs," in league with foreign capitalists. The harrassment extended from engineers to the "bourgeois" intelligentsia as a whole. Most professional and special-purpose organizations and associations were either closed entirely or placed under closer party control at this time. The Russian intelligentsia's traditional pretensions to moral leadership were subjected to harsh criticism, and a crash plan came into effect to train a new cohort of "proletarian intelligentsia" whose lower-class origins, youth and commitment to the revolution were supposed to make them more reliable supporters of the party's goals.

The "cultural revolution" of the First Five-Year Plan period (similar in many substantive respects, as well as in name, to the one Communist China was to experience in the 1960s) left the old Russian intelligentsia intimidated, demoralized and, within a decade, numerically overwhelmed by an influx of new young professionals, many of lower-class origins and dubious educational backgrounds, a large proportion of whom were members of the Communist Party. But the episode left a deep psychological scar on the professionals who identified with the old intelligentsia, and was particularly daunting to them in their exercise of initiative in any field, for fear of being accused of sabotage.

Stalinism and the Question of Societal Initiative

The totalitarian model, which has often been applied to the Stalinist system that emerged in the 1930s in the wake of upheavals of the First Five-Year Plan and collectivization, depicts it as innately and systemically opposed to any form of societal initiative. Society, according to the totalitarian model, is something to be manipulated, molded and mobilized by the regime. It has no power of independent action, and the regime has "atomized" it, destroying all accessible associational bonds except the universal bond of state citizenship, in order to maximize control and achieve the regime's goals.

While this picture is doubtless overdrawn,[10] there can be little doubt that Soviet society in the 1930s and 1940s was incoherent and lacked strong associational groups and capacity for internal organization. This was partly a result of the state's coercive actions (for example, the removal of the most active stratum of the peasantry in the kulak deportations and the intimidation of the intelligentsia in the cultural revolution). But it was also the product of the great social and geographical mobility accompanying rapid industrialization and urbanization in the 1930s, and, in the late 1940s, the enormous demographic upheavals associated with the Second World War.

During the period 1929 to 1953, the Soviet Union was transformed from a population that was more than four-fifths rural to one not much more than half rural. By the beginning of the 1960s, the urban population had risen above 50 percent. Urban society itself experienced an abnormally high rate of upward mobility from blue-collar to white-collar, professional and administrative jobs as the country rapidly industrialized.[11] Under these circumstances, it is not surprising that institutions such as trade unions were weak, and that the new professional and administrative elites were non-assertive vis-à-vis the regime.

State coercion, although not the only factor contributing to social passivity, must be seriously considered in attempting to identify the impediments to individual and group initiative in the Stalinist system. For the peasantry, collectivization imposed many restraints and created new rigidities that were not wholly dissimilar to those that had existed for the enserfed peasantry in Russia before the 1861 Emancipation. Peasant out-migration was even restricted by law (although by no means eliminated in fact) from December, 1932, when peasant flight to the towns to escape famine in the countryside led the regime to introduce the requirement of internal passports and a restrictive registration system for urban residents.

Arrest, jail and sentences to labor camp were common experiences in all sectors of the population, and it was also common for individuals to be arrested or fired from their jobs without any connection with a specific criminal act but because of membership in a particular social group. As Solzhenitsyn has described in *The Gulag Archipelago,* Stalinist terror came in waves, and the waves broke over different segments of the population at different times: Nepmen, kulaks and, to a lesser extent, the old intelligentsia at the end of the 1920s; members of the elite, particularly Communist officials but also non-Communist professionals, in the Great Purges of 1937–38; the returning POWs and members of various non-Russian nationalities after the Second World War.

Freedom of association (even in the qualified sense in which it had existed during NEP) disappeared at the beginning of the 1930s, and the so-called voluntary organizations for youth, sports and cultural activities were under firm state control, and often used for purposes of mobilization. Censorship was severe, with adverse effects on initiative in the cultural and intellectual sphere. Public life in all its aspects became increasingly ritualized and artificial. The borders of the Soviet Union were tightly closed against the outside world, and citizens needed special permission to enter frontier zones.

The end of the cultural revolution of the First Five-Year Plan period seemed for a short time in the early 1930s to promise relaxation and greater tolerance of cultural diversity. These hopes, however, were quickly dashed. Almost all creative and intellectual fields developed their own "orthodoxies" of style and content—not necessarily specifically Marxist, but no less stultifying for that. Some fields found themselves under the rule of local intellectual dictators like Lysenko. In the mid-1930s, a campaign against formalism and Western modernism foreshadowed the anti-Westernism of the postwar period and emphasized the increasing isolation of Soviet cultural and intellectual life from the West.

The intelligentsia, severely intimidated by cultural revolution at the beginning of the 1930s, received a second dose of terror in the Great Purges of 1937–38. True, the professional elite as a whole—engineers and artists, Communists and non-Communists, former "proletarians" and former "bourgeois"—gained status and material privileges in the course of the 1930s, and this meant that the taming of the old "bourgeois" intelligentsia was achieved by a mixture of carrot and stick. But the process left the group with an uneasy conscience, isolated in its privileged but dependent position, and no longer confident of the moral authority to which it had traditionally laid claim.

Despite the general rigidity and restraints on initiative of the 1930s, however, certain types of initiative were extravagantly celebrated, while others were functionally necessary either for survival or for success in certain kinds of jobs. The press celebrated the daring exploits of aviators and polar explorers, whose adventurous spirit was held up for emulation. "Stakhanovite" workers were applauded not only for over-fulfilling their quotas but also for finding ways of breaking out of routines and making production more efficient. Peasants, especially peasant women, were encouraged to become Stakhanovites of the collective farm, which often involved well-publicized defiance of the conservative authority of husbands and fathers.

Although the party's administrative and managerial cadres were under slightly less pressure to meet unrealistic production targets after 1932, their jobs still required the kind of aggressive, entrepreneurial qualities that had emerged during the First Five-Year Plan. Management, especially industrial management, was the real focal point of initiative and enterprise in the Stalinist system.[12] The big Soviet industrialists of the 1930s were larger-than-life figures, lauded in the Soviet press as *bogatyri* (knights) of Stalin's industrialization, who were fired with devotion to Stalin and the building of socialism, ready to perform heroic feats and overcome seemingly impossible obstacles to fulfill the Plan.

Economic entrepreneurship in the strict sense of individual profit-oriented activity took place within what has come to be called "the second economy" during the Stalin period, as it had done during War Communism. The "second economy" included the black-marketeering and speculative buying and re-selling that were not only widespread but also inevitable in an economy where basic goods were rationed (as they were in Soviet cities from 1929 to 1935, and again from 1941 to 1947) or in extremely scarce supply. Almost everyone working in the official trading network was involved to some extent in the second economy (indeed, many were former private traders from the NEP period). This same type of wheeling and dealing, on behalf of enterprises rather than individuals, also took place within state industry, which was part of the "first economy." State industry could not have functioned without the "fixers" (*tolkachi*), whose job it was to find and procure (by whatever legal or informal means) the raw materials, machines, spare parts and other goods that the plant needed. (In principle, these were allocated under the Plan, but in practice the enterprises often had to use their own ingenuity.)

Change in the Post-Stalin Period

Stalin's death in 1953 produced an almost immediate relaxation and policy changes in a number of spheres. Concessions were made to the collectivized peasantry, tentative overtures made to the West, and the release of political prisoners from the gulag began. The change of atmosphere, known as "the thaw" after the title of Ilia Ehrenburg's novel, was most evident in intellectual and cultural life. Writers and other members of the intelligentsia began to speak out against the artistic constraints and intellectual dishonesty that had prevailed under Stalin, especially in the postwar campaign against "cosmopolitanism" and Western influences in culture. Despite a series of setbacks and rebukes, *Novyi mir,* a journal edited by the poet Tvardovsky, took the lead by publishing works like Dudintsev's *Not by Bread Alone,* which described the trials of an innovative scientist in conflict with an oppressive and self-satisfied bureaucracy.

In 1956, Khrushchev made his famous Secret speech to the Twentieth Party Congress denouncing Stalin's crimes. Although the scope of Khrushchev's criticism was essentially limited to the victimization of Communists in the Great Purges and Stalin's failings as a wartime leader, the effect on the Soviet and other Communist elites was dramatic. In Eastern Europe, news of the Secret Speech plunged Hungary and Poland into turmoil. In the Soviet Union, Communists were forced to confront issues from the past that many of the older generation of cadres (whose promotions had come in the wake of the Great Purges) might have preferred to forget.

Educated professionals, particularly those who identified with the moral traditions of the old Russian intelligentsia, were heartened and excited, and threw themselves with fervor into the campaign of de-Stalinization that followed Khrushchev's speech. For students and other young people, this was a period of intense excitement and enthusiasm, epitomized by the mass poetry readings at which daring young poets such as Voznesensky and Yevtushenko read from their works.

The mood of the intelligentsia, its cultural heroes and even many of the controversial issues raised in the late 1950s and the first half of the 1960s were, in many respects, remarkably similar to those that have reappeared in the mid 1980s.[13] One important difference, however, was that the forces *resisting* change in the Khrushchev period were either much stronger or much more frightening to the supporters of change than are their counterparts in the 1980s. Another difference was that in the Khrushchev period only a minority of the mass media and thick journals was firmly in the camp of the reformers, in contrast

to the present pro-*glasnost'* majority, if not monopoly, in the media
of the 1980s.

In the early 1960s, the best-known of the thick journals, *Novyi mir,*
battled to expand the sphere of permissible discussion. Under the
editorship of Tvardovsky, it published works such as Solzhenitsyn's
One Day in the Life of Ivan Denisovich, thereby opening public discussion on the labor camps, and the memoirs of the writer, Ilia
Ehrenburg, which were the first to use NEP as an image of cultural
freedom and discussion of NEP as a way of condemning Stalinist
repression. But *Novyi mir* came under heavy attack from other journals
and newspapers as well as from the cultural bureaucracy and part of
the political leadership. It was unable to publish Solzhenitsyn's later
works, despite bitter and protracted struggles.

A dissident movement, using *samizdat,*[14] emigre journals and contacts
with the Western press instead of official Soviet publications to dis-
seminate its message, emerged within the intelligentsia, partly in response to the difficulties encountered by such reform-minded journals
as *Novyi mir* operating within the normal Soviet context. Needless to
say, the dissident movement was viewed with great alarm by the Soviet
authorities, and with an equal degree of excitement and encouragement
in the West. Because of the dissidents' Western and émigré links, and
their gilded-youth reputation, there was never a realistic possibility of
their gaining wide popular support in Russia, even before the movement
was compromised by association with the Jewish emigration issue in
U.S.-Soviet relations in the early 1970s.

Nevertheless, some of the dissidents' feelings were widely shared by
educated Russians, frustrated by cultural constraints and insufficient
access to the West. Even *Novyi mir* found it increasingly difficult to
maintain its stance of Communist "loyal opposition," especially after
Solzhenitsyn, *Novyi mir*'s most controversial author, crossed over to
the dissident side. In a remarkable description of the plight of the
intellectuals of the late 1960s and 1970s who were critical of the regime,
but not open dissidents, Evtushenko writes that although the reformers
"penetrated the fortress," they then found themselves isolated from
contact with their fellows:

> Foreign helicopters began circling over our heads, hospitably lowering
> rope ladders that swayed enticingly over our heads. But only the weak
> ones clambered up them, exchanging the struggle for liberty in their
> fatherland for Radio Liberty.[15]

In matters of government and administration, Khrushchev himself
was a reformer. But his reforms appeared to his critics to be "hare-

brained schemes"; and he alienated a large part of the Communist bureaucratic elite by his efforts to change the administrative structure: first, through the creation of regional economic administrations (a blow to the entrenched government economic ministries, as well as bringing the threat of relocation to the provinces to many of their personnel), and later by his scheme to bifurcate the party, state and trade-union bureaucracies into parallel industrial and agricultural lines. Many older Communist officials doubtless resented his dethroning of Stalin and the threat to their own positions and the values inherent in de-Stalinization.

Khrushchev's reforming impulses included an effort to increase popular participation in government and to stimulate societal initiative. He tried to revitalize the soviets, announced his intention of taking some functions away from the state, launched a partly successful volunteer-mobilization drive for settlement and cultivation of the virgin lands, and encouraged the creation of volunteer groups (*druzhinniki*) for the maintenance of public order, with the ultimate aim of turning over all police functions to such bodies.

But these attempts to stimulate societal initiative were unsuccessful. In the first place, the Stalinist tradition of highly formalized "voluntary" activity cast a shadow over Khrushchev's initiatives in this area: for many educated Russians, the very term "voluntary organization" had come to suggest something fake, a regime project fraudulently represented as popular participation. Khrushchev had little sympathy for the idea that different sectors of society might want to organize groups to fit their own individual interests, let alone defend or promote them. As one Western scholar has remarked, he had a monolithic sense of popular participation,[16] and continued to assume that the basic purpose of a voluntary organization was to further the state's goals or, in the parlance of Khrushchev's youth, "to serve the Revolution."

After Khrushchev's fall in 1964, and particularly after the ineffective economic reforms of the mid 1960s associated with Kosygin's name, the pace of change slackened. Retrospectively, the Brezhnev era has been labelled a period of social and economic stagnation, bureaucratic corruption (which apparently emerged for the first time since NEP as a major problem and source of popular indignation), and cynicism and demoralization within the intelligentsia.

Yet standards of living improved markedly (although rates of economic growth began to drop), and luxuries such as private cars, dachas, television sets and washing machines became much more widely available than before. The second economy, or black market in goods and services, flourished in the 1970s, and was granted a surprising degree of tolerance by the regime.[17]

Small groups of dissidents from the intelligentsia remained in contact with Western journalists throughout the Brezhnev period, and there was a steady rise in circulation through *samizdat* of literary, historical and other manuscripts not approved by the censor. The dissemination among the younger generation of Western-style popular culture, from blue jeans to rock music, also increased markedly in the 1970s.

Less noticed in the West, but perhaps equally significant in the long term, were signs of change in the professional elite and its relationship with government. There was a great expansion of the group known as "scientific workers" (meaning non-teaching scholars, researchers and professionals in all fields, including the social sciences).[18] Public debate by specialists on policy issues became more prominent in the mass media as well as the specialized journals, and experts from social science research institutes began to play a more prominent and visible role as consultants to government and party agencies. The 1970s also saw the rise of special interest movements and groups of professionals concerned about issues such as environmental protection and restoration of historic buildings, including churches.

In addition, World War II veterans, who had had no official association until 1956, became increasingly active in the 1970s, apparently largely as the result of spontaneous organization[19] at the local level, among men who had served in the same units. This was a movement that cut across class, rather than being associated specifically with professionals. Unlike the environmental and historic restoration movements, it was patriotic in spirit and had no quasi-dissident overtones.

Reinterpretation of Soviet History
Under *Glasnost'*

One of the leading advocates of *glasnost'*, the historian Iurii Afanasev,[20] identifies two periods of Soviet history as having special relevance and exemplary force for the present. The first is the period he calls "under Lenin," designated 1917–1929 by Afanasev (although Lenin died in 1924) in order to extend Lenin's mantle over the entire NEP period. The second is the period "after Stalin," designated 1956–65 by Afanasev, and thus roughly covering the Khrushchev period.[21] Notably absent from Afanasev's discussion is the quarter century between "under Lenin" and "after Stalin."

This focus on NEP and the positive evaluation of it is not new in Soviet historical debates. In fact, it was the chief characteristic of the historical revisionism of the early 1960s, although that revisionist trend was interrupted and partly silenced in mid course. Then, as now, the thrust of the revival of NEP was anti-Stalinist. In the 1960s, there was talk of an official rehabilitation of Bukharin, Stalin's political opponent of the late 1920's, although this never came about. In connection with the debate on economic reform of the mid 1960s, there was also much private discussion about the "NEP alternative" and the "Bukharin alternative."[22]

Bukharin has still not been officially rehabilitated,* but in terms of historical discourse this now seems less important than in the past, since not only Bukharin but also other previously unmentionable leaders of the political oppositions of the 1920's have reappeared on the historical stage.[23]

Meanwhile, the "Bukharin alternative" has been presented in detail for readers of the widely disseminated weekly, *Literary Gazette*. In a recent issue, the magazine's political commentator, Fedor Burlatsky, a leading advisor under Khrushchev, wrote an extended dramatic dialogue between an imaginary Stalinist and Bukharinist at the end of the 1920s which gives the Bukharinist the best of the argument and allows him to lay plausible claim to Lenin's heritage.[24]

There are a number of reasons why NEP should attract particular attention from policymakers in the 1980s. First, NEP represents market relations and the legalization of the second economy. Gorbachev has already moved in this direction with the laws on individual and cooperative enterprises. In addition, NEP, cherished by the intelligentsia as a golden age of intellectual freedom, is an appropriate symbol of *glasnost'*.

Despite its symbolic value, one might suspect that the actual historical NEP of the 1920s—economically primitive, survival-oriented, already partly cut off from the West—is less interesting to Soviet economists of today than are the NEP-type reforms that have taken place in the past two decades in socialist states such as Hungary and China.

This, however, is vehemently denied by one economist, Nikolai Shmelev, whose bold article in the June 1986 issue of *Novyi mir* aroused much attention and controversy in the Soviet Union. Shmelev is an uncompromising advocate of "the 1980s model of the New Economic Policy." "Without acknowledgement of the fact that rejection of the Leninist new economic policy complicated the building of socialism in the USSR in the severest way, we will once again, as in 1953 and in 1965, doom ourselves to half-hearted measures, and, as is well known, half-hearted measures are often worse than none at all,"

---

*Bukharin's official rehabilitation occurred in February 1988, just before this book went to press [Ed.].

he writes. Two kinds of socialism have been attempted in the Soviet Union—a socialism based on administrative coercion (as in War Communism and the Stalin period), and a socialism based on cost-accounting that recognizes the significance of the "human factor" (NEP). It is time to recognize the superiority of the second, according to Shmelev, and decisively reject the elements of "Stalinism in action" that remain embedded in the Soviet system.[25]

Assessment of the Stalin period in the *glasnost'*-oriented press is almost universally negative. As is often the case in Soviet intellectual life, novelists and poets have led the way in recent criticism of Stalinism.[26] Works such as Rybakov's long-awaited *Children of the Arbat* and Trifonov's *Disappearance,* both dealing with the Great Purges, have aroused widespread comment, admiration and enthusiasm among the educated public. As befits the 1980s, film has also played an important de-Stalinizing role. The Georgian director Tengis Abuladze's *Repentance* (a condemnation of Stalin's terror and the Great Purges) was given mass release in cinemas throughout the Soviet Union in the first half of 1987.[27] The Great Purges are not the only Stalinist topic to be subjected to critical examination and condemnation. Other literary works that have recently appeared deal critically with such subjects as collectivization, repression in the cultural and intellectual field, and the deportation of ethnic groups during World War II.

Journalists and historians have begun discussing the theme of Stalinist bureaucratization, often taking literary-sociological works such as Aleksandr Bek's novel *New Appointment* (finally published after many years of *samizdat* existence) and Rybakov's *Children of the Arbat* as their point of departure.[28] This theme is familiar to the Western public as the leitmotif of Trotsky's *The Revolution Betrayed,* published in 1937 after his expulsion from the Soviet Union. In the post-1956 period, it became popular with European Marxists, including members of Western and Eastern European Communist parties, who have no doubt helped its dissemination (until now, mainly through *samizdat*) in the Soviet Union. Current Soviet treatments of this theme often legitimate their arguments by citing Lenin as an early critic of Stalin's bureaucratic tendencies.[29]

The Khrushchev period is often recalled sympathetically by pro-*glasnost'* writers. As Aleksei Adzhubei (Khrushchev's son-in-law, and influential editor of *Izvestiia* in the Khrushchev years) comments, "many people now believe that the 20th Party Congress and the 27th Party Congress (1986) have common characteristics"; he is currently writing his memoirs on the period which will be published next year.[30] A writer in *Pravda* recently stated that Khrushchev initiated a drive for democratization, although it lacked "system and purpose." Its failure was the result of opposition to reform on the part of conservative bureaucrats.[31]

Those who write on the Khrushchev era, especially in its de-Stalinization aspect, often dwell on the excitement they felt as students in the 1950s and their nostalgia for the hopes and idealism of their youth. The theme of "thirty lost years" between the first post-Stalin thaw and the Gorbachev era of *glasnost'* is a recurrent one.[32] Some, like the poet Evtushenko, note that the students of the 1950s and early 1960s who grew up with de-Stalinization have now become middle-aged officials, as well as middle-aged intellectuals, and hope that this generation of senior bureaucrats has a different psychology from its predecessors.[33] But this is an unusually optimistic view of the bureaucracy, which is generally portrayed as a bastion of conservatism and inertia, and the main obstacle to reform in the 1980s as well as the 1960s. Recalling the period after the Twentieth Party Congress in 1956, the political commentator Aleksandr Bovin writes:

> My generation and I watched with bewilderment, pain and a disgusting sense of our own impotence, as the ideas of one of the most historic congresses of our party kept seeping through the bureaucratic sand.[34]

The new interpretations of Soviet history cited above come from intellectuals: historians, social scientists, journalists, writers. They speak in the name of *glasnost'*; and without *glasnost'* they would not be speaking as they do. But even those who are political commentators or expert consultants to the political leadership are not necessarily spokesmen for Gorbachev and the Politburo. They respond to signals from the political leadership, but they are also trying to influence its course.

The Soviet intellectuals who have taken the initiative under *glasnost'* probably sympathize with Gorbachev's political agenda. But they also have a particular agenda of their own: in the tradition of the prerevolutionary Russian intelligentsia, they want to assert their right to be society's moral leaders and truth-tellers.[35] This is a major theme in the film *Repentance,* in which the artist Sandro (who looks and behaves very much as a Christ figure) stands up to the tyrant Varlam in the name of truth and beauty. It is also present in Dudintsev's new novel *Robed in White,* which takes a similar theme to his 1956 success *Not by Bread Alone* but portrays the positive heroes in even more exalted terms. In an interview with Adzhubei, Dudintsev explained his title:

> Throughout the long history of human culture the morally superior people, the heroes who saved the city, the cloister of humanity, from evil forces,

were always robed in white. It is written in the Apocalypse: 'These men that are robed in white—who are they and from where do they come?' The answer comes—they 'have passed through the great ordeal'. . . . [36]

For Dudintsev and those who think as he does, *glasnost'* is the mechanism by which the intelligentsia is able to robe itself in white once again and challenge the Stalinist-bureaucratic forces of evil. History, in this Manichean view, is a battlefield of the forces of good and evil, illustrated in the Soviet period as the NEP principle and the Stalinist principle. The historian has the choice of robing himself in white and telling the truth about Soviet history, or succumbing to evil pressures and endorsing "non-truth" (*nepravda*).

This approach to history is uncongenial to many Soviet citizens who are not of the intelligentsia. Judging from the summaries of letters to the editor published from time to time in the press, ordinary Russians are uneasy about the new *glasnost'*. Letters to the editor rarely mention NEP (which is too distant for most people to remember), but often protest against undue denigration of the achievements of the 1930's and 1940's, mentioning enthusiasm, heroic struggle and sacrifice, and a sense of national purpose among the characteristics of the Stalin period.[37] Soviet politicians, accordingly, are likely to be more cautious in their reappraisal of Soviet history than the intelligentsia would prefer.

Retrospect on the Seventieth Anniversary of the Revolution

In his major speech on Soviet history for the seventieth anniversary of the revolution, Gorbachev devoted relatively little attention to the NEP period. While noting that "these days, we turn more often to the last works of Lenin, to Lenin's new economic policy," and recommending the NEP food tax as a policy worth contemporary study and possible emulation, he seemed less excited about NEP as a model than many Soviet commentators. "Certainly," he stated (implicitly disagreeing with NEP's most enthusiastic recent advocates), "it would be a mistake to equate the new economic policy and what we are doing now at a fundamentally new level of development."[38]

Contrary to many intellectuals' hopes before the speech, Gorbachev did not give Bukharin a full rehabilitation, and said that in the economic debates of the late '20s "Bukharin and his followers had . . . underrated the practical significance of the time factor in building socialism in the 30s."[39] Indeed, modernization "at a snail's pace" (Bukharin's phrase of the 1920s) seems out of keeping with Gorbachev's sense of urgency about the move into high technology of the 1980s and '90s. Gorbachev's calls for an economic breakthrough and dire warnings about the consequences of delay[40] have been more reminiscent of the First Five-Year Plan—even of Stalin's warning that the Soviet Union must catch up or go under[41]—than of NEP.

As far as the Stalin period is concerned, Gorbachev had already expressed unqualified condemnation of the Great Purges: "I believe that we can never and must never forgive or justify what happened in 1937–1938. Never. Those who were then in power are responsible for it."[42] He had also condemned the "authoritarian assessments" of the 1930's and 1940's that stifled "lively discussion and creative thought."[43] But he had spoken positively of some aspects of the Stalin period, for example, the initiative and enthusiasm of the early Stakhanovites (workers exceeding their norms) of the 1930s,[44] and repeatedly suggested that the Stalinist period left a mixed legacy, with pluses as well as minuses.[45]

In the seventieth anniversary speech, Gorbachev noted the "atmosphere of intolerance, hostility, and suspicion" in the country under Stalin, and deplored "the absence of a proper level of democratization in the Soviet society that made possible . . . the wanton repressive measures of the '30s." These were "real crimes stemming from an abuse of power," he stated; and, moreover, Stalin knew about the crimes. As he had done before, Gorbachev went further than Khrushchev in identifying the intelligentsia as well as the Communist Party as a target of the Great Purges,[46] and he announced that the Politburo had set up a fact-finding commission on the Purges to complete the work interrupted in the mid-1960s. But Gorbachev had warm words for Khrushchev: "it required no small courage of the party and its leadership, headed by Nikita Khrushchev, to criticize the personality cult and its consequences and to re-establish socialist legality."[47]

One of the most interesting parts of Gorbachev's assessment of the past in the seventieth anniversary speech dealt with collectivization. The Stalinist method of centralized command which produced results in industry "was impermissible in tackling the problems of refashioning rural life," Gorbachev said. There were excesses in collectivization; "there was a departure from Lenin's policy towards the peasantry." Nevertheless, collectivization remained a cornerstone of the system in Gorbachev's analysis, which relegated individual peasant farming firmly to the past.[48]

Comrades, if we assess the significance of collectivization as a whole in consolidating socialism in the countryside, it was in the final analysis a transformation of fundamental importance.[49]

Stalin was "an extremely contradictory personality," Gorbachev said. "We have to see both Stalin's incontestable contribution to the struggle for socialism, to the defense of its gains," and "the gross political errors" and abuses committed by him and his associates.[50] But the Stalin period, despite those errors, remained basically a time of achievement.[51] "That was when the world's first socialist society had its beginnings, when it was being built. It was an exploit on a historical scale and of historic significance."[52]

Notes

1. Openness in culture and access to information.

2. Non-specialist journals for the educated public, publishing articles on social, historical, economic and current-interest topics as well as fiction and poetry.

3. Speech of Gorbachev to the 18th Congress of Trade Unions, *Pravda,* February 26, 1987.

4. Speech to January plenum of the Central Committee of the Soviet Communist Party, January 27, 1987, published in *Pravda,* January 28, 1987.

5. See, for example, articles in *Literaturnaia gazeta,* 24 June 1987, p. 10, and 8 July 1987, p. 10; and *Moscow News,* 1987, no. 22 (June 7–14), p. 12. Note also the recent statement of Soviet interest in publishing Lee Iacocca's inspirational memoirs of a life in capitalist management (*Newsweek,* September 7, 1978, p. 5.).

6. "In comparison with the Khrushchev era, much has changed," Zaslavskaia recently told Western reporters (The *New York Times,* 28 August 1987, p. 4). "There are no longer the dark masses which could be ruled easily, whose minds could be controlled. There are thinking people, who have been educated in how socialism ought to be, and they want it that way."

7. In a Russian intellectual context, this view owes much to the Russian historians of the late Imperial period, who saw state monopolization of initiative and societal passivity as a national characteristic, manifested particularly in the Petrine reforms of the early eighteenth century. The totalitarian model (see the section on "Stalinism and the Question of Societal Initiative"), popular with Western Sovietologists of the postwar period, applies a more extreme version of this concept to Soviet history, especially the Stalin period. Although still basically unacceptable in public Soviet debate about Soviet history, the totalitarian model is not unknown to Soviet intellectuals, and in some circles has acquired a certain radical chic in the age of *glasnost'.*

8. For a discussion of contemporary Soviet "protectionism" in historical context, see Jerry F. Hough, *Russia and the West: The Politics of Gorbachev's Reform* (New York: Simon and Schuster, forthcoming 1988).

9. During NEP, as (illegally) under War Communism, the most profitable forms of private enterprise involved working across the boundary line between public and private sectors, and moving goods and materials from one part of

the public sector to another. To facilitate these activities, Nepmen cultivated contacts and sometimes even held appointments in state industrial trusts and marketing syndicates.

10. For a discussion of the recent arguments against the use of the totalitarian model in Soviet studies, see Abbott Gleason, "'Totalitarianism' in 1984," *Russian Review*, vol. 43 (1984), pp. 145–59.

11. On the general question of upward mobility in the Stalin period, see my article "The Russian Revolution and Social Mobility: A Re-examination of the Question of Social Support for the Soviet Regime in the 1920's and 1930's," *Politics and Society*, Fall, 1984.

12. On the qualities of Soviet managers and the context in which they operated in the Stalin period, see two excellent Western studies: Joseph Berliner, *Factory and Manager in the USSR* (Cambridge, Mass., 1957) and David Granick, *Management of the Industrial Firm in the USSR* (New York, 1954). For a lively fictional representation of a postwar Soviet industrial manager, see Vera Panova's novel, *Kruzhilikha*, first published in 1947.

13. This similarity is often noted by commentators on *glasnost'*. For an example of 1960s nostalgia, see the interview with culture heroes of the Khrushchev period—the poets Evtushenko and Voznesenskii and the chansonnier Okudzhava—published with cover picture in the popular illustrated magazine *Ogonek*, 1987, no. 9 (Feb.), p. 30.

14. *"Samizdat"* is the term for unofficial reproduction and circulation of manuscripts that came into common use in the Khrushchev period.

15. *Ogonek*, 1987, no. 9 (Feb.), p. 30.

16. George W. Breslauer, "Khrushchev Reconsidered," *Problems of Communism*, vol. 25, no. 5 (September-October 1976), pp. 28–29.

17. This has been described as Brezhnev's "little deal" with the administrative and professional middle class: see James R. Millar, "The Little Deal: Brezhnev's Contribution to Acquisitive Socialism," *Slavic Review*, vol. 44, no. 4 (Winter, 1985), pp. 694–706.

18. There are now almost 1.5 million persons classified as "scientific workers" (meaning scholars, researchers and professionals in all fields of learning) in the Soviet Union. Their numbers almost quadrupled in the course of the 1960s and 1970s. *SSSR v tsifrakh v 1983 g. Kratkii statisticheskii sbornik* (Moscow, 1984), pp. 76 and 172; *Narodnoe obrazovanie, nauka i kul'tura. Statisticheskii sbornik* (Moscow, 1971), pp. 233 and 248.

19. Official recognition and praise for the veterans' movement came much later, starting in the early 1980's. The creation of a new All-Union Organization of War and Labor Veterans, evidently intended to build on the existing foundations, was announced at the end of 1986 (*Moscow News*, 1986, no. 52, p. 3).

20. Afanasev was appointed Rector of the State Historical-Archival Institute toward the end of 1986. Not a Soviet historian himself (his field is historiography), he has been highly critical of existing work on Soviet history. According to S. G. Wheatcroft, who has given the fullest account to date of developments in the historical profession, Iurii Afanasev is the brother of the

present editor of *Pravda,* V. G. Afanasev: Wheatcroft, "Unleashing the Energy of History: Moscow, 1987," *Australian Slavonic and East European Studies,* vol. 1, no. 1 (1987), p. 95.

21. Interview with Afanasev by T. Menshikova, *Sovetskaia kul'tura,* March 21, 1987, summarized in *Current Digest of the Soviet Press,* vol. 39, no. 12 (1987), p. 1.

22. See Moshe Lewin, *Political Undercurrents in Soviet Economic Debates. From Bukharin to the Modern Reformers* (Princeton, 1974).

23. The metaphor can be taken literally in this case: Bolshevik leaders of the revolution and Civil War period who later became Oppositionists are among the chief *dramatis personae* in Mikhail Shatrov's plays, the most recent of which is *Dictatorship of Conscience,* currently playing in Moscow. For a signal from Gorbachev on the resurrection of former oppositionists, see his remarks that "we must not forget names" and there should be no more "blank pages" in history (*Pravda,* 14 February 1987).

24. *Literaturnaia gazeta,* 22 July 1987, p. 11. Burlatsky's article, along with the Afanasev interview (see n. 20), the article by Shmelev (see n. 25) and the general trend towards a Bukharin revival are criticized by N. Melnichenko, deputy director of the Ukrainian Institution of party history, in *Pravda Ukrainy,* 31 July 1987.

25. Nikolai Shmelev, "Credits and debts," *Novyi mir,* 1987 no. 6, pp. 142–158.

26. The professional historians who specialize in the Stalin period seem less prepared, though not necessarily less willing, to illuminate subjects like the Great Purges. See, for example, the report of historian Iu. S. Borisov's lecture "Stalin—man and symbol" and the much more informative comments on the Great Purges from the floor in the emigre newspaper *Russkaia mysl',* 29 May 1987, pp. 5–6.

27. For a sample of the enthusiastic reaction of reviewers to Abuladze's film and the socio-political significance attached to it, see *Current Digest of the Soviet Press,* vol. 39, no. 5, pp. 1–7.

28. For example, the review of Bek's *Novoe naznachenie* by G. Popov in *Nauka i zhizn', 1987 no. 4,* and the review of Rybakov's *Deti Arbata* by A. Turkov in *Literaturnaia gazeta,* 8 July 1987, p. 4.

29. See, for example, the interview with Dr. A. Butenko in *Moskovskaia pravda,* 7 May 1987, p. 3.

30. Publication of Adzhubei's "Those 10 Years" in the journal *Znamia* was announced in the journal's August 1987 issue.

31. G. Smirnov, *Pravda,* March 13, 1987, pp. 2–3.

32. See, for example, Igor Dedkov, "A Discourse about One Generation," *Moscow News,* 1987, no. 16 (April 19), p. 2; Aleksandr Bovin, quoted in *New York Times,* 30 January 1987, p. 1.

33. *Ogonek,* 1987, no. 9, p. 30. See also Evtushenko's interview with an Italian journalist, reported in Foreign Broadcast Information Service, *Daily Report—Soviet Union,* 29 Jan. 1986, p. 6.

34. Quoted by Bill Keller in *New York Times,* 30 January 1987, p. 1.

35. See A. I. Volodin, "On the traditions of our country's intelligentsia," *Pravda,* March 10, 1987, p. 3. Volodin identifies civic spirit and moral commitment as the essence of the "true" Russian intelligentsia. "Philistine" and "petty-bourgeois" attitudes are its antonym.

36. *Moscow News,* 1987, no. 1 (Jan. 11–18), p. 11.

37. See, for example, L. Kurin, "The people will tell the truth," *Pravda,* 23 July 1987, p. 3.

38. Speech of 2 November 1987, *New York Times,* 3 November 1987, p. 5.

39. Speech of 2 November, *loc. cit.,* p. 6. In an interview with correspondent Bill Keller (*New York Times,* 3 November 1987, p. 4), Burlatsky struck a positive note and said that he was now 90 percent sure that the dramatization of his dialogues between a Stalinist and a Bukharinist (see the section on "Reinterpretation of Soviet History Under Glasnost'") would be approved for television showing. Nevertheless, it is hard to believe that Burlatsky and other Bukharin advocates were not disappointed by Gorbachev's treatment of the issue.

40. See, for example, Gorbachev's speech "The basic question of the country's economic policy," 11 June 1985, in M. S. Gorbachev, *Izbrannye rechi i stat'i* (Moscow, 1985), pp. 108–36.

41. See the section on "The Stalinist Model of Change."

42. Speech at meeting with leaders of media and creative unions in Central Committee, *Pravda,* 16 July 1987, p. 2.

43. Speech to the January plenum of the Central Committee, *Pravda,* 28 January 1987, translated in *Current Digest of the Soviet Press,* vol. 39, no. 4, p. 3.

44. Speech to veterans of the Stakhanov movement, 20 September 1985, in Gorbachev, *Izbrannye,* pp. 281–93.

45. See, for example, speech to meeting of media chiefs, reported in *Pravda,* 14 Febraury 1987. This evenhanded position seems more compatible with that of Gorbachev's Politburo colleague Ligachev than has been suggested by some Sovietologists, who see basic disagreements between the two on *glasnost'.* Ligachev has warned against picturing Soviet history as nothing more than "a chain of unrelieved mistakes" and recommended that the country's achievements in the period in which it "became world leader" should also be remembered: speech to Conference of USSR State Committee for Television and Radio, as reported in *Current Digest of the Soviet Press,* vol. 39, no. 12 (1987), p. 4.

46. Speech of 2 November, 1987, *loc. cit.,* p. 6. See also speech at meeting in Central Committee reported *Pravda,* 16 July 1987, p. 2.

47. The *New York Times,* 3 November 1987, p. 4. Gorbachev also praised Khrushchev for "changes for the better in Soviet society and in international relations," though faulting him for "capricious behavior" and failure to back up his reforms with democratic mechanisms.

48. *Ibid.,* p. 5.

49. *Ibid.,* p. 6.

50. *Ibid.,* p. 6.

51. The areas of achievement in the 1930s specifically mentioned by Gorbachev were industrialization (including the fact that "a heavy industry, including engineering, a defense industry and a chemical industry abreast of the times were built in short order practically from scratch, and the general electrification plan was completed"), collectivization, cultural revolution (meaning primarily raising the literacy rate and introducing universal and compulsory primary education), strengthening of the multi-national state, consolidation of the Soviet Union's international position, and development of new forms of economic management and social relations. *New York Times,* 3 November 1987, pp. 5–6.

52. *Ibid.,* p. 5.

PART TWO

Russia After Stalin

3

The Soviet Economic Model

Robert Campbell

The purpose of this chapter is to describe and interpret the economic model bequeathed to the present leadership by the past. This model is a kind of "living legacy," many features of which still operate to control the behavior of the economy. This model, originally constructed under Stalin, has already been worked over by two generations who have tried to refashion it to serve contemporary needs. The Soviet leadership has had roughly a quarter century of experience of modifying the Stalinist economic model, and this experience will be useful in our understanding of what features of the model constitute its essence and what would have to be changed to reconstitute it as a new model.

To appreciate the various dimensions of the Soviet growth model, and to understand what constraints may limit change, we must first understand what the "model" is.

My premise is that the Soviet economic model must be understood primarily as a growth strategy matched with a supporting institutional system. By "strategy" I mean policy choices of a macro character, and of long duration, such as the choice between extensive and intensive growth, or the decision to rely on investment as the main force for economic growth. By "institutional system," I mean the institutions and procedures of central planning, or to use another term I find more useful, the institutions and procedures of the administrative approach to running an economy. That administrative system includes not only such familiar features as controlling the output and allocation of producer goods such as steel and lumber by means of centrally set targets and a system of rationing these goods in physical terms, and vertical flows of information, but also less conspicuous characteristics, such as a reporting and evaluation system operating on a fairly short time cycle, uniform for all functions.

An important element in this definition of the model is that these institutional features and the strategy are reasonably consistent with each other and mutually supportive. For example, the high rate of investment that is the hallmark of the strategy is supported by the unequivocal control over the allocation of national output between consumption and investment which planning in physical rather than money terms by such central organs as the Gosplan makes possible.

It is probably also useful to distinguish a third element in the model, *i.e.,* a realm of policy that is less aggregative than strategy, and is less rigidly embodied in or supported by institutional arrangements. This class of decisions is not fully addressed by the macro strategy, or fully constrained by the micro mechanisms built into the institutions. It includes, for example, a choice concerning the degree of exploitation of agricultural producers, such allocational choices as the division of Gross National Product (GNP) between defense and other uses, or policy regarding the degree of openness permitted in international economic relations. These policy decisions involve dimensions of economic choice which could be varied, and through which the leaders express preferences beyond their strategic choices and the micro detail. The dividing line between strategy and policy is not clearcut, and one might ask whether something like regional development policy represents a strategic commitment or a variation of policy. But it is a useful distinction, nevertheless, because it alerts us to the fact that change, perhaps even significant change of policy, is possible without changing the strategy or the institutional system. Stalin's coercive (as distinguished from merely exploitative) price policy toward agriculture was preordained neither by the strategy, nor by the structure. Similarly, although Stalin followed a strongly autarkic policy, Khrushchev was able to expand the importance of international economic relations significantly with virtually no adjustments in the system or of the basic strategy.

These three elements of the model are formed under the influence of, and are to some extent constrained by, doctrinal and theoretical propositions touching on economic matters. Like many economists specializing in Soviet economic affairs, I am disinclined to emphasize doctrine as a major determinant of economic choices, but ideological predispositions have distorted the perspective of the creators and operators of this model in a number of ways, particularly if one thinks of doctrine not only as Marxian ideology, but also as Stalinist dogma. Examples are the Marx-inspired idea that in reckoning cost and signalling worth the pricing system should not include interest or rent charges, or the dictum that obsolescence did not exist under socialism. In Stalin's day, there was once a major controversy over whether commodity production existed in a socialist economy, and whether the law of value operated in that economy. In my view, no major feature of the system or the strategy depended on what answer one gave to this question, but the existing doctrine on the point meant that whenever anyone attempted to improve economic calculation, or to enhance lateral interactions between firms, like those characteristic of markets, this doctrinal point provided a language for attacking the suggestion.

Finally, we should remember that this economic model operates within a political environment. A distinguishing feature of the Soviet social order is the high degree to which politics and economic management are fused in a single system. The political environment creates powerful restraints on what can happen in the way of economic reform. We might argue about which way causation runs in this relationship, but my view is that the two realms are mutually interactive. Finally, the economic model, conceived as I have described it, in interaction with the economic environment, produces economic outcomes. I consider the subject of how the Soviet economic model performs to be one of the areas in which we are interested, and which should be considered at each stage of its evolution.

These elements of the economic model interpenetrate and reinforce each other, and if change is to occur, *all* must change together in a mutually consistent way. Some of the linkages are more confining than others, and specifically, some aspects of the interdependence of system and strategy more important than others. One of the tasks confronting anyone who studies and predicts change in the Soviet system is to assess the relative latitude for maneuver in these various linkages.

A Brief Description of the Stalinist Model

Growth Strategy

Today we have a widely used shorthand label for the Stalinist growth model, *i.e.,* the "extensive growth" model. But that term is the invention of a later era to dramatize a hoped-for alternative, *i.e.,* "intensive growth." The term reflects some aspects of the old model better than others, and, in any case, it only labels conveniently a complex of features characterizing the Stalinist approach to economic growth that was thoroughly understood under a variety of older terms.

One of these older labels is the "mobilization approach" to growth. Growth depended on high rates of capital accumulation to make possible a rapid rate of growth of the capital stock. One way to think about this strategy at its most abstract and aggregative level is to remind ourselves of the growth model created by G. A. Fel'dman.[1]

Central to his model is the relatively simple idea that the primary determinant of the rate of growth is the rate of investment. But he added a special twist to this by noting that how rapidly investment could be increased was constrained by the capacity of the sector producing investment goods. The strategic variable to be manipulated was therefore the allocation of whatever investment goods could be produced between expanding the capacity of the investment sector itself, and expanding the capacity of the economy to produce final goods that would satisfy directly the wants of consumers. In a stark over-simplification, the choice was between using steel to produce equipment to go into more steel mills, or to produce equipment to be invested in facilities to produce final products that people could use. Fel'dman was involved in the invention of the Soviet model for only a short time, and was a victim rather than an architect of the Soviet indus-trialization model. But he has a memorial to his appreciation of the crucial allocational choice in the steel mills the Soviet model has created and in its reliance on capital stock growth as a major pillar of Soviet economic expansion.

A second feature of the mobilizational approach was gross shifts of the country's labor resources. Labor whose productivity was low in agriculture was moved out of that sector into higher productivity occupations in other sectors. There was no hope that the Soviet Union could become a modern country without a huge investment in human capital, and so millions of people were given at least a primary education. This educational effort was partial and in some way elitist, but it was carried out on a massive scale nonetheless. Another form of mobilization was to raise the rate of participation of the able bodied population in the labor force.

The Stalinist strategy also depended on massive technology transfer through the importation of capital goods with varying emphasis at different times. But this was generally envisaged as a short-term ex-pedient. Even at its most open, in the early years of the industrialization drive, Stalinist trade policy was aimed at import substitution.

Other dimensions of the classic Stalinist approach have been cap-tured in Grossman's characterization of it as the antithesis of the three M's—mobility, money, and marketization—whose growing importance played so important a role in economic growth in the economic history of the West.[2] The Soviet formula shifted people on a massive scale, but in a way that differed from what we usually mean by mobility, since it involved highly centralized control, and limited individual choice. It restricted the mobility of material resources, placing extraor-dinary obstacles in the way of anyone who might want to trade su-perfluous equipment or materials with some other enterprise. The

Soviet growth model strongly de-emphasized the power of money. American veterans complained that their veteran's pin (the famous "ruptured duck"), along with a dime, could buy a cup of coffee. In the USSR, for most goods, the connection worked the other way around—the dime alone could not command resources. Finally, in the form of highly centralized decisions and physical allocation, the Soviet model was the antithesis of markets. The Soviet authorities downgraded the importance of markets, money and mobility because of their distrust of fine calculation, their fear of decentralized values and perspectives, and their unwillingness to see leverage in the hands of individuals and decentralized economic actors.

The mobilizational approach also created institutional instruments for mobilization and direction of resources, as, for instance, the collective farms in which individualistic peasants were forced to enroll so that they might be more easily directed, or mass organizations that were to provide the vehicle for transmitting the policies of the regime and supporting its goals, such as labor unions. The most important of these structures, of course, was the bureaucracy—the "structure designed by geniuses to be run by idiots"—which reconciled dynamic change in the large with individual passivity.

Institutional Structure

The institutional structure of the Soviet administrative approach to running the economy was designed to support this strategy. The structure was highly centralized. It fused political and economic life. It put into the hands of the leadership control over the central variable of the strategy, *i.e.,* the division of the nation's output between investment and consumption. It reinforced the strategy's preferences regarding sectoral output priorities by the direct allocation of investment to create the capacity for those outputs. This institutional structure also supported the de-emphasis of money, markets, and mobility in many familiar ways: guiding enterprise behavior through an elaborate structure of plan indicators, de-emphasizing prices, introducing the labor booklets which were used to tie workers to jobs, making money and banks passive actors in the process.

Innumerable corollaries to these central features of the model add to its distinctive character. Physical quantities were emphasized as the measure of success at the expense of quality, variety, and satisfying the client. The feature of vertical ties inherent in any hierarchical system was reflected in numerous concrete ways—vertical integration of production versus specialization and co-operation, and inattention to regional integration. Most lists of these corollaries would include a preference for repair over replacement; replication of existing facilities at the existing level of technology, with whatever technical upgrading took place only at the extensive margin; a temptation to think big and to seek solution of complex problems through undifferentiated panaceas; a penchant for strategic flanking maneuvers, gigantomania, and brute force solutions rather than patient efforts seeking refinement, adaptation, and variation. This list of exotic behaviors could be made very long, but it is more interesting to ask how tightly these corollaries are linked to the central features of the strategy and structure. Do they fall in the policy area, or are they mandated by the institutions and strategy? Most of the features listed do seem persistent, and I think that most of us would incline to the view that they are what the Russians would call *zakonomernye* (*i.e.,* law-governed) rather than *sluchainye* (accidental) corollaries.

Doctrine

In the doctrinal sphere, the classical Stalinist model operated with a simplistic and rigid set of ideas. Stalin did not want to be constrained by any concepts that seemed to imply objectivity in economic analysis or by professional experts relying on them. Anything that smacked of the economist's traditional warning that "you can't afford to do that because of resource constraints" he couldn't stand. His solution was to rid himself of the professionals who might ground their theories in such cautions. He especially distrusted the mathematical economists, and drove them into exile.[3] The spokesmen for the classic model glorified some simpleminded and fatuous ideas, as in calling material balances a "scientific tool for planning." And Stalin felt it his responsibility to criticize and clarify discussions on economic theory, as he did in his booklet on *Economic Problems of Socialism,* in which he declared erroneous some notions entertained by the textbook writers.

Performance

This model worked. It enabled the USSR to overcome at least some aspects of economic underdevelopment, to exploit the "advantages of backwardness," and to make significant progress toward the goal of catching up with the advanced capitalist countries. GNP grew between 1928 and 1955 at an average annual rate of 6.7 percent according to Bergson's calculation.[4] The capital stock did indeed grow at a high rate. Rapid growth of employment, especially in the nonagricultural economy, was achieved, and the system did manage to increase participation and average hours worked. Demographic dynamics worked in favor of the policy in the sense that the share of the population in the working ages increased.

But in evaluating the performance of the Stalinist growth model, we must remember that although it was successful, it succeeded in a very special environment. When the process began, there was an extraordinarily large pool of underutilized labor which could be mobilized. The uneducated population represented a potential opportunity for a high yield from investing some of society's resources in human capital. The West had achieved a level of technological advancement that could be borrowed directly, or whose successes showed the paths the USSR could follow with little risk. The leaders were able to exploit the enthusiasm of a populace aroused by doctrine. The USSR was endowed with a rich patrimony of natural resources, especially mineral resources, that had been little explored and still less exploited. When those conditions changed, the effectiveness of this system was bound to decline. The decline had not yet begun when Stalin died, although he had certainly created problems that needed urgent attention, most notably the condition of agriculture.

Against this background my central concern is to review what happened to the effectiveness of this growth strategy after Stalin died, and to examine the tasks his successors faced in trying to alter it to improve performance. In tracing these changes it will be useful to distinguish between the Khrushchev period and the later period under Brezhnev and Kosygin. Let us first look at each of these two periods separately, and then return to consider some persistent problems and continuities that seem to carry over from one period to another.

Khrushchev's Efforts to Change the Model[5]

Economic Performance

In attempting to interpret what the first generation of reformers tried to do to remodel the Stalinist system they had inherited, we must remember that the traditional strategy and institutions were still working. The economy presented some urgent problems, but it would be an error to project current perspectives backward and to conclude that the Stalinist growth model had lost its viability or even its vitality by the time Stalin died.

The best systematic long-term record we have for following Soviet economic performance since the 1950s is the computations of Soviet GNP prepared by the Central Intelligence Agency.[6] These follow the methods and conventions developed and applied by Bergson and his RAND associates for evaluating the first quarter century of Soviet growth. For the years 1953 to 1965, *i.e.*, from Stalin's death to the year after Khrushchev was removed from the leadership, the CIA data show GNP growing at an annual average rate of 5.6 percent per year, not much below the average during Stalin's rule. Industrial output was growing at 7.9 percent per year. That is not as high as it had been in the heyday of forced-draft industrialization (Moorsteen and Powell calculated that it was over 11 percent in 1929–55) but still impressive. And a series of policy repairs in agriculture, makeshift though they finally proved to be, made it possible to elicit much better performance from agriculture than had occurred under the model as it had operated under Stalinist policies. Although there were ups and downs, agricultural output grew on the average during the years from Stalin's death to Khrushchev's ouster at more than 4 percent per year.

This was still extensive growth, based on rapid increases in the labor force, and on a growth rate for the capital stock that outpaced the growth of the labor force and of output. The stagnation in productivity had not yet occurred, so that increments in productivity were still adding to the continued mobilization of larger inputs of land, capital, and labor to production. Moving from sector to sector in this period, one can find reasonably impressive measures of technical progress. I have in mind such changes as improvement in size, efficiency, and utilization of power generating equipment, substitution of diesel for steam locomotives, improved indicators for equipment in the ferrous metals industry, and the introduction of entire new branches of industry, such as fertilizer production. These were sometimes based on technology imports, or in any case still represented catch-up along established, proven, paths.

The continued efficacy of the basic Stalinist model is attributable to the fact that the environment had not yet changed to any serious degree. It was still possible to increase the labor force at rates much like those in Stalinist times—between 1950 and 1965, the nonagricultural labor force was growing at more than four percent per year, for a total increment of 30.6 million persons. The total labor force grew less rapidly than its nonagricultural component because of an appreciable attrition in the collective farm labor force, which fell from approximately 39 million to 26 million.[7]

This economy was still capable of diverting into investment the high share of the economy's output required to sustain the contribution of the second pillar of the extensive pattern, *i.e.*, the rapid growth of the capital stock. According to the CIA study, investment grew at 9.4 (new fixed investment) or 9.8 percent (all investment) in those years, and the capital stock was still growing at between nine and ten percent per year, according to the official Soviet statistics.

Admittedly there were some problems urgently requiring attention, and both in the succession period, and after Khrushchev had consolidated his power, numerous changes were attempted. Some of these were rejected, and some successfully executed. These were mostly policy changes—changes in the proportions in resource allocations to different sectors, changes in agricultural policy, and the opening up of the economy to more foreign trade. Other examples include gains from expanding fertilizer use and the Soviet formula of "chemization," which involved substituting chemical processes for mechanical processes; major structural changes of a typically top-down kind, such as Khrushchev's heavy emphasis on corn and swine; a reorientation of fuel policy away from solid fuel toward hydrocarbons. Many of these policy changes generated substantial yields, and the continued viability of the system is attributable to its capacity for flexibility in the policy area if nowhere else.

One of the new departures considered on Stalin's death was a major allocational shift to improve living conditions for the population. The standard interpretation seems to be that Malenkov proposed a consumer-oriented allocation policy, with significant cuts in the allocation of resources to defense. Khrushchev was able to win out over Malenkov in the succession struggle partly over this issue. But then following an old tradition, Khrushchev himself stinted military expenditure to some degree even as he sought modernization of the armed forces.

I think it is accurate to say that Khrushchev defended the major elements of the traditional strategy—such as activist party intervention, a high rate of investment, counting on initiatives from the top rather than from below. Overall, he maintained Stalinist priorities in gross allocation decisions.

Khrushchev was an activist reformer on a large scale, and it is worth cataloguing some of the major actions. The most serious problem created in the Stalinist period, and the one that threatened the continuation of the system by the time he died, was the problem of agriculture. This was an area which all party factions agreed required remedial action. Agriculture was the area in which Khrushchev did most both in terms of policy and institutional change. He instituted a real revolution in the terms of trade between agriculture and the rest of the economy by raising agricultural prices roughly threefold. He abolished the machine-tractor stations (MTS), which had been an important agency of state interference in collective farm decisionmaking. He instituted the virgin lands program.

One of the most celebrated of Khrushchev's changes was the shift to a regional administrative structure. Because of the branch-organized structure, potentially important resource-saving interactions at the local level were ignored. Possibilities for economies of scale through specialization and co-operation in the production of intermediate goods such as castings were shunned by enterprises distrustful of getting co-operation from enterprises in alien ministries. By redesigning the hierarchy to place the administrative boss at the regional level, these enterprises would have a common boss only one rung up the ladder, who would see that the interaction was accomplished. Unfortunately, this is one of those changes where what is gained on the swings is likely to be lost on the roundabouts—a common feature of administrative tinkering in general. The benefit of greater attention to local interactions was offset by a lessened ability to manipulate those aspects of performance that depend on a branch-wide perspective. For example, innovation or specialization within the tractor industry probably gains from having all the tractor plants under a unified vision and control. But the relevance of this experiment to the issue of Khrushchev as a reformer is that it is fully in the tradition of the Stalinist model.

One feature of the original Soviet development model was a regional development policy that did little to equalize the uneven levels of development across regions in the empire inherited by the Communists. Development planners face a dilemma in this matter: development resources, such as investment or managerial attention, are likely to be most effective in stimulating growth if allocated to regions where a solid economic infrastructure already exists; unfortunately, that means perpetuating regional inequality. Generally, Stalinist policy chose development effectiveness over equalizing levels of development, which was stated as a goal, but slighted in practice. This history has left Siberia, Central Asia, the South generally, still appreciably behind the European heartland. All regions have been pushed forward, but without the kind of differential push that would equalize their relative levels of development. The problem acquired a new dimension after the Second World War, when the addition of the Baltic regions added more variance at the upper end of the distribution. Because the regional structure is closely correlated with ethnic divisions, regional inequality has implications for perceptions of how different ethnic groups are being treated. Since the demographic transition in the Slavic areas of the USSR, the problem has become more complicated because of the much higher comparative rate of population growth in the Muslim areas. The dilemma sharpens between using investment to provide jobs and incomes for these people and using the same investment in other regions where it could be more productive.

The Khrushchev regime appears to have attempted a more vigorous policy of equalizing levels of development and incomes among regions, giving the goal more prominence as a target in the five-year plans, and using various methods for redistributing income. I interpret the Western studies on the matter as indicating that he had some minor success in this goal.[8] But the problem has by no means been overcome. Siberia is still a wasteland, and since the one-time jolt given it by the Second World War, the East has not advanced its relative standing on the major dimensions.[9] All the usual indicators of output per capita, levels of living, income per capita or other measures of welfare, investment per capita, and so on, suggest that there is still a disparity. For example, in 1970, Tadjikistan had a per capita income of 57 percent of the national average and Estonia 35 percent above it. And differentials in the 1970s did not favor the less developed areas.[10]

Since there seems to have been no significant policy or performance shift between the two regimes in this area, we ought to follow this topic into the Brezhnev era here. Without having changed the situation, Brezhnev simply declared that the goal of equalizing the regions had been achieved, and that development policy could now focus on other goals. That is typical Brezhnev head-in-the-sand talk, and the problem of regional inequality remains on the agenda for Gorbachev to deal with.

This is an interesting problem in the context of Gorbachev and reform because it presents a peculiar mixture of structure and policy. As long as the administrative structure of the economy is organized along branch rather than regional lines, it is difficult to raise the importance of regional development above locational choices taken to optimize growth from a national or branch perspective. The corrective comes through the regionally organized Party hierarchy, in which local interests assert their regional claims. This phenomenon has not been carefully studied, but there must be an interesting interaction between institutional reform and the fundamentals of the political structure. The desire to build a coalition of local support might well coincide with a desire to break the power of the Moscow-dominated industrial branch hierarchy. This is a feature of the current situation to which reform-watchers should be alert.

Khrushchev invested considerable effort and political capital in educational reform. This was a first attempt to adapt a mass educational system to the changing realities of demand for labor after three decades of intensive industrialization. Levels of general education were rising, and there had been a rapid expansion of higher education. But the mix of graduates did not match the economy's needs very well, and Khrushchev's goal was to correct that through "polytechnical education." But the proposed changes prompted resistance both by educators and by parents, who saw education through the general education track

as the path to social advancement. Educational reform was postponed
as unfinished business.

Khrushchev was able successfully to attack some institutionalized
aspects of the old system. An outstanding example is the system of
labor camps and the hydraulic cancer that Thane Gustafson describes
in his book on reform in Soviet politics.[11] The KGB had created a
massive empire based on using political prisoners to carry out such
labor-intensive activities as building dams, hydroelectric plants and
roads in underdeveloped areas. Both the projects themselves, and this
approach to using labor, tended to be economically wasteful. Cutting
down that empire was an interesting case of institutional change which
did involve a powerful vested interest and a political battle. But Khrushchev was able to carry it off, and this is one of those historical
experiences we need to absorb in order to understand the political
aspects of the process of change. I attribute his success in part to the
fact that the camp system had been an excrescence on the main system.
The camps were antithetical to the central institutions of the system,
which were rational-bureaucratic and sought economic effectiveness,
however clumsily. This is an example of the kind of reform that favors
removing some eggshell, rather than unscrambling the whole omelet.

Another institutional change during Khrushchev's administration was
the reorganization of the research and development establishment, although I do not know how much Khrushchev himself was involved
in it. The institutes heavily oriented toward applied science were
removed from the Academy of Sciences, and put in the industrial
network, and the Academy was permitted to become more fully focused
on basic science. He continued the policy of generous allocation of
resources to expand the research and development establishment. Employment in the "science and science services" sector grew at about
nine percent per year, and the number of "scientific workers" (the
measure, probably exaggerated, which the USSR uses to track personnel
engaged in research and development) grew at almost ten percent per
year.

Doctrine

Looking back on the Khrushchev era, I am impressed with how
active a period it was in the doctrinal sphere. Khrushchev permitted,
even sponsored, far-reaching doctrinal relaxation. It was a period when
some of the elite came to understand their system. It witnessed the
publication of a classic analysis of its problems in the book by the
aircraft designer, Antonov.[12] Mathematical economics was permitted to
reemerge; Kantorovich's book on linear programming, which offered

an alternative to the Marxian theory of value, was published at long last;[13] Kantorovich, Novozhilov and Nemchinov were awarded a Lenin prize. Liberman published his famous article on profit.[14]

Unfortunately, none of this doctrinal and theoretical innovation culminated in a vision of reform. The economists were stymied in an effort to reconcile the insights of the Kantorovich school with the commitment to centralization. This took the form of a complicated argument about a "system of optimal functioning of the economy" (*sistema optimal'nogo funktsionirovaniia ekonomiki* or SOFE), about which I will say more below. Khrushchev was thus an extremely activist leader, trying to change things in a great many areas. Most of his actions, however, worked the policy angle rather than changing the strategy or the fundamental institutions of the administrative system. As far as I can tell, all the initiatives we associate with him share this quality: opening up the economy; changing industrial structure by creating a chemical industry; complaining about the structural implications of the "steeleater" line of thinking; shifting the basis of military power to more modern weapon systems; moving away from coal to oil.[15] In his major policy initiatives—the virgin lands program is an example—he went along with the highly centralized style. This was a choice of policy thoroughly consistent with the centralized institutional structure, and a quintessential expression of the extensive Soviet strategy of growth. He reorganized the hierarchical pyramid of administration in the industrial sphere from its branch principle to the regional principle, but it was still hierarchical. With the important exception of agriculture, little was accomplished in price reform, even though the last general overhaul of prices had been in 1955. (There were some price changes in 1962, but general overhaul was put off to the next regime, *i.e.,* the reform of 1967.)

Many of Khrushchev's initiatives ultimately failed. After a short period of success, his quick fix to the problem of getting more grain produced—the virgin lands program—turned into a quick failure. I have already mentioned education policy as an example. Some of his ideas never came to fruition. At one point he offered a vision in which the state would one day simply announce prices for agricultural produce, and let the agricultural producers compete for the business. But that idea never took concrete form, and the agricultural sector remained under burdensome central direction.

What are the lessons to be learned from the Khrushchev period? I am struck with how long it took for any vision of reform to emerge from the increased theoretical sophistication. It takes a long time for doctrinal change to be transformed into changes of institutions and policy, and this process advanced scarcely at all in the Khrushchev period. It is possible that in working primarily on the policy dimensions of the model, Khrushchev faced a different, perhaps simpler, problem than trying to change fundamental institutions. The premise of an extensive study of Khrushchev as a political leader[16] is that his major task was to win authority largely at the higher levels of the Party and the apparatus. He had to outflank his rivals and win acceptance for his policy initiatives in an intra-Party power struggle, whereupon he proceeded to impose policy change. In two of the examples I have discussed—agriculture and the camp system—he was dealing with components that were only peripherally related to the basic institutional structure. When his efforts at agricultural reform placed him at odds with the basic power structure (in trying to bifurcate the Party apparatus into separate industrial and agricultural branches), he was in trouble.

The Experience of the Brezhnev-Kosygin Period

Performance

During the Brezhnev-Kosygin period the deficiencies of the Soviet model began to show up dramatically in the form of a steady slowing of economic growth. The average annual rate of growth of GNP fell from 3.7 percent in the Ninth Five Year Plan to 2.7 percent in the Tenth, to 2.2 percent in the Eleventh.[17] During this entire period, the reduced growth of inputs of capital, labor, and other resources was exacerbated by a diminishing contribution from productivity gains. According to CIA calculations, output per unit of combined factor inputs rose at 0.82 percent per year in the 1960s and 0.7 percent per year in the 1970s, but by the end of the 1970s was *negative*.[18]

Generally declining growth culminated in a real debacle in the late 1970s—in 1979, GNP grew by less than one percent. In contrast with some other annual fluctuations, this stagnation was a reflection not only of agricultural problems, but of sharp slowing in other sectors as well. There were years in the late 1970s when output of important industrial commodities such as steel actually fell, a development previously all but unheard of.

In general, poor performance in agriculture contributed significantly to this discouraging record. In its first years the new regime took some vigorous steps to improve the performance of agriculture which, after significant growth during the early part of the Khrushchev period, declined after 1958. Procurement prices were raised, and agriculture was favored in the allocation of resources for investment. There was some early response to these measures, but it was short-lived and, for the period as a whole, agriculture remained a problem. From 1965 to 1980, according to official figures, agricultural production grew at about two percent per year. This was achieved, however, by a substantial expansion of inputs from outside agriculture such as fertilizer and fuel, and the CIA calculates that *net* output (in the sense of value added) grew at less than 1 percent per year. Moreover, because of the increasing relative importance of animal products, an increasing share of crop output was consumed within agriculture to feed animals, so that the other concept of net output, *i.e.,* deliveries of consumable goods to the rest of society, grew much less rapidly than gross output.

Environment

The decline in growth may be explained to a large extent by adverse changes in the environment for growth. This change is particularly evident in labor supply. During Khrushchev's tenure, the nonagricultural labor force had grown by *annual* increments of 2.3 million persons, or at average increases of 4.4 percent per year. In the Tenth Five-Year Plan these increments were still at the level of about two million persons per year, but by the Eleventh they were down to one million and the annual growth rate down to 0.9 percent. A half century of rapacious exploitation of natural resources had resulted in a rapid rise in the investment expenditures needed to expand production of energy and natural resources to meet the needs of the economy. The USSR discovered the problem of pollution, and had to begin allocating some resources to combat it. Growth in production and technical progress in the rest of the world, by which the Soviet leaders had always defined their own aspirations, seemed more of a challenge than they had in previous decades. The Japanese were approaching the USSR in terms of total output and surpassing it in technical achievement and productivity. The military challenge had become more complex, raising the standard of performance required of the Soviet economy. It is a cliche today to say that the Soviet leaders see the Strategic Defense Initiative as likely to generate rapid military-technical progress that they must match, but the implications of such an advance by their adversaries was already being felt earlier.[19] As procurement policy shifted to try to compete in technical sophistication as well as in numbers of weapons, Soviet producers found themselves at a disadvantage. It is now widely believed that their inability to deal with the technology as they sought to move into more sophisticated areas was very important in the slowdown in military procurement.[20]

The changing conditions that made the old model obsolete are partly an expression of success and maturity. The relentless accumulation of capital created production facilities that had to be supplied with raw materials and labor, and had to be repaired and replaced both for reasons of physical depreciation and technical obsolescence. Urbanization and the proliferation of industrial occupations made the problem of medical and health care a greater challenge than it had been in a simpler society. Murray Feshbach is persuasive in his argument that there has been a serious deterioration in health conditions, and it is plausible to hold that this is an expression of industrial arrival.[21] But health care policy failed to adjust to the new circumstances either in terms of adaptation or resources. It is remarkable that the health services sector, which had grown so rapidly in the Stalinist period, has since been left to languish. If employment in health services had grown at more than 7 percent in the period from 1928 to 1953, it grew at only 2.5 percent per year after 1965.

I think that health care exemplifies a common failing of the Soviet model, *i.e.,* a tendency on the part of policy makers to think that they have "solved" some problem and to turn their attention away from it, without realizing that there must be constant adjustment as conditions change. The creation of a huge educational establishment engaged in churning out a mass of degree-holders whose relevance to the changing structure of manpower needs is declining is another example.

As education expanded to achieve virtually universal secondary education in the 1970s, its past focus on producing highly trained elites and the corollary popular perception of education as the high road to social advancement were no longer appropriate.

As the Soviet economy narrowed the gap between its structure and level of technological maturity and that of the advanced industrial nations, the benefits that accrued from technological borrowing and catching up along well trodden paths were bound to diminish. Innovation has come to require more push from internal assessments of needs and potentials, internal motivations, and the nation's own resources.

Strategy

In the Brezhnev-Kosygin era, the deteriorating performance of the Soviet economy began for the first time to be diagnosed as a failure of the extensive growth strategy. Soviet commentators began to accept the diagnosis and terminology already current in Eastern Europe that the task was to shift from an extensive to an intensive growth strategy, to create conditions in which growth of productivity could compensate for slower growth of resource inputs. The Tenth Five Year Plan had been called "The Five Year Plan of quality and effectiveness." But for the Eleventh Five Year Plan the ritual slogan was "getting the economy onto the rails of intensive growth." It is remarkable, however, that even as the period continued, I find in the talk about a new strategy very little understanding of the many-faceted nature of strategy, or of how meaningless the slogan "intensification" was in the absence of institutional change.

Under Brezhnev and Kosygin no significant progress was made in creating a new institutional base that could give vitality to the new strategic conception of intensive growth. In a situation that was in many ways far more threatening than Khrushchev had faced, and one in which the bankruptcy of the old strategy was ever more frankly acknowledged, the leaders exhibited little vision or boldness in devising changes to deal with the problem.

Systemic Reform

In the institutional sphere, this was not a period of significant change in the basic institutions of the administrative model. The new leadership began with an elaborate agenda of institutional changes, agreed upon at a Plenum in September 1965.[22] The reform can be described as a series of measures intended to give the managers of enterprises more freedom in decisions about their use of resources, and to provide a set of signals and incentives that would encourage them to use this new freedom in socially desirable ways. The number of indicators covered in the enterprise's plan was reduced, new incentive funds were authorized, and the price system was reformed. The price reform included the introduction of interest and rent payments, and gave more attention than before to the issue of utility to the consumer as a consideration in setting relative prices. In terms of organizational charts, the most important change was the reintroduction of the ministries, often with the introduction of a new mid-level organization in the hierarchy, called the production association. At the time of the introduction of the reform, it was stated that the system of material-technical supply would be retained, but that there would eventually be a transition to a system of "wholesale trade," which was widely interpreted as an abandonment of the system of physical allocation. Some experiments with the wholesale trade idea were undertaken, as in the use of a no-limit system for the distribution of petroleum products in one of the Soviet regions (Voronezh oblast). Use of such "experiments" to try a new organizational form or incentive structure or planning practice in a limited jurisdiction became a common approach. Other examples were experiments in self-financing (introduced in Minpribor), placing some research and development organizations "on khozraschet," that is, financing them through contracts with clients rather than grants, and in some cases giving them their own endowment of working capital to replace advances from the client. An important feature of reform during the Kosygin-Brezhnev period is that following the original set of measures there were successive waves of reform, in which an idea was modified on the basis of experience, or one that had been introduced on a piecemeal, experimental basis was extended to a broader arena.

Many economists would probably share my feeling in looking back on the original reform movement in the 1960s that we were somewhat taken in. There is no denying that a great deal was happening. Gertrude Schroeder calls this continuing set of changes and experiments, which ultimately stretched out over a decade and a half, "a series of measures unprecedented in scope and intensity."[23] Many of us wrote articles dissecting these reforms, assessing how they might help or in what respect they were flawed. We saw this or that measure as a step forward, or a sensible correction. Using a smaller number of more general success indicators would indeed give the manager more latitude in decisionmaking. The changes were not complete, and some particular combination of measures seemed not fully coherent. For example, the *Bol'shevichka-Maiak* experiment of letting the assortment of products produced by a consumer goods plant be determined by customer orders would not work, since fixed prices might make the mix of products the customer wanted disadvantageous for the producer, given the formula that governed his bonus. We also sagely pointed out that it did not help that many of the reforms were scuttled in the process of implementation.

But it took a while for us to realize that these changes were not just incomplete and marred by internal contradictions, nor was it just that they were scuttled in the process of implementation. The changes did not even begin to get at the basic flaw in the system, in that they did not touch the main operating principles of the administrative approach. The essential weakness of these measures as an effort at reform has been permanently captured in Gertrude Schroeder's description of them as a "treadmill of reforms," and in the now familiar dismissal that all they involved was "administrative tinkering." Schroeder went on to express what was wrong with this tinkering: "As long as incentives are tied to meeting plans for whatever indicator, and other essentials of the system are not altered, the relationship among all units . . . will remain administrative rather than economic in nature. The behavior of each link will continue to be oriented toward meeting its own particular plan targets and satisfying its own superior organizations."[24] Another critic of this kind of reform, Janusz Zielinski, drawing on the extensive experience of similar reforms in Eastern Europe, drew the same conclusion. As long as the rewards of the enterprise were tied to the cyclical goal setting and evaluation of performance by a superior organ, the enterprise would have no interest in meeting the needs of its customers, or concern with standing up to its suppliers to receive better inputs or service.[25]

Policy

Significant initiatives in the policy area were undertaken in the Brezhnev-Kosygin era. Perhaps most important were two serious allocational commitments, *i.e.,* to strengthening Soviet military capabilities, and to providing more investment resources for agriculture and higher incomes for its participants. In the accelerated military buildup after 1965, procurement grew preferentially, at a rate higher than GNP. In retrospect, I view that commitment of resources to the military as having had deleterious consequences. The result was that one of the traditional pillars of the standard model, *i.e.,* continued rapid increases in the capital stock of the economy generally, was neglected. This neglect was reflected not only in the quantitative dimension of capacities, but also in the technological level of the equipment that went into these facilities. To the extent that the economy had some capabilities for generating advances in technology, they were lavished on the production of military hardware rather than on the production of equipment to raise the technological level of the economy. Gorbachev and his supporters have made this one of their major charges against the previous leadership,[26] and we should perhaps discount it as a self-serving evaluation. But it has been advanced extensively and convincingly in the Soviet economic literature for some time, and I think the data supports it. Even according to official statistics, which there is good reason to believe have become increasingly upward-biased, the stock of fixed productive capital grew at more than 8 percent per year from 1965 to 1975. But this rate then fell to 7 percent in the Tenth Five Year Plan and to only 5 percent in the Eleventh. It would be complicated to disentangle the factors that contributed to this slowdown. But I believe that Gorbachev is correct in thinking that an excessive commitment of the economy's capacity for producing equipment to producing military hardware was an important factor.

The regime made a major commitment to agriculture in the form of large investment allocations and increases in procurement prices for agricultural output, and then to a broader set of goals in the form of the food program in 1982. Since the late 1960s, 27 percent of all investment has gone to agriculture, and then under the food program, the "agro-industrial complex" (or APK, which in addition to agriculture includes sectors producing inputs for it and processing its output) was to receive about one-third of all investment resources. In agriculture they gave more latitude for the private plot, especially in livestock operations.

A third important policy change was a further opening to international trade with the advanced industrial countries in connection with *detente*. Use of technology transfer was extended to many sectors, in contrast to the lopsided emphasis on chemicals under Khrushchev. Notable additions were large import programs for the automotive and energy sectors. Another new departure was a decision to import feed to foster the expansion of livestock operations and meat production. During the 1970s, Soviet trade grew at about 6.5 percent per year in real terms, well above the growth of the economy as a whole. In 1965 the share of industrially advanced countries in Soviet foreign trade turnover was only 19 percent, but by 1980, it had reached 33 percent.[27]

Foreign trade illustrates the link between policy change and systemic change. As I stated earlier, changes in the various parts of the model are linked, and there is a limit to the gains that are possible from improvements in policy that are unsupported by corresponding systemic changes. The relationship is an ambivalent one. A policy change can compensate for weaknesses in the system, but it can be deprived of much of its potential benefit by the recalcitrance of systemic obstacles. Productivity in Soviet livestock operations has traditionally been undercut by an inefficient feed mix, and one of the gains from expanded imports has been an increased supply of the concentrates that the clumsiness of the system makes it impossible to produce domestically. As an example from the other side, the contribution of imported technology to breaking domestic technological bottlenecks is often hindered by systemic obstacles. To cite an example I have looked at in detail, pumps imported from the West to increase production from aging Soviet oil wells have been used ineffectively by the oil industry.[28]

One of the puzzling aspects of the Brezhnev period is the presence of a kind of drift in important policy dimensions, which, while neither intended nor controlled, had serious consequences. For example, the effectiveness of the wage system as an incentive mechanism appears to have been seriously undercut by the spread of *uravnilovka,* a kind of leveling of wages.[29] The apparent growth in the importance of the second, unofficial and illegal, economy, with all the repercussions that it had for the effectiveness of the system, is another case in point.[30] A third is the loss of control over the supply of money, leading to repressed inflation.[31]

Doctrine and Theory

Nothing stands out as exceptional during the period in terms of doctrinal change. With the exception of writings by some of the mavericks sheltered in Abel Aganbegian's institute in Novosibirsk,[32] this was not a fertile period for insights into the causes of ineffective performance. Nor did there seem to be any imaginative exploitation of the potential of the new ideas concerning micro efficiency, or of the calculational tools they spawned, to make the economy work better. A great deal of the energy of the economics establishment went into controversies over SOFE and its relationship to a political economy of socialism.[33] Such new tools of micro-optimization as linear programming surely continued to make their way into specific uses here and there. But there is extensive commentary in the Soviet literature to the effect that decisionmakers at lower levels rejected the potential gains for the economy from better data handling capacities and optimizing models because they were disadvantageous under the existing incentive system or incompatible with existing practice.

We arrive at the paradox that in the 1970s, the Soviet leaders experienced for the first time the bankruptcy of the old strategy. It was demonstrated in terms they could not ignore, but they brought less imagination and boldness of thought to the problem than had the first generation after Stalin. Why was there so little institutional change and why was policy improvement so unhelpful and at times even out of control? We can certainly find support for the idea that institutional stasis is attributable to the conservatism of the bureaucracy. We particularly see their hand with respect to the 1965 reforms and their implementation. The reform intended to diminish the power of the ministries, but was unsuccessful. Many changes legislated at the top were never translated into practice, and this is most likely explained by footdragging by those charged with implementing them. The Soviet literature is full of complaints about how the ministries ignored the provisions of the reforms, and continued their old habits of "administrirovanie," that is trying to run things by unilateral, unknowing and unsympathetic *diktat* from above. The ministries are powerful organizations against whom other bodies have a difficult time prevailing. One of the studies sponsored by the Soviet Interview Project (an extensive survey of former Soviet citizens who emigrated in the 1970s), details how unsuccessful the Central Statistical Administration was in realizing, against the interests of the ministries, the enhanced roles it was supposed to have in shaping and controlling the reporting function in the reformed system.

But in the final assessment, much of the blame must be assigned to ineffective leadership at the top. Much of the fecklessness of the

Brezhnev leadership in improving the system is adequately explained in political, rather than in bureaucratic and institutional terms. In my view, this was a period when the state establishment, and the planners themselves, were willing to entertain more ideas about reform than was the political leadership. I see a near consensus in the Western political literature that Kosygin wanted more economic reform than Brezhnev would allow.

Persistent Problems

Two problems that have persisted through the entire history of the Soviet economic model and remain today as a legacy of the Stalinist model are the poor performance of agriculture and the problem of innovation and technical progress.

Agriculture

In Stalin's day it was customary for Western commentators to speak of agriculture as the Achilles' heel of the Soviet economy. That seems a much less apt metaphor today, which I suppose is a tribute to the reform efforts of the first two generations of post-Stalin leadership. Nonetheless, agriculture remains *the* problem sector, the ineffectiveness of which leads to distortions in the allocation of resources, and is an obstacle to the USSR's attaining the status of a modern society. There has been some useful institutional change, but the major approach has been to reverse the exploitative relationship of the nonagricultural sector to agriculture that Stalin established in the original version of the model. Stalin's success in turning the terms of trade radically against agriculture so damaged agriculture that his successors could coax more from it only by offering terms of trade far more favorable to agriculture than exist almost anywhere else in the world (with the possible exception of Japan). The leaders have boxed themselves into a situation in which they must pour ever more resources into agriculture to coax out additional output, on terms that are increasingly disadvantageous for the nonagricultural sector. The subsidy reconciling consumer prices with agricultural procurement prices is today more than 80 billion rubles. The leaders have tried a great many variations of policy— easing conditions for the private plot, juggling the price structure, and introducing various technical improvements. But Soviet agricultural policy in its grosser contours has retained features that stultify the power of these modifications to transform it. Although my knowledge of Soviet agriculture is limited, I am perfectly comfortable with the conventional wisdom. D. Gale Johnson, for example, has said that

Soviet agricultural policy continues to operate under a presumption that agricultural producers cannot make correct decisions on their own. Agricultural decisionmaking is still highly bureaucratized and centralized, with the majority of the important decisions still made or influenced from Moscow. The instrument that might pass decisionmaking power downward—the price system—is still perverse in its incentive effects.[34] What makes the regime's reluctance to take decisive action so puzzling is that this is an area in which radical institutional change could be introduced on a broad scale in an isolable context without changing the traditional central planning system elsewhere. That is exactly what the Chinese have done, and largely on this rationale. The Soviet Union could bring about a rapid and significant improvement in agricultural productivity by withdrawing administrative interference, and by trusting the price link to be the motivating and directing device. To explain what has prevented the Soviet planners from initiating these changes is not a question an economist can answer. The answer must be found in the cultural, historical and political realms. As with the American Civil War, so much has been invested in the terrible struggle with the peasant half of Soviet society that even today the leaders are unable to approach the problem with objectivity.

Innovation and Technological Progress

The Soviet system of central planning has never been able to institutionalize a system of widely supported, self-sustaining innovative behaviors on the part of producers. The designers of the system created institutional arrangements for innovation that were consistent with the original model of Stalinist economic growth and with the environment within which economic development was occurring. In the original model, the premise was probably valid that it was impossible to rely on local initiative and local innovative behavior. The society lacked the managerial, entrepreneurial and technical elites who could perform that function. And given the level of Soviet development compared with that of the rest of the world, technological borrowing from abroad, which the Soviet system did on a large scale, presented major advantages over domestic innovation. In building the system, its architects accordingly placed the function of technical policy and innovation at a very high level in the structure. Technical administrations of the ministries and the research and design establishments they administered were given the responsibility for establishing technical policy, designing new equipment, approving such importation as was considered appropriate, and so on. Innovation was simply not seen as an enterprise function. Local decisionmakers had neither authority over it nor responsibility for it. An enterprise was told to introduce a new process, was assigned the task of producing a new product designed by someone else, told to create a new production line using new technology, and so on. Arthur Alexander's classic description of how this process worked in the aircraft industry illustrates the principle. Major scientific institutes at the center with research and development facilities and the best personnel had responsibility for airfoil testing, testing of materials, creating approved designs for subassemblies, and so on. By and large, even powerful designers were supposed to work within that framework, and when approved designs were finally produced, the task of producing them in large runs was assigned to production plants that had little hand in their development.[35]

This high degree of centralization was appropriate to the conditions in which development was taking place. It minimized variety and competition (which was no big loss under the circumstances), and concentrated the limited technical skills, vision, and decisionmaking power at a high level in the hierarchy in order to give it leverage. The related phenomena of institutional separation of the function of research and development from producers and the generally weak connections among those involved with innovation—the research and development people, the producer, and the customer—were unlikely to impose too costly a burden.

Apart from the considerations of level of development and potentials for borrowing just discussed, this kind of centralized system works much better for some activities than others. It may still work for large, well-defined missions that can be given a high degree of priority, that require the mobilization of large amounts of resources. It works best in innovations that exploit the existing state of knowledge, but there are examples in which it works even at the frontier of technological development, as in space exploration. Indeed, it is in that kind of task that we have most often seen Soviet successes—the space program, rocketry, development of the atom and hydrogen bombs. The Soviet system is much clumsier when adapting a fundamental breakthrough to a variety of applications, developing its inherent capability and differentiating it to realize its potential in multifarious applications. Computers are an example.

As conditions have changed the balance of costs and advantages of this structure has also changed. This is a system in which a function conceived too narrowly as "science" or "research and development" (*nauchno-issledovatel'skii i opytno-konstruktorskie raboty* or NIOKR in the Russian terminology) is torn away from the other functions required for innovation. The changes that Soviet reform in this area have introduced seek to join research and development with production under one roof: the scientific-production associations (NPO's) created in the Brezhnev-Kosygin era are an example. But I think there is a more fundamental problem. Joining research and development to production is not enough. The Soviet administrative structure is deficient in having few nodes that bring together the other ingredients for innovation—knowledge of needs, the resources, the marketing knowledge, and the *motivation* to innovate—and to which the research and development function could be attached.

Apart from the organizational weaknesses that make it difficult to find a home for the innovation function, it is interesting to raise the issue of how the existing institutional structure in science, with its monopoly power and social and political privileges may involve a vested interest that will resent efforts to change and perhaps resist effectively. There certainly are such vested interests, reflected in the reaction of the research and development establishment in the face of competition from imported technology. The argument has been made by some groups in the Soviet Union that the USSR should not be importing technology when it has its own research and development capacities. I have found no evidence that this community has been a potent defender of its interests. Here again we are moving into a discussion of issues of political processes best left to others. But it is my impression from the entire history of relations between the Party and the science establishment, from Stalin's subjugation of the Academy of Sciences to Gorbachev's current pruning of the research and development network, that the weak link here is not Party power, but a poverty of understanding about innovation.

Lessons

Are there any conclusions from this retrospective review? Let me sketch a few that are partial and oversimplified, but in which I believe, and which may be relevant in considering the prospects for change under Gorbachev.

First, I think it is crucial to bear in mind the interconnectedness of the various aspects of the Soviet economic growth model. Doctrinal and theoretical ideas, political context, institutional structure, strategy, and policy, all constrain one another. One of the most fascinating questions is which connections are tightest, and which less so. An associated issue is in which area to start the reform process, and how to shift among the various kinds of reform. It is clear to me that it is impossible to realize a new "intensive" strategy without changing the central institution of the Stalinist legacy, *i.e.,* the hierarchical administrative machinery that makes management responsive to higher level officials rather than to those with whom they interact in the social process of using resources and producing their outputs. This central institution and the extensive strategy were designed to work together, and they will have to change together. You can't have intensive growth in the old structure.

There are a few cleavages in the structure of the economy that make it possible to work on some areas without changing the system as a whole. Khrushchev had the idea of cutting agriculture loose from the rest of the economy to govern itself, guided only by prices. Although he never seriously tried to implement that vision, it remains an option available to the leaders if they have the wit and will to use it.

There is a great deal of room for maneuver in policy within the established strategy and institutions of the centrally planned economy. The first two generations of reformers have made good use of this option. Much of the slack in that domain has been taken up, although there are still options in the areas of wage policy, on the issue of allocation, on foreign trade, for improving performance.

Doctrine, as either a constraint or an impetus, is tied more loosely to the model. While there was tremendous progress in doctrinal matters and growth of insight in the Khrushchev period, it had little impact on either strategy or on institutions.

Despite my skepticism about specific doctrinal obstacles to change, it does seem to me that economic policy changes require increased sophistication in social thought generally. This interaction is well illustrated by the failure of Liberman's advocacy of profit as a success indicator to have much impact on reform in the 1960s. Even when seen against the momentous shift from Marxian to modern conceptions of economics that occurred in the 1960s, the much wider ranging understanding of social forces and mechanisms emerging today is impressive.[36]

There are a few doctrinal constraints that I think will continue to be significant. Comparing the USSR with other socialist societies, I am impressed with how little the Russians have been willing to enlarge the sphere of the private sector. Its only significant place in the system is the private plot in agriculture. And they have always been most reluctant to move in a consistent direction there—periods of relaxation have alternated with periods of tightening. Moreover, even where the system necessarily resorts to market mechanisms, as in the labor and consumer goods markets, the leaders are reluctant to let markets be markets. Outsiders find it easy to offer useful prescriptions in this area: to enhance incentives, let wages vary in accordance with productivity and scarcity, and price goods at cost. They have refused to consider proposals for market clearing prices for meat or housing, although such proposals would solve many problems and result in more efficient allocation of resources. Another prescription offered by outsiders has been to legalize some black markets and to open more activities to private initiative. Private economic activity has strong advantages in stimulating performance and it infringes on socialist values only slightly wherever three conditions exist. These are that the activity be labor intensive, so that it will not need to draw much on the central system for material inputs; that it involve great adaptability in satisfying the heterogeneous tastes of purchasers; and that it produce consumer goods for households rather than producer goods for the central system.[37] A great variety of services, such as repair, tailoring, housing maintenance, and restaurants, fit these conditions, and socialist experience elsewhere demonstrates the efficacy of private activity in such activities. But this is one sphere in which doctrine and ideology still appear to hold sway. The Soviet leaders prefer to accept black markets and corruption rather than to legalize that activity and let those incomes be open.

It is interesting to speculate on what deep-seated forces may exist, either in the values of the leadership, or in a (quite possibly correct) perception on their part that the populace thinks it has an implicit contract with the leadership not to upset current understandings about what is fair. Strongly felt ideas about *spravedlivost'*, or justice, are only now being brought into the arena of open discussion in the USSR, but even in the Brezhnev period there was some rudimentary discussion about social justice and implicit contracts with the people.

Much of the institutional reform (administrative tinkering) has been neither coherent nor guided by any sense of a new design toward which change is directed. One possible paradigm of a new system would be that of administrative decentralization, in which various kinds of functions and decisions are delegated downward in the hierarchy. In such a system managerial behavior would be monitored and controlled through more general indicators, so that choices would be increasingly made on the basis of information held locally or gathered in lateral interaction with others, rather than from above. Three variables to be considered in decentralization are where a decision is made, what criterion is used to guide it, and what information is needed to make it. It is difficult to find coherence among these three variables short of decentralizing all the way, at which point there occurs a qualitative change to marketization. If the decision criterion is simplified to the point of being the single number profit, if all the choices about how to maximize this performance variable are left to the firm, and it is guided solely by information it draws out of its interactions with other firms in market-like bargaining, the three variables that have to interact in guiding decisionmakers to efficient choices are once again coherent.

Much of the experience with reform tinkering shows the limitations of administrative decentralization as the approach to improving the behavior of enterprise management.

Can the system be revitalized without giving up the main instrument of administration, the administrative hierarchy? Has the model inherited from the Stalinist era finally outworn its usefulness? Is there life left in it still? Might it be possible to so modify it by more consistent administrative decentralization, or by some ingenious hybridization of the administrative principle and the market principle that producers will be interested in innovating, develop an interest in serving clients, become cost conscious, and so on? I am dubious. For me, the bottom line is that the administrative hierarchy connecting the central planners to the producers must be so shrunken and undercut that producers lose interest in its dictates. Without that change, there will be no change in the behavioral defects that now debilitate the system. It is impossible to make the administrative approach to running the economy so flexible and so capable of absorbing and using information that the principal-client relation on which it relies can elicit appropriate behavior from its enterprise directors. As S. S. Shatalin, one of the more perceptive Soviet economists says, " . . . our directors live not only in the real world of economic effect and responsibility which they recognize as determining their own objective interest, but above all in a world of administrative subordination. This distorts the true economic relations appropriate to a more efficient use of resources."[38]

I do not think that the efforts of two major cycles of reform policies over the 30-odd years since Stalin's death help us understand the vested interests that would fight these changes; the kind of maneuvering that would be effective in buiding coalitions to support radical change in the economic model; or whether the fight against vested interests can be successful on a broad front. We have seen many political victories that cleared the way for specific reform measures. But those have often been policy battles in the upper reaches of Party politics, without extensive engagement of parties-at-interest at lower levels. Gorbachev must therefore move into unfamiliar territory, and there is little experience that we can rely on for predicting how successful he will be.

Notes

1. See "A Soviet Model of Growth," in Evsey Domar, *Essays in the Theory of Economic Growth* (New York: Oxford University Press, 1957), pp. 223–261, and John E. Elliott, *Comparative Economic Systems* (Englewood Cliffs, NJ: Prentice-Hall, 1973), pp. 471–476.

2. Gregory Grossman, "Soviet Growth: Routine, Inertia and Pressure," *American Economic Review,* May 1960.

3. For some this was literal exile, as in Fel'dman's banishment to Central Asia. For others it was professional exile, as exemplified by Eugene Slutsky, the only Russian world-class economist of the period, who spent the rest of his life in meteorology.

4. Abram Bergson, *The Real National Income of Soviet Russia since 1928,* (Cambridge: Harvard University Press, 1961), p. 217. (There are theoretical problems in this measurement that exercise economists, but that we need not concern ourselves with.)

5. One source for this section is George W. Breslauer, *Khrushchev and Brezhnev as Leaders: Building Authority in Soviet Politics* (London: George Allen and Unwin, 1982). Breslauer's is a political rather than an economic study, but I have depended on it heavily for chronology and some political interpretations. Another is Carl Linden, *Khrushchev and the Soviet Leadership 1957–1964* (Baltimore: Johns Hopkins Univ Press, 1966).

6. *USSR: Measures of Economic Growth and Development, 1950–80,* Studies prepared for the Joint Economic Committee, Congress of the United States (Washington, DC: United States Government Printing Office, 1982).

7. Here, and in many other cases, I simply cite Soviet data from the statistical handbook TsSU, *Narodnoe khoziaistvo SSSR,* various years, without refinement.

8. This is a very complicated set of issues to follow conceptually, and it is made even more difficult by the fact that the Russians publish very little of the information we need to really judge what is happening. But this seems to be the conclusion of several studies, among which I would cite Martin Spechler, "Regional Developments in the USSR," in U.S. Congress, Joint Economic Committee, *Soviet Economy in a Time of Change* (Washington, DC: United States Government Printing Office, 1979), pp. 141–163; Gertrude Schroeder, "Regional Differences in Incomes and Levels of Living in the USSR," in V. N. Bandera and Z. L. Melnyk, *The Soviet Economy in Regional Perspective* (New York: Praeger, 1973), updated in "Soviet Regional Development Policies in Perspective," in NATO, *The USSR in the 1980s* (Brussels: NATO, 1979), pp. 125–141; Matthew Sagers, "The Development of the Soviet Periphery," *Soviet Economy,* volume 1, July/September, 1985, pp. 261–284; Elizabeth Clayton, "Regional Consumption Expenditures in the Soviet Union," *Bulletin of the Association for Comparative Economic Studies,* Vol XVII, nos. 2–3, 1975, pp. 27–46.

9. Robert Campbell, "Prospects for Siberian Economic Development," in Donald Zagoria, ed., *Soviet Policy in East Asia* (New Haven: Yale University Press, 1982), pp. 229–254.

10. Gertrude Schroeder, "Soviet Regional Development Policies in Perspective," in NATO, *The USSR in the 1980s* (Brussels: NATO, 1979), pp. 126–127.

11. Thane Gustafson, *Reform in Soviet Politics: Lessons of Recent Policies on Land and Water* (New York: Cambridge University Press, 1981).

12. O. K. Antonov, *Dlia vsekh i dlia sebia* (Moscow: Ekonomika, 1965).

13. L. V. Kantorovich, *Ekonomicheskii raschet nailuchshego ispol'zovaniia resursov,* Moscow, 1959.

14. E. Liberman, "Plans, Profits, and Bonuses," *Pravda,* 9 September 1962.

15. This shift was one of the rationales for scrapping the 6th Five Year Plan (1956–60) and substituting the Seven Year Plan which ran from 1959 through 1965. (It was generally said that newly discovered mineral wealth of Siberia had to be taken advantage of in a new plan.) And in fact, oil and gas which had accounted for 31 percent of the increment in mineral fuel production between 1950 and 1955, accounted for 89 percent in the Seven Year Plan period.

16. George W. Breslauer, *Khrushchev and Brezhnev as Leaders* (London: George Allen and Unwin, 1982).

17. "The Soviet Economy under a New Leader," in JEC, *Allocation of Resources in the Soviet Union and China,* Hearings before the Subcommittee on Economic Resources, Competitiveness and Security Economics of the Joint Economic Committee, March 19, 1986, p. 80. This exaggerates the slowdown a bit, since the growth rates for the Ninth and Tenth are based on GNP in 1970 prices, and for the Eleventh on 1982 prices. Measured in the same, 1982, prices, there was only slight deceleration between the Tenth and the Eleventh.

18. *Ibid.*

19. This line had been pushed by Marshall Ogarkov from the early 1980s in his dispute with the political leadership.

20. See, for instance, CIA testimony in JEC, *Allocation of Resources in the Soviet Union and China,* Hearings before the Subcommittee on Economic Resources, Competitiveness and Security Economics of the Joint Economic Committee, Nov 21, 1984, and January 15, 1985, pp. 56–57.

21. Murray Feshbach, "Issues in Soviet Health Problems," in *Soviet Economy in the 1980's: Problems and Prospects,* Selected Papers submitted to the Joint Economic Committee, Congress of the United States (Washington, DC: United States Government Printing Office, 1982) Part 2, pp. 208–227.

22. A comprehensive collection of laws, regulations and commentaries covering the changes is available in an addendum to *Ekonomicheskaia Gazeta,* called *Khoziaistvennaia reforma v SSSR,* Moscow, 1969.

23. "The Soviet Economy on a Treadmill of 'Reforms,'" *Soviet Economy in a Time of Change,* A Compendium of Papers Submitted to the Joint Economic Committee, Congress of the United States (Washington, DC: United States Government Printing Office, 1979), pp. 312–340.

24. *Ibid,* p. 337.

25. This is well developed in Janusz Zielinski's *Economic Reforms in Polish Industry* (New York: Oxford University Press, 1973).

26. This is in his speech to the June, 1985, conference on questions of accelerating scientific-technical progress. M. S. Gorbachev, *Izbrannye rechi i stat'i,* (Moscow: Politizdat, 1985), p. 118.

27. Ministerstvo Vneshnei Torgovli SSSR, *Vneshniaia torgovlia SSSR,* various years.

28. Robert W. Campbell, *Soviet Energy Technologies: Planning, Policy, Research and Development,* (Bloomington: Indiana University Press, 1983), pp. 221–225.

29. S. S. Shatalin, "Effektivnoe ispol'zovanie resursov: interesy i stimuly," *EKO,* 1986:12, pp. 3–22 gives some cogent illustrations.

30. This is perhaps an arguable point. We have certainly become much more aware of this phenomenon and its corrosive effect on discipline, though maybe I am mistaken in describing it as peculiarly a Brezhnev-Kosygin period phenomenon.

31. Gregory Grossman, "A Note on Soviet Inflation," in U.S. Congress, Joint Economic Committee, *Soviet Economy in the 1980's: Problems and Prospects,* Part 1 (Washington, DC: United States Government Printing Office, 1982), pp. 267–286.

32. This is the *Institut ekonomiki i organizatsii promyshlennogo proizvodstva* of the Siberian Division of the Academy of Sciences of the USSR.

33. The fullest account of the ins and outs of this controversy and the roles of various institutions in it is Pekka Sutela, *Socialism, Planning, and Optimality: A Study in Soviet Economic Thought.* Commentationes Scientiarum Socialium, 1984, no. 25.

34. A convenient summarization of the Johnson diagnosis is available in D. Gale Johnson and Karen Brooks, *Prospects for Soviet Agriculture in the 1980's* (Bloomington: Indiana University Press, 1983).

35. Arthur J. Alexander, *R and D in Soviet Aviation.* The RAND Corporation, R-589-PR, Santa Monica, 1970.

36. The kind of issues that Tatiana Zaslavskaia and the sociologists have brought up are Exhibit A, of course, but one finds similar sensitivity to novel aspects of social processes across the disciplinary map. A couple of interesting examples are S. S. Shatalin in economics, and B. P. Kurashvili in law.

37. This is not an absolute set of requirements. Private enterprises servicing state production can also work fairly well, as in contract labor and in the industrial activity that progressive agricultural units have developed even in the USSR.

38. S. S. Shatalin, "Effektivnoe ispol'zovanie resursov: interesy i stimuly," *EKO,* 1986:12, pp. 3–22.

4

War, Weapons, and Soviet Foreign Policy

Robert Legvold

For a people so worried about Soviet military power, we have a strangely confined way of framing the issue. Most of the time we dwell on how much of it they have. Occasionally we add a word about the menacing side of Soviet military doctrine. And always in the background there is the simple, settled faith that Soviet leaders believe greatly in the power of the sword. But hardly ever do we push beyond, do we try to explain why the Soviets arm as they do or what fears, hopes, conceptions, and misconceptions drive them. For this most central of all issues we carry on without much sense of, and apparently without much interest in, the sources of Soviet defense policy, military practice, and notions of security.

Like all countries, however, particularly the large and ambitious ones, the Soviet Union has become the military challenge that it is for enormously complex reasons. Unraveling the puzzle requires one to travel through a maze of connections linking historical biases, strategic concepts, images of war, the process by which weapons are acquired, and even the prism through which our military efforts are viewed (and those of NATO and China and now Japan). These and a few more elements are the puzzle's pieces. Cause and effect join most of them, but by devious paths leaving the pursuer perplexed and nearly overwhelmed.

For example, the way Soviet military and political leaders picture a Third World War obviously shapes the strategy by which they intend to fight it, and this strategy in turn creates requirements for certain forces rather than for others. But how many additional factors play a role? To what extent is Soviet strategy also the product of tradition, inertia, and the lessons of the last war and to what extent is it the creature of the other side's manifest strategy? To what degree are the character and structure of Soviet forces the outcome of a political process within the Soviet military or among various domestic Soviet economic interests of which the military is only one? To what degree are they fashioned by political leaders with aggressive peacetime foreign policy objectives in mind?

And then there are the more fundamental issues. What is the impact of Soviet notions of security? Or of Soviet beliefs about the role of force in international politics? Or, for that matter, of Soviet views on the nature of military power and its relationship to a nation's overall sources of strength?

To reduce the analytical challenge to size, I shall divide the relevant aspects of Soviet behavior into three parts: First, the Soviet approach to the question of war—how Soviet leaders think about war, how they prepare for it, and how they are likely to act if it comes. Second, the Soviet approach to the use of military force in peacetime, including Soviet intervention in Third World crises. And, third, the Soviet approach to arms control. These categories, while not exhaustive, incorporate most of what matters to us when we think about arms and the Soviet Union. They arch beyond the narrower questions of the Soviet Union's wartime strategy, peacetime force posture, and the competitive arming of the superpowers. They extend to the active use of force and to the diplomacy of arms control—to the intersection of foreign policy and security policy. They, therefore, require more broad-based explanations appropriate to all aspects of Soviet behavior, which brings me to the second half of my analytical framework.

Understanding any state's behavior abroad means tracing the impact of two basic influences: that of the international setting and that of domestic politics and process. When theorists deal with the first, they ordinarily have in mind the character of the international political system and, in particular, the structure of power within it. States are said to behave in one way in a bipolar system and in another in a multipolar system. But that raises the issue to too high a level of abstraction. To understand the impact of the external setting on foreign and security policy, a notion at once more diffuse and mundane is required, one sensitive to the effect of the lesser changes in context, those that, while leaving the system unaltered, do affect the range of alternatives available to national leaders.

The other influence, the internal factor, poses even stiffer analytical challenges. Not only is it difficult to conceive a framework capturing the enormously ramified domestic political background to foreign policy; it is also usually next to impossible to know who gets what, when, and how in a shrouded system like that of the Soviet Union. My solution in this essay is to avoid any pretense of completeness in reconstructing the dynamic by which Soviet internal politics shapes external behavior, and to introduce the domestic factor only where it has been or *may* have been decisive.

Neither of these two influences, however, works its effect directly. For the most part each is mediated by perception, by the way people comprehend international realities, and by the competing images of reality infused, as a result, into the domestic political process. This is not to dispute that people and institutions act out of institutional and self-aggrandizing reasons; it is, rather, to reintroduce the notion that politics is frequently about genuinely held differences of view.

In sum, what follows is an effort to explain why the Soviets think about and prepare for war the way they do, why in times of peace they use force as they do, and why they seek what they do from arms control. For the explanation, it examines two main sources—the external and internal settings of policy—but as filtered by the perceptions of people who make or influence decisions.

The real interest, however, is not simply in why things are as they appear to be, but in the changes they undergo and in the reasons they do. And, amidst the changes, whether there are traces of what might be called learning, a concept I will define later when I return to the issue.

The Historical Background

One can never go straight to the heart of the matter where the Soviet Union is concerned. A dense, often unexpressed set of assumptions stands in the way, or shows the way, depending on one's analytical predilections. In the case of this topic, two assumptions are central. The first involves the place of military power in the Soviet—indeed, in the Russian—world view. Prevailing wisdom is fairly straightforward on this score: The Soviets, like their Russian forebears, are thought to cherish military power far more than most national leaderships, to define their status and well-being by their store of it, to trust it as the means they know best for securing and enlarging their rule, and to judge others, respecting or dismissing them, according to their share of it.

The second assumption relates to the Soviet approach to the pursuit of national security. Again, conventional wisdom is straightforward. Henry Kissinger was only saying a little better what many others had said before him when he wrote in his memoirs that "Russia's rulers—Communists or tsars—," perhaps because of an "insecure history, perhaps from a sense of inferiority," have responded "by identifying security not only with distance but also with domination. They have never believed that they could build a moral consensus among other peoples. Absolute security for Russia has meant infinite insecurity for all its neighbors."[1]

Convictions so widely and deeply held usually have some foundation, and so it is with these. Soviet leaders from Stalin's time have indeed placed great stress on the importance of military power, compelling their society to sacrifice mightily in order to possess it. Celebrating the virtue of military strength is, in fact, a tradition long antedating them. One thinks of Harold Nicolson's Russian general who, when discussing the approaching Congress of Vienna, boasted, "Well, so far as that goes, one does not need to worry much about negotiations when one has 600,000 men under arms."[2] Or one recalls Sergei Witte, Prime Minister to Nicholas II, asking his readers rhetorically, "Who created the Russian Empire, transforming the semi-Asiatic Moscovite tsardom into the most influential, most dominant, grandest European power?" And then answering: "Only the power of the army's bayonet. The world bowed not to our culture, not to our bureaucratized church, not to our wealth and prosperity. It bowed to our might."[3]

Russia's rulers through the centuries did more than venerate the idea of military power: beginning with Tsar Peter, they recast their entire society to guarantee its growth. Peter's military reform, after all, served as the inspiration for nearly all of his savaging of the old social and administrative order. "Everything undertaken by the great Tsar," writes one historian, "whether in administration, education or economics, was, in a very direct sense, derived from or consequential upon his singleminded battle for the creation of an efficient military machine."[4] Those who followed him preserved a bureaucratized nobility, organized along lines entirely of service to the state, beginning with military service, a home industry created by the state to address its requirements, chief among which was the elimination of military weakness, and a society divided into an enslaved, backward peasantry and a westernized elite, created to meet the challenges of Europe, the first of which was the war waged by Sweden's Charles XII against Peter's Russia for the first twenty years of the eighteenth century.

Lenin and those with whom he made the 1917 revolution said that the purpose of their handiwork was to destroy this subordination of society to military need. They were dedicated to smashing the old order and with it the primacy of the military imperative. Lenin even opposed the preservation of a standing army, favoring a people's militia as the proper way to avoid undue militarization. However, not only did this moment of idealism pass quickly during the Civil War and the intervention of 1918–22, but also, when Stalin imposed his own harsh revolution on the country a decade later, the historic combination of politico-economic transformation and military preoccupation re-emerged. This time, however, it was reinforced by a military leadership that stood for the concept of a nation in arms, organized for war, whose industry was designed to produce for the military and keyed to providing the advanced technologies that someone like Mikhail Frunze believed would decide the outcome of the next war. " 'Red militarism,' " David Holloway has written, "is an apt term for many aspects of Soviet life in the 1930s. The creation of military power was one of the main objectives of the industrialization drive, and military requirements had an important effect on the pattern of industrial development."[5] By the mid-1930s, the Soviets had embarked on a vast armament program that, with only momentary exceptions, has not slackened since.

But to leave matters here would be to ignore an equally important aspect of the issue. While it is beyond doubt that Soviet leaders assign a high value to military power, at the heart of their beliefs is an essentially economic, rather than military, notion of power. They assume that the crucial dynamic in international politics is, in their phrase, the "correlation of forces," and they measure progress by the pace at which it changes. The concept, when understood as they understand it, has a grand sweep, vastly exceeding our more narrow version of it. In their minds, it stands for all the major trends in an historical age, not merely the growth of Soviet power, or the growth of Soviet military power. It is as much dependent on the problems affecting Western society as it is on the Soviet capacity for bringing revolution by bayonet. It incorporates everything from the momentum of the so-called national liberation struggle in the Third World to the vigor of the peace movement in the West and even to the militancy of capitalist trade unions. To the degree that the correlation of forces reflects the strength of the socialist camp, the notion of strength has far more to do with the basic (or comparative) dynamism of these societies than with the size of their armies or the collective throw-weight of their intercontinental ballistic missile (ICBM) force.[6]

Khrushchev's exuberance stemmed from this notion of power. When he launched his frontal assault on the West's position in the Berlin crises (1958–61), he acted from a conviction that the underlying balance of power was shifting; but for him, the balance of power did not mean only, or even primarily, the military balance. His arrogance of power may be traced directly to his confidence in the dynamism of the Soviet economy and the momentum of Soviet science—symbolized in the launching of Sputnik in the fall of 1957. He actually thought that the Soviet economy was outpacing the American economy, and, in his euphoria, went so far in the 1961 Party Program as to pledge that by 1970 the Soviet Union would surpass the United States in *per capita* Gross National Product. The growth of Soviet military might would follow naturally, and it would have its own utility, not the least of which would be to contain any intemperate Western reaction to this fundamental shift in fortunes. But military might was to be the result of other societal events, rather than their source.

Gorbachev shares Khrushchev's perspective on power, although in Gorbachev's case the tables are turned. He, too, places great emphasis on the economic underpinning of Soviet power, but, because he is worried about Soviet economic performance, his themes are different. Gorbachev has said since he came to prominence that, unless something is done to correct current economic trends, the Soviet Union will not enter the twenty-first century a great power worthy of the name. Military might will not do it alone. Indeed, as he continually reminds his military leadership, the economy must be attended to if the base of Soviet military power is to be preserved.

The same can be said of the Soviet concept of security. It, too, has more than one side. On the one hand, Russia's leaders over the centuries did seek their nation's security through the absorption of others' lands—as Richard Pipes has noted, at the rate of "every year the territorial equivalent of modern Holland for 150 years running"—and their Bolshevik successors have emulated them by striving to control, albeit not to absorb, a still wider band of neighboring states.[7] Long before World War II, Stalin had established as the standard of security for his country the appearance of a "ring of brother states."[8] He did this in the 1920s when championing the concept of "socialism in one country," the notion by which the Soviet Union came to be the garrison of revolution rather than its instrument or spark.

Some would maintain that this expansionism was predatory, and for the most part neither induced by fear, nor a matter of seeking greater security. Pipes, for example, has written that Russia's agricultural poverty and the opportunity to plunder neighboring lands, unprotected by natural geographic barriers, were a driving force behind Russian imperialism.[9] Whether one accepts this interpretation or another stressing the ebb and flow of invasion and counterthrust across the unhindering plains of Eurasia, the other side of the story is how contemporary Soviets understand their country's past. From Solzhenitsyn to the most loyal regime intellectual, they see these military strivings as responses to an imperative. To borrow the words of a contemporary Soviet historian: "Whether defending itself or taking the offensive, on the whole Russia waged just and unavoidable wars. . . . It had no other choice. If the country wanted to live and develop, then for five centuries it had to cast aside its scabbards as useless and take up the sword to prove its right to life and development to its neighbors. To a certain extent these wars were people's wars."[10]

To this sense of historical rectitude, Soviet leaders add a deeply emotional image of the threats that have beset their regime since 1917. In their view, their enemies have not been merely competitors or even aggressors, but rather haters of their revolution, obsessed with a determination to smother it, ready to strike an alliance with any movement or government, no matter how odious, capable of doing it harm. Until the late 1950s, Soviet leaders portrayed their country and their socialist allies as on the defensive against this threat, indeed, as literally encircled by such adversaries.

But here, too, there is more to the story, and this additional dimension has recently begun to assume a special significance. In the late 1950s, the Soviets stopped complaining of their country's encirclement. (Khrushchev said that no longer could anyone tell who was encircling whom.) Then, during the next two decades they entirely let go of their fear for the territorial integrity of the Soviet state. If, through the military accomplishments of his tenure, Brezhnev has left one major legacy, it has been to make Soviet leaders and elites at last believe in the security of their country from any plausible threat of military attack. They can at last be sure that no combination of adversaries would, except from sheer desperation, contemplate striking the Soviet Union.

Gorbachev is the first Soviet leader to benefit from this dimension of the Brezhnev legacy. Perhaps it is already apparent in the strikingly different way he frames the question of national security. For Gorbachev has begun to speak about the link between Soviet national security and the security of other nations—the link between national and mutual security. He is the first Soviet leader to say that his country cannot pursue its own security at the expense of others, particularly that of the United States. There can be, he remarked in an interview with *l'Humanité* in February 1986, "no security for the USSR without security for the United States."[11] Since then this acknowledgment has become a frequently repeated theme.

Whether Gorbachev's new language represents a genuine rethinking of old biases and whether it has or will manifest itself in changed behavior are topics to which I will return later. First, however, I wish to address the related and more concrete matters of the Soviet approach to war, to the peacetime use of force, and to arms control, not the least because they bear directly on the subject.

War

Great powers arm for war. When they amass vast quantities of armaments and raise large standing armies, they are readying themselves for general war or its obverse, preventing general war. They are not preparing themselves for local wars or other violent events in the Third World. Nor are they merely trying to give their foreign policy teeth. These other considerations may be by-products of the arming they do—consciously produced and valuable by-products—and, at times, even consciously sought objectives, for which some of the country's men and arms are specifically designated. But the bulk of the tanks, artillery, aircraft, ships, and missiles that are manufactured and deployed, and the bulk of the troops that are trained and organized exist either to fight or to deter a general war.

This has been true throughout the twentieth century and it remains true today even for the superpowers and even in the nuclear era. It remains particularly true for the Soviet Union, which, while more interested now in the secondary uses of military power, has never devoted a fraction of the attention the Americans have to raising forces for purposes short of war. Measured against the effort to prepare for general war—a Third World War—Soviet attention to lesser conflicts has been trifling. Counter-insurgency warfare, Green Berets, Marines, rapid deployment forces have not significantly diverted Soviet military planners, not, at least, until the Afghan war. Soviet force projection capabilities, growing steadily over the last twenty years, are largely derivative from forces intended for a general war in Central Europe and not expressly created for another mission. (As a result, when judged against the projection capabilities of American forces, which have been, they suffer great gaps.) And nuclear doctrine remains the responsibility of military leaders, rather than civilian strategists given to calculating the finer foreign policy implications of nuclear imbalances.

As a result, any understanding of Soviet military might that begins anywhere but with the place of war in Soviet thinking will miss the mark. The kinds of weapons the Soviet Union has, in the quantities in which it possesses them, and how they are deployed, are overwhelmingly the product of what the military believe they require to wage war in Europe or in Europe and Asia. The evolution of their beliefs on this score, therefore, is a critical part of any assessment of the meaning of shifts in Soviet military strength.

How the Soviets approach the question of war—what they think war will require, either to wage or to prevent—is very much a function of context. That is, features of the international setting play a major, often a decisive, role in establishing the Soviet view of war, and none more so than the arrival of the nuclear era. Nuclear weapons are a great divide separating one era of Soviet concepts of war from another. Where before Soviet leaders accepted, indeed, proclaimed the inevitability of war, after the nuclear era had begun and the implications of the new weapons had sunk in, they declared war to be nothing of the kind. Not only could war be avoided, but Soviet policy was taxed to ensure that it would be.

Because we have so long lived with the recognition of the folly that nuclear weapons have made of war—a realization that came readily to the non-Leninist West—we have never quite appreciated the watershed that it represented to the Soviets. For them, by contrast, until the 1950s war had not merely been a possibility but a certainty. Their dogma made it such, as did their instincts and emotions. From the earliest days of the Bolshevik regime, Soviets leaders took it for granted that sooner or later a war with the imperialists would engulf them. This was the premise of the theses on military doctrine prepared for the Tenth Party Congress in March, 1921.[12] It remained the assumption of Stalin and his comrades in the aftermath of the Second World War. In David Holloway's phrase, the postwar years were for them "a prewar period."[13]

Reversing these many ingrained assumptions and replacing them with the imperative of avoiding war, therefore, represented a far more wrenching adjustment for the Soviet leaders than for their Western counterparts. That it did can be seen in the delayed and tortured transition to a new view of war in the years after Stalin's death. Stalin himself failed to understand the implications of the nuclear revolution, a point made by a number of authors, but obscured by a wider tendency to feature Stalin's affected indifference to America's new atomic bomb, a reaction rightly interpreted as the opposite of his real feelings.[14] The proof of Stalin's blindness was in his clinging to the utterly obsolete notion of the "permanent operating factors" as deciding war's outcome. The permanent factors included the stability of the home front, the morale of the armed forces, the quantity and quality of military divisions, their armament, and the abilities of commanders. These, rather than technology or surprise, were what counted.

What is important, however, is to understand the reason for Stalin's blindness. When he denied that nuclear weapons had transformed war, when he insisted that the next war would be decided by the same factors that had decided the last one, he was not simply whistling past the graveyard or attempting to make the best of a weak hand. He was betraying the hold that powerful assumptions concerning the nature and sources of war had on his generation.

Not until two years after his death did Soviet military leaders begin to acknowledge the dubious sanity of Stalin's ideas in a nuclear world. Even when they began to confess that the first, surprise blow with nuclear weapons might "be one of the decisive conditions for the achievement of success, not only in the initial period of a war, but in the war as a whole," they still felt obliged to defend the notion of the permanent operating factors.[15] Several more years would pass before they could completely free themselves of the Stalinist legacy, formally banishing all trace of old concepts, and putting in their place a thoroughly revamped notion of what the next (nuclear) war would be like.

The sequence is interesting, and, if sequence reveals cause, important in assessing developments in our own day. Long before the Soviet political and military leadership had come to understand the new features of war in the nuclear age and officially introduced their concept of what war now entailed—a stage reached only at the very end of the 1950s—Khrushchev had cast aside the old notion of war's inevitability. He did so at the Twentieth Party Congress in February, 1956. He and the military leadership may not yet have determined what war had become, but the awful implications of nuclear weapons had convinced them that it could never be.

Thus, a radical revision of the setting (the advent of nuclear weapons) led to a repudiation of an old and entrenched concept (the notion of the inevitability of war), which, in turn, was followed by a redefinition of the phenomenon (the nature of war). And, to finish the sequence, this altered understanding of the phenomenon then produced a different approach to it—that is, produced a different military strategy and forces to support it. By 1960, Khrushchev had announced that the next war would be inexorably a nuclear one, and would be so from its opening moments. He had created a new service, the Strategic Rocket Forces (1959), and subordinated all other services, including the ground forces, to it. He had pronounced the surface navy and aviation to be obsolete, overtaken by the new requirements of war. And he had begun a large-scale demobilization of military personnel.

In the 1970s, Soviet concepts changed once again (in 1977 the notion of strategic superiority was set aside and in 1981 the notion of victory in war). Again, shifts in the setting had occurred beforehand (the achievement by the Soviet Union of nuclear parity, the slow construction of an arms control regime consolidating the reality of mutual assured destruction, with the simultaneous collapse of detente and an accelerated American defense effort). It seemed not too much to suppose that further adjustments in the Soviet image of the phenomenon of war itself would follow. And then in their train was it not to be expected that the thrust of military strategy and the character of Soviet military power would soon change as well? I will come back to the question.

Between the 1950s and the 1970s, however, there had been other modifications of the external setting—less dramatic than the introduction of nuclear weapons, but of vast consequence nonetheless for the Soviet approach to war. It is now commonly agreed that in the second half of the 1960s, after Khrushchev's ouster, the Soviet image of war, the military objectives to be sought in war, and the requirements for Soviet forces began to undergo a massive reworking.[16] Gradually, Soviet military planners would come to believe that war need not be an instantaneous and convulsive eruption of nuclear attacks, but rather one with a lengthy conventional phase, or perhaps a decisive conventional phase. In effect, where Khrushchev had rejected the inevitability of war, his successors now rejected the inevitability that war must be nuclear.

The causes were once more in the external setting. Michael MccGwire, who has offered the starkest and most far-reaching version of the transformation, proposes two such causes.[17] The first and lesser cause, indeed, more catalyst than cause, was de Gaulle's decision to withdraw France from the NATO military organization. By thus diminishing NATO's capabilities, first in depriving the alliance of military resources and second in reducing its defensive depth, the French, says MccGwire, stirred the thought in the Soviet military that conventional forces— indeed, their conventional forces—could prevail in a war. But the inspiration depended on another primary cause: the adoption of the concept of flexible response by the Americans in the period after 1961. Whatever may have been Soviet assumptions about nuclear weapons and war, once the Americans began to speak and act as if they believed war could and should be kept beneath the nuclear threshold, the Soviet Union suddenly had a conventional option.[18]

From this shift, originating in these sources, a whole series of consequences followed, affecting the whole of Soviet military power. First, to continue with MccGwire's version of the argument, the Soviet Union's basic military objectives underwent fundamental change. Freed from the specter of inevitable escalation, the Soviet leadership could now take seriously the wartime objective of avoiding nuclear devastation. But, if this were achieved in part through a strategy sparing the United States from the same fate, the other long-standing Soviet wartime purpose of seizing Western Europe intact required that the Soviets keep the Americans from gathering their forces, reattacking, and driving the Soviet Union back.

To pursue these revised objectives, the Soviet leadership had to fundamentally alter Soviet military strategy. To put itself in a position to implement an altered strategy, it had to adjust not only the structure of forces but also the operational concepts by which they were to be employed. For example, nuclear strategy could no longer be predicated on preemptive use: launching nuclear missiles on the *presumption* the other side was about to strike. Instead, strategy left the initiative to the other side and assumed the Soviet Union would fire only after U.S. missiles were already on their way. In the jargon of nuclear strategy, this is a posture of "launch under attack." But a launch-under-attack policy required missiles that could be readied and fired in the comparative instant that it took U.S. missiles to reach the Soviet Union. And the execution of the policy required that nuclear-release decisions, down to the sequence of attack, be transferred from the military leadership, where they had been based during the earlier era, back to the political leadership.[19]

Or, to take another example, the new objectives led to a strategy stressing not only a rapid breakthrough with conventional forces and an attack in depth but also the suppression of NATO's theater nuclear capability by conventional means. This in turn imposed the need for important structural changes in Soviet ground forces. Not only was it necessary to find a conventional firepower substitute for nuclear weapons in effecting the initial breakthrough, but enormously enhanced requirements were also placed on modernized conventional means to ensure a rapid penetration into the rear areas. Destroying a theater nuclear capability by non-nuclear means created a whole new set of demands for Soviet aviation.

These examples scarcely scratch the surface. Literally every Soviet service, every aspect of force structuring, every element of operational doctrine, and the whole of military strategy was touched and, more often than not, transformed by these new military objectives, which were the result of a new image of war, itself the result of changes in the external setting.

The international setting, as I suggested at the outset, however, is only one of two principal influences on Soviet behavior in the military sphere. The other is the domestic setting. Of the two, the domestic setting seems to me to be the less decisive influence, but at times it has nevertheless had a significant effect. In the early postwar days, for example, the strength of Stalin's personality and biases, not to mention his hold on political power, contributed significantly to the delayed adaptation by the Soviet Union to the nuclear era. The peculiar lessons that Stalin (though not he alone) drew from the Second World War—and one can only guess at the enormous psychological commitment that he must have made to them—almost guaranteed a blindness to the ultimate implications of nuclear weapons.

Even when the adjustment began in the first years after his death, domestic politics intervened, encumbering the process. Georgy Malenkov, Stalin's heir apparent, who seemed to have grasped the revolution that war had undergone, made the case for giving up on old ideas, and presented a version of what Khrushchev would put before the Twentieth Party Congress three years later. Khrushchev fought him at the time, successfully it turned out, in a fight which contributed both to making him Stalin's actual heir and to a further delay in the Soviet Union's historic accommodation to nuclear weapons.

It was not the first time that a basic disagreement among Soviet leaders had profoundly affected the direction of Soviet thinking about war and its imperatives. In the early 1920s, the great debate between Trotsky and Frunze over the need for and content of military doctrine— proletarian military doctrine, they would say—cut to the very heart of the Bolshevik regime's fledgling efforts to set a military course.

And it was not the last time that Khrushchev, as a political force, would make a critical difference to Soviet military practice. When he made his peace, so to speak, with nuclear weapons, he clearly took their implications much farther than the majority of the Soviet military found congenial. His extreme version of what one Soviet officer would call "one-variant war," by which was meant a war that went immediately nuclear, fought largely with nuclear weapons, belittled conventional forces and a combined-arms approach, much to the distress of the professional military. Their essentially open opposition sped the quick decision in 1961 to halt the reduction of military manpower and to rehabilitate the combined-arms approach. But in this instance, as in the others, the real impact of the domestic factor was more on the timing and the degree of change than on change itself.

Today, we face the prospect that this complex mesh of cause and effect—deriving from both politics at home and a changing world beyond—may be advancing toward another historic leap forward. Slowly under the old leaders who ruled in the late 1970s and now, tumultuously, under Gorbachev, Soviet conceptions of war and how the Soviet Union should ready itself for one are in motion. By the late 1970s, Brezhnev, Gromyko and the others had already begun to alter some of the most enduring notions underlying Soviet military planning. First came the repudiation of strategic superiority as a goal of Soviet arming. In a speech in early 1977 in Tula, Brezhnev undid what had always been presented as an honorable and openly professed aim of Soviet policy, the achievement of "superiority in arms."[20] Four years later, at the Twenty-sixth Party Congress, Brezhnev denied that there could be victory in nuclear war, a sensible admission which, as it happens, Soviet leaders had not been able to bring themselves to make until

1981, not the least because their military did not want to concede the point. In 1982, the last year of Brezhnev's life, the Soviet leadership announced a no-first-use doctrine: a pledge not to fire nuclear weapons before nuclear weapons had first been launched by the other side.

All of this, of course, could be viewed as simply word play—an effort to say what would appeal to anti-nuclear groups in the West and, in particular, what would take the wind out of the sails of Western critics who were using to good effect the frightening aspects of Soviet military doctrine. Thus, while in one sense a direct response to the external environment, these reformulations could hardly be said to represent conceptual changes bearing on the Soviet image of war or on what Soviet military leaders still intended to do should one occur. Instead, from this vantage point, they were a rhetorical ploy, designed to conceal the absence of any real change in Soviet thought or deed.

Others would be more inclined to see these adjustments as the logical culmination of the post-Khrushchev evolution in the Soviet concept of war. MccGwire, for example, treats the disavowal of strategic superiority as a goal, the debunking of victory in war, and the pledge of no first use as the corollary of a posture whose purpose is to avoid the nuclear devastation of the Soviet Union in the course of a war waged in Europe and Asia by conventional means. In this case, Soviet leaders could be said to be simply updating basic political concepts to reflect the revolution that had already taken place in the Soviet image of war.

My own impression is that the process was more intricate and diffuse, but, as a result, a still more powerful agent of the change to come later in the Gorbachev era. By the early 1980s, several changes in the international setting directly threatened the late-1960s and early-1970s Soviet image of war. Soviet cynics or worst-case analysts—many of whom were doubtless in the military—could hold that the Americans had ceased to disbelieve in nuclear escalation, had stopped working to raise the nuclear threshold, and had set as their goal the ability to fight and win in a nuclear war.[21] An arms control program designed to destroy the heart of the Soviet Union's (land-based) nuclear deterrent; a modernization of NATO INF designed to demolish the C^3 of the Soviet theaters of military action (TVDs), allowing virtually no warning time;[22] the development of counterforce on land and at sea, designed to give the United States a large-scale damage-limiting capability; capped off by SDI, designed not to render nuclear missiles "impotent and obsolete" on both sides but rather more secure and more effective on one side, and doctrinal statements reintroducing the idea of successfully waging a protracted nuclear war—these, the cynic or worst-case analyst might think, would raise doubts about the realism of the war for which Soviet leaders had been preparing over the last decade and a half.

Even leaving the Americans out of the picture, other developments were pounding relentlessly against prevailing Soviet assumptions. The most powerful of these was new technology, which, when incorporated into NATO defense, threw into doubt the ability of the Soviet Union to execute its conventional-war strategy. Thanks to radical technical advances, new and more potent means of tracking, targeting, and destroying Soviet troops and hardware were entering NATO force structures, significantly reducing the advantage of the offense over the defense. If these innovations did not in themselves rectify the balance between the Warsaw Pact and NATO, they did begin to destroy any serious confidence Soviet military planners could have in their ability to slice through NATO's front lines, and with great dispatch envelop the rear areas.

The skirmishing between Marshal Nikolai Ogarkov and the Soviet political leadership in the early 1980s must be understood in this light. He was not, it appears, so much raising a cry over the rubles he could not get for defense as he was expressing his exasperation with an image of war that was changing too slowly. He seems to have had a clear sense of how rapidly the old premises were being eroded, a clearer sense than his political superiors. He also evidently had fairly definite notions about what should be done.[23] When in the fall of 1984 the Soviet leaders got him out of their hair, they did not free themselves from the dilemma behind his impatience. The challenge was not in a person but, rather, in a situation. Having exerted themselves for a decade and a half to equip their country for a war that well might not go nuclear, they now faced American leaders who seemed less interested in playing by those rules and new trends in technology that threatened to help NATO even if they were to play by them.

In fact two quite separate impulses may have been converging at about this time. For political leaders, in a vague and half-acknowledged fashion, a new moment of truth was arriving. At last they had reached a point of genuine nuclear parity with—and in some respects superiority over—the other superpower, only to discover that the ensuing dynamic was not one of quiet American acceptance. On the contrary, frightened by what they took to be the momentum of Soviet nuclear programs, the Americans had restored an older image of the Soviet threat and recommitted themselves to an ambitious arms buildup of their own. Even before the election of Ronald Reagan, in the last two years of the Carter Administration, in Soviet eyes, the Americans were reverting to an older ethos that held that the Soviet Union was not entitled to real military equivalence. In an earlier phase, indeed, up to the 1970s,

Soviet leaders were so fixed on overcoming the disparity between their nuclear forces and those of the United States that little reason existed to contemplate what came after the discrepancy was overcome. But, once rough parity was achieved by the early 1970s, they had more reason to address the effect of one side's military effort on the other or, at least, to contemplate an ongoing military competition and an adversary scarcely ready to throw in the towel.

If in Brezhnev's day this was only a dawning awareness, still too weak to prompt clear shifts in Soviet behavior, under Gorbachev the traces of rethinking are far more impressive. In Brezhnev's day, the new formulas seemed at best a vague acknowledgment of the need to approach the military contest differently once the goal of nuclear parity had been achieved. Gorbachev, however, not only talks as though he has grasped the hopelessly unending nature of the nuclear arms race, but he is also beginning to do things directly impinging on the Soviet role in it. Thus, he not only offers ideas that are, for a Soviet leader, fresh, such as the relating of one country's security to another's— which is, after all, a way of admitting that one country's arming has an impact on the other. He also seems to be moving toward a far more restrictive set of criteria for determining the Soviet defense effort. In the press, in his speeches and in what he has said privately to the military, he seems to be groping toward a concept of sufficiency as a basis for allocating resources to defense. He speaks of ensuring Soviet security, but not by imitating the United States or attempting to match every feature of its military establishment. We will do what is necessary to defend ourselves, he tells his audiences, "but we will not take a single step beyond the demands and requirements of sensible, adequate defense."[24] To his military he maintains that struggling to keep in perfect step with the Americans is playing the game as the other side wants it played. When the underlying justification of new programs and systems is to keep up with the Joneses, rather than clearly de-monstrable military need, Gorbachev is said to be saying no to his defense planners. His supporters in intellectual circles have even begun to spell out the features of what he and they call "reasonable suffi-ciency." Reasonable sufficiency, they say, consists of pared-down nuclear arsenals capable only of launching a secure second strike; conventional forces capable only of defending, not conducting major offensive op-erations, and interventionary forces capable of deterring an aggressor in regional crises but insufficient to prop up a regime incapable of defending itself.[25]

Soviet leaders are not merely beginning to confront the kind of world they want now when nuclear parity is theirs, yet accompanied by a reflexive readiness on the part of the Americans to answer anything that looks like a Soviet desire to outmatch them. It is now beginning to appear that they, along with their military leadership, are also struggling to deal with the disintegration of their prevailing image of war. The manifestation of this is a slow stirring of interest in strategic defensive operations. For half a century the Soviets have emphasized the offense: a swift, massive forward thrust through the enemy's front lines, overwhelming his secondary forces, and devastating the infrastructure of war in his rear areas. But three or four years ago, even before Gorbachev's arrival, certain items began appearing in military literature exploring the role of strategic defense in war, implying that the concept deserved a more prominent place in Soviet thinking.

It is not yet clear from where the new interest comes. It may reflect the force of the new technologies, which, if developed and exploited by NATO, once more favor the defenders in the perennial battle between offense and defense. If, contrary to Soviet assumptions of the last twenty years, war probably cannot be waged and won on the other side's soil, at least not with odds that a cautious betting man would find satisfactory, then where does one turn? Logic and prudence suggest that the potential weaknesses of an offense-based strategy be offset by paying greater attention to a defense-oriented one. The incentive to do so grows if, as has been the case over the last five years, some on the other side begin to plan modifications of their own strategy, proposing early offensive operations deep behind Warsaw Pact lines in a war on the central front.

Maybe the explanation is considerably less far-reaching or reassuring. Maybe Soviet military leaders are not in the least rethinking a basic defense posture, but simply looking for ways of introducing elements of defense to strengthen what remains a decidedly offensive orientation. As several leading American specialists on Soviet military thinking would point out, defense in depth—the focus of the discussion—has more to do with offsetting new NATO capabilities and doctrines so that the Red Army can go over to the offensive as soon as possible or maintain the offensive once launched than it does with thoughts of abandoning the notion of offense altogether.[26]

Michael MccGwire, however, believes the explanation for the new Soviet defense emphasis stems from a far more fundamental upsetting of preexisting views. He would argue that Soviet leaders, sometime after 1979, suddenly let it sink in that a war with the United States need not be fought only in Europe. Events in the Persian Gulf region after the Shah of Iran was driven from power and the Soviets had chosen to intervene massively in Afghanistan made war thinkable elsewhere to the south of Soviet borders. But should this come to pass, MccGwire reasons, Soviet leaders would have a major stake in preventing the conflict from escalating. To do so, they would require a strategy to retain their military positions in Europe and Asia, not to overrun the other side. MccGwire sees this as precisely the direction of current Soviet thinking. The new emphasis on strategic defense, the new organizational forms such as the Western "theaters of military action" created in 1984, and, more recently, the shifting Soviet approach to conventional arms control in Europe, he believes, all point in this direction.

Which of these two explanations is correct is difficult to say. But either way, the powerful influence of setting on the Soviet image of war is apparent, as is the certain impact on Soviet arms and strategy. However distinctive Gorbachev's personal effect on the course of trends has been, it is to accentuate, not to create, change. The deeper impulse to change arises from a constantly evolving external setting. By the same token, the quest to find the sources of Soviet military programs and war plans in some permanent set of foreign policy objectives—the "Finlandization" of Western Europe, for example—seems to me even more misguided. If one cares about primary causes, the place to begin is with the world outside and what it does to the Soviet image of war.

Arms Control

In theory, the other way to change the Soviet image of war is through arms control. Arms control, in theory, also bears on a second crucial consideration—the likelihood of war. It does the first by readjusting the wherewithal of war, and, therefore, the possible course of war. It does the second by rearranging the military balance in ways that reduce the temptation to fire nuclear weapons impetuously in times of crisis, by helping to build confidence among distrustful military competitors, and by easing the general political atmosphere.

American arms control policy has not successfully altered the Soviet image of war, except more recently for the worse (by seemingly adding evidence of a desire to develop a capacity to fight a protracted nuclear war). During the period of detente in the early 1970s, American approaches to arms control did encourage Soviet observers to worry less about the likelihood of war. At the time, they were ready to concede that the progress achieved in arms control, beginning with the upgrading of the hot line in 1971, owed much to an evolution in U.S. arms control policy. During these years, American attitudes were said to be undergoing "enormous changes," leading to a much fuller recognition of the "danger of nuclear war," thereby, in fact, diminishing the danger of nuclear war.[27] But this did not last, and by the end of the decade

Soviet commentary had stopped suggesting U.S. arms control initiatives were impeding the risk of war.

When one looks for a cause, again, the influence of the international setting looms large. Soviet observers located the sources of the earlier more productive American approach in a changing set of international imperatives. Shifts in the external setting of U.S. policy, namely, the unpromising drama in Vietnam, the growth of Soviet military power, and, flowing from that, the increasing madness of nuclear escalation were said to have left the United States with no choice. (Later, however, when the Americans demonstrated that they, indeed, did have a choice, the turn for the worse in American arms control policy was attributed to the pathology of American politics, not to the international context of American policy.)

More to the point, Soviet arms control policy responded to the international setting. Indirectly the external context influenced Soviet arms control policy by shaping the Soviet image of war. At the beginning of SALT, in particular, the Soviet position derived almost entirely from the needs of its military, and these, in turn, reflected the needs of war. Thus, for example, in the period after 1969, the essence of the Soviet approach was to leave Soviet military programs untouched, even if, in leaving them untouched, U.S. programs, too, were left to run free. To the extent the military had a stake in strategic arms control in the early stages of SALT, it was to avoid unleashing a competition in ballistic missile defense. For, given Soviet notions of how to deter the Americans from climbing the nuclear ladder, the Soviet military cared more about Soviet missiles reaching their targets than about attempting, rather futilely, to obstruct U.S. missiles from reaching theirs. Nor did the Soviet military relish a competition in a new arena in which the Soviet Union might find itself at a technological disadvantage. Not surprisingly, the Soviet position in SALT, therefore, never went much beyond the campaign to curb ABMs.

Inasmuch as Soviet political leaders had a stake in nuclear arms control as a means of averting war, it was as a part of foreign, as distinct from security, policy. On this issue, from the start Soviet leaders have had a more political notion of how one reduces the likelihood of war than their American counterparts. It is not the refined structuring of deterrence that matters most to them, but rather the management of the political environment. To the degree that arms control seemed a plausible way to go about this task, Soviet leaders made room for it. Because, however, they were more interested in affecting the character of U.S.-Soviet relations than the structure of the military balance, they naturally had a greater stake in affecting the dynamic and politics of the East-West competition than in rescuing a concept of deterrence. Or, as the phrase goes, they cared more about arms race stability (for political reasons) than about crisis stability, a psychological, not a political, concept that has to do with the abstract imperatives of nuclear escalation theory.

They also, however, had both a more general and a more specific (*i.e.*, political) stake in arms control. The more general stake was in altering the atmospherics of U.S.-Soviet relations. Arms control—the act of reaching agreements—was thought likely to have a salutary effect on the temper of the adversary. As long as the practical impact of arms control on the military balance remained limited by their own preference, the process mattered more than its product.

At the same time, Soviet leaders had a more specific interest. Arms control, they supposed, could help them cope with the particular challenge raised by China. Again not surprisingly, at the height of detente (1972–74), Soviet leaders put a good deal of energy into cajoling the Americans into an agreement uniting the two superpowers against any "third power" whose recklessness risked nuclear war.[28] American leaders took this as an attempt to isolate and menace the Chinese— as it may well have been. But more probably Soviet leaders thought they were, in their own fashion, reducing the risks of war.

Over the 1970s, as SALT moved from one negotiating phase to another, the Soviet position evolved. Gradually, Soviet leaders came to seek ways of constraining a wider array of U.S. nuclear programs through arms control. By the early stages of SALT II, they were clearly interested in using the process to deter the deployment of a new generation of U.S. strategic systems (Trident I and II and MX). But little had changed in their reluctance to consider constraints on their own plans in order to succeed. When SALT II was finally worked out in 1979, it introduced greater predictability into the future force structures of the two sides—and, hence, met the needs of the Soviet military— but it did not materially alter these structures. It certainly did not address the problem of the vulnerability of ICBMs, which by now was driving American preoccupations. But the issue of ICBM vulnerability mattered so much to the Americans because they took seriously their own theories of crisis stability, and, throughout the 1970s, Moscow was not on the same wave length.

By the end of the 1970s, the most that one could say is that Soviet leaders had moved beyond arms control as a mere mechanism for lobbying against new American programs. In SALT II, they had built, with the Americans, a regime providing predictability in the force composition of the two sides. The overall quantitative limitations on delivery systems, reinforced by the subceilings on particular kinds of systems (such as MIRVed ballistic missiles) and by the limits on the number of warheads permitted on MIRVed missiles created an element of certainty for military planners contemplating future force requirements. To achieve this regime, Soviet leaders had been willing to pay a price: They had sacrificed a degree of unilateral control over deployment decisions and a degree of secrecy in weapons development. The counting rules of SALT II compelled them to do other than they had planned in some missile categories and the verification provisions compelled them not to do what they might to impede U.S. monitoring of their missile tests.

But all this was a far cry from the kind of arms control that would affect the shape of a future war and, along the way, the shape of national nuclear establishments. Change of that kind awaited the arrival of Gorbachev. With a swiftness that would be notable in any society, but downright startling in the case of the Soviet Union, the new leadership has launched ideas, proposals, and measures that dramatically alter the Soviet stance in all three of the central areas of military competition: strategic nuclear weapons, theater nuclear weapons, and conventional weapons. In some of these, Soviet notions are noticeably more advanced than in others, *e.g.,* in the area of theater and intermediate-range nuclear arms control. But in all three, fundamental change has begun to appear.

Not surprisingly, the ideas soonest translated into reality are in the sphere least central to Soviet assumptions about war—that of short- and intermediate-range nuclear weapons in the European and Asian theaters. Beginning with his visionary arms control speech of January 1986, Gorbachev moved with bold strides to the virtual repudiation of the rigid INF arms control stance of his predecessors. True, the existence of these weapons is not crucial to the execution of the Soviet Union's strategy for fighting a war in Europe or Asia, since they are a reserve force intended to deter NATO from using what nuclear weapons escape the Warsaw Pact's conventional attack—and, where they have a more immediate role, other nuclear arms can substitute. But no Soviet leader before him had ever so completely reversed direction, and so quickly. Nor had any Soviet leader ever agreed to scrap not merely a whole generation of new weapons but also a whole category of weapons, and then offered to eliminate still another category of shorter-range systems when the Americans and their allies fretted over the dangers of agreeing to do away with only INF.

Perhaps Soviet military men were pacified by the knowledge that, in sacrificing the modernized intermediate-range forces for which they had waited twenty years, they were rolling back the new threat posed by short-warning systems such as the Pershing II. But, it should be underscored, that is not the way they had thought or behaved under

Gorbachev's predecessors. Maybe they were comforted, as some in Western Europe have come to fear, by the prospect of moving toward a de-nuclearized Europe in which their conventional advantage would loom larger. But that had not been a priority for which Soviet military leaders had ever before been willing to sacrifice the entirety of their own weapons.

Here the force of Gorbachev's personality appears to have been decisive. Gorbachev, for overriding political reasons, decided that he wanted an agreement in this area, and—again, for the first time in memory—set aside military criteria. To him, it would appear, the value of reaching some kind of arms accord with the Reagan Administration, perhaps in order to break the log-jam of arms control or to ease the way to the Washington summit or to lobby with Western publics, outweighed the specific objections that might be raised on military grounds alone. So, in uncharacteristic Soviet fashion, he set out to negotiate an agreement, even on overwhelmingly U.S. terms.

In the area of strategic arms control, cause and effect have been different. Here, too, Gorbachev's approach has diverged from that of his predecessors. But, in this case, he has been much more the agent of pressures from the world of these weapons. As early as October, 1985, seven months into his tenure, Soviet negotiators in Geneva tabled a proposal to cut in half Soviet (and U.S.) strategic forces. Still more strikingly, this offer included sublimits that would significantly reduce the largest Soviet ICBMs, the once untouchable portion of the Soviet force. Since then the Soviets have added other elements to their proposal, each involving a more substantial restructuring of Soviet strategic forces, the decisive effect they had previously always dodged.

In this case, however, the international strategic environment itself has motivated Gorbachev. At a minimum, the American interest in twenty-first-century strategic defense technologies, with all their ramifications for a whole array of weaponry, gives Gorbachev reason to want a way out of a disadvantageous excursion in the arms race. Gorbachev or anyone else in his shoes has reason to consider unprecedented limits on Soviet offensive nuclear forces, if that be necessary to slow down the American effort. At a maximum, Gorbachev's initiatives reflect a more general and profound rethinking of the dynamic of the superpower nuclear competition, stirred by the experiences of the late 1970s and early 1980s.

It is still too early to say whether Gorbachev's increasingly far-reaching concessions in the area of strategic arms control will carry the Soviet Union over the last and crucial threshold: beyond a restructuring of Soviet forces to a restructuring of nuclear deterrence, either by depriving the two sides of their large and growing capacity to strike the other's land-based missiles or by introducing a greater measure of stability through some mutually acceptable combination of defense and offense. Because of the distance Gorbachev has traveled in less than two years, he is not so far from crossing the threshold in either direction.

The latest and, ultimately, the most consequential evolution is in the Soviet approach to conventional arms control. Since early 1986, Gorbachev has shown an interest in tackling the hardest and most central military issue between East and West: the character of the conventional balance in Europe. The heart of the problem, of course, is the nature of Soviet forces and the strategy the Soviets intend to implement in the event of war. Only by transforming this posture, diminishing the Soviet capacity for a swift *blitzkrieg*-like offensive, and substituting a more clearly defensive stance will the problem be solved. During the long MBFR negotiations, since 1973, the Soviets' approach has been to reduce their own forces but not to restructure them. Reductions, however, offer no solution, for, by preserving the current configuration of the balance, albeit at lower levels, they leave the essence of the problem untouched. What is new about Gorbachev's rhetoric is an apparent willingness to consider the restructuring of forces.[29]

With gathering emphasis, the Soviet leader has begun to cast the issue in fresh and constructive terms. Where there are imbalances, he says, let the advantaged side shed its superiority. Where weapons favoring surprise attack abound, let them be removed. Where warfighting strategies stress offensive operations, let them be turned in more defensive directions. Indeed, he argues, the rule should be that each side retain only what it takes to defend, not what permits the conduct of large-scale offensive operations.

Gorbachev and his allies have scarcely begun to translate these good-sounding words into concrete action. From all appearances, they have no practical notion of how talk of an equilibrated balance in Central Europe is to be brought to life in altered orders of battle and reconstituted fighting units. And almost certainly they have no clear image of a coherent and specific arms control agenda leading in this direction. What is more, the Soviet military seem not yet to have gotten the message. Much of what they write and say preserves the past, sometimes by echoing Gorbachev's exhortations but then giving them an old-fashioned meaning.[30]

If, however, words do in the end lead to deeds, what will be the explanation for this metamorphosis? Part of the answer will have to do with Gorbachev's nuclear agenda: to achieve the kind of nuclear regime he wishes, an intricate network of linkages ultimately brings him back to the state of the conventional balance in Central Europe, and compels him to consider what relief he is prepared to offer the West. Ultimately, Gorbachev cannot advance toward the denuclearization of Europe nor can he hope to reform the strategic nuclear balance with the United States freed from the threat of the Strategic Defense Initiative, unless he is prepared to tackle the conventional imbalance in Europe's heart. But this becomes easier if, at the same time, the Soviet military for quite separate reasons are beginning to rethink the way that a war might actually be fought, leading them to relax their attachment to the primitively offensive posture of the past. So, in this last and decisive dimension of the military competition, the character of Gorbachev's leadership and the imperatives of a changing setting merge to create a powerful new effect.

Learning and the Evolution of Soviet Concepts

Learning, in the everyday use of the word, means the process of acquiring knowledge. Psychologists tend to use the word even more broadly, meaning the process by which opinions change in response to a compelling experience or communication. I am interested in a two-tiered process by which, on the one hand, people shift from simple generalizations to more complex ones and, on the other, achieve greater efficiency in aligning ends and means. The two need not always appear together; either part of the process will fulfill my definition, a definition I have partially borrowed from two pioneers in this area of thought. Lloyd Etheredge and Ernst Haas both stress the progression from starker to richer representations of reality as the essence of learning, and Haas also includes, indirectly, progress toward a more effective reconciliation of ends and means.[31]

Within this particular definition of learning, there are additional distinctions that will help us grasp the significance of the evolution in the Soviet approach to war, arms control, and the use of force in peacetime. Joseph Nye offers two of these. The first is between simple and complex learning.[32] Simple learning involves an adjustment of behavior in the face of failure, but without altering basic aims or values.[33] "Complex learning involves recognition of conflicts among norms and goals in complex causal situations and leads to new priorities and adjustments of trade-offs."[34] In any society, most learning is of the first sort, but the more important learning is of the second kind.

Nye's other distinction is between incremental and discontinuous learning. As the term implies, incremental learning is the slow, step-by-step adjustment of ideas or attitudes, propelled by the gradual accumulation of experience or insight. Discontinuous learning is the great leap, when under the impact of one dramatic development or event, the mind changes. Discontinuous learning is the rarer of the two, but the more interesting, because when it occurs it is often also accompanied by complex learning. The effect of nuclear weapons on Soviet thinking is an illustration. Not only did this one revolutionary development radically alter the Soviet approach to war, but it did so by transforming basic values and assumptions. (With the advent of the nuclear era, Soviet leaders stopped believing war to be inevitable, stopped believing war could be the engine of revolution, and started believing that war's implications made cooperation with the other side imperative, rather than merely a convenience.)

I would add a third distinction. It also matters whether learning is independent, joint, or interactive. Independent learning is the kind that occurs apart from or even contrary to the learning taking place in other societies. Joint learning occurs when two or more societies learn simultaneously. Interactive learning occurs when one society learns from another. If the Soviet leadership in general, and Gorbachev in particular, have learned that national security cannot be divorced from mutual security, this would be an important instance of independent learning. Over the years, American leaders have attempted to tutor their Soviet counterparts on this point, but never successfully. Now, in a period when American leaders have placed less emphasis on mutual security and shown less sensitivity to Soviet national insecurity, Gorbachev seems to have been persuaded.

As for joint learning, the recognition among leaders of both super-powers of the folly of war in the nuclear age serves as a case in point. Each reached the same conclusion, and neither needed the other's help or instruction to do so. It may be that the gradual acceptance of the importance of having secure second-strike or retaliatory nuclear forces on both sides is also an example of joint learning, although, because the principle was accepted later by the Soviets, it may be that it was learned from the Americans, and is, therefore, an illustration of in-teractive learning.

This last kind of learning holds special importance for us outside the Soviet Union, because it is the sphere in which we can most influence the Soviets. Were the Americans to persuade Gorbachev and his colleagues that the world would be safer under a nuclear regime combining offense and defense, *i.e.,* one that made room for the Strategic Defense Initiative, an important measure of interactive learning would have taken place. But, at the same time, if that interactive learning does not occur, and the Americans nonetheless go forward, the results will be fateful for the nuclear balance in the future. The crucial shift in the Soviet image of war in the late 1960s, from an early and inevitable nuclear spasm to a potentially protracted conventional struggle, almost certainly involved interactive learning: it was almost certainly in part the product of the Kennedy Administration's concept of "flexible response." The Soviet leadership's more recent willingness to accept on-site verification in key arms control accords seems to be another instance of learning from the Americans. This is surely the argument some Soviet commentators now offer against their country's penchant for secrecy, a habit, they say, which diminishes Soviet security by encouraging the other side to judge Soviet capabilities and intentions always in worst-case terms.[35]

The trouble with interactive learning is that it is not always beneficial: the other side can learn both unwanted and unintended lessons. The challenge, therefore, is not merely to understand how to "teach" the other side—that is, how to overcome the obstacles to interactive learning—but also to comprehend precisely what kind of interactive learning is taking place, and, therefore, to avoid its pitfalls.

If we reexamine the last thirty years' evolution in the Soviet approach to arms and arms control using some of these standards, we may gain a better understanding of change. Compared with the early, primitive Soviet notion of war in the first years of the nuclear era, Soviet assumptions have grown constantly more complex and discriminating. And, so, too, has the matching of ends with means. The Soviet Union's elaborate capacity to wage conventional war and to cope with a variety of nuclear contingencies built since the mid-1960s contrasts sharply with the situation in the late 1950s and early 1960s, when Soviet leaders tried to supplement a rudimentary nuclear force with raucous claims of crushing strategic superiority.

Recently, the Soviet image of war has grown more confused. The response of Soviet military planners to a general war in Europe, refined and comprehensive as it is, begins to look less and less persuasive to friend and foe alike. Consequently, the Soviets are once more forced to consider the appropriateness of their strategy and to face the difficult choices involved in modernizing their forces. Some would argue that Soviet leaders are also learning that war may not be primarily or exclusively a European affair. What Soviet leaders have never learned to do, however, is to conceive of war and the prevention of war as a matter of precisely calculated scenarios derived from game theory. This is a peculiarly American proclivity, perhaps because of the role of civilian strategists in designing the U.S. nuclear posture. Much of what the Soviet Union learns about war is what its military learn, because the Soviet military continue to dominate war planning. And Soviet military leaders continue to believe that war is an unpredictable affair, the unforeseeable twists of which are best anticipated through large and redundant forces, a strong industrial base, and superior morale.[36]

The Soviets have also made strides in the area of arms control. They have moved in a slow but steady evolution from a shallow, circumscribed, one-dimensional vision of arms control to a far more ambitious, sensitive, and flexible arms control program. For the most part, the learning has been incremental. During the twenty years of strategic arms negotiations, the Soviets have advanced from a position of avoiding significant constraints of any sort, except on ballistic missile defense, to a tentative acceptance of broad quantitative limitations, then quantitative reductions, to proposing the elimination of entire categories of new and deployed weapons and compelling a considerable restructuring of offensive strategic forces, along with severe limitations on a new area of competition, strategic defense.

Over the years, Soviet learning has also been simple and independent. That is, for the first half of the history of SALT from 1969 to 1979, Soviet leaders adjusted their negotiating posture, but usually with no effect upon their basic values, such as their image of war and the character of their war planning. They also went about their agenda largely unpersuaded by the concerns motivating the Americans; they seemed to be neither listening to nor willing to adopt any part of American reasoning. Gradually, however, in the course of SALT II, they began to accept fragments of the American argument—for example, the need to reduce the threat of MIRVed missiles to fixed land-based missiles (the heart of each side's strategic deterrent), the need to reduce secrecy in order to enhance verification, the need to accept equal numerical limitations, rather than asymmetrical limits reflecting the asymmetries in the two sides' forces, etc.

The striking departures under Gorbachev may also be seen as a manifestation of the beginning of complex learning. When he subordinates military values in choosing an arms control posture, as he apparently has in negotiating the INF agreement and in discussing strategic arms cuts at Reykjavik, he is altering basic Soviet *priorities.* The fifty-percent reduction in offensive strategic arms urged by the Soviet side since October, 1985, when combined with subceilings for heavy missiles, would perforce diminish the large counterforce capability of the Soviet Union. Were this agreed upon, the Soviet Union would, for the first time, be accepting limitations changing the essence of its strategic forces and, therefore, presumably its plans for the use of nuclear weapons.

Even if one does not take seriously Gorbachev's appeals for denuclearizing the world and eliminating nuclear deterrence (he, in ways that are startling to an American audience, speaks of deterrence as a misbegotten notion), the Soviet leader has already said and done enough to open Western minds to the possibility that in coming years he could change much in the Soviet approach to the East-West military competition. Should the Soviet Union, for example, engage in a serious restructuring of the conventional military balance in Europe, Gorbachev and his colleagues would have transformed the problem at the heart of the postwar East-West controntation. Nothing has been more basic to the institutions and preoccupations of the Cold War than the conventional military balance in Europe, and to cut the Gordian knot would be a vast and historic revision of values. Similarly, should Gorbachev, because of domestic economic priorities or foreign policy considerations, accept a far-reaching modification of Soviet strategic forces as a way of attaining a new and more stable nuclear regime, he would have utterly reversed the initial Soviet approach to strategic arms control. What once had been a relatively trivial adjunct of Soviet security policy would have been transformed into a major mechanism for setting the terms of Soviet security.

The concept of learning is but one way of framing an issue central to Western debates over the nature of the Soviet challenge. No dispute has been more fundamental among Western, and particularly American, observers than the one concerning the degree to which the Soviet Union adapts its military policy to an ever-changing international environment. Those on one side tend to see Soviet international behavior as largely a function of the Soviet system, or Marxist-Leninist ideology, or of two hundred years of Russian history. While not denying that Soviet leaders modify their behavior in dealing with other nations, for the most part, change is seen as one of tactical accommodation. Those on the other side recognize the force of history and the impact of the Soviet political order, but concentrate more on the character and scale of the Soviet adjustment to a changing environment. For them, the interaction of Soviet inclinations with a complex and often contrary international political system bulks as large as the historical, ideological, and political givens of Soviet foreign policy.

The concept of learning can help to make this argument more lucid and systematic. Much of Soviet learning when it is simple does deserve to be seen as tactical accommodation, although, in the long run, as one accommodation is added to another, the cumulative effect may be substantial. On the other hand, complex learning, by any fair-minded judgment, involves a significant adaptation to environment. When the Soviet Union changes not only its strategy and tactics, but also its priorities and values, surely adaptation has occurred. That is true even if backsliding follows at some later point.

Learning and the Use of Force in Peacetime

Nowhere in the fusion of arms and Soviet policy was more damage done to U.S.-Soviet relations over the last fifteen years than in the Soviet exploitation of force in Third World crises. True, when the Soviet Union has used arms, until the war in Afghanistan, it has not been with its own combatants in Third World areas or against the United States or its allies, but instead within its own alliance, against the collapse of orthodoxy. But these recourses to military might have never roiled East-West relations nearly so much as the lesser uses of force in places like Angola, Ethiopia, and ultimately Afghanistan. Thus, when it comes to the problem of Soviet military action in peacetime, the primary instance is Soviet interventionism in areas of regional instability.

As a result, Western governments have a major stake in what the Soviet Union has or has not learned on the subject. Fifteen years ago, Soviet leaders began with a complex and compartmentalized set of assumptions concerning change in the Third World and the military role of the superpowers. On the one hand, they were enormously impressed by America's failure in Vietnam, not the least because military superiority had been insufficient to decide the outcome. In the last years of the Vietnam War, a number of Soviet commentators even began to echo Americans who wrote of the decreasing usefulness of force as a means of dealing with most of the problems facing the modern nation-state, including the challenge of violent change when national interests are thought to be at stake. On the other hand, Vietnam was seen as a particularly chastening experience for the United States that would make the Americans less prone to interfere with what the Soviets call "national liberation revolutions." Defending national liberation revolutions, moreover, was put forward as one of the peacetime missions of the Soviets' blue-water navy by its architect, Admiral Gorshkov, in a celebrated series of articles on seapower published in 1972. And, in the decade between 1965 and 1975, the Soviet ability to project force far from Soviet shores grew exponentially.

When the Caetano regime collapsed in Portugal in the mid-1970s, southern Africa seemed suddenly filled with revolutionary fervor, and Soviet leaders seized the opportunity. To Henry Kissinger and others who protested the Soviet and Cuban role in Angola, they smugly responded that detente had nothing to do with their commitment to the "national liberation struggle." What happened in the Third World and what the Soviets did to foster the chances of their revolutionary friends, they argued, should not be linked to the superpower relationship, nuclear arms control, or economic cooperation. Detente, according to them, concerned things too important to jeopardize simply because Washington was troubled by change in one corner of the world or another.

A decade later, many of the same issues came to look different to Soviet leaders. Not that Soviet "learning" had begun only in these years. Through difficult experience going back at least to the 1960s, they had grown steadily more sophisticated about the obstacles to social and political change in much of the Third World. Thus, if more recently they have reconsidered their own part in helping to bring about change, it is not that they have suddenly come to understand the complexity of this milieu. They have known of it for some time. Nor is the reconsideration due to the fact that the economic burdens of involvement are for the first time weighing heavily upon them; Soviet leaders, since the mid-1960s, have acknowledged their economic limits in dealing with the Third World.

The new learning is of a different sort, although earlier lessons continue to resonate. It manifests itself in four ways: First, and most importantly, Soviet leaders have learned that U.S.-Soviet relations cannot be separated from Soviet actions in Third World troublespots. Grudgingly, they have come to recognize that the Americans will inevitably react to what they perceive as a Soviet attempt to exploit instability in order to extend Soviet influence and displace that of the United States. As a result, Soviet leaders appear ready to put the issue of superpower behavior in regional crises on the agenda of a renewed detente, and non-official Soviet experts are already discussing with their American counterparts ways of managing this dimension of U.S.-Soviet competition.

Second, since 1979, the Soviets have learned that they, too, have reason to care about how the other side conducts itself in regional crises. They have learned how complex and, at times, downright perverse the turn of fortunes can be in the Third World. Since 1979, the Soviet Union has found itself more of the time defending frail and threatened regimes—from Nicaragua to Mozambique, Angola to Kampuchea—from virulent counterinsurgencies, many of them assisted by the United States, than helping "national liberation movements" to power.

Third, Soviet authors have begun openly confessing that the source of regional instability is not that which they once claimed it to be and that which provided a simple rationale for Soviet involvement. Conflicts in the Third World, they now acknowledge, arise from many causes, many of them indigenous and particular, rather than from the ubiquitous machinations of imperialism. Sometimes the problem is in multi-ethnic societies where separatist movements seek to break away from the center. On other occasions, segments of society rebel against privileged postcolonial elites who dominate the state bureaucracy, the army, and other positions of power. Sometimes conflicts will flare up within a country because of the exploitation of poorer regions by the richer, or because of the need of local elites for an "external enemy" to distract discontented populations. And so on.[37] Viewed in this light, much of the turbulence and conflict in the Third World does not produce easy choices (or rationalizations) of good against evil, nor does it create clear-cut imperatives for Soviet policymakers.

Finally, there is the experience of the Afghanistan War. It now becomes apparent that Gorbachev not only regards the original decision to invade as a mistake, but the time to cut Soviet losses as upon him. From a fairly early moment in his tenure, he had taken little trouble to conceal his impatience with the war and his eagerness to be free of it. But it is a large and historic step to pass from this stage of ruefulness to the actual decision to abandon the effort and take the consequences. Never has a modern Soviet leader done so, and the effect is likely to be profound.

Already one finds intellectuals advancing extraordinary lessons. Write three of them: "The history of the last decades shows that in none of the regional armed conflicts . . . has the aggressor succeeded in achieving a military victory, not to speak of a political one. Judging by everything conflicts of the scale of the U.S. invasion of Grenada can be regarded as the upper limit of effective use of armed force in modern conditions."[38] One should have learned well, they suggest, the folly of acting "as military guarantors of Third World regimes that have no broad social base and are incapable of defending themselves." What the vicarious lesson of the American experience in Vietnam failed to teach, the more direct experience of Afghanistan has imprinted more deeply on Soviet minds.

It is too soon for us to judge whether all or any of this amounts to complex learning. This shift in Soviet perspective does not mean that the Soviet Union has renounced an active role in the Third World nor that it has decided to avoid assisting what it considers revolutionary forces. But it is a good illustration of how powerful even simple learning can be when layer is added to layer. It is almost certain that, as a result of these four developments, the Soviet Union will behave differently in the future when confronted with the question of whether to use force in the Third World.

The implications of this line of analysis are profound. If the basis of the Soviet military effort and the impulse that more than any other determines the scale and content of this effort are the Soviet image of war, then our concern must be with that image. To focus instead on Soviet military capabilities is to mistake effect for cause. (To focus on military capabilities, even when supplemented by imputed Soviet intentions, is still to mistake effect for cause.) To focus on the foreign policy purposes of military power is to confuse secondary with primary causes. Focusing on secondary causes, of course, is not entirely useless, but, obviously, neither is it an optimum strategy. For the United States and its allies to put themselves in the best position to respond to the Soviet military challenge, they must concentrate squarely on the single factor that most accounts for the accumulation of Soviet military power and its planned uses: namely, the evolving Soviet image of war. That becomes particularly consequential when one image is evolving into another, as may be true in the current Gorbachev era.

Because the international setting plays a central role in shaping the Soviet image of war and the United States is an important part of that setting, we are not without influence. Several problems flow from this, however. First, U.S. foreign and security policy remains only an aspect of the international setting, although granted a vitally significant one. China and its policies, other players in the East-West context, including our major allies, and the politically neutral force of technological advance also have their parts to play. Thus, the effect of the setting on the Soviet image of war is not entirely within our control.

Second, to the degree that setting *is* within our control, our choices are neither simple nor often even very real. Were one to draw lessons from the last thirty years along purely theoretical lines, John Foster Dulles would be proved right. The best of all worlds would be one in which the Soviets could not hope to emerge from any major test of arms unravaged by nuclear war. Then, regardless of their capacity to wage conventional war, as long as nuclear disaster were sure to follow, they would not dare to venture forth. But, for Dulles to be right in the real world, disaster would assuredly have to follow, requiring in turn an unmistakable U.S. superiority in nuclear arms *and*—and this is the more difficult requirement—a certainty that these weapons would be used. Failing either, the choice is to continue the conventional arms competition, struggling to patch up deficiencies in the West's effort by invoking the possibility, only the possibility, of nuclear escalation.

In this less than ideal circumstance, the United States and its allies have a considerable stake in knowing when, how, and why Soviet leaders learn. If, as suggested in this essay, the process is long, slow, and cumulative; if, moreover, learning in one area is connected with learning in another (for instance, if learning in the sphere of arms control depends on learning in the sphere of war and vice versa); and, most of all, if the dominant influence is an ever-changing external reality, then the Western policymaker who thinks in terms of directly compelling the Soviet Union to give up this or that part of a threatening military capability or to cease this or that upsetting action has framed the problem incorrectly. He or she, in the long run, will be more productive by striving to alter the Soviet image of war, concept of arms control, and notion of the use of force. And this can only be done indirectly by recognizing what in the larger setting is at work on Soviet minds. The policymaker will contribute most, first, by being alert to the way our strengths and weaknesses, words and deeds figure in the Soviet definition of the problem, and then by attempting to reshape that definition more in accord with Western national interests. Second, he or she will do so by paying more attention to Soviet opportunities than choices, worrying more about reducing incentives and temptations to act than coercing the act itself.

The trouble is, American habits push us in the opposite direction. We have a natural tendency to want to instruct the Soviet Union: To teach its leaders what their goals should be, and how they should go about achieving them; where they should involve their country, on whose behalf, and by what means; what they should think about war, and how they should deter it, prepare for it, and fight it. Nearly all of this instruction is utterly wasted. The Soviets, like most people, learn primarily from their own involvement in a changing international environment. To the extent that interactive learning is important, and to the extent that the Soviets learn from the United States, whether about a safe and sound nuclear regime or about restraint in the peacetime use of force, it will result far more from U.S. behavior than from U.S. pedagogy, far more from the way the United States interacts with a changing international environment than from the quality of the seminars in which it offers to enroll the Soviet Union.

Notes

1. Henry A. Kissinger, *White House Years* (Boston: Little, Brown and Co., 1979), p. 118.

2. Harold Nicolson, *The Congress of Vienna* (New York: Harcourt, Brace and Co., 1946), p. 120.

3. Sergei Witte, *Vospominaniya,* Vol. 2 (Moscow: 1960), p. 380.

4. Tibor Szamuely, *The Russian Tradition* (New York: McGraw-Hill, 1974), p. 94.

5. David Holloway, *The Soviet Union and the Arms Race* (New Haven: Yale University Press, 1984), p. 9.

6. This and the next paragraph are drawn from my paper "The Soviet Union and the Issue of Military Power," in Dick Clark, ed., *United States-*

Soviet Relations: Building a Congressional Cadre, Second Conference, January 14–18, 1987 (Wye Plantation: Aspen Institute for Humanistic Studies, 1987), pp. 17–21.

7. Richard Pipes, *Survival Is Not Enough* (New York: Simon and Schuster, 1984), p. 37.

8. From J. V. Stalin's *On the Opposition,* as noted by Condoleezza Rice, "The Making of Soviet Strategy," in Peter Paret, ed., *The Makers of Modern Strategy* (Princeton: Princeton University Press, 1985), p. 661.

9. In addition to his book, *Survival Is Not Enough,* pp. 37–44, see also his *Russia Under the Old Regime* (New York: Scribner, 1974).

10. F. N. Nesterov, *Svyaz vremen: Opyt istoricheskoi publitsistiki* (Moscow: Molodaya Gvardiya Publishing House, 1980). For an approving review, see, V. Kargalov in *Nash Sovremennik,* no. 1 (January 1981), pp. 187–91.

11. As reprinted in *Pravda,* February 8, 1986, p. 2.

12. See Condoleezza Rice's account of the theses drafted largely by Sergei Gusev in her "The Making of Soviet Strategy," pp. 261–62. On the same theme, see Dimitri Fedotoff White, *The Growth of the Red Army* (Princeton: Princeton University Press, 1944), p. 168, where he takes from M. Frunze, *Izbrannye proizvedeniya* (Moscow, 1934), p. 7.

13. Holloway, *The Soviet Union and the Arms Race,* p. 27.

14. The authors who did understand include: Herbert S. Dinerstein, *War and the Soviet Union* (New York: Frederick A. Praeger, 1959), pp. 36–63; Raymond L. Garthoff, *Soviet Strategy in the Nuclear Age* (New York: Frederick A. Praeger, 1958), pp. 61–91; Thomas W. Wolfe, *Soviet Strategy at the Crossroads* (Cambridge: Harvard University Press, 1964), pp. 26–37; and J.M. Mackintosh, *Strategy and Tactics of Soviet Foreign Policy* (London: Oxford University Press, 1962), pp. 88–104.

15. The famous initial retreat occurred in Marshal of Armored Forces P.A. Rotmistrov's article in *Krasnaya Zvezda,* March 24, 1955.

16. Foremostly, see Michael MccGwire, *Military Objectives in Soviet Foreign Policy* (Washington: The Brookings Institution, 1987); but also, Stephen M. Meyer, "Soviet Theater Nuclear Forces," *Adelphi Papers,* no. 187 (Winter 1983/ 84), and Phillip A. Petersen and John G. Hines, "The Conventional Offensive in Soviet Theater Strategy," *Orbis,* vol. 27, no. 3 (Fall 1983), pp. 695–739.

17. MccGwire, *Military Objectives in Soviet Foreign Policy,* pp. 28–35.

18. In MccGwire's analysis, the effect of this apparent reluctance to escalate to nuclear war was reinforced by a new American emphasis on a secure nuclear second-strike capability, implying that the Americans were not committed to launching an early nuclear first strike.

19. This is MccGwire's argument in *ibid.,* pp. 52–54. He asserts the transfer but does not supply evidence, and the most thorough treatment of the subject does not deal with the historical evolution of the Soviet approach to nuclear release. (Stephen M. Meyer, "Soviet Nuclear Operations," in Ashton B. Carter et al., eds., *Managing Nuclear Operations* [Washington: The Brookings Institution, 1987], pp. 470–531.)

20. *Pravda,* January 19, 1977.

21. Even those who cannot be regarded as cynics or worst-case analysts began to argue such by 1980. See the particularly thoughtful and elaborate analysis of M.A. Milstein, "Nekotorye kharakteristiki sovremennoi voennoi doktriny v Soedinennykh shtatakh," *SShA: Ideologiya, politika, ekonomika*, no. 5 (May 1980), pp. 9–18.

22. C³ is an abbreviation of Command, Control, and Communication.

23. See the points made by Arnold Horelick, "Security," in Abraham Becker, et al., eds., *The 27th Congress of the Communist Party of the Soviet Union: A Report from the Airlie House Conference*, Rand/UCLA Joint Notes Series, JNS-01, December 1986, p. 49. "Marshal Ogarkov seemed to have been calling in May 1984 for a radical and early shift in investment priorities away from strategic nuclear systems based on well-developed technologies toward new technologies for conventional warfare and for weapons based on 'new physical principles.' "

24. Speech at the 18th Congress of the Trade Unions of the USSR, *Pravda*, February 26, 1987, p. 3.

25. See Igor Malashenko, "Reasonable Sufficiency and Illusory Superiority," *New Times*, no. 24 (June 22, 1987), pp. 18–20; Vitaly Zhurkin, Sergei Karaganov, and Andrei Kortunov, "Reasonable Sufficiency," *New Times*, no. 40 (October 12, 1987), pp. 13–15; and, by the same authors, "O razumnoi dostatochnosti," *SShA*, no. 12 (December 1987), pp. 11–21.

26. See Stephen Meyer, "Paths for Soviet Security Policy in the 1990s," forthcoming, as well as the work in progress of Condoleezza Rice.

27. G. A. Trofimenko, "Na sterzhnevom napravlenii," *Mirovaya ekonomika i mezhdunarodnye otnosheniya*, no. 2 (February 1975), pp. 6–7.

28. For a firsthand account, see Kissinger, *The White House Years*, pp. 548, 554–55. A good analysis is in William G. Hyland, *Soviet-American Relations: A New Cold War*, Rand Report, R-2763-FF/RC (May 1981), and Raymond L. Garthoff, *Detente and Confrontation* (Washington: The Brookings Institution, 1985), pp. 242–43.

29. I have explored the Soviet Union's evolving position on conventional arms control in greater detail in "Gorbachev's New Approach to Conventional Arms Control," *The Harriman Forum*, vol. 1, no. 1 (January 1988).

30. On this, see *ibid.*, pp. 5–6.

31. See Lloyd Etheredge, *Can Governments Learn?* (New York: Pergamon Press, 1985), p. 143. The second element appears in Ernst Haas, "Why Collaborate? Issue-Linkage and International Regimes," *World Politics* (April 1980), p. 390, a citation I have taken from Joseph S. Nye, Jr., "Nuclear Learning and U.S.-Soviet Security Regimes," paper presented to the American Political Science Association, 1986 Annual Meeting, August 28, 1986, p. 12.

32. Nye, "Nuclear Learning and U.S.-Soviet Security Regimes," pp. 12–13. The labels are his, but the idea in turn he borrows from Chris Argyris and Donald Schon, *Organizational Learning: A Theory of Action Perspective* (Reading: Addison-Wesley, 1978).

33. Jack Snyder calls this "tactical learning." See his article, "Science and Sovietology: Bridging the Methods Gap in Soviet Foreign Policy Studies," *World Politics* (January 1988).

34. Nye, "Nuclear Learning and U.S.-Soviet Security Regimes," p. 12.

35. V. Zhurkin, S. Karaganov, and A. Kortunov, "Vyzovy bezopasnosti—starye i novye," *Kommunist,* no. 1 (January 1988), p. 45.

36. Freeman Dyson has contrasted the two approaches by noting that the American "objective of deterrence comes with a demand for absolute assurance, while the objective of victory [the instinctive and only lately eschewed Soviet preference] comes, if at all, only at the end of a long road of incalculable chances and immense suffering. From a Soviet viewpoint, the objective of victory may be considered the more modest, since it is based only on hope and faith while the objective of deterrence is based on calculated threats." (*Weapons and Hope* [New York: Harper and Row, 1984], p. 190.)

37. This list is taken from G. Mirsky, "K voprosu o vybore puti i orientatsii razvivayushchikhsya stran," *Mirovaya ekonomika i mezhdunarodnye otnosheniya,* no. 5 (May 1987), pp. 80–81. Mirsky, an exceedingly sophisticated and nuanced analyst of Third World issues, is not altogether representative. He has understood these other factors to be important for many years. What is significant in his case is not the existence of these views, which are longstanding, but that he is now able to express them.

38. Zhurkin, et al., "Reasonable Sufficiency," p. 15.

5

Human Rights: A Thaw Imperiled

Robert Cullen

On September 14, 1987, jailers at a Soviet prison in Omsk opened their doors and released a 28-year-old inmate named Aleksei Magarik. Magarik, a slight, shy man, aspired to be a cellist. More to the point, he aspired to play the cello in Israel. In 1983 he had applied to emigrate, been rejected, and found himself a refusenik. He persisted in his demand for freedom and became a teacher of Hebrew for the refusenik community in Moscow, where he lived in a communal apartment with his wife and infant son. In March, 1986, Magarik went to visit a friend in Tbilisi. At the airport, he was arrested. The KGB said it found narcotics in his luggage, although Magarik denied ever having seen the drugs. He was sentenced to three years at hard labor, a term later reduced to 18 months. Magarik's case was not unique. For years, the KGB had carefully monitored the refusenik community for signs that it was organizing itself. When a refusenik organized and taught a Hebrew class, a reaction from the authorities was all but inevitable. Not infrequently, the reaction took a form like the drugs in Magarik's suitcase. What was unique about Aleksei Magarik was his status at the time of his release. He was, according to the records kept by Israel and the National Conference of Soviet Jewry, the only remaining Jewish refusenik jailed by the Soviets for political reasons. He was the last "Prisoner of Zion" in the Soviet Union.

It is a measure of the changes Mikhail Gorbachev has wrought that the minor milestone represented by the release of Aleksei Magarik went all but unnoticed in the West. To be sure, Gorbachev has not changed the Soviet Union into a liberal democracy. Amnesty International's most recent report on Soviet human right's practices "observed no improvement in the harsh and arbitrary treatment of prisoners of conscience in 1986."[1] But since the middle of 1986, Gorbachev's policies have changed the world's perception of the human rights issue in his country. By releasing famous prisoners like Anatoly Shcharansky and Yuri Orlov, by allowing long-term refuseniks like Ida Nudel and David Goldfarb to emigrate, by permitting Andrei Sakharov to return to Moscow, Gorbachev has transformed the discussion of Soviet human rights from an angry examination of repression to a hopeful question of how far reform can go. Under Leonid Brezhnev, the Soviet Union contributed the word "gulag" to the world's languages. In the era of Gorbachev, as he himself proudly noted, the Russian word that has entered the world's lexicon is "glasnost'."[2]

But, less than a year into Gorbachev's human rights thaw, signs of trouble began appearing. Demonstrations shattered the facade of unity in Kazakhstan, Lithuania, Latvia and Estonia. Crimean Tartars, seeking to return to the homeland from which Stalin drove them, demonstrated at the walls of the Kremlin. These events suggested that the limits of liberalization may be tested by minorities whose grievances have long been suppressed. Within Russia itself, the new openness produced not only helpful suggestions for reform, but the open appearance of a Russian nationalist group whose ideology has strong anti-Semitic and fascist overtones. By the fall of 1987, influential members of the Politburo clearly felt that the movement toward openness, democratization, toward freer emigration, and toward religious freedom had gone quite far enough. Gorbachev and his colleagues were groping through uncharted territory, and neither they, nor anyone else, could predict where their journey would end.

Within the West, as well, the thaw produced uncertainty. During the two decades preceding Gorbachev's accession to leadership, a demand that the Soviet Union honor certain fundamental human rights became embedded in the politics of the United States and, to a lesser degree, Western Europe. The steady stream of released prisoners and emigrants satisfied many longstanding Western demands. But it raised questions, as well. Were the manifest changes in Soviet human rights policy largely cosmetic, or did they reflect real change in the way the Soviet leadership looked at its own people and the world? Were there policies the West might adopt that would encourage further liberalization? Conversely, by failing to respond with gestures of its own would the West risk stifling the Gorbachev human rights reforms in their infancy? Was there any way out of the cycle of brief thaws and long periods of repression that has dominated so much of Russian history?

The uncertainty on both sides was understandable, for the experience of both Russia and the Soviet Union offered little hope that a thaw could be sustained. From its earliest days, Russia has been a country with harsh leaders. That was, perhaps, inevitable in a country that struggled to defend an open plain against attackers from East and

West, a country that fell under the domination of the Mongol hordes at roughly the same time Western Europe was launching its Renaissance. From the days when the hooded riders of Ivan the Terrible's oprichnina terrorized the boyars to the nights when Stalin's NKVD came knocking on the doors of old Bolsheviks, the first emotion felt by Russian rulers in the face of dissent has been fear—fear that dissent might become rebellion, that emigration might become the mass defection of the most talented. "We were scared—really scared. We were afraid the thaw might unleash a flood which we wouldn't be able to control and which might drown us," Nikita Khrushchev wrote of the liberalization he introduced after Stalin's death.[3] And, prompted by fear, the eventual response of Russian leaders to dissent has been cruel repression. What the West would recognize as liberal reform ideas surfaced only rarely— in the program of the Decembrists in the 1820s, in the reign of Tsar Alexander II in the 1860s, in the avant-garde of the early 1920s, and in the convergence theories of Andrei Sakharov in the 1960s. When they did surface, such ideas were either snuffed out by the police or smothered by the bureaucracy. The only "reformers" who ever succeeded in Russia were the Bolsheviks; and they won because they were prepared to be as secretive, and as tyrannical, as the government they overthrew.

This heritage was particularly onerous to the minorities of both Russia and the Soviet Union. Those who failed one or more of the tests posed by the three pillars of Tsar Nicholas I's official ideology— nationality (Russian) orthodoxy (adherence to the Russian Orthodox Church) and autocracy—had even less protection from repression than the Russian peasantry. Russian Jews were particularly vulnerable. The empire required Jews, when the rules were strictly enforced, to live within the so-called Pale of Settlement in Eastern Russia and Western Poland. Their access to higher education was controlled by rigid quotas. Periodically, they suffered the sanctioned terror of pogroms. The best for which many Russian Jews could hope from the tsars was permission to emigrate. Not surprisingly, the Russian Revolution initially appealed to many of them. Lenin, at least, condemned anti-Semitism and ethnic prejudice as a tool used by the ruling class to divide the workers. The Jews, in the early days of Soviet power, had their own schools and a special department within the government. But those rights evaporated under Stalin. In the 1930s, the special Jewish schools and many synagogues were closed. After World War II, as his paranoia deepened, Stalin seemed to select the Jews as special targets. Leaders such as Solomon Mikhoels were murdered. Only Stalin's death in 1953 saved Russia's Jews from a scheme to exile them en masse to Siberia.

The human rights legacy left to Gorbachev, however, was the work not only of Stalin, but also of the men who led the Soviet Union throughout most of his adult life—Khrushchev and Leonid Brezhnev. As Gorbachev was completing his studies at Moscow State University, Stalin died and Khrushchev took over. He freed thousands of political prisoners from Stalin's camps. His "secret speech" denouncing Stalin's tyranny to the 20th Party Congress in 1956 was the central event of the 1950s in the Communist world. Gorbachev's reaction to it has never been published. But some of his contemporaries have described those times as a period of hopeful ferment among Soviet youth, times when it seemed that the party might yet find its way toward a more humane vision of socialism. This was the atmosphere as Gorbachev began his party career and it was the atmosphere at his first congress, in 1961, when Khrushchev again attacked the moldering old dictator.

But Khrushchev's was a highly idiosyncratic, erratic approach to human rights. He was capable of ordering the publication of Aleksandr Solzhenitsyn's "One Day in the Life of Ivan Denisovitch"—and of permitting the persecution of Boris Pasternak. Although he nearly emptied the Gulag, he was also a man who referred to Jews as "Yids" and ordered the closing of more synagogues and more Orthodox churches. As a young party official in his native Stavropol, Gorbachev saw this damaging erraticism as well. Years later, talking to a Soviet journalist, Gorbachev observed that Khrushchev's agricultural reforms had been "half-baked," and damaging to the agricultural productivity of the region. He might well have thought the same of Khrushchev's entire effort at reform and de-Stalinization. After Khrushchev's ignominious ouster in 1964, there could be no doubt in anyone's mind that the legacy of Khrushchev's brand of reform was failure.

The Brezhnev era also bequeathed to Gorbachev a legacy of failure in the human rights area, but failure of a different kind. Superficially, Brezhnev and the general secretaries who succeeded him briefly, Yuri Andropov and Konstantin Chernenko, managed to keep a lid on dissent. The tone for the new era was set in 1965, when the KGB arrested authors Andrei Sinyavsky and Yuli Daniel for anti-Soviet agitation and propaganda. Their crimes, apparently, consisted of publishing their works abroad, under pseudonyms, and circulating them in samizdat at home. They were sentenced to seven and five years, respectively, signalling the end of the Khrushchev thaw. Nevertheless, many dissident groups arose in various parts of the Soviet Union over the ensuing 20 years. Some attracted the attention of the world; others operated in provincial obscurity. But their fates were almost all similar. Sooner or later, their members were arrested and sent off, either to jail or into exile. By the time Gorbachev came to power, the Nobel laureate,

Sakharov, was in internal exile in Gorky; Shcharansky, Orlov, and dozens of others were in jail; Solzhenitsyn, Georgii Vladimov, Vasily Aksyonov, Vladimir Voinovich and other dissident writers were living in exile; as were less openly political artists such as Yuri Lyubimov and Mstislav Rostropovich. The status of dissent was symbolized by a sad spectacle in Moscow's Pushkin Square on International Human Rights Day, December 10, 1983. Within the remaining fragments of the dissident community, word had passed of a plan for a silent protest: the removal of hats in front of Pushkin's statue. But no dissidents got the chance for even this innocuous demonstration. Anyone who paused in front of the statue and reached for his hat that evening was immediately surrounded and hustled away by burly plainclothes policemen.

The persistence and spread of dissent during the post-Khrushchev era was probably due to the fact that the policies of Brezhnev, Andropov and Chernenko were a half-hearted kind of Stalinism. The Brezhnev leadership, seeking economic gains and international legitimacy, left the country partially open to outside influences and signed the Helsinki Final Act, which encouraged dissidents. Most important, the Brezhnev leadership had no stomach for two of the principal tools of Stalinism: terror and the censorship of foreign correspondents. Without the acute fear that characterized Stalin's time, the fear of the anonymous denunciation and the midnight knock on the door, more and more Soviet citizens began to test the limits of dissent. They found a willing audience for their complaints in the foreign press corps resident in Moscow. Ludmilla Alexeeva, in her history of the various Soviet dissident movements, describes the birth of this new phenomenon at the trial of Sinyavsky and Daniel. Outside the courtroom where the trial was taking place, foreign correspondents stood in one group. The two authors' friends stood in another. There was no mixing, out of fear of the old taboo against associating with foreigners. But when the authors' wives emerged from the courtroom each day, their friends gathered round them to hear what had transpired in court. The correspondents listened in. Their accounts of what they heard were publicized around the world and broadcast back into the Soviet Union by Western radio stations.[4] A new medium of communication was discovered, and it soon grew into a force that embarassed the Soviet government and encouraged the dissidents by drawing the attention of the world to their efforts and their plight.

This new medium eventually raised the cost of repression for the Soviet leadership. In addition to stifling creativity at home, the repression of human rights meant the loss of sympathy and support from intellectuals abroad. In the West, intellectuals increasingly spurned the

Soviet model, turning instead to Eurocommunism or to various forms of neoconservatism. Repression of human rights and emigration, along with the Soviet military buildup of the 1970s and Soviet thrusts into the Third World, became one of the chief arguments used against detente in organs of the intelligentsia such as "Commentary." Within the Soviet Union, intellectual antipathy manifested itself in different ways: the intense popularity of the anti-Stalinist plays of Yuri Lyubimov at Moscow's Taganka Theater; the cult surrounding satiric bard Vladimir Vysotsky; and a general apathy. These were intangible costs, but costs nonetheless. Abroad, they contributed to the elections of conservative governments in the major Western nations that soon challenged the Soviet Union with new weapons deployments and the threat of an unrestricted arms race. At home, they limited the leadership's options. After Brezhnev's death, when Andropov, and then Gorbachev, sought ways to reinvigorate the economy, they found that their legions of academics were producing precious few innovative ideas.

In no area was the failure of the Brezhnev human rights policy more apparent than in the area of emigration rights. Brezhnev inherited a policy that generally denied Soviet citizens the right to leave their own country. Khrushchev had considered the idea of allowing Soviet Jews to go to Israel, only to reject it. But in the late 1960s, two new factors came into play. The Six-Day War galvanized many Soviet Jews to begin demanding emigration to Israel. And, when Richard Nixon came to office in Washington and the first negotiations about detente began, Americans who sympathized with Soviet Jewry injected their demands for emigration rights into the bargaining. As a result, the emigration question was posed to the Soviet leadership with new urgency. Brezhnev eventually accepted a tacit deal with the United States: in return for trade and arms control, the Soviets would allow at least some emigration for purposes of "family reunification." In the 1975 Helsinki Final Act, he committed his government to look favorably upon requests for emigration to reunite families, and, by reference, he accepted the provision of the U.N.'s Universal Declaration on Human Rights which stipulates that every person has the right to enter and leave his own country.

Consequently, the 1970s saw some 265,000 Soviet Jews leave, along with lesser numbers of ethnic Germans and Armenians. But the implicit bargain with the United States was not kept. There were arms control agreements. But Congress did not approve granting the Soviets the status, for tariff purposes, of a most favored nation (MFN),[5] and access to Export-Import Bank credits. Instead, in 1974, it enacted the Jackson-Vanik amendment, which denied both those benefits to communist countries that did not permit free emigration. The Soviets responded to this perceived intrusion into their internal affairs by slashing emigration for the years 1975 through 1977. Then, in 1978 and 1979, emigration went up again. Those were years in which the SALT II treaty was being completed. They were also years in which the Carter administration, the Congress, leading American Jewish organizations, and the Soviets engaged in serious discussions about a presidential waiver of the Jackson-Vanik amendment in return for the Soviets' improved performance on emigration: 28,864 Jewish emigres in 1978 and 51,320 in 1979. But the late Senator Henry Jackson refused to support a waiver unless President Carter could get explicit assurances from the Soviets that they would continue to permit high levels of emigration. The Soviets refused to give such assurances, again insisting that emigration rates were an internal matter. Without Jackson's approval, the American Jewish community was unwilling to support a waiver. Thus, in the summer of 1979, the Carter Administration decided not to waive the amendment for the Soviet Union; adding insult to the injury, from the Soviet point of view, it granted a waiver to the People's Republic of China. In short order, the Senate shelved the SALT II treaty and the Soviets invaded Afghanistan. Detente was over, as was the period of high emigration. It sank to an average of about 1,000 people per year by the early 1980s.

Gorbachev's inheritance on the emigration issue was a host of unsolved problems. Despite the release of hundreds of thousands of emigrants, the Brezhnev policy had failed to obtain favorable trade terms from the United States. From the standpoint of the Soviet image, it was an unmitigated disaster. Throughout the 1970s, the Soviets never clearly stated why some people and some ethnic groups might be permitted to emigrate and others not. Although their Helsinki commitments suggested that anyone could leave, particularly to join family members abroad, in practice the Soviets allowed only three groups to go: Jews, whose homeland was Israel; Germans, descended from colonists invited to Russia by Catherine the Great; and Armenians whose families had entered the Soviet Union after World War II. This left the entirely reasonable impression that Soviet policy was arbitrary and capricious, that it favored some ethnic groups above others, and that Moscow did not live up to its international obligations. Then, by opening the gates to some emigration, and shutting them again, the Kremlin had created a new class within Soviet society: the refuseniks. These were people stranded in a particularly cruel limbo. Their presence in Moscow and other major cities only served to call attention to the inhumanity of Soviet policy. That cost the Soviets on many fronts. In the United States, influential American Jews increasingly began supporting conservative, anti-Soviet policies. In the Middle East, the Soviets were all but frozen out of the peace process, and Israel made renewed emigration a precondition for their readmission.

Gorbachev needed time to make changes. His initial speech as general secretary contained a call for "glasnost'" in party affairs. It seemed, at the time, an odd statement from a man who had just been selected by a secret process. During the next year, Gorbachev eased some of the warhorses of the old order out of the party and government. In February, 1986, the Soviets released Shcharansky. By the late summer of 1986 signs of real change began to appear. The first harbingers were Soviet officials who spoke quietly to diplomats and journalists in the corridors at events such as the Reykjavik summit. Their message was that Moscow had decided on some major human rights reforms. First, the rules and regulations regarding emigration would be published for the first time. Second, these sources suggested, the Kremlin had decided that the roughly 11,000 refuseniks were a propaganda liability and should be released. Third, they said, there would be a general liberalization of travel restrictions, fulfilling a desire common to most Soviet citizens for the opportunity to travel abroad. The strategy behind this, one Soviet source told me, was co-opting dissent through glasnost'. Under the new order that Gorbachev was creating, dissidents would want to channel their criticism into the system. The demand for emigration would dry up as living conditions improved; in the end, these sources said, the Kremlin estimated, only 30,000–40,000 people would leave. The whole society would be reinvigorated.

Within a few weeks, some of these predictions began to come true. In December, 1986, Gorbachev personally called Andrei Sakharov at his place of exile in Gorki and invited him to return to Moscow and resume his work as a physicist. Sakharov accepted. In January, 1987, KGB chief Viktor Chebrikov announced that an agent had been fired for harrassing an investigative reporter in the Ukraine. The dissident psychiatrist, Anatoly Koryagin, was freed and allowed to emigrate. In February, 1987, the Soviets announced an amnesty for prisoners who were jailed for violating one of the political statutes in the Soviet criminal code; some 150–200 were released. Then, the Kremlin disclosed that a review commission was overhauling the criminal code.

Throughout 1987, the authorities permitted small steps toward greater freedom of religion. Jews were allowed to restore the ritual bath, or mikvah, at the Leningrad synagogue and to open a carry-out kosher restaurant near the synagogue in Moscow. In August, the Ukrainian Catholic Church emerged from underground and sought legal status. Rev. Gleb Yakunin, a dissident Russian Orthodox priest who had been suspended from his duties for 20 years, was granted a new parish in a village outside Moscow. Protestant groups were permitted to import thousands of Bibles donated by their co-religionists abroad. The state was still promoting atheism, but there was a feeling that the authorities were coming to the realization that religion could be an ally, rather than an opponent, in their struggle for an upright, sober society. Lenin's dictum that "the eradication of religion is our government task" seemed to have been put aside, at least for a while.[6]

The most intriguing change of all was the sudden appearance of thousands of quasi-political "clubs" in Moscow, Leningrad and other cities. In the atmosphere of 1987, they sprang up like desert flowers after a rain. Some were devoted to environmental issues. Some were "perestroika" clubs and discussed economic reforms. The authorities tolerated them, and even assisted them in finding places to meet. One Soviet official, in October, 1987, told me they signalled a fundamental change in the attitude of at least some of the party's top echelon: the clubs' activities were presumed to be innocent and constructive until shown otherwise. In previous years, there had been a presumption of guilt by the authorities whenever citizens tried to organize themselves. In any event, the clubs represented a new phenomenon in Soviet society—tolerated political activity outside the party structure. To optimists, they looked like the first buds of pluralism in the Soviet Union.

The Supreme Soviet published a decree spelling out the new rules for leaving the country, effective January 1, 1987. In March, the flow of emigrants began to rise, reaching an average of about 800 per month by summer, a rate which promised that nearly all of the 11,000 long-term refuseniks would be out sometime in 1988. But there remained a great deal of deliberate ambiguity in Soviet emigration policy. The January decree specified that only close relatives—siblings, children or parents—could invite a Soviet citizen to emigrate for purposes of family reunification. The closeness-of-kinship criterion was a device that the Soviets used like a faucet in the 1970s to control the flow of emigration. When more emigration was desired, the Soviets loosened or ignored the rules about the closeness of relatives who could invite a Soviet citizen to emigrate, permitting people to go abroad to join aunts, uncles, or cousins. When they wanted to reduce emigration, they tightened both the rules and the enforcement of them. That pattern continued in 1987. In order to get rid of the long-term refuseniks, the Soviet authorities frequently waived the requirement that an applicant be invited by close relatives. But, in an apparent effort to deter new applicants, the Soviets generally, but not always, enforced the rule for those who were not already refuseniks. Of the 4,687 people who left in the first eight months of 1987, the State Department counted fewer than 200 who were not long-term refuseniks.

At the same time, however, other travel restrictions were liberalized in intriguing ways. In July, in an interview with the Soviet weekly "New Times," Rudolf Kuznetsov, head of the visa and registration department of the Ministry of Internal Affairs, stated that the rules for private travel abroad "have been amended to include (trips at the invitation of) other relatives besides next of kin, as well as acquaintances."[7] And in late September, 1987, Gorbachev made a sweeping statement to a delegation of visiting French citizens: "As far as departures from our country are concerned, there is only one obstacle and restriction on that score: If a person has been connected with state secrets . . . the person is permitted to leave when the secrets become outdated."[8] Gorbachev and Kuznetsov did not mention that a character reference from a would-be traveler's local or workplace party unit was still an essential part of an application to travel abroad, a requirement which effectively denied travel to anyone the party did not deem a good representative of the Soviet Union. And, they seemed to be talking about the rules for temporary departures from the Soviet Union, not about the rules for permanent emigration. American officials reported in September a sharp increase in the number of Soviets applying for tourist visas to the United States. Even if this aspect of the liberalization is limited to temporary visits by party-approved people, rather than permanent emigration, the opportunity to see the rest of the world at first hand would be a dramatic and welcome reform for millions of Soviet citizens.

The result was a muddled emigration situation in the autumn of 1987. On the one hand, the regularity of the emigration numbers since March, 1987—as well as private comments by some Soviet officials— suggested that the Soviets wanted to maintain a steady, modest outflow, without the sharp peaks of the 1970s. On the other hand, the decree of January 1, 1987 laid the legal groundwork for shutting off the flow once the long-term refuseniks are out. If the demand for emigration were to become suddenly chaotically intense, if other ethnic groups, such as the Ukrainians or Lithuanians, suddenly began demanding to leave, or if the reaction abroad did not suit the Politburo in the future, the rule requiring an invitation from a close relative could be used to stifle most emigration requests. This raised the prospect of renewed tension with the West. According to Israeli estimates, as many as 400,000 of the roughly two million remaining Soviet Jews would like to emigrate. That figure is impossible to verify, since it is based on the number of invitations sent by Israelis to the Soviet Union, not on initiatives taken by Soviet Jews themselves. Soviet officials themselves continued to estimate privately in 1987 that no more than 50,000– 60,000 Jews wanted to leave. But it seems reasonable to believe that if emigration were really free, many thousands more, in addition to the 11,000 refuseniks, would try to go, if only to better themselves economically. The true test of the new Soviet emigration policy seemed likely to come in 1988 or 1989, when, with the long-term refuseniks gone, the Soviets would face the choice between letting new applicants go or shutting off the flow. They seemed to be feeling their way on the issue and keeping their options open.

The new limits of dissent were easier to discern in the reaction to protests by minority groups and nationalities. In August, 1987, authorities in the three Baltic republics, Latvia, Lithuania, and Estonia, surprisingly gave permission for demonstrations to mark the anniversary of the signing of the Molotov-Ribbentrop Pact, which led directly to the annexation of the Baltic states by the Soviet Union. In Tallinn, Estonia, the demonstrators were allowed to gather in front of the city hall and march, several thousand strong, to a nearby park. There, speakers urged publication of the pact's secret protocols, which have never been published in the Soviet Union. They called for self-determination for the Baltic peoples. Sixty-two people joined a group dedicated to erecting a monument to the victims of Stalin. But two weeks later, one of the organizers of the protest, Tiit Maddison, was summoned by the local authorities and told he had a week to choose between exile and possible prosecution. He chose exile to Sweden.[9] In other Baltic states, as well, there were indications that the new policy might allow occasional demonstrations to let off nationalist steam, but it would not permit dissident leaders to arise. In Latvia, several organizers of Riga's August 23 protest reported that a few days thereafter, they were kidnapped separately by KGB agents, taken to remote areas, and threatened. One of them, the Catholic activist, Robertas Grigas, was beaten and then forced to dig a grave—with the clear message that it might be his own.[10]

Nevertheless, the human rights thaw of 1987 had some obvious payoffs for the Soviets. Their image improved dramatically around the world. Foreign Minister Eduard Shevardnadze, who once had to listen in international forums to protests about the treatment of Andrei Sakharov, was able to stand at the rostrum of the U.N. General Assembly in September and quote Sakharov—in opposition to the Reagan administration's Strategic Defense Initiative.[11] In the Middle East, the Soviets were able to position themselves to play an equal role with the United States in any future peacemaking process, in part because they mollified Israeli opinion by permitting some Jewish emigration. A nation's image is an intangible factor, and its impact in international affairs is impossible to gauge precisely. But it would seem to be a safe assumption that the miserable Soviet human rights image in 1983 had something to do with Moscow's utter failure to deter West Germany from electing a conservative government and deploying Pershing II missiles. Four years later, in the summer of 1987, the West German government could not withstand Soviet pressure for removal of its Pershing I-A missiles. The new and favorable Soviet image in Western Europe doubtless contributed to that signal success.

But the new human rights policy had its costs, as well. Minority nationalities, sensing that the rules were changing, began pressing grievances which Moscow had traditionally repressed, rather than resolved. Kazakhs rioted when Moscow tried to put a Russian in control of their corruption-ridden republic. Crimean Tartars demanded the right to return to their homeland. To Moscow, the most disturbing protests no doubt were those in the Baltic states, particularly Lithuania, where the population was united by both ethnicity and Catholicism. The Soviets had only to look at Tibet or Poland to see what a combustible mixture frustrated nationalism and religion could be.

Shortly after the Baltic demonstrations, one very influential Politburo member bluntly warned that things had gone far enough. Viktor Chebrikov, chief of the KGB, chose to deliver a speech on the 110th anniversary of the birth of Feliks Dzerzhinskii, founder of the Soviet secret police, and to paint a nasty picture of the results of liberalization. He spoke of "the carriers of alien ideas, ideas hostile to socialism. Some of them are well on their way to committing anti-state and anti-social acts. Some are even ready to cooperate directly with the special services of imperialist states, to betray the Motherland." Recent emigrants, he charged, were being used in the West for anti-Soviet propaganda. Political prisoners released under the amnesty were trying to "inspire anti-social demonstrations" in order to provoke a crackdown. Part of the population, he warned, was already infected with "the virus of nationalism." "We can't forget," Chebrikov concluded, "about the organic unity of socialist democracy and discipline."[12]

Chebrikov's was not the only voice calling for discipline. Another senior Politburo member, Yegor K. Ligachev, had spoken during the summer of the "scum and debris" brought to the surface of Soviet society by glasnost'.[13] The ouster of Boris Yeltsin from the leadership of the Moscow party organization in November showed the strength of the reactionary forces. The true factors behind Yeltsin's dismissal remained a secret. But it seemed clear that, while the conservative forces in the party were behind Gorbachev's efforts to improve discipline and efficiency, their support for other aspects of the reform program—widespread cadre replacement, genuine competition in elections—was conditional at best. If the conservative backlash continued to gather strength, the human rights thaw was also a likely casualty.

Whatever the Soviets' internal deliberations about human rights were, there did not seem to be much Western governments could do to influence them. Gorbachev's tentative liberalization on emigration and political rights differed fundamentally from the policy under which Brezhnev allowed two big waves of emigration in the 1970s. Brezhnev opened the gates in order to pay for specific trade and arms control measures he wanted from the West; he tolerated no internal dissent. Gorbachev had foreign audiences in mind as well, but his basic policy purpose was domestic. He wanted to unleash the stifled energies of the Soviet people by allowing them more freedom to discuss their ideas, more access to the rest of the world, and a greater sense of control over their collective destiny. He wanted to claim the loyalty of the intelligentsia and to forestall any union of disgruntled workers and intellectuals, such as Poland saw in the Solidarity period. Human rights reform was, in contrast to economic reform, a quick change that could be accomplished by fiat in Moscow. With its roots in domestic concerns, Gorbachev's thaw was less susceptible to influence from outside.

Insofar as it affected foreign policy, Gorbachev's liberalization was the cornerstone of a broad—and quite successful—Soviet effort to appeal to both intellectual elites and mass opinion in the West. That effort included a much more sophisticated Soviet approach to public relations. Given the freedom of the news media in the West, there was nothing any Western government could do to thwart this Soviet effort to appeal to Western opinion, as long as the liberalization continued.

Because Gorbachev was playing the human rights issue to benefit the overall Soviet image, rather than seeking specific concessions, the levers the United States tried to use in the 1970s became increasingly irrelevant. In the Brezhnev period, the United States dangled—then jerked away—MFN status and Export-Import Bank credits as carrots to promote freer emigration. That policy was largely counter-productive in the 1970s,[14] and the carrot looked quite shopworn by 1987. Because of budgetary restrictions, the Export-Import Bank had little or no money for easy financing of Soviet-American trade. MFN may retain some symbolic value, but the Soviets know that whether they get MFN or not, they will get no assurances about the reliability of the United States as a trading partner or about access to American technology. An annual waiver of Jackson-Vanik would still require the Soviets to listen to a humiliating debate in Congress each year over their emigration record. There was merit in arguing, in 1986, for changing or waiving the Jackson-Vanik amendment as an initiative to break the deadlock on emigration. Once Gorbachev decided to break that impasse anyway, that rationale was gone. The Jackson-Vanik Amendment's repeal might be mildly useful as a gesture of recognition, if the Soviets were to maintain an acceptable level of emigration after the long-term refuseniks are out. But whatever the United States chooses to do or not do about MFN status, it will not weigh very heavily in Soviet calculations.

The Soviets do have a strong interest in access to Western technology, an interest which could provide leverage on the human rights issue. The United States maintains a cumbersome set of export controls to thwart Soviet efforts to obtain technology with military applications. A panel of experts commissioned by the National Academy of Sciences reported in 1987[15] that the controls had grown beyond useful size. They covered thousands of items of dubious military value and seemed to penalize American exporters more than the Soviets. American efforts to control the re-export of American technology to the Soviet bloc give Western European firms an incentive not to buy American products. The panel estimated the annual cost in lost American exports to be at least $9 billion. Export controls are not precisely suitable for use as a human rights lever, because no administration could risk removing controls which are vital to the national security to reward improved Soviet performance on emigration. Nor should American businesses which are losing Western European markets be penalized for poor Soviet performance by the retention of ill-advised controls. But, given the persistence of the American trade deficit, the possibility of streamlining the controls will no doubt be on the agenda of the next administration. It would be a mistake to link this issue directly to Soviet human rights performance. But it would do no harm to remind the Soviets of the practical reality that their performance will affect the climate in which reform is considered. That consideration could have a marginal impact on Soviet behavior.

The most effective course for the West lies in accepting Gorbachev's tacit realization that the real human rights leverage of the Western democracies is the power of public opinion. Western governments can make clear to the Soviets, in word and deed, that a continuing thaw will be acknowledged and a crackdown will be condemned. They must be more skillful in this than the Reagan administration was in November, 1987, when it rewarded a long period of improved Soviet human rights performance by allowing a minority of conservative congressmen to humiliate Gorbachev by blocking a proposal that he speak before a joint meeting of Congress. Western human rights advocates can continue loudly to call attention to the plight of Jews and dissidents. At the same time, they must demonstrate that a good human rights performance will contribute to an atmosphere that encourages economic and security policies beneficial to both East and West. Western governments can insure that their radio broadcasts to the Soviet Union are as fair and objective as possible, playing the role of reporter, not cheerleader, for Eastern Europe and the Soviet minority nationalities. They can let the Soviets know that the West wants steady progress on human rights, not the overthrow of the Soviet system.

No outside influence, however, will ultimately determine the limits of the liberalization Mikhail Gorbachev has begun. The Politburo's bottom line is self interest. It wants a strong, vigorous nation, but a nation still firmly under the control of the Communist Party and its precepts. Gorbachev and his generation differ from Brezhnev and his cohorts in their realization that the same hand that disciplines the people can also stifle them. They will relax their grip as long as relaxation appears to be paying off in a more productive and creative society, in what Ligachev has called "constructive glasnost'." But Gorbachev will have to be smarter, or luckier, than his predecessors to make that payoff continue. He may find that opposition within the party forces him to return to the human rights policies of Brezhnev and Andropov. If he avoids that, history suggests that grievances long suppressed will, somewhere within the Soviet purview, sooner or later, bubble over into open defiance of the party. It may be in Eastern Europe, as Khrushchev encountered in Hungary in 1956. It may be in one of the Soviet Baltic states. It may be elsewhere. History further suggests that, if and when he confronts this challenge, Gorbachev will ultimately see it as a choice between crushing the dissent or risking the disintegration of the socialist world. Western preferences and Western leverage will hardly affect his calculations. Unfortunately, history also suggests what his decision will be.

Notes

1. "Amnesty International Report, 1987," London, Amnesty International Publications, p. 320.

2. "Druzheskaya Vstrecha M.S. Gorbacheva s Gabrielm Garcia Markesom," *Izvestiya,* 17 July 1987.

3. *Khrushchev Remembers, The Last Testament,* p. 79 (Little, Brown & Co. Inc., Boston, 1974).

4. Ludmilla Alexeeva, "Soviet Dissent," Wesleyan University Press, 1985.

5. In reality, this term is a misnomer. More than 150 countries have MFN status with the United States, meaning that countries which do not have it are subject to unusually high tariffs.

6. These developments were reported in summer, 1987 by the Keston News Service in its biweekly reports, nos. 282, 283, and 284.

7. "Getting an Exit Visa," *New Times,* No. 28, 1987.

8. Gorbachev's remarks were reported by TASS and distributed by the Soviet Embassy Information Department in Washington, D.C.

9. Testimony of Tiit Maddison before the U.S. Commission on the Conference on Security and Cooperation in Europe, Washington, Oct. 6, 1987.

10. Keston News Service, No. 284, Sept. 24, 1987.

11. From Shevardnadze's prepared remarks, distributed by the Soviet mission to the U.N., Sept. 23, 1987.

12. *Izvestiya,* Sept. 12, 1987, p. 2.

13. *Sovietskaya Kultura,* July 7, 1987.

14. See "Soviet Jewry," *Foreign Affairs,* Winter 1986–87.

15. "Balancing the National Interest: U.S. National Security Export Controls and Global Economic Competition." National Academy of Sciences, Washington, D.C., Jan. 14, 1987.

PART THREE

Gorbachev's Russia

6

Gorbachev and the Politics of System Renewal

Timothy J. Colton

Mikhail S. Gorbachev has pledged himself to the lofty goal of revitalizing a society of nearly 300 million people. After a hesitant start, he has cast himself as an advocate of far-reaching reforms in the Soviet economy, in communications and culture, and, most fascinatingly, in political institutions. In pursuing change, he generates an electricity absent from the main circuits of Soviet politics for a generation. As supporters rhapsodize about being "born anew in this exciting time of triumph of truth," Gorbachev has gone so far as to profess that the USSR has entered a "Renaissance epoch."[1]

We know, however, that, in Russia, as elsewhere, things are not always as they appear. We also know that it is far too soon to reach a final judgment on Gorbachev. The best we can do for now is explain how he and the Soviet elite arrived where they are, examine the main elements of his platform, and assess its prospects.

Change, Succession, and Crisis

*Gorbachev and the Action
Cycle of Soviet Politics*

Gorbachev is best placed in the cycle of action and reaction repeated by the Soviet regime since 1917. Revolutions from below and above, with a lapse in the 1920s, built the Soviet system roughly as we know it. Joseph V. Stalin in the mid-1930s wrenched the Soviet elite toward maintenance of the system. Nikita S. Khrushchev in his ebullient way strove to humanize and adapt Stalin's construction, after which Leonid

I. Brezhnev's approach was one of conservative restoration. Now, under Gorbachev, the reform impulse returns to the fore.

Historical circumstances have made it difficult for Gorbachev to pick up where Khrushchev left off. The institutions Gorbachev intends to modernize were bolted into place by a single-minded tyrant a half-century ago. Stalin's "great retreat" into policy and organizational conservatism coincided with a singularly brutal purge of the Soviet elite. The more plebeian and more malleable managers whom he substituted for the builders of the system were so young that many were to remain in place until the 1980s. Just enough of a relic to be tinged with revolutionary idealism, Khrushchev possessed the decency to begin a reformation after 1953 but lacked the shrewdness and the power to bring it off. He undeified Stalin and emptied the Gulag, only to be entrapped by his own contradictions and humiliated by his own lieutenants. His premature departure left the field to the very managers, then in middle age, whom Stalin had groomed to run his machine without asking questions.

For sheer consistency, Brezhnevism was without equal in Soviet history. Brezhnev had eighteen years in power to Stalin's twenty-nine, but Stalin used up and cast aside his creatures at will, whereas Brezhnev swore by "respect for cadres" and was content to let associates carry on almost into dotage. In policy, where Stalin moved by lurches, Brezhnev inched along one line, conservative and technocratic. From top to bottom, his establishment entered the 1980s in a state of physical exhaustion, fixed in its ways, and vulnerable to attack.

Gorbachev is thus seizing a golden opportunity when he accuses his predecessor of fostering "an artificial stability" and putting in abeyance "the inflow of fresh forces . . . the constant renewal . . . demanded by life." In both personnel and policy, Gorbachev has been able to say that a "forced change" has become unavoidable and that he, Gorbachev, is its agent.[2]

The catalyst of change, as has been the case so often in the past, has been political succession. The choice of a leader is fraught with uncertainty in a one-party state that lacks such institutions as free elections, constitutional limits on terms of office, and impartial courts to settle disputes. The rivals' need to vie for support makes it easier for muffled voices to be heard and for policy to be redirected. With Brezhnev in the 1960s the turn was to no-change. With Gorbachev, as with Khrushchev, the change is to change.

The three mini-successions of 1982 to 1985, and the complications arising from the lingering deaths of Brezhnev, Yurii V. Andropov, and Konstantin U. Chernenko, shrouded the transition in conspiracy and suspense. But this counted less in the end than that power was grabbed by a younger, stronger General Secretary who was eager to act on the problems that beset his country.

The Crises of Effectiveness and Coherence

Gorbachev has come to portray those problems in stark terms indeed. In speeches in early 1987, he spoke of "the danger of the growth of crisis phenomena" in the USSR and of "a condition of stagnation and somnolence, threatening society with ossification and social corrosion." He has since used a clinical analogy that implies a Soviet pathology: "Problems have to be solved and diseases have to be cured. If you drive a disease into an organism's depths, the disease only worsens."[3]

At its origin, "crisis" is a medical term, referring to a turning point at which the patient's health either snaps or recovers. If, strictly speaking, a crisis calls into question survival in the short term, the Soviet Union is not in critical condition. The party has had little cause to fear overthrow by army coup or crowds in the streets. There has been nothing comparable to the Gulag mutinies of the 1950s or the Polish outbreaks of 1970, 1976, and 1980.[4]

Seweryn Bialer identifies a different phenomenon, one much closer to what Gorbachev seems to have in mind, when he writes of the regime's "crisis of effectiveness."[5] The Soviet system may be said to face such a crisis in several senses. Many of its practical problems have worsened in recent years. There has been a growing awareness of the seriousness and the interrelatedness of the problem, but the response of most Soviets has been apathy rather than outrage. And the ineffectiveness of the regime has been weighed not against the traditional aspirations of its citizens alone but also against the performance of other countries, particularly the capitalist democracies.

Ineffectiveness is most easily measured in economics. The familiar story of two decades of waning rates of growth of Soviet national income, technology and productivity, and living standards, with a steeper fall after 1975, need not be repeated here. "Social corrosion," also highly visible, takes forms from alcohol abuse to higher infant mortality, anomie of the Soviet youth, and ethnic conflict. Internal ailments have implications for national security, power, and prestige, so much so that proponents of reform almost always appeal to these values. It is becoming more difficult for the Soviets to sustain their present foreign commitments, much less to expand them as did Brezhnev at his height.

If Western analysts have been alert to the crisis of effectiveness, they have said less about what I would call the emerging "crisis of coherence" of the regime. The issue here is neither the robustness of core institutions nor their efficiency as policy instruments. The crisis of coherence is about integration. It is manifested in the decline in the Soviet state's capacity to bring consistency to disparate behaviors and attitudes, to prevent the transfer of citizens' affection and effort to alternate structures, and to exercise collective wit. It is as slow to ripen as the crisis of effectiveness and as insidious in the long run.

Liberal historians have long identified "two Russias," one official and attached to the mighty state and the other unofficial and popular. Even high Stalinism could not stamp out society's underground life, some of which then gained acceptance during de-Stalinization.[6] In Brezhnev's time, it could be argued, the duality of Soviet society was reasserted. The rulers, eschewing mass terror but unwilling to make the adaptations needed to keep in step with the ruled, permitted, stimulated, and at times forced them to ply extra-systemic channels in order to gratify individual and group desires. By default and stealth, the USSR acquired the rudiments of a civil society, but one nestled in the interstices of the state.

The slide toward dualism under Brezhnev might be thought of as a recourse to what Albert Hirschman in his well-known study *Exit, Voice, and Loyalty* calls the "exit option" for dealing with stressful social or political situations. As Hirschman shows, disaffected individuals and their leaders alike may see in escape from such a situation (by migration, for example) an attractive alternative to both passive acquiescence and political action to amend the status quo. The exit option, however, has paradoxical effects. It may keep the peace, yet at the price of depriving the dominant system of the talents of many able persons and of postponing a reckoning with the source of stress.[7]

In the Soviet Union in recent decades, the most egregious displays of exiting behavior have been the spread of the "second economy" (which operates through black markets and non-monetary exchanges) and of official corruption (which feeds on the second economy). The world of ideas saw the rise of dissent in the 1960s and, following its muzzling by the KGB, the creation of a shadow culture, the emigration of leading writers, and the souring of the young on politics. In personal relations, critics write of a seeping increase in "double morality" (*dvoinaya moral'*) and "divided consciousness" (*razdvoyennoye soznaniye*), in which individuals pay lip service to approved values while scoffing at them in action.

A more elusive symptom of the incoherence of the Soviet system has to do with the system's ability to understand itself and its problems. The crux of the matter is the impoverishment of communication by means of secrecy, compartmentalization, oversimplification, and sometimes lies. Carried out in the name of political control, this was a badge of Stalinism, decreased but not eliminated afterward. The Brezhnev oligarchy, to be fair, gave experts in the bureaucracy and in think tanks more latitude than before to study and debate discrete issues. Yet it may have made overall coherence less by impeding the aggregation of such issues into larger patterns. It reconciled itself to the microscope of policy analysis but not to the telescope of social debate. Nor did it ever outgrow the reflex to cover up unpalatable facts bred into it under Stalin. When problems flared up in the mid-1970s, one of the Politburo's first reactions was to suppress the most damning statistics, such as those on infant deaths.[8]

The USSR's best and brightest have not reacted well to receiving only snippets of the truth. Most galling under Brezhnev was that, despite the greater technical proficiency and material privileges of the intelligentsia, the rationing of information remained at bottom arbitrary. A Soviet writer in 1981 pictured the intelligentsia as entangled in a web of "magical silences" and uncodified taboos more nettling than those in any primitive society. "They are slippery, and depend on the tastes, temperament, and tactics of the latest 'boss.' . . . They are capable of coming together into a system, but the system so far is incomplete and changes whenever the situation changes."[9]

The point is not so much that thinking persons feel unfairly treated as that haphazard and redundant checks sap their ability to work creatively, and thereby rob the Soviet state itself of the capacity to manage an increasingly complex environment. New technologies jar with old methods of control—as in the laboratories where researchers wait for weeks to photocopy materials indexed in seconds on computer screens.[10] The porousness of national frontiers and the globalization of knowledge creates its own kind of anomaly, making it harder to suppress inconvenient truths or to sustain some of the more preposterous myths once accepted unquestioningly.

The art of autobiography is as important to self-knowledge in societies as it is in individuals. By this criterion Brezhnevism let the country down badly. Although nostalgic fiction about the old Russia and memoirs of the Great Patriotic War of 1941–45 were equally in vogue, discussion of many facets of the country's history under Soviet rule was smothered. The halting of de-Stalinization made it virtually impossible to probe the politics of any period from Lenin's death in 1924 to the installation of Brezhnev forty years later. Stalin's barbarisms could be mentioned only elliptically, and the highest clearance was needed to print even the name of Khrushchev, whose years in power were encapsulated in buzzwords such as "subjectivism" and "voluntarism."

Only in art could a Soviet citizen allude to what many feared to be a tragic loss of societal memory. This theme was expressed in some of the best fiction of the late Brezhnev period, most movingly in *And the Day Lasts Longer than a Century,* the 1980 novel by the Kirgiz writer, Chingiz Aitmatov. His hero, Yedigei Zhangel'din, has partial amnesia because of a war wound, only dimly recalling that he came to live at a Kazakhstan whistle stop because his peasant parents were uprooted by Stalin's farm collectivization. Aitmatov tells the fable of ancient inhabitants of the area who acquired robot-like slaves by torturing prisoners until their memories were erased. Astride a local burial ground is a launch pad for space vehicles, but the military-manned site is off limits to civilians and its rockets blast off unannounced. State secrecy is thereby reproducing the same kind of cognitive gap that has disabled Yedigei and, in its extreme form, reduced the slaves to a subhuman existence.[11]

Memory damage, literary taboos, and the severe limits on social science were all testimony to how the Soviet system in the latter part of the Brezhnev era was being held back by a kind of failure of intelligence. The adaptations required by a mature industrial society were being retarded by the equivalent, for an entire society, of an individual's mental blockages and neuroses. Political innovation, as Hugh Heclo points out, has as a mainspring the ruminations of "men collectively wondering what to do."[12] Whatever its other merits and demerits, Brezhnev's Soviet Union was not good enough at wondering what to do.[13]

The Evolution of Gorbachev's Vision

If Mikhail Gorbachev has begun to deal with Soviet ills, he did not begin from a cogent blueprint for reform. A close ally, Aleksandr N. Yakovlev, has written that when the new rulers asked themselves which course to steer, they found themselves "unprepared to answer, either practically or theoretically."[14] This applies as well to Gorbachev as to anyone.

Gorbachev surely did have qualms about the *status quo.* They arose, he later said, while he was still the party leader of Stavropol' province in the 1970s. Like many who were then working "on the periphery," he said, he "saw the real processes taking place in society and came to feel that it was impossible to go on this way."[15] That negative judgment, however, did not spell out a definite alternative. Had Gorbachev sought one openly, the aging Brezhnev would never have inducted him into the party Secretariat in 1978 or into the Politburo two years later. Informal meetings with policy advisers may have helped with Gorbachev's education. So may have Andropov's fumblings toward change in 1982–84, though it is striking how little credit Gorbachev has since given Andropov for anything. But all these experiences were only preparatory. Gorbachev's real apprenticeship in reform occurred on the job.

"Acceleration" and "Putting Things in Order"

It is no slur on Gorbachev to say that at the time that he became General Secretary he was what the Hungarian economist, Janos Kornai, writing of economic change in communist countries, calls a "naive reformer," one who desired improvement yet bandied concepts about without working them through.[16] His main watchword in March, 1985, "acceleration" (*uskoreniye*), was partly meant to exude a new, vigorous style after the pathetic interregnum of Chernenko and the preceding years of plodding government. In substance, it conveyed more interest in society's speed than in its destination.

Gorbachev spoke of acceleration in mostly economic terms: "The main question is how and at what cost the country can attain an acceleration in economic development . . . a quickening of growth tempos."[17] The achievement of his economic goals, he said, would depend primarily on technological modernization, which would be bought by shunting investment into civilian engineering. Since it would take some time for state-of-the-art machinery to be available, the government would have to make efficient use in the meantime of existing human and material resources: "During the first phase of the struggle for more rapid economic development, we can and must get an essential lift by putting things in order, by heightening labor, technological, and state discipline."[18]

"Putting things in order" meant enforcing and intensifying Andropov's crackdown on tardiness and sloppiness at work and on unauthorized revisions of state plans. It was strongly reflected in the May, 1985 decrees curbing the sales of alcohol. The virtues of orderliness and *uskoreniye* were joined with power politics in Gorbachev's personnel policy. Leaders who had been in place for too long, he asserted, had become fat and complacent. They should either fall into line or "simply get out of the way."[19]

Gorbachev's reed-thin margin of victory in the Politburo dictated that his changes begin there. He scored a breakthrough at the April and July, 1985 plenums of the Central Committee, which ushered four new members into the Politburo. Fortified by their votes, he picked off his adversaries one by one. Grigorii V. Romanov, Premier Nikolai A. Tikhonov, and the Moscow party leader, Viktor V. Grishin (evidently his main rival in March, 1985), fell in the first year. Dinmukhammed A. Kunayev of Kazakhstan and Geidar A. Aliyev, the top-ranking first deputy premier, were retired from the Politburo in 1987. As members of the party old guard were evicted, allies of Gorbachev were moved in. By the time of Aliyev's retirement in October, 1987, eight of the thirteen full members of the Politburo had been brought into it during Gorbachev's tenure as General Secretary. At intermediate levels, Gorbachev had had oversight of staffing since 1983. Once in power, and assisted by a protege (Georgii P. Razumovskii) who was now head of the party's personnel section, he began the biggest cold purge since Stalin.

The early Gorbachev invited innovation in economic and social policy. He was also vaguely receptive to institutional change, at least in the economy. Beginning in April, 1985, he called for "restructuring (*perestroika*) of the economic mechanism," which would marry better central planning with administrative decentralization, along the lines of experiments begun by Andropov. That summer he asserted that a new mechanism could be functioning by the end of the year, an innocent notion that mercifully sank without a trace.[20] Ideas and politics occupied but a small niche in Gorbachev's early rhetoric. The major exception was his fervent advocacy of *glasnost'*, or openness of reporting and discussion, but even this took a back seat to the economy. In one speech, he saluted "our locomotive, our enormous state," hardly an image that suggested responsiveness by the state to the citizen.[21]

The Greening of Gorbachev

Scholars who surveyed Gorbachev's first year could be forgiven for seeing some modest potential for economic change but little else.[22] Only the Twenty-seventh Party Congress, which convened in February, 1986, gave an inkling that this view was premature. Gorbachev was now willing to mount a frontal attack on Brezhnev and his illusion of "improving matters without changing anything." He broke new ground by tying *perestroika* to all manner of institutions, not only economic, and by alluding cryptically to improvements in "socialist democracy." On his main subject, the economy, he used far tougher language than before: "Our situation now is such that we cannot limit ourselves to partial improvements—a radical reform (*radikal'naya reforma*) is necessary." To this end, he demanded re-examination of ideological teachings about property, planning, and prices.[23]

Gorbachev's most interesting changes of direction occurred after the party congress, although most were foreshadowed at it. They were evidently the outgrowth of both private reflection and interaction with events and forces in the public realm.

Two environmental triggers in particular stand out. The first was what Gorbachev came to see as the selfish opposition to his proposed reforms by a bureaucracy that he increasingly characterized as a homogeneous class. The theme surfaced at the June, 1986 plenum of the Central Committee and at a private audience three days later with Soviet literary figures. To the writers, Gorbachev expounded bitterly on the stalling tactics of the entire "managerial stratum" (*unpravlencheskii sloi*), which "does not want to lose rights connected with their privileges."

The very existence of a meeting with writers is related to the second change in the environment: Gorbachev's honeymoon with intellectuals whose hopes were being buoyed by *glasnost'*. In May, 1986 an impromptu insurrection from within the ranks toppled the executive of the Union of Cinematographers and elected as head of the union Elem G. Klimov, a director whose best films had been bottled up by the censors under Brezhnev. Gorbachev's first personal intervention was his audience in June with the writers, at which he made a spirited pitch for their support. Several days later, the Union of Writers' congress selected a new, mostly reformist board.

From this point on, several new strands attained prominence in Gorbachev's rhetoric. Most noticeably, he adopted a far more exuberant vocabulary to portray reform, maintaining that change must be nothing short of "revolutionary." He also said with growing conviction that transformations must embrace all segments of society, encompassing "not only the economy but . . . social relations, the political system, the spiritual and ideological sphere."[24]

When he addressed a national conference of social scientists in October, 1986, Gorbachev emphasized yet another far-reaching point, that "new thinking" was a precondition of economic and social advance. Gorbachev's column of revolutionaries needed a road map, and his— and here we have a crucial synapse—could be drawn only in a climate of greater intellectual freedom. "The search for truth must be carried out through the juxtaposition of different points of view, through discussion and debate, through the breaking of former stereotypes. . . . It is necessary that everywhere things be arranged so that the people who are searching, creative, and in the vanguard of restructuring breathe more easily, work more fruitfully, and live better."[25]

The greening of Gorbachev, as it were, culminated in his marathon speech on political change to the January, 1987 plenum of the Central Committee, perhaps the most significant by any Soviet leader since Khrushchev's 1956 "secret speech" about Stalin. He now argued explicitly that the malaise in the Soviet Union stems, not just from the country's state of hibernation after 1964, as had been the nub of his statements in 1985, but from genetic defects in the Stalinist model that were solidified under Brezhnev. "Theoretical notions about socialism remained largely at the level of the 1930s and 1940s, when our society faced quite different problems"; such "authoritarian" appraisals finally had to be re-evaluated. Another high point of his report was his articulation of the idea of *demokratizatsiya,* democratization. "Only through democracy and thanks to democracy," he said in recommending electoral and other reforms, "is reconstruction possible."[26]

In sum, Gorbachev's diagnosis of Soviet problems has become increasingly biting and his prescriptions more ambitious. In a short time, he has moved from a preoccupation with growth rates, discipline, political staffing, and small policy adjustments to endorsement of much more comprehensive changes. *"The business of restructuring,"* he said in January 1987 of his plans, *"has turned out to be more difficult, and the causes of the problems embedded in our society more profound, than we had imagined earlier."* The more he and the party examine the situation, "the more there move into view new, unresolved problems, left over as a legacy from the past."

Gorbachev in Action

Although Gorbachev has been scrupulous about telling the Soviet people that relief from their problems will come only after years of effort, he is well aware that the litmus test of leadership is deeds and results, and not high-flown words.[27] It is appropriate to ask how he is faring thus far at converting his slogans into real reforms. The Gorbachev record is mixed. It blends traditional nostrums with *ad hoc* innovations and, in some fields, with bold attempts to alter major Soviet realities.

Wielding the Personnel Weapon

Aggressive exploitation of the General Secretary's prerogatives in the personnel area may be the least original of Gorbachev's achievements. But it has been indispensable to the creation of a reliable political machine and, in his eyes, to the reinvigoration of Soviet government.

So many heads had rolled by the time the Twenty-seventh Congress opened that 41 percent of the members of the Central Committee were newly elected. By Gorbachev's second anniversary in power, in March, 1987, he had removed 38 percent of the full and candidate members of the Politburo who had been in place when he began. Turnover over two years was 76 percent among the Central Committee secretaries and department heads, 64 percent in the Council of Ministers (73 percent in its Presidium), and 39 percent among regional first secretaries of the party.[28] Almost all members of the "Dnepropetrovsk mafia" and of the several other subgroups of Brezhnev's coterie were pensioned off. In local districts and towns, some first secretaryships changed incumbents three or more times by early 1987.[29]

The shakeup has been rude by any measure, but it has been especially so when compared to the leisurely pace of elite transition during the previous two decades. In every sector, Gorbachev's rate of hiring and firing has been far more intense than during the Brezhnev-Chernenko eras, and has considerably exceeded turnover during the brief Andropov interlude, when Gorbachev himself was already behind many of the changes, particularly at the provincial level.[30]

Although Gorbachev has behaved deferentially toward some veteran Soviet politicians, he has also brought significant numbers of younger men into positions of responsibility. It is no small accomplishment that in two years the mean age of full and candidate members of the Politburo dropped from sixty-nine to sixty-five years (and to sixty-three years by October, 1987), of Central Committee secretaries and department heads from sixty-eight to sixty-one, and of members of the Council of Ministers from sixty-five to sixty (from sixty-nine to fifty-nine on the Presidium of the Council of Ministers).[31] There has been little rejuvenation at the provincial level, but one survey finds new district and town first secretaries to be on average only forty years old and adds that old-timers' places "are being taken by individuals who would do as their sons."[32]

A final aspect of personnel policy after March of 1985 was its intrusiveness. Gorbachev's new men were not only younger, more energetic, and better educated than the old guard, but they tended to have had fewer involvements with the organizations being placed in their hands. In terms of government departments, this meant that Gorbachev's new managers were either transferred laterally from other agencies or, more typically, had vaulted over several rungs on the job ladder. For positions of authority outside Moscow, Brezhnev's habit of promotion from within the locality was now said to be conducive to the establishment of independent satrapies. Gorbachev made more of an effort to import well-qualified outsiders, the majority from an expanded pool of "Central Committee inspectors." Soviet-style carpetbaggers, they were given marching orders to uproot local "protectionism," graft, and sloth.[33]

Gorbachev may take satisfaction from battering the bureaucracy, but this alone has not solved his problems. The data on turnover suggest, indeed, some second thoughts. When one analyzes Gorbachev's staffing changes over time, in every category they abruptly decline after the spring of 1986.[34] Gorbachev may also be having doubts about the practice of bringing in outsiders. Among regional party bosses in the Russian Republic, 63 percent of those appointed in his second year came from posts within the region and only 25 percent from Moscow; in the first year, only 12 percent were recruited locally with 81 percent coming in from Moscow.[35]

What accounts for this shift? The thinness of Gorbachev's own patronage base has been one reason, attributable to a career dominated by service in a single region (Stavropol') and a single policy area (agriculture). With few exceptions, he has had little luck at installing cronies in positions of influence.[36] He has thus had no alternative to striking accords with relatively independent politicians, most frequently from one of the provincial party organizations. The newly prominent officials promoted from the Urals and western Siberia form the most conspicuous such group, numbering among them Tikhonov's successor as head of government (Nikolai I. Ryzhkov), the second-ranking Communist Party secretary (Yegor K. Ligachev), and new local party chiefs in Kazakhstan (Georgii V. Kol'bin) and Moscow (the ill-fated Boris N. Yel'tsin).

Some degree of slowing down the pace was inevitable as Gorbachev moved down his "hit list" and established commitments to new appointees. He may well have reminded himself that Khrushchev antagonized his own men by constantly holding the threat of disgrace over their heads. He may also have discovered that new agents create enemies as well as enforce dictates—as happened most vividly with the Alma-Ata riots of December, 1986, the aftershock to Kol'bin's replacement of Kunayev in Kazakhstan. The backlash has been greatest when there is an ethnic component (Kunayev is a Kazakh, Kol'bin a Russian) or when the interloper "pushes his way through like a tank," to quote an article on the new breed of local party secretary.[37]

It now appears that Gorbachev appreciates the danger that a harsh staffing policy can demoralize his entire bureaucracy. He continues to threaten to sack derelict officials "in front of the whole country"— and his May, 1987 ouster of Defense Minister Sergei L. Sokolov for negligence demonstrates his seriousness even toward the military. Gorbachev, however, now also admonishes his supporters that there shall be no "disrespectful attitude toward cadres in general" and no mechanical purging to please superiors or in order to meet artificial circulation quotas.[38] He seems to have come to the conclusion that officials will not do better work simply out of fear and if public policies and larger structures are not also changed.

Economic Activism and Reform

The new leaders' first response to Soviet economic decay was a burst of policy activism that is quite respectable by recent Soviet and comparative yardsticks.[39] After an early emphasis on punitive measures—the most draconian having been the prosecution of corrupt officials and the May, 1986 prohibitions on "unearned income"—emphasis has shifted to more affirmative measures. Gorbachev's Politburo has increased capital investment, given priority to non-military technological modernization, and begun to supply schools and factories with microcomputers. Planners and managers are being pressed harder to deliver goods and services to the consumer. A single inspectorate now performs quality control for 1,500 large manufacturing plants. New rules allow farms to sell at market prices all produce above the requirements of the plan and even 30 percent of their prescribed quotas of meat, milk, eggs, fruit, and vegetables.

The most innovative policies have been those affecting small enterprise, foreign economic ties, and incomes. As of May, 1987 economic activity by individuals and family firms has been legalized for twenty-nine varieties of consumer goods and services. New regulations make the establishment of cooperative businesses easier; they can hire non-relatives and include up to fifty members. Decrees of September, 1986 and January, 1987 authorize a number of industrial entities to trade directly with foreign partners and establish the legal framework for joint commercial ventures on Soviet soil. The first moves were made in September, 1986 to force steep wage differentials based on productivity.

For all its vigor on policy specifics, the Gorbachev leadership in its first two years did not perform a general overhaul of the economic system or breach the traditional canons of state socialism in the manner of marketizers in Hungary and China. Many of the early decisions bore the mark of political compromise—the relaxation of controls on individual enterprise, for instance, requires most entrepreneurs to work normal hours at a state enterprise and allows them to take up their own work only in their spare time. On grand options for reform, a government commission on economic restructuring, chaired by Nikolai V. Talyzin, the new head of Gosplan, did work behind the scenes. The public debate over reform intensified in 1987, some participants even calling for a quick transition to a mixed economy, with minimal state planning, a large private sector, and integration into the global market. But Gorbachev concluded in June, 1987 that only "the first steps at assimilating new management methods" had been made.[40]

Beyond doubt, part of the problem has been with Gorbachev himself. In 1985–86 he forcefully called for higher economic quality, economic decentralization, and new ideas on planning, while simultaneously stressing rapid quantitative growth, administrative recentralization, and orthodox approaches to the plan. Conversely, Gorbachev's expressed views on the economy, as on so many issues, have become steadily more radical and his impatience with halfway solutions has grown. Policy aides, especially his chief economic adviser, Abel G. Aganbegyan, have helped bring greater rigor to his economic approach.

After two years of delay, economic reform was given a large boost at a plenum of the Central Committee in June, 1987. It adopted a position paper on reform, approved the first major reform legislation (a "law on the socialist enterprise"), and promoted the new party secretary for planning, Nikolai N. Slyun'kov, to the Politburo. Most importantly, Gorbachev's outline at the plenum of a "new management mechanism" marked a watershed in leadership thinking about economic change.

Gorbachev's statement was novel for its detailed timetable for the introduction of a reform package, all of the pieces of which are to be in place by 1991. It goes further than before in blaming the Soviet Union's economic stagnation on the Stalinist formula of mobilization from above, rather than only on poor tactics in the 1970s. It grants that reform might produce a temporary diminution of growth rates and observes that much of the low-quality growth in the unreformed system is useless. It dwells at length on agricultural decentralization through "family contracting" and on cooperatives, one of Gorbachev's genuine enthusiasms. Most remarkably, it makes the first forthright admission by any General Secretary of the need to incorporate market relations, based on the uncoerced interplay of supply and demand forces, into the core operations of the Soviet economy. The Soviets, he said, must achieve "the *systematic mastery and management of the market, with due regard for its laws,* and the strengthening and increase in the authority of the ruble," an objective which would be incalculably "more difficult than issuing commands and directives."[41]

There can be little doubt that Gorbachev remains ardently attached to a few irreducible economic components of socialism, chief among them being the predominance of state ownership, some type of planning, and a social safety net. While continuing to urge debate, he has also indicated that there must be limits to debate and change: "Some people have been suggesting things that go beyond the bounds of our system, and in particular that abandon the instrument of the planned

economy. We have not gone that road and will never do so, because
we are getting ready to strengthen socialism and not to replace it with
a different system."[42]

Accordingly, Gorbachev's embrace of the market and its "laws"
remains grudging, almost as if he finds it as distasteful a tonic as it
is necessary. Although he may have provided a broad template for
reform, much of its content remains unclear. It is far from certain
what the real roles will be for powerful institutions such as Gosplan,
the industrial ministries, and the banks. This is also true of the share
of prices to float with supply and demand (there are to be centrally
fixed and "negotiated" prices along with market prices), the volume
of economic activity to be covered by the state orders (*zakazy*) that
will replace physical plans, the place of the so-called state "control
figures" (which some suspect will be the old physical targets smuggled
in the back door), and the means of inducing competition among
producers. It remains to be seen whether Gorbachev fully accepts the
ramifications of the tradeoffs—between quality and quantity, individual
and collective rights, and dynamism and security—built into his proposals.

As we watch the Soviets wrestle with these enormous issues, we
must remember that changes short of total reform can nonetheless
make a difference. Manipulations of policy such as the anti-egalitarian
decrees on wages will affect tens of millions even if they do not change
the economic system. The potential of marketization in the provision
of consumer products, services, and food is also important, even if it
is unmatched in other sectors. Gorbachev's interest in such a liberalization seems to have grown apace, regardless of where he stands on
heavy industry, and he has justified it by invoking Lenin's New Economic Policy of the 1920s, which tolerated private farming and trade.
Some spokesmen predict that individuals and cooperatives could account for 15 percent of the Soviet national income within a decade.[43]

As for comprehensive reform, the battle over it is probably barely
joined. In Hungary, the most reformist of the East European countries,
radical reform was discussed for fifteen years before being introduced
in 1968, and two decades later it is still being debated and improved.
In China, controversy has been continuous over the last decade and
shows no signs of abating. In the Soviet Union, therefore, we can
expect the struggle to go through numerous rounds in the 1990s and
beyond. The removal of Talyzin from Gosplan in February, 1988, only
one month after the new enterprise law began to take effect, is but
the opening bell.

The Gorbachev Thaw

The precipitous thaw in communications, intellectual life, and the arts has already had greater impact than the episodic relaxations of the Khrushchev years. Gorbachev's *glasnost'* has been directed in part at placating interest groups—particularly the cultural and professional elites—and at using "the weapon of openness," as it is unabashedly described, to expose mismanagement and apply pressure to officials and others who resist his program. But the campaign has also been oriented to the neuropsychology of the Soviet system as a whole, to its collective capacity for comprehending its flaws and problems. *Glasnost'* short-circuits the unofficial communication networks which arise, as Gorbachev said in 1985, when citizens "hear one thing [in the official media] but see another in real life."[44] Most importantly, it gives the regime better antennae for tuning in to the society it governs, recognizing that, as Aleksandr Yakovlev puts it, "contemporary socialism must as a first priority get to know itself."[45]

Gorbachev's opening gambit in this area was to promote less hidebound officials, from Yakovlev (now a Central Committee secretary and member of the Politburo) down to magazine editors and studio directors.[46] In the media, the newcomers have made tangible improvements in coverage of current events and social issues. The decision, albeit belated, not to stonewall on the Chernobyl' tragedy of April, 1986 was a turning point in the government press's treatment of natural and man-made disasters, about which Soviet citizens were always thought too immature to read. The press now provides more data about who officials are and how they make their decisions. In investigative reporting, taboo after taboo has been shattered—on describing drug addiction, unemployment and hoboism, statistical fraud, police brutality, neglect of invalids and orphans, emigration, and the special stores and clinics for officials, to name only a few. Subjects that were open to public discussion under Brezhnev, and there were many, are now examined with a less wooden protocol. Information about the world outside the Soviet Union can now be presented in a more neutral light.

The leaders have also sought to elicit greater candor and empiricism in the social sciences. Yakovlev has not minced words about the muzzling of sociology and other disciplines under Brezhnev: "enclaves closed to criticism," primitive techniques, the laying waste of theory by "a megatonnage of dogmatism."[47] Social scientists are now promised better statistics, both to improve their work and, as a *Pravda* essay said after the January, 1987 plenum, to win the trust of the public: "If you hide from people information about the general conditions of their own lives . . . you cannot expect their activation either in production or in politics."[48] Even the pages of *Kommunist,* the party's dishwater-dull theoretical organ, have been opened to real-life controversies.

The effervescence under Gorbachev has been greatest in the arts, where pressure from below has played a greater role. Party policy here now ranges from keen approval of new currents to benign neglect. At Klimov's initiative, a number of movies suppressed by the Brezhnev regime have now been reviewed by a "conflict commission" of film makers and industry management and given commercial distribution. In literature, works that had been consigned "to the drawer" for years, even decades, have been released in journal and book form. The 1986 upheavals in the cinematographers' and writers' unions have found lesser echoes among composers, architects, and painters.[49] Nor is the ferment only in high culture. Melodiya, the main state studio, now records rock bands reviled only a year or two earlier as the embodiments of Western decadence, and the party youth league books them on tours. Some of the teenagers attending their concerts now sport purple hair and "heavy metal" gear.

The most stunning product of the thaw is the outburst of historical revisionism. Gorbachev, evidently out of both conviction and political calculation, was at first highly reluctant to encourage it. He implored intellectuals at his June, 1986 meeting with leading writers to stay away from Soviet history, saying it would only "set people at one another's throats." By early 1987, however, he had reluctantly accepted the need to fill in "forgotten names and blank spots" in the country's past.[50] In a carefully crafted speech on the seventieth anniversary of the Russian Revolution in November, 1987, Gorbachev proclaimed Stalin's "enormous and unforgivable" guilt for "wholesale repressive measures and acts of lawlessness," while also noting his "incontestable contribution to the building of socialism." He spoke with respect, if not total approval, of opponents of Stalin such as Nikolai I. Bukharin, whose economic and political program in the 1920s bore certain similarities to Gorbachev's.[51] In February, 1988, in a decision of vast symbolic value, the Soviet Supreme Court legally rehabilitated Bukharin and the other victims of Stalin's last great show trial, in 1938.

The first works in two decades to confront the dark chapters of Soviet history began to appear in 1986, even before Gorbachev expressed his support. "Repentance," Tengiz Abuladze's brilliant antitotalitarian film, shocked viewers with its surrealistic rendering of a dispute over disinterment of the body of a dead dictator, a powerful allegory of de-Stalinization. In February, 1987 the Union of Writers announced that Boris Pasternak had been posthumously reinstated in the union and that his great novel about the Russian Revolution, *Doctor Zhivago,* would finally be published in the USSR in 1988, thirty years after it won for its author a Nobel Prize (for which Pasternak was hounded to his death at home). In October plans were revealed to publish in 1988 the late Vasilii Grossman's novel about World War II, *Life and Fate,* which explicitly compares Stalinism to Nazism.

Less sensational, but of enormous moment to Soviet audiences, have been other examples of the new history. A play by Mikhail Shatrov about the 1918 Brest-Litovsk treaty shows Bukharin and other Bolsheviks later to be liquidated by Stalin (and never rehabilitated by Khrushchev) as competent and honest; Stalin is portrayed as a boorish anti-intellectual who wants the party to be "a closed order of sword-bearers." The terror of the 1930s is brought to life in Anatolii Rybakov's *Children of the Arbat,* which recounts arrests and fear in Moscow, and in Anna Akhmatova's posthumously published poem, "Requiem," telling of her vigil under "the stars of death," in front of the Leningrad prison in which her husband was executed. Vladimir Dudintsev's first novel in thirty years, *White Robes,* chronicles the persecution of geneticists in the late 1940s.[52]

Nikita Khrushchev is also emerging from the shadows. Gorbachev's November, 1987 speech for the first time lauded his role in debunking Stalin and promoting liberalization. Yevgenii Yevtushenko and other literary lions of the 1950s have recalled Khrushchev's courage and warm heart as well as his petulance and shallowness. An account of his 1957 dismissal of Marshal Georgii K. Zhukov reveals that officers eager to please him stooped so low as to try to slaughter the marshal's horse.[53]

It would be wrong to think that journalists, social scientists, and writers have been given complete freedom of expression. Few of them really believe this to be so. Important areas of taboo have survived— Kremlin politics, the contemporary KGB, and the saintly Lenin head the list. Censorship has not been abolished, and the works of most living emigre writers remain unpublished.[54] Publications in the provinces, under the thumb of local bosses, remain far inferior to Moscow. Episodes such as the exclusion in July, 1987 of most reporters from the Chernobyl' trial underline the fact that, when it so wishes, the regime still decides what news is fit to print. And free assembly, a form of expression taken for granted in the Western democracies, continues to have few defenders in the USSR.

Glasnost' has also given rise to a predictable backlash. At least a substantial minority of the population—24 percent in one sample of workers—believes it "does more harm than good."[55] Even some liberals are edgy, primarily out of fright that conservatives will be provoked.

They have reached, as did Gorbachev in remarks to editors in July, 1987, for the old bromide of anathematizing "antisocialist" views. Critics, Gorbachev said, should question and probe, but "must not undermine socialism" and must seek answers to problems "within the limits of socialism."[56] Such remarks are less a guide to the boundaries of debate than a reminder that boundaries continue to exist and, as in the past, it is up to the individual to find them by bumping up against them.

Most worrisome to the leadership has been the inflammatory tone of some of the journal and newspaper articles and letters, as well as television programs, in which participants have traded insults and impugned one another's motives. The problem, as Gorbachev not inaccurately told the editors, is largely one of culture: "We still do not have enough political culture, we still do not have the culture to carry out discussions, to respect the point of view even of a friend or comrade. . . . We are an emotional people."[57] As he surely realizes, a civic culture cannot be built by decree.

Supply Side Politics

Every political system enables some participation and also contains it within agreed-upon limits. In the Soviet Union, the regime's emphasis has always been on the latter part of the equation. Without eliminating restrictions, Gorbachev now wants to shift emphasis. He sees participation in much the way some pro-market economists saw the task of economic recovery in the United States in the early 1980s: as a matter of encouraging increased output by reducing state taxation.

Gorbachev, who gave short shrift to political change in his first months in office, had by 1987 moved "democratization," as he called it, to the top of his agenda. Gorbachev's political reforms, it must be emphasized, would not replicate Western-style democracy. The expansion of political competition and of the involvement of the populace in political decisions would take place, as he envisages it, within the framework of continued single-party rule. Like *glasnost'* in the media and the arts, Gorbachev's proposed political changes seem to have mostly instrumental value for the new Soviet leadership.

According to Gorbachev, his political changes would heighten the population's sense of identification with the regime and galvanize it to work hard. Order and discipline would be attained "at a higher level, based not on mindless or blind execution of orders but on participation of the members of society in all things." Participatory reform would also provide the authorities with new channels of information about community opinion and subject lower-level administrators to "control from below." Finally, it would act as "a guarantee of the irreversibility of restructuring." This is the most radical rationale, for it can only mean that Gorbachev sees the diffusion of power as a constraint on the regime: it will prevent a future Brezhnev from turning back the clock.[58]

The new approach is being put into effect in more than one way. To telegraph its seriousness, the regime has several times bowed to what it calls, in pre-1917 phraseology, *obshchestvennoye mneniye*, best translated as "educated public opinion." While some of the first concessions were symbolic, as with the August, 1986 decision to hold a contest to redesign an unusually ugly war monument in Moscow, some had real costs. The best example would be the discarding the same month of "the project of the century," the planned southward diversion of Siberian rivers, which was highly unpopular with Russian intellectuals but had been kept alive for twenty-five years by economic ministries.

A major aspect of Gorbachev's "supply side politics" is his encouragement of political activity by non-bureaucratic organizations based on voluntary effort. The party itself has taken the initiative to establish new, foundation-like associations to foster popular involvement with causes such as preservation of historical buildings, contact with foreign cultures, and care of orphans and war veterans. It has tolerated the proliferation of non-political and political clubs in Moscow and other large cities, some of them with their own publications, without having decided whether to give them permanent legitimacy.[59] The regime has also shown new interest in resuscitating certain state organizations, especially those with a wide discrepancy between ceremonial and actual roles. In this category is the pyramid of government legislatures or "soviets"; a number of suggestions have been aired to make them livelier and less subservient to their executives. A related initiative is the June, 1987 law providing for public discussions and referenda on major issues, while leaving the final say on referenda to the government.

Gorbachev has been most supportive of electoral reform, a major deviation from precedent but one supported in the past by some Soviet scholars and tried in several other communist countries.[60] Gorbachev's wish, unveiled tentatively at the January, 1987 plenum, is for multi-candidate elections, conducted by secret ballot, of deputies to the soviets, party secretaries, and factory directors and other economic supervisors.

The "economic democracy" provisions are the first to have been enacted. The June, 1987 enterprise law mandates that Soviet employees choose their own bosses, subject to confirmation by higher authority. It was adopted over publicly stated objections that it was legally suspect and politically pretentious.[61] In the soviets, a national experiment with multiple candidates—but not, to repeat, with multiple parties—was conducted in selected districts in June, 1987. Election of secretaries in the party has been carried out thus far only at the prompting of such strongly pro-Gorbachev local leaders as Boris K. Pugo in Latvia. Intraparty democracy will be the main agenda item of a special Nineteenth Party Conference, the first since 1941, which is to open June 28, 1988.

If even partial political reforms are to go ahead, changes must be made in the Soviet system of justice. Arbitrary treatment by the police and courts is hardly an incentive to voluntary participation in public affairs, as the rulers fully understood when they politicized justice after the revolution.

It is intriguing, therefore, to see that a brisk debate about legal and judicial reform has erupted under Gorbachev, with a pronounced intensification, as in so many other fields, after mid-1986. Scholars and journalists (led by two combative legal correspondents, Yurii Feofanov of *Izvestiya* and Arkadii Vaksberg of *Literaturnaya gazeta*) have called for "legal *glasnost'*," including the publication of crime statistics and of departmental regulations that have the force of law. They have asked probing questions about the virtual disappearance of acquittals from the courts and about sentencing and release procedures, including what one called "telephone law," decisions made by judges after being pressured by officials.[62] At an emotional round table between legal bureaucrats and Moscow writers in late 1986, it was agreed that, "considering the sad experience of the past," legal reform was no less needed than economic reform.[63] More recently, Aleksandr Yakovlev, of the inner leadership, has disparaged the presumption in Soviet theory that the rights of the individual are "a benefaction from on high."[64]

The results to date are inconclusive, although not disheartening. A November, 1986 party resolution on "socialist legality" gave few details, but only weeks later the USSR's best-known political dissident, Andrei Sakharov, was released from exile. Some 200 more dissidents were pardoned over the next few months. In an extraordinary rebuke, *Pravda* on January 8, 1987, printed an announcement by the head of the KGB, Viktor M. Chebrikov, that KGB agents who had tampered with a journalists' inquiry into corruption in the Ukraine had been fired and the journalist, Viktor Berkhin, exonerated.[65] In early 1988 the "special psychiatric hospitals," in which many dissidents have been confined, were switched from the police to the Health Ministry.

More substantial legal change has not yet progressed beyond the study stage. Gorbachev, a law school graduate who never practiced law, told the January, 1987 plenum there should be a revision of the penal code so as to "defend more effectively the interests and rights of citizens." A panel of legal scholars, criminologists, and judges is said to be pondering dilution or excision of the clauses covering "anti-Soviet propaganda" and similar offenses. Also under consideration are proposals for elimination of the death penalty, lifetime appointment of judges, early provision of defense counsel to the accused, and adoption of a quasi-jury system for trials for serious crimes.

As with economics and culture, there is only so much that moderate reformers can do in the area of law without changing the essence of the institutions they wish to save. Gorbachev's assurance in January, 1987 that he would not "break up our political system" will not lay the question to rest. The "mindless obedience" deprecated in his report has been a standing feature of Soviet life since the rise of Stalin, as have mute legislators, snooping policemen, and pliable judges. These things will not be easily superseded, and conservatives will be alarmed if they are. Even reform-minded Soviets have a deeply ingrained fear of the mob and a nervousness that an unraveling of political controls will lead to anarchy.[66]

It may be easier to achieve a consensus of the elite on legal reform than on other measures, since this would extend a trend toward predictability and professionalism in law enforcement that had begun in the 1950s and would benefit more people than it would harm. Multi-candidate elections, however, will detract from elite security and place a strain on many time-honored procedures. Boris Pugo, among others, has argued that meaningful elections in factories and local governments cast doubt on "certain fossilized canons of party practice," most directly the *nomenklatura* system of prior clearance of all staffing decisions by the party organs.[67] Although he did not say so, it is self-evident that open elections within the party would not be readily squared with the principle of hierarchy. Gorbachev, who has ruthlessly used appointment from above, has so far brushed the problem aside, declaring that "democratic centralism" will not be tarnished.

As with *glasnost'*, organizational problems probably pale before psychological and cultural ones. An account of the experimental election of a district party secretary in Moscow is one of many that illustrates the point. Most of the voters were bewildered by the experience, not knowing whether to express themselves and expecting the election to "roll down the rut worn over the decades," whereby "They ask us to vote, and we vote" for the approved candidate. "We are only beginning to learn," the story concluded, "how to nurture our own opinions and to voice them openly and without fear."[68] Mastering that lesson will take as long as any of the changes Gorbachev has set in motion.

Political Dynamics

The Soviet scene several years into Gorbachev's reign abounds in mirage effects. A stroll down a Moscow street turns up signs of change everywhere, but along with it so much that remains as before. Gorbachev has grumbled about those who only talk of reform, creating merely "the illusion of restructuring." It is politics, operating on several levels, that will determine how much progress is real and how much illusory.

Gorbachev's Reform Tendencies

Mikhail Gorbachev has maintained that if he had not happened along, "there would have been someone else" to spearhead reforms.[69] Yet there is no denying his pivotal role thus far. The future of reform will be very much shaped by how he deals with what he thinks and what he learns.

As should be apparent, since coming to power Gorbachev has spoken with more than one voice. If we examine the spectrum of his policies for general principles of action, his program can be seen to incorporate three main tendencies: *policy activism, system reintegration,* and, most weakly, *system change.* All are broadly reformist in spirit, although they entail different kinds of reform.

Pragmatic *policy activism,* the least demanding, has been directed mainly at the regime's crisis of effectiveness. Taking the system's basic machinery as its point of departure, it pulls every available lever and pushes every button to get things done. Typical are Gorbachev's adroit use of the personnel weapon and, in the economy, his Politburo's policy innovations on issues of corruption, technology, foreign trade, and distribution of wages.

System reintegration addresses the Soviet system's crisis of coherence. It is concerned with institutions rather than policies alone, believing the main defect in both to be the inability to unite attitudes and behavior in Soviet society into a logical and functional whole.[70] Gorbachev has been especially troubled by two related manifestations of incoherence under Brezhnev: poor self-knowledge and exiting behavior.

The remedy offered to correct the first flaw has been a strategy of intellectual and cultural *self-discovery.* It has been achieved primarily through a relaxation of political controls over the media, the arts, and the social sciences. To cope with the incoherence that has been expressed as exiting, Gorbachev's response might be seen as an exercise in *system extension.* He seeks to make legitimate, and to coopt into the official system, a variety of activities that the rigidity of the state during the last generation has driven out to unofficial structures. The lost souls now being reclaimed include many (although not all) black-market entrepreneurs—who can now work legally and become subject to government licensing, inspection, and taxation—underground artists, and dissidents and semi-dissidents. Supply side politics fits equally well with self-discovery and system extension, inasmuch as it is directed both at finding out about citizens' opinions and at luring some of them into public life.

System change would bring the modification of fundamentals of the Soviet order. On this level, progress under Gorbachev has been slight and the prospect of more is most uncertain. This is a man, when all is said and done, who believes fiercely in the worth of Soviet state socialism, trumpeting it to have "repeatedly and in many ways demonstrated its superiority over capitalism"[71] He has time and again insisted that he wants to modernize the system, not scrap it, and has made the motto "More Socialism!" (*Bol'she sotsializma!*) a propaganda staple. It is abundantly clear that he stands by the Soviet Union's single-party political system, state-dominated economy, and collectivist approach to rights, in which the needs of society and the state take precedence over those of the individual.

This does not mean, however, that Gorbachev is imparting no impetus to change anything essential. If one must accept at face value his reiterations of his faith in "socialism," we must do the same with his assertions, equally plaintive, that major surgery is needed for Soviet socialism to compete and thrive in changing circumstances. These statements have become more common as his education in power has proceeded since March, 1985.

Therefore, while continuing to expound the core values of the regime, Gorbachev has come to interpret some of them, and to connect them to practical considerations, in ways that may point to structural change. His Marxist economics have made room for a more accommodating attitude toward individual and cooperative enterprise and a recognition that forms of market coordination must be grafted onto government planning. His Leninist politics have not prevented him from issuing a searing critique of Soviet political culture or from proposing major changes in rules affecting participation. His organic view of society coexists with other convictions—about the reliance of the whole on the well-being of the individual cells—that are pulling him away from Stalinist absolutism.

If the regime were to institutionalize policy changes that Gorbachev has already made, it is possible that some change would take place in the system. A party directive decreeing slacker censorship is one thing;

While most of the present leaders will probably defer to Gorbachev on routine issues, on matters of consequence they will make their views heard. The situation, it ought to be underlined, is far from static. Several in the leadership seem to have drifted toward greater radicalism, much as has Gorbachev.[74] And Gorbachev will have a freer hand once he has completed the renovation of the Politburo and brought in more enthusiastic supporters. His early pace suggests that he will not dawdle with this. Gorbachev-era promotees are already more dominant among the Politburo candidates and non-ranking secretaries (four of six and five of five, respectively) than among the voting members of the Politburo.

There is no reason to doubt Gorbachev's contention, persistently made, that the main obstacles to his reforms have been raised, not in the Politburo, but in the bureaucracy below. Resistance is found, he said in April, 1987, "at the level of the Central Committee and the government, in the ministries, republics, and regions."[75] The Soviet press today overflows with anecdotal evidence of economic and other administrators dragging their feet on innovations. Lucid evidence is the difficulty Gorbachev had in arranging the January, 1987 plenum of the Central Committee, which is overwhelmingly composed of party and government bureaucrats. It had to be postponed three times, Gorbachev said, until the necessary "clarity" could be reached—a revelation made all the more astounding by his statement at the plenum that the committee had been for years an inert rubber stamp.[76]

One should be skeptical, however, of any simplistic image of a bureaucratic monolith, or of Gorbachev and his Kremlin allies as fighting a lonely battle against all odds. Gorbachev himself favored such an image in some of his early statements about the "bureaucratic stratum" and its crassly self-interested hostility to him. But he has since begun speaking of administrators in more differentiated terms. He now identifies bureaucratic supporters as well as nay-sayers, and allows that the latter include "people who are honorable and unselfish but remain the prisoners of old concepts."[77]

This is not to trivialize bureaucratic obstructionism but rather to argue that it be kept in perspective. Absent a crisis in the party leadership, most bureaucratic foes of reform will work to absorb rather than repel it. Their resistance will take the form of a multitude of uncoordinated, localized actions. They will be motivated, not only by prejudice and privilege, but also by a conviction that they are doing their duty and, more often than not, by a sincere befuddlement about what is expected of them.[78]

Gorbachev is not without an arsenal he can deploy in the bureaucratic arena. He can scold laggards from his bully pulpit and remove them outright if they are defiant. At the Nineteenth Party Conference to be held in 1988 he can be expected to purge the Central Committee of those members who have been least cooperative. He can also bribe individual bureaucratic supporters with offers of promotion and can appeal to them collectively by playing to interests beyond those related to their jobs. The salaried middle class to which they belong should be well served by the stratification of incomes and greater availability of personal services that Gorbachev promises. Like intellectuals, administrators also stand to benefit from a greater leniency and predictability in political control, especially if they are applied to foreign travel.

A perceptive Soviet publicist, Fedor Burlatskii, has noted that the administrator who shuns change is more to be feared than the man in the street, "since he has more influence and more depends on him." Yet the Soviet bureaucracy, as Burlatskii said, has no monopoly on conservatism. "A part of the mass [public], passive toward changes, must be considered as a factor braking restructuring."[79]

In understanding this, as other, aspects of Gorbachev's policies, we should avoid black-and-white thinking about support and resistance. Gorbachev has more than any previous leader looked at Soviet society as having needs that must be respected: "We cannot make our society dynamic and vital if we do not take interests into account, if there is not a reciprocal link through which interests influence both policy and society."[80] The interests of which Gorbachev has been most solicitous are those of the Soviet middle class, broadly defined, and most emphatically of the intelligentsia, the main beneficiary of cultural liberalization. At the same time, he has tended to look at social interests in highly specific terms, rather than in the crude class categories that pervaded Soviet theory in the past. In addition to his general middle-class bias, Gorbachev's early actions suggest that he is intent on appealing to substrata within large social constituencies.

The multinational character of Soviet society, in which Russians comprise a bare majority, presents Gorbachev with particular problems. Gorbachev's personnel and anti-corruption policies have had greatest effect in the outlying areas, and it is no accident that the most violent outburst against him, in Kazakhstan in 1986, was fueled by grievances over such policies. *Glasnost'* also is evoking non-Russian (and Russian) resentments on a variety of issues. The demonstrations in the summer of 1987 by Crimean Tatars in Moscow, and by local nationalists in the Baltic republics, would not have been possible without Gorbachev's liberalization. On the other hand, when it comes to the advantages of cultural and political change, most members of the minority groups are not likely to think much differently from the Russian majority. In economics, local politicians of all backgrounds are apt to see a larger role for themselves, mostly in terms of promoting consumer welfare, if management is decentralized. And certain aspects of economic reform, including the toleration of small businesses, may actually be of less profit to most Russians than to modernized minorities with a strong entrepreneurial tradition, such as the Baltic peoples, the Armenians, and the Georgians.

Among socioeconomic groups, it holds as a gross generalization that white-collar employees have the most to gain, and blue-collar workers the most to lose, from Gorbachevism. It is the workers who have been most offended by the rationing of vodka, who will complain most vociferously about increases in food prices, and who have gained the least from the cultural thaw. Surveys show that the bulk of Soviet workers have seen little improvement from economic change thus far and "feel restructuring only in the greater pressure at work."[81] Radical economic reform, if consistently pursued, is certain to bring plant closings and retraining programs. In June, 1987, Gorbachev promised that no workers would be left unemployed, but he also announced the necessity of a "regrouping of the work force," which would redeploy workers out of smokestack industries and into advanced manufacturing and services.[82]

If all these points apply here and now, Gorbachev's reforms have the potential of eventually urging the USSR down a path long since travelled by the West, on which economic modernization blurs rather than reinforces class boundaries. Soviet peasants stand to benefit economically from economic reform, and many Soviet workers still have ties with the village. Economic dislocation will affect the middle class as well as the working class—high officials now speak of deep cuts in the administrative staffs of economic agencies and of closing hundreds of unproductive research institutes. Most significantly, the regime's approach to wages and welfare promises to increase stratification and differentiation within class groups, not only between them: "It is precisely the most qualified part of the population, the 'wagons' on which society rides, that will come out ahead of their present situation."[83] These wagons are found in all social classes, including the industrial proletariat.

Gorbachev has on several occasions said (making a point familiar to political sociologists in the West) that attainment of higher levels of education and income magnifies an individual's aspirations for political rights. It should follow that the best schooled and most affluent groups will most appreciate political reforms. It is interesting that the Soviet leadership seems not entirely comfortable with this logic. How else to explain the totally unexpected provision for election of factory directors and foremen? Better a dose of workplace democracy, Moscow's attitude seems to be, than a working-class revolution.

No Room to Retreat?

Gorbachev, like politicians everywhere, likes to dramatize political choices. Putting on his best television evangelist's face at the January, 1987 Central Committee plenum, he stated that the course he had charted was absolutely necessary, "for we simply have no other way." "It is impossible for us to retreat and we have nowhere to retreat to."

Many in the Soviet elite, however, assuredly do think it possible to retreat, perhaps to a revivified Stalinism. Nor is the decision as simple as whether to go backward or forward, or even whether to go full- or half-throttle. Doubtless, there are those with influence in the Soviet Union who would prefer to strike off on an entirely different tangent, or to accept some parts of Gorbachev's program and reject others, or even to subside into a reasonably intelligent conservatism, such as that represented by Leonid Brezhnev in the first half of his administration. The longer Gorbachev and his allies are able to exploit the immense organizational resources at their disposal, and the more success their changes bring, the worse it will be for their detractors. Yet Gorbachev can never be rid of them entirely, and he will never be able to forget what the enemies of change did in October, 1964 to another reformist leader, Nikita Khrushchev.

The basic question is whether *perestroika* will work. Fedor Burlatskii, a Khrushchev reformer for whom Gorbachev has been a godsend, has said that the worst thing for the Soviet Union would be inept and indecisive "microreforms," the creation of "something that is half horse and half grouse, some kind of dinosaur that can neither jump nor fly."[84] Gorbachev clearly fears this as well, and intends to carry out macroreforms, but his own inhibitions and the many constraints in his political environment may keep him from going far enough. Herein lies a real danger for him. Had he been unambitious, Gorbachev could have gotten away with Brezhnev-style band-aid solutions for quite some time. Now that he is being almost reckless in the way he challenges elites and vested interests, he probably cannot survive reforms that fail to deliver the goods, especially economically.

Will the Gorbachev reforms be sufficient to alleviate the regime's crisis of effectiveness? In the short term, over the next five years, the odds are overwhelming that they will not. Gorbachev seems conscious of his vulnerability here, as I have noted, and has braced the public for a long wait for improvement and even, most recently, for a dip in economic growth before new structures begin to pay dividends. As time goes, it will be essential to Gorbachev that he continue to show the impressive ability to learn in office he has exhibited so far. This is because, as has been convincingly demonstrated in other communist countries, serious economic and other reforms must constantly be adjusted and affirmed. If Gorbachev persists with his more enlightened cultural policy, and with the ginger political reforms begun in 1987, he will not be alone in being educated by experience. His changes make a credible beginning on curing the Soviet system's crisis of coherence. At a minimum, they will give the leadership and the whole Soviet elite superior intelligence as well as feedback about what they are doing. The dinosaur, finally, will know better whether it can jump or fly, and that knowledge itself is a crucial condition of getting off the ground.

If Gorbachev's economic and other reforms fizzle, if after a period of adjustment things do not improve, if there is an unforeseen policy disaster (most likely to occur in foreign policy)—if worse comes to worst, the balance of political forces may conceivably tip enough to force a retreat. If that happens, two things may be predicted. First, a radical change of compass would be impractical without a change of leader. If it is debatable whether the Soviet system has room to retreat, there is no question that Mikhail Gorbachev has left himself very little. Second, a retreat would not come easily. Gorbachev is giving many in the elite, and millions outside it, a stake in a broadly reformist strategy. Overcoming his coalition would not be impossible, nor would it be but a day's work, and it probably could not be achieved without violence. The possibility cannot be excluded that an enforced retreat, polarizing the political elite and attempting to remobilize a partially emancipated society, would bring about what has so far eluded the Soviet system, a crisis of survival.

Notes

1. Quotation by Teimuraz Mamaladze in *Izvestiya,* January 31, 1987, p. 3, and by Gorbachev in *Pravda,* May 20, 1987, p. 3.

2. *Pravda,* January 28, 1987, pp. 3–4.

3. Ibid., p. 1; February 26, 1987, p. 1; May 20, 1987, p. 1.

4. For further discussion, using crisis in the narrow sense of a crisis of survival, see Timothy J. Colton, *The Dilemma of Reform in the Soviet Union,* rev. ed. (New York, Council on Foreign Relations, 1986), pp. 57–61. The terrible camp battles of the 1950s are described in Aleksandr I. Solzhenitsyn, *The Gulag Archipelago 1918–1956,* vol. III (New York, Harper and Row, 1978), chaps. 10–12.

5. Seweryn Bialer, *The Soviet Paradox: External Expansion, Internal Decline* (New York, Alfred A. Knopf, 1986), p. 75.

6. See especially Robert C. Tucker's classic essay on "dual Russia," in his *The Soviet Political Mind,* rev. ed (New York, W. W. Norton, 1971), pp. 121–142.

7. Albert O. Hirschman, *Exit, Voice, and Loyalty* (Cambridge, Mass., Harvard University Press, 1970).

8. The frequency of exiting behavior, in defiance of system canons, might be another cause of the denial of reality. Corruption is an especially good example. As in eighteenth-century Russia, collective repression of the truth about corruption was resorted to because Russians lived in a world "where no one could maintain moral identity or sense of purpose without denouncing bribery but where no one could function without taking and giving bribes." George L. Yaney, *The Systematization of Russian Government* (Urbana, University of Illinois Press, 1973), p. 34.

9. Yefim Etkind, "Sovetskiye tabu," *Sintaksis* (Paris), no. 9 (1981), p. 8.

10. See the account in *Pravda,* September 10, 1986, p. 3.

11. Chingiz Aitmatov, *Sobraniye sochinenii,* 3 vols. (Moscow, Molodaya gvardiya, 1982–84), II, 195–489. In the 1960s Soviet literature as a whole lost the sense of personal wholeness and harmony typical of Stalinist "socialist realism." Novelists now wrote of alienation, disintegration, and confusion. Katerina Clark, *The Soviet Novel: History as Ritual* (Chicago and London, University of Chicago Press, 1981), p. 232.

12. Hugh Heclo, *Modern Social Politics in Britain and Sweden* (New Haven and London, Yale University Press, 1974), p. 305.

13. A suggestive parallel might be the plight of Jimmy G., the strong but passive and "unconcerned" amnesiac described by the neurologist Oliver Sack in *The Man Who Mistook His Wife for a Hat and Other Clinical Tales* (New York, Summit Books, 1986), p. 36. It is interesting that some of the best work on memory loss has been done by Russian psychologists.

14. A. Yakovlev, "Dostizheniye kachestvenno novogo sostoyaniya sovetskogo obshchestva i obshchestvennyye nauki," *Kommunist,* no. 8 (May, 1987), p. 4.

15. *Pravda,* May 20, 1987, p. 1. On the other hand, the unofficial transcript of Gorbachev's June 19, 1986, audience with Soviet writers contains a surprisingly warm reference to the economic situation in Stavropol' in 1969. See Arkhiv samizdata, "Beseda chlenov SP SSSR s M. S. Gorbachevym," AS No. 5785, prepared by Radio Liberty, Munich. All quotations from his remarks in this chapter are from this Russian-language version.

16. Janos Kornai, "The Hungarian Reform Process: Visions, Hopes, and Reality," *Journal of Economic Literature,* 24 (December, 1986), pp. 1724–1726.

17. *Pravda,* April 24, 1985, p. 1.

18. "Nastoichivo dvigat'sya vpered," *Kommunist,* no. 8 (May, 1985), p. 32.

19. Ibid., p. 32.

20. This claim was made in remarks in Minsk, only a summary of which was given in *Pravda,* July 12, 1985, p. 1.

21. "Nastoichivo dvigat'sya vpered," p. 34.

22. See, for example, the statement that Gorbachev's reformism "has nothing in common with liberalism . . . stresses authoritarian rule, discipline, and

predictable conformist behavior. Cultural experimentation, not to speak of expanded political rights, has no place in his world." Seweryn Bialer and Joan Afferica, "The Genesis of Gorbachev's World," *Foreign Affairs*, 64 (America and the World issue, 1985), p. 620.

23. Quotations from the congress speech are taken from *Pravda*, February 26, 1986.

24. Ibid., August 2, 1986, p. 1.

25. Ibid., October 2, 1986, p. 1.

26. All quotations here from ibid., January 28, 1987, p. 1; emphasis added.

27. As an example of Gorbachev's cautioning about the time needed to deliver on reforms, see his claim that the population "understands that there are problems with restructuring that will take one, two, and for certain of them even three five-year plans to resolve." Ibid., July 15, 1987, p. 2.

28. I define turnover here as the proportion of all office holders at the beginning of the measured period who left office during the period due to retirement, demotion, liquidation of the office, or death. Death accounts for less than 5 percent of turnover in every category except the Politburo under Andropov. In a small number of cases, an official moved from one position in a given category to another; these were included in turnover totals. This rule was waived for the membership (including candidate members) of the Politburo, since a seat there confers political status over and above one's administrative position.

29. This last point is in *Pravda*, January 14, 1987, p. 1.

30. Average yearly turnover under Gorbachev, as of March 10, 1987, was 19 percent among Politburo members and candidates, 38 percent among Moscow party secretaries and department heads, 32 percent in the Council of Ministers, and 20 percent among regional party bosses. Under Brezhnev (between his last party congress in March, 1981 and his death), annual turnover was 3, 2, 2, and 6 percent, respectively, and under Chernenko 5, 6, 10, and 10 percent.

Under Andropov, annualized turnover in these four groups was at 15, 25, 16, and 18 percent, far closer to Gorbachev's. But three of the four exits from Andropov's Politburo were by death, and the only outright removal (of A. P. Kirilenko) had apparently been settled when Brezhnev was still alive; all four under Gorbachev were political demotions.

Gorbachev appears to regard his purge as a continuation of the changes begun under Andropov. Officials appointed under Andropov and Chernenko have been far less vulnerable than others. In the Council of Ministers, for example, 76 percent of the Brezhnev holdovers were removed in Gorbachev's first two years, as compared to only 11 percent of those selected after November, 1982.

31. I lack ages for five of the twenty-nine March, 1987 secretaries and department heads, but have them for all others.

32. *Pravda*, January 14, 1987, p. 2.

33. See Colton, *Dilemma of Reform*, pp. 104–105; and Thane Gustafson and Dawn Mann, "Gorbachev's First Year: Building Power and Authority," *Problems of Communism*, 35 (May-June, 1986), pp. 8–11.

34. If turnover is grouped into six-month intervals ending in September of 1985, March and September of 1986, and March of 1987, the pattern is striking. In the Politburo, turnover rates (annualized) are 13, 47, 0, and 11 percent in those subperiods; in the Central Committee apparatus 62, 85, 7, and 14 percent; in the Council of Ministers 28, 63, 32, and 28 percent; and among regional party leaders 26, 30, 10, and 13 percent. Invariably, the most rapid change was in the second half of Gorbachev's first year. There was some recrudescence of change in the second half of his second year, but never to anything like the peak level.

35. Based on information available on the twenty-six new first secretaries named in Gorbachev's first year and the eight in the second year. It should be noted that, although only 12 percent of the first year's secretaries came directly from a position in the region, 54 percent had once held such a position. The pattern in the Council of Ministers is quite different. Of the nine branch economic ministers appointed in Gorbachev's second year, only two were deputies of the outgoing minister, the standard Brezhnev pattern; four held field positions in the ministry and three had most recently been party officials. For a related discussion, see Thane Gustafson and Dawn Mann, "Gorbachev's Next Gamble," *Problems of Communism,* 36 (July-August, 1987), pp. 10–16.

36. Four Stavropol' colleagues have been named to the Council of Ministers, but only one (V. S. Murakhovskii, first deputy premier in charge of agriculture) to a major portfolio. None has been named a national party secretary or department head or to an important position in the KGB. Brezhnev, with his much wider experience, was a far more effective patron in the mid-1960s.

37. *Pravda,* January 14, 1987, p. 2.

38. Quotations from ibid., July 15, 1987, p. 2.

39. Changes up to mid-1986 are summarized in Colton, *Dilemma of Reform,* chap. 4. A good overview by an economist is Philip Hanson, "The Shape of Gorbachev's Economic Reform," *Soviet Economy,* 2 (October-December, 1986), pp. 313–326. A fine socioeconomic analysis is Peter A. Hauslohner, "Gorbachev's Social Contract," ibid., 3 (January-March, 1987), pp. 54–89. Political variables are discussed in Timothy J. Colton, "Approaches to the Politics of Systemic Economic Reform in the Soviet Union," in ibid., 3 (April-June, 1987), pp. 145–170.

40. *Pravda,* June 26, 1987, p. 3.

41. Quotations from ibid., June 26, 1987, pp. 1, 3; emphasis added.

42. Ibid., July 15, 1987, p. 2.

43. Hanson, pp. 319–320.

44. *Pravda,* April 24, 1985, p. 2.

45. Yakovlev, p. 10. Compare to Gorbachev's comment to the writers in June, 1986: "We have no [political] opposition, so in what way can we monitor ourselves? Only through criticism and self-criticism and above all through openness. There cannot be a society without openness. We are learning about this."

46. Yakovlev was made head of the party's propaganda department in July, 1985, secretary for propaganda and cultural affairs in March, 1986 (his re-

sponsibilities broadened to include science and social science in January, 1987), and a full member of the Politburo in June, 1987. Other key appointments, all in 1986, included those of V. G. Zakharov as Minister of Culture, Yu. P. Voronov as head of the Central Committee's culture department, M. F. Nenashev and A. I. Kamshalov as chiefs of the publishing and film industries, and I. T. Frolov as editor of *Kommunist*. Frolov in 1987 became one of Gorbachev's personal assistants.

47. Yakovlev, pp. 8, 13.

48. T. I. Zaslavskaya in *Pravda*, February 6, 1987, pp. 2–3.

49. Many younger painters in Moscow, impatient with their conservative union and with state studios and galleries, have begun experimenting on their own. Since May, 1987 individual painters, other artists, and artisans in Moscow have been allowed to sell their wares at a large weekend arts fair in Izmailovo park. A painter with whom I spoke in September, 1987 said that the opening of the fair was the first time he had felt proud to be a Soviet citizen.

50. *Pravda*, February 14, 1987, pp. 1–2.

51. This speech is in ibid., November 3, 1987.

52. The Shatrov play is in *Novyi mir*, no. 4 (April, 1987) (quotation at p. 27); Rybakov's novel started publication in *Druzhba narodov*, no. 4 (April, 1987); Akhmatova's poem is in *Oktyabr'*, no. 3 (March, 1987); Dudintsev's novel is in *Neva*, no. 1 and 2 (January and February, 1987). As with the better-known *Doctor Zhivago*, it is bizarre to think how long some of the literary works here have gone unpublished. Shatrov's was written in 1962, Rybakov's was first slated for printing in 1967, and "Requiem" was completed in 1940!

53. The details about the purge of Zhukov are in "Marshal Zhukov," *Ogonek*, no. 49 (December, 1986), p. 7, and no. 51 (December, 1986), p. 27.

54. See on this point Nancy P. Condee and Vladimir Padunov, "Reforming Soviet Culture/Retrieving Soviet History," *The Nation*, June 13, 1987, p. 816. The newspaper *Moscow News* was reprimanded in September, 1987 for publishing a sympathetic obituary of the emigre novelist, Viktor Nekrasov. And yet, plans seem to be afoot to publish some of the poetry of Joseph Brodsky, the 1987 Nobel Prize laureate in literature, who has been living in exile in the United States for some years.

55. *Izvestiya*, May 5, 1987, p. 2.

56. *Pravda*, July 15, 1987, p. 2.

57. Ibid., p. 1. For particularly acrid press exchanges, see *Izvestiya*, April 20, 1987, p. 4 (about river diversions), and *Sotsialisticheskaya industriya*, May 24, 1987, p. 3, and June 14, p. 3 (concerning Stalin's poor preparations for World War II).

58. *Pravda*, January 28, 1987, p. 2, and February 26, 1987, pp. 1–2.

59. There were said to be 30,000 such clubs by the beginning of 1988.

60. See Werner G. Hahn, "Electoral Choice in the Soviet Bloc," *Problems of Communism*, 36 (March-April, 1987), pp. 29–39.

61. See especially *Sotsialisticheskaya industriya*, February 17, 1987, p. 2.

62. Quoted in "V pol'zu spravedlivosti," *Literaturnaya gazeta*, no. 47 (November 19, 1986), p. 13.

63. Arkadii Vaksberg, "Komu eto nuzhno?" ibid., no. 4 (January 21, 1987), p. 12.

64. Yakovlev, p. 17.

65. The party first secretary in Voroshilovgrad region was then dismissed in February, 1987, and the chief of the Ukrainian KGB, Stepan N. Mukha, several months later.

66. See the essay by the reformist intellectual, Fedor Burlatskii, in *Pravda,* July 18, 1987, p. 3. While strongly defending political liberalization, he argues against an unrestricted right of assembly, warning of "how quickly democracy and mob rule interpenetrate." His main example is the activities of *Pamyat* (Memory), a group of ultra-nationalist Russians who have staged several demonstrations in Moscow, but he also mentions gatherings of Jewish "refuseniks."

67. Ibid., July 8, 1987, p. 2.

68. *Moskovskaya pravda,* July 18, 1987, p. 2.

69. *Pravda,* May 20, 1987, p. 1.

70. This is nothing new. Many in Russia before the revolution worried over essentially the same problem, as is brilliantly argued in Yaney, *The Systematization of Russian Government.*

71. Gorbachev remarks to Margaret Thatcher, *Pravda,* March 31, 1987, p. 2.

72. Ibid., June 13, 1987, p. 1. Compare to his statement to the writers in June, 1986 that "clashes and arguments do occur" in the Politburo.

73. Ibid., November 13, 1987, pp. 1–2. Yel'tsin's speech and resignation threat were at first considered too explosive to be publicly reported. A TASS bulletin was sent out to Soviet editors, but revoked within minutes.

74. The best example of this is probably Premier Ryzhkov, who in mid-1987 strongly endorsed economic reforms quite a bit more thorough than those he seemed to favor a year or two before.

75. *Pravda,* April 17, 1987, p. 1.

76. Ibid., February 26, 1987, p. 1.

77. Ibid.

78. Soviet surveys suggest that such confusion may be most serious in the administrative apparatus of the party. See ibid., June 17, 1987, p. 2, which reports that 79 percent of party secretaries polled in one region "imprecisely understood the distinction" between new and old kinds of economic leadership.

79. Ibid., July 18, 1987, p. 3.

80. Ibid., July 15, 1987, p. 2.

81. *Izvestiya,* May 5, 1987, p. 2.

82. *Pravda,* June 26, 1987, p. 5.

83. Zaslavskaya in *Sotsialisticheskaya industriya,* February 7, 1987, p. 2.

84. *Pravda,* July 18, 1987, p. 3.

7

The Crisis of the Soviet System of Power and Mikhail Gorbachev's Political Strategy

Thane Gustafson

Mikhail Gorbachev's politics are a tough act to follow. When after one year in office he had not yet produced the millenium, Western reviewers were ready to dismiss him as a conservative and a technocrat. Then as he unveiled one radical measure after another over the next year-and-a-half, the critics called him naive and rash and began forecasting his fall. The latest reviews, following his dismissal of Moscow Party chief Boris Yeltsin in the fall of 1987, now bring us Gorbachev the Party opportunist, trimming to the conservative wind. Yet the man must have an underlying strategy. What is it?

When Gorbachev became General Secretary of the Central Committee of the CPSU in March 1985, he appeared to believe that the problems he faced were essentially economic. To the extent that they were political, this was because of Brezhnev's mistakes, not because of basic flaws in the political system. The key word of Gorbachev's first major policy speech in April, 1985, was "acceleration" ("*uskorenie*"), and the changes he proposed were confined mainly to the "economic mechanism."[1] But within a year Gorbachev had begun to speak of "restructuring," "radical reform," "revolution," and "democratization." By the first half of 1987 his diagnoses of the past, his initiatives for the present, and his proposals for the future raised fundamental political issues, many of which had not been touched since the 1920s.[2]

Naturally, in analyzing any politician's moves it is extremely difficult to separate the tactical from the strategic and the improvised from the premeditated. Was Gorbachev planning radical reforms from the start and only biding his time, or has his thinking evolved along the way? At this point we cannot say. But whatever his path, by the beginning of 1987 Gorbachev had concluded that the real crisis facing him was not only economic but political. His recent actions, therefore, should be seen not only as an attempt to revitalize the economy but also the political instruments and resources by which power and authority are generated and maintained.

It is logical, on reflection, that economic and political crisis should go together, because the political and economic systems created by Stalin were together the embodiment of a single development strategy.[3] What Gorbachev is now telling us is that as the strategy is outgrown, both its economic and its political sides are in crisis, and one cannot reform one without reforming the other. For Gorbachev, the "crisis of effectiveness" that Western scholars speak of is indeed a "crisis of survival."[4]

But is the political system any more reformable than the economic system is, short of wholesale systemic change? Just as there has been a treadmill of economic half-reforms since Stalin's death, has there not been a treadmill of political half-reforms as well? What, if anything, stands to make Gorbachev different from previous "reforming" General Secretaries?

Part I of this chapter describes the causes and consequences of the political crisis. Part II describes how Gorbachev's political strategy appears designed to respond to it. Part III evaluates the consistency of the strategy and its appropriateness as it has evolved so far.

The Crisis of the Soviet System
of Power and Authority

On the surface, the Soviet system of power appears remarkably unchanged from what it was thirty years ago, after Khrushchev had gathered the reins back into the hands of the Party leadership. The power of the General Secretary and the collective power of the Politburo over the classic instruments of rule remain formally unopposed, unchallenged, and undivided. This small group of men still holds nominally total control over personnel, political agenda and economic priorities, organizational structures, official means of communication and sources of information, and instruments of coercion.

This point may have seemed in doubt under Brezhnev, especially in the first half of his reign. There was speculation in the West that patronage and clientelism were declining, that various interest groups were gaining power, that decision-making in Soviet politics was becoming incremental and consensual, and above all, that the powers of the General Secretary were in decline. But Brezhnev could move the traditional levers firmly enough when he chose to, as he showed by making sharp changes from time to time in investment shares (in agriculture, energy, and defense) or in personnel (as in Georgia and Azerbaijan). Indeed, under Brezhnev the office of the General Secretary became more of a formal institution than ever before. Since his death, the whirlwind of changes in personnel, institutions, and resource flows— all unleashed from the General Secretary's office—shows clearly that there is power in the old levers yet.

Neither has there been any deterioration in the Politburo's capacity to manage the politics of succession and power entirely within its own ranks, or to defend its prerogatives from potential encroachers. All three post-Brezhnev successions were handled within the closed club of the Politburo, and there is no sign that the Central Committee played any role other than the purely formal one of endorsing the choices of the Politburo. Even Iurii Andropov's care to have himself re-appointed a Party secretary in the spring of 1982 was a tacit acknowledgment on his part that the succession, as always, would be a matter of Party insiders choosing one of their own. The meager evidence available suggests that Gorbachev's election as General Secretary was no different.[5]

As for encroachment by other elite groups, Marshal Ogarkov's summary dismissal in the fall of 1984 showed that the Politburo, even under a feeble General Secretary, remained as able and determined as in the past to deal with high-ranking irritants. Despite talk in the Western media of the military as "king-makers" in the Andropov succession, the subsequent systematic humbling of the uniformed military under Gorbachev brings their apparent influence lower than it has been in decades.[6]

Thus the powers of the General Secretary and the Politburo remain awesome; yet, paradoxically, over the last generation they have also grown subtly weaker. Within the elite (which one might define very roughly as the top thousand positions in the system) political resources have broadened and the players—including the leaders themselves— have apparently accepted certain tacit rules. Among the former is an expansion of multilateral communication and information within the top elite, the emergence of "opinion" not controlled by the General Secretary, and the development of individual prestige attached to leading figures.[7] Among the latter is a greater freedom to discuss policy issues in public and to take dissenting positions without being accused of political disloyalty. These new features have not disappeared under Gorbachev; indeed, *glasnost'* favors them; and they undoubtedly help to explain Gorbachev's difficulties in dealing with resistance in the Central Committee, his deliberateness in personnel changes, or his care in dealing with the leadership of the KGB or the military-industrial ministries (and with the military hierarchy, for that matter, until the Rust affair), or with senior Brezhnev veterans such as Gromyko, Kapitonov, Ponomarev, and Baibakov, all of whom have been given prominent positions upstairs.

Such a subtle erosion of absolute power in elite politics one might call *le petit mal.* But alongside it there is a *grand mal,* which affects the leaders' control of the mass of officialdom and of the population at large. The leadership increasingly finds that its awesome power will not serve its goals; it is less and less able to carry out its political agenda; and the more it attempts to control events the more real control eludes it. As a result, the leaders' power fails to build authority, in the sense of enhancing their standing as problem-solvers or their credibility as spokesmen for society's values. The fundamental reason is not the character of General Secretaries or the dynamics of power at the top, but rather the evolution of Soviet society as a whole and the consequent changes in people's minds. These make the traditional levers less effective and their objects less responsive. This is the real source of political crisis; it is a crisis of power and authority.

Two Sources of the Decline in the Leaders' Power and Authority

Before going on, let us pause briefly to look at what we mean by power. Power is not a physical force, although we often talk as though it were; it is a relationship between a subject and an object, and it always involves two aspects. If A wishes to move B, he must first transmit his will to B. The classic levers of transmission in Soviet politics are familiar: control of political organization, personnel, and agenda; education, indoctrination, and control of information; rewards, punishments, and threats, etc. But these are not the things that will actually move B; what actually moves B is what we call (aptly enough) B's "motives": fear, faith, norms, beliefs, habits, hope, greed, etc. These are inside B, which means that B must ultimately move himself for A to have power over him. Power, in all its varieties (coercion, influence, authority) thus always involves a lever acting at a distance on some resource in people's minds.

The reason for stressing this distinction is that the traditional Soviet system of power faces problems with both the levers and the motives: its traditional levers are too crude for the more delicate tasks they must now perform; they have increasingly harmful side-effects that act against the leaders' own goals,[8] and they are less and less able to manipulate the resources in people's minds—their motives, beliefs, habits, and perceptions—in the ways the leaders require. It is as though the leaders were trying to drive a tractor with reins and a whip.

The Leaders' Weakening Command of the Resources in People's Minds: Motives, Beliefs, and Habits

In the Soviet state in its third generation, mass terror has receded, social mobility has declined, and ideological elan has faded. Job security is taken for granted, and for a growing fraction of the population, privileges and amenities are as well. Therefore, what resources remain that will move either elite or population? Stalin's successors have gradually found themselves limited to a choice between faith and greed, and both pose growing problems.

The decline of ideological faith among the Soviet people is an old theme in Western sovietology. One may question how deep that faith was to begin with, but the long sclerosis of official thought has made ideology ineffective as a means of moving people. It would be hard to express the reasons for present-day apathy and cynicism more strikingly than Gorbachev himself did in his plenum speech in January 1987:

> The theoretical concepts of socialism remained to a large extent at the level of the 1930s–40s, when society was tackling entirely different tasks.

> The causes of the situation go far back into the past and are rooted in that specific historical situation in which, by virtue of well-known circumstances, vigorous debates and creative ideas disappeared from theory and social science, while authoritarian evaluations and opinions became unquestionable truths.

> There occurred a sort of absolutization of the forms of organization of society that had emerged in practice. Moreover, such ideas were essentially equated with the core characteristics of socialism, viewed as unchangeable and elevated as dogmas.

Gorbachev himself is manifestly a true believer in Marxism-Leninism, determined to revive faith and pride in a just, cleansed, and modernized socialism. But how many are there like him? Many Soviet citizens undoubtedly share his sense of shame over the country's stagnation and his disgust over the corruption and anomie of the 1970s, but those are emotions born of injured national pride and offended puritanism, not necessarily of faith in socialism. Gorbachev may be too late.

Indeed, one of the most remarkable recent developments in Soviet society is the rise of competing values that, potentially, pose strong obstacles to the leaders' efforts to appeal to ideology. Gail Lapidus sums them up in a recent essay:[9] (1) a growing preoccupation with universal moral concerns, which provide a broader basis for values than *partiinost'* and the moral categories of Marxism-Leninism; (2) a shift away from exclusive emphasis on collectivism toward increasing acceptance of diversity and individualism (including private and cooperative forms of property), as well as recognition of the legitimacy (and inevitability) of contending interests in society;[10] (3) an evolution away from insistence on single truths toward growing acceptance of the legitimacy of diverse opinions and of debate; (4) a weakening of the idea of human perfectibility and of the conviction that one can create a perfect society, free of human vice or failing. These changes appear to have two broad sources: first, the re-emergence of alternative values from private life into public view (and simultaneously, many people's increasingly open withdrawal from public life into private values);[11] and second, the alteration of people's beliefs and expectations as a result of their experiences over the last generation.

This evolution in public values and beliefs complicates immensely the task of the Soviet leaders, because it amounts to nothing less than a spontaneous reassertion of the norms of civil society, after two generations of absolute dominance by the state. By and large, the response of the state under Brezhnev was to accommodate itself, grudgingly and piece-meal, to society's evolving values, so long as they remained private, lashing out against them only when they became too public. The result was a tacit deal, which made it increasingly difficult for the leaders to mobilize people's energies by invoking official values. Gorbachev may find the intelligentsia of little help to him here, since it is precisely among them that the evolution of values has gone furthest.[12]

As a result, General Secretaries have gradually been thrown back on economic self-interest as the one popular resource on which they could really act, but that resource too has become more difficult to mobilize than in the past. As the sociologist Tat'iana Zaslavskaia argues, citizens' living standards have now risen so high that minor economic incentives will no longer force them to work hard at their jobs.[13] To get a bigger response, the leaders would have to increase both rewards and penalties, allowing some to get rich and others to lose their jobs. Both Khrushchev and Brezhnev shrank from the implications.

What about a return to mass coercion? The passing of mass terror has been more than simply a change in the style of coercion; a generation after Stalin's death, people's perceptions and expectations have gradually adjusted to a saner life. The results of surveys of recent Soviet emigrants are especially striking: they suggest that the habit of fear and the mistrust of others that still reach deep inside older people have largely faded among younger Soviet citizens.[14] The young see the pattern of KGB political repression as graduated and predictable rather than random; and provided one conforms outwardly the probability of trouble is perceived as low. More important, younger people do not fear to speak their minds to a wider circle of people than their immediate families. Along with mass terror, intimidation and atomization are fading as well.

As a result, while the state is still able to deter overt political nonconformity, it has lost the more general power over the population that mass insecurity once provided, and it is doubtful that that power could be recovered under any circumstances. People are losing the habit of doing the regime's bidding simply because they fear the consequences of not doing so, and as they lose their fear, they share their perceptions with one another, and the effect is multiplied. In short, while the regime's negative power to intimidate individuals or specific groups still remains, the threat of terror as a mobilizing force is gone.

In sum, the range of motives, habits, and beliefs on which the Soviet leadership can act has narrowed, while a number of competing ones, which they do not control, have reappeared. Bolshevik fervor has almost entirely disappeared as a motive force; acquiescence in the official values of the state is still widespread but largely passive. Fear can deter, but it can no longer mobilize. The leadership is driven to rely on economic self-interest, but they are deterred by their own ambivalence from making effective use of it. The result, at least under Brezhnev, was the slow emergence of a sort of tacit social contract that required the leaders to accept, without admitting it even to themselves, a decline in their active power over society.

It is possible to argue—and, as we shall see, Gorbachev does indeed argue—that what has changed is not people's motives but their circumstances, and therefore what is needed to move them is more vigorous and intelligent use of the levers. But here we come to the second cause of the deterioration of the leaders' traditional powers— the increasingly awkward side-effects of the traditional instruments of rule.

Declining Effectiveness of Traditional Levers

The traditional Soviet system operated with a surprisingly narrow array of political instruments,[15] of which the most important was the control of personnel, particularly within the Party organization. This was possible because the leadership confined itself to a narrow range of goals—essentially internal security, industrial growth, and military power—and concentrated its power on those.[16]

But since Stalin's death the list of objectives pursued by the leaders has broadened to include consumer welfare, agricultural modernization, and broad technological innovation, and simultaneously each of the main objectives has grown more complex than before. Consequently, side-effects that were once acceptable as the leaders sought to maximize a handful of objectives regardless of cost, have now become less tolerable to them.

1. The Personnel Weapon. Control of cadres remains the key to power in the Soviet system, but the weaknesses and drawbacks of the weapon of personnel have become more apparent in recent years. First, from the standpoint of the formation of power, General Secretaries since Stalin have learned that mere hiring and firing does not guarantee the loyalty or responsiveness of subordinates. Previous work associations produce the strongest bonds,[17] but simply appointing one's long-time proteges (assuming one has them) has disadvantages of its own, especially if one's cronies do not happen to be particularly competent. Second, the personnel weapon is a poor instrument for stimulating effective performance, because the wielder, particularly if located far away, is tempted simply to fire scapegoats instead of finding out the facts or looking for more precise remedies.

Third and most serious, the use of the personnel weapon leads to backlash. Since rank is the key to a whole system of graduated state perquisites that are taken for granted by the holders (such as deficit goods, travel, and access to information or "in" entertainment) efforts by all levels of leaders to use the broom as a routine instrument provoke bitter resentment and demoralization, lessen the cadres's experience and effectiveness, and make them less willing to speak out or keep their superiors accurately informed. This leads in turn to resistance from below; fired officials resurface in other high offices; ministry and party officials resist removal or transfer; pointed articles appear in the local press on the need for trust in cadres and the harm done by excessive turnover. Such resistance is nothing new; the phenomenon of the "family circle" (*"krugovaia poruka"*) of local officials conspiring to support one another against the center is more ancient than the Soviet regime. But as the decades go by the bureaucracy increasingly regards job security and orderly promotion as its prerogative.

As a result, those with political resources to trade use them to resist the personnel weapon. The most valuable and professional elements of the elite—the military, the scientists, the secret police—have sought and gained a measure of control over their own promotion systems. Under Brezhnev regional party leaders successfully bargained for job security for themselves—while retaining the personnel weapon for their own vigorous use. Far from declining in importance (as some Western observers thought at the time), patronage sank to the regional level, producing local satrapies, "zones beyond criticism," and family circles.

These the Gorbachev leadership is now struggling to undo; but having purged most of the Brezhnev-era appointees from the government and party apparatus, Gorbachev's men in the Secretariat are discovering that local patronage networks are re-forming around the new appointees. In the Party apparatus, in particular, few local officials are named from outside their own districts.[18] Thus the personnel weapon increasingly confronts the leaders with delicate problems of dosage: if you overuse it, it has toxic effects; but if you underuse it, others at middle levels will do so in your place. Appointing outsiders helps to produce loyal officials, but increases local resentment and resistance, and the outsiders' lack of familiarity with local conditions can make them less effective. There is no satisfactory balance, yet so long as cadres policy remains one of the principal powers of the party apparatus at all levels, the dilemma will remain.

2. Checkers and Watch-dogs. Another important traditional instrument is the use of multiple checkers and watchers and the practice of denunciation raised to a national art, the system that Merle Fainsod called the "institutionalization of mutual suspicion." This system engenders much the same toxic side-effects as the overuse of the personnel weapon, but in addition it is very labor-intensive. In a typical province there are thousands of paid local *revizory* and hundreds more who descend from Moscow, not to mention tens of thousands of volunteers nominally enrolled as People's Controllers.[19] It is not uncommon for half the personnel of a Soviet enterprise to belong to one or more of the innumerable bodies that exist to check up on one another.[20] Indeed, nearly every Soviet citizen ends up being involved in one way or another, since entire bureaucracies are deliberately set to check up on each other, not to mention the ubiquitous army of secret-police informers. As tasks throughout society grow more complex, the cost of the watch-dog system grows, because it absorbs vast numbers of people with scarce skills who are thus lost to production.[21]

From the beginning, the response of the watched has been to subvert the system, whether by co-opting the watchers on a grand scale,[22] or forming local "family circles" of mutual protection at the local level,[23] or watering down the control system by turning it over to the least qualified and poorest equipped, as with quality control in most civilian industry or enforcement of environmental-quality laws. Only the tasks of the highest priority—such as military production and political security—warrant elite snoopers;[24] the rest are distinctly lackadaisical.

The result is that the leadership gets the worst of both: the waste of time and energy produced by multiple meetings, reports, inspections, etc., and the corruption, misreporting, concealment, and resulting loss of control engendered by the family-circle response. The system produces negative criticism more than helpful advice, and it typically works best after it is too late, when all that remains is for the checkers to inform their superiors.[25]

Indeed, keeping higher-ups informed is the central purpose of the system in the first place. Unlike a conventional regulatory system, which is intended to encourage law-abiding behavior by providing clear rules, orderly adjudication, and fair punishment, the Soviet multiple-watchdog arrangement is part of a system in which the rules themselves are deliberately allowed to remain inconsistent and illegal behavior is tacitly recognized as necessary for the economic and administrative systems to function. The purpose of the checkers is to contain and inform more than to regulate, except during the relatively exceptional periods when the leaders mount a campaign or make examples. But as policy grows more complex and technical, an outside watchdog (particularly one such as the People's Control Commission), operating through periodic raids, is usually unable to report intelligently on what it has discovered or to recommend positive action. As an instrument of rule and a source of information, therefore, the traditional system is increasingly ineffective.

3. Controls Over Information. A third example of weakening levers with growing side-effects is the leadership's use of controls over the flow of information and discussion. By tightly limiting information from outside the country and managing it inside, the regime has tried to shape the population's perceptions and to ward off competing ideas. But information about the outside world is reaching the Soviet population in greater abundance, and above all in more convincing packaging, than ever before. Through videocassettes, attractive consumer goods, increased foreign travel, and even models passed on by the Soviet media themselves, Soviet citizens are now in daily contact with different ways of thinking and with standards of living far higher than their own. The models may not always be lofty ones (one sometimes sympathizes with Gorbachev's grumpings about "bourgeois mass culture"), but they are undeniably influential, and the old system is less able to control what the people see and think.

Yet graduated control over information is a central part of the regime's system of rationed privileges. "High-coercion systems are low-information systems," the political scientist David Apter once wrote, but he may not have foreseen that information itself would become a tool and a perquisite in the leaders' hands, so that once coercion declined the flow of information would not necessarily rise again in proportion. The consequences are increasingly apparent. By treating access to information and the freedom to discuss policy as political and institutional perquisites to be allocated according to individual rank or institutional prestige, the rulers have created a system of compartmentalized information which gives them poor protection against false data, little avail against professional monopolies of advice, and small opportunity, short of the very top, to debate the "big picture." Colleagues in neighboring ministries cannot get the information they need for policy, while hierarchical superiors are overloaded.

One result is policy mistakes. Official review commissions lack the detailed data necessary to resist bureaucratic pressures in favor of unsound projects, while whistle-blowers are prosecuted for exposing inside information.[26] Many laws and most of the innumerable agency regulations are unpublished and inaccessible, although many of them are obsolete or contain mistakes.[27] The lack of pertinent information as well as the lack of practice in using it to think about policy hinders learning and the formation of new consensus when old policies fail, and surely helps to account for the negative-mindedness, naivete, and impracticality of much of the Soviet literature of reform until recently.

As a result, the leaders end up once again with the worst of both worlds—the side-effects of an overdeveloped control system, combined with a gradual loss of real control. Gorbachev has frequently noted that one result is a great deal of strain for the top leadership, and any reader of the weekly summaries of Politburo meetings will agree. But report after report, decision after decision, still fail to produce action. Not surprisingly, the Brezhnev leadership responded to this by calling for fewer and fewer reports, and the pattern spread to lower levels, contributing to the famous "zones beyond criticism."[28]

4. Economic Incentives. We noted earlier that because of the declining effectiveness of other motives, Stalin's successors have been forced to rely more heavily on economic incentives. Ironically, though, Stalin made more effective use of economic levers than they. Scorning egalitarianism with such withering phrases as "petty-bourgeois levelling," he created a steep scale of glittering rewards and chilling penalties, both tightly tied to performance. So extreme were the resulting inequalities that after his death his successors moved quickly to temper them.

But in the process they blunted their instrument. Under Brezhnev especially, the connection between performance and reward weakened and then virtually disappeared, as salary scales narrowed and the rules governing bonuses grew so cumbersome that in practice the same amounts ended up being given to all. Wages outstripped productivity, with the result that money in circulation grew faster than the goods to spend it on. Massive subsidies kept the prices of housing, basic services, and staple foods far below cost, further eroding the workers' sense that their supply was tied to their work; while subsidies to state enterprises (not only direct but indirect, as in the form of credits that were never repaid) had the same effect on managers.

Vast quantities of cash built up in bank accounts,[29] creating buying power that inevitably found an outlet "on the left," as the Russians say, while the authorities looked through their fingers (to use another Russian expression) at the moonlighting, mass theft, and bribery that grew up all around them. In addition to weakening the moral fabric of the system, the growth of the second economy undercut the state's own economic levers by creating powerful competitors to them.

In sum, all of the principal levers of the system—the personnel weapons, the checkers and watchers, the control of information, and economic incentives—have all weakened. Incidentally, it is not for lack of sophistication on the part of the wielders. The KGB's coercion of dissidents under Andropov, for example, was a sophisticated exercise in selective dosage. The careful rationing of official rewards (access to information and travel, allocation of professional status and participation in policy advice, and even the allocation of what one might call standing to official dissent) has become exceedingly refined. Even the Soviets' response to the information revolution shows creative thinking to fit the new opportunities with the old mechanisms.[30]

But the results remind one of Joseph Berliner's observation about Soviet economic reform: one eventually gets diminishing returns from tinkering with obsolete technologies. And like the command economy, the traditional system of levers is increasingly obsolete, because it gives the leaders forms of political power that are negative, blunt, or counterproductive, consisting mainly of the ability to prevent things from happening (if the leaders lean hard enough), or to secure the appearance of compliance and the absence of organized opposition. In political as in economic matters, the leaders are frequently deprived of timely, accurate information; they find themselves forced to resort to campaigns to overcome inertia; and they must reckon with the side-effects of their own actions. Despite their seemingly unlimited ability to hire and fire, to reward and to punish, to allocate, initiate, and block, Soviet leaders must increasingly be content with a limited degree of control over the everyday behavior of the mass of their citizens.

For Gorbachev, this paradox threatens crisis, because with such resources for power a General Secretary is virtually limited to caretaker government or possibly to some return to crude repression. Since Gorbachev intends neither, he cannot simply rely on firing people or spying on them; he must give them a stake in change. He cannot simply orate to passive crowds; he needs an active constituency. Therefore he has been attempting to draw on new resources in people's minds, to revive old levers and create new ones.

I. GORBACHEV'S APPARENT POLITICAL STRATEGY

Gorbachev's political strategy, as it has developed to date, combines old and new. On the one hand, as he must, he has vigorously grasped the classic levers: control of personnel, organizational structure, media, policy agenda, and allocation of resources. Turnover of personnel has been unprecedentedly high, and like his predecessors, Gorbachev uses mass public campaigns and political pressure applied through the party. Large parts of Gorbachev's economic and social program rely heavily on these traditional devices. The new quality-control program, *gospriemka,* for example, is operated by a new layer of checkers.[31] The law on individual economic activity, though it frees private enterprise with one hand, binds it with the other by promising two more bureaucracies, one to check individual incomes, the other to tax them. The reformed planning system adds a new horizontal layer, the regional "production-economic administrations," to the maze of vertical authorities that local managers must reckon with.[32] The anti-alcohol campaign, the war on corruption, the law on illegal incomes, and the drive to restore labor discipline, are all based on familiar coercive techniques. Gorbachev has redrawn organization charts and rejuggled performance indicators as enthusiastically as Khrushchev ever did; his speeches define the boundaries of official orthodoxy on history, culture, and dissent; and he is the vigilant guardian of party discipline. His rhetoric is filled with Bolshevik exhortation and familiar military metaphors. In short, in many ways Gorbachev is a very traditional Soviet politician.

But since his first days as General Secretary Gorbachev's political strategy has also contained strong elements of innovation, and these have become more prominent over time, especially after mid-1986. They fall into six general categories: (1) new ways of reaching the Soviet public; (2) measures to improve the availability and quality of information; (3) experimentation with various forms of voter power; (4) more systematic legislation and expanded legal guarantees; (5) a revival of economic levers; and (6) ideological innovation and the cautious beginnings of reflection on the roles of the party apparatus.

Taken together, the innovative elements in Gorbachev's strategy appear designed to provide him with new ways of appealing to people's motives and influencing their perceptions. They also appear—and this is potentially far more daring—to be aimed at providing lower levels of the system with what one might call "delegated levers" of their own, to be used to bring pressure to bear on resistant middle-level officials and to provide protection to those who take risks on his behalf. Gorbachev's aim thus appears to be to build a mass constituency for his program, giving citizens not only economic but also political incentives to support his program, as well as providing them with information, protection, and even a measure of local power. In the process he is attempting to revitalize some classic levers, develop new ones, and use them to move people more powerfully than any Soviet politician has managed to do in a generation.

After discussing these six directions of change, we shall attempt in a later section to evaluate the Gorbachev strategy as a whole. As we shall see, it is still tentative, ambiguous, contradictory, and changeable. The biggest question is how the new is supposed to coexist with the old. Nevertheless, Gorbachev has already gone beyond previous General Secretaries in his ambitions as a political reformer, opening up issues, ideas, and options that have been closed since the 1920s.

Revitalizing Political Resources and Renewing Political Levers: Six Directions of Change

Improving Communication with the Public

Traditional Western thinking about Soviet politics has long emphasized the importance of "transmission belts" (although the phrase is actually Lenin's) as conveyors of the leaders' will to the people, but in the last couple of decades the transmission belts have become badly frayed. Soviet people discount the media as sources of information; they attend official meetings as a tiresome obligation; and the politicians find it difficult to reach them. It is here that the phenomenon of "exit," described in the chapter by Timothy Colton, has become most striking, and nowhere more so than among young people. As Gorbachev observed to a group of editors and writers in mid-1987:[33]

> When you and we painted life in pink colors, the people saw it all and lost interest in the press and in public activity. They felt humiliated and insulted when such phoney stuff was palmed off on them.

Therefore, Gorbachev has been trying to revitalize communications with the population. He has been tireless in making appearances throughout the country, bringing his message to every major city and

TABLE 1
The Spread of Television Since Khrushchev's Day

	1965	1985
TV sets per 100 families	24	97
urban	32	101
rural	15	90
TV sets per 1,000 population	68	293
urban	94	314
rural	37	255
Annual output of TV sets	3,655	9,371
of which color	0	4,024

Source: *Narodnoe khoziaistvo SSSR v 1985g*, pp. 169 and 446; *Narodnoe khoziaistvo SSSR 1922–82*, p. 448.

region. He is an outstanding orator, if not as earthy as Khrushchev (so far he has refrained from homilies about milkmaids or whistling shrimps), but clearly he is his own best ambassador.

The most striking aspect of Gorbachev's efforts to improve communications has been his aggressive, inventive, and abundant use of television. This reflects a basic change in Soviet life in the last generation: compared to Khrushchev's day, television has become a true mass medium which now reaches into nearly every Soviet home, reaching 97 percent of all families in 1985, compared to 24 percent in 1965. Annual output of television sets has nearly tripled since 1965, and nearly half of all TV's now produced in the Soviet Union are color sets. But what is most remarkable is their distribution: while in 1965 it was primarily the city-dwellers who owned TV sets, by 1985 rural families were rapidly drawing even (see Table 1). (In this respect as in others, the Brezhnev era prepared the way for Gorbachev.)

As a result, Gorbachev is the first Soviet TV politician and TV is one of the major tools of *perestroika*. Mass television opens the possibility of making a populist approach to authority-building work as it could not in Khrushchev's day.

But a populist politician is helpless if he cannot tell how his message is being received, and a necessary corollary of better communications downward is better communications upward. Khrushchev in his day had encouraged cautious experimentation with opinion research, but systematic surveys of public opinion are developing rapidly under Gorbachev. A new Center for the Study of Public Opinion is about to open and an Institute of Socio-Economic Problems is being formed. Soviet sociologists are being asked to supply the leadership with more abundant information about popular wages, incomes, health, consumption patterns, etc., as a basis for policy.[34]

To some extent, such information was being gathered before, by a variety of groups that had sprung up in the 1960s, including sociological teams inside the KGB, but the more significant findings were either classified or censored. The difference this time is that much more of what is being gathered now will be made public, giving the leadership an additional political lever. This brings us to the political significance of *glasnost'*.

Making Communication More Attractive and Credible: The Progress of Glasnost'

The most startling development of the last two years has been the extraordinary flowering of *glasnost'* in all the Soviet media. This is not a new device for Soviet leaders, of course; nothing could be more traditional in Soviet politics than the use of the media, the arts, and the social sciences to further the leaders' policies. *Glasnost'*, on one level, is no more than a selective relaxation of controls on public expression and information. But its real importance is that it marks a growing understanding of the roles of information in a modern society. Gorbachev has been trying to do three new things: first, to broaden access to existing information; second, to improve the quality and quantity of information; and third, to make better use of it to inform policy at all levels.

For the last two years journalists, artists, and scholars have been pushing back long-established barriers and asserting their right to explore previously forbidden zones. Few social issues are taboo any longer, and previously untouchable historical and ideological subjects are being opened up, often with a daring and frankness that would have sent their authors to prison only a few years ago. The next frontier is coverage of the military, space, foreign affairs, justice, and the environment, which have long been protected from criticism by special ministry-based systems of censorship.[35] The statistical system is being criticized as never before, and the range (if not always the reliability) of publicly available statistics is broadening.[36] The Party apparatus, up to the level of province committee or non-Russian Central Committee, is fair game for criticism,[37] and even the local offices of the KGB are no longer entirely immune.[38]

Natural and man-made disasters are now being reported promptly in the Soviet press. The nuclear disaster at Chernobyl' in the spring of 1986 was an important test of the *glasnost'* policy, which the leadership passed impressively, though after stone-walling at first. The media have reported on political incidents as well, including riots in Alma-Ata in December 1986, nationalist demonstrations in the Baltic Republics, Armenia, Azerbaijan, and elsewhere since 1986, the demands of the Crimean Tatars in July 1987, and the marches of Pamiat' and other groups.

The coverage of Chernobyl' illustrated the political payoff to be had from *glasnost'*: through its unprecedentedly frank coverage[39] the leadership was able to turn a catastrophe to some political advantage, especially since for once the Soviets' own coverage was more accurate than that of foreign radio services. Gorbachev skillfully used the Chernobyl' episode to bolster his case for arms control, discipline in the work place, and, of course, for *glasnost'* itself. Later in the year, he made similar use of the riots in Alma-Ata, when he told the Central Committee that national tensions only worsened when allowed to fester out of sight.

But so far *glasnost'* has spread unevenly. While it would be an exaggeration to say that it is confined to the Moscow intelligentsia or to the foreign community, one serious problem from Gorbachev's standpoint is that some Moscow editors are racing ahead, testing the limits of official tolerance with each new issue, while in the provinces the local press hangs back, frequently under pressure from local politicians. This is a new twist on a familiar Soviet story: in the traditional Soviet system of information, the circulation of ideas and news worsens as one moves from higher levels to lower, and the most striking expression of that is the dismal state of the local press. One of the aims of the *glasnost'* policy is to improve local reporting to keep local officials on their toes, but there is little on which to build. Long neglected and despised, local reporters are underpaid, undertrained, and easily intimidated. Defense of the local media has been a prominent theme in the central press and in Gorbachev's own speeches over the last two years, but there is little progress to show for it yet. At this point, citizens who wish to sound off about local issues still have little choice but to write a letter to the editor of a central newspaper.

Still, the improvement in the central media, particularly in Soviet television and in major dailies such as *Izvestiia,* has been so remarkable that Soviet citizens have begun paying much more attention to them. The circulation of *Izvestiia,* which had dropped off by 3 million during the Brezhnev era, by 1986 had recovered to over 7 million.[40] If one of the achievements of *glasnost'* is to get the people to listen to and contribute to the official media, then Gorbachev will have taken a long and essential first step toward reviving a political lever that has been losing power for half a century. But there is still a long way to go, beginning with the extension of *glasnost'* to publicity about decision-making within the central government itself. In this respect, Gorbachev still falls short of Khrushchev; despite rumors that Gorbachev wanted the proceedings of the January and June 1987 Central Committee meetings published, that has not yet happened; and the proceedings of the tumultuous session of October 21, 1987, which led to Boris Yel'tsin's downfall, will not soon be released.

Tampering with the Powers of Officialdom:
Gorbachev's Electoral Experiments

Accountability is a favorite word in Soviet political vocabulary, but in practice, of course, it has always meant accountability to higher authority, even when it was applied to officials theoretically elected from below. That is why the most startling measures Gorbachev has proposed to date are changes in elections and voting, possibly supplemented by fixed terms of office and new rules on compulsory retirements. If implemented fairly, these measures could indeed introduce a measure of accountability to voters below, giving citizens at all levels of the system quite new sorts of incentives.

Thus, multiple candidacies were introduced on an experimental basis in elections to the local Soviets.[41] Leadership positions in major enterprises, including the post of director, will also become elective under the new law on the socialist enterprise. But the most controversial idea advanced by Gorbachev is that secret ballots and multiple candidacies should be extended to positions in the Party apparatus itself, to levels as high as the first secretaries of republic central committees.[42]

Secret balloting is not an entirely new practice in Party organs, nor is it new as a reform proposal. The secretary of a local Party organ or large primary party organization (PPO) is typically elected by open ballot, but the bureau (or committee) of which he is a member is elected by the whole organization in a secret ballot "that usually seems to be truly secret."[43] Yet clearly the election of the secretary is what really matters, and in 1961 Frol Kozlov, then second secretary and heir apparent to Khrushchev, advocated secret ballots at the 22nd Party Congress. The idea is clearly controversial within the present Politburo. Thus Ligachev, writing in *Kommunist* in 1985, called for voting by show of hands as a more "democratic" procedure.[44]

Right behind the issue of electoral changes comes that of fixed terms of office and compulsory retirements. Gorbachev is thought to have attempted on at least two previous occasions to re-introduce fixed terms of office into the Party rules. The USSR Academy of Sciences has already adopted a rule requiring its members to surrender their administrative positions at 70, possibly a deliberate model for other officials.[45] Khrushchev's previous efforts in the same direction were praised by a former Gorbachev aide in *Pravda,*[46] and Gorbachev may intend to try again at the Party Conference planned for June 1988.[47]

A related theme introduced by Gorbachev in June 1987 is that of strengthening "elective" bodies over "executive" ones:

> An excessive growth of the role of executive bodies to the detriment of elective ones has occurred. At first glance everything proceeds as it should. Plenary meetings, sessions, and meetings of other elective bodies are regularly held. But their work is often overformalized. Secondary questions or even those decided in advance are brought up for discussion. (. . .) Let's face it, some comrades started to view elective bodies as a burden which brings only difficulties and hindrances.

Typically, of course, executives lightened the burden by not reporting to the electoral body at all; thus the Moscow *gorispolkom,* we are told, prior to spring of 1987 had not reported to a full session of the Moscow City Soviet in over 30 years.[48] Nothing surprising here, except that Gorbachev then went on to draw startling implications for the Central Committee itself:

> Let us say honestly: there were many crucial questions of concern to the Party and the people that remained outside plenum agendas for several years. Comrades will remember that plenums of the CC were brief and formal. Many members had no opportunity throughout their membership term to participate in debates or even to put forward proposals.

Gorbachev was careful to cover himself, though, by adding that the decisions of higher party committees would continue to be binding on lower ones.

At the January 1987 plenum Gorbachev justified the idea of multiple candidacies as a means of enabling the Soviets and the Party organs "better to know the mood and will of the population." The recent experience of East European countries suggests that such measures can be implemented without threatening the essence of the traditional distribution of power or the *nomenklatura* system.[49] Higher authorities will focus their efforts on controlling nominations instead of elections, assuming they do not rig the ballot box outright. But East European experience also suggests that secret ballots and multiple candidacies give the voters a weapon against the least-qualified candidates and introduce an element of uncertainty with which local officials must reckon, making them more responsive to the voters' wishes. This is democracy on the shortest of leashes, but from the leaders' point of view, it could rouse the citizens' interest in political participation and provide an added lever over middle-level officials, all at an acceptably small political risk.

More Systematic Legislation and Legal Guarantees:
Encouraging Countervailing Forces
and "Kontrol'" from Below

In the summer of 1986, the Supreme Soviet created a stir by announcing a five-year plan for new legislation.[50] Since then, a stream of new laws has appeared, more or less on schedule, providing an elaborate legal foundation for *perestroika*. Two aspects of this policy are of special interest. First, one of its apparent aims is to bring legislation into conformity with the 1977 Constitution, consistent with Gorbachev's avowed goal of closing the gap between public words and deeds. Thus a new law announced in July 1987, giving citizens the right to sue officials for illegal acts, was originally promised in Article 58. Another law published on the same date, which extends and codifies the practice of conducting national debates on proposed legislation, implements Article 114. It is noteworthy, however, that a law providing for national referenda, which was announced in the 1986 five-year program to implement the Constitution's Article 108, has not yet appeared, although it would not seem to pose a threat to the leadership.[51]

Second, the new legislation reflects a concern to give individual citizens and individual enterprises means of defense against arbitrary and illegal acts by middle-level bureaucracies. Thus the law permitting suits against officials, though it does not provide for recovery of damages, would if implemented bring the Soviet Union up to the level of most other countries except the United States. Similarly, the new law on the socialist enterprise, also enacted in July 1987, enables enterprises to go to court to appeal unjustified plan targets. Needless to say, for such laws to have any practical meaning, they must be applied by the courts, and in the past the courts have had no way of withstanding outside pressure brought against them, usually by local Party authorities.

The prominent role of legislation in *perestroika* presumably reflects the legal background of the new General Secretary and the progress of the law and the legal profession in Soviet life in recent decades. But it also appears to represent part of a larger strategy to strengthen countervailing forces at the local level and to bring them to bear against unresponsive or abusive officials. This strategy includes the courts, but other bodies as well, such as the local Soviets, the Komsomol, and the labor unions. Thus in February 1987, speaking to a congress of trade-union leaders, Gorbachev proposed legislation to give labor unions the power to stand up to management.[52] His suggestions come close to granting the unions veto power over managers' plans, over prices of major consumer goods and services—a startling change indeed for an institution that has spent most of the last sixty years "dancing the krakowiak" (as Gorbachev put it) with management.

One of Gorbachev's purposes here is clear enough. By giving local citizens and institutions protection and authority, he hopes to unburden the party apparatus and leadership from the load of *kontrol'* (i.e., checking and oversight) from above. Gorbachev frequently cites the endless meetings at the top, the burden of returning again and again to the same questions, the "literal avalanche of check-ups and inspections that descends on institutions, enterprises, and organizations." "For all the importance of *kontrol'* from above," he told the Central Committee in January 1987, "we must raise the level and effectiveness of *kontrol'* from below."

> If we achieve such *kontrol'* [from below], there can be no doubt that many causes for complaints and messages to higher authorities will disappear, and the majority of the questions raised in them will be decided at the local level.

But Gorbachev's thinking evidently goes beyond raising the efficiency of *kontrol'* and unburdening higher authority. A legislative framework, legal guarantees, and countervailing powers are logically an essential part of any coherent strategy to revive the political system, both to protect citizens against pressures and reprisals from local officials, and to introduce a measure of consistency and predictability, strengthening popular faith in the legitimacy of the system. That will require, of course, not only new and more public legislation, but a systematic effort to improve the administration of justice, particularly to strengthen independence of the judiciary against intervention by local authorities.[53]

'Raising the Authority of the Ruble': Strengthening Economic Levers

In one of the best-read classics of the Soviet period, *The Golden Calf* by Il'f and Petrov, the con-man hero, Astap Bender, has made a fortune through blackmail but is unable to find anything to spend it on. Under the classic command system, the market shrivelled up and money lost much of its importance; economic signals were displaced by administrative ones.

Gorbachev is now attempting to "raise the authority of the ruble," by increasing the role of economic signals and instruments throughout the system. Gorbachev's economic reforms are discussed elsewhere in this book, but what is important here is to point out the political implications: the new emphasis given to economic levers promises to add considerably to the regime's ability to move people. This has a positive side: citizens are being encouraged to form cooperatives and private businesses, farmers to sell up to one-third of their produce as they see fit, and managers to earn hard-currency abroad. But the "economization" policy also has a negative side: by raising the prospect that workers can be laid off or enterprises go bankrupt, the new leaders are reviving the potential for mass coercion, substituting the "icy water of economic calculation" for physical threats.

It isn't simply incompetent or undisciplined workers who stand to lose their jobs; once managers have to meet their own payrolls out of their own profits, they will have an incentive to move quickly—if allowed by the local party authorities—to cut back their overgrown workforces. So far, they have the blessing of the leadership. In one widely publicized experiment, begun under Andropov, the Belorussian railroads have released 13,000 railroad workers, with over 14,000 more to follow from the republic's metro, auto pools, and civil aviation.[54] Similar reports are becoming common throughout the country.

But there is more: if the center successfully unburdens itself by switching from administrative to economic methods, a large fraction of the 18 million people who work in bureaucratic and clerical jobs nationwide will become redundant,[55] particularly the 1.5 million who work in the supply system.[56] A vast slimming campaign is already under way: policemen, agricultural administrators, ministry officials, even the apparatus of the USSR Council of Ministers—all are in danger of losing their jobs. This has aroused understandable anxiety, and the leaders and their publicists have been at pains to reassure the citizenry that there will be no unemployment,[57] but the reports of mass layoffs continue.

Reinterpreting Basic Ideological Tenets

One definition of reform is that it is a reassertion of a political community's fundamental values and an attempt to bring political life back into conformity with them. The result is inevitably more like a reinterpretation, but it requires, to succeed, a common core of values on which most of the community's members and leaders can ultimately agree. In the case of the Soviet Union, if the political culture of the people has drifted so far from the state ideology that no such common core exists, then reform is impossible.

Therefore, at the base of Gorbachev's political strategy is, first, his belief that whatever the ossification of the system, whatever the decline in the Soviet people's faith in the leaders and their words, the people continue to embrace the fundamental values of socialism. Gorbachev professes that faith in every speech. Second, *perestroika,* while advertised as a restatement of those fundamentals, is necessarily a reinterpretation of them, an attempt to reconcile official values with the emerging culture (or more exactly, cultures) of Soviet society. Thus, one of the essential aspects of Gorbachev's reform strategy has been the beginnings of a review of basic ideological tenets.

Such a review necessarily begins with Lenin himself, since any reinterpretation must receive his posthumous blessing. The Lenin that has been emerging from the leaders' speeches and the literature of *perestroika* in the last two years is the Lenin of his last years,[58] the Lenin of the New Economic Policy,[59] the author of "On Cooperation," a Bukharinist Lenin of economic gradualism and political moderation. He is also the Lenin of the "Last Testament,"[60] a defender of legal rights, democracy, and national cultures to whom the crudeness and Great Russian chauvinism of a Stalin are foreign. The New Lenin is also a man of the market, a believer in money-commodity relations over administrative methods. Such a Lenin would have opposed forced collectivization, while supporting the use of various intermediate forms of cooperative economic activity for generations to come.[61] In short, Lenin is indeed *zhivee vsekh zhivykh* ("more alive than all the living"— a standard slogan over the decades) and as politically useful as ever.

Behind the official and semi-official re-imaging of Lenin is an attempt to rethink socialist property, the acceptable limits of social conflict and expressions of interest, the place of money and economic levers, the meaning of equality, and even, very cautiously, the roles of the Party itself. The first obstacle along this road, of course, is the utter novelty of it to most Soviet citizens, and especially to the keepers of ideology themselves. Addressing a meeting of social-science faculty department heads in the fall of 1986, Gorbachev criticized the dogmatism and scholasticism of most Soviet social science and called for an "activation of the theoretical front," buttressing his appeal, inevitably, with a quote from Lenin:[62]

> The first obligation of those who wish to seek "the paths to human happiness" is not to pull the wool over their own eyes, but to have the daring to acknowledge openly what is.

Accompanying Gorbachev's calls for doctrinal *aggiornamento* is the increasingly prominent theme that it is the people and their society who define "what is," which implies that the party and its theoreticians, if they are to justify their continued role as the leading elements of the system, must learn how to enlist the people's cooperation and support.

Yet at the same time Gorbachev is attempting to impose a personal vision of "what is," a vision that over time has grown more and more radical. In the fall of 1986 he began using the word, "revolutionary," to describe his program. But there is no revolution without contradictions to provoke it, and indeed the word, "contradiction," has recently become a prominent part of Gorbachev's vocabulary.[63] Gorbachev evidently takes these words most seriously; his portrayal of what is at stake in *perestroika* has grown more urgent. Thus his words in June 1987:

History has not left us much time to resolve this task. . . . Depending on how *perestroika* goes, according to its results, the potential of socialism will be judged, what it gives to man, how socially effective a socialist society is. . . . There may be no "sweet tomorrows" if we don't work by the sweat of our brow today, changing our way of thinking, overcoming inertia, and mastering new approaches.

This vision is evidently sincere, but it is not clear how widely or strongly it is shared beyond a narrow circle of Gorbachev's followers. Hence one of the most serious potential contradictions in Gorbachev's own approach is between his instinct to look to the "mood and will of the people" (as he put it in January) and his conviction that he speaks from a higher consciousness. This point brings us to the next question: What are the aims of Gorbachev's political strategy and how likely is it to work?

II. IS GORBACHEV'S STRATEGY AN EFFECTIVE RESPONSE TO CRISIS?

The first part of this essay described the crisis of the Soviet system of leadership as a weakening hold over the resources in citizens' minds and a deterioration of the traditional political levers, analogous to the crisis of the command economy, indeed, the political face of the same crisis. Is Gorbachev's political strategy an appropriate response? Can new or revived political instruments supplement and reinforce the old, or only conflict with them? Does Gorbachev's strategy presage a new "political contract" with a population that will share his goals, or is he unleashing forces that he will be unable to control? It is clearly too early to do much more than raise these questions; but at least one can begin thinking how Gorbachev's latest moves fit with the traditional system of power, and how appropriate they are to the problems he faces.

The Possible Logic of Gorbachev's Political Strategy: Is It Really Anything New?

Gorbachev's political strategy appears designed to serve four objectives: (1) to strengthen Gorbachev's own hand by weakening that of his opponents; (2) to create a strong constituency for change; (3) to make his program irreversible; and (4) as an ultimate objective, to revive and strengthen the regime's legitimacy. Each of these, of course, serves the others, yielding an increase of power and authority for Gorbachev himself and for the political system as a whole. This last point is especially important: just as Gorbachev can argue that economic reform is a positive-sum game, because the resulting increase in wealth will benefit everyone, he might also justify political reform as a positive-sum game, because it will halt the dissipation of power and authority, the turning away of the people from the regime, that had reduced the latter years of the Brezhnev regime to the appearance of control, but with less and less of the reality of it.

It is clear, at any rate, that in Gorbachev's mind the traditional resources and levers are inadequate for his purposes. Consider for example the use of the personnel weapon. Despite the sweep of Gorbachev's "cold purge" since March 1985, it is striking to note that Gorbachev has been very careful not to challenge officials appointed since Brezhnev's death,[64] and he has shown some sensitivity lately to charges that cadres are being replaced too freely. Thus in August 1987 he suggested to a group of agricultural managers that in the future most of the personnel turnover would come through attrition:[65]

If you ask me whether in order to carry out *perestroika* it is necessary to replace every one of our cadres, [I would answer] no. I think we must resolve the tasks of *perestroika* with the people and the cadres we have. . . . But in addition there is a natural process: there are those who have already come to the end of their working life, and that is understandable. Or some people simply don't have the strength to take on new tasks. That's understandable too, and there is no cause to dramatize the situation. . . . In principle we assume that basically the existing personnel will be able to handle these tasks. We do not intend to break our cadres.

The message is deliberately ambiguous, but its essence is clear: Gorbachev knows he must make do with the human material he has.

Hence the key to his strategy is motivation. But Gorbachev is reluctant to rely on economic interest alone; on the contrary, one of his chief complaints about the Brezhnev era is that it tolerated the spread of consumerism, individualism, "private-property mentality," and materialism (which Gorbachev calls "thingism"). He appears to take some comfort, however, in the thought that consumer wants have also become more advanced, creating new demands that can be satisfied through collective and cooperative mechanisms.[66] And although he has condemned the tendency toward "levelling" (i.e., excessive egalitarianism in salaries and bonuses) that took place under Brezhnev and has begun increasing income differentials, Gorbachev, like Andropov before him, stressed that collectives, not individuals, should be the main beneficiaries to be rewarded in proportion to their work, and that the rewards themselves should be primarily collective as well (although more recently he has been fudging on this point, by treating families as acceptable "collectives"). Thus he apparently hopes to limit the destabilizing effects of economic inequalities and the moral corrosion of individualism.

Not only is economic self-interest an ideologically inadequate motive in Gorbachev's eyes, it is also politically insufficient, because it will not protect citizens who take initiative at the local level from being harassed by middle-level bureaucracy. This is one strong reason for Gorbachev's experimentation with *glasnost'*, improved legal guarantees, and democratization. Gorbachev does not use the term, "constituency," but beginning with the January 1987 plenum, he began talking about the need to guarantee that *perestroika* would be irreversible and that the mistakes of the past would not be repeated. There is ultimately only one way to do that: by reallocating political powers, not just economic ones, to the local levels, so as to weaken permanently the various apparatus on which the Stalinist system rested.

Is that really what Gorbachev intends? Until recently one could argue that Gorbachev's political strategy was not essentially different from that of his predecessors. Every General Secretary since Stalin, after all, has seen his power and authority erode relative to the man before him, and each one has fought back with a strategy of "reforms," described very well by George Breslauer.[67] They have always seen the middle of the bureaucracy as the main obstacle; they have invariably dwelt on the crucial importance of cadres; they have all manipulated history and have all invoked a "grandfather figure" against their immediate predecessor; and they have always started out sounding like populists—indeed, populism is a natural response in an authoritarian system. In the end, their political strategies have ended up much alike; as George Breslauer observes, "party activism, political intervention, and pressure are the constant winners in post-Stalin politics."[68] What makes Gorbachev different?

A comparison with Khrushchev yields some interesting answers. At first glance, their styles and techniques are similar in many ways. Gorbachev wields the broom as energetically as Khrushchev; he hectors the bureaucracy and exhorts the population in the best Khrushchevian manner, peppering his speech with proverbs and earthy examples; and Gorbachev has shown some of the same zest for raising the stakes when opposed. Both advertise themselves as reformers and men of the people, and both enjoy getting out of the office for a walkabout. Above all, Gorbachev is the same enthusiastic man of action, who would rather stir things up than sit safely by. Napoleon's "On s'engage et puis on voit" would do nicely as a motto for both.

Some differences, of course, are obvious too, particularly at the early stages of their careers as General Secretary. The Khrushchev of 1953–57 was an artful political tactician, who resembled the Stalin of the 1920s more than the Gorbachev of 1985–86. Khrushchev in those years staked out a conservative policy position against Malenkov's more liberal pro-consumer and pro-agricultural proposals, and this played a major part in his consolidation of power.[69] In contrast, in some respects he was far more vigorous in his early years than Gorbachev has been so far, firing a larger share of the obkom leadership of the Party and putting in his own proteges (of whom he had far larger numbers than Gorbachev, stemming from a longer and more varied political past). Khrushchev postponed announcing a reform program until he was fully in a position to challenge the old guard in the Politburo. In the process, he created a "constituency" in the Party elite. Gorbachev, facing less opposition in the Politburo and more of a consensus for change, has done the opposite, announcing a reform program before his constituency is fully consolidated.

The more one examines the two men, the more deeper differences appear. Khrushchev was a man of the years just after Stalin's death— "a quintessential Stalinist, if with a difference," Harry Rigby calls him.[70] He did not doubt that the Soviet economic system would catch up with the capitalists or that the political system could govern effectively. If he rejected mass terror, he had no compunctions about using coercion. Having restored the Party apparatus to the leading position in the Soviet political system, he pushed it deep into economic administration, and when that did not work he pushed it even deeper.[71] Khrushchev's "populism" was never more than half a policy, because no matter how much he might rouse people on the stump, he was never willing to grant the local level real power; the people had no meaningful political currency to contribute, other than their obedience. His efforts to promote "public" bodies and "non-salaried" participants were aimed strictly at increasing his mobilizational reach; and the notion that labor unions, for example, might attempt to veto managers' decisions would have horrified him.

Khrushchev invoked Leninist norms against Stalin's arbitrary lawlessness, but his main intention was to reassure the Party apparatus and the elite that henceforth it would be physically secure. His de-Stalinization campaign drew a careful line at about 1934; the later Stalin was dethroned, but the earlier one was not, and still less the system he created. Gorbachev, in contrast, is not only challenging Stalin as a leader but also the system he created; and this time it is Lenin who is being divided in two, to support notions of socialist property and economic policy that Khrushchev would not have approved of.

Khrushchev did not challenge the fundamentals he had inherited: if he tried to revive agriculture, for example, it was largely through administrative means, and not through investment at the expense of heavy industry and defense. (Only in his last years, in 1962 and after, did Khrushchev move toward the big-investment agricultural strategy for agriculture that subsequently became the hallmark of Brezhnevian policy.)[72] He did not doubt his authority to speak on all technical subjects, whether agronomy or nuclear strategy, and to raise up or humble technical experts as he pleased, largely according to whether they supported his latest technological gimmick. Meeting frustration, Khrushchev reacted by making ever more vigorous use of traditional instruments of power—more hiring and firing, more reorganization, more and more policy initiatives, and more administrative pressure.[73]

Gorbachev comes a generation later, after many a campaign and many a "reform," and both he and his colleagues have long reflected on the limits of the traditional system. (Indeed, the Gorbachev program as it has evolved to the present must be seen not only as the result of Gorbachev's learning on the job since 1985, but also of three decades of collective learning—and unlearning—in Moscow and especially in the provinces. The changes of the last two years would not have been possible if the new leaders had truly been "naive reformers.")[74] Coercion has its place in Gorbachev's panoply, but primarily to restore order and discipline; he has no illusions about its power as an instrument of change. Consistent with his stress on the importance of economic levers over administrative ones, Gorbachev is ambivalent about the role of the Party in economic management (more on that below). Technology alone will not perform miracles; Gorbachev does not pretend to know more than the experts, but neither does he expect them to bring about the millenium within the existing structure. He is more than willing to question fundamental investment priorities; indeed, he states openly that the long imbalance in favor of military programs has been one of the main causes of today's troubles.

The most important difference, which drives all the rest, is the two men's differing assessments of the situation facing them: for Khrushchev the word "perfecting" (*sovershenstvovanie*) was truly the one that applied. Gorbachev questions the very viability of the system.

Consequently, one can make the case that Gorbachev's political strategy, especially since the beginning of 1987, does indeed go farther in challenging the fundamentals of the system and attempting to devise new political instruments than that of any Soviet politician since the 1920s. But does he stand a chance? In the next section we examine the coherence, consistency, and realism of Gorbachev's approach.

Contradictions and Dangers in Gorbachev's Strategy

Three Contradictions

A politician's strategy develops piece-meal, the product of improvisation, opportunity and tactics, good or bad advice, and insights that may be more intuition than logic. In the case of a Soviet politician, the process is further complicated by an extreme need for discretion. If Gorbachev's ideas on economic reform, we learn, began taking concrete shape after 1980 in informal discussions at country houses outside Moscow,[75] his thoughts on political reform must have evolved even more privately. Snapshots of Gorbachev and Andropov walking together in short sleeves through the woods, deep in conversation, suggest one source of his thinking, but how much of Gorbachev's early mullings would he have wished to discuss with his patron?[76]

At any rate, it is not surprising that Gorbachev's strategy, only two years after his accession, is full of inconsistencies. But three of them stand out as so fundamental that no mere process of thought can resolve them; as we shall see, they are inescapable constraints and basic political issues.

The first is that Gorbachev is forced to use the old to build the new, and consequently his program is in constant danger of being subverted, exhausted, or defeated. *Glasnost'*, for example, is being carried out by a media system that is more centralized than ever before, especially because of the prominence of TV. The printed essays and articles that are the most supportive of Gorbachev's program come almost entirely from Moscow journalists and media, causing Gorbachev to complain of "usurpation" and to wonder out loud, "Where is the rest of the country?"[77] But despite well-meaning phrases at the top about reinforcing the local media, it is clear that local journalism is so decrepit that it cannot possibly play a strong role for a long time to come. Assiduous protection from the center may ward off its enemies but will not make it competent or independent. Self-financing through advertising would be a long-term step in the right direction, but that is frequently opposed by the local Party apparatus;[78] and besides, money is the least of the resources which local journalists require.[79]

The weapon of *glasnost'* is being managed entirely from above, and no real measures have been taken so far to change the traditional structure of media control. Despite rumors in the summer of 1986 that the censorship agency, *Glavlit,* was about to be abolished, the fall brought instead an announcement of a new head. Discussion of censorship itself is still forbidden;[80] and to my knowledge there has been no public mention of the existence of the *Perechen',* the censors' list of forbidden facts and topics. The ministerial visa system, too, is still intact.

What is true of structures is also true of people. Despite the extraordinary turnover in personnel in recent years, Gorbachev can hardly avoid conducting *perestroika* with people who have long pasts in high places under Brezhnev. Undoubtedly largely by necessity, he has filled most of the top positions in the Party and government with people who are older than he, and with the exception of a handful who were clearly out of favor in the Brezhnev years (such as Politburo member Aleksandr Iakovlev and Gorbachev's new aide Ivan Frolov, *Ogonek*'s Vitalii Korotich, and *Novyi mir*'s Sergei Zalygin), most of them had to make their compromises before 1982. *Literaturnaia gazeta* is still in the hands of Aleksandr Chakovskii, an accomplished literary survivor; *Pravda* is in those of Viktor Afanas'ev, who held the same post under Brezhnev; cinema is under veteran Central Committee apparatus man Aleksandr Kamshalov; culture under Vasilii Zakharov, once in charge of ideological affairs under Romanov in Leningrad. There are many other examples. How dedicated to *glasnost'* would they be if the reforming energy at the top were to weaken? Gorbachev's real allies at the top are still few, yet reform still depends entirely on them and on their chief.

The second contradiction is that the *objectives* pursued by the new strategy must co-exist with the old—indeed, in most respects, they *are* the old objectives. *Glasnost'* is supposed to tell the "whole truth," but not, of course, if that truth tarnishes the 70th anniversary of the October Revolution. Local elections are supposed to reinforce the authority and responsiveness of local officials, but the program they must carry out is that of the center just the same. As one manager observed about the prospect that his post will become elective:[81]

In any case we will be not be electing a program—especially since the program is assigned to us, it's the plan—but an individual capable of carrying it out. But let's say that a higher organ, the ministry or the *glavk,* keeps throwing new targets at us in the middle of the year, adds to our targets (which in fact happens all the time). Will that please the personnel? Hardly. What I am supposed to do then, resign?

The third contradiction flows from the second. It is that the reformers have barely begun to face up to the ambiguity that lurks in *perestroika,* namely, Who rules? Though he may talk about listening to the "mood and will" of the people, one may be sure that Gorbachev has no intention of dividing power; on the contrary, the main argument of this essay is that his aim is to regain the real control that his predecessors were losing. But Gorbachev is like the puppet-maker who dreams of giving life to his carvings: what will he do when they start to move on their own? He cannot go very far toward deconcentrating, delegating, and decentralizing, before he is obliged to reassert his hand. This is already clear in the case of elections. If enterprise directors are elected by their workers, who will choose the candidates? As a skeptical Moscow brigade leader commented in *Izvestiia,* after observing that all seven of his past directors had been "Varangians," that is, appointed from outside:

This system is hardly likely to change after the new law is adopted. They may present us with a total unknown and say, "Here is your director, vote for him." Or, if we elect our own, he will in any case have to be approved higher up. One of two things is bound to become a formality: either the election or the approval [by higher authority]. It's not difficult to guess which one it will be.[82]

There is, in addition, a tactical reason why Gorbachev cannot "surrender control to regain control": if he fails to use the traditional instruments himself he will find that others will do so in his place— local Party leaders, in particular, who will rebuild the local patronage networks that Gorbachev is now having so much trouble dismantling. Control not exercised at the top will tend to be recaptured at middle levels, and the central leadership will need all its power to prevent that from happening.

Twin Dangers

As a result of these three contradictions Gorbachev's strategy faces two principal dangers. The first is that Gorbachev's reforming energy, in response to resistance from officialdom and passivity from the people, could degenerate into Khrushchevism, that is, an increasingly frantic use of the General Secretary's traditional powers over cadres and structure. Gorbachev is a willful man, and there is a hint of such a tendency in his words to an audience in Estonia in early 1987:

> I must tell you straight out: today we can still discuss these questions, exchange opinions, and seek approaches on how to bring to life the decisions of the January Plenum. Today perplexed questions are still in order, because we must think everything deeply through. But tomorrow those who remain stubborn and those who will not understand the demands of the present time, will simply have to get out of the way.[83]

By the time of his fall, Khrushchev had succeeded in alienating every major group in the political system, including the provincial party apparatus, which had saved him seven years before. So far, Gorbachev has been far more cautious and more skillful, not only in his dealings with the provincial party apparatus but also with the KGB. But from the summer of 1986 on he began hectoring and scolding officials at every level, and his attacks have escalated steadily since. The June 1987 plenum marks an even more aggressive phase, as Gorbachev attempts to use the build-up to the Party Conference of 1988 as a means of bulldozing opponents out of the way. Even now Gorbachev may be making more powerful enemies than friends.

We may be sure that as *perestroika* is implemented, it will face the classic problems of previous reforms, and the center will be forced to intervene, using the "administrative methods" that are now out of fashion. There will be "localism," the tendency of regions to look to their own priorities first. If managers produce what is profitable, awkward shortages and surpluses will result. If there is real price reform, there will be inflation; if real incentives, unforeseen inequalities. The experience of reforms in China, in particular, suggests how strong the pressure will be to intervene from the center, in effect returning to old ways.

The other danger is political disorder. To the extent that Gorbachev's strategy succeeds it will unleash forces that have been dormant in Soviet politics since the Revolution, breeding instability and disorder. A handful of essential conditions has kept the Soviet political system remarkably stable over the thirty-five years since Stalin's death.[84] The leaders have taken care to manage the population's expectations, partly through massive propaganda and the exclusion of competing ideas. But a program of reform that now aims at promoting new ideas is bound to cause popular expectations to soar; and indeed Gorbachev has already observed as much.[85] Another factor in stability has been the fact that formal organization from above has traditionally displaced social organization from below, and this has helped to keep the aspirations of different segments of the population from coalescing, preventing instabilities in one sector or region from spreading to the rest. But now the deliberate mobilization of local social forces may weaken the traditional bulkheads. Lastly, both the elite and population have traditionally been obsessed with maintaining order. Yet the Gorbachev policies are already threatening disorder and the signs of conservative backlash can already be seen.

What Becomes of the Functions of the Party Apparatus?

If even a fraction of the Gorbachev political strategy comes to pass, then what becomes of the functions and powers of the local Party apparatus? This is clearly the most crucial issue.

Statements by local Party officials during the last two years sound understandably confused. On the one hand, some are clearly attempting to rethink their traditional duties; others are clinging to their familiar roles.[86]

Beginning in January 1987, Gorbachev himself took up the issue. He sounded at first as though he envisioned the Party apparatus as a sort of ombudsman of *perestroika*. But in the same breath he denied that he had any intention of changing the apparatus's leading role in economic management;[87] indeed, in a subsequent speech he criticized those who might have misunderstood that the local apparatus should confine itself to "some sort of pure politics."[88] But under a reformed economic mechanism there should be no need for the Party apparatus to worry about contract fulfillment or supply bottlenecks; since the "economic organs" will be doing their job, they should get on with it without petty intervention by the Party:

> The raikom cannot act as the organ of economic management—that is what must be understood. That is not its function.[89]

The Party's chief instrument, as always, must be the selection and assignment of cadres and control over organization. In short, the Party's traditional basis for power remains intact and unchallenged. But needless to say, this ducks the real question, which is, Who is ultimately responsible for plan fulfillment? If it is ultimately the Party apparatus (as Gorbachev still insists it is), then the result will be the same merry-go-round of local hiring and firing as before. Just as Janos Kornai argues that in economic reform the ultimate question is whether the manager looks up to the planner or down to the customer for his orders, so also in political reform the final issue is whether local officials look upward to the Party for their jobs or downward to their voters. So far, Gorbachev's answer, for all its ambiguities, is clear enough on the basics.

Meanwhile, not surprisingly, the press reports that not much has actually changed in practice. In one recent article, a *Pravda* correspondent observes that in a group of *obkoms* (provincial committees) he surveyed, the branch departments of the *obkom* tend to be staffed by newly co-opted officials from the corresponding economic branches, who bring over with them their habits of mind unchanged: "My job as head of the construction department," they say, "is to oversee 'my' factories and meet 'my' plan." (This theme, of course, is not new; the new twist is that Salutskii asserts most instructors are brought in essentially "raw," and that such co-optation is the rule, not the exception.)[90] Another *Pravda* correspondent observes that the same point applies to many new *raikom* (district committee) first secretaries in rural areas: they are co-opted "specialists," as opposed to their predecessors, who were frequently generalists. One might have thought that Gorbachev's policies would call for precisely the opposite, but the Party's cadres departments probably had little choice: the "ossification" (*okostenenie*) that prevailed in cadres policy under Brezhnev meant that the new Party officials did not punch their career tickets in the time-honored sequence. Consequently, the Party is drawing on what is available, and that means economic specialists.[91]

With new personnel such as this, it is not surprising that the local Party apparatus may be moving in the opposite direction from what Gorbachev says he wants, that is, toward more *podmena* and petty tutelage, rather than less.

III. CONCLUSIONS AND SPECULATIONS

This essay has developed three themes: (1) The Soviet system faces not only an economic crisis but also a political one; indeed, they are two faces of the same problem, the exhaustion of the Stalinist strategy of development. (2) This is increasingly Gorbachev's own perception of the situation; accordingly, he has begun developing a strategy of political reform aimed at renewing the state's resources for reaching and moving its citizens. (3) Though he has already gone beyond previous general secretaries, Gorbachev has barely begun to confront the contradictions and dangers inherent in his approach. What are the chances that Gorbachev will manage these contradictions and dangers, keep himself in power, and forge ahead with *perestroika*?

Gorbachev is compared to the great reformers of Russian history. But Gorbachev must hope the analogy is false, because it assumes an enlightened ruler pushing a backward people into modernity. Instead, Gorbachev and allies have staked their chances for success on the opposite proposition: that the Soviet people have outgrown the Stalinist structures and beliefs; indeed, that the people have become more modern than the institutions. That is a positive way of saying that after three generations of the unique Stalinist mixture of repression, mobilization, nationalism, and social conservatism, there has somehow evolved a new society. It is not the society that Lenin or Stalin had in mind; and it is clear that today's leaders do not fully understand it or accept it even though they come from it. But Gorbachev's approach suggests a growing (if still tentative) understanding that this new society cannot be dominated by the state as it was in the past, and that politicians must come to new terms with it, using different instruments and policies.

To say that Gorbachev is prepared to come to new terms with Soviet society is not to say that he is prepared to let society dominate the state, despite his occasional references to the "will of the people." He still considers himself to be the source of initiative; and he still considers that the state will continue to shape the evolution of society.[92] If there is a formula from Russian history that Gorbachev himself might borrow, it is that of the "wager on the strong." But how optimistic Gorbachev is about this society's strengths and about its willingness to obey him! He is wagering that passivity and political apathy will give way to initiative and commitment—but that these will serve his purposes; that communal and cooperative values can co-exist with individualistic ones—and that neither will generate disruptive inequalities; that the population is "responsible" enough that democratization will not degenerate into disorder; that the intelligentsia will play a constructive role in *perestroika* instead of simply testing the limits of official tolerance; and finally that the rising consciousness of national groups will reinforce the Soviet community rather than the reverse. Does Soviet society really offer so solid a foundation on which to build? Can it really be so strong and yet so meek?

Probably not, at least not for years to come. Gorbachev is already being forced to strike out at excesses of *glasnost'*, to label some people dissidents and arrest them, to put down demonstrators, to limit enterprise autonomy, to limit private incomes. He is being driven, in short, to define and enforce new boundaries between orthodoxy and heterodoxy, between approved participation and dissent, between autonomy and plan, and between popular wishes and the will of the state. *Perestroika* until recently has been at the stage when flowers bloom from rifle barrels and everything seems possible; but that stage is already over.

Does that mean that Gorbachev is fated to fail? Many economists, arguing that nothing short of wholesale systemic reform stands to make the Soviet economy efficient, tend to dismiss everything short of that as "tinkering." But tinkering is precisely what reformers do; it is what distinguishes them from revolutionaries; and Gorbachev, for all his rhetoric, is not a revolutionary. Whether his reform program can succeed, therefore, depends on where the new boundaries just named are ultimately drawn, and whether they produce a reconciliation of official and popular values, of "word and deed," or only disillusionment, cynicism, and continued "exit" by the population.

Notes

1. "O sozyve ocherednogo XXVII s"ezda KPSS i zadachakh, sviazannykh s ego podgotovkoi i provedeniem." Speech to the Plenary Meeting of the CPSU Central Committee, 23 April 1985, reprinted in M. S. Gorbachev, *Izbrannye rechi i stat'i* (Moscow: "Politizdat," 1985), pp. 7–23.

2. See in particular Gorbachev's speeches to the Central Committee in January and June 1987: "O perestroike i kadrovoi politike Partii," *Pravda,* January 28, 1987; and "O zadachakh partii po korennoi perestroike upravleniia ekonomikoi," *Pravda,* June 26, 1987.

3. This idea is ably developed by Peter Hauslohner in "Gorbachev's Social Contract," *Soviet Economy,* vol. 3, no. 1 (January-March 1987), pp. 54–89.

4. Gorbachev himself used the expression, "crisis phenomena" in his January 1987 speech to the Central Committee. Since then he has retreated to the formula, "pre-crisis," but he has grown ever blunter in his analysis of the symptoms.

5. Bohdan Nahajlo, "Mikhail Shatrov on the Treaty of Brest-Litovsk" (Radio Free Europe Bulletin, no. 14, April 8, 1987).

6. See Timothy J. Colton, *The Dilemma of Reform in the Soviet Union* (New York: Council on Foreign Relations, 1986), pp. 98–100.

7. Grey Hodnett, "The Pattern of Leadership Politics," in Seweryn Bialer, ed., *The Domestic Context of Soviet Foreign Policy* (Boulder, Colorado: Westview Press, 1981), pp. 92–93, 104.

8. This part of the argument is analogous to Charles Lindblom's metaphor of the "thumbs" of centrally planned economies. See his *Politics and Markets* (New York: Basic Books, 1977), pp. 65–75.

9. Gail W. Lapidus, "Gorbachev and the Reform of the Soviet System," *Daedalus,* vol. 116, no. 2 (Spring, 1987), pp. 8–9.

10. One of the most revealing changes is the growing use of the term, *interesy*. Initially, this was the property of liberal thinkers (see for example T. Zaslavskaia, "Chelovecheskii faktor rasvitiia ekonomiki i sotsial'naia spravedlivost'," *Kommunist*, no. 13 (September 1986), 63, 65–66), but more recently the word has been adopted by Gorbachev himself and has become widely used in Soviet publications.

11. Thus Zaslavskaia writes of the "alienation of a portion of the working class from public goals and values." Zaslavskaia 1986, op. cit., p. 66.

12. In an excellent presentation at the AAASS annual meeting in New Orleans in 1986, Gordon Livermore of the *Current Digest of the Soviet Press* suggested that Gorbachev is likely to find today's intelligentsia more constructive-minded than Khrushchev did in his day, because the corruption and decay of the 1970s repelled intellectuals just as much as it did the Party reformers and technocrats, while the main disruptive issues of the 1950s, Stalinism and the camps, have largely been vented. Nevertheless, my argument suggests that behind the seeming congruence of aims there may lie a more fundamental potential divergence of values between Party reformers and intellectuals than ever before.

13. Zaslavskaia 1986, op. cit., pp. 62–63.

14. Donna Bahry and Brian D. Silver, "The Intimidation Factor in Soviet Politics: The Symbolic Uses of Terror," Soviet Interview Project Working Paper no. 31 (February 1987).

15. The clearest and best-known statement of this is Samuel Huntington and Zbigniew Brzezinski, *Political Power: USA/USSR* (New York: The Viking Press, 1963), pp. 194–195.

16. See the discussion of this point in Seweryn Bialer, *Stalin's Successors* (Cambridge: Cambridge University Press, 1980), p. 37.

17. T. H. Rigby, "The Soviet Regional Leadership: The Brezhnev Generation," *Slavic Review* (March, 1978), pp. 9ff.

18. For a discussion of this point, see Thane Gustafson and Dawn Mann, "Gorbachev's Next Gamble," *Problems of Communism*, vol. 36, no. 5 (September-October, 1987), pp. 1–20. Under Andropov and during Gorbachev's first year, several provincial party chiefs served a "tour" in the Central Committee before being re-appointed to their provinces. This pattern has faded, however, since the 27th Party Congress.

19. These estimates come from an article by-lined by Gennadii Kolbin shortly before he was reassigned to Kazakhstan from Ul'ianovsk ("Vzyskatel'nost'," *Pravda*, December 2, 1986). A recent estimate from Lithuania is that there are 90 different services with responsiblity for *kontrol'* ("Prostor initsiative," *Pravda*, August 8, 1987).

20. S. Maniakin, "Perestroika i kontrol'," *Pravda*, September 24, 1987.

21. This argument is developed by Tat'iana Zaslavskaia in "Chelovecheskii faktor . . . ," op. cit., pp. 61–62.

22. Thus throughout its history the Main Political Administration of the military has consistently failed the four basic tests of an effective watchdog agency, as Timothy Colton demonstrates in *Commissars, Commanders and*

Civilian Authority: The Structure of Soviet Military Politics (Cambridge, Mass.: Harvard University Press, 1979).

23. That this response was present from the earliest days of the command system is evident from the work based on the Harvard Project of the 1940s and 1950s. See in particular Joseph Berliner, *Factory and Manager in the USSR* (Cambridge, Mass.: Harvard University Press, 1957).

24. In a speech in Murmansk in the fall of 1987 Mikhail Gorbachev paid a rare public tribute to the system of "military representatives" posted in military-industrial plants: "Take defense," he said. "There we do not lag in any way. So we do know how to work. But there, I must tell you, the quality-control officers make it hot for everybody: for the workers, the designers, the engineers, and the managers. That is how *gospriemka* must work. ("Nemer-knushchii podvig geroev Zapolar'ia," *Pravda,* October 2, 1987.)

25. Thus one of the lessons of the nuclear disaster at Chernobyl' in the spring of 1986 is that the presence at the site of representatives of all the major offices concerned with nuclear power (including safety officials) did not prevent the foolish experiments that caused the accident, but it guaranteed that news of it reached Kiev and Moscow very quickly, since no one wanted to be the last to report.

26. See for example an interview with Academician Boris Paton, "Bezo-pasnost' progressa," *Sotsialisticheskaia industriia,* October 10, 1986. An interesting recent case of whistle-blowing involves construction defects at the Minsk nuclear powerplant, caused by systematic neglect of design specifications. A Ivakhnov, "Nuzhny li stroikam Makaevy?" *Izvestiia,* October 24, 1986.

27. I. Kaz'min and A. Pigolkin, "Podzakonnyi akt," *Izvestiia,* October 17, 1986.

28. Thus, Ligachev observed in January 1987 that the Kazakh and Ukrainian Central Committees had not been summoned to report to the Politburo in twenty years.

29. Total savings in individual bank accounts grew 20-fold in a generation, from 10.9 billion rubles in 1960 to 220.8 in 1985. Revealingly, while the savings of the average city-dweller grew 5-fold during this period, those of the average rural resident grew nearly 9 times, reflecting both the improved earnings of peasants but also the scarcity of goods in the countryside. (Source: *Narodnoe khoziaistvo SSSR v 1985g* [Moscow: "Statistika," 1986], p. 448.)

30. The latest example is "Akademset'," the computer network of the Academy of Sciences, and similar experimental networks pioneered by INION. See O. L. Smirnov and Iu. A. Savostitskii, "Dialog cherez kontinenty," *Ekonom-icheskaia gazeta,* no. 13 (March 1987), p. 9.

31. Implemented at the beginning of 1987 in a select number of enterprises drawn mostly from the machine-building sector, the *gospriemka* system differs from the traditional quality-control system in that it is operated by an independent watchdog agency subordinated to the State Committee for Standards, whereas this function was traditionally exercised by offices belonging to each producing enterprise.

32. The functions of the new regional administration are described in an interview with the chairman of the RSFSR Gosplan, N. N. Maslennikov,

"Perestroika upravleniia territoriei," *Pravda,* September 11, 1987. The new regional dimension added to the planning system is described in the 1987 planning decree, published in *O korennoi perestroike upravleniia ekonomikoi* (Moscow: Politizdat, 1987), pp. 76–80. The regions and republics, in particular, are to have extensive authority over the planning of all construction.

33. "Prakticheskimi delami uglubliat' perestroiku," *Pravda,* July 15, 1987.

34. Interview with I. I. Gladkii, chairman of the State Committee for Labor and Social Questions, "Po trudu, po spravedlivosti," *Pravda,* September 2, 1987.

35. At the Sixth Congress of Journalists in March 1987 *Pravda* chief editor V. G. Afanas'ev criticized the constraints on coverage of space and ecology, describing the "visas" required from the agencies concerned before anything negative can be published. Only direct support from a Central Committee secretary enabled *Pravda* to print material about the pollution of Lake Baikal or the need to review plans to divert northern rivers—and even then, Afanas'ev added, only with great difficulty. At the same Congress *Izvestiia* commentator Aleksandr Bovin criticized the restrictions under which foreign-affairs correspondents still work: "I envy my journalist colleagues who write on internal affairs," he said. Sure enough, *Pravda* did not publish his following words, which took the Ministry of Foreign Affairs to task. ("Na pul'se perestroiki," *Pravda,* March 14, 1987.) But foreign observers rubbed their eyes in disbelief over Bovin's public polemics with the General Staff over the deployment of the Soviet SS-20's, and his barbs at unnamed politicians who brought about the "relinkage" of Soviet arms-control positions at Reykjavik and after (*Moscow News,* no. 10, March 8, 1987), and over *Pravda*'s publication of numbers on the US-Soviet strategic balance on March 17. In early 1988, Soviet revelations related to the INF Treaty became more remarkable still.

36. For example, in the fall of 1986 the statistical annual *Narodnoe khoziaistvo SSSR,* for the first time in many years, published detailed figures on crop yields for 1985, and *Kommunist,* in a new statistical section that began in its first issue for 1987, revealed data on infantile mortality. On the other hand, in other respects the reliability of Soviet statistical reporting has actually declined, most notably the national-income statistics for 1986. See Jan Vanous, "The Dark Side of 'Glasnost'": Unbelievable National Income Statistics in the Gorbachev Era," *PlanEcon Report,* vol. III, no. 6.

37. Thus the Belorussian CP Central Committee and its apparatus were criticized in Pravda for slow implementation of perestroika, especially in light industry, for which the relevant secretary and department head were singled out by name. A. Simurov and A. Ulitenok, "S pozitsii trebovatel'nosti," *Pravda,* March 29, 1987. This clearly comes under the heading of "routine glasnost'" rather than Aesopian politics aimed at the Belorussian leadership, since the previous head of the Belorussian CP, Sliun'kov, had just been promoted to CPSU Central Committee secretary in Moscow and a new Belorussian first secretary, Ye. Sokolov, had just been installed a few months before.

38. On January 4, 1987 *Pravda* published an account of persecution of a local Ukrainian correspondent, V. B. Berkhin (M. Odinets and M. Poltoranin,

"Za poslednei chertoi"). On January 8 KGB Chairman Chebrikov signed a brief note in *Pravda,* announcing that the responsible officials, who turned out to belong to the Ukrainian KGB, had been punished.

39. See especially Jonathan Sanders, "The Soviets' First Living Room War: Soviet National Television's Coverage of the Chernobyl' Disaster" (Paper prepared for the Program on Global Disasters and International Information Flows: The Annenberg School of Communications, Washington D.C., October 8–10, 1986).

40. N. I. Efimov, first deputy editor of *Izvestiia,* in an interview in *La Repubblica,* June 21, 1986. In 1987 *Narodnoe khoziaistvo SSSR za 70 let* (Moscow: "Finansy i Statistika," 1987), pp. 582–584, published selected circulation figures of major periodicals. They do not quite bear out Efimov's claim, but they do show a sharp drop in circulation for both *Izvestiia* and *Ogonyëk.*

41. Not in the form of direct competition in single-member districts, evidently, but in the form of multiple-member lists in newly consolidated districts. With more candidates than seats available, seats will be awarded in the order of votes received.

42. Much has been made of the fact that the final resolution of the Central Committee plenum of January 1987 did not adopt this idea. But Gorbachev introduced it in strikingly tentative language, so that it appears not to have been a formal proposal. Recall his singularly crab-like formulas: "It appears advisable to take counsel about the refinement of the mechanism of forming leading Party bodies. Many different proposals have come in to the Central Committee in this connection. Allow me to report on the conclusions which have been drawn on the basis of the generalization of these proposals." And so forth in the same style. In short, the issue has not yet been joined. Gorbachev did not return to it at the June 1987 Central Committee meeting.

43. Jerry F. Hough, *The Soviet Prefects* (Cambridge, Mass.: Harvard University Press, 1969), p. 162.

44. Ye. Ligachev, "Sovetuias' s partiei, s narodom," *Kommunist,* no. 16 (1985), p. 83.

45. So far without much success, apparently. An interview with Academician Nikita Moiseev, one of the few to submit his resignation on time, reveals that most senior figures in the Academy have petitioned for extensions "on an exceptional basis." N. Il'inskaia, "Pochemu v otstavku?" *Pravda,* August 17, 1987.

46. G. Smirnov, "Revoliutsionnyi sut' obnovleniia," *Pravda,* March 13, 1987.

47. The device of a Party Conference is itself an innovation, or rather the revival of an institution long unused. None has been held since 1941 and its powers are naturally vague, but distant precedents suggest that a Party Conference can amend Party rules and remove members of the Central Committee, although not elect new ones. See Dawn Mann, "Party Conferences as Political Tools," *Sovset' News,* vol. 3, no. 3 (March 1987).

48. Iu. Kaz'min, "Litsom k cheloveku truda: zametki s sessii Moskovskogo gorodskogo Soveta narodnykh deputatov," *Pravda,* March 17, 1987. Kaz'min

adds: "Deputies had to make their way into the ispolkom as petitioners, not as the plenipotentiary elected representatives of the people—and they still do."

49. Werner Hahn, "Electoral Choice in the Soviet Bloc," *Problems of Communism,* vol. XXXVI, no. 2 (March-April 1987), pp. 29–39. The Polish experience is in many ways the most interesting. It is analyzed in greater detail in the same author's *Democracy in a Communist Party: Poland's Experience Since 1980* (New York: Columbia University Press, 1987).

50. *Vedomosti Verkhovnogo Soveta SSSR,* no. 37, 1986.

51. I am indebted to Professor Peter Maggs of the University of Illinois, whose analyses of recent legislation have been appearing regularly on *Sovset'.*

52. "Perestroika—krovnoe delo naroda," Speech by M. S. Gorbachev to the XVIIIth Congress of the Labor Unions of the USSR, *Pravda,* February 26, 1987.

53. Such "telephone justice" has been widely discussed in the Soviet press recently and has drawn many letters to the editor. See Peter H. Solomon, "Soviet Politicians and Criminal Prosecutions: the Logic of Party Intervention" (Soviet Interview Project, Working Paper no. 33, March 1987).

54. Interview with the First Secretary of the Belorussian CP, Ye. Ye. Sokolov, "Vremia uchit'sia," *Pravda,* September 3, 1987.

55. This figure comes from Gorbachev's speech in Murmansk in October 1987, "Nemerknushchii podvig," op. cit.

56. *Pravda,* August 21, 1987. This figure does not include employees of the ministry supply systems, the so-called "glavsnaby."

57. See for example the pair of articles by V. Kostakov, "Zaniatost': defitsit ili izbytok?" *Kommunist,* no. 2 (1987), pp. 78–89, and "Polnaia zaniatost'. Kak my ego ponimaem?" *Kommunist,* no. 14 (1987), pp. 16–25.

58. That this is the explicit intent of the new leadership can be seen from the guidelines issued to the new editorial board of the Central Committee's official theoretical journal, *Kommunist,* in August 1986. These specified that the journal should pay particular attention to the works of the last years of Lenin's life. (*Pravda,* August 22, 1986.)

59. See particularly Lev Voskresenskii, "Along the Road to the Socialist Market," *Moscow News,* no. 48 (November 30, 1986), p. 121. For background on the handling of the NEP theme, see Elizabeth Teague, "Symbolic Role Ascribed to the NEP," *Radio Liberty Research Bulletin,* RL 415/86 (November 3, 1986).

60. Egor' Iakovlev, "Farewell," *Moscow News,* no. 3 (January 18, 1987), p. 13.

61. Danilov, "Istoki i uroki," op. cit.

62. *Pravda,* October 2, 1986. The major speeches delivered at the meeting, together with summaries of participants' major points, will be found in *XXVII S"ezd KPSS i zadachi kafedr obshchestvennykh nauk* (Moscow: "Politizdat," 1987).

63. Thus in his speech to the Central Committee in June 1987, Gorbachev used the word "contradiction" again and again to describe the current situation in the country. For example, the "contradiction between the requirements of

renewal, creativity, and constructive initiative, on the one hand, and conservatism, inertia, and mercenary interests (*korystnye interesy*) on the other." (1/5) Gorbachev also referred to "contradictions between the interests of various groups of the population, collectives, agencies, and organizations," (1/5) and particularly to "the contradiction between the near-term, narrow-minded interests, even egotistical motivations of particular individuals and the interests of the whole society, the long-term interests of the working people." (1/5) Later on, he said, "We must learn the complex, dialectically contradictory art of perestroika." (3/4) In his analysis of the Stalinist system, he referred to its "ever-growing contradiction" with the requirements of economic growth today. (3/6) (The numbers in parentheses refer to page and column respectively of the *Pravda* version.)

64. For details on this point, see Gustafson and Mann, "Gorbachev's Next Challenge," op. cit.

65. Remarks to a meeting of managers of the "Ramenskii" Agro-Industrial Kombinat ("Perestroika izmeriaetsia delami," *Pravda*, August 6, 1987).

66. As Gorbachev observed in one of his earliest speeches, people are increasingly interested in good housing and amenities, leisure, and tourism. See "O sozyve ocherednogo XXVII s"ezda . . . ," op. cit., p. 15. Since then he has given steadily stronger emphasis to social programs, health care, and housing, all of which are amenable to collective and cooperative approaches.

67. George W. Breslauer, *Khrushchev and Brezhnev as Leaders: Building Authority in Soviet Politics* (London: George Allen and Unwin, 1982).

68. Breslauer 1982, op. cit., p. 278.

69. See Rigby, op. cit., and Breslauer, op. cit.

70. Rigby, op. cit.

71. See Barbara A. Chotiner's summing up of the lessons of the 1962 bifurcation of the Party in her *Khrushchev's Party Reforms: Coalition Building and Institutional Innovation* (Westport, Conn.: Greenwood Press, 1984), pp. 273–290.

72. George Breslauer argues this point convincingly in *Khrushchev and Brezhnev as Leaders*, pp. 61ff. Khrushchev's evolution toward what became the Brezhnevian agricultural policy is described in my *Reform in Soviet Politics* (Cambridge: Cambridge University Press, 1981), pp. 16–25.

73. See especially Michel Tatu's description of Khrushchev's reaction to frustration in his *Power in the Kremlin* (New York: Viking Press, 1970).

74. For a discussion of the process of learning and innovation in Soviet policy-making, see "Bringing New Ideas into Soviet Politics" in my *Reform in Soviet Politics*, op. cit., Chapter 6.

75. From Philip Taubman's interview with Abel Aganbegian, "Architect of Soviet Change," *New York Times*, July 8, 1987, p. D1.

76. One such photo, seemingly from an amateur's camera, is reproduced in Dusko Doder, *Shadows and Whispers* (New York: Random House, 1986).

77. "Prakticheskimi delami uglubliat' perestroiku," *Pravda*, July 15, 1987.

78. V. Fedotov, "Kogda razgovor ser'eznyi," *Pravda*, October 26, 1986. Fedotov's account describes local press in the province of Lipetsk, which has been repeatedly featured as a showcase for *perestroika*.

79. One of the more potent threats is to deny new housing to the staff of a troublesome local newspaper. For a good description of the dynamics of intimidation of the local press, see N. Shabanov, "Za chto sulili gazetu?" *Pravda,* August 6, 1986.

80. *Pravda* chief editor V. G. Afanas'ev came as close as anyone I have seen when he referred at the 6th Congress of Journalists to the widespread practice of "self-censorship." (*Pravda,* March 14, 1987, op. cit.)

81. M. Berger, "Predpriiatie i perestroika: obsuzhdaem proekt Zakona SSSR," *Izvestiia,* March 4, 1987.

82. Berger, op. cit.

83. "Rech' M. S. Gorbacheva na vstreche s partiinym, sovetskim i khoziaistvennym aktivom Estonskoi SSR," *Pravda,* February 22, 1987.

84. See Seweryn Bialer's discussion of the conditions of stability in Bialer 1980, op. cit., pp. 145–182.

85. As Gorbachev commented to the XVIII Congress of Labor Unions, "The high goals set by the Party, the growing changes in the economy and in the social and political spheres have led to what one might call a 'revolution of expectations.'" ("Rech' M. S. Gorbacheva na XVIII s"ezde profsoiuzov SSSR," *Pravda,* February 26, 1987, p. 1.

86. See in particular the remarkable fictional conversation between Shirokov and Streshnev in Fedor Burlatskii, "Conversation Without Equivocation," *Literaturnaia gazeta,* October 1, 1986, p. 10. (Trans. in FBIS, *Daily Report/ USSR,* October 8, 1986, p. R6.)

87. "I want to emphasize that no one can relieve the Party committees of their concern and responsibility for the state of affairs in the economic field."

88. Tallinn speech, op. cit., February 21, 1987.

89. Ibid.

90. Anatolii Salutskii, "Svoi i chuzhie," *Pravda,* December 21, 1986.

91. Iu. Makhrin, "Obnovlenie," *Pravda,* January 14, 1987.

92. One recalls here Seweryn Bialer's words at the end of the 1970s: "One can agree that the post-Stalin era witnessed a decline in the role of the political, a decrease in the extent of its relative autonomy from the social environment. At the same time, however, the political factor continues to affect the evolution of Soviet society to a greater extent than it does other industrial societies on a similar level of industrial development. The shaping of the political factor by social influences continues to be low in comparison to the shaping of the social environment by the active, mobilizing, and directing influence of the political factor." (Bialer 1980, op. cit., pp. 124–125.)

8

Gorbachev's Program of Change: Sources, Significance, Prospects

Seweryn Bialer

We bind a man hand and foot with all kinds of agreements; we drive him into a bottle, cork it up and put a government stamp on it; and then we go around saying: "Why doesn't this man show any energy or any initiative?"
—from a speech by S. I. Syrtsov,
Chairman of the Council of Peoples' Commissars
of the Russian Republic, February, 1930,
O Nedostatkakh i Zadachakh (Moskva-Leningrad, 1930, p. 15)

In the Fall of 1987, the Soviet Union had become the most interesting country in the world. What is happening there is nothing less than a gigantic experiment, now only in its infancy. The massive changes initiated in the Soviet Union call to mind Robespierre's observation that one week in the life of a revolution may produce more significant events than an entire year of normalcy. But to change the Soviet system, the new course initiated by Mikhail Gorbachev needs far more than a single year. It will require at least a decade.

In one of the world's most secretive countries, there is now official talk of openness. In a society that has known not a single day of genuine democracy, the leadership preaches democratization and grass roots participation in the institutions of governance. A state that has put an extraordinary premium on stability and conformity is shifting toward innovation and individuality. Today, authorities promote clashing views where once a single truth was proclaimed the only truth. While continuing to emphasize patriotism, the authorities no longer equate it with a cult of the military. They are retreating from the idea of a "perfect society," from the goal of a secular Utopia that they invoked in the past to justify the shortcomings of Communist rule. They are now beginning to recognize the errors of the past in order to avoid perpetuating or repeating them. In this sense, the new mood reflects what was best in the critical and searching spirit of the old democratic Russian intelligentsia, which Stalin virtually extinguished.

Gorbachev's greatest plans for the change are in the economic sphere. Yet the most startling developments of his two-and-one-half years in office are not economic: they are in the political and cultural areas. If they endure, these measures will profoundly change the system he inherited.

In short, a major program of planned change, of reform in almost all aspects of life, has been initiated by the new leader and has struck a responsive chord in the Party and in the society. But this process has only scratched the surface of Soviet life. Its impact on the massive country, on the everyday life of its citizens and on the standard behavior of the ever-present bureaucracy is still modest.

The "new" dominates top level decision making, the media, and official declarations about the future direction of the country. But the "old" is dominant in the everyday lives of Soviet citizens. Thus the key question is not primarily how much further Gorbachev will go with his iconoclastic ideas, but rather how deeply the process that he has initiated will penetrate Soviet society.

The Sources of Change in the Soviet Union

Why does this type of change occur in the Soviet Union? Major change in other societies is often described as inevitable. But in political life, all that is inevitable is what has already happened. This is particularly true in a country such as the Soviet Union, where social, economic, and cultural forces are largely subordinated to political considerations. The simplest answer to the question, therefore, is that these changes in the Soviet Union are taking place because a new leader took the reins of power and found them either desirable or necessary or both. If Brezhnev or Chernenko had lived several years longer, the Soviet "reconstruction" would probably not now be taking place.

Although the transition in leadership was a necessary cause of the changes, it was far from sufficient. Six major factors combined to bring them about: the domestic performance of the Soviet system in the Brezhnev era; the new requirements for Soviet economic growth; the changed nature of Soviet society and the conditions for its stability; the character and consequences of the technological revolution in capitalist societies; the deterioration of the international position of the Soviet Union; and finally, the ascent not only of a new individual but of an entire political generation to leadership.

The Crisis of the System Under Brezhnev

One phrase used by the new General Secretary at the June, 1987 Plenum of the Central Committee succinctly sums up the present leadership's assessment of the Brezhnev era; it was characterized, he said, by the appearance of "pre-crisis phenomena." The implication is that, without the urgent actions undertaken by Brezhnev's successors, the Soviet Union would have found itself today in an acute crisis that would endanger the stability of the regime. The new leadership also makes it amply clear that the "pre-crisis" conditions were present in almost all fields of domestic endeavor. By the end of the Brezhnev era, Soviet society was chronically ill. The system was not functioning well.

In the political arena, the most significant development was the alienation not only of the population at large but also of the party, from both the rulers and the regime. Political stability was achieved through coercion, mass political apathy, and a lack of civic spirit. The Party and the administration became highly bureaucratized, penetrated throughout by a corporate spirit that expressed a lack of interest in anything but its own well-being and power and controlled in several regions by Mafia-like informal associations.

While the people of the Soviet Union are highly literate and deeply interested in music, ballet, and literature, the officially sanctioned culture was wooden and banal and the most creative and independent spirits were suppressed or exiled. Even the enforced artistic standard of "socialist realism," with its hollow, relentless optimism could no longer hide the sense of deep cultural pessimism permeating the educated strata of the society. This was the artistic expression of the feeling of hopelessness prevalent among the workers. The Soviet Union has probably been the only major country in the world where the youth neither rebelled nor expressed any youthful enthusiasm that could be channeled into creative public endeavors. The heroes of the youth were their own "private" poets and balladeers (in particular, Vysotsky) who were barely tolerated by the authorities, and their major public expression of dissatisfaction was the flaunting of the artifacts of Western mass culture, such as blue jeans and popular records, officially permitted but never encouraged.

Major reforms, as well as revolutionary transformations grow out of major crises. The Soviet Union is no exception. The new leaders who took power in the Soviet Union in the mid-1980s, and at least a part of the Soviet political elite, knew that they had inherited a country and a system in a state of material and spiritual crisis.

The Economy

Soviet economic performance depended on the viability and efficacy of two things: the Stalinist model of the economy and the model of economic growth. The first has been the organization of the Soviet economy as engineered by Stalin and largely retained by his successors until recently. The second defines the sources and the nature of Soviet economic growth.

The functioning of the Stalinist model of the economy depends on administrative activity and regulation—for this reason it is sometimes described as a "command economy"—and not on self-generating and self-enforcing market forces. The Bolshevik fear of *political* spontaneity found its extreme *economic* expression in the Stalinist model. The Polish economist Oscar Lange aptly characterized this economic model as a "war economy," a definition that has found its way into Soviet economic discussions in the Gorbachev years.

In one discussion in 1986, at which I was present, a member of the Central Committee characterized the Stalinist economic model, which he made clear still existed in the Soviet Union, as "war communism." The use of this term is important in understanding present Soviet thinking on this subject and its attitude toward the Stalinist model. The term describes a short period in Soviet history, during the Civil War roughly from 1918 to 1920, and the economic policy imposed by Lenin during this period. Lenin's "war communism" eliminated both market and money, made wide-ranging use of coercion to confiscate without compensation almost the entire production of the peasantry, nationalized industrial and service units of any kind and size, and regimented labor in a military fashion. "War communism" was the ultimate expression of administrative socialism. The Stalinist economic model was a somewhat less extreme variant of "war communism," but applied on a much larger scale to the expanding Soviet economy. Moreover, while the Leninist model was basically egalitarian in that it distributed poverty equally among the working people even including the party members, Stalinist "war communism" decreed poverty only for the working class and abundance for the party elite.

The model of economic growth that accounts for the enormous expansion of the economy, by now the third largest in the world, from the late 1920s through the Brezhnev era was neither Stalinist nor anti-Stalinist. It was one of extensive growth, which in one form or another characterized other societies at an early or intermediate stage of their modern industrial and agricultural development during their "First Industrial Revolution." Economic expansion was achieved by ever increasing contributions of labor, capital and land into the process of production. The extensive model of growth has persisted in the Soviet Union until the present, making it unique among countries of a similar or even a lower level of industrialization. According to the estimates of the economist Clark Kerr, 90 percent of the economic growth of the United States in the twentieth century was achieved through intensive growth—that is, through technological progress, and only 10 percent through capital investments. For the Soviet Union, these figures are reversed.

The extensive method of growth has its limits, and in the early 1970s these limits were being reached in the Soviet Union. The Soviet political leadership, not to mention Soviet economic experts, were aware that the Soviet economy had to switch to an intensive growth that would rely on productivity of labor and capital through technological progress and better incentives, declining relative costs of production, conservation of raw materials, improved quality of products and a build-up of the infrastructure. The many resolutions, decrees, and exhortations to this effect that emanated from the political leadership in the Brezhnev era bore witness to this.

Yet the understanding of Brezhnev and his associates of the gigantic task facing the Soviet economy in its conversion from extensive to intensive growth was at once superficial, abstract and inconsistent. They had overlearned the lessons of the Soviet Union's initial industrialization. While their speeches and decrees spoke of the necessity of intensive growth, their five-year plans still put the greatest stress on extensive factors. Even when they were making serious efforts to emphasize intensive factors, they were determined, because of inbred conservatism and political and ideological reasons, to attain it without any major changes, through the Stalinist model of the economy.

There existed reasonable compatibility between the Stalinist economic model and the extensive model of growth, especially in a country as large and as rich in labor and natural resources as the Soviet Union. Moreover, this compatibility was largely effective because the Soviet Union was a latecomer to the international process of industrialization and was able for a sustained period to utilize the advantages of its backwardness by borrowing heavily from the technological advances of more developed industrial countries. The First Industrial Revolution—that of heavy industry and basic light industry (e.g., textiles, mining, electrification, and railroads)—can be started and can reach relatively high levels by different methods of growth and within diverse dominant models of the economy. To go further, however, requires methods for which the Stalinist system does not provide an effective framework.

Before it assumed power, the new leadership had already recognized elements of the unhappy economic reality hidden behind Brezhnev's bombastic phrases about "advanced socialism." They had reached the conclusion that what was required was a simultaneous change of the model of the economy from the Stalinist administrative, command economic organization to an as yet undefined system in which market forces would play a much more significant role. It must be distressing for the Soviet leaders to recognize that Marx's dictum that the relations of production become a fundamental obstacle to the development of productive forces—that is, the prevailing economic system can stifle economic growth—applies not to the capitalist, but to the socialist countries, and particularly to the Soviet Union.

The New Soviet Society

The society over which the new Soviet leadership presides is in many respects different from the one of 20 to 30 years ago. It is a younger society, where those between the ages of 18 and 35 constitute about 60 percent of the urban labor force, and those born after Stalin's death in 1953 account for two thirds of the total population. It is a society in which the level of skills of industrial workers and employees has risen markedly. It is a society socially dominated by a large new middle class, which may be politically fragmented and powerless but which sets the lifestyle for the society at large. It is a far more highly educated society than in Khrushchev's time, in this respect fully comparable to other industrial nations. It is a society with a professional class that is, numerically, the largest in the world. It is also a society in which the previous high rates of upward mobility have declined significantly and, thus, where the structure of class, status, and power has become more settled and permanent than before. The superimposition of a stagnant, conservative political leadership and a system where politics is in full command, on a society that was changing significantly, created a chasm between the regime and the society at large.

The socio-political stability of the Soviet regime was not entirely predicated on the regime's highly coercive character, or on the harshness of the Soviet police state. The regime passed several significant tests of stability for which the level of coercion alone could not account. The victory in the Second World War, the abolition of Stalinist mass terror after 1953, the ineffectiveness of dissent in the 1960s and its isolation and the decimation of its practitioners in the 1970s, and the lack of major disorders in the non-Russian republics in the post-Stalin era are the most notable examples.

The changing Soviet social landscape diminished the effectiveness of many of the traditional non-coercive sources of stability and introduced new destabilizing forces. It is ironic that, in a country with an official vision of a secular Utopia, the people's actual expectations were, for many decades, very modest. These modest political, social, cultural, and economic expectations were the result of bitter experience, of dashed hopes, and of perenially unfulfilled promises.

The last decade, however, has been different. The expectations of the peasantry as a whole and of the older generation of the working class have remained modest, since their point of comparison has been a more difficult past. But the economic expectations of the *younger* working class have been much higher, and their dissatisfaction with their status, particularly with their economic conditions, more overt. *Their* point of comparison has not been the past, but rather the much higher current status of the middle class, the economic conditions of the politically privileged, and, especially in the large metropolitan areas, second- or third-hand knowledge or suspicions about conditions in the West or in Eastern Europe.

To make matters worse, the urban working population and the members of the middle class who are now in their late thirties grew up during the Khrushchev period, with its unrealistic promises of heaven on earth. In other societies bad conditions alone do not necessarily promote instability; it is conditions of improvement and raised hopes, followed by visible deterioration, that are potentially destabilizing. Such a pattern can be discerned in the Soviet Union. In the decade of 1965–1974, the Soviet Union began the process of the Second Industrial Revolution and significantly improved the level of consumption throughout the society, especially in durable consumer goods and housing. By the beginning of the next decade, however, this process had ended, and stagnation and even decline far outweighed any improvements.

The Soviet middle class felt increasingly frustrated by the discrepancy between its social status and its political and economic position. Politically, it was entirely powerless. Its substrata were fragmented and politically vulnerable, isolated from one another and from the political elite, which was characterized by a closed network of friendship, and from the working people below, whom they regarded with ill-concealed disdain.

The middle class was particularly frustrated by its economic position. Its members were the victims of the policies of economic leveling and egalitarianism, practiced by both Khrushchev and Brezhnev, which resulted in the middle class being paid salaries lower than those of highly skilled workers or cotton growers. Moreover, their salaries were deliberately frozen beginning in the early 1970s. The middle class was moving into a state of social anomie.

The case of the Soviet upper-middle class is of special importance here. This upper segment is composed of two groups, which are distinguished by the Soviets as the "creative intelligentsia" (including writers, film makers, journalists, artists, and scientists) and as the "technical intelligentsia" composed of engineers, agronomists, economists, and statisticians. In Western terminology, both of these groups would be referred to as "professionals." Not all of the elements of middle class dissatisfaction were felt by every part of the professional strata; scientists, for example, were better paid than economists.

Many significant causes of the professionals' frustration and alienation from the system first appeared during the Brezhnev era. The essence of their alienation was a single fact: most professions in the Soviet Union are treated by the political rulers as no different from occupations such as plumbers, carpenters, or tractor drivers. Professions in the West generally enjoy a high degree of autonomy: in the Soviet Union professionals are not at all independent.

In addition to being treated no differently than plumbers or tractor drivers, Soviet professionals are beset by both practical and political problems, as the following examples will illustrate: the doctor who has neither syringes nor needles available for necessary injections; the playwright whose play is transformed beyond recognition by constant "advice and suggestions" from cultural officials; the economist who is without accurate information about the Soviet economy, in fact knowing less than Western economic specialists on the Soviet Union; the filmmaker whose film, which has been made only after major concessions have been made to the system, then disappears into the vaults of the Ministry of Culture; the professor of Renaissance history who is unable, even once, to visit Italy; the physicist who is cut off from contacts with his Western colleagues working on projects similar to his own; the journalist who is forced to deny in print an outrage that he himself witnessed; and the poet who is forced to write the same Party line as the general, but the general always says it before him.

The Soviet professional strata have now attained a socially critical mass. They are indispensable to the smooth running of the Soviet system. Most of them aspire to a truly professional status, which conflicts with the role assigned to them by their government, which is characterized by a lack of independence and freedom for self-expression. The fact that they are more aware than before of the possibility of better conditions only serves to intensify their frustration and alienation.

Moreover, in contrast with the middle class as a whole, its upper crust, the professionals, have been able to develop social networks, centered on individuals like the Moscow theatrical director, Yuri Lyubimov, or an institution (*e.g.,* the Novosibirsk branch of the Soviet Academy of Science). Much of the current analysis of the Soviet "precrisis situation" emanating from the Gorbachev administration, and many of the policies that he initiated, were discussed among professional groups during Brezhnev's rule. There can be little doubt that the stirrings of the professionals in the late 1970s and early 1980s prepared some of the ground for the Gorbachev policies. The new leadership was able to identify the growing tensions between the new society and the antediluvian socio-political and economic system. It recognized, furthermore, that the system's sources of stability had seriously deteriorated in the late Brezhnev era and in the period of interregnum in the early 1980s. Gorbachev's policies are intended to rescue the Soviet system from this growing and potentially explosive destabilizing social force through far-reaching directed change. In this limited sense Gorbachev's function is similar to that of President Franklin D. Roosevelt during the Great Depression: to save the system from its own follies by a process of evolutionary reformation.

It is clear that the new leadership is also beginning to understand that plans must take into account the new character of Soviet society, which is far less malleable than it was in the past. The circumstances that made possible the accomplishment of the past "revolutions from above," especially the one imposed by Stalin—a peasant society vulnerable to mass terror—are no longer present. Gorbachev's task is not to crush any class or group but rather to create conditions that will stimulate and engage the energies of all of them. What is needed is the creation of conditions that will promote the self-interests of the various strata in modernization. What is necessary is to create a coincidence of interests between the modernizing interests of the state and the society. Gorbachev hopes for a reconciliation of the interests of the state with those of the society, which is the new requirement of stability in the Soviet Union.

The Technological Challenge from the West

The Soviet population, particularly outside the major metropolitan areas, measures Soviet economic progress by comparing their present conditions to those of the past. For the Soviet leadership and political elite as well as larger professional groups, however, the key measure of progress was and continues to be that of the industrially advanced capitalist countries. This is a Soviet tradition. Beginning with Lenin and intensifying under Stalin and afterward, the slogan of "catching up and surpassing" the principal capitalist countries was at the center of attention.

Three causes are responsible for this tradition, which is as strong today as it was in the past: Soviet ideology, Soviet security and foreign policy, and the psychology of the Soviet leadership. The official ideology proclaims the superiority of the socialist over the capitalist system. This superiority is to be primarily, although not exclusively, demonstrated in the economic sphere. To do so the Soviet Union must grow faster than the main capitalist countries, surpass the main "capitalist bastion," the United States, in the absolute size of its Gross National Product (G.N.P.) and eventually in the per capita size of the G.N.P., and then to move beyond the capitalist world in technological sophistication. As Lenin wrote, "In the final analysis the competition and struggle between capitalism and socialism will be resolved in favor of the system that attains a higher level of economic productivity."

The close relationship between a country's economic strength and its military power and international influence is a truism in the modern era, one which has been elevated by the Soviet leadership to be the central premise of their economic policy. Their fear of "capitalist encirclement" assumed undying enmity between the Soviet and imperialist states, with the ever-present danger of war. They assumed also, particularly with the growth of Soviet military power, an unending and unrelenting Soviet-capitalist competition in the international arena for control and influence, for strategic bases and economic advantages. For Lenin, "peaceful coexistence" meant only a *peredyshka,* a "breather," between the inevitable clashes with imperialism. This attitude was reinforced by Stalin and tempered, but not abandoned, in the post-Stalin era with the advent of the nuclear age.

The economic strength of the Soviet Union relative to the capitalist states has played a major role in the leadership's thinking about foreign policy in at least three ways. First, to be effective as a model for others the Soviet Union had to be more successful than its capitalist adversaries economically, and in particular, more technologically successful. Second, to conduct an active, and increasingly global, foreign policy, to have allies and friends, the Soviet Union has had to be able to protect major resources abroad. The cost of these resources was high and required a strong and dynamic economy. Third, the stability, loyalty, and control of the Soviet empire in Eastern Europe, Cuba, and Vietnam could not depend exclusively on the presence of Soviet military power. The Soviet Union had to be able to offer these countries economic resources and technological progress to assure their sociopolitical stability and loyalty.

The importance to the Soviet leadership of measuring their own economic-technological progress by Western standards has had a psychological dimension. It has often been noted that the Soviets, even in high places, suffer from feelings of inferiority toward the West. Their often blustering, arrogant behavior is intended to compensate externally for their inner feelings. One might expect that, with the advent of strategic parity and recognized global power status, these feelings of inferiority would disappear. Nothing of the sort has happened. The persistent Soviet demand to be recognized as "equals" by the Americans expresses a psychological need for reassurance about their position in terms of world power, as if they themselves did not believe it.

This insecurity would radically diminish were it not for the fact that by the standards of contemporary Western civilization the Soviet Union is not at all the equal of the United States. It lags behind the West not only by material standards, but also in the relationship between the state and society, the civic culture, and indeed, the very concept of citizenship. The comparative perspective then serves as a reference point for the self-evaluation of the Soviet leader.

In the last 15 years, almost all capitalist countries entered the era of the Third Industrial Revolution. The Soviet Union has yet to create many of the requisites for this revolution, from reliable telephone networks to the much more complicated production of such primary electronic components as super-miniaturized microchips. By the end of the 1970s, some members of the Soviet political class and the professionals were well aware of the revolution that was sweeping the West and the Far East, but the Soviet leadership apparently did not understand the nature of the challenge nor did it contemplate a realistic Soviet response to it.

The Third Industrial Revolution of the capitalist world was gearing up at the same time that Soviet economic growth was slowing down. The simultaneity of these two developments was calamitous for the domestic and international aspirations of the Soviet rulers. Excluding the Second World War, the decade from mid-1970s to the mid-1980s was the first prolonged period in Soviet history when the Soviet Union was falling behind the capitalist nations according to the key economic indicators of growth. Most importantly, the technological gap between the Soviet Union and the advanced capitalist countries was sharply widening.

Yet even these comparisons do not tell the main story. The most important comparisons concern factors that can seldom be quantified. The major physical indicators of Soviet production, which were once the most visible signs of its accomplishment and a matter of great pride to the Soviet leadership, political elite and people, now seemed either irrelevant or even an expression of backwardness. A few examples will illustrate this point:

The Soviet Union produces twice as much steel as the United States, with a G.N.P. one-half the size, but still encounters chronic shortages of steel. The reason is simple: the Soviet Union is wasting steel. The amount of steel in Soviet capital and consumer goods is far too high by world standards. Furthermore, Soviet steel mills overproduce low-quality steel and underproduce steel of high caliber.

The Soviet Union is the largest producer of shoes in the world. But an average shoe may fall apart within a few weeks and enormous inventories of shoes that no one wants to buy, at any price, rot in Soviet warehouses.

Soviet educational facilities graduate each year three times as many engineers as do American universities. But we know now from the experience of Soviet-Jewish emigration to the United States that only a few of them can qualify to work in American industry because of their extremely narrow specialization and the severe limits on their knowledge of contemporary production technologies and methods.

The Soviet Union is the world's largest producer of lumber, but Soviet industrial utilization of lumber constitutes only 30 percent of its weight, while in America, Canada, or Sweden, the rate of utilization is 95 percent. More than one-half of the Soviet production of lumber does nothing but rob future generations of their inheritance of natural resources.

What counts economically in the contemporary world is not the quantity but the productivity of the production process, the modernity of the product mix, and the costs, quality and the ready availability of the products. In all of these respects, in the last 15 years the Soviet Union has regressed relative to the West.

The present Soviet leaders are well aware of this state of affairs. They feel that their sense of purpose is endangered. Their patriotic pride is hurt. The progress of Japan and the modernization of the newly industrial nations in Asia must be a particularly bitter pill for them to swallow. More importantly, what they understand as their destiny of international greatness has been called into question. Their sense of urgency in countering the economic and technological challenge is reinforced by their fears of its potential military consequences. They recognize that their international aspirations cannot be reconciled in the long term with their relative economic weaknesses and the narrow range of their foreign policy resources. In the final analysis, this is the deepest source of the present Soviet leaders' commitment to real change.

The Soviet International Position

Toward the end of the 1960s and during the early 1970s, the Soviet international position significantly improved. It appeared to the Soviets that a great change in international politics was taking place, the fulfillment of a dream for which generations had been sacrificed. The Soviet leadership began to regard the favorable change in the correlation of forces as a secular trend with the potential of becoming irreversible. Soviet leaders expected favorable consequences from American public recognition of a state of strategic parity with the Soviet Union. The *Ostpolitik* and the *detente* of the early 1970s were increasingly considered by the Soviet leaders to be an offensive strategy. *Detente* seemed to guarantee the avoidance of dangerous confrontations with the United States, the stabilization of Europe including the recognition of Soviet domination of East-Central Europe, the expansion of economic relations with the West including the large-scale technology transfers needed by the Soviets, and at the same time a free hand for Soviet expansion in the Third World.

By the late 1970s and early 1980s, however, the Soviet international position had deteriorated significantly. While *detente* with Western Europe was still alive, the Soviet invasion of Afghanistan in 1979 put an end to Soviet-American *detente*. American defense policies in the late 1970s, and particularly in the early 1980s, ended the deterioration of the strategic balance against America. The Soviet deployment of SS-20s in Europe backfired by bringing the Atlantic Alliance closer together. The Soviet anti-Intermediate Nuclear Force (I.N.F.) campaign was a textbook example of diplomatic clumsiness following a major military blunder.

While still weary of international military involvements, the United States had largely abandoned its post-Vietnam nihilistic attitude toward international activism, and had regained much of its sense of confidence. It increased its military budget and began a new stage in the modernization of its conventional forces. At the same time, the Soviet Union found itself overextended. Its international commitments were a drain on Soviet resources and held no promise of short-term victories. Indeed, the so-called national liberation movements that in the 1970s were a symbol of increased Soviet influence, became by the early 1980s anti-Soviet forces. The Soviet Union found itself without major friends abroad and with a troubled empire at home.

The Soviet Union's relative international decline combined with its domestic crisis led to an urgent reassessment of the strategic direction of Soviet security and foreign policies. The unimaginative Soviet leadership, tactically inflexible and strategically frozen in old concepts and traditional policies, could not even begin to redress the situation. The obvious seriousness of the Soviet predicament provided a forceful stimulus for change. As Gorbachev and his associates have argued, the most important Soviet foreign and security policy statement consists of the program of domestic renewal and radical reform.

The Soviet Succession

The five factors examined thus far explain why, in the early 1980s, a powerful force for change was building in the Soviet Union. Yet such radical, multidimensional change was not at all inevitable. What *was* inevitable was that without such change the crisis of effectiveness that had gripped the Soviet Union in its domestic and international roles would deepen, and at some point might become a crisis of the nation's very *survival.* The powerful need for change had to find a historical agent to transform it from a potential into a reality. This historical agent emerged during the Soviet succession, confirming once again the central role of leadership in human affairs.

It was inevitable that the leadership succession after Chernenko's death in March, 1985, when the pressures for change were particularly strong, would have become a catalyst for reform. That these reforms, however, became so broad in scope and fundamental in nature was the result of four characteristics of this particular succession: it involved not one but three changes in the position of the General Secretary; it involved a major turnover in the top leadership and upper levels of the elite in all spheres of Soviet life; it both overlapped with and facilitated generational change within the Soviet political elite; and it placed in the position of General Secretary a reform-minded and headstrong leader whose personality and mindset are decidedly different from those of the members of the party apparatus from which he emerged.

In its entire history the Soviet Union has had only four top leaders— Lenin, Stalin, Khrushchev and Brezhnev. In the present succession, however, within the span of less than three years, four leaders consecutively occupied the position of General Secretary—Brezhnev, Andropov, Chernenko and Gorbachev. Moreover, those four leaders were very different from one another and each represented a different base of power. This had a number of consequences. The personal loyalties within the top leadership and between elite groups and top level leaders, established through decades of association, were now weakened or broken.

This pattern of succession permitted a leader who did not have a developed political machine, who was a newcomer and a relative outsider to the top leadership, and whose pro-reform orientation was known well before his victory, to win the top prize. Brezhnev, when he assumed power, had been a member of the Politburo for 13 years and of the Central Committee for 20. Andropov had been a member of the Politburo for almost 15 years and of the Central Committee for 17 years before 1982. Chernenko had been a member of the Politburo for 10 years and of the Central Committee for 15 years. Gorbachev had been in the Politburo, of which he was the youngest member, for less than five years, and a member of the Central Committee for only 10 years. A contender for the top position, regardless of his real preferences concerning the substance of policies and patterns of politics, normally cannot disclose any tendencies toward reform as long as the old leader is in charge. That Gorbachev was in the Politburo for a relatively short time increased the likelihood that he might be an innovator. Moreover, he assumed power under highly unusual, almost emergency, conditions. Under these circumstances, and with a powerful patron, Yuri Andropov, Gorbachev was identified as a reform-minded leader as early as 1982.

Gorbachev was, to a large extent, an outsider in the top leadership until he assumed power. In all probability, he was designated by Andropov to be his successor and was denied the position by Chernenko. In the period between Brezhnev's death in 1982 and Gorbachev's election in 1985 he was not adopted by the Old Guard nor did he seek an alliance with them. In fact, Gorbachev was selected for the top position because there was a large enough mass of members in the Politburo who did not dare to oppose his candidacy and again select another member of the Old Guard such as Chernenko. The mood of frustration among the elite and the Party unmistakably favored the selection of a new man. But his margin of victory was actually quite narrow. For Gorbachev the outsider, the Politburo's dirty trick of electing Chernenko in 1984 and the struggle and estrangement from the Old Guard in the period of 1984–1985 clearly reinforced his reform tendencies and nontraditionalist approach.

In retrospect, one should not underestimate the significance of the Chernenko "Incident": the selection for the top leadership position, in a situation of deep crisis and growing expectations, of a nonentity, a second-rate Party hack. The anger, disgust and shame in segments of the political elite, or the educated strata and parts of the population, significantly weakened the power of the Old Guard. This made the election of Gorbachev when Chernenko died easier than it otherwise would have been and undermined the prestige of the Old Guard. On the other side of the ledger, in one respect the Chernenko interlude increased the difficulty of the job of new leadership. The election of

Andropov in 1982 to succeed Brezhnev met with enthusiasm within the elite and, it appeared, overall support and growing expectations among the professionals and the population in the large metropolitan centers. The let-down, to put it mildly, that set in with Andropov's death and the election of Chernenko, muted the enthusiasm, the expectations and people's willingness to commit their active support to Chernenko's successor.

Succession can, in a narrow sense, be understood as the simple act of replacement of the top Soviet leader. In a broader sense, however, it includes the change of the top leadership *group* and even large segments of the political elite. In this broad sense, the succession is even today not entirely finished at the top leadership level and far from complete at the level of the political elite. For practical purposes the Politburo, the Party Secretariat, and the Presidium of the Council of Ministers are institutions of the top leadership, and the Central Committee of the Party is the institution that defines the Soviet top political elite.

Still, the turnover of the leadership and top and intermediate level political elite during Gorbachev's short tenure in office has been very high. At the Twenty-seventh Party Congress that convened one year after Chernenko's death about 40 percent of the Central Committee members were replaced. (A similar percentage was replaced at Khrushchev's Twentieth Party Congress, which took place three years after Stalin's death.) In the entire Secretariat of the Central Committee there remains only one person who occupied the same position in the Brezhnev era. In the Politburo, including both full and candidate members, only three leaders have been held over from the Brezhnev era, one of whom is on his way out (the boss of the Ukraine, Shcherbitsky), and the other two, Andrei Gromyko and Mikhail Solsmentsev, occupy largely symbolic positions. The replacements in the elites of all major hierarchies and almost all Republics is accelerating, and will probably reach an apogee at the Nineteenth Party Conference in June 1988. This is the result not simply of the reforming character of Gorbachev's leadership, or of the extent of his power, which is still circumvented, but of the actuarial tables as well. Gorbachev inherited from Brezhnev a leadership group and a political elite that was much older than at any point in Soviet history, and with the exception of Mao's China, probably the oldest in the world. Demographics helped to reinforce Gorbachev's ability to push his reform initiatives.

The post-Brezhnev succession coincided with the change of political generations in the Soviet political elite and the leaderships of the major bureaucratic hierarchies. In all of Soviet history there has been only one comparable period—between the Seventeenth and the Eighteenth

Party Congresses, from 1934–1939. In this period, Stalin's great purge replaced the revolutionary Bolshevik generation with a new elite composed of people who had come to political maturity since the revolution and who owed their promotions to Stalin himself. The post-Brezhnev succession is now replacing this political generation.

During the first year of Gorbachev's succession I characterized the newcomers to elite positions, as a group, in the following way:

> These new leaders seem to be less ideological and more interested in efficiency in domestic policies. They believe that the economic system should be improved by reforms that will stress increased managerial rights, greater efficiency, and technological progress, more rational methods of planning, and the use of pricing and cost-effectiveness considerations. But they do not believe in changing the fundamental principles of the system. They seem to think that a thorough overhaul of the system with its existing structures, conducted by the new Party and state managers, will exploit enormous reserves of productivity that were left fallow by the old, tired, and complacent leadership. The primary requirement they believe is discipline. They feel that in the long run partial reforms and enforced demands for greater work discipline and greater responsibility of managers of basic production and service units will produce an upsurge in economic growth. (Seweryn Bialer, *The Soviet Paradox* [New York: Alfred A. Knopf, 1986], pp. 119–120)

In light of what has happened in the Soviet Union in the last two years, was my characterization accurate? In my opinion, it was correct when it was written, and to a large extent remains so even today, but with three important reservations. First, the new political generation is much less homogeneous than it seemed at that time; even as Gorbachev came to power, an important segment of the new elite stratum was already far more critical of the system and convinced of the need for deeper changes than those initiated in 1985. Second, under the influence of Gorbachev and his close associates, many in the new elite accepted the need for more profound changes, and not only in the economy, than they had sought when the succession process had just begun. Third, the main actor in the succession, Gorbachev himself, had a vision of change in the Soviet Union that went further than his initial policies and speeches had suggested. Gorbachev and his close associates moved well ahead of the mood and temper of the overall new elite generation.

Finally, the person and character of Gorbachev himself looms very large. When he took power he was an almost unknown quantity in the West. Today, after having been in office for more than two-and-one-half years, we can speak with some confidence about key aspects of his personality and his style of leadership, and the extent of his commitment to change—although the deepest motivations for his plans and actions may well remain hidden.

Gorbachev has demonstrated that he is a leader in the strict sense of the term: that he has the "capacity or fitness for drawing others, for guiding them, for giving a particular quality or character to a movement." This was not always the case with the Party's General Secretaries in the post-Stalin era. Khrushchev had strong elements of it, which, however, other elements of his character and his pattern of behavior either counteracted or nullified. In his short tenure in office, Andropov showed clear promise as a leader. Neither Brezhnev, nor, of course, Chernenko, were leaders in the sense in which I use the term here. The second was a puppet to whom even the extremely strong paraphernalia of his office afforded little stature and dignity. The first was primarily a "Chairman of the Board," a corporate chieftain who reconciled bureaucratic interests, but utterly without personal dynamism. By contrast, Gorbachev is admired, is being emulated, and has stamped the imprint of his own personality on the powerful position he holds. Even people who do *not* believe in the ultimate success of his program admire him. Among his close supporters and aides he has been able to create in this very short period of time an aura of exceptionality, of charisma.

It is also clear that Gorbachev is an astute politician. He came into office lacking a personal political machine of his own. His bureaucratic power base is still extremely frail. He came to power at a time of domestic and international difficulty, with exaggerated expectations of what he could achieve and how quickly he could accomplish it. And yet, without producing any visible material improvements at home, he was able to consolidate his power at the top and prepare conditions for a similar consolidation at the upper-middle levels of the political elite at the Party Conference scheduled for June, 1988. He established himself as an international statesman and has taken the initiative in arms control.

As a politician he is, unlike Khrushchev, quite cautious, but at the same time he can make decisive personnel and policy decisions. By Soviet standards, he is well educated. Where Khrushchev was primarily emotional, he is cerebral. He can both plan ahead and improvise. His previous experience was quite limited, but he is a quick learner. More importantly, he is critical and skeptical. He has a questioning mind. At heart he is an innovator who does not accept answers just because they come from an authoritative source, or reflect past experience. He shows great determination to implement his views, and by all accounts has a forceful personality. He is probably driven by patriotism and historical personal ambition to reverse the decline of his country.

Gorbachev is the first Soviet leader since Lenin who does not read his speeches but actually talks to his audience. As a speaker he is both exciting and convincing. He is adept at informal exchanges, at telling jokes, and at working a crowd. He is learning to use television; in his televised appearances, he is a serious, powerful, and sincere personality. People respond to him partly because he appears to show genuine curiosity about their work and lives. One has the impression that even if the majority is still skeptical about the durability and success of his "new course," Gorbachev is nevertheless able to ignite in them a spark of interest and even excitement. He is a modern leader in the sense that he has begun to conceive "modernity" not as a thing, an object, but primarily as a set of attitudes or approaches that is innovative and dynamic in all spheres of activity.

When we examine the question of the origin of the present cycle of change in the Soviet Union, the question leads to an answer that stresses the confluence of a number of critical objective and subjective factors, both domestic and international, but that cannot attach specific weights to each of these factors. The centrality of each of these factors is unquestionable. Yet what was decisive for the cycle of changes to take hold in the Soviet Union was not their individual weight but rather their confluence.

First, the multidimensional Soviet domestic crisis incubated for a long period of time. Its scope and depth was magnified by the inaction of the past leadership. By the end of Brezhnev's rule the crisis constituted a virtual emergency.

Second, the technological progress in the capitalist world, combined with Soviet stagnation, reawakened fears for Soviet security and global status. It unleashed in the political elite the deepest motivating force, Russian patriotism, in favor of reform.

Third, changes in the structure of the Soviet society coincided with the determination of the new Soviet leadership to pursue modernization at almost any cost. The necessity to mobilize the intelligentsia to support reforms combined with bureaucratic opposition to change created the need to fuse economic reform with political democratization and cultural liberalization.

Fourth, and finally, the existence of a man like Gorbachev, with his talents *and* independent thinking, within the Party apparatus, and his elevation to a position of top leadership was an accident of history. In his almost three years in office, Gorbachev has grown in stature and shown impressive qualities of leadership and a growing determination to reform the Soviet Union. He became, indeed, a central factor in the attempt to modernize the Soviet Union politically, socially, culturally and economically.

The Significance of Changes
in the Soviet Union

Neither Western statesmen and experts, nor the Soviet educated stratum, have formed a consensus on the significance of the changes in the Soviet Union that Gorbachev has already wrought or that he plans to effect. It could hardly be otherwise when the process of change in the Soviet Union has just begun and when the political and expert community in the West is divided by ideological predispositions that influence their analyses. This threshold question, thus, emerges: what yardsticks apply when evaluating the present changes in the Soviet Union and their apparent directions, and what expectations are realistic and what are not?

Economically, the Soviet Union is not becoming a capitalist country. Markets and capitalist economic instruments existed before the advent of capitalism and are potentially compatible with diverse economic models including nationalized, socialist economies. Yet the marriage of the market and capitalist economic mechanisms with socialism is, and will probably remain, very far from complete in the Soviet Union. Economic rationality will certainly expand and grow. But major economic decisions will remain under the administrative control of the political authorities.

Politically, the Soviet Union is not becoming a Western democracy. Nor are there any indications that this is a goal toward which the Soviet leadership desires to move. Probably some institutions of Western democracy will develop in the Soviet Union, but these will not lead to a Western system in the foreseeable future. The Western democratic model is not the birthright of every nation or society nor is it the natural state for all societies. The odds of a Western-style democracy developing in an immense, multi-national country that has never in its entire history known a single day of political democracy are very long.

Socially, the Soviet Union is not becoming an open society with few restrictions on the free flow of information. It is not becoming a society in which the relations between the state and the society are bridged by authentic participation and a network of voluntary, independent associations or in which the prerogatives of the state are sharply curtailed. Freedom of religious belief and practice is not being restored, or rather created, in the Soviet Union. The freedom to abstain from political participation, to develop legal forms of employment free from state control, to earn private incomes are as yet only marginally enhanced by the reforms. Nor is the dominance of the Russians and to some extent other Slavs over non-Russians in almost all fields of endeavor now being abandoned in the Soviet Union.

In my opinion, the critical benchmark for the evaluation of change in the Soviet Union is the Russian and Soviet historical experience itself. It is as unwise to dismiss changes within this framework as unimportant for Russia and the West and irrelevant to our assessment of the convergence of Gorbachev's reform as it is unwarranted to see them as forerunners of the convergence of the two kinds of systems.

There are two recurring patterns of Russian and Soviet history within which Gorbachev's experiment can be understood. One is simple: it refers to Russia as the eternal latecomer, trailing behind the West in industrial, technological and scientific progress. This analysis invariably notes that Russia tried cyclically to catch up by borrowing from the West and engaging in revolutions from above and in revitalization movements. Peter the Great and Alexander II are invariably cited as examples of these cycles. From such a historical perspective, the Bolshevik Revolution could *also* be seen as another such movement of revitalization. Gorbachev fits perfectly into this pattern. While in the most general way true, this pattern tells us little about the substance and relative significance of the reforms begun by Gorbachev. It offers no guidance, concerning the nature of the borrowing from the West under Gorbachev as compared with that under his predecessors.

The second pattern, one that I prefer, emphasizes the ebb and flow of change in the Soviet system that occurs initially in one sphere of public life and is then carried to other spheres. The Soviet Union has gone through four primary cycles of change and two transitional periods, all associated with the person and program of a specific leader. The first cycle, with Lenin in power, performed a *political* revolution and consolidated it in the victorious Civil War. "War Communism" (1918–20), as it was called, an attempt to use political power for the transformation of the society, the economy and the culture, was based on the unrealistic assumption that the Bolshevik Revolution would spread to Europe. The restabilization of the advanced capitalist countries of Europe forced a Soviet retreat and the limitation of the Bolshevik Revolution to the political sphere.

Stalin's accession to supreme power in the Party, and his policies in the decade of 1928–1939, brought about a social, cultural, and economic transformation through the use of political power. This cycle ran its course when the political system that Stalin inherited was itself transformed into a personal dictatorship based on mass terror. Stalin's economic and social revolution was much deeper and more difficult for the Soviet people, and had more important consequences than the strictly political revolution of Lenin. However, without Lenin's political revolution Stalin's transformations would have been impossible. But it was Stalin's program of change that decisively shaped the Soviet system as we know it today.

When Stalin died, the choices open to the successor leadership, which until mid-1957 was collective, were in some respects wide and in others quite narrow. They were narrow with regard to two key characteristics of Stalin's rule: unlimited personal dictatorship and mass terror as the basic method of rule. The entire political elite and the top echelons of all bureaucratic hierarchies, including the K.G.B., and the custodians of the means of violence, the Soviet High Command, yearned for an end to both. They simply wanted to enjoy the privileges granted to them by Stalin without the fear associated with the all-pervasive mass terror and the arbitrariness of Stalin's personal dictatorship. Only a leader who would fulfill these yearnings had a realistic chance of ruling Russia.

The choices, however, open to Khrushchev in the social, political, economic and cultural fields, and in foreign and security policy, were quite broad. During his rise to power, Khrushchev embraced a number of policies in these areas that broke with Stalin's policies and that served him well in his struggle with his powerful, conservative opponents. He continued to move away from Stalinism even after he consolidated his power in 1957 with the defeat of the "anti-party" group and the dismissal of Marshal Zhukov. The Khrushchev era clearly marks a separate cycle. It partially dismantled the Stalinist political system. In other areas some of Stalin's major policies and many organizational arrangements were significantly changed (*e.g.,* the immense growth of investments in agriculture, the abolition of the Machine Tractor Stations [M.T.S.], the Sovnarkhozy structure, etc.). Yet, the key Stalinist institutions outside the strictly political field remained intact. Most importantly, the Stalinist model of the economy entirely survived Khrushchev's reforms.

Gorbachev's rule begins a fourth new cycle of change. It already touches almost every sphere and field of public life—just as Stalin's revolution did. Its centerpiece, however, its dominant element to which changes in other fields are subordinated, is economic. Gorbachev's program amounts to an attempt to dismantle the Stalinist model of the economy. The logic of Gorbachev's dismantling effort, however, also requires major social, cultural, ideological and eventually political reforms.

The pattern of the ebb and flow of transformations in Soviet history contains, therefore, two phases in which the system was created, Lenin's and Stalin's on the one hand, and two phases, Khrushchev's and Gorbachev's, in which Stalin's system is being dismantled on the other. In both cases the political cycle of change was followed by a socio-economic crisis; in both cases political change was the point of departure for the socio-economic changes; in both cases different major leadership figures presided over the political as compared to the socio-economic cycle of transformation; and in both cases the political and socio-economic cycles were separated by periods of transition.

On the surface, the two transitional periods—the years of the New Economic Program (N.E.P.) and the Brezhnev era—appear to be sharply different. Yet in some ways they were similar, particularly in the function that they served in the process of change in the Soviet Union. In both periods modifications of the system were incremental rather than sweeping. In both periods the internal contradictions of the system accumulated and led finally to a crisis. Both periods provided conditions for the gestation of ideas that eventually led to a new cycle of changes.

Gorbachev's actions and programs are thus of potentially historical significance. They may already be more important than the transformations in the Soviet system wrought by Khrushchev. In the same way that Lenin paved the political way for Stalin's revolution, Khrushchev established the minimal political conditions for the social, economic, cultural (and ultimately political) revolution that Gorbachev is attempting to force on Russia. His goal seems to be the dismantling of the entire Stalinist legacy, particularly in the socio-economic sphere, which was left largely untouched by Khrushchev.

Gorbachev's post-Stalin predecessors—Khrushchev, Brezhnev, Andropov, and Chernenko—all took Leninism as their ideological touchstone and as the source of legitimacy of the Party's role in Soviet society. Gorbachev and his associates are doing so as well. They are attempting to trace their current reforms and their programs for the future to the period of Lenin.

However, Gorbachev's attempt to revert to Lenin raises a major question: to which Lenin is he reverting? What is his understanding of Leninism? Lenin's political and sociological theories were far from homogeneous, as were his practical policies. There can be no doubt that the Lenin to whom Gorbachev refers so often as his inspiration and as the legitimizer of his reforms is the Lenin of the N.E.P. and the last year of his life.

It is the Lenin who declared a truce with the peasants, restored the "capitalist" institutions of market, money, and small private enterprise, who saw taxation as the main form of regulating private economic activity and cooperatives as the chief form of economic transition to socialism, who sought joint ventures with foreign capital, permitted a very high degree of cultural pluralism, opted for a reconciliation with "bourgeois specialists," and who defined the economic system of N.E.P as "state capitalism." It is the Lenin of the last year of his life who was besieged by doubts about the future, and troubled by many features and patterns of development in the system that he created, who declared the necessity of a slow process of social and political change, who was desperate about the fast-growing bureaucratization of the Soviet state and the growth of bureaucracy in general, who in a private letter to Stalin broke personal relations with him, and who criticized Stalin as the People's Commissar for Nationality Affairs for the excesses and brutality of its dealings with Transcaucasian nations.

Gorbachev's commitment to *this* Lenin seems genuine. This is confirmed by the serious attempt of Soviet historicans and ideologues, at Gorbachev's request, to rethink the experience of N.E.P., and to reevaluate Soviet history from the October, 1917 revolution until Lenin's death. In fact, some of Lenin's views and concerns are relevant to Gorbachev. The most obvious example is the N.E.P. A second example of equal importance and relevance concerns the issue of bureaucratization and bureaucracy which obsessed Lenin toward the end of his life.

The steps Gorbachev has taken during his first three years in office have been directed at important changes in the traditional configuration of the Soviet political, economic, social and cultural institutions. Some of these changes have already proved significant, and partly unexpected. As one Western author has remarked, "We knew that Gorbachev was going to be different. We did not know that he was going to be *that* different." But this is only the beginning. The longer range significance of Gorbachev's changes is primarily in their potential.

Thus far, Gorbachev has been reluctant to publicly express a coherent, integrated vision of what he is working to realize. His slogans— "new ways of thinking," "acceleration," "renewal," and "reconstruction"—resist clear definition. This approach, of course, avoids meaningless promises and emphasizes the pragmatic character of his reform activities.

Soviet officials and economists have a clear appreciation of the existing ills. They also understand, more or less, what they want to achieve. The confusion, unclarity and indecision, however, concerns the question of how to get from here to there. There is nothing unusual about this. Gorbachev, after all, has set a course well outside of his own and his nation's experience.

Three elements constitute the major components of Gorbachev's *political* vision of the future. The first is the curtailment, decentralization and change of the political orientation of the Soviet bureaucracies. The second element is the democratization of Soviet life. The third is the enhanced role of law and legality.

The question of bureaucracy is one of the central problems faced by Gorbachev in his effort to implement his program of transition to modernity and at the same time a key component of his vision of modernity. Gorbachev's policies seek to curtail the bureaucracies, reducing them in size, bringing them closer to the production process, and most importantly, changing their political orientation.

As the Israeli sociologist, Eisenstadt, has demonstrated, from ancient empires to modern days, bureaucracies have displayed three types of political orientation. They are either ruler-dependent, corporatist (that is, centered on their own collective interests), or client-oriented. In reality, particular bureaucratic organizations have seldom conformed precisely to any of the three configurations; rather, they have exhibited combinations of all three. From the time of Stalin's ascension to power to the beginning of Gorbachev's rule, the principal Soviet bureaucratic organizations have experienced two changes.

Under Stalin's personal dictatorship they became more ruler-dependent than those of any modern state (including prewar Nazi Germany). Under Khrushchev, the ruler-dependent orientation of major Soviet bureaucracies slowly eroded. When Khrushchev, during his last two years in office, attempted to build a power base independent of the bureaucracies, the alliance of leaders of *all* major bureaucracies ousted him without difficulty. Brezhnev's rule signaled the transformation of the major bureaucracies into corporatist-oriented bodies, presided over by an oligarchy within which the interests of every principal bureaucracy were represented. The corporatist nature of Soviet bureaucracies, their strength, their ability to escape control from above and pressure from below was only reinforced by the prolonged interregnum between Brezhnev and Gorbachev.

The political logic behind Gorbachev's program of reforms is to suppress the corporatist spirit of Soviet bureaucracies, and to make them at once more leader-oriented and client-oriented. Gorbachev's most important method of dealing with the bureaucracy is his wide-ranging replacement of personnel. This may be effective to some degree in the short run. Yet every bureaucracy has an inherent tendency to become corporatist. The new appointees will in time build their own machines. The real challenge will be to create conditions that will preserve their different political orientation.

Gorbachev confronts the same paradox that faces every major reformer. He has no choice but to use most of the people who broke the machine to repair it. Gorbachev's economic program will reduce the actual power of all bureaucracies, including the all-powerful party *apparatus.* Yet these bureaucracies are indispensable in his efforts to implement far-reaching reforms. The Party *apparatus* is particularly necessary to mobilize an army of Party activists behind his program. He then wants the bureaucracies to work actively against the privileges to which they are accustomed, to work against their own interests.

He is attempting to achieve this through *glasnost'* and grass-roots democratization. The new independence of the media, and particularly of investigative reporting, serve Gorbachev's anti-corporatist purposes by putting pressure on recalcitrant bureaucrats, as does the growing freedom of the creative intelligentsia in the cultural fields. The grass roots democratization of communal affairs, the increased participation of the working people in the life of their economic units, a greater attention to complaints against the abuse of the power and privileges of the local leaders are all intended to restrain the bureaucracies. Yet today in the Soviet Union, these developments, encouraged by the General Secretary, resemble guerrilla warfare against entrenched interests. They are marginally effective hit-and-run raids rather than frontal assaults.

The place of Gorbachev's program of democratization in his vision of the new Soviet Union is intriguing. What the General Secretary says and does suggests that what may emerge in the Soviet Union is something that might be called "inverted democracy." In capitalist democracies, democratic institutions and behavior are primarily those that affect large groups of people; they are macro-institutions. Smaller units, especially those concerned with economic life, are in most cases far from democratic in intent, structure and behavior. Businesses are to a greater or lesser degree authoritarian in nature; workers do not elect their bosses, although they do, of course, have many rights in the workplace and are free to change jobs. Nor are most trade unions democratic.

Gorbachev's "democratic" vision seems to be the reverse of this. He envisages elements of a "grassroots" democracy at the micro-societal level—election by the workers of the enterprise director, election of members of the local soviet, perhaps even genuine elections of local trade union leaders, the accountability of industrial enterprise management to the workers and of local officials to their constituencies, and probably also the genuine election of leaders in primary, *i.e.,* the lowest level, party organizations.

In the society at large, however, Gorbachev's initiatives do not envision democratic patterns in either state or party institutions either now or in the foreseeable future. It would be unjust to assert that Gorbachev anticipates no democratic elements whatsoever here. There is already a greater openness on the part of the Soviet government in dealing with its peoples, an increased flow of information from the top down and a frankness in the public discourse that was previously unknown. Another such element is the attempt to create institutional constraints on officials that will make their abuse of power more difficult. This will also include greater scope for the Soviet citizen to criticize unjust behavior of lower and middle rank officials with less fear of retaliation. Yet, the basic thrust of Gorbachev's program is not in the direction of developing democracy on the macro-level.

Gorbachev seems to be conscious of the unusual nature of the "democracy" he is trying to bring to his country. He has spoken from time to time of the pioneering, innovative role of his efforts and of the Soviet Union becoming a unique international model. On the basis of our observation of efforts to install this sort of "inverted democracy" in capitalist *and* socialist states (such as Yugoslavia), Gorbachev's concept would appear to have little chance of success.

However far Gorbachev stands from Khrushchev's Utopianism, the hopes he attaches to micro-democratic reforms nevertheless contain a strand of Utopian thinking. His efforts are likely to prove futile for at least two reasons. First, historically, modernization neither requires nor is it associated with this kind of democracy. Indeed, the reverse is true. The vertical line of organizational authority, the line-staff division, the need for technological discipline, for steep stratification of responsibilities and rewards all contribute to the authoritarian nature of the modernization of economic institutions. Second, Western sociology has established the validity of the "iron law of oligarchy" in formal organizations: trade unions, governmental bureaucracies, cooperative movements, and religious associations demonstrate, even if their origins are genuinely democratic, that they soon become authoritarian and oligarchic. If this is true within a macro-democratic order like the United States, how much more likely will it be in the Soviet Union, with its traditions.

What is true of Gorbachev's program of democratization in the society at large is equally true of the Communist Party itself. "Democratic centralism" was always identified in the West, and rightly so, as the guiding principle of the Communist Party's internal life and as the pillar of the authoritarian nature of the Party. The principle itself, even if truly adhered to, has nothing in common with our Western understanding of a democratic order. We often forget, however, that the perniciousness of the principle was particularly associated with its breach in practice when the "democratic" disappeared entirely and what was left was the unvarnished and uncompromising "centralism." The pursuit of the principle of "democratic centralism" in Party life

as it was initially intended would constitute a grass roots democratization of the Party.

The restoration in practice of the prefix "democratic" into the centralized principles of Party behavior seems to be exactly what Gorbachev is striving for. Yet even if he achieves this goal, the Soviet
Communist Party will remain a highly authoritarian organization and
not only because of the preservation of its monopolistic position in
the Soviet Union. Even if some individuals whom the upper Party
authorities do not desire are selected to the Party committees at the
lower levels, the professional Party bureaucracy that represents the
Party and oversees its everyday activity will be appointed from Moscow
or from the republican centers. The Party Bureaus and Secretariats on
the local and republican levels, that is, the Party's decision-making
and executive institutions, will be composed of individuals who were
selected by Moscow; the Central Committee of the Party that is empowered to elect the Politburo and Central Secretariat will remain in
fact selected by the Politburo and Secretariat; and the General Secretary
and his closest associates will select the individuals whom they want
to be members of the Politburo and Secretariat, when they consolidate
their power.

Finally, Gorbachev's reforms in the political realm address the question of the role and substance of law and legality in the Soviet Union.
It is not entirely clear how important legal questions are deemed to
be in Gorbachev's program of change. The legal reforms that are
officially contemplated, however, are extensive in design and move
decisively away in substance from the Soviet tradition. They include
the preparation of new criminal and civil codes, as well as a new
code of legal procedures. There is also consideration being given to
the feasibility of separating the office of public prosecutor from the
courts, which are now a part of a single institution, the Ministry of
Justice. This Soviet review of the legal system is also addressing the
changes that would be necessary to bring about the greater independence
of the courts, and greater rights for the accused. Also under consideration are plans to revamp the office of the public defender and to
significantly increase the rights and the independence of the office.
Finally, the Soviets are seeking a reformulation of legal statutes to
codify the actual and proposed changes in the economy, in cultural
life and in communications.

In the discussions concerning the legal system, which are extraordinarily outspoken, and which include not only academics but also
prosecutors, public defenders, judges, Ministry of Justice officials, writers, managers and ordinary citizens, a consensus is emerging about
the role of law in the society and about the rule of law. It bears a

certain resemblance to the German concept of "Rechtsstaat" as it was initiated by Frederick the Great and took shape in nineteenth-century Prussia. This concept conferred enormous prerogatives on the state and favored the state in conflicts with citizens. At the same time, it stressed the sanctity of legal norms, the predictability of legal procedures and the limits of the rights of the State in its relations with citizens or legal entities. While the Prussian legal system may not appeal to Americans, an approximate equivalent of it would constitute a major improvement for the Soviets.

In the economic sphere, Gorbachev seeks to introduce change of two types. The first is the replacement of the Stalinist economic model with one in which market forces and economic instruments would play a major role. The second is a decisive change from an extensive strategy of growth to an intensive one. The issue raised by the second group of changes is not what Gorbachev intends to do, but how successful can he be and how quickly. The first group of changes, however, requires some elaboration.

All Western analysts of communist societies distinguish among various types of reform in a centrally planned economy. The distinction that I have most frequently applied in my own writings are those among policy reforms that redistribute resources; organizational reforms that redistribute authority; and structural reforms that abolish or create basic institutions. The first two types occur within the parameters of the existing system, while the third changes the parameters themselves. Very often these distinctions are expressed by distinguishing between changes "within the system" and changes "of the system."

The Soviet Union is now in a period of rapidly occurring and far-reaching economic change, both in terms of policy and organization, which touches its institutional structure and behavior. The decisions of the Central Committee Plenum in June, 1987 and the State decrees that followed it are, at the time of this writing, the most far-reaching steps taken by Gorbachev in the economic sphere. Gorbachev's proposals to the Plenum were presented as a plan of "fundamental reconstruction of the management of the economy." They mark a radicalization of his vision of the proposed economic future of the Soviet Union.

Can the new system, in its proposed form, fulfill the promise of radical improvement in capital and in labor productivity, in the quality of goods and in the rate of growth? This seems doubtful. In the crucial areas of economic activity, such as price formation, quality control and competition, it is not the market forces that will play the decisive role, but rather the administrative structures. And yet the proposed reform is of great importance. Its significance is that it established the organizational and psychological conditions for a series of reforms to come later. These reforms will introduce the market mechanism into price formation, quality control and competition. The reform announced at the Plenum makes sense only if it is understood as such a prelude.

The *social* domain is of immense importance to Gorbachev's program for the modernization and the transformation of the Soviet Union. The new leadership seeks reconciliation between the regime and society, a relationship endangered during the second half of Brezhnev's leadership. It also seeks to create conditions in which the modernizing impulse will penetrate the society. These aims are not always compatible. Gorbachev's social policies and reforms are oriented toward both. The most important of these policies concern social discipline, welfare, alienation and stratification.

Gorbachev's first acts after assuming power were directed at strengthening social and particularly work discipline. These steps were not intended to be a short-term campaign but rather a long-range, continuous effort. Normative appeals, new laws, but most importantly stricter enforcement of existing laws succeeded in part in improving social discipline. A Soviet official put it into perspective: "A modern society is first of all a society where by and large people are honest and work honestly." The initial aim of these policies was a radical improvement in the working, or rather non-working, habits of the blue and white collar workers. At the time Gorbachev took power the reality was very gloomy, indeed, for both the Soviet leadership and society.

Almost from the beginning, Gorbachev's policies were also directed at strengthening the discipline of the bureaucracies and fighting official corruption. Proper—from the point of view of the interest of the state—bureaucratic behavior can be reduced to two types of behavior: accurate, honest reporting to superiors and a just and thoughtful attitude to the public. On both scores the Soviets created a bureaucratic monster.

Under Brezhnev, the control of the bureaucracies by the political leadership was superficial. Many of the controlling individuals or institutions were coopted by the bureaucracies. The flow of information to the top was outrageously manipulated and misleading, forcing the leaders each year to produce ever more grandiose lies to cover up those of the year before. Officials of lower units provided false documentation to buttress the rosy reports sent upward by their superiors. This reporting pattern created in every bureaucracy a criminal system of mutual interdependence and protection from top to bottom.

Corruption has probably less potential to harm Gorbachev's plans and vision of the future than the bureaucratic ills of dishonest reporting and indifference toward the Soviet public. A modern society cannot tolerate a notoriously high-level flow of false information. Yet, within a highly centralized and coercive system, this may be unavoidable. Research has firmly established that high-coercion systems are low-information systems. Gorbachev does seem to understand that, along with better control and less tolerance, this bureaucratic scourge can be reduced to tolerable levels only if the administrative apparatus is drastically cut in its middle levels, radically decentralized, given new rights and responsibilities on the managerial level, and finally, made more accountable to the public.

In the post-Stalin era, the Soviet Union developed a welfare state of enormous scope, if not of great quality. At the present, this welfare state is facing a most serious crisis. The problem is two-fold. On the one hand, the welfare state fails to perform many of its functions well, is underfinanced and backward. On the other hand, it is far too large, attempting to provide many services it should not, and it is far too expensive. It suffers simultaneously from a crisis of underdevelopment and a crisis of overdevelopment.

The Soviet welfare state performs many services that all welfare states offer, such as retirement pensions, medical care, day care for children, summer camps, and environmental protection. Gorbachev's anti-alcoholism campaign is a good example of a desperately needed program that falls within the purview of a welfare state. Yet most of the traditional functions of a welfare state are seriously underfinanced in the Soviet Union and, in many areas, are of a quality that even the Soviets themselves now describe as scandalous.

The most serious and tragic example of the Soviet welfare state scandal is medical care. An indirect indication of its low priority is the fact that about 70 percent of Soviet doctors are women. This is certainly not intended to imply that women make worse doctors than men, but rather than medicine is a low-paying and thus low-status job and, therefore, it is reserved mainly for women. What occurred in Soviet medical services may be described as de-professionalization. The educational level of medical schools is low. Pharmaceuticals are scarce and of poor quality. Hospital equipment dates from the Second World War. The problems in health care are so serious (as reflected in mortality statistics), that they were singled out as a target for major changes by Gorbachev himself at the June 1987 Plenum.

The crisis of underdevelopment of the Soviet welfare state concerns the quality of the services it provides and the level of financial support it receives. The average pension of 60 rubles a month is not enough for survival.

The underdevelopment crisis is serious, but from the political point of view and from the point of view of socioeconomic development, the overdevelopment crisis of the Soviet welfare state is equally serious and more difficult to tackle. In essence, it is the consequence of a conscious decision by past Soviet leaders, beginning with Khrushchev, to include in welfare services offerings that can be better dealt with through other approaches. Those services include ridiculously low apartment rents under conditions of major housing shortages, very low prices for basic foods, transportation, telephones, and a variety of other goods and services. The complete job security of Soviet workers, regardless of their performance, is also an aspect of social welfare. It is the Soviet equivalent of Western unemployment benefits, but it probably includes a much higher percentage of the work force than does the Western average. All the Soviet welfare services and entitlements are financed by truly enormous state subsidies; the agricultural subsidies, for example, are more than double the retail price of agricultural products in state stores.

Gorbachev is apparently aware of the two-fold crisis of the Soviet welfare state. He is attempting to deal with the crisis of underdevelopment as part of his program to resume the Second Industrial Revolution. Gorbachev also clearly intends to deal with the crisis of overdevelopment, but this is a difficult task. The immense subsidies for housing, food and transportation have a deleterious effect on the Soviet economy. They drain resources from the state investment fund. There is a direct connection between the very low apartment rents and their rapid deterioration, because of their lack of upkeep and maintenance. There is also a direct connection between the low prices for basic food and the constant shortages (except of bread) in supplying the state retail stores and the long lines in front of the stores.

Gorbachev will have great difficulty in cutting the subsidies and thus increasing the prices, because by doing so he will undercut the basic unwritten agreement between the Party and the workers. Moreover, the standard of living of the working class is so low that major price increases may be dangerous and will have to be gradual. Finally, the working class has become accustomed to the existing scope of the welfare system. It is convinced, partially by the words and actions of previous leaders, that there is a "free lunch" under socialism. Of course, the "free" education, housing, transport, and the like are not clearly free. They have, however, become associated in the minds of Soviet workers with Soviet-style socialism. Reeducation will be most difficult, both politically and economically.

Gorbachev clearly opposes the psychology of the "free lunch." He knows that his market reforms require the sharp decline and eventual elimination of most state subsidies. He has not yet faced, however, the popular reaction to major cuts in subsidies. He will probably have to show some visible improvements in people's lives before he can risk a wholesale cut in subsidies. This will complicate his program. He must simultaneously preach the need for austerity and the imperative of raising people's living standards. Without doing both, without resolving the two-fold welfare crises of underdevelopment and overdevelopment, the modernization that Gorbachev seeks will remain largely unattainable.

One of the most disquieting socio-political phenomena for the Soviet leaders must be the almost palpable alienation of a large part of the society from the Soviet regime. It is expressed in the skepticism that greets government promises and the cynicism about the system itself. It combines apathy with indifference to reform. It is manifest in the lack of pride in work and in the neglect of state property. This alienation cuts across generational lines, but some Western studies of recent emigrants from the Soviet Union to America conclude that the younger the people are, the more intense their alienation.

The major source of alienation is the deep sense of injustice shared by large segments of the population. The experience of other societies, as well as of the Soviet Union and Russia, show that a shared sense of injustice may be a more important cause of unrest and declining stability than materially unsatisfactory living conditions. This was the case in Poland in 1980. This phenomenon does not threaten the survival of the Soviet regime, but it does endanger its stability and the success of Gorbachev's reforms.

The main source of the widespread sense of injustice is the typically indifferent, negligent, and sometimes brutal treatment the average citizen receives from the lower level bureaucrats with whom he must interact. Regardless of how rapid and profound the changes at the upper level of the establishment turn out to be, it will take a very long time before they trickle down to the local bureaucracies. In the meantime, the sense of injustice and the anger that it produces among the rank-and-file citizens is, if anything, increasing. The average citizen now hears everywhere the openly expressed views of how bad things have been and how everything is changing for the better. But his everyday experience has not changed at all, rendering him even angrier; and he can express his anger more openly now because it is much safer to do so.

Gorbachev's goal of modernizing the Soviet Union will have an enormous impact on the society, especially its stratification. Some tenets of stratification always seem to be associated with modernization. Common sense, if nothing else, would argue that two such tenets are that people should be rewarded according to the quality and complexity of the work they perform and that businesspeople in the main should be the ones who take care of business.

If the second tenet was never adopted in the Soviet Union, the first was elevated to a doctrinal canon of the Socialist society. According to Marx, in socialism, the lower phase of communism, each contributes to society according to his abilities, and each is rewarded according to his work. In practice, however, this canon was honored in the breach.

The Soviet pattern of stratification includes the worst possible combination of traits. It is highly elitist in its correlation of political power to economic rewards. It is the powerful who get rich: politics governs the distribution of economic rewards. But it is distinctly egalitarian in its correlation of the quality and complexity of work performed to real rewards. An enterprising, efficient worker does no better than a lazy one. Thus, there is no incentive for enterprise and efficiency. This is a deadly combination for a country that has set out to modernize, a fact that Soviet leaders are beginning to realize.

Yet change is difficult. The Soviets are caught in a Catch-22 predicament. In order to raise economic incentives and increase pay scales, the productivity and quality of available goods must also improve. This is likely, however, only when material incentives improve. The transition to a more functional economic stratification is therefore extremely difficult. It must be Gorbachev's plan to fill this transitional void, partially at least, with exhortations, calls to patriotism, and other such substitutes.

Perhaps no less difficult than the economic aspects of the shift are the socio-political ones. They may even become explosive. In the post-Stalin period the party entered into an unwritten contract with the Soviet working class, which is expressed in the workers' saying, "They pretend they pay us, and we pretend we work." This was far more than a joke. One party to the contract, those in power, raised minimum wages, increased average wages, promised and delivered a modest but steady growth in the standard of living, kept the differential between wages and salaries low and even lowered them, and, crucially important, provided the workers with an almost complete job security. (They also started to treat the collective farmer as a citizen.) In addition they expended enormous subsidies on commodities such as bread, lard, potatoes and services such as rents and transportation to keep prices low. On the workers' side, docility, low expectations and aspirations, and participation in the farce of the propaganda double-talk were their contributions to the social contract. The contract became rather frayed at the edges when, from the mid-1970s, the economy experienced stagnation.

It is this contract (and other, similar, "equilibrium contracts" with managers and administrators) that Gorbachev seems set to break, and which he must break if he wants his plans of modernization to become more than mere slogans. Such a policy, potentially of great value for the modernization program, carries with it, however, major threats to stability. These are greatest in the transition from the old social contract to a new one, the benefits of which can be promised but not yet delivered.

The changes that have already occurred, or are intended, in the cultural sphere, broadly understood, were the most surprising of Gorbachev's actions. *Glasnost'*, and the entire range of freedom of expression for the creative intelligentsia, are instruments of Gorbachev's effort to break the resistance of the bureaucracy and to mobilize broad support for his leadership and his program. But these steps are much more than cultural instruments in the service of socio-political change. If they continue, expand and endure, their consequences for Soviet culture, for Soviet society and for the nation at large may be enormous. Three such potential consequences are of particular importance. They concern civil society, ideology and the understanding of the very term "modernity" in the Soviet Union.

From Hegel to de Tocqueville to Gramsci, social thinkers have been concerned with the relations between state and society, and particularly with one of its aspects that they have defined as "civil society." This concept refers to the independence of such social units as community organizations or professional associations from direct supervision, control and management by the state. Totalitarianism eradicates all vestiges of "civil society." Populist capitalist democracy, as exemplified by the United States, is the best illustration of the other extreme, in which civil society is widespread, legitimate and dominant.

Gorbachev's program for the future of the Soviet Union seems to envision the creation and cultivation of selected elements of "civil society" never before known in Soviet or Russian history. If Gorbachev is serious about, and successful in abolishing cultural censorship, in permitting freedom for investigative reporting, encouraging participation in local community life, in giving workers a voice in enterprise management, and in holding free elections in the party's primary organizations, he will be granting relative autonomy to selected segments of the population, and thereby creating elements of "civil society" in the Soviet Union.

This process may be reversed, perhaps triggered by economic troubles. The ebb and flow of encouraging then limiting *glasnost'* will be controlled by the vicissitudes of Soviet domestic politics. Zig-zags are inevitable. The longer the process of *glasnost'* survives, however, and the greater its scope becomes, the more difficult even its partial reversal may become for the Soviet leadership to manage. The members of the creative intelligentsia who have committed themselves, in growing numbers and with increasing intensity, to Gorbachev's reforms, will not return with docility to their former function, to use Stalin's phrase, of being "engineers of human souls" in the service of the leader. What is happening today in the Soviet Union in the cultural sphere is not simply a thaw, one of the many of the post-Stalin era. It is potentially a sea change, the consequences of which are unpredictable.

The public criticism of Stalinism is broader in scope and deeper, albeit less dramatic, than that of the Khrushchev era. It is gaining momentum. It also includes a revisionist interpretation of the pre-Stalin period and of the Brezhnev era. In contrast to the critique of the past under Khrushchev, which concentrated on Stalin himself and ascribed all evils to his personality, the current criticism centers on the policies and structural characteristics of the Stalinist system. Gorbachev's decision to give vent to criticizing of the past is necessary for establishing his credibility with the intelligentsia. The key weakness of the Khrushchevian criticism of Stalin is, to a lesser degree, present now: no interpretation is given to explain how Stalin and Stalinism were possible in the Soviet Union.

Marxism-Leninism, adapted to Soviet conditions and supplemented by the experience of seventy years of Soviet history, still constitutes the conceptual framework, the political culture within which Gorbachev, his associates and the political elite think and operate. (This is no longer true for a large part of the creative intelligentsia, a fact that has caused a potential chasm to develop between them and the leadership.) But Gorbachev and his associates also operate according to the tenets of Russian nationalism, or, if one prefers, patriotism, and by the managerial ethos. Both in domestic and foreign policy the Soviet leadership is moving away from doctrinal principles. Their approach to ideology is becoming far more instrumental than in the past. This is reflected in their ideological eclecticism, which selects from the Marxist-Leninist menu those elements that suit Gorbachev's line.

Gorbachev's power base within the various bureaucratic hierarchies is not solid. Yet the alliance he is trying to forge through his program of "reconstruction" is broad and heterogeneous, and shows signs of both growth and consolidation. The alliance includes purist Marxists or Leninists who think that the original goals of the revolution, which they idealize, were perverted by Lenin's successors, and hope that at last they can return to what they consider the original sources of the revolution. It also includes people who consider themselves very far from Marxism-Leninism and adhere to democratic and liberal principles, following in the tradition of the democratic, non-revolutionary intelligentsia of the nineteenth and early twentieth centuries. It attracts Russian patriots who bemoan the decline of their country and believe that Gorbachev represents the final chance to make Russia great once again. It encompasses those within the military and the industrial-military sector who fear for the security of the Soviet Union if its relative technological decline continues. It attracts scores of careerists who increasingly believe in Gorbachev's survival and want to hitch their futures to his rising star.

Gorbachev's alliance appeals to the instincts and interests of the professional groups who are convinced that the General Secretary's new course will provide greater scope for them. It invites those who are beginning to believe that the Gorbachev policies will, in fact, reward hard work and skill. It draws those in the non-Russian republics who hope that the program of modernization and democratization will create a new deal for their nations more favorable than past practices. In fact, Gorbachev's reforms, and the alliance that is evolving to support and implement them, constitute an attempt to create a new social contract between the regime and various social groups and strata. The essence of a binding contract in socio-political life is the trust each party to the agreement reposes in the other. Thus far, the trust on either side is still limited. The groups that have committed themselves to the new contract in the upper political class and in the subordinate strata still constitute a minority. This is not unexpected. Major revolutionary and reform movements in the Soviet past, as in other countries, were initially propelled for a protracted period by active minorities that attained legitimacy only much later.

It is apparent that the new Soviet leadership understands the concept of modernity differently than did their predecessors. For Stalin, Khrushchev and Brezhnev, modernity meant new factories, new construction, a larger labor force, improved technology, and above all, increased production of basic resources and products. Stalin's speech of March, 1946, in which he discussed the future of the Soviet Union, and Khrushchev's and Brezhnev's speeches, in 1959 at the Twenty-first Party Congress, and in 1971 at the Twenty-fourth Party Congress, respectively, are almost identical in their understanding of modernity, and of their nation's progress to achieve it. They emphasized the production of tangible "things" rather than the modernizing process itself. They focused on quantifiable growth in the economy. This kind of approach was typical of the First Industrial Revolution and its mechanistic approach to the creation of wealth, of the economic macro-theories of the early capitalism of Adam Smith and David Ricardo, which led Marx to develop his mechanistic "labor theory of value" and his distinction between "productive" and "nonproductive" labor. Stalin, Khrushchev, and Brezhnev were all schooled in the principles of Soviet prewar industrialization, the industrial mobilization of the

Second World War, and the postwar reconstruction. Marxian principles of economic thinking, characteristic of the First Industrial Revolution, corresponded to their own experience. The cult of technology characteristic of the Soviet ruling circles throughout Soviet history focused primarily on its material aspects. The Soviet technological *ethos* was that of an engineer, a mechanic, an inventor of industrial improvements on the one hand, and of the robber baron on the other. It was, in a way, a replication of the American industrial experience from the post–Civil War period to the First World War, adjusted to Russian and Soviet conditions. The meaning of modernity for Gorbachev and many in the political elite, as well as for many scientists and economists, is quite different. They recognize the importance of high technology, but their perception of the *process* of modernization, however, centers not on *things* but on people, their attitudes and skills, and the conditions necessary for their creativity and their commitment. This is the basic reason why Gorbachev should be recognized as the first modern leader of the Soviet Union.

Many questions about Gorbachev's vision of the new Soviet system cannot yet be answered, partly because the requisite evidence is lacking, but also, and more importantly, because Gorbachev himself probably has something less than a comprehensive view of the system that will emerge from his reforms. We do not know, for example, the answer to such a major question as the role of the mass party and of the professional party *apparat* in the new system, although we know from Gorbachev's speeches what he does *not* want their role to be. We do not know how central the market will be in the reformed economic system and what weight the separate sectors will have in the mixed economy yet to emerge. We cannot be certain of the new long-range policy pertaining to the non-Russian nations of the Soviet Union and the degree of autonomy they will enjoy. Such questions can be multiplied, but one thing we do know with certainty: the answers will emerge in a bitter struggle for high stakes. Both for Gorbachev and his opponents, what is at stake is not only their personal fate, but the future of Russia and of the Soviet Union.

The significance of what is happening in the Soviet Union may be summarized by the following conclusions:

1. In the post-Stalin era many reforms were initiated and accomplished. They dealt, however, with only one or another aspect of politics, economics, or culture. Gorbachev's program constitutes the first *comprehensive* reform of the system since the advent of Stalinism.

2. The Soviet leadership has begun to dismantle the Stalinist socioeconomic and cultural systems and is modifying the political system bequeathed by Khrushchev and Brezhnev. The potential significance

of this process for the evolution of the Soviet Union and its transformation is as great as was Stalin's revolution from above in the 1930s. If successful, it will conclude the cycle of anti-Stalinist changes initiated by Khrushchev in the political field.

3. Gorbachev's economic reforms move in the direction of a rather eclectic model of "market socialism." This dramatically reverses the trend of Soviet history, with the exception of the nine years of N.E.P. In two respects the current reforms seek to move beyond N.E.P. The New Economic Policy initiated by Lenin and ultimately destroyed by Stalin permitted private farming, small private enterprise in industry, craftsmanship and services. The industrial, construction, mining, transportation, finances and foreign trade areas were, however, highly centralized and based on the principles of strict planning and state distribution of goods. Today these sectors are all being decentralized in varying degrees and are gradually being exposed to market forces. Moreover, the N.E.P. moved in the direction of stricter limits and higher taxation of private economic activity. Gorbachev's reforms, of course, seek to encourage such activity.

4. The personality and character of the General Secretary has been crucial to his program of change. Gorbachev's personal importance to the cycle of reforms cannot be over-emphasized. The accidental confluence of a deep crisis of the Soviet system, the exhaustion of the old guard, the patronage of Andropov, and an unusual period of succession put Gorbachev in power. His talents, determination, political orientation, and the fact that he is the first modern leader of the Soviet Union all give shape to the direction, scope, and dynamism of the reforms. But it was important that he was a member in good standing in the association of professional party functionaries, that his career was typical of that of an *apparatchik* of his generation. It has been said that only a rabid anti-Communist such as President Nixon could have succeeded in initiating an opening to the People's Republic of China and a Soviet-American *detente*. Similarly in the Soviet Union, only a party *apparatchik* could succeed in initiating significant liberalizing reforms. This is because he is recognized by the closely knit brotherhood of the party *apparat* as one of them, and because he knows well the tactics and the values of party politics and has developed the instinct to survive and to strike decisively when necessary. The purely managerial types such as Malenkov or Kosygin or, today, Prime Minister Ryzhkov, could not have pulled off what Gorbachev did.

5. Gorbachev's reforms are associated with a widespread change of leading cadres. The extent of this change already surpasses the turnover initiated by Khrushchev over a longer period of time. Moreover, the new leading cadres seem to be more favorably disposed to reforms

because they all belong to a new, post-Stalinist generation. While experience shows that major changes in a political system can occur even when the composition of a political elite is stable, it also shows also that a major turnover in personnel, especially when accompanied by a generational transition, facilitates the program of reforms and increases the chances of success.

6. The Soviet leadership's analysis of its own society implicitly recognizes the bankruptcy of the concept of the "new Soviet man," the model "Homo Sovieticus." Entrepreneurship, initiative, spontaneity, and social discipline are among the traits in short supply in the Soviet Union but typical of modern societies. It is essential that the regime introduce significant changes in the process of socialization and education, as well as in terms of the rewards and indices of Soviet success.

7. Gorbachev's reforms in the cultural and communication fields, known as *glasnost'*, mark the beginning of the political and professional emancipation of the Soviet creative intelligentsia. Their significance can only be compared to the emancipation of the Russian peasants from serfdom in the 1860s—and, indeed, the two developments share some of the same limitations. This process of emancipation serves not only Gorbachev's needs of the moment but is also a recognition of the indispensability of the intelligentsia for the program of modernization of the Soviet Union, and thus is likely to represent more than a short-term thaw.

8. The implementation of Gorbachev's reforms would lead to the development of elements of a "civil society" in the Soviet Union. Trade unions, professional groups, cultural associations and other similar institutions may gain a significant degree of autonomy from the political authorities. This will not only reverse the Stalinist and post-Stalin pattern but will also signify a retreat from some highly authoritarian aspects of Leninism.

9. Gorbachev's reforms go beyond policy and organizational changes. They promote structural, institutional changes in the Soviet system. Institutional reforms attempt to change permanently the behavior patterns of individuals, social groups or organizations. Traditional organizational features of the system may in important respects remain unchanged while the functions of these organizations could be altered as could the behavior of individuals within the organizations.

10. In the broadest sense, what Gorbachev seeks is nothing less than a redefinition of Soviet socialism. His aim is to make socialism more attractive both at home and abroad, and perhaps even restore some unity and vigor to the nearly defunct international communist movement. The "new" socialism will abandon opposition to *all* capitalist institutions, especially economic micro-institutions and what the Soviets

still call capitalist "formal democracy"—that is, democracy in political life. When Gorbachev visited Prague in the spring of 1987, his official spokesman, Genadii Gerasimov, was asked at a press conference: "What is the difference between Gorbachev and Dubcek?" Gerasimov replied, "Nineteen years." In fact, Gorbachev's thinking is beginning to resemble the views of those reformers in Eastern Europe who have not wanted to abandon Marxism but rather to reinterpret it and adapt it to contemporary realities.

Plausible Outcomes of Changes
in the Soviet Union

What are the likely outcomes of the sweeping changes in the Soviet Union? While many are possible, some are more likely than others. There is much speculation over whether Gorbachev will succeed or fail. One meaning of "success," as defined by Webster's Third International Dictionary is a "favorable termination of a venture." Another is "the degree or measure of attaining one's desired end." The second is the more pertinent to our inquiry because it views success as a relative, as opposed to an absolute, state.

Seldom in human affairs is the outcome of a venture either a total success or a complete failure. This will be most likely the case as well with the present process of change in the Soviet Union. It is likely that it will partly succeed and partly fail. Gorbachev's central goal is the modernization of the Soviet Union. The dismantling of the Stalinist system and the redefining of socialism is less an intrinsic goal than a means to achieve the central goal.

Can the Soviet Union become modern in the contemporary sense of the term, and if so, how soon? The Soviet Union has already developed many of the material prerequisites of modernity. It possesses a skilled labor force, an educated urban population, advanced science, a very large professional class, pockets of high technology; it is rich in natural resources; its economy is gigantic; the rate of capital formation is high. It has, in short, the proverbial bootstraps by which to pull itself up. But the Soviet Union's transition to modernity will depend on how effectively those resources are developed and used. Here, optimistic predictions are not warranted.

The power of attitudes that are dysfunctional for modernity, the commitment of the managerial strata to the irrelevant or harmful lessons of early industrialization, the political constraints imposed by oligarchic rule, the existence of a political elite that is loathe to abdicate its privileges, and the constraint of multi-ethnicity will make the process of changing attitudes in the Soviet Union difficult, prolonged and probably ultimately inadequate to replicate the current phase of modernization in many capitalist countries.

If Gorbachev's revolution continues, the Soviet Union may create large pockets of modernity outside the military-industrial sector. Yet to become truly modern, it is not enough to have a modern *sector* in the economy: it is necessary to change the way of life of the society at large. The creation of a large high-tech sector in the Soviet economy would be a major achievement indeed, but it is still a far cry from modernity.

There is no disagreement in the Soviet Union or in the West that modernization will require the abandonment of central planning, and the introduction of some sort of "market socialism." Yet we should remember that economists still consider Hungary a centrally planned economy, inasmuch as political authorities continue to make the macroeconomic decisions. And there are very few Sovietologists who would consider a retreat from central planning as extensive as in Hungary applicable to Soviet conditions, or who would not consider a thoroughly "Hungarianized" Soviet Union a virtual miracle.

Gorbachev's own timetable for Soviet modernization is clear: time and again, he has referred to the turn of the century, the year 2000. Yet, his evaluation of the difficulty of the task at hand has steadily increased and continues to increase. In discussions with Soviet officials and economists, the "catch-up" deadline of the year 2000 is almost invariably discounted. I asked a high Soviet official whether if, by the year 2000 the Soviet Union is not falling further behind the advanced capitalist countries, he would consider that a major victory for Gorbachev's program. His answer was an unqualified "Yes." Thus, if Gorbachev's revolution is continued, it may well achieve enough in 10–15 years to improve significantly the Soviet standard of living. It will achieve enough to decrease the *rate* of Soviet technological *decline* relative to the West or—which is less likely—perhaps even *stop* the decline. It will not achieve enough to fulfill Gorbachev's program of making the Soviet Union modern.

The second of Gorbachev's goals, and at the same time the means to reach the goal of modernity, is a thorough de-Stalinization and liberalization of the system. The difficulty of carrying out such a cycle of reforms in diverse spheres of Soviet life is complex beyond imagination. As Professor Samuel Huntington of Harvard University has remarked, "Reforms are more difficult than revolutions." In the Soviet Union, this is certainly the case. The victory in the Russian revolution in October, 1917 and in the civil war that followed were far easier to achieve than the tasks of Stalin or Gorbachev.

Revolutions like the Russian one of 1917 occur in political systems and social orders that are on the verge of disintegration. The ensuing political vacuum is filled by the revolutionary organization and consolidated by political mobilization. Major reforms that grow out of crises are substitutes for revolution; they are meant to *prevent* developments that could lead to revolutionary situations. The system within which they take place is far from the brink of revolution. Its institutions are still solid; there is no power vacuum. Revolutions develop from crises of survival; major reforms take place and are intended to counteract crises of effectiveness. Revolutions tend to devour their children, expel from leadership and even annihilate the originators of the revolution and abandon their Utopian goals; in reforms, the great danger is that they will be absorbed and neutralized by the system that still displays a powerful instinct for survival. New structures and processes created by major reforms may still shelter old behavior.

It is hardly surprising that in the conceptualization and implementation of his "new course" Gorbachev is facing major obstacles. These barriers to the implementation and success of Gorbachev's strategy of reforms are multi-dimensional, and can be divided into socio-political, structural, and international categories.

Political and Social Obstacles

Gorbachev faces organized political opposition to his policies from individuals or groups at the high political level in Moscow and in some capitals of the Republics, as well as from groups outside the official power structure. This opposition is partly submerged in the Byzantine court politics in Moscow and can only be deduced, and its individual participants identified, through the inexact art of Kremlinology. The opposition has taken advantage of *glasnost'* to express unmistakably its enmity to Gorbachev's new course. Its tactic is not to deny the need for reforms but rather to protest their breadth, scope, intensity, and the speed with which they can be implemented. In its propaganda, the opposition conveys the fear that these reforms may destroy Russia and the Soviet way of life, and endanger the survival of the system.

The existence of opposition, even at the very highest level, was indirectly confirmed by Gorbachev himself when he publicly mentioned that because of differences of opinion in the Politburo, the crucial January, 1987 Central Committee Plenum, which gave the major impetus to the socio-political and cultural reforms, had to be postponed three times. At the highest Party and government levels, the people who are most often identified in Moscow political circles with opposition to Gorbachev can be divided into two groups: the first consists of the remnants of the Old Guard who are, however, on their way out; the second, more important group is formed by contenders from Gorbachev's own generation. The figure generally recognized as Gorbachev's principal foil is Yegor Ligachev, the titular second secretary of the Party. Ligachev is deeply respected in the Party apparatus, in which he served longer and probably enjoyed a higher standing before the final succession than Gorbachev. His prominence in the affairs of the party remains great. His skills as a politician are said to be considerable. In his speeches to Party activists he supports Gorbachev's political course, but he always manages to sound a strong note of caution and to insert passages that warn against excesses of the "new course" and stress the value of the experience accumulated by the Party apparatus.

The political base of Ligachev and whoever is allied with him at the top is the powerful Party apparatus, the conservative part of the cultural intelligentsia, the lower-level managerial stratum, and nationalistic Russian groups who were brought into the open by Gorbachev's *glasnost'*.

An extreme example of the fierceness of the opposition is provided by the vicious attack on Gorbachev's political course at the meeting of the leadership of the Union of Writers of the Russian Republic (R.S.F.S.R.). One of the leaders, Yurii Bondarev, said in his speech, published in the newspaper "Literary Russia":

> I am being asked by foreign correspondents whether a civil war has broken out in our literary circle. No, comrades, what has developed is not a civil war. It can be rather compared to the brutal onslaught of our country in the summer of 1941 of the forces of barbarism. If this onslaught is not halted it will endanger the very existence of our great Russian cultural heritage and of our Soviet way of life.

Many of the participants in the meeting quoted Ligachev in their speeches.

Still another example of opposition is provided by an association that was created last year in Russia under the name *Pamyat'* or "Memory." Its members may be divided into two groups. The first is composed of those who are concerned with the preservation of Russian folklore and monuments. The second group brings together the worst kind of Russian chauvinists with a very pronounced anti-Semitic bent, who see in Gorbachev's policies some sort of Jewish-Masonic conspiracy. They have resurrected the notorious "Protocols of the Elders of Zion." In the spring of 1987, this group organized a march on the

Kremlin in which a few hundred people participated, carrying posters proclaiming the need for the "Rebirth of Russia" and demanding an audience with Gorbachev. The unquestionable existence of opposition to Gorbachev does not, however, constitute a real present danger to his leading position. The struggle at the top concerns the extent of Gorbachev's power. It is also extremely unlikely that the history of Khrushchev's initial years in office will be repeated, with Gorbachev facing his own "anti-party" group with a majority in the Politburo, as Khrushchev did in June 1957.

Moreover, Gorbachev's personal power is steadily on the rise. One can discern, for example, his hand in events affecting Ligachev. His position traditionally carried with it the supervision of personnel policies (the "nomenklatura") and of ideological matters. Yet without touching Ligachev's formal position, Gorbachev transferred personnel policy to his loyal Central Committee secretary, Georgii Razumovsky, and made Ligachev share the top ideological position with the man who is personally closest to Gorbachev, the Central Committee Secretary Alexander Yakovlev.

In June 1987, a plenary session of the Soviet Communist Party's Central Committee took place in Moscow. This meeting marks the end of the first act in the drama of domestic transformation initiated by Mikhail Gorbachev. In almost every dimension of his domestic program and situation—political, economic, cultural, social, and psychological—it constitutes the beginning of a new phase of his reforms. In the mid-summer of 1987 the General Secretary demonstrated his grasp on the levers of political power in the Kremlin.

Gorbachev's position within the leadership improved. The advancement of his right-hand man, Alexander Yakovlev, the Secretary of the Central Committee for Economic Affairs Nikolai Slyunkov and the Secretary for Agriculture, Viktor Nikonov, to full membership in the Politburo has for all practical purposes ended the ability of his high-placed opponents to challenge his power position, or the speed of his reform activities, in this top decision-making body. It also underscored the dominance of the General Secretary over the Central Party Secretariat, the executive arm of the Party. Yakovlev's promotion placed him on equal footing with Gorbachev's main competitor, Yegor Ligachev. His position is potentially as important in Gorbachev's regime as was that of Mikhail Suslov, the chief ideologue and *éminence grise* in Brezhnev's era. By now the Politburo contains only two holdovers from Brezhnev's days; close to two-thirds of its members, and more than three-quarters of the members of the Party Secretariat, were appointed by Gorbachev. This shift is especially remarkable when one considers that from July 1985 until the June 1987 Plenum, a full two years, Gorbachev was able to appoint to the Politburo only a single individual.

Another aspect of Gorbachev's consolidation of power concerns the military. His control over the Soviet Armed Forces has been visibly strengthened. The ludicrous affair of the 19-year-old West German Cessna pilot who landed harmlessly on Red Square provided the opportunity for a decisive shake-up of the High Command. The former Commander of the Far Eastern Military District, General of the Army Dimitrii Yazov, who attracted Gorbachev's attention during his visit to Khabarovsk about a year earlier, was promoted in an unprecedented manner over 40 marshals and senior Generals, appointed Minister of Defense, and coopted to candidate (non-voting) membership of the Politburo. His Deputy for Political Affairs, the Chief Commissar of the Armed Forces is General A. D. Lizichev, an old friend of Gorbachev. Apparently almost two hundred generals of the rank of Lieutenant General and below were retired or dismissed. At no other time since the Khrushchev era has the political clout of the Armed Forces, its visibility, prestige and credibility within the elite and the population, been as low as seems to be the case today.

A notable victory for Gorbachev was the resolution of the Plenum to convene in June, 1988 the 19th All-Union Party Conference, a resolution that he was unable to achieve only six months earlier at the January, 1987 Plenum of the Central Committee. The purpose of the conference is to evaluate the progress of managerial reform and "democratization," but most importantly it will be empowered to make massive changes in the composition of the Central Committee. By announcing the convening of the Conference Gorbachev is, in effect, putting the second echelon of the Soviet elite on probation. He is warning them to shape up or face the consequences. While the June, 1987 Plenum consolidated Gorbachev's power in the top hierarchy beyond challenge, the June 1988 conference is intended to reshape the Central Committee, which consists of more than 300 full members, depending on the needs of his power and his policies.

Yet, Gorbachev's power is, to a large extent, policy defined. That is to say, when one considers how much power he has, one should ask "power for what?" Gorbachev understands this very well and tried hard to build up a political machine that will not simply support his policies but be personally loyal to him. He has placed in high positions about a dozen individuals with whom he worked in Stavropol, or from the adjacent Krasnoyarsk and Northern Caucasus. One of them is the previously mentioned Central Committee Secretary Razumovsky, another is the head of the entire Agro-Industrial complex, Vsevolod Murakhovsky.

Finally, the question of opposition and Gorbachev's power must take into consideration an area about which information is scant: his institutional power base. It would appear that none of the traditional power bases of the top leader are as yet available to Gorbachev. The Party apparatus, the bedrock of Khrushchev's and Brezhnev's power, is controlled in Moscow by the General Secretary and his loyal followers. But many of the key figures of the Party apparatus outside Moscow, the Secretaries of some republics, provinces, cities, and districts and their 200 thousand-strong army of subordinate, full-time Party functionaries, have developed neither bonds of personal loyalty to the General Secretary, nor a deep commitment to his reforms.

The high level party apparatchiki constitute the largest bloc in the Central Committee and their support is absolutely vital to the General Secretary. In normal circumstances the symbolic power and prestige of his office keeps them at bay; but in an unexpected crisis, their support may not be forthcoming. It must have been disconcerting to Gorbachev at the Party Congress in March 1986 that despite the turnover of the provincial secretaries, who are members of the Central Committee, about 40 percent failed to create a sufficiently loyal power base in this body. It is therefore not surprising that Gorbachev is systematically replacing the local Party secretaries, old and new alike, and selecting their successors with particular attention paid to their loyalty and policy orientation. The State administration and the economic bureaucracies, especially in the Moscow and republican ministries, can hardly be considered Gorbachev's power base. It is among them that the most vociferous dissatisfaction with his policies is being voiced.

The greatest riddle with respect to Gorbachev's power and his power base concerns the KGB. Rumors in Moscow suggest entirely contradictory situations. Some say that there are plans to split the KGB into two parts—one to deal with intelligence and one to deal with domestic secret police work. This would weaken the domestic secret police, whose authority and prestige largely derive from their association with tasks of foreign intelligence. According to other rumors, the head of the KGB, Politburo member Viktor Chebrikov, is committed to the General Secretary and fully supports his policies.

Logic may not be the best guide in this case, but the KGB hierarchy and its chief would seem to have no particular reason to be Gorbachev's loyalist followers and helpers. The process of democratization and *glasnost'* is antithetical to the precepts of the KGB. The new stress on legality, the tolerance of some dissent, the freeing of political prisoners and other elements of the new course would appear not to be to the KGB's liking, not unlike some recent cases in which KGB officials have been accused of abuse of power. Chebrikov is not a Gorbachev appointee and no close past ties between the two men are known in the West. The past loyalties to Andropov of both Gorbachev and Chebrikov may have created a bond of mutual loyalty, and the fact that Gorbachev elevated a man respected in the KGB, Eduard Shevardnadze, to be Foreign Minister and his close associate in the Politburo, may have pleased the organization. But there is no evidence for either proposition known in the West. Still, at a time of major change, of a general loosening of the rules of social and political behavior, the KGB may be even more important than in the past. It may serve as the regime's last line of defense against a loss of control. In these circumstances a Gorbachev-Chebrikov alliance is fully consistent with Soviet-style political logic. My own guess is that Gorbachev has close ties with the Soviet intelligence community which deals with other countries, but is harsh and forbidding in his attitudes to the domestic secret police sector of the KGB.

The analysis of Gorbachev's power base leads to some curious conclusions. His position as General Secretary now and in the near future is safe. A coup against him is most improbable. Yet aside from the central Party apparatus, it is extremely difficult to identify a structural power base for him. His most loyal allies are in the ranks of the creative intelligentsia. But the creative intelligentsia hardly constitute a power base in the Soviet Union. The symbolic value and prestige of his office are a key asset. But now, and probably in the near future, his greatest strength probably lies in skillful and convincing manipulation of public relations. His power and influence are personalized. He is an intelligent and clever statesman, an instinctive natural leader of a sort rarely found in the Soviet Union. His public persona is that of a celebrity, a TV performer whose dynamism and charisma attract growing popular sympathy, attention and perhaps support. Gorbachev's non-traditional power base and sources of support could be sufficient if his new course proceeds smoothly. But if he does not expand his power base, he could be severely hurt by a crisis of the type that Khrushchev faced in Hungary in 1956, a major defeat abroad, or, most importantly, a serious domestic crisis growing out of the unintended consequences of his new course, like the massive student demonstrations in China.

The greatest obstacle to Gorbachev is not opposition, but resistance. Unlike opposition, resistance is neither organized nor open. Its practitioners are the intermediate-level administrators in the ministries in Moscow and the capitals of the Republics, the lower level Party and State officials, the managers of enterprises and the local Mafias, particularly in the non-Russian republics.

In resisting Gorbachev's orders, the ministerial administrators in Moscow and the high-ranking Party and State officials in the republics and provinces are defending their privileges and ways of life. As one government official put it, behind every one of the almost 200 economic targets that are transmitted to the enterprises by the planners, there stands an army of 30 thousand officials who will become superfluous if *their* target is abolished.

All of Gorbachev's economic reforms, even those that fall far short of fundamental change, require two contradictory conditions for their success. The intermediate-level officials must begin to implement the reform; but in the process of reform the intermediate level of administration must lose its importance, be reduced in size, and perhaps eventually disappear.

It is too much to ask of large armies of officials to participate voluntarily in their own elimination. So officials will fight rear-guard battles in the hope that, as before in Soviet history, these reforms too will pass. It is interesting to note that Gorbachev's wrath has recently been directed not only at state officials but also against Party functionaries. This would indicate that it will be difficult for the General Secretary to overcome the resistance of the state and economic officials by using "assault teams" from the Party apparatus. The middle and lower level Party apparatus gained power and independence during Brezhnev's rule and particularly in the period of interregnum. It will require greater doses of control, increased pressure from Moscow, and certainly additional personnel changes to make these strata more supportive of Gorbachev's line.

Many in the West believe that Soviet managers, directors of enterprises and firms are supporters of economic reforms. In reality, the majority is probably among the most determined opponents. In general, Soviet managers have learned to live with the traditional Stalinist economic system and to take advantage of it. They are geared to the traditional way of doing business. They have a limited capacity to learn new skills and new patterns of work. They are afraid of the new environment that major reforms are supposed to create. They are afraid that they may be replaced by younger and more flexible people. Most of them are not eager to exchange what they have for the promise of larger monetary rewards and greater independence from the middle-level economic bureaucracy and the planners in Moscow. Nor do they like Gorbachev's proposals for electing heads of enterprises and for increasing the participation of workers in the administrative affairs of their enterprises. (The resistance of the managers seems uncharacteristic of the attitudes of the technical intelligentsia, who chafe at the condition of technological stagnation. These are the technocrats who support economic change.)

The best organized and fiercest resistance to Gorbachev's ideas and programs comes from the Soviet-style "Mafia families" who live in some Russian provinces, but particularly in the non-Russian republics. They are formed by all types of officials—party, state, economic and police—who have long worked together and become accustomed to concealing one another's mistakes and crimes. The term "families" is apt, because these Mafias usually include people with family ties to key officials.

The most powerful Mafias seem to be located in the non-Russian republics. Their chieftains were among the main beneficiaries of the relaxed control from Moscow and the security in office that were characteristic of the Brezhnev years and the interregnum. These men became uncrowned kings, ruling their fiefdoms with an iron fist, corrupting officials and inspectors from Moscow, and keeping their doings well-camouflaged from their nominal superiors. Some of them were members of the Politburo or had close personal and sentimental relations with Brezhnev, and therefore could not be touched by any control organization.

The party boss of Kazakhstan, Dinmukhamed Kunayev, was one notorious example, Vladimir Shcherbitsky of the Ukraine is another. For the last 30 years, Shcherbitsky occupied in sequence the three most important positions in the Ukraine—Republican Party Secretary for Personnel, Prime Minister and First Secretary of the Ukrainian Party. For the last 20 years he has been a member of the Politburo in Moscow. It is difficult even to imagine the depth and the scope of the personal machine that Shcherbitsky was able to build up during three decades in the Ukraine. It is also difficult to imagine the extent of the difficulty that Gorbachev is facing in purging a political machine in a Republic that is bigger and more populous than France. It will not be enough merely to expel Shcherbitsky from all of his positions, although the majority of the Politburo will certainly agree to such a step. In light of Shcherbitsky's connections, friendships, and alliances, this will create considerable ill will against Gorbachev in the second most important part of the Soviet Union. Gorbachev must proceed cautiously. Shcherbitsky's dismissal must be preceded by, or coincide with, a thorough purge of high- and middle-level officials in the Ukraine. Even more difficult, their replacements must be found primarily in the Ukraine (where the pattern of selecting Russians for the key top positions, which is followed in the non-Russian republics, is unthinkable), among individuals who have sufficient experience for high office but who are not closely identified with Shcherbitsky and therefore promise to become loyal to Gorbachev and supporters of his policies. Gorbachev is clearly preparing for a showdown with Shcherbitsky and his machine. He has made frequent trips to the Ukraine and substantial personnel changes have taken place. In Moscow it is said that Shcherbitsky is for the moment still useful to Gorbachev because he plays a stabilizing role in the Ukraine, and tries to balance the nationalistic pressures evoked by *glasnost'* against the interests of the Russified Ukrainians.

Yet purges alone, however extensive, cannot eliminate resistance to Gorbachev's policies. New people must be found, with inclinations far different from those they have learned under the tutelage of the Old Guard. From top to bottom, new officials will have to adopt new ways of party, state, and economic work. This process of change will be a long and difficult one at best. Yet it is a process absolutely essential for breaking the resistance to Gorbachev's programs, for the success of his new course, and for economic policies that will probably be more radical in the future.

A major barrier to Gorbachev's policies is socio-political inertia. It is present everywhere in Soviet society. Its most important expressions are apathy, routinization, non-involvement and deep skepticism about anything new. It emerged from the many tribulations of Soviet history and the ever present distinction, even among officials, of "they," the authorities, and "we" the ruled. Inertia is a state of mind that puts personal security and safety, caution and private preoccupations ahead of social obligations, a sense of social responsibility, or aspirations for public recognition. It constitutes the main obstacle to Gorbachev's economic innovations and political and cultural reforms. They have not yet made a substantial dent in the widespread fear of commitment and involvement, in the passivity expressed in the phrase, "this too shall pass," and in the predominance of purely private preoccupations and concerns.

Research conducted by Soviet television's public opinion poll concluded that the new programming substantially increased viewer interest across all strata. But it succeeded only minimally in stimulating active participation in the new course. A Moscow University professor reports that about 20 percent of his class actively joins in discussions of the "new course," another 20 percent limits itself to asking questions, and the remaining 60 percent remains silent.

When Gorbachev took power he thought that he would be facing a brick wall of conservatism that his hammer blows would destroy. He has encountered instead a sponge of resistance and indifference that bounces back whenever it is hit. Inertia and indifference predominate even among the educated strata and the creative intelligentsia, from whom the most active and effective supporters of Gorbachev's policies have been recruited. Few editors and journalists and even fewer scholars use their writings to test the limits of what is possible under the new conditions.

For every editor such as Vitaly Korotych of the now-exciting mass weekly *Ogonek,* the courageous editor Yegor Yakovlev of the daily *Moscow News,* and the pioneering editor of the monthly *Novy Mir,* Sergei Zalygin, for every path-breaking sociologist and economist, such as Tatyana Zaslavskaya and Abel Aganbegyan, there are hundreds and thousands of editors and journalists, social scientists and economists who do only the required minimum to avoid being classified as opponents of the "new course." For every active supporter of Gorbachev's line there are hundreds of Party members who are indifferent to the new policies and pay only lip service to them. Many admire Gorbachev and follow his policies with great interest, but still do not trust him.

The most widespread emotion evoked by Gorbachev's "new course" is probably neither opposition nor resistance but simply confusion. There is a lack of coherent understanding of what he wants to achieve, combined with instinctive skepticism in the broadest strata of the population. The only way Gorbachev can successfully overcome the resistance to his program is to combine two components: first, an attack from above through an intensive use of the media, support from that part of the creative intelligentsia that is willing to commit itself to the struggle, and pressure from the party and state officials who are loyal to Gorbachev; second, major, consistent and intensive efforts to mobilize commitment and support for Gorbachev's program from below. It is impossible to know whether this necessary combination of pressures from above and from below can be created on a large scale in the near future. But it appears clear that a major crisis may make such a combination necessary for Gorbachev's survival. Even without such a crisis, the implementation of his program will depend on his ability to reduce inertia and mobilize active mass support.

The task is complicated by the fact that the Soviet people of all strata, but particularly the urban working class and the peasantry, do not trust or believe their leaders on any level in domestic affairs, and particularly where grandiose plans for improvement are concerned. Popular trust in the Soviet leaders' foreign and international security policy is a different matter.

Throughout Soviet history, the government has repeatedly lied to the people about the conditions in which they live and the prospects for change. The lack of trust in the political leadership has been passed from generation to generation. It affects the Communist Party itself (almost 8 percent of the population), which has evolved from an authentic political movement, an association of idealistic believers in an exalted and common cause, into a loose organization in which opportunists and careerists hold court, well versed in the Soviet double-talk. Moreover, the minority who remain idealistic is primarily composed of dogmatists and fanatics whose views are rooted in the Stalinist past.

The alienation of the Soviet people, and the mind-set of the bureaucrats who run their lives, are part of the moral crisis of the Soviet people. The Russian writer and journalist Volkov speaks of a "moral degradation" of the society, brought about by the fact that open discussion of problems has long been forbidden. Another writer, Kunitsyn, in an interview on Moscow Radio unprecedented for its harsh openness, asserts that almost everybody in the Soviet Union has fallen victim to "a loss of honesty . . . and any real concern for other people." For Gorbachev the most painful expression of this alienation and decay, and his most immediate concern, is the far-reaching erosion of the work ethic. It may take quite some time before even real material incentives will take hold of the working class. As far as the peasantry is concerned, it ceased to exist as a class, and probably even the implementation of wide-spread market reforms would evoke a response infinitely weaker than that of the Chinese peasantry.

Gorbachev's new course will require perseverance, continuity and honesty to reverse the process of alienation. It will require much greater *glasnost'*. The criticism of the reality of Soviet life under Gorbachev has clearly gone further than under Khrushchev. But it has a crucial shortcoming: by and large *glasnost'* does not explain, and most often does not even attempt to explain, *why* Soviet society has reached a stage of such deep crisis. It raises the question whether Gorbachev himself has the insight, to say nothing of the power and the necessary time, to address these basic questions.

The bureaucratic resistance to the implementation of Gorbachev's program is closely connected to two other trends within the bureaucracy: the chronic distortion of information and widespread corruption. The gross falsification of reports has already been noted. Its scope is not, however, fully understood, nor its destructive consequences adequately appreciated in the West. The fact is that in the Soviet Union nobody tells the truth to his superiors. The entire bureaucracy, from the lowest clerk to the highest government minister, regardless of the area of responsibility, is engaged in unending deception.

Corruption has long been considered characteristic of the Soviet Union. Its scale and range are unknown in any capitalist industrial society. It is not confined to the occasional bribe, or even the regular and customary "baksheesh." It is rather an entire "culture of corruption," a way of life. The Soviet writer Kunitsyn complained in a radio interview in Moscow that moral decay has penetrated a sphere in which honesty had flourished for centuries—that of medicine. Kunitsyn said that "in recent years such an atmosphere has been created in some medical organizations . . . that sick people have simply begun to feel that they are doomed if they do not give bribes not only to doctors, especially surgeons, but also to nurses." He ended with a grotesque description of the state of Soviet medicine: only if a person pays a bribe will he be permitted to live.

The enormity of the theft that goes on in the Soviet Union every day involving both the lowest worker and the government minister has assumed such proportions that it significantly skews the official figures on the distribution of the national income. There are heated discussions in the Soviet Union among specialists about what proportion of the G.N.P. is simply stolen; a conservative figure is 15 percent. To cover corruption honest people are sent to jail and authority is abused.

There are numerous reasons for Gorbachev to fight this corruption. The income from theft of state property is a disincentive to hard work. The corruption of officials is one of the root causes of the alienation of the people from their government. Corruption corrodes the spirit of discipline, the work ethic and the devotion to duty that are central in Gorbachev's plans of renewal. The effectiveness of Gorbachev's battle against corruption will be a test of his promise to have an honest and truthful government and to bring justice to society. How can he win this battle? Harsher punishment will certainly help, as will closer control over the coercive apparatus itself. Will it not be, however, a situation in which the little fish are caught and the big fish are permitted to continue to swim? Here again, *glasnost'*, grassroots democratization, and other elements of the new course are expected to carry the burden of the struggle. On what basis should one conclude that this burden, on top of other burdens, will not be too heavy?

Finally, another obstacle to Gorbachev's success concerns the near-term prospects for his regime. Before the June 1987 Plenum some officials said that a mistake had been made in the last half year when too much effort and attention had been centered on democratization and the "*glasnost'*" process and not enough *directly* on economic matters. This view seems justified. Before the Plenum, a gap was beginning to open between the increasingly unorthodox (for Soviet conditions) activities in the socio-political and cultural "superstructure," and the visibly slow economic progress and the modesty of edicts proclaiming the transformation of the economic "base." Democratization and *glasnost'* were, in the design of the leaders, to serve as the battering ram against bureaucratic resistance to Gorbachev's economic reforms and social inertia and apathy. But without visible economic improvements, their very existence was endangered. The key reason for the Party leadership to support them would disappear. The opposition to their continuation by the Party traditionalists would have gained momentum. A country with Russian and Soviet traditions, in the absence of dynamic economic thinking and the hope of better economic conditions, has no place for the "luxury" of democratization. Democratization can occur only if it goes hand in hand with economic development and not as its substitute. In fact, the continuation of harsh economic conditions without the prospect of their radical change calls for steps in the political arena that are the precise opposite of democratization. The June Plenum, in its reforming economic thinking and hope of economic improvements, closed the gap between the economic "base" and the political and cultural "superstructure." The instrumental role of democratization and *glasnost'* in the service of economic modernization has been again established.

Yet, another domestic gap is now in the process of developing in the Soviet Union: a gap between what Gorbachev preaches and what he can deliver in the short run. The Soviet population, and, most importantly, the working class in the large metropolitan areas, has yet to see a single improvement in its situation. Their hopes have been raised. Their sense of injustice (because of their treatment by the bureaucracy) is now stronger than their sense of deprivation (the lack of consumer goods). Their rising expectations on both counts, however, focus on the short term, and their anger will rise if Gorbachev cannot deliver on his promises.

The deliberations of the June 1987 Plenum attest to Gorbachev's understanding that he must deliver, and deliver fast, if he wants his reform program to take hold. The reason for the pressure on Gorbachev's plans is as important from the economic point of view as they are from the political. If, in the next two to three years, he is not able to provide real material incentives to the working force and the managerial strata—that is, more money to buy more consumer goods—his entire reform program may fail.

The Plenum centered on the restructuring of the managerial and planning systems—a long-range task that has only begun. Gorbachev made it amply clear, however, that some immediate economic tasks are pressing and must be accomplished at the same time that the reform is taking place. The priorities that he emphasized were: major increases in agricultural production and in the marketing of produce, an improvement in services with special attention to health care, the acceleration of housing construction, greater emphasis on industrial consumer goods. Gorbachev is a man in a hurry who wants to inculcate his subordinates with the same sense of urgency that he feels. Yet, every major reorganization is bound to produce disorganization. Restructuring the planning and management system and immediate increases in consumer goods production may, in the short run, be incompatible goals.

The Soviet economic model is, of course, the prime obstacle to reform: it discourages innovation, initiative, entrepreneurship and risk-taking; it does not stimulate technical progress; it emphasizes quantity over quality. Gorbachev's edicts on improving productivity and the quality of products, on bringing scientific-technological institutes closer to the production units, and on a strict accounting of costs, can have only a marginal effect. For the director, the engineer, the foreman, and the worker to change their long-established behavior, they will have to be satisfied with the answer to the question, "What's in it for me?" Moreover, they will have to believe that the changes will endure. As yet they do not have a satisfactory answer to the question and are skeptical about the durability of Gorbachev's initiatives.

The Soviet economy lacks a key incentive for modernization—competition. Soviet industry exists in a seller's market. The new Soviet leaders recognize this. It is not clear, however, what they are planning to do about it, and how they can find a functional equivalent of competition. In the Hungarian economic model, a strong element of competition was introduced by extensive participation in the world market. This is scarcely possible for the Soviet Union.

It is not yet proven that Gorbachev is a convinced radical "marketizer." In a meeting in the spring of 1987 with a Yugoslav delegation, according to Yugoslav sources, Gorbachev is said to have castigated the Yugoslav system and questioned its socialist character. The potential for liberalization in the Soviet economy within its present parameters is great. But its ceiling without structural marketing reform is not as high and flexible as Gorbachev evidently believes.

Not the least of the obstacles to Gorbachev's program is the multinational character of the Soviet state. Gorbachev's policy toward the non-Russian republics contains two elements that illustrate the complexity of the issues involved. The first is to root out the tightly knit Mafias of party-state officials who ruled their republics as fiefdoms during the Brezhnev period and the interregnum.

The second element of Gorbachev's policy toward the non-Russian republics is a measure of glasnost' and democratization: open discussions of nationality relations in the Soviet Union will occur. There may be greater cultural autonomy for the intelligentsia and the populations of those republics and perhaps even a somewhat greater toleration of their religions. It is probably clear to the Soviet leaders that transplanting *glasnost'* and democratization to the non-Russian republics carries with it a greater danger of producing unintended negative consequences than in Russia itself. The cohesive glue of Russian patriotism is missing in these republics. It is quite probable that the "new course" will reinforce native nationalism, centrifugal tendencies, and demands for much greater autonomy.

Recent examples are the riots in Alma-Ata, the capital of Kazakhstan, when its leader, Kunayev, was replaced by a Russian, Gennadi Kolbin; the Tatar demonstration in Moscow to press for a return to their Crimean homeland, from which Stalin had evicted them; the far from frivolous dispute in the Ukraine about whether menus in restaurants should be printed in Ukrainian or Russian; and a letter from 38 Byelorussian intellectuals to the General Secretary asking for radical changes in the teaching and use of the Byelorussian language in the Republic in place of Russian.

Many Western and Soviet analysts see the rise of national friction and discord in the Soviet Union as a major danger to Moscow. They may be right. The anti-Russian demonstrations in Alma-Ata may have been a taste of things to come. National disintegration is not, however, imminent; nor will Russian authorities be unable to deal with the unrest. Of key importance here is the course of events in the Ukraine. The Ukraine is treated by Moscow less as an imperial province than as a junior partner in ruling the Soviet Union. As long as the bond of the Slavic nations of the Soviet Union is not drastically weakened, the national aspirations and even unrest among the non-Slavic elites and peoples can be contained.

Yet there is another aspect of the ethnic national question in the Soviet Union that may have an even greater impact on the fate of Gorbachev's reforms. The very fact of the multi-national nature of the Soviet Union will affect the scope and depth of any plans by Gorbachev to institute structural reforms. Such potential reforms, and even some that are already underway, would inevitably involve a devolution of power and greater local autonomy. Knowing well the potential dangers that this would create, the new leadership may be unwilling to go far in such reforms in the Soviet Union as a whole. The multi-ethnicity would act as a powerful brake on any reforms desired or contemplated by Gorbachev. How the General Secretary proposes to reconcile greater freedom, more *glasnost'*, more autonomy, while striving at the same time for greater cohesion of the multi-national state is not at all clear.

From the inception of the Soviet Union, its domestic development was closely related to its international conduct. It is therefore not surprising that a number of obstacles to the implementation of Gorbachev's program are international in nature. The most obvious are the costs of the Soviet role as a global power "equal" to the United States and the burden of an arms race that, despite some progress in arms control negotiations, does not yet show signs of abating. The most important international obstacle is the Soviet East European empire and the likely impact of Gorbachev's domestic reforms on the socialist satellites.

The new leader is committed to the preservation of Soviet domination in its empire. This is not only for the sake of Soviet security but also, and primarily, in the interest of the leader's and his party's legitimacy within the Soviet Union itself. Gorbachev's East European policy is still not fully formulated, and contains much of the improvisation so typical of him.

These policies may be characterized as centrist. When he took power Gorbachev moved swiftly to reestablish Moscow's control over the East European Communist elites, which was weakened in the last years of Brezhnev and during the interregnum. At present his policy has three major components: to preserve socio-political stability in these countries; to assure the closeness of the empire to its metropolitan power; and to extract a greater contribution from Eastern Europe to the modernization of Russia itself.

Gorbachev is personally neither for nor against socio-political and economic reforms in Eastern Europe. He will speak in Rumania about the need for more democracy under this most oppressive European regime. To the Hungarians he will speak about the need for greater discipline. To the East Germans he will press for a greater contribution to the common cause and warn about the necessary limitations of their flirtation with West Germany. In the approaching succession of the top leaders of virtually all of the East European countries, he probably wants the conservative Czechoslovak leader, Gustav Husak,* to be replaced by someone more liberal, and the liberal, Janos Kadar of Hungary by someone more conservative.

By all accounts Gorbachev's favorite East European leader is General Wojciech Jaruzelski of Poland. Obviously, this cannot be because of the modernizing programs or initiatives in Poland. The country is economically stagnant and lacks a realistic plan for economic reform. But Jaruzelski saved the Russians from the terrible political and economic costs of invasion. A Polish nationalist, he showed himself in Gorbachev's eyes to be committed to a close relationship with his Russian "elder brother." He restored political stability. Yet his kind

---

*Gustav Husak was replaced by Milos Jakes just before this book went to press [Ed.].

of stability is not that of Ceausescu and Husak. It goes hand in hand with what are enormous private freedoms by Communist standards.

However flexible Gorbachev's policies toward Eastern Europe may be, potential developments there could threaten his reform program within the Soviet Union. There are two reasons for deeming this threat to be serious: incongruities in Gorbachev's policies toward the East European countries and the probable effect on these countries of the course of reform in the Soviet Union.

The East European governments do not have the legitimacy of traditional, democratic or authentically revolutionary regimes. Their legitimacy and stability is shallow and critically depends on the economic performance of their regimes and, of course, on coercion and the threat of it from the Soviet Union. Their economies are faring badly. The primary goal of Gorbachev's policy towards these countries, socio-political stability, requires an improvement in their economic performance. This, in turn, requires closer economic ties with capitalist countries. Such ties are far more difficult to establish today than in the 1970s because of higher unemployment, stiffer competition, tighter credit in the West and growing protectionism in the global economy. Closer political relations are often the condition for better economic ties. The second and third goal of Gorbachev's East European policy—greater cohesion of the empire and a more significant European contribution to Russia's modernization—are at odds with his first goal of stability.

Equally as important is the potential impact of events within the Soviet Union on Eastern Europe. The potential domestic risks and dangers of Gorbachev's policies in the Soviet Union pale in comparison to their potential consequences in Eastern Europe. There is simply no way to prevent the Soviet example from encouraging the democratic and nationalistic aspirations of the elite, the liberal intelligentsia and the dissatisfied workers in Eastern Europe, aspirations that cannot but take an anti-Soviet course. This potential danger is well understood in Moscow. It may affect the fate of Gorbachev's domestic reforms in two ways.

First, the recognition of the danger by the Soviet leadership may restrain the changes that are planned. Quite a strange situation has developed, in which the conservative regimes in Eastern Europe, primarily Czechoslovakia and East Germany (as well as Castro's regime in Cuba), are unhappy about Gorbachev's reforms, particularly in the political and cultural areas. A recent East European joke illustrates their concern. It refers to the Brezhnev Doctrine, which the Soviet Union invoked in 1968 to justify its invasion of Czechoslovakia to keep it Communist. The current joke has the East German and Czech armies preparing to invade the Soviet Union in defense of the Brezhnev Doctrine.

Second, the spark in Moscow may create a fire in Eastern Europe that will create the necessity as the Soviets see it for an internal invasion like the one in Poland in 1981, or a direct Soviet military intervention, as in Czechoslovakia in 1968. It is at least possible that Dubcek's course in 1968 would be acceptable to Gorbachev; but Poland of 1980–81 and Hungary of 1956 certainly would not be. It is well to remember that reforms in the post-Khrushchevian Soviet Union were for all practical purposes cut off by the Soviet invasion of Czechoslovakia in 1968.

It is unfortunate for Soviet reforms that *all* socialist countries that have chosen to move away from the traditional Stalinist model are in deep economic as well as political trouble. Yugoslavia is now economically in the worst situation of its postwar history. Politically, it is a country torn by deep, sometimes violent, strife. It faces a long period of economic austerity and social ethnic unrest.

Hungary, the major success story of the Soviet East European empire, is also in serious trouble. Two elements of the Hungarian crisis are worth emphasizing. First, the Hungarian model of market socialism has reached the limit of its effectiveness. To sustain a healthy economy the Hungarian leadership must cross the border between state-regulated economic policies and true freedom for market forces. This will require the recognition of the legitimacy of unemployment and of failure (i.e., the bankruptcy) of many of its economic units. Such measures will not be easy. Second, at the center of the Hungarian model of socialism has been the country's close relation to and dependence on the capitalist world trade and credit market. Neither is particularly healthy at present. A declining capacity to sell its goods to the West and past credit commitments have left Hungary in deep economic difficulty.

In his struggle for radical reform, Gorbachev must therefore face the failures and difficulties of reform in other socialist countries. This cannot but help those who urge caution in the Soviet Union. Of course, the radical reformers can point to what Hungary has achieved in the past two decades and to the success of China's agriculture. But the troubles of socialist reform elsewhere certainly serve as persuasive arguments in the internal Party disputes and struggles in the Soviet Union.

Forces that Favor Gorbachev's Success

Seventy years after the Bolshevik revolution, which signalled the start of an enormous effort to achieve equality at any price with its capitalist enemies, the Soviet Union is again at the starting gate of another attempt at modernization. The Soviet Union's survival from foreign enemies is no longer at stake. What is at stake is the country's ability to achieve long-lasting domestic stability, to secure its imperial domain, and to attain a level of international power and influence commensurate with the aspirations of its leadership and political elite.

The Soviet Union today possesses many of the prerequisites of another successful modernization process. What it lacks, and what calls into question the success of its latest efforts at catching up with modern countries, are systemic social, economic, political and cultural prerequisites of modernity as they are understood when the end of our millennium approaches.

It is probably futile for the Soviet Union to attempt to become another United States, Japan or West Germany. But it does not have to remain backward. Many of the factors that prevent the country's modernization were created by purposeful human action or are the unintended consequences of such actions. They are man-made and can be un-made. The progress that the Soviet Union makes will depend on will and faith, trust and cynicism, divisiveness and justice, self-interest and compassion, routine and innovation, and above all else, the element in human activity with the greatest potential for both creativity and destructiveness—leadership.

Gorbachev's progress in his quest for modernization can be attained only if many of the dominant, insidious and dark sides of the system over which he presides can be overcome. The foregoing review of his progress has not led to an optimistic conclusion. Yet the strength of a creative and goal-centered leadership rests exactly on its belief in success against all odds. What are the most significant forces in Gorbachev's favor? What are his chances of igniting the spark that will lift his nation to a new level? What are the chances that the human factor will once again give the lie to "objective" odds?

Our discussion of the obstacles to Gorbachev's plans for reform of necessity also pointed out the major elements of his relative strength. Not much more can be said about the General Secretary's assets. The most important of them are the actual and potential powers and authority of his office. If he plays his cards right, and is both cautious and determined, what happened to past General (or First) Secretaries will happen to him. His power, up to a point, will increase.

Gorbachev's mettle as a strategist has yet to be tested. His tactical skill in political infighting, however, is now clear beyond question. His power is increasing visibly, but so is the resistance to the implementation of his plans. In the top echelons of the leadership the power of his opponents is declining. The power reserves of his office are far from being depleted, and after the Party Conference in June 1988 his personal position within the top leadership and in the Central Committee will probably be even more secure than it was six months earlier.

The tangible and symbolic assets of the position of General Secretary are considerable, especially when the post is occupied by a dynamic and tactically skillful personality. The Soviet Party and State still remain highly centralized and the circular flow of power still provides major reserves of stability for the top leader. He can hire and fire, he can induce required behavior by a combination of carrots and sticks. He can build, as Gorbachev is building, in the higher echelons of the elite a political machine that is loyal to him personally and has acquired an ever-increasing stake in the success of his endeavors.

The Central Committee of the Party (over 300 full members) has in the past simply reflected the balance of power in the Politburo and in the Secretariat. Gorbachev may not yet have an automatic majority in the Central Committee, but it is immensely difficult, however, for his opponents to control a Plenary meeting of the Central Committee, establish its agenda, and manipulate its membership while they are a clear minority in the Politburo, and an insignificant part of the Central Committee Secretariat. In the era of *glasnost'* and democratization it is possible that the Central Committee will become more important. As of now, however, democratization has not yet reached the top decision-making, executive and symbolic institutions of the Party and the State.

The office of the General Secretary has also traditionally had immense symbolic power. The General Secretary is statutorily elected by the Congress of the Party, not by his colleagues in the Politburo and Secretariat or even the Party's Central Committee. He alone speaks *for* the Party. He is the incarnation of the Party's power and of its infallibility. In an ironic way, the traditionalism of Gorbachev's opponents makes it clear, however, that the General Secretary is not engaged in "experiments" but rather in the early stages of comprehensive reform. In the economic area, every element of the Stalinist model is being called into question. There is almost no sphere of public life in the Soviet Union that is not a target of reform. The political danger to a Soviet leader who initiates such comprehensive changes is much greater than the instituted "experimentation" and incremental reforms. But the chances that the reforms will succeed are also significantly higher.

All the elements mentioned above that favor Gorbachev's program are important. But the most important factors in his favor are psychological. There is a feeling in the Soviet Union that there exists no alternative to Gorbachev. In part this feeling refers to Gorbachev as a person and a leader. In part it refers to his program and the direction in which it is moving. The program may be imperfect, but it is the only one available. The alternatives of tyranny, stagnation, social miasma, and hopelessness are worse. The question, "Are you for or against Gorbachev?" requires the answer, "Compared with what?" In this respect the mood of the country supports change. Most of the people who do not actively support Gorbachev do not trust him yet, and are skeptical that he will bring about change. Stalinism and Brezhnevism have few supporters.

The active public may not constitute the majority of Soviet society. Yet it is the active minorities that are always harbingers of change and a decisive force in effecting it. However, until such reforms are tested and recognized as effective, the determination necessary for bold action will be lacking. Past Soviet experience tells us that the response to this contradiction tends to be largely self-defeating. From the range of possible reforms, the leaders usually select a compromise that will cause the least disturbance and require the least cost and effort. They usually introduce it as a limited experiment, virtually ensuring that the results will be far from conclusive and often disappointing. This outcome in turn fuels the arguments of the reform's opponents, who block its further implementation. The leadership soon reverts to the traditional way of doing business, tinkering with the system and thereby allowing it to absorb and nullify the well-intentioned, piecemeal reforms. This pattern explains the inherent stability of the traditional economic system and the failure of recurrent attempts at reform.

A variation of this pattern, the "hothouse phenomenon," constitutes yet another instance of counterproductive experimentation. In this variation, the leadership initiates reform on a carefully restricted scale under conditions that have been selected to encourage success. When the leadership attempts to expand the reform to different geographic areas or to other economic units, however, these conditions simply cannot be duplicated.

At the beginning of Gorbachev's rule it looked as if the incremental pattern of reforms would be repeated. By now it is working in his *favor,* just as it worked for Stalin in the late 1920s. The traditional view is that one does not fight against the Party, and Gorbachev *is* the Party. These factors work, of course, only up to a point, but they work in Gorbachev's favor. Moreover, the mood of the Party elite and activists in the last years of Brezhnev's rule and during the ensuing interregnum was increasingly one of embarrassment, impatience and a desire for greater dynamism and openness to change at the top. (This was initially true of Stalin and Khrushchev as well, but not true of Brezhnev, whose leadership responded to the widespread desire for stability and retrenchment.)

Many of the people and groups who supported Gorbachev's coming to power oppose his policies today. Yet it would be a mistake to assume that the general belief in the need for change has suddenly disappeared. Ironically, *glasnost'* makes the opposition to change more apparent today than at any time since Khrushchev's ouster. Yet the widespread desire for change persists. Other than the ideologues who condemn Gorbachev and his entire program, most people dislike one or another aspect of it. They do not necessarily overlap or reinforce each other, and the restrictive conditions of the Soviet system make it difficult for them to form an alliance.

Moreover, the investment that the party's *aktiv* has in Gorbachev is increasing the longer he stays in power. In this respect his status in the international arena influences his domestic status. The disarmament causes with which he closely identified himself are popular in Russia. Prime Minister Thatcher's symbolic recognition of Gorbachev as an historical figure strengthened his position in the Soviet Union. Similarly, his meetings with President Reagan have had the same effect.

Gorbachev's *social* power base may be broader than his base in the bureaucracy. Those to whom his program offers most, and most immediately, is the Soviet middle class. While this class is educated, it is not powerful. It lives better than the workers, but not dramatically so; and its aspirations are greater than those of the working class. As much has been suggested by the sociologist Tatiana Zaslavskaya, of the Academy of Social Sciences at Novosibirsk, who is closely identified with Gorbachev, when she wrote this year "the most qualified (*i.e.* professional) part of the population, which carries the burden of the movement of the society as a whole, is precisely the one that will come out ahead in the present situation." As of now, this stratum may not want to risk total support of Gorbachev's program. But the longer he stays in power the more active and supportive they will be.

Major reforms in Communist countries display two basic patterns—the incremental and the comprehensive. The Soviet Union and Poland in the 1960s were examples of the first; Hungary and the People's Republic of China are examples of the second. The incremental pattern is characterized by experimentation. Experiments are the enemies of major reforms. Far-reaching reforms must be carried out without hesitation. This is especially so within the generation that will decide the political fate of Gorbachev—his own generation. Most of them entered politics during Khrushchev's anti-Stalinist campaign with great hopes of renewal and then saw their hopes dashed. They are now being given a second lease on life. Their mood, their determination, are a major factor in Gorbachev's progress.

Another emotion that is widely represented in the politically active circles in Moscow has an apocalyptic element to it. "This is our last chance," many say. For some, the "last chance" is an expression of patriotic feeling, of the need to make Russia great. For others it is of a last chance to break the dominant pattern of Russian and Soviet history. For still others, it involves the conviction that the Soviet people have suffered too much and too long for the sake of the "glorious future" that never came, and that they are presented with the "last chance" to live better during their own lifetimes.

The apocalyptic element is almost always present in the "this is our last chance" feeling. Not for the first time in Russian history, a large part of the intelligentsia—and this time joined by a part of the political elite—is filled with apocalyptic feelings and visions. They believe that, in the next decade and a half, the choice will not be between radical change supervised by the leadership and reform segments of the Party, on the one hand, and bureaucratic inertia, conservatism, in a word, Brezhnevism, on the other. For them, the most likely alternative to reforms is a new tyranny.

Yet another sentiment was best expressed to me by a middle-ranking member of the Soviet elite. When presented with the irrefutable evidence of the dramatic obstacles to radical change in his country he responded, "This may all be true, but psychologically I cannot even consider the possibility that Gorbachev will fail, will be defeated." The intensity of commitment to Gorbachev's plans of the relatively small band of his supporters may ultimately carry a greater weight than the majority, which is simply apathetic, skeptical, and uncommitted.

Similarly, another supporter of Gorbachev, when urged to face the probability of upheaval in Eastern Europe, angrily retorted, "Eastern Europe has already once in the past, in 1968, (in Czechoslovakia) cut off the possibilities of reform in our country. This time we will not let the East Europeans dictate whether we have or do not have a chance to modernize Russia. We will defend, if needed, our security interests, but they will not stop our efforts." It was useless to try to convince this party intellectual that Soviet policies in Eastern Europe should be dramatically changed, if only because they may derail the reform movement in the Soviet Union itself.

There can be little doubt that for the leadership, segments of the Party, and the educated class, the greatest source of commitment and determination for change is patriotism—or, if one prefers, Russian nationalism. It is by now a cliche that the Soviets are insecure and that their relations with the West are influenced by this insecurity.

But the strongest feeling one now encounters in the Soviet Union is shame; shame at the country's backwardness, at the brutality of Soviet life, at the lack of beauty, at the militaristic order at a time of worldwide revolution of democratic participation, at the drunkenness and social pathology that is everywhere. This feeling is encountered not only among the elite and the intelligentsia, but also among ordinary people. Sometimes in discussions with Westerners the shame is camouflaged by artificial arrogance or bitter humor, but it is nonetheless an angry, deep, and uncompromising shame, and a quest for respectability by the standards of civilized countries.

It is a shame that is most fully expressed in typically Russian heart-to-heart talks with friends that last long into the night. Such a deep, almost desperate shame is a powerful weapon in Gorbachev's arsenal. It provides a major psychological basis for his efforts.

Revolutions or sweeping reforms very often succeed when they fail, and very often fail when they succeed. The Russian Revolution of 1917 succeeded beyond the wildest imagination of its most ardent supporters. Yet it failed in the sense that it abandoned a major part of the Bolshevik program, for which the revolution was made and the Civil War was won. The Hungarian Revolution of 1956 clearly failed. Yet some of the beliefs for which Hungarians risked their lives came into being in the next three decades.

Whether Gorbachev's reforms succeed or fail, their ultimate outcomes will amost certainly be different from what Gorbachev expects and Western observers of the Soviet Union predict. He may succeed in modernization but not radically transform the Soviet political system. He may fail in ambitious goals and indicators of modernization but may still bring enormous and lasting changes to the Soviet socio-political system. This is because two variables intervene between the goals and the outcomes of reforms and revolutions. The first is the relative autonomy and importance of the "process" as opposed to the "product." The second concerns the unavoidability of unintended consequences of actions directed toward specific reform goals.

In Gorbachev's revolution the "process" is the social democratization, political liberalization and economic decentralization. The "goal" is modernity. The process may well make possible major improvements in the Soviet Union. It is at the same time unlikely that changes in the Soviet Union's *relative* level of modernization compared with the West will be significant by the twenty-first century. It is entirely reasonable to expect that the changes in process, if they continue for more than a decade, will become *normative* rather than mainly *instrumental.* The Soviet political, economic, and cultural elites may elevate political necessity to a self-evident truth. It is also plausible, however, that the concentrated effect of the utilization of the Soviet Union's enormous objective reserves of growth and qualitative improvements, which have been so under-utilized by past regimes, will create a positive, if not long-lasting, result sooner than expected and "freeze" the Soviet process at an earlier point than one would predict, based on the present speed of Gorbachev's reforms.

Brezhnev's conservative rule, and its prolongation beyond the patience of the political class by Chernenko's year in office, contributed decisively to an unintended consequence, the radicalism of the reforms proposed by Gorbachev. The development of *glasnost'* led to the unintended consequence of a reactionary backlash symbolized by the "Memory" group. In discussing the plausible outcomes of Gorbachev's "reconstruction that will lead to revolutionary transformation," what are the likely unintended consequences? Two are worth considering.

First, if Gorbachev does not succeed in injecting dynamism into the Soviet economy within a reasonable period of time, he may be ousted and his regime replaced. Depending on the domestic and international circumstances, which are impossible to predict, a successor regime could represent one of three orientations: it could be more radical in its program for change in the Soviet Union, it could return to the Brezhnevian equilibrium and settle for a slow decay and declining international position, or it could revert to a modernized version of strict authoritarianism, or even some form of despotism. The first outcome is most likely at a relatively early stage of Gorbachev's reform, in perhaps five to six years; the second is most likely when the Gorbachev regime becomes tired—in eight to ten years; the third is most likely to evolve if an international catalyst of major proportion is introduced, such as major revolts in Eastern Europe. The third outcome, a strict authoritarianism with elements of despotism, is the most likely consequence of Gorbachev's visible failure.

A second unintended consequence of Gorbachev's program of reforms concerns the Soviet Union's international goals and position. The major source of Gorbachev's determination to make his country modern is his own, and the political elite's, growing recognition that Soviet and Russian international aspirations to greatness will rest on an inadequate foundation without modernization. Soviet patriotism and Russian nationalism are the sources of the domestic creative turmoil that is gripping the country. As Gorbachev said in his first major speech, in the fall of 1984, before he took power: "What is at stake today is the ability of the Soviet Union to enter the new millennium in a manner worthy of a great prosperous power. . . . Without the hard work and complete dedication of each and every one it is not even possible to preserve what has been achieved."

The most probable outcome of Gorbachev's efforts is, as noted, major domestic improvements and the elimination of a widening East-West technological gap (although not of the gap itself). Were such an outcome to occur by the turn of the century, it could affect Soviet international aspirations in one of two ways. The more likely would be a more active but less military Soviet Union. The less likely, but quite plausible, would be an eventual displacement or reduction of the international goals and aspirations, the international rationale, of Gorbachev's revolution.

What factors argue for the plausibility of the second outcome? First, the Soviets have achieved strategic parity with the United States and there is nothing on the horizon that can change this. Never in their history have the Russians been as secure from external danger as they are now and will remain in the foreseeable future. The dangers to the Soviet regime are internal and imperial. With domestic progress, the Soviet insecurity that contributed so significantly to the arms race since the achievement of parity may diminish. The arms race was not, of course, the primary cause of the Soviet-American, or East-West, conflict, but it contributed significantly to the virulence of the conflict. A Soviet Union that understands that it is externally secure may be less hostile to the West. The intermediate-range effects of Gorbachev's program of "reconstruction" may also partly redirect Soviet ambitions and aspirations from the international to the domestic arena. At the present such redirection is to a large extent strategic and tactical, but it may become permanent. The Soviet Union may become more a traditional great power than it had been, preoccupied internationally with the factors *directly* influencing its domestic security, and with its status rather than its power in the global arena. Such an outcome is plausible if Gorbachev is only partly successful in his modernization program. If this happens, however, the Gorbachev enterprise, which has begun to enhance Soviet foreign policy resources, may end, as a result of the unintended consequences of his reforms, with a Soviet Union that is much less belligerent and ambitious in the international arena.

After the Revolution and Civil War in Russia, Lenin defined his vision of the future in a now-famous phrase, "Socialism equals electrification plus Soviet power." Gorbachev has not yet given us his definition of what combination of technological level of development and political, social and cultural characteristics is socialism. It is clear that "electrification," the symbol of the First Industrial Revolution, will not suffice on the technological side of the equation. But it is also becoming clear that "Soviet power" will not suffice in the political, economic, social, and cultural field, if it is represented by the Stalinist or Brezhnevian model.

The countries where Communist Parties rule have, with some ex-
pections, notably Cuba and Rumania, begun to move away from the
traditional Soviet model. While in the 1950s and 1960s, the discussion
within the Communist world examined the "different roads *to* socialism," today the focus is on "different roads *from* socialism."

Russia was a latecomer to the process of modernization. The Soviet
Union has continued in this position throughout its history. From
almost the beginning of the Russian revolutionary regime, its leadership
borrowed on a vast scale, consciously, not only technology, but also
methods of organization and technological culture from capitalist countries. Stalin's Soviet system fused the capitalism of the sweat shop
with Oriental despotism. Gorbachev's vision of the new Soviet system
is likely to be a combination of modern capitalism with enlightened
authoritarianism.

PART FOUR

Russia and the West

9

The Evolution of U.S. Policy Goals Toward the USSR in the Postwar Era

John Gaddis

One of Sigmund Freud's acknowledged—if, by today's standards, somewhat sexist—frustrations was his inability "despite my thirty years of research into the feminine soul" to answer the question: "What does a woman want?"[1] Analogies between psychoanalysis and geopolitics are usually best not made, but it does seem reasonable to surmise that the great Viennese physician might have nodded sympathetically had he lived to witness the difficulties more recent generations of researchers have had in trying to fathom precisely what the United States government has wanted in its relations with the rest of the world.

To be sure, the foreign policy objectives of most great nations are rarely immediately apparent. They reflect, first of all, state interests, and these can exist in both explicit and tacit forms that parallel closely the conscious and sub-conscious motivations of Freud's patients. It is not at all unusual to find interests concealed behind the same facades of self-deception, over-simplification, bias, myth and legend that impede the diagnosis of individual psychoses in a clinical setting; further complicating the problem is the fact that when it is the behavior of governments that is under scrutiny, it is normally multiple clinicians who are doing the analyzing. Then, too, there is the difficulty that what one intends is not what one always winds up doing: that is a problem for individuals but even more so for governments, obliged as they are to filter policy through complex and often discordant bureaucracies without losing the support of vociferous but often clashing constituencies.

Nor have those who write about foreign policy done all that much to clarify objectives: one difficulty here is the academic propensity for methodological compartmentalization. Political scientists tend to focus on the *processes* by which policy is made;[2] but they give little attention to the effects those processes are supposed to produce, or to whether we would even recognize the intended destination were we ever to arrive there. Historians concern themselves with the *evolution* of policy over time;[3] but rarely make explicit the assumptions underlying it at any point, or the manner in which these differ from what has gone before and from what is to follow. Most journalists, when they write about such matters at all, do so in an anecdotal style that leaves tasks of generalization almost entirely to their entertained—but not always profoundly enlightened—readers.[4]

What is needed if we are to understand what the United States has really sought in world affairs—if we are to overcome the official reluctance to define objectives, the methodological bog with which scholars have surrounded them, and the tendency of journalists cheerfully to assume that "truth will out" if enough "facts" are assembled—is an approach that combines generalization with careful examination of the historical record. Theory has the value of suggesting a *range* of possible policy goals: it can facilitate both the specification of underlying assumptions and their systematic comparison. But the results must then be matched up against historical reality to see which among possible objectives Washington has actually sought, when, and for what reasons. Both positive and negative findings are of interest in such an analysis, because the rejection of otherwise plausible options can reveal as much about ultimate goals as can their implementation.

There are, of course, problems with this kind of approach. It proceeds deductively rather than inductively, thereby running the risk of imposing upon the past an analytical structure that exists only in the mind of the analyst. It can distort and, at times, even reverse chronology, thus obscuring obvious relationships between cause and effect. But chronological empiricism, too, has its weaknesses, not the least of which is the awkwardness of attempting to generalize in any meaningful way from it. Historians have long realized—as their colleagues in the physical and biological sciences now are coming to[5]—that change is not always a gradual process: it can take the form of sudden and even dramatic shifts from one state of equilibrium to another, with extended periods of continuity in between. If one thinks of these theoretically derived options, therefore, as "paradigms,"[6] and considers not only the assumptions upon which they rest but the historical context in which they flourish, fail to flourish, or shift from one to another, then perhaps one can make a certain amount of progress toward unravelling "what the United States wants" in its relations with the rest of the world.

This essay applies that approach to a particular problem: what have been the objectives of the United States in its relations with the Soviet Union since the formation of that state seven decades ago? I have organized it around five theoretically plausible alternatives: (1) overthrowing the Soviet regime altogether; (2) containing Soviet influence within the boundaries of the U.S.S.R.; (3) changing that country's internal structure; (4) competing selectively within a framework of overall co-existence; and (5) cooperating generally within a framework of shared interests. I will then compare these options against the historical record of American policy toward the Soviet Union since 1917 with a view to determining: (a) which of them were seriously pursued, by whom, for how long, and with what results; (b) what the assumptions behind these options were; and (c) whether a comparison of those assumptions with the results they produced can provide a useful standard for evaluating current and future policy toward the U.S.S.R.

Option One: Overthrowing the Regime

The United States could have sought, as an objective, to reverse the consequences of the Bolshevik Revolution altogether: to seek the overthrow of the Soviet government, to remove the Communist Party of the Soviet Union from its position of authority inside that country, and possibly even to break up the U.S.S.R. itself into its constituent parts. The assumptions underlying such an objective would be: (1) that the government that came to power in 1917 is and has always been illegitimate; (2) that the United States can have no interests in common with such a government; (3) that Washington is obliged, because of American national interests and the interests of legitimate states elsewhere in the world, to take the lead in eliminating that government; and (4) that there can be no stability in world politics until that goal has been accomplished.

The abstract formulation is clear enough. But what historical evidence is there that the United States government—or even isolated officials within it—have ever regarded overthrowing the Soviet regime as a serious objective? Has there been a point at which all of the assumptions that would have to inform such a goal have been in place?

It was the administration of Woodrow Wilson that came closest to seeking the overthrow of the Soviet government as a deliberate objective. The year 1917 witnessed not only the triumph of Bolshevism in Russia but also the abrupt—if temporary—emergence of the United

States from its long-standing tradition of non-involvement in European affairs. What happened in Petrograd in November of that year appeared to threaten a conception of American interests that had abruptly and dramatically expanded; Washington's response, in turn, appeared to threaten Bolshevism itself as President Wilson refused to extend diplomatic recognition to the new regime, initiated an ambitious ideological campaign against it, and in the summer of 1918 actually authorized military intervention by the United States—alongside that of its wartime allies—in Siberia and North Russia.

But the fact that Wilson considered the new Soviet government illegitimate and saw the United States as having no interests in common with it does not mean that he was prepared to regard that government's elimination as an overriding priority. Intervention took place, it is important to remember, within the larger context of a world war: the Bolsheviks' separate peace had endangered prospects for an Allied victory, and Wilson, like the British and the French, was determined to prevent Germany from taking advantage of what had happened by transferring troops and supplies to the Western Front. Painful experience in Mexico had made the President sensitive to the danger that foreign intervention might actually *strengthen* a revolutionary regime by conferring the legitimacy of nationalism on it; significantly one of his motives for authorizing American participation in the Siberian and North Russian operations had been to ensure—or to attempt to ensure—that they did not become so overtly anti-Bolshevik as to produce that effect.[7]

What Wilson wanted was a "nonpartisan" intervention: he hoped to keep German troops tied down in the East while at the same time creating a political arena in which the various forces in Russian society—Reds as well as Whites—could compete democratically for the favor of the Russian people.[8] It was to be intervention *on behalf* of self-determination; not intervention to *crush* revolution. Admittedly, this may have been a naive approach. Certainly it reflected little sense of Russian historical realities, or of the conditions that existed inside that country at the time. The Bolsheviks themselves clearly regarded it as a scheme aimed at their own destruction, and with good reason, for as their own actions in dissolving the freely elected Constituent Assembly had already shown, they were incapable of winning popular support and had no intention of trying to do so.[9]

But there is a difference between hoping that something will happen as a serendipitous by-product of a praiseworthy effort, and resolving to do whatever is necessary—however unpraiseworthy—to bring the intended consequence about. Wilson's policy fell into the first rather than the second category. He clearly hoped that the Russian people, given the opportunity, would overthrow Bolshevism; but he was at no point willing to commit his own or his country's energies single-mindedly to that purpose. Victory over Germany and the creation of a stable postwar order were his major priorities; with the American people yearning for a return to their normal state of disengagement from world affairs, the possibility of engineering anything as purposeful, costly, or *internationalist* as an anti-Bolshevik crusade was simply out of the question. And even if that had been possible, there is reason to believe Wilson himself would have regarded such a crusade with profound ambivalence: he had used force to promote democracy in unprecedented ways—that had been his avowed objective in getting into the war in the first place—but he never ceased to agonize over the contradictions involved in resorting to coercion to bring about freedom from it.[10]

"The existing regime in Russia is based upon the negation of every principle of honor and good faith, and every usage and convention, underlying the whole structure of international law; the negation, in short, of every principle upon which it is possible to base harmonious and trustful relations, whether of nations or of individuals." This is how Bainbridge Colby, Wilson's last Secretary of State, justified making "non-recognition" the official policy of the United States toward Soviet Russia in 1920.[11] But although this statement emphasized in the strongest possible terms the illegitimacy of the Soviet regime and the impossibility of having normal relations with it, the Colby note also reflected Washington's quiet acknowledgement that Bolshevism was now soundly entrenched and not likely soon to go away. One rarely proclaims policies toward governments one does not expect to survive.

Non-recognition had evolved, under Wilson, as a means by which the United States could make clear its dislike for what was happening beyond its borders without at the same time feeling obliged to do anything about it.[12] Colby made this point clearly enough: American officials would welcome the overthrow of Bolshevism, but they were not prepared to take active measures—beyond denying normal diplomatic relations—to bring that event about. Instead they would rely upon the effects of isolation and the passage of time to produce the desired results.

As it happened, events proceeded in just the opposite direction. Most other nations had established diplomatic ties with Moscow by the mid-1920s; even more remarkably, American trade, investment—and, at a critical moment in 1921–22, famine relief—had by that time played a major role in stabilizing the new Soviet government. Far from contributing to the overthrow of Bolshevism, the Republican administrations of the 1920's inadvertently helped to stabilize it through their own commitment to the idea—based on the principles of limited government and free enterprise—that they had no authority to force private individuals and corporations into compliance with official policy.[13] The contradictions of capitalism, as Lenin would have been the first to acknowledge, can move in mysterious ways.

Another opportunity to seek the overthrow of the Soviet government—but one never acted upon—came during the first two years of World War II. There was nothing automatic about the Roosevelt administration's forebearance toward Moscow during the early months of that conflict. Goodwill generated by the establishment of diplomatic relations six years earlier had largely dissipated by 1939; the Nazi-Soviet Pact and the invasion of Finland caused it to disappear altogether.[14] Contemplating counterfactuals is always risky, but given the persistence of isolationism in the United States together with the consequent political dangers of aiding Britain and France, it would not have been inconceivable for Roosevelt to have yielded to the geopolitical logic of Neville Chamberlain and Joseph P. Kennedy: that Russia posed the greater ultimate danger than Germany, and that the Western democracies should accordingly seek to channel Hitler's aggressive tendencies toward the east, thereby turning one repugnant adversary against another while sparing themselves.[15]

What Roosevelt actually did, of course, could hardly have been more different: he took the consistent position that Germany posed the greater threat to world order than did the Soviet Union; he resisted pressures to break diplomatic relations with Moscow following the pact with Germany and the attack on Finland; he ran considerable risks both politically and constitutionally to get military assistance to Britain for use against the Germans; he went out of his way to share with Stalin intelligence pointing to the likelihood of a German attack; and when that attack finally came, in June, 1941, he immediately embraced the Russians as allies and within months made them eligible for Lend Lease, on the grounds that defense of the Soviet Union was now vital to the security of the United States.[16] These are not the actions of a nation determined to exploit the vulnerabilities of another.

To be sure, once the United States itself had entered the war, it was content to allow Russians to bear the main burden of ground fighting in Europe, a strategy that carried with it the obvious danger—some Soviet scholars have suggested the deliberate intent[17]—of exhausting Stalin's regime, or even bringing about its collapse. But it is not at all clear that the United States and Great Britain could have created a successful Second Front much earlier than in fact they did; a failed Second Front would only have helped Germany. It is worth recalling, as well, that the United States as this time was carrying virtually the entire weight of a not insubstantial war against Japan, a war from which the Soviet Union—for its own good reasons—had remained aloof. Nor should one forget the simple fact that Roosevelt expected to win: he knew full well that victory would ensure even a severely weakened Russia a significant expansion of political influence over the postwar world, especially if the United States reverted to isolationism thereafter, as the President thought it might.[18]

There is simply no evidence, then, that the Roosevelt administration at any point contemplated taking advantage of what in retrospect was the most obvious opportunity since 1917 to eliminate the Soviet regime: alignment, whether openly or surreptitiously, with the geopolitical objectives of Adolf Hitler.

Hitler's demise, of course, changed things drastically. The attainment of victory not only dissolved the chief bond that had held the Grand Alliance together; it also left a power vacuum in Central Europe with increasingly suspicious super-powers glaring at each other from opposite sides of it. The condition of those two powers would appear, at least on the surface, to have been very different. Whatever gains it had made in political influence as a result of the war, the Soviet Union was a crippled giant in 1945: it was in no condition to engage in any kind of protracted economic or military competition with its American rival. The United States, in contrast, was at the apex of its strength: its participation in the war had been, by comparison, relatively painless in terms of casualties suffered or civilian dislocation sustained; it had emerged from that conflict with an undamaged industrial plant twice the size of what it had been five years earlier; and it now possessed, as impressive products of that capacity, a monopoly over atomic weapons and the means to deliver them.

The question therefore arises: why did the United States not exploit these advantages in the wake of World War II to eliminate, or at least to neutralize, its only possible competitor for influence in the postwar world? With a succession of crises in Iran, Turkey, Greece, Czechoslovakia, and Berlin between 1946 and 1948, there was no absence of provocations that could have been seized upon as plausible justifications for such a policy. Stalin's totalitarianism was no less objectionable in American eyes than Hitler's had been; had not one of the "lessons" of the war just ended been that internal repression breeds external aggression? The wartime strategy of "unconditional surrender" had emphatically reinforced the principle of eliminating adversaries, not compromising with them. And there were prominent individuals—most conspicuously General George Patton—who urged immediate preventive war against the Soviet Union before it had had time to recover its strength.[19]

As had been the case with its predecessor, though, the Truman administration never seriously considered taking advantage of Soviet vulnerabilities in so cold-blooded a way. There were several reasons for this:

(a) However things may have appeared in retrospect, it was not all that clear *at the time* that the United States enjoyed so decisive a military edge over the Soviet Union. Both nations had demobilized substantially after the war, but American demobilization proceeded at twice the pace, in effect leaving the Soviet Union with at least the appearance of conventional force superiority in Europe.[20] Atomic bombs provided only a partial counter-balance: there were so few as late as 1949 that American military planners were expressing serious doubt as to whether the United States could prevail in a war with the Soviet Union, even if it used all available atomic weapons.[21] There also existed within the Truman administration, at least until the summer of 1950, the emphatic if misguided conviction that further increases in defense spending would almost certainly bankrupt the country.[22]

(b) Moral considerations—and their very realistic political implications—also discouraged any serious thought of initiating military action against the Soviet Union. Advocates of that alternative had to overcome the deeply engrained and widely held presumption that "Americans don't start wars."[23] It was a simple-minded and, in the light of history, at least a debatable proposition, but the political reality that lay behind it was inescapable: the American people would not support what they perceived to be aggression. For statesmen who had just emerged from fighting a war that had commanded almost universal approbation—but who remembered another two decades earlier that had not—the need to ensure public support was critical. And, at least for strict constructionists, there was also an interesting constitutional dilemma: how could a democracy plan—and secure necessary Congressional authorization for—a preventive war without giving away the fact that it was doing so?[24]

(c) Then there was, as well, the growing realization that the total elimination of adversaries can cause more problems than it solves. The experience of "unconditional surrender" during World War II had not been a happy one. It had left power vacuums in Europe and Northeast Asia that the United States had been obliged, within three years of victory, to attempt to fill. It had imposed upon Americans and their allies the complex and often distasteful burdens of military occupation. Given the size of the territory that would have to be occupied, forcing "unconditional surrender" on the Soviet Union in the event of war appeared to be a wholly unrealistic option. Nor could there be any certainty, as George F. Kennan pointed out, that a successor regime in Russia, following in the wake of a defeated or discredited Soviet government, would be any easier to deal with. As a result, contingency plans for war made no automatic provision for overthrowing the regime, but rather assumed, as Kennan put it, "a *political* settlement, *politically* negotiated."[25]

Underlying these arguments against preventive war and unconditional surrender was the sense that the Soviet government—unlike the adversaries of World War II—was not irredeemable: the whole idea of "containment" was based, after all, on the assumption that it is sometimes better to live with adversaries than to seek to destroy them. It is significant this viewpoint existed *prior* to the Soviet Union's acquisition of atomic weapons and of a retaliatory capacity that could be used directly against the United States. Even before the threat of nuclear annihilation had forced Americans to acknowledge the stake they had in the survival of their adversary, the idea of trying to overthrow the Soviet government had been discarded—if it had ever been seriously considered in the first place.

But international relations are not just a matter of what nations *plan*; they revolve as well around what nations *perceive*. Soviet leaders appear over the years to have *perceived* an intention on the part of the West to overthrow them, even if that intention has not—at least in the case of the United States—in fact been there. Given the conspiratorial background from which Bolshevism emerged, the existence of such suspicions would hardly be surprising. We even have Khrushchev's account of Stalin's warnings that "we'd never be able to stand up to the forces of imperialism, that the first time we came into contact with the outside world our enemies would smash us to pieces; we would get confused and be unable to defend our land."[26] The fact that Soviet fears have been exaggerated does not make them any less significant, nor has it lessened the Soviet government's deep and persistent preoccupation with the question of its own legitimacy.

Rarely—if ever—has a regime required such constant acknowledgement by others of its right to rule. It was vital to the Soviet leaders, not only to have won the war and to have gained enormous influence thereby, but also to have that victory and that influence explicitly *recognized* by the United States and the other Western powers. Hence, the Soviet Union's long and curious campaign, sustained over two decades, to have the international community officially confirm World War II boundary changes in Eastern Europe: it was as if the Russians had inherited the same propensity for "legalism" once thought to be characteristic of the American approach to international affairs.[27]

The great irony of the 1975 Helsinki agreements—which did at last recognize the "inviolability" of the World War II European settlement—

is that they reinforced as much as they relieved Moscow's anxieties by introducing into the dialogue on "security and cooperation" in Europe the issue of "human rights." This happened for a simple enough reason: the West's price for acknowledging the legitimacy of boundaries was Moscow's acknowledgment that concerns about human rights were also legitimate, not only in Eastern Europe but within the Soviet Union itself. What the Russians had not anticipated was the intensity and persistence with which these concerns would manifest themselves over the next several years: the Carter administration would make human rights a central issue in its relations with the U.S.S.R.; the Reagan administration during its first three years in office appeared to expand this indictment into an attack on the legitimacy of the Soviet regime itself. From Moscow's perspective, the path from Helsinki to the "evil empire" speech was straight, and all downhill.[28]

But from an American perspective, one can only be struck by the extent of the misunderstanding that was involved here. Even without access to still-classified documents, it seems quite safe to insist that at no point did either the Carter or the Reagan administration give anything like serious attention to how they might undermine the Soviet regime, or to what they would do in the unlikely event that such a thing should come about.[29] What the Russians perceived to be challenges to legitimacy have in fact been calls for liberalizing the *existing* system in the Soviet Union, or, more often, bids for domestic political support within the United States through the easy tactic of exaggerating an adversary's iniquity.[30] If one wanted to test the extent to which there has existed within this country during the past decade any real enthusiasm for overthrowing the Soviet system, there could be no better way than to contrast the acclaim with which Americans received Alexander Solzhenitsyn's eloquent accounts of the horrors that system has perpetrated, on the one hand, with the embarrassed silence that has greeted his unique ideas on what might replace it, on the other.[31]

The United States government has at no point committed itself wholeheartedly to the objective of overthrowing the Soviet regime. It has not, since 1933, overtly or systematically challenged that government's legitimacy. It has not, since the earliest days of the Bolshevik Revolution, regarded itself as having no interests in common with the Soviet Union: such interests existed—especially in the economic field—even during the period of non-recognition. Although the United States did, after 1945, take the lead in seeking to "contain" the expansion of Moscow's influence in the postwar world, it did not seek nor was it prepared for any effort to remove the Soviet government from its position of authority inside Russia. Nor has official Washington ever claimed that postwar global stability requires elimination of the Soviet regime; instead the intention has been to incorporate that regime in some way *within* the framework of stability.

The issue of "legitimacy" persists, one suspects, because of the extraordinary sensitivity the Soviet leadership continues to feel on such questions, and the extraordinary imprecision of political rhetoric in the United States. That suggests, in turn, several implications for policy:

(a) While retaining the right to criticize Soviet policy, the United States government should avoid any appearance of challenging Soviet legitimacy, for the simple reason that it has never considered itself to have a vital interest in replacing that regime. Given Soviet sensitivities on this point, even the *intimation* of such an intent could well thwart genuine policy objectives.

(b) The United States should encourage greater understanding on the Russians' part of American pluralism in general, and of the con-stitutional separation of powers in particular, so that the criticisms of the Soviet system that will inevitably be made are not regarded as reflecting any official determination to destabilize that regime.

(c) The United States might well consider—in precisely this context—reminding the Russians that their own concept of "peaceful coexistence" insists that struggles between systems can take place within limits that imply tacit acknowledgements of legitimacy on both sides.

Option Two: Containing Soviet Influence Within the Boundaries of the U.S.S.R.

A second theoretically-plausible objective of United States policy with respect to the Soviet Union could be to restrict Moscow's ability to wield influence in the world at large. This policy would rest on the assumptions: (1) that the Soviet regime shares no interests in common with the United States; but that (2) the United States has neither the obligation nor the resources to attempt to eliminate it; therefore (3) Washington's objective should be to frustrate the expansion of Soviet influence *beyond* the boundaries of the U.S.S.R.; with the expectation that (4) repeated foreign policy failures will in time cause Soviet leaders themselves to modify their system and to moderate their ambitions.

It was Kennan, of course, who first suggested "containment" as an objective, implicitly in his classic "long telegram" of February, 1946, and then explicitly in the equally influential public elaboration of that dispatch, the "X" article on "The Sources of Soviet Conduct," published in *Foreign Affairs* in the summer of 1947. Three years later, Paul Nitze and the other authors of NSC-68, the first major reassessment of postwar national security policy, reaffirmed Kennan's conclusion that the United States should assign first priority to the containment of

Soviet expansive tendencies. There were, to be sure, major differences between Kennan and Nitze over *how* to achieve containment; those disagreements would continue for decades afterwards, and through them one can trace many of the difficulties that have arisen in seeking that objective.[32] But it is important in this context to stress what Kennan and Nitze had in common, and to note the success both men had in making containment—broadly understood—the goal of early postwar American policy toward the U.S.S.R.

Kennan based his argument on what he saw as the unique characteristics of the Soviet state under Stalin's rule: Because of its need for external enemies to justify its own domestic oppression, the regime in Moscow could never be reassured about other governments' intentions through traditional diplomacy. The unimaginative bosses of the Kremlin needed excuses "for the dictatorship without which they did not know how to rule, for cruelties they did not dare not to inflict, for sacrifices they felt bound to demand." Only by picturing the outside world as hostile could Soviet leaders sustain their own precarious legitimacy: nothing that the West could do would disarm their suspicions, nor was it worthwhile even to try.[33]

But neither was the Soviet leadership insane: if confronted with repeated foreign policy failures, Kennan insisted, it would in time learn from experience and moderate its own aggressiveness from within. "[T]he Soviet leaders are prepared to recognize *situations,* if not arguments," he wrote in 1948. "If, therefore, situations can be created in which it is clearly not to the advantage of their power to emphasize the elements of conflict in their relations with the outside world, then their actions, and even the tenor of their propaganda to their own people, *can* be modified."[34] Kennan concluded from this that the task of American diplomacy should be to ensure that Moscow's attempts to widen its influence were unsuccessful, and by those indirect means to persuade Soviet leaders to moderate their unrelenting hostility toward the outside world.

Kennan sought to accomplish this goal in two ways, one that was made clear at the time, the second one obvious only in retrospect. The first was to build countervailing centers of power along the periphery of the Soviet Union: if one could have strong and self-confident societies in vulnerable areas, capable of resisting intimidation from Moscow whether in military, ideological or psychological forms, then the Soviet sphere of influence could hardly expand. That was the assumption that lay behind the Marshall Plan, together with simultaneous decisions to end punitive occupation policies and to seek the economic revival of Germany and Japan. But it is clear now that this was only the first stage of Kennan's strategy: he sought not just to contain Soviet influence within its existing boundaries, but also to roll it back by encouraging the emergence of nationalism among Moscow's satellites. "[T]here is a possibility," Kennan noted in 1949, "that Russian Communism may some day be destroyed by its own children in the form of the rebellious Communist parties of other countries. I can think of no development in which there would be greater logic and justice."[35]

If these two things could be made to happen—if the Soviet Union could be prevented from expanding its influence beyond the point at which it then existed, and if Moscow's control over its own satellites could be eroded—then, in time, Kennan thought, this succession of failures would compel Kremlin leaders to moderate their internally driven suspicion of the outside world; to recognize "that the true glory of Russian national effort can find its expression only in peaceful and friendly association with other peoples and not in attempts to subjugate and dominate those peoples."[36]

Much the same set of assumptions informed NSC-68, the sweeping revision of national security policy that took place early in 1950 under the direction of Paul Nitze. If one could succeed in "frustrating the Kremlin design," that document concluded, then "it might be possible to create a situation which will induce the Soviet Union to accommodate itself, with or without the conscious abandonment of its design, to coexistence on tolerable terms with the non-Soviet world." This would not require overthrowing the Soviet government or attempting to impose punitive conditions on the Russian people: even in the event of war itself, American objectives would "not include unconditional surrender, the subjugation of the Russian peoples or a Russia shorn of its economic potential." Rather, the goal would be to bring about "Soviet acceptance of the specific and limited conditions requisite to an international environment in which free institutions can flourish, and in which the Russian peoples will have a new chance to work out their own destiny."

The authors of NSC-68 foresaw, like Kennan, the possibility of exploiting potential fissures within the international communist movement. "The Soviet monolith," they concluded, "is held together by the iron curtain around it and the iron bars within it, not by any force of natural cohesion. These artificial mechanisms of unity have never been intelligently challenged by a strong outside force." If confronted by an adversary "which effectively affirmed the constructive and hopeful instincts of men and was capable of fulfilling their fundamental aspirations, the Soviet system might prove to be fatally weak."[37]

Kennan and Nitze differed emphatically over how to implement containment. Because Kennan viewed the international balance of power as relatively stable and American resources (as well as wisdom) as limited, he favored efforts to contain Soviet expansionism only in areas deemed vital to American interests, only by means consistent with American capabilities, and only to the extent that success appeared likely. Nitze, conversely, saw the balance of power as decidedly unstable but he also regarded American resources as virtually unlimited; as a consequence, he favored efforts to contain Soviet expansionism wherever it appeared, by whatever means necessary, at whatever the cost, and whatever the prospects for success.[38]

But the existence of these differences, substantial though they were, ought not to obscure the *common* assumptions behind what Kennan and Nitze were trying to do: (1) that it was up to the United States to act in some way to maintain the balance of power in the face of Soviet expansionist pressures; (2) that this would not require war with the Soviet Union, and that if war with a Soviet proxy should occur— as it did in Korea—the war would be kept carefully limited; (3) that internal change within the Soviet Union itself was not a prerequisite for the success of containment, but that the success of containment might in turn bring about internal change; and (4) that, once such changes had occurred, the assimilation of the Soviet Union into the established international order might be possible.

There were, admittedly, difficulties with the Kennan-Nitze approach:

(a) It left unresolved the tension between credibility and capability: how does one contain challenges to the balance of power without spreading one's resources so thinly around the world as to invite them, as the Truman administration seemed to be doing prior to the outbreak of the Korean War? But, alternatively, if one chooses to boost the resources allocated to containment, how does one do this without sacrificing solvency, a concern that was much on the minds of Truman's critics once the United States had decided to intervene in Korea?

(b) It raised the dilemma of ends versus means: how does one resist Soviet "imperialism" without taking on "imperialist" characteristics oneself?[39] By what right did the United States seek widely dispersed spheres of influence of its own—as in Latin America, East and Southeast Asia and Western Europe—when it denied to the Russians the right to do the same thing in those parts of the world adjacent to it? How did one build coalitions without dominating them, as Washington hoped to do with the Marshall Plan? How did one seek allies—as in NATO—without turning them into puppets?

(c) It ran the risks, as well, of self-fulfilling prophecy: was not the perpetual "frustration" of Soviet designs likely to produce greater, not lesser, antagonism toward the West? How could one expect negotiations to take place when the United States had reached a "position of strength" if, for the Russians, this meant a "position of weakness"?[40] How did one know when containment had been achieved, and one could then safely grant the mutual recognition of interests upon which a true balance of power must be based?

The Soviet Union has not, to this day, fully accommodated itself to the existing international order in the way that Kennan and Nitze hoped it would: even though it has grown noticeably in sophistication, the Kremlin leadership still functions on much the same basis—and still views the outside world with much the same mixture of suspicion and envy—as it did in Stalin's day.[41] But internal change has taken place: the "terror" has been largely dismantled, the "cult of personality" has been solidly condemned, and life for the average Russian—though by no means approaching Western standards—is measurably freer and more comfortable than it was when Kennan first expressed the hope that foreign policy failures would induce Soviet officials to embrace domestic reform.[42]

It is also the case that the international system itself has demonstrated far greater resilience than either Kennan or Nitze expected. The prospect of the Soviet Union's coming to dominate other vital centers of industrial-military power—a possibility that seemed very real in the late 1940s—has obviously not come to pass. Instead, the past four decades have seen greater stability in the positions of the great powers relative to each other and to the rest of the world as well than at any other point since the eras of Metternich and Bismarck. It is true that this balance of power has been purchased in large part by creating a balance of terror based on nuclear weapons. But those devices have hardly been the *only* component of postwar stability: if by some magic they were to disappear tomorrow there are non-nuclear stabilizing mechanisms that might still keep the system intact,[43] although one must acknowledge that—apart from the old triumvirate of Jonathan Schell, Mikhail Gorbachev and Ronald Reagan—few these days seem brave enough to want to risk that experiment.

Nor has international communism given Moscow the capacity, once deeply feared in the West, to dominate other countries solely through ideological means. As Kennan and Nitze anticipated, the Soviet model has had little appeal to those who have enjoyed the freedom to choose or reject it; in those countries where communism has taken hold, nationalism has rendered it so diverse a phenomenon as to be virtually meaningless. Any movement that encompasses within it the likes of Kim Il-sung, Fidel Castro, Nicolai Ceaucescu and Deng Xiaoping is not a movement at all; it is an opaque fog. The West has long since prevailed in the ideological Cold War, and it has hardly had to lift a finger to do so.

One can argue, to be sure, that these things would have happened in any event, even if Washington had never committed itself to containment: the sun does not really rise because the rooster crows. Whether these successes came about *because* of that goal or *in spite of* it are questions that cannot be answered until we gain access to relevant Soviet and Chinese documentation. Still, one test of an effective strategy is the extent to which it associates itself with what is likely to happen in any event: alignment with inevitability, after all, is not a bad way of ensuring that one's objectives are met. The idea of containment, as Kennan and Nitze understood it, did just this: it assumed that Soviet efforts to destabilize the international system would in time generate their own resistance, and it defined the goal of American policy largely as one of helping that process along.

What lessons for policy might be derived from the experience of containment?

(a) One might be to recognize that, while national *interests* may be there forever, specific *strategies* in pursuit of those interests should probably not be. Containment, as described above, was intended for a particular situation at a particular time: it was never meant to inform American policy toward the Soviet Union for all time to come.[44] It by no means excluded the possibility of more flexible approaches should more flexible leadership appear in the Soviet Union. What this suggests is the need for a "sunset" law on strategies that would ensure their relegation to the history books—or, at the very least, their reconsideration—when the circumstances that gave rise to them have changed.

(b) There is a fine line to walk, in strategy, between flexibility and credibility. If one seeks, as Kennan did, to retain the initiative—defining interests narrowly, perceiving threats conservatively, and formulating responses selectively—then one risks leaving flanks exposed and encountering unpleasant surprises. But if one takes the opposite approach, as Nitze did—defining interests so broadly as to perceive any hostile act anywhere as a mortal danger—then one risks losing control of how and where one deploys one's resources, for the simple reason that perceptions of threats are infinitely expandable, but resources never are. There is no easy answer to this dilemma, but an awareness of its existence cannot hurt.

(c) Means need to be monitored regularly to keep them consistent with ends. There is the danger that in the process of *containing* one's adversary one can come—at least in the eyes of much of the rest of the world—to *resemble* one's adversary. This is to be guarded against, not only because it is apt to provoke unnecessary resistance, as the United States discovered during the Vietnam War, but also because there are still eminently self-interested reasons for entertaining "a decent respect for the opinions of mankind."[45] A balance of power, after all, need hardly preclude the toleration of diversity; indeed diversity may well be the most effective (and certainly the cheapest) way to maintain a balance of power.

(d) There needs to be some recognition of the principle of reciprocity. If what one really wants is a stable international system, then it has to offer roughly equal advantages to the major participants in it. Where these do not exist, or where they exist in obviously unequal proportions, threats to systemic equilibrium are almost certain to follow.[46]

(e) Finally, it might be worth elevating to the level of strategy the principle of serendipity: if one can associate one's goals with what is likely to happen in any event, one can then be reasonably certain of attaining them. Or, to put it another way, it is a short-sighted strategy that requires one always to be shoveling unpleasant substances uphill.

Option Three: Changing
the Soviet Union's Internal Structure

The principal objective, in this approach to dealing with the Russians, would be to remove the threat posed by the Soviet government *principally* by seeking to alter its internal character. The assumptions would be: (1) that foreign policy is ultimately a reflection of internal political structure; (2) that although the Soviet regime is legitimate by the standards normally required for diplomatic recognition, it is also an autocratic government and, because of this, a destabilizing force in world affairs; (3) that without changes in the domestic character of the Soviet regime, one cannot expect changes in its external behavior; but (4) that the United States has the capability, through a judiciously applied combination of pressures and inducements, to bring about such changes.

The historical origins of this line of thought predate the Bolshevik Revolution: they go back to the point at which Americans first began inferring the *behavior* of governments on the basis of the *form* governments take. That linkage had not played a prominent role in American thinking about world affairs during the first century after independence: the United States, as a republic, maintained normal and for the most part uneventful relations, after all, with an array of autocratic monarchies. But toward the end of the 19th century—whether because of increasing awareness of events overseas, or because of increasing foreign immigration into the United States, or both—Americans began to associate the absence of democratic institutions internally with aggressive behavior on the international scene.[47] The marked deterioration in relations with imperial Germany and tsarist Russia in the years that preceded the outbreak of World War I best illustrates the pattern: Woodrow Wilson was only reinforcing it in April, 1917, when he welcomed the overthrow of the Russian tsar as a victory "for freedom in the world, for justice and for peace," and—in the same address— justified American entry into the war against imperial Germany as a "fight to make the world safe for democracy."[48]

The implications were clear, if far-reaching: international stability appeared to depend upon transforming the nations of the world into democracies based on the American model. Certainly the League of Nations, Wilson's main preoccupation after victory, involved imposing a structure derived principally from the American constitutional example upon the post–World War I international system. One of Wilson's rationales for intervention in Russia was, as has been seen, to recapture opportunities for democratic reform he thought had been lost with the overthrow of the Provisional Government. For Wilson, the boundaries between domestic reform and foreign policy were, at best, indistinct: in an impressive expansion of the American progressive tradition, he seemed to be arguing that the powers of government should be enlisted, in both realms, to produce democracy as a result.

But the nation's enthusiasm for seeking stability through democratization has proven sporadic, at best. Wilson himself made only halfhearted efforts along these lines in Russia, and his countrymen's ardor for the League quickly cooled as well. As the domestic reform impulse waned, so too did support for reform in the world at large. Nor did it revive when economic distress brought new reforms a decade and a half later in the shape of the New Deal. It would take another war to resuscitate the view that peace required democracy and justice, and even then a fair amount of un-Wilsonian skepticism persisted, not least in the mind of Franklin D. Roosevelt himself.

It is true that, like Wilson, Roosevelt sought to justify American participation in world war in reformist terms: the Atlantic Charter was, after all, little more than a restatement of the Fourteen Points. And, of course, Roosevelt did strongly support creation of—and American membership in—the United Nations. But the President's aspirations for international reform were more superficial than substantive: it was useful to articulate them—if for no other reason than to cloak the realism that in fact shaped his policies[49]—but those policies would not stand or fall upon prospects for a global New Deal.

For Roosevelt, cooperation in international affairs required no necessary congruence of domestic institutions and priorities: states with very different systems could have common interests. Nor did most Americans at the time question the wisdom of cooperating with one dictator to defeat another: some even reversed the traditional equation, deducing from the effective *behavior* of the Russians in fighting the Germans the conclusion that their *form* of government had already evolved toward democratic capitalism.[50] Certainly the attraction of defeating adversaries with minimal casualties and maximum effectiveness was sufficient to override whatever qualms might have existed, as Roosevelt himself once put it, about "hold[ing] hands with the devil."[51]

One statesman who did worry deeply about the gap between American domestic institutions and those of the Soviet Union, though, was Roosevelt's Secretary of War, Henry L. Stimson. The chief difficulty in Washington's postwar relations with Moscow, the old progressive warned President Harry S. Truman in July, 1945, was likely to be the contrast

> between a nation of free thought, free speech, free elections, in fact a really free people, [and] a nation which is not basically free but which is systematically controlled from above by secret police and in which free speech is not permitted. . . . [N]o permanently safe international relations can be established between two such fundamentally different national systems. With the best of efforts we cannot understand each other.

Stimson wrote these words with the recently-tested but still secret atomic bomb very much in mind, and in the weeks that followed he toyed with one of the most remarkable ideas in the history of American reform: that the bomb might be used as an instrument with which to induce—or even to compel—Soviet leaders to abandon the totalitarian character of the system they had imposed upon the Russian people.

No sooner had he articulated this thought, though, than Stimson backed away from it; the reasons suggest something of the difficulties involved in making domestic reform a foreign policy goal. First, Stimson found that although his own close advisers—notably John Mc-Cloy—shared his concern about prospects for postwar cooperation with the Russians, they did not see domestic incompatibility as a necessary barrier to it. Second, W. Averell Harriman, a man of vastly greater experience than Stimson's in dealing directly with the Russians, insisted that Stalin would regard as a hostile act any attempt to use the bomb to extract reforms: the old dilemma of how to encourage change from outside without provoking nationalism from within remained as real as it had in Wilson's day. In the end, Stimson departed from Truman's Cabinet with the recommendation that the United States try to win Stalin's trust by offering to share information about the bomb without preconditions, on the grounds that "the only way you can make a man trustworthy is to trust him."[52]

The Truman administration did not follow that recommendation either, but it did put forward during the next two years two imaginative proposals that would—if implemented—have produced changes of a sort inside Russia, if not the thoroughgoing reforms Stimson had in mind. One of these was the Baruch Plan for the international control of atomic energy, which would have resulted in the transfer of American atomic weapons to the United Nations in return for Soviet willingness to allow international control over all sources of fissionable material within the U.S.S.R. The second was the Marshall Plan, which the Russians were invited to join on the condition that they reveal detailed information on their internal economic situation. Neither of these initiatives originated as attempts to alter the Soviet system; the goals rather were to control atomic energy and to revive Europe. But the conviction did exist that Moscow's cooperation in either of those efforts would require internal changes within the Soviet Union; predictably, the Russians rejected them both.

Stimson's brief consideration of how one might seek to reform the Soviet system from the outside, together with the less sweeping requirements for change stipulated in the Baruch and Marshall plans, were the only significant examples of such thinking in Washington for many years: it would not be until the 1970s that American officials would return to the goal of attempting, as a conscious policy objective, to modify the internal political structure of the U.S.S.R. To be sure, it became a staple of both public and private rhetoric during the height of the Cold War to stress the obvious differences between American democracy and Soviet totalitarianism, but few concluded from this that coexistence between the two systems required their convergence. The Kennan-Nitze strategy of containment had anticipated evolution within the Soviet system, but never to the point of correspondence with Western democratic principles and certainly not as the result of any open American crusade to bring such a thing about. There were those within the Nixon administration who suggested that increasing economic and cultural contacts with the West would render Soviet society more "permeable," and hence more relaxed and tolerant;[53] but these changes were always seen more as a consequence of improved relations than as a prerequisite for them.

The major postwar effort to make reform in Russia an objective of policy in the United States arose, during the early 1970s, outside the Nixon administration: it took the form of attempts by Senator Henry Jackson and his Congressional colleagues to transform Kissinger's concept of "linkage" into a Stimson-like instrument with which to secure greater respect for human rights inside the Soviet state. Kissinger's intentions with regard to "linkage" had been modest: he had held out the prospect of trade, investment, and technology transfers to induce Moscow's cooperation in limiting arms and in managing crises, but he doubted whether the Russians needed economic concessions badly enough to relax internal controls in order to get them.[54] But Jackson wanted to use such American economic leverage as existed to make life more tolerable—and departure from the U.S.S.R. more feasible— for Soviet Jews and dissidents; he was also profoundly skeptical about Kissinger's detente strategy and not at all reluctant to see it held "hostage" to the issue of human rights inside the Soviet Union, par- ticularly if this might advance Jackson's own 1976 presidential am- bitions.[55]

As it turned out, this mixture of principle with expediency did little to help Jackson: he was never a strong contender for the Democratic nomination. But his injection of "human rights" into the campaign did provide his rival, Jimmy Carter, with a potent means by which to attack Kissinger simultaneously from the Right and the Left: Carter could appeal both to critics of detente and to supporters who none- theless worried about its perceived "amorality." It was a clever political gambit, but it worked less well when the new administration attempted to apply it officially, early in 1977, to the realm of geopolitics. De- termined to assert independence from his predecessors but convinced as well of the need to improve Soviet-American relations, Carter os- tentatiously announced the demise of "linkage," combined an offer of "deep cuts" on strategic missiles with highly public expressions of sympathy for Andrei Sakharov and other Soviet dissidents, and then appeared surprised when the offended Russians themselves established a "linkage" and refused to budge on either point.[56]

It was Carter's unfortunate habit to think in compartmental but not integral terms. He combined Kissinger's emphasis on arms control with Jackson's emphasis on human rights, but he failed to see—as both Kissinger and Jackson ultimately had—the contradictions in these two approaches: Soviet leaders were unlikely to extend the trust upon which arms control has to depend to an administration they perceived as challenging their legitimacy. The fact that what Carter had in mind was reform, not revolution, made little difference from the Soviet perspective: in an inversion of the American "domino" theory, the Russians took the view that if the United States gained *any* capability to effect change within the Soviet Union, this would only encourage it to seek more; better, therefore, to resist such efforts from the start. As a result, Carter wound up achieving the objectives of *neither*

Kissinger nor Jackson: his accomplishments—or, more precisely, the absence of them—were uniquely his own.

The Reagan administration, too, gave thought to how it might change Soviet society during its first years in office, but here the emphasis was more on exhaustion than on reform: convinced that the Soviet economy was in serious trouble, the new President and his advisers talked frankly of engaging Moscow in an all-out arms race, with the expectation that this would force an increasingly hard-pressed Kremlin leadership to choose between economic collapse at home or acknowledging a resurgent American military superiority in the world at large.[57] The administration's enthusiasm for reviving the MX missile and B-1 bomber programs, for building a 600-ship Navy, and for upgrading conventional ground force capabilities all can be understood in this context, as can President Reagan's own imaginative contribution to this effort, the Strategic Defense Initiative.

But, with the passage of time, the idea that one can force the Soviet system to change by exhausting it has come to seem about as plausible as earlier efforts to remind Kremlin leaders of their obligation to respect human rights. The Soviet economy seems no nearer collapse today than it did in 1981; certainly the ability of those who direct it to allocate resources more or less as they choose has not been impaired. At the same time—and despite impressive initial successes in winning appropriations for rearmament—the Reagan administration has run into increasing resistance in the last several years from a Congress curiously impervious to the logic of trying to exhaust the Russians by tripling our own national debt. Who, Lenin used to ask, does what to whom?

The infrequent attempts that have been made since 1917 to "reform" the Soviet Union have suffered from an exaggeration of the American ability to influence events inside the U.S.S.R., and a corresponding underestimation of the extent to which the Russians resist carrying out reforms they might otherwise undertake for fear of seeming to yield to external pressures. They have neglected the tendency of a still highly defensive Soviet regime to confuse calls for reform with challenges to legitimacy. They have failed to take into account the persisting strength of Russian nationalism, a force rarely sympathetic to outside ideas, however praiseworthy the rest of the world might find them to be. They have miscalculated the capacity of the Congress—and of the American people—to sustain the consistent action necessary to effect change within the limited range in which it might be possible.

But Americans have also tended to overlook or to deprecate the reality of reform in the Soviet Union when it does take place. That country today is very different in character—and a very much more "liberal" place for those who inhabit it—than it was in Stalin's day.[58] And yet, official Washington rarely comments on this phenomenon: it has given far more attention to justifiably condemned abuses inflicted upon small groups of dissidents than to the genuine progress that has been made since Stalin's death in improving the lot—and the liberties— of the majority of Soviet citizens. One reason for the omission may be that those Americans who have sought changes in the Soviet system have not always done so for wholly disinterested reasons: they may have been sincere in their concern for victims of abuses in that country, but in reviewing the history of these campaigns, one cannot avoid the unsettling impression that other self-interested motives have been at work as well, not least the domestic political advantages that are so easily derived from attacking the Soviet Union.

What lessons for policy follow from all of this?

(a) One might be to recognize, once and for all, the difficulty of trying to alter the internal institutions of another country unless one is in total occupation of it, as the United States and its allies were in Germany and Japan after World War II. Otherwise, the nationalism that is sure to be offended by what is perceived as interference in internal affairs tends to overcome whatever possibilities may exist for reform. Changes have come more easily within the Soviet system when the United States has *not* been trying to obtain them, rather than the other way around.

(b) A second lesson should be to clarify the reasons why we want change inside the Soviet Union in the first place. Is it to make that country, over the years, more like us, and, if so, is that a necessary prerequisite for international stability? Or is it to make the U.S.S.R. a more efficient—or less efficient—rival? Or is the objective simply one of placating domestic constituencies by embarrassing Moscow, in which case one can again legitimately ask with what larger interests such an objective might correspond?

(c) The third and most basic question is this: are we willing to give up or significantly to reduce prospects for agreement with the Soviet Union in the international arena in order to bring about change within its domestic system? And are we certain that such changes, if carried out, would necessarily produce a government more sympathetic to the interests of the United States and its allies than the one that exists there now? There is, after all, such a thing as appreciating one's adversaries: they could be worse. Or, to invoke what appears to be the only geopolitical aphorism to have emanated from the Carter administration: "If it ain't broke, don't fix it."[59]

Option Four: Competitive Co-existence

A fourth possible objective the United States could have in its relationship with the Soviet Union would be to compete for influence within a framework of shared systemic interests. Such an approach would be based on the assumptions: (1) that great nations can have both cooperative and competitive interests at the same time; (2) that the United States shares with the Soviet Union an interest in avoiding mutually destructive war or any dramatic shifts in the status quo that might lead to it; but (3) that, for both geopolitical and ideological reasons, Moscow intends to compete with the United States for influence in the world by means that do not risk war; therefore (4) the task of American statesmen must be to find ways of countering that Soviet influence without upsetting the overall structure of international relations that has evolved since 1945.

Until the Eisenhower administration came into office in 1953, most Washington officials had regarded the Cold War as a transitory phenomenon. However tense the confrontation with the Russians might be, it would not last indefinitely: either war would bring it to an end, or, more likely, the Kremlin leaders' realization that they were not going to have their way would push them toward more moderate policies, making continuing efforts at "containment" unnecessary. Kennan himself had regarded that strategy as appropriate only for Stalin, and had expected new situations—and new American policies—to emerge upon the dictator's death.[60] Nitze, less optimistic, worried that growing Soviet military strength might tempt Stalin or his successors into irresponsible actions that could risk war; but he expected that American rearmament, if implemented along the lines advocated in NSC-68, would prevent that from happening and would then open up possibilities for a negotiated resolution of differences on terms favorable to the West.[61]

Eisenhower and his advisers, in contrast, anticipated a long-term competitive relationship with the Soviet Union for two reasons: First, Moscow's progress in developing nuclear weapons and the means to deliver them meant that war could now destroy the United States itself; with this fact in mind, Eisenhower quietly ruled out direct military confrontation as a viable option.[62] Second, attempts to end the Cold War through containment—by building centers of resistance to the Russians in those parts of the world threatened by them—ran the risk, Eisenhower thought, of bankrupting the United States and ultimately undermining its way of life.[63] For these reasons, the President neither expected nor sought a quick end to Soviet-American competition; rather he concentrated on finding ways to sustain that rivalry without war over an extended period of time.

His preferred strategy was, of course, the so-called "New Look," an approach that relied heavily upon the prospect of nuclear "retaliation" to deter Soviet expansionism while at the same time conserving limited American resources. But that strategy did not depend wholly upon the deterrent effect of nuclear weapons: an integral—if overlooked—aspect of it was the use of negotiations to establish limits within which competition would be carried on. Just because the Russians insisted on attaching the adjective "peaceful" to the noun "co-existence" did not make it "appeasement," Eisenhower told a press conference in 1955: "To my mind, coexistence is, in fact, a state of our being as long as we are not attempting to destroy the other side."[64]

Several considerations led Eisenhower to endorse negotiations as a way of reducing the danger of war while lowering the costs of confrontation: The death of Stalin in March, 1953, provided grounds for expecting greater flexibility on Moscow's part than had been present in previous years. European allies—and particularly Winston Churchill—were strongly encouraging Washington to test Soviet intentions in this regard. Eisenhower himself believed that the West would be negotiating from a position of strength, both because of the military rearmament that had taken place since Korea, but also because, like Kennan and Nitze before him, he saw signs of developing ideological fragmentation within the international communist bloc.[65] It was, as well, the President's strongly held conviction, based on his reading of Clausewitz, that strategies without objectives made no sense:[66] since surrender was unthinkable, military victory impossible, and the cost of containment unacceptable, it seemed logical to explore possibilities for incorporating Soviet-American rivalry—which was certain to continue—within a mutually acceptable framework of co-existence.

The idea that one could negotiate with the Russians without appeasing them was by no means widely accepted in the United States at the time Eisenhower took office: even so experienced (and tough) a diplomat as Charles E. Bohlen came close to being denied Senate confirmation as ambassador to the Soviet Union in 1953 for the simple reason that he had been present at the Yalta conference eight years earlier.[67] All that had changed by the end of Eisenhower's term: despite a decidedly mixed record of accomplishment, three summit meetings, a succession of foreign ministers conferences, and extended bilateral contacts at lower levels had, by 1961, legitimized the idea that one could talk to the Russians without at the same time being taken in by them.[68] This was an important legacy for the incoming Kennedy administration, burdened as it was by the memory of past Democratic foreign policy humiliations and by a paper-thin electoral mandate: had Eisenhower not made negotiations with the Russians "respectable," the new President and his advisers might well have found it impossible to pursue contacts with them—as indeed happened with regard to the Chinese.[69]

In fact, Kennedy continued Eisenhower's objective of seeking competitive co-existence. As Walt Rostow put it in a 1962 internal memorandum, "we should try to work over the longer run toward tacit understandings with the USSR as to the ground rules covering our competition." If the Russians "are convinced of our capacity and will to deal with their efforts to extend power into the free community, it may become increasingly possible to make them feel that we share a common interest in the exercise of restraint."[70] Kennedy himself made much the same argument in his American University address of June, 1963: the idea, he stressed, was to convince Kremlin leaders "that it is dangerous for them to engage in direct or indirect aggression, futile for them to attempt to impose their will and their system on other unwilling people, and beneficial to them, as well as to the world, to join in the achievement of a genuine and enforceable peace."[71]

What did the strategy of embedding competition within co-existence actually achieve? In fact, quite a lot, if one reviews the record of the Eisenhower and Kennedy administrations:

(a) The establishment of personal contact between American and Soviet leaders. It is a bit of a surprise to recall that four summit conferences took place between 1955 and 1961 (one of them, that of 1960, broke up in disarray). This compares with a record of no Soviet-American summits during the preceding decade (except for Potsdam, which was really a wartime summit), and only one—Glassboro, 1967—in the decade that followed. Students of international relations are, with reason, skeptical about summits: they are thought to lead to exaggerated expectations, unforeseen confrontations, and unnecessary misunderstandings, a perception amply reinforced by the ill-prepared Reykjavik summit of 1986.[72] But they probably also moderate perceptions on both sides: it is difficult to view one's adversary as the embodiment of evil once one recognizes him to be human, and quite probably a grandfather as well. To the extent that personal relationships create a basis for cooperation among nations—and the extent of this is admittedly limited—then summits are an important mechanism for bringing that about.

(b) Achievements in arms control. The decade preceding 1955 had seen no progress whatever toward the control of nuclear weapons. But during the next ten years, Soviet and American officials would reach several significant agreements: an informal moratorium on atmospheric nuclear testing that lasted from 1958 until 1961; the Limited Test Ban Treaty of 1963; and, later that year, a United Nations resolution banning the placement of nuclear weapons in outer space. Easily as important as these public accords was a tacit understanding that had also emerged by 1963: that neither the Russians nor the Americans would attempt to shoot down each other's recently launched and—because of their role in preventing surprise attacks—critically valuable reconnaissance satellites.[73] To be sure, these accomplishments fell well short of hopes for progress toward general and complete disarmament. But they did reflect the emergence of an avowed common interest in limited arms control, and that in itself was progress when compared to what had gone before.

(c) Successes in crisis management. The fact that World War III had not occurred by the time Eisenhower became president suggests that Moscow and Washington had not wholly failed in managing crises prior to that time. But the 1950s and early 1960s did see a remarkable sequence of potentially dangerous confrontations—Dienbienphu, 1954; Quemoy-Matsu, 1955; Hungary-Suez, 1956; Lebanon, 1958; Berlin, 1958–59; the U-2 incident, 1960; Cuba, 1961; Berlin, 1961; Laos, 1961–62; the Cuban Missile Crisis, 1962—*every one* of which was resolved without major military involvement by either superpower: the same could not be said of Korea in 1950, or of Vietnam and Afghanistan later on. This is, in retrospect, an impressive record of Soviet and American accomplishment in restraining competition where it seemed likely to lead to war; it was consistent with a pattern of rivalry conducted within mutually understood limits.

Why, then, did the "competitive co-existence" regime not survive? In one sense, it did, at least for a time: Lyndon B. Johnson saw himself as continuing and even building upon Kennedy's strategy; nor did Khrushchev's deposition in 1964 bring dramatic shifts in Moscow's approach to the West. And yet, in more subtle ways, the pattern of Soviet-American relations was changing: Washington was becoming preoccupied to the point of obsession with the war in Vietnam, which meant that relations with the Russians attracted proportionately less attention than in the past. Simultaneously—and perhaps with this fact in mind—the new Soviet leadership was devoting its energies to the quiet but steady accumulation of strategic military hardware, thus reversing Khrushchev's habit of ostentatiously rattling rockets he did not possess.

These events suggest a major difficulty in pursuing "competitive coexistence": the point at which competition ends and cooperation begins is not always similarly perceived. The Johnson administration discovered this—belatedly—when it sought to enlist the Soviet Union's help in ending the Vietnam War: that assistance was not forthcoming, and in retrospect one is hard pressed to think of anything that could have been more to Moscow's advantage at the time than to have had the United States distracted by, and bogged down in, such a costly, indecisive and vastly unpopular guerrilla war.[74] Nor, to the apparent surprise of the Kremlin, was Johnson prepared to cooperate on strategic arms control after the Soviet invasion of Czechoslovakia and the simultaneous proclamation of the "Brezhnev Doctrine" in the summer of 1968.[75]

No one in Washington had explicitly repudiated the goal of "competitive coexistence" by the time Johnson left office in 1969, but the conditions of competition had dramatically changed by then, and not to the advantage of the United States. The nation had severely weakened itself, both at home and in the world at large, through its unsuccessful quest for a military solution in Southeast Asia. The Soviet Union had used the resulting opportunity significantly to strengthen its own military position, and with somewhat less success—events in Czechoslovakia having done little to enhance its external image—to widen its influence in the rest of the world. The incoming Nixon administration saw the Kennedy-Johnson approach as having produced something new and decidedly unpleasant in the history of the Cold War: a situation of approximate military parity between the United States and the Soviet Union. Its determination to reverse this trend—or, in the eyes of its critics, to accommodate itself to it—would lead it to embrace yet another objective in relations with Moscow: "cooperative co-existence."

What are the lessons for policy from the experience of "competitive co-existence"?

(a) One might be to acknowledge frankly—applying a geological image to geopolitics—the "stratified" character of the Soviet-American relationship: that neither competition nor cooperation wholly defines it, but rather that both elements are present in patterns allowing competition to proceed at certain "levels" alongside the cooperation simultaneously taking place at others.

(b) Precisely because of this "stratification," there can be, on both sides, a strong interest in maintaining the status quo at the systemic level—that is, doing nothing to destabilize the overall structure of international relations—while simultaneously pursuing competitive advantages within it.

(c) A major task for Soviet-American diplomacy then becomes that of defining in a mutually acceptable way the boundary that separates competitive from cooperative interest; or, to put it another way, distinguishing competition that has the potential to destabilize the international system from that which does not.

(d) That distinction can be either explicit or tacit: explicit distinction has the virtue of clarity and precision, but as arms control negotiations have shown over the years, it is difficult to bring about; as the reconnaissance satellite experience demonstrates, tacit distinction is easier to arrange, but one is never quite sure what has been agreed to, or how long the resulting agreement will last.[76]

(e) Agreed-upon distinctions, whether derived tacitly or explicitly, can become "rules" of the super-power "game": they provide the means by which competition can take place between rivals in the absence of a referee, without leading to the elimination of either competitor or to the destruction of the arena within which they compete.[77]

Option Five: Cooperative Co-existence

A final objective the United States might plausibly identify in its relationship with the Soviet Union could be to enlist the assistance of that country in the joint task of preserving world order. The assumptions underlying such an approach would be: (1) that geopolitical interests tend to override ideological interests; (2) that the United States and the Soviet Union, despite conflicting ideologies, share interests that go beyond simply perpetuating the international system; (3) that these interests involve a *balancing* of power rather than its unilateral expansion; and (4) that the United States can therefore best secure its own interests by seeking the Soviet Union's cooperation at multiple levels of activity within that system.

Historical evidence for the existence of this approach to the Russians can be located in two very different periods and under two very different administrations whose similarities turn out to be greater than one might have suspected: those of Franklin D. Roosevelt and Richard M. Nixon.

We have already seen how Roosevelt refrained from exploiting opportunities presented by the rise of Nazi Germany to seek the elimination of the Soviet regime; nor did he make any serious effort, either before or during World War II, to change its character. What, then, did Roosevelt really want in his relationship with the Russians? With the passage of time and the gaining of perspective, it appears that the President was pursuing a consistent—if mostly unarticulated—policy throughout his term in office, and that it was aimed toward securing Moscow's assistance in the preservation of a global balance of power.

The idea appears first in Roosevelt's decision to establish diplomatic relations with the Soviet Union in 1933, an action that the President took for several reasons: There was the obvious fact that the 16-year policy of non-recognition, proclaimed at the end of Wilson's administration, had neither weakened nor isolated the Soviet government. Soviet-American economic contacts had flourished despite non-recognition, and could be expected to increase still further—a point of no small importance in the midst of a depression—if that policy were changed. But the strongest justification, in Roosevelt's mind, for normalizing relations with Moscow was the need to counter the rise of potentially aggressive regimes in Berlin and Tokyo. Soviet Foreign Minister Maxim Litvinov, who negotiated the recognition agreement with Roosevelt, reported back to Moscow that the President had even gone so far as to suggest signing a non-aggression pact with the Russians, aimed at deterring the Germans and the Japanese.[78]

Even to have raised that possibility, given the domestic and international situation Roosevelt confronted in the mid-1930s, now seems irresponsible. American isolationism, which became more intense as the depression deepened, imposed obvious limits on the extent to which Washington could do anything more than maintain minimal diplomatic contacts with the Russians. With the Western European democracies themselves appeasing Hitler, there was little prospect of establishing any common basis of resistance to him. And the nature of the Soviet regime itself militated against the kind of cooperative relationship Roosevelt had envisaged: Moscow's refusal to honor the admittedly loosely negotiated agreement establishing diplomatic relations conveyed a strong impression of duplicity; with the onset of Stalin's purges the idea that common interests might exist with such a government became so distasteful to most Americans as to preclude even thinking about it.

What is interesting about Roosevelt's policy is the persistence with which he tried to preserve prospects for cooperation, despite these unpromising circumstances. His appointment of the egregiously pro-Soviet Joseph E. Davies as ambassador in 1936, together with the "purge" the following year of the allegedly anti-Soviet East European Division in the Department of State, can be understood in this context;[79] so too can Roosevelt's surprising receptivity to Stalin's equally surprising idea of having the United States construct warships for the Soviet Navy.[80] Then there is also the President's handling of Soviet-American relations after the Nazi-Soviet Pact and the invasion of Finland, already discussed above. All of these actions grew out of Roosevelt's conviction that Germany and Japan posed greater threats to American interests than did the Russians, and that, despite differences on other points, Moscow and Washington had a common interest in opposing those aggressors.

That assumption was critical to the success of the World War II Grand Alliance. The effectiveness with which Russians fought Germans made the joint Soviet-American interest in victory over the Third Reich obvious to all but the most obtuse observers: certainly these considerations influenced the speed with which Roosevelt made Lend-Lease available to the U.S.S.R. in the fall of 1941; the special treatment granted the Soviet Union by attaching no political or economic conditions to the aid it received; the President's sincere—if, given the target, misguided—efforts to win Stalin's trust during the war; and Roosevelt's sensitivity to postwar Soviet security interests, even to the point of—temporarily—supporting the Morgenthau Plan for the destruction of German industry as a means of relieving Stalin's insecurity about his western border.[81]

One should not conclude from this, though, that Roosevelt was naive about the Russians. He did foresee the possibility that Soviet and American interests might clash after the war, particularly in connection with the question of self-determination in Eastern Europe. He quietly withheld from the Russians potential instruments of "linkage"—information about the atomic bomb, postwar reconstruction assistance, reparations from the American zone in occupied Germany—that could be used to exert pressure if they became difficult. But he did hope that the combined Soviet-American long-term interest in maintaining a mutually beneficial postwar international system would override whatever short-term differences existed; certainly he was prepared to explore, to the maximum possible extent, opportunities for integrating the Soviet Union into that system.[82]

Why did Roosevelt's effort fail? Insofar as the war was concerned, it did not: Russian assistance against Germany was forthcoming in abundance and proved to be decisive; similar help would have been available against Japan as well had the atomic bomb not so abruptly removed the necessity for it in August of 1945. But the President had expected more: he assumed that Stalin shared his interest in constructing a stable postwar order, and would participate in a great-power condominium—the so-called "Four Policemen," made up of the United States, the Soviet Union, Great Britain and Nationalist China—to maintain it.

This proved not to be the case, as Roosevelt himself was coming to realize at the time of his death.[83] In order for a condominium to succeed, each participant must define individual security requirements conservatively, taking care not to infringe upon those of the others. Stalin showed no such restraint; his paranoia was so abiding as to render him congenitally incapable of specifying where, if at all, Soviet security interests ended.[84] The effect could only be to compel the other "policemen" to expand their own security requirements beyond what they otherwise would have been, and to end any prospect that wartime cooperation against Hitler could survive without Hitler.

A similar effort to find common ground with the Russians in sustaining the status quo occurred three decades later under Richard Nixon and Henry Kissinger. Like Roosevelt before and during World War II, the Nixon administration confronted the unpleasant reality that the United States could not, acting on its own, ensure its security requirements. Just as the Soviet Union's assistance had been required to defeat Nazi Germany, so now in the wake of the Vietnam War— a period that had seen American power weaken while that of the Soviet Union had grown—cooperation with the Russians appeared necessary if the international balance of power was to be maintained. It was a matter, in each instance, of accepting what could not be avoided, but at the same time attempting through innovative and frequently personal diplomacy to influence the results.

This approach differed from the "competitive co-existence" sought by Eisenhower and Kennedy in its pessimistic assessment of American power. There had been little question during the 1950s and 1960s that the United States enjoyed military superiority over the Russians: under those circumstances, one could confidently expect a competitive relationship to preserve American interests, so long as limits existed that would avoid escalation to nuclear war. But Nixon and Kissinger had no such confidence: the Russians' attainment of strategic parity, together with the blow to American credibility and self-confidence inflicted by the Vietnam War, left them worried that even competition *within* such limits could leave the United States at a substantial disadvantage.[85] Moscow's cooperation beyond the joint goal of avoiding war would be needed if the balance of power was to be maintained.

But if Nixon and Kissinger were pessimistic about American strength, they were at the same time optimistic about their own ability, through skillful diplomacy, to secure Soviet cooperation. They sought to do this in several interrelated ways:

(a) Explicit acknowledgement of the Soviet Union's status as one of the world's two super-powers. Nixon and Kissinger recognized—and were prepared elaborately to defer to—the Soviet government's determination to be treated with respect. They shared Roosevelt's view that personal contacts could often achieve what exchanges between foreign offices could not; moreover, they had the advantage—unlike Roosevelt— of dealing with a Soviet leadership that was prepared to respond to such treatment. It was, perhaps, appropriate that the third Nixon-Brezhnev summit in as many years took place, in 1974, just outside Yalta.

(b) The creation, through such direct contacts, of Soviet-American "regimes"—rules and procedures defining the limits of acceptable behavior—in the important fields of arms control and crisis management. The intent here was to restrain Soviet action that might upset the status quo, whether through the additional deployment of strategic weapons or the exploitation of Third World crises, but to do it by negotiating understandings to govern each side's behavior in such matters. The resulting agreements—SALT I and the statement on "Basic Principles" to govern Soviet-American relations, both concluded at the 1972 Moscow summit—went well beyond the earlier "competitive co-existence" pattern, which had assumed a continuation of rivalry in these areas, limited only by the restraint necessary to avoid war.

(c) The use of "linkage"—carefully-arranged combinations of inducements and constraints—to secure these agreements. The inducements lay primarily in the economic realm: Nixon and Kissinger were prepared to offer the Russians access to the trade, technology and investment capital they would need to modernize their economy in return for cooperation on arms control and crisis management. But there were constraints as well, not the least of which was the prospect of improved relations between the United States and the People's Republic of China.

The Nixon-Kissinger search for comparative "cooperative co-existence" was a thoughtful and sophisticated attempt to make the best of a bad situation. To the extent that American influence in the world was higher when the Republicans left in 1977 than it had been eight years earlier—and it probably was—they can be said to have succeeded: certainly the "opening" to China more than compensated for the "loss" of South Vietnam. But the long-term objective of "cooperative co-existence" proved as elusive in the 1970s as it had in the 1940s and, once again, the Russians bear much of the responsibility for this.

Just as Stalin had never accepted Roosevelt's view that Soviet interests would best be served by a cooperative rather than a unilateral search for security, so Brezhnev and his associates three decades later, despite the fact that they had welcomed the SALT I and "Basic Principles" agreements, could not bring themselves to refrain from exploiting opportunities as they arose, whether by stretching the occasionally value language of SALT I to justify new strategic weapons deployments, or by taking advantage of post-Vietnam/post-Watergate passivity in Washington to intervene in a succession of otherwise unrelated crises ranging from Angola to Afghanistan. Both the Roosevelt and the Nixon administrations made the mistake of assuming that Soviet willingness to cooperate extended much farther down in the "strata" of Soviet-American relations than in fact it did.

There were, to be sure, mitigating circumstances. Even as they pushed for the "Basic Principles" agreement, the Russians made it clear that they would not feel inhibited about supporting "wars of national liberation" in Third World areas, a reservation Washington incautiously ignored.[86] The Russians could also claim, with good reason, that the Americans had failed to deliver the economic inducements that were to have accompanied agreements on strategic arms: as has been noted, these fell prey to a sudden and ill-conceived enthusiasm on the part of Congress for promoting reform inside the Soviet Union. It is also the case that the United States itself was pursing unilateral advantages in its efforts to destabilize the Marxist government of Salvadore Allende in Chile and in its determination to deny the Russians a role in Middle East after the 1973 Yom Kippur War.[87]

But the fact remains: there was an American administration in the early 1970s—as there had been in the early 1940s—that was prepared to accord the Soviet Union the legitimacy, the respectability, and the great-power status its leaders have so persistently sought. In both instances, the temptation of short-term unilateral gains caused Moscow to squander the potential that existed for long-term cooperation. In both instances, the results were ultimately to the Russians' disadvantage: it is difficult to see how American rearmament in the late 1940s and early 1950s made the Soviet Union any more secure than did American rearmament in the late 1970s and early 1980s. Confronted twice with "windows of opportunity" for building a cooperative relationship with the United States, the Russians both times blew it.

What lessons can be drawn from these experiments in "cooperative co-existence"?

(a) Soviet-American contacts are likely to remain, for the foreseeable future, more "competitive" than "cooperative."[88] This suggests that policy-makers should concentrate on finding ways to make that competition less dangerous instead of attempting to resolve all conflicts of interest that underlie it. If the history of postwar Soviet-American relations has demonstrated anything at all, it is that harmony is not necessarily a prerequisite for stability or, indeed, for peace.

(b) Where agreements to cooperate—tacit or explicit—are reached, they are unlikely to be observed unless grounded firmly in respective national interests on both sides. Whatever the attractions of personal diplomacy in moderating suspicions, overcoming inertia, and exploring possibilities, no one's interests are served by a cosmetic papering over of cracks.

(c) Linkages should be pursued only when administrations are certain that they can control fully the combination of inducements to be offered and constraints to be imposed. Given the American constitutional mandate for multiple hands on the steering wheel, caution in proceeding is highly advisable.

(d) Assessments of power in world affairs are tricky things: because of the difficulty of knowing what *kinds* of power are likely to be decisive at any point, it is probably a bad idea to base one's policies on the assumption either that one's own power is declining, or that one's adversary's is.

Conclusion: The Present and the Future

It is easy to *say* that one should have coherent objectives in conducting foreign policy; but it is not so easy in fact to decide what they should be, or to implement them once they have been chosen. Goals, after all, reflect interests, and interests can exist in multiple and not always congruent forms. It is not unusual to find policy-makers simultaneously pursuing objectives theoreticians would find contradictory; nor do they always suffer pangs of conscience—or of violated logic—as a result.

Thus, Woodrow Wilson (who did suffer) balanced his desire to overthrow Bolshevism against his commitment to the right of peoples everywhere to determine their own form of government. The Republican administrations of the 1920's reaffirmed officially the compromise Wilson finally reached—non-recognition—but then tacitly sanctioned a lively economic relationship with the Soviet Union because of their respect for the principle of *laissez faire.* Franklin D. Roosevelt, the president who is supposed to have elevated inconsistency to a high art, was in fact the most consistent of pre–Cold War chief executives in dealing with the Russians if one considers his efforts to enlist their aid against Germany and Japan, but that consistency is more apparent in retrospect than it was at the time.

All postwar administrations have embraced—in a loose sense—the goal of keeping power balanced in the world, but they have gone about this in different and at times apparently contradictory ways.[89] The Truman administration hoped for an eventual moderation of Soviet ambitions, but concentrated on building Western strength as a means of bringing that about. Eisenhower legitimized negotiations—and with them the idea of competitive co-existence—but linked it to a hair-raising strategy of nuclear retaliation that left few options in between. Kennedy and Johnson, too, sought competitive co-existence, but allowed their pursuit of it to be distracted by a disastrous effort to prove American "credibility" in, of all places, Southeast Asia. Richard Nixon and Henry Kissinger redefined the objective as something approaching a cooperative condominium with the Russians, but they allowed that goal to be compromised by Congressional efforts to liberalize internal conditions within the U.S.S.R.

Objectives became even less clear under Jimmy Carter, who managed somehow to agree with both Henry Jackson *and* Henry Kissinger at the same time. That indecisiveness came through clearly in Carter's choice of advisers: an administration capable of installing Zbigniew Brzezinski as Assistant for National Security Affairs and Cyrus Vance as Secretary of State obviously was going to have difficulties identifying priorities with regard to the Russians. (The President solved the problem at one point by reflecting the quite opposite views of both men in the same speech.)[90] The invasion of Afghanistan, by Carter's own admission, opened his eyes to Moscow's true intentions;[91] only then did he clearly abandon the Nixon-Kissinger cooperative co-existence approach—which he had modified (and confused) by linking it to efforts to change the internal nature of the Soviet system—and revert to the older and more modest alternative of competitive co-existence.

Ronald Reagan would, in the end, continue that approach, but not before obfuscating it in his own way by appearing, in his early rhetoric as president, to call into question the very legitimacy of the Soviet regime, and by embracing quite openly the idea of forcing changes within it by exhausting the Russians in a new arms race. When the administration finally got around to producing an approved National Security Council policy statement on relations with the Soviet Union, in December, 1982, the resulting document—NSDD-75—confused things even further by coming down in favor simultaneously of containing Soviet expansionism while moderating Soviet behavior, encouraging the liberalization of Soviet society, and negotiating agreements with the Russians when they were in the interests of the United States.[92]

The 1984 re-election campaign brought about a further moderation of Reagan administration rhetoric and an intensified interest in negotiations;[93] by the end of 1985 the White House was proudly citing the first summit with Mikhail Gorbachev as a triumph for personal presidential diplomacy. And, of course, at Reykjavik in October, 1986, things went a good deal further: in the most remarkable display of improvisation in high places since the Tsar Nicholas II and the Emperor William II attempted to settle their nations' differences on the yacht off Bjorko,[94] the President and the General Secretary managed to agree—depending on one's version of events—upon the elimination of all strategic land-based missiles, or of all strategic missiles in total, or of all strategic missiles and bombers, or of all nuclear weapons, within the next decade and a half, or thereabouts. The world was saved from this imprecision only by the President's last-minute refusal to compromise on the equally imprecise Strategic Defense Initiative.

Deciding on objectives has never been easy for American presidents, but this succession of events suggests that it is getting harder all the time. It is not completely clear why this should be so, but certain possible explanations come to mind:

(a) Presidential administrations appear increasingly inclined, when confronted with conflicting objectives, to "split the difference"; to compromise by embracing even mutually exclusive alternatives in the hope that one of them will work. What this procedure neglects is the phenomenon of "fratricide": the fact that the simultaneous application of conflicting approaches to the same target is more apt to produce the failure of all than the success of one.

(b) Whether this inability to decide reflects a lack of courage, or of intelligent advice, or simply of a serviceable attention span, is not at all apparent: all of these probably have had a hand in varying degrees. It may also be that our generation's well-documented preoccupation with image over substance makes it more difficult than it used to be to concentrate on a single clearly defined objective and to stick to it.

(c) Certainly it has been the case—even before Lieutenant Colonel Oliver North lent unaccustomed color to its proceedings—that the National Security Council, whose purpose it was both to convey and to analyze options for the President, has not been fulfilling its original mandate. Instead it has developed a bureaucratic—and in recent years, an ideological—perspective of its own that leaves it ill-equipped to provide the objective advice for which it was intended.[95]

(d) It is also ironic that, alone among major agencies of government dealing with foreign and national security affairs, the N.S.C. lacks an institutional memory: there is no permanent staff presense, and no mechanism for reviewing systematically the experiences of previous administrations as a standard of reference against which to compare current options. It is as if, at the top, all history begins with Inauguration Day.

What is to be done? It may seem odd for a historian—a representative of the most determinedly *inductive* of the social sciences—to recommend greater attention to *deduction*. But an abstract categorization of potential objectives can be a useful way, in advance, of comparing the benefits and anticipating the problems involved in projected courses of action; it can also ease the task of learning from past experience. "Theory exists," Clausewitz wrote a century and a half ago,

> so that one need not start afresh each time sorting out the material and plowing through it, but will find it ready to hand and in good order. It is meant to educate the mind of the future commander, or, more ac-

curately, to guide him in his self-education, not to accompany him to the battlefield; just as a wise teacher guides and stimulates a young man's intellectual development, but is careful not to lead him by the hand for the rest of his life.[96]

Whether Freud would have found this perspective useful in dealing with his patients is difficult to say. But the White House could certainly afford to try it.

Notes

1. Quoted in Charles Rolo, *Psychiatry in American Life* (Boston: Little, Brown, 1963), pp. 70–71.

2. Two excellent examples are Joseph S. Nye, Jr., *The Making of America's Soviet Policy* (New Haven: Yale University Press, 1984); I. M. Destler, Leslie H. Gelb and Anthony Lake, *Our Own Worst Enemy: The Unmaking of American Foreign Policy* (New York: Simon and Schuster, 1984).

3. See, for example, John Lewis Gaddis, *Russia, the Soviet Union, and the United States: An Interpretive History* (New York: Wiley, 1978).

4. For examples, see Strobe Talbott, *Deadly Gambits: The Reagan Administration and the Stalemate in Nuclear Arms Control* (New York: Knopf, 1984); and Walter Isaacson and Evan Thomas, *The Wise Men: Six Friends and the World They Made: Acheson, Bohlen, Harriman, Kennan, Lovett, McCloy* (New York: Simon and Schuster, 1986).

5. See Stephen Jay Gould, *The Panda's Thumb: More Reflections in Natural History* (New York: Norton, 1980), pp. 179–85; and, for a related argument, James P. Crutchfield, J. Doyle Farmer, Norman H. Packard and Robert S. Shaw, "Chaos," *Scientific American*, CCLV (December, 1986), 46–57.

6. I use this term in the now widely accepted sense originally proposed by Thomas S. Kuhn in *The Structure of Scientific Revolutions* (Chicago: University of Chicago Press, 1962).

7. See, on these points, George F. Kennan, *Soviet-American Relations, 1917–1920: The Decision to Intervene* (Princeton: Princeton University Press, 1958), pp. 379–80, 403–4; and, on the lessons of intervention in Mexico, W. B. Fowler, *British-American Relations, 1917–1918: The Role of Sir William Wiseman* (Princeton: Princeton University Press, 1969), pp. 185, 196; also John Milton Cooper, Jr., *The Warrior and the Priest: Woodrow Wilson and Theodore Roosevelt* (Cambridge, Mass.: Belknap Press and Harvard University Press, 1983), p. 268.

8. Arthur S. Link, *Woodrow Wilson: Revolution, War, and Peace* (Arlington Heights, Ill.: Harian Davidson, 1979), pp. 96–97.

9. Robert V. Daniels, *Russia: The Roots of Confrontation* (Cambridge, Mass.: Harvard University Press, 1985), pp. 114–15.

10. See Cooper, *The Warrior and the Priest*, pp. 319–23.

11. For the Colby note, see U.S. Department of State, *Foreign Relations of the United States* [hereafter *FR*]: *1920*, III, 463–68.

12. Non-recognition had been applied previously in Mexico, after Huerta overthrew Madero in 1913, and in China as Washington's response to Japan's "twenty-one demands" in 1915.

13. See, on this point, Gaddis, *Russia, the Soviet Union, and the United States*, pp. 98–105.

14. Thomas R. Maddux, *Years of Estrangement: American Relations with the Soviet Union, 1933–1941* (Tallahassee: University of Florida Presses, 1980), pp. 27–101; also Edward M. Bennett, *Franklin D. Roosevelt and the Search for Security: American-Soviet Relations, 1933–1939* (Wilmington, Del.: Scholarly Resources, 1985), pp. 69–187.

15. It would be stretching a point to suggest that the policies of appeasement favored by Chamberlain and Kennedy had as their *primary* motive the military entanglement of Nazi Germany with Soviet Russia. But both men did worry deeply that one consequence of abandoning appeasement—if the result was war with Hitler—would be to leave the way open for the Soviet domination of Europe. See, on this point, Telford Taylor, *Munich: The Price of Peace* (Garden City, N.Y.: Vintage Books, 1979), p. 982; Robert Dallek, *Franklin D. Roosevelt and American Foreign Policy, 1932–1945* (New York: Oxford University Press, 1979), p. 213.

16. Maddux, *Years of Estrangement*, pp. 102–62.

17. See Nikolai V. Sivachev and Nikolai N. Yakovlev, *Russia and the United States*, translated by Olga Adler Titelbaum (Chicago: University of Chicago Press, 1979), p. 163; and, for a more moderate formulation, Vilnis Sopols, *The Road to Great Victory: Soviet Diplomacy, 1941–1945*, translated by Lev Bobrov (Moscow: Progress Publishers, 1985), pp. 41–42.

18. It is important to recall, in this connection, Roosevelt's comment to Stalin at Yalta that public opinion would not allow American troops to remain in Europe for "much more than two years" after the war. (Bohlen minutes, Roosevelt-Churchill-Stalin meeting, February 5, 1945, U.S. Department of State, *Foreign Relations of the United States: The Conferences at Malta and Yalta, 1945* [Washington, D.C.: 1955], p. 617).

19. Ladislas Farago, *Patton: Ordeal and Triumph* (New York: 1964), p. 806. See also, on the question of preventive war, Burton I. Kaufman, *The Korean War: Challenges in Crisis, Credibility, and Command* (Philadelphia: Temple University Press, 1986), pp. 56–57.

20. Total U.S. military personnel on active duty as of mid-1948 were 1.4 million, down from 12.1 million in mid-1945. (U.S. Bureau of the Census, *Statistical History of the United States from Colonial Times to the Present* [Washington, D.C.: 1960], Series Y 763, p. 736). The best comparable Soviet figure for 1948 is now believed to be that given by Khrushchev in 1960: 2.9 million, down from 11.3 million in 1945. (Matthew A. Evangelista, "Stalin's Postwar Army Reappraised," *International Security*, VII (Winter, 1982/83), 115.) These statistics in no way invalidate the major point of Evangelista's article—that the Soviet Union was not capable of invading Western Europe during the years immediately following World War II. But they do suggest strongly that the United States was in no position to launch a preventive war against the Soviet Union either.

21. See the conclusions of the 1949 Harmon Committee report, in Thomas H. Etzold and John Lewis Gaddis, eds., *Containment: Documents on American Policy and Strategy, 1945–1950* (New York: Columbia University Press, 1978), pp. 360–64.

22. Warner R. Schilling, "The Politics of National Defense: Fiscal 1950," in Warner R. Schilling, Paul Y. Hammond, and Glenn H. Snyder, *Strategy, Politics, and Defense Budgets* (New York: 1962), pp. 1–266.

23. See, on the historic durability but possible current erosion of this tradition, Arthur M. Schlesinger, Jr., *The Cycles of American History* (Boston: Houghton-Mifflin, 1986), pp. 84–85.

24. For the objections of George F. Kennan and Dwight D. Eisenhower on this point, see John Lewis Gaddis, *Strategies of Containment: A Critical Appraisal of Postwar American National Security Policy* (New York: Oxford University Press, 1982), pp. 49n, 174n.

25. NSC 20/1, "U.S. Objectives with Respect to Russia," August 18, 1948, in Etzold and Gaddis, eds., *Containment,* p. 193. The conclusions of this document were later approved by President Truman as NSC 20/4 in November, 1948.

26. Nikita S. Khrushchev, *Khrushchev Remembers: The Last Testament,* translated and edited by Strobe Talbott (Boston: Little, Brown, 1974), p. 375.

27. George F. Kennan, *American Diplomacy: 1900–1950* (Chicago: University of Chicago Press, 1951), pp. 82–83.

28. See, on this point, Seweryn Bialer, *The Soviet Paradox: External Expansion, Internal Decline* (New York: Knopf, 1986), p. 322.

29. *Ibid.,* p. 239. There was, to be sure, a tendency on the part of certain early Reagan advisers—notably Richard Pipes—to picture the Soviet Union as being on the verge of collapse, and to suggest that slight pushes in the right direction might cause it to. But this position did not command wide support in the Reagan administration; it also suffered from the difficulty that too much emphasis on it could paradoxically lull the West into a sense of complacency and undermine efforts at rearmament. See, on this point, Michel Tatu, "U.S.-Soviet Relations: A Turning Point?" *Foreign Affairs* LXI (America and the World, 1982), 594–95.

30. The tactic is not unknown in the Soviet Union as well. Indeed, there is a curious asymmetry in the Russians' tendency to regard American anti-Soviet rhetoric as an expression of official intent, but to express astonishment and dismay in the relatively rare instances in which we reciprocate.

31. See Schlesinger, *The Cycles of American History,* pp. 111–17.

32. For the individuals involved, see Gregg Herken, "The Great Foreign Policy Fight," *American Heritage,* XXXVII (April-May, 1986), pp. 65–80.

33. Kennan to State Department, February 22, 1946, *FR: 1946,* VI, 700. See also Kennan's dispatch of March 20, 1946, *ibid.,* pp. 721–23.

34. NSC 20/1, August 18, 1948, in Etzold and Gaddis, eds., *Containment,* p. 187.

35. Joint Orientation Conference lecture, September 19, 1949, George F. Kennan Papers, Box 17, Seeley Mudd Library, Princeton University.

36. Kennan unpublished paper, "The Soviet Way of Thought and Its Effect on Foreign Policy," January 24, 1947, *ibid.,* Box 16.

37. NSC 68, "United States Objectives and Programs for National Security," April 14, 1950, *FR: 1950,* I, 242, 247.

38. A more thorough comparison of the Kennan and Nitze approaches to containment appears in Gaddis, *Strategies of Containment,* pp. 90–106.

39. For a good discussion of this problem, see Schlesinger, *The Cycles of American History,* pp. 141–62.

40. The classic discussion is, of course, Coral Bell, *Negotiation From Strength: A Study in the Politics of Power* (New York: Chatto and Windus, 1963).

41. For the persistence of Stalinism in the Soviet Union today, see Bialer, *The Soviet Paradox,* pp. 3–18; also Stephen F. Cohen, *Rethinking the Soviet Experience: Politics and History Since 1917* (New York: Oxford University Press, 1985), pp. 141–57.

42. See, on this point, Jerry F. Hough and Merle Fainsod, *How the Soviet Union Is Governed* (Cambridge, Mass.: Harvard University Press, 1979), especially pp. 518–55; also Bialer, *The Soviet Paradox,* pp. 19–26.

43. John Lewis Gaddis, "The Long Peace: Elements of Stability in the Postwar International System," *International Security,* X (Spring 1986), pp. 99–142.

44. Despite the fact that some authors appear to insist on treating all of postwar American national security policy as a series of variations on the containment theme. See, for example, Gaddis, *Strategies of Containment, passim.*

45. See Number 63 of *The Federalist Papers* (New York: New American Library, 1961), p. 382.

46. There is a good discussion of this point in Raymond L. Garthoff, *Detente and Confrontation: American-Soviet Relations From Nixon to Reagan* (Washington, D.C.: Brookings Institution, 1985), pp. 1106–16.

47. See, on this point, Gaddis, *Russia, the Soviet Union, and the United States,* pp. 27–41; also Manfred Jones, *The United States and Germany: A Diplomatic History* (Ithaca: Cornell University Press, 1984), pp. 35–64.

48. Wilson speech to Congress, April 2, 1917, Arthur Link, ed., *The Papers of Woodrow Wilson* (Princeton: Princeton University Press, 1966–), XLI, pp. 524–25.

49. For Roosevelt's realism, see Dallek, *Franklin D. Roosevelt and American Foreign Policy,* pp. 321, 533–34.

50. John Lewis Gaddis, *The United States and the Origins of the Cold War* (New York: Columbia University Press, 1972), pp. 34–42.

51. Quoted in Keith David Eagles, "Ambassador Joseph E. Davies and American-Soviet Relations, 1937–1941" (Ph.D. dissertation, University of Washington, 1966), p. 328.

52. Stimson's brief flirtation with "atomic reform" can be traced in Henry L. Stimson and McGeorge Bundy, *On Active Service in Peace and War* (New York: Harper, 1948), pp. 638–46.

53. See Henry A. Kissinger, *American Foreign Policy,* Third Edition (New York: Norton, 1977), pp. 124–26, 158–9, 172–3; also Stanley Hoffmann, *Primacy*

or World Order: American Foreign Policy Since the Cold War (New York: McGraw-Hill, 1978), pp. 57–58.

54. "We were convinced that Jackson was acting like a man who, having won once at roulette, organizes his yearly budget in anticipation of a recurrence. Inevitably, his approach would backfire sooner or later." (Henry A. Kissinger, Years of Upheaval [Boston: Little, Brown, 1982], p. 987).

55. Garthoff, Detente and Confrontation, pp. 412, 456.

56. Ibid., pp. 563–68. For an alternative point of view, see Gaddis Smith, Morality, Reason and Power: American Diplomacy in the Carter Years (New York: Hill and Wang, 1986), pp. 67–68.

57. See, on this point, Seweryn Bialer and Joan Afferica, "Reagan and Russia," Foreign Affairs, LXI (Winter, 1982/83), especially pp. 261–67.

58. See, on this point, the works cited in note 42.

59. The formulation is that of former Budget Director Bert Lance.

60. George F. Kennan, Memoirs: 1925–1950 (Boston: Little, Brown, 1967), pp. 365–67.

61. NSC-68, April 14, 1950, FR: 1950, I, pp. 272–76.

62. Stephen E. Ambrose, Eisenhower: The President (New York: Simon and Schuster, 1984), pp. 38, 93, 122–23, 148, 169, 206, 248, 295, 313.

63. Gaddis, Strategies of Containment, pp. 132–36.

64. Eisenhower press conference, February 2, 1955, Public Papers of the Presidents: Dwight D. Eisenhower, 1955 (Washington: U.S. Government Printing Office, 1959), p. 235.

65. See, on this point, David Allan Mayers, Cracking the Monolith: U.S. Policy Against the Sino-Soviet Alliance, 1949–1955 (Baton Rouge: Louisiana State University Press, 1986), especially pp. 115–25.

66. Gaddis, Strategies of Containment, p. 135.

67. Charles E. Bohlen, Witness to History: 1929–1969 (New York: Norton, 1973), pp. 309–36. See also T. Michael Ruddy, The Cautious Diplomat: Charles E. Bohlen and the Soviet Union, 1929–1969 (Kent, Ohio: Kent State University Press, 1986), pp. 109–24.

68. Gaddis, Strategies of Containment, p. 228.

69. Roger Hilsman, To Move a Nation: The Politics of Foreign Policy in the Administration of John F. Kennedy (New York: Doubleday, 1967), pp. 344–57.

70. Rostow draft, "Basic National Security Policy," March 26, 1962, Lyndon B. Johnson Papers, Vice Presidential—Security File, Box 7, Lyndon B. Johnson Library.

71. Kennedy American University address, June 10, 1963, Public Papers of the Presidents: John F. Kennedy, 1963 (Washington, D.C.: U.S. Government Printing Office, 1964), pp. 461–62.

72. Stanley Hoffmann, "An Icelandic Saga," New York Review of Books, XXXIII (November 20, 1986), 15–17.

73. See, on this point, Gerald M. Steinberg, Satellite Reconnaissance: The Role of Informal Bargaining (New York: Praeger, 1983), pp. 39–70; and Paul B. Stares, The Militarization of Space: U.S. Policy, 1945–1984 (Ithaca: Cornell University Press, 1985), pp. 62–71.

74. For an interesting argument to this effect, see Janos Radvanyi, *Delusion and Reality: Gambits, Hoaxes, and Diplomatic One-Upmanship in Vietnam* (South Bend, Ind.: Gateway Editions, 1978).

75. John Newhouse, *Cold Dawn: The Story of SALT* (New York: Holt, Rinehart and Winston, 130–32.

76. For an illuminating discussion of the respective virtues of tacit and explicit cooperation, see Steinberg, *Satellite Reconnaissance*, pp. 175–78.

77. See, on this point, Gaddis, "The Long Peace," pp. 132–39; also Stanley Hoffmann, "Superpower Ethics: The Rules of the Game," *Ethics and International Affairs*, I (1987), 37–51.

78. Maddux, *Years of Estrangement*, pp. 13–15; Bennett, *Franklin D. Roosevelt and the Search for Security*, pp. 21–24. Litvinov's reports are printed in the Soviet Foreign Ministry publication, *Dokumenty vneshnei politiki SSSR* (Moscow: 1957–), XVI, especially pp. 658–59.

79. See Bohlen, *Witness to History*, pp. 39–41; also Kennan, *Memoirs: 1925–1950*, pp. 82–85.

80. Thomas R. Maddux, "United States–Soviet Naval Relations in the 1930's: The Soviet Union's Efforts to Purchase Naval Vessels," *Naval War College Review*, XXIX (Fall, 1976), 28–37.

81. For Roosevelt's wartime policy toward the Soviet Union, see Gaddis, *Russia, the Soviet Union, and the United States*, pp. 147–68.

82. See, on these points, Gaddis, *Strategies of Containment*, pp. 4–13.

83. Dallek, *Franklin D. Roosevelt and American Foreign Policy*, pp. 533–34.

84. See, on this point, Vojtech Mastny, *Russia's Road to the Cold War: Diplomacy, Warfare, and the Politics of Communism, 1941–1945* (New York: Columbia University Press, 1979), especially p. 306.

85. Gaddis, *Strategies of Containment*, pp. 285–86.

86. Garthoff, *Detente and Confrontation*, pp. 41–42.

87. Garthoff argues strongly (if, to my mind, somewhat unconvincingly) in *Detente and Confrontation* that for these reasons the United States bears the chief responsibility for the collapse of detente.

88. See, on this point, Zbigniew Brzezinski, *Game Plan: A Geostrategic Framework for the Conduct of the U.S.-Soviet Contest* (Boston: Atlantic Monthly Press, 1986), pp. xiii–xiv.

89. For a detailed examination of reasons for these contradictions, see Gaddis, *Strategies of Containment, passim.*

90. Carter speech at Annapolis, Maryland, June 7, 1978, *Public Papers of the Presidents: Jimmy Carter, 1978* (Washington, D.C.: U.S. Government Printing Office, 1979), pp. 1052–57. For an analysis, see Garthoff, *Detente and Confrontation*, pp. 602–4.

91. Smith, *Morality, Reason and Power*, p. 224.

92. The actual document is still classified, but its substance is briefly summarized in Garthoff, *Detente and Confrontation*, pp. 1012–13.

93. See, on Reagan's gradual abandonment of ideology for pragmatism, Schlesinger, *The Cycles of American History*, pp. 57–59.

94. In 1905. As at Reykjavik, it didn't stick.

95. See, on this point, Destler, Gelb and Lake, *Our Own Worst Enemy,* pp. 265–66.

96. Karl von Clausewitz, *On War,* edited and translated by Michael Howard and Peter Paret (Princeton: Princeton University Press, 1976), p. 141.

10

Western Influence on
the Soviet Union

Michael Mandelbaum

In the society of sovereign political communities influence, like wealth and power, is unevenly distributed. Some countries are more influential than others. Influence has passed from west to east in much greater volume than in the opposite direction. There have always been centers, or "cores" of economic innovation and cultural dynamism, whose influence has radiated outward to the less advanced periphery.

The locus of the world's centers of learning, productivity, and military power has shifted as civilizations have risen and fallen from the time of the ancient Greeks to the present. Since at least the 16th century, what is generally known as the West—encompassing Western Europe and, since the 19th century, North America—has constituted a core. Its epicenter, however, has moved. France in the 18th century, Great Britain in the 19th, Germany and the United States in the 20th have had more influence than the other Western countries. Since the 16th century, Russia has been part of the periphery. It has been the object, the recipient, of influence emanating from the West.

The West has been consistently more advanced than Russia in economic terms, which are relatively easy to assess. New products and processes have originated in the West and made their way east. What is advanced and what is backward in cultural terms is far more difficult to judge. These are matters of opinion. But Western cultural forms have been adopted by Russians to a greater extent than the West has drawn on those forms indigenous to Russia. Historically, the court and the intelligentsia in Moscow and St. Petersburg looked to Paris, Berlin, London and Vienna. Russian artists, musicians, writers and architects borrowed more from the West than their German, French and British counterparts took from them.[1] Some of the arts, literature in particular, flourished in Russia in the 19th century and afterward. But even the great Russian writers felt compelled to see the West at first hand. Turgenev studied in Berlin and lived much of his life abroad; Pasternak, to take another example, made an early pilgrimage to Germany. Thomas Mann, by contrast, apparently never felt the need to visit Russia.

Advances in the art of war, too, usually originated in the West and were later adopted in Russia. Particularly during periods of rapid progress in military techniques, this handicapped the Russian state. But the tsars, and later the Communists, often managed to compensate for the relative backwardness of their country by concentrating their society's resources, especially its manpower, on military tasks. The West has generally had the more sophisticated forces; Russia's armies have almost invariably had the advantage of sheer size. Russian regimes have used quantity to offset quality.[2]

While admitting the material advantages of the West, Russians have often asserted that the Russian people hold higher, purer spiritual values.[3] The Soviet regime has contended that the 1917 revolution gave Russia and its imperial holdings the most advanced political system in the world, the one toward which history was driving all other societies. But that revolution was made in the name of a man, Karl Marx, who emphatically considered Russia to be peripheral to the main theater of history, and as such hardly a candidate for the sort of revolution that he had in mind. And the man who did most to make the revolution in Marx's name, V. I. Lenin, was enough of a Marxist to expect that the seizure of power in Russia by the Bolshevik Party would be simply a prelude to the main act in the historical drama of the worldwide proletarian revolution—the overthrow of capitalism in the most advanced countries, notably Germany.

Still, in the years after 1917 the Soviet regime held itself out as a model for the rest of the world, and some outside Russia were ready to take it as that. There were numerous sympathizers, indeed sizable Communist parties, in the West. A Communist movement partly inspired by the Soviet example seized power in China. After 1945, however, and especially after 1956 and Nikita Khrushchev's denunciations of Stalin's crimes, the ranks of those who took Soviet revolutionary claims seriously steadily declined. By the decade of the 1980s, the idea of the Marxist-Leninist state as the vanguard, the model, the glowing image of the future was dead in the West and far from thriving in the Soviet Union itself.

There, in fact, the historical pattern had reasserted itself. Soviet political and economic institutions had begun to be compared unfavorably—albeit implicitly or privately—with those of the West. Just as the Decembrist rebels, the small group of officers and nobles that launched an abortive coup against the tsar in 1825, drew inspiration from Montesquieu and Adam Smith, so Andrei Sakharov looks to the Western example of parliamentary democracy and reformers within the Soviet establishment—the economist Abel Aganbegyan and the sociologist Tatiana Zaslavskaya—are guided by the Western experience and by the work of Western social scientists and economists. Influence is again traveling from west to east.

The Anatomy of Influence

The Western impact on Russia and the Soviet Union is difficult to gauge. It has been prominent, and undoubtedly significant. But it has taken many forms over a long period of time. Customs, beliefs, theories, values, products and techniques—the whole array of things that make up what anthropologists call human culture—have passed from west to east. The array is so broad as to make any classification arbitrary. Still, one distinction is both obvious and important. It is the distinction between Western influence on external and on internal Russian behavior.

The external influence of one country or a group of countries on another is the easier of the two types to describe. The object of that sort of influence is a single entity—a state. The range of behavior that is affected is modest. The sovereign state, as a member of the international system, behaves in a limited number of ways: it expands, retreats, fights and negotiates. Moreover, what each state does in the international system is *inherently* a response to the other states. The basic fact of international politics is that there *are* others. The foreign policy of any state is a deliberate effort to influence those others. International politics is an exercise in mutual influence.[4]

Internal influence is more difficult to trace. The object of that influence can be an entire society. Millions of people may be affected in dozens, even hundreds or thousands of ways—their customs, institutions, beliefs and the like—often over long stretches of time.

The two types of influence are obviously very different from each other. One is the subject of deliberate efforts by governments. External influence is the aim of foreign policy. The other takes place for the most part outside the boundaries of governmental activity; governments often try to channel it but they do not always succeed. It is a process more than a policy, the age-old process of cultural transmission.

Foreign policy is deliberate, calculated, and subject to retrospective assessment. Success and failure can be weighed. Cultural transmission is more like a phenomenon of nature than a deliberate undertaking. It is broad and diffuse, the subject of millions of transactions and decisions. It is deeply significant but difficult to record in other than impressionistic fashion. To summarize, foreign policy affects what states *do*; cultural transmission affects what societies *are*.

The difference between the two types of influence may be illustrated by a pair of analogies. Foreign policy resembles an act of teaching. One individual addresses another with an explicit purpose in mind, a purpose that both understand. Cultural transmission is more like what students of society call "socialization." This is the process by which people acquire habits, attitudes, and assumptions from their surroundings, usually without even realizing that they are being affected. People are bombarded with cultural signals and messages every day. Over time these have an impact. So it is with societies.

Russia has been the recipient of both kinds of influence from the West from the 16th century through the Soviet period. Only the first has been the result of conscious Western policy. There has, it is true, been recurrent Western interest in changing the Soviet political system since 1917. The United States has shown greater interest than Western Europe. The interest arises from the American political tradition. The belief has been widely held in the United States, particularly in the 20th century, that aggression and international conflict are the work of undemocratic regimes. It follows that if the offending regime can be reformed, international conflict will subside. This is a view most closely associated with Woodrow Wilson, but hardly confined to him or to the first part of this century in the United States. Americans considered the post-revolutionary Soviet Union an undemocratic regime and, particularly after 1945, a dangerous state. Accordingly, it was a frequently expressed American hope and an occasional aim of American foreign policy to make the Soviet political system more Western, more democratic; this, in turn, it was thought, would make the Soviet Union a more peaceful member of the international community.[5]

At the outset of the Cold War the United States offered several proposals that, if accepted, would have transformed the Soviet Union. The Marshall Plan would have tied the Soviet economy much more closely to the economies of Europe and North America. The Baruch Plan for the control of atomic energy would have opened Soviet military facilities to the international community and ultimately diluted the sovereign powers of the Soviet state.[6] The Soviet Union rejected both.

During the 1970s, Soviet internal political practices again became a target of American foreign policy. The United States launched an effort to promote human rights. By signing the Helsinki Accords of 1975, the Soviet regime committed itself to respecting the liberties of its citizens as Western governments do theirs as a matter of course. This would have required a drastic—indeed a revolutionary—change in the way the Soviet Union is governed. No such change occurred. Moscow ignored the provisions of the Helsinki agreements that conflicted with the norms of Leninist rule.[7]

It would be a mistake, however, to conclude that the Soviet internal order has remained unchanged since World War II. If it has not moved appreciably closer to Western practices it has at least gone some distance away from those of the Stalinist era.[8] But there is no basis for imputing the changes that have taken place inside the Soviet Union to Western policies.

The Europeans have been less confident than the Americans that reformed regimes will be good international citizens and less optimistic about the prospects for transforming the Soviet Union. They have generally subscribed to the tradition of "realpolitik," according to which it is the external behavior rather than the internal order of other countries that is the legitimate objective of foreign policy. So while the United States has occasionally tried, and largely failed, to shape what the Soviet Union is, the Europeans have scarcely tried.

The West has in fact exerted both internal and external influence on the Soviet Union since 1945, although in the first case not as the result of deliberate policies. Yet, ironically, it is the United States alone that has had the greatest effect on Soviet foreign policy, which the canons of realpolitik take to be the most promising target of the policies of other countries. The United States has been the central member and the driving force of the Western coalition that has opposed the Soviets in Europe. Although NATO is a joint European-American undertaking the United States has acted as very much the senior partner. Outside Europe the American government has often acted without its European allies. The United States, along with the Soviet Union, has been a global military power and the anchor of a major coalition. The process of cultural transmission from west to east has also proceeded over the last 40 years, as over the last 400. But this kind of influence on the Soviet Union has come from the West as a whole rather than from its single strongest country.

Specifically, since 1945, the West has influenced the Soviet Union in three distinct ways. Each of these three was a pattern that was a familiar part of international politics in other eras, with other countries. The first is an example of external influence. It is the Western, and in particular the American policy of containment, which has been central to international politics and to the foreign policies of the two great nuclear powers for four decades.[9] The arms race, the second pattern, involves both foreign policy and cultural transmission. The Soviets have adopted Western technical and industrial innovations. They have done so, however, not through the slow, random diffusion of ideas and techniques, but rather as the result of governmental policies rooted in the competitive realities of the international system.[10] If containment is a case of the West exercising influence on the Soviet Union through confrontation, the arms race is an example of influence through imitation. Cultural transmission might be called influence through infiltration, and the third predominant pattern of influence in the relations between the West and the Soviet Union is a purer instance of cultural transmission. As in the past, Soviet society has absorbed influence from the West. And as did the tsars, the Soviet government has tried, with some success, to regulate what the Russian people receive. It has sought the material advances of the West without the social and political forms that go with them. Like the tsars, the Soviet leaders have wished to import Western "hardware" while keeping out Western "software."

By the 1980s, the first two patterns, containment and the arms race, had reached a stalemate. Neither side could dislodge the other from its most important geopolitical positions. Neither side seemed likely to gain a decisive advantage over the other in weaponry. The first was the consequence of the second. The internal institutions, practices and beliefs of the Soviet Union, by contrast, after three decades of immobility, seemed, with the coming to power of Mikhail Gorbachev, to become suddenly fluid and much more susceptible to Western influence. The third pattern of influence showed signs of change, and therefore had the greatest potential of the three for reshaping relations between East and West.

Containment

The relations among sovereign states are sometimes described in the language of physics. Each state strives to expand, to gain power and territory, to assert itself. International politics is the collision of assertive, opposing forces. States may therefore be seen as vectors, or, to use a more quotidian metaphor, as billiard balls. When they meet, the strength of one modifies the direction and the momentum of the other. The international system at any particular moment is the sum of all of these colliding forces. There is more to international politics, to be sure, than the conflict of self-seeking states, but that image does describe the most successful Western effort to influence the Soviet Union: containment.

The West sought to prevent the advance of Soviet power into Western Europe by building economic and military strength to serve as a barrier against it. In the early years of the Cold War, Washington sought to contain the Soviet Union, to keep it from expanding beyond the lines that the Red Army had reached in April, 1945, by giving economic assistance and political support to countries close to the Soviet sphere of influence. After 1950, the chief instrument of containment became military power. The United States stood at the center of a military coalition whose purpose was to resist attack from the east.

For the first decade of the East-West conflict American officials spoke from time to time of going beyond containment to "roll back" Soviet power. The idea was to evict the Soviet Union from the part of Europe, stretching from the middle of Germany in the west to the new Polish border in the east, that the Soviet Army had occupied during the course of World War II. The goal was never seriously pursued. After the failure to give any assistance to the Hungarians when they rose against the Soviets in 1956, it was dropped even from American rhetoric.

The policy of containment is a familiar part of European history. It has a long pedigree. The European powers periodically joined together to resist one or another of their neighbors that was threatening to dominate the continent. Continental coalitions blocked the Spanish Habsburgs, Louis XIV of France, Napoleon, Wilhelmine Germany and Hitler. In the wake of World War II, the Soviet Union emerged as the strongest European state. The Western Europeans feared that Stalin might try to follow in the footsteps of the would-be conquerors of the past. They banded together to prevent him from doing so.

They were joined, and ultimately led, by the United States. American policy in Europe also had historical precedents. It was descended from the British practice of assisting defensive coalitions on the continent. Since the 16th century, the British had reckoned that a hegemonic power in Europe would threaten not only its immediate neighbors but ultimately the British Empire and the British Isles themselves, despite the safety provided by the English Channel. The United States was separated from Europe by a much larger body of water than the Channel. But in the 20th century American governments made much the same calculation. They decided that events in Europe affected their own security. They first supplemented and then effectively replaced the British as the offshore guardian of the continental balance. American armed forces went to Europe twice, in 1917 and 1944, to keep Germany from achieving dominion there. In 1947, the United States committed itself to keeping the Soviet Union from moving further westward.

The policy of containment has been successful. The Soviet Union has not moved west. Western Europe, an entity that has come to be defined as encompassing the countries from Denmark to Greece and from Britain to Austria, is a community of free, liberal, prosperous states with close ties to North America. The power of the United

States has served as the ballast for a postwar dispensation in Europe that has proved remarkably stable and popular, at least in the western part of the continent.

It may be asked whether this state of affairs is the result of direct American influence on the Soviet Union. It can be argued that it would have come to pass without the various measures that together constituted the policy of containment. The Soviet Union, it is sometimes said, having been devastated by World War II, was far too weak to push beyond the ceasefire lines. Even today, when it is much stronger, the argument goes, it has no incentive to extend its domain to Western Europe, which would only bring economic disadvantage and political danger.[11]

It is true that the Soviet Union was battered in 1945, although it is also true that it deployed a huge, victorious army in the center of Europe. Still, the Soviets have good reasons to respect the *status quo* in Europe, not the least of which is the fact that it keeps Russia's historic nemesis, Germany, divided. That does not prove, however, that the American role in Europe has had no effect. The Soviets are not well served, at least in economic terms, by controlling Eastern Europe, or by adopting as clients distant radical regimes in Cuba, Angola, South Yemen and elsewhere; yet they do. Soviet foreign policy since 1945 has not been in conspicuous thrall to economic logic.

Moreover, in international politics, power abhors a vacuum. A vacuum of power existed in Western Europe in 1945. Something was bound to fill it. A logical candidate was the Soviet Union. Dean Acheson's metaphor for Soviet behavior—"You cannot argue with a river; it is going to flow. You can dam it or deflect it but not argue with it."[12]—may have overstated the case. Stalin's divisions were not poised to strike west in 1947. But power can seep as well as gush.

Without countervailing force of some sort, the temptation for the Soviet Union to try to exercise some measure of political control in the rest of Europe would have been strong, perhaps irresistible. While Stalin was cautious, he was not inherently reticent. His ambitions, and those of his successors, were limited by what they thought it would cost to pursue them, not by some independent sense of the proper scope of Soviet power. The Soviet leaders never, as far as we know, came close to launching an attack with the aim of subduing all of Europe after 1945. Within the Kremlin archives there may exist no document presenting a master plan for conquering or subverting Western Europe. But there was never a good opportunity to do so; and it is opportunities that inspire plans.

If the United States had remained aloof from Europe, the vacuum in the western part of the continent would have been filled in some other way. Perhaps the historic great powers, Britain, France, and Germany, would have rallied themselves, banded together, and assembled sufficient military and political counterweight without help from the other side of the Atlantic. If they had not, Soviet influence almost surely would have reached beyond the middle of Germany. Just what form it would have taken is difficult to say. The term that has gained currency for an unseemly Soviet role in the affairs of a Western country is "Finlandization." The coinage is, in a sense, unfair. Finland's lot is not a particularly distasteful one. The Finns do show a certain amount of deference to Moscow, but in almost every way theirs is a fully independent state.

It is one thing for Finland to work out such an arrangement with the Soviet Union, however, and quite another for Germany—a more strategically located, powerful, and in every way important country—to do so. A "Finlandized" Germany would make for a very different Europe than the one that has evolved since 1945. Moreover, Finland's benign status is possible in part precisely because Germany is *not* Finlandized. A necessary condition for Finlandization is the presence of a countervailing force to Soviet power on the continent, which gives even formally neutral countries a measure of protection.

Containment, therefore, is a case of successful Western influence on the Soviet Union. The result of this success has been a tolerable, stable relationship between the Soviet Union and Western Europe.

The United States endeavored to contain the Soviet Union outside Europe as well. The contest between the two was played out, often through allies and clients, in Korea, Indochina, Central and South America, the Middle East, Africa and Afghanistan. The instruments of the competition were the same as in Europe: political support, economic and military assistance, and sometimes the armed forces of the United States and the Soviet Union themselves.[13]

The policy of containment has enjoyed less success beyond Europe than on the continent. In some places American efforts, together with local forces, did succeed in resisting those aligned with Moscow. The southern part of the Korean peninsula, for example, was kept from Communist control in the Korean War. Egypt, once aligned with the Soviet Union, switched sides and established close ties with the United States. In other places, however, American efforts failed. Cuba moved into the Soviet camp. Fifteen years later, all of Indochina fell to Communist armies.

Not every development outside Europe was the result of the exertions of either the United States or the Soviet Union. The People's Republic of China, once the junior partner of the Soviet Union in what was called the Sino-Soviet bloc, shifted its geopolitical position closer to the United States. The development was welcome in the West and was assisted by deft American diplomacy but it was hardly the consequence of the policy of containment. In general, the capacity of the two great nuclear powers for shaping events outside Europe has declined in the postwar period, as the techniques for producing military strength diffused from the world's core to its periphery, and especially to places even more distant from the core than Russia.

Nor was every setback for the American policy of containment an unmixed blessing for the Soviet Union. Cuba proved to be an expensive client, requiring large annual subventions. Vietnam was similarly costly. Soviet-supported regimes in Angola and Afghanistan found themselves under seige from guerrilla insurrections that they could not defeat. Still, Moscow evidently regarded Cuba, Vietnam, and Angola as gains, showing no sign of being prepared to abandon the friendly regimes that hold power in these countries. In the ongoing contest with the United States, however, these gains were of limited significance. The regimes with close ties to the Soviet Union in the farther reaches of the Third World were poor, distant from the center of great power concerns, and generally far less consequential than Europe.

The contest for the Third World, such as it was, and thus the American policy of containment there, had reached a kind of equilibrium by the latter half of the 1980s. Unlike Europe, some regions remained politically unsettled. In a few, wars were being fought. But there seemed little prospect that, whatever happened in the individual countries, either the United States or the Soviet Union could gain a decisive advantage over the other. Although less plainly successful, the policy of containment had more or less the same effect elsewhere as in Europe: a stalemate.

Containment was a straightforward policy. It involved the application of force or economic and political assistance in a particular place to block or discourage Soviet advances there. It was a direct approach to the task of exerting influence on Soviet foreign policy. In the 1970s, the United States tried to exert influence indirectly as well. It made an effort to connect different arenas of the competition, to use pressure or concessions in one to produce desired Soviet policies in another.

It was the Nixon Administration that attempted to link different issues and different parts of the world. Initially the Administration tried to enlist Soviet assistance in settling the war in Vietnam. Washington hinted that if the Soviets persuaded the North Vietnamese to be cooperative the United States would be forthcoming in the arms talks that were just getting under way, but that there would be no arms control accord while the war continued. Later, Washington's dramatic *rapprochement* with the People's Republic of China was partly aimed at pressing the Soviets to be more accommodating in their relations with the United States. Both initiatives enjoyed modest if temporary success. The Soviet Union was apparently helpful in getting Hanoi to sign the 1973 Paris Peace Accords although not to observe them thereafter. Moscow seemed more anxious to improve relations with the United States after the Nixon visit to Beijing in 1972.

Linkage eventually came to be seen as an effort to involve the Soviet Union in a series of political, cultural, and above all economic relationships with the West that would encourage the Soviets to practice restraint abroad, particularly in the Third World. Enmeshed in a "web of interdependence," it was hoped, Moscow would abandon the project of spreading its political influence abroad by force and subversion for fear of rupturing its profitable connections with the West.

Just who thought this, and with what degree of confidence, is not easy to say. The official claims were hedged and guarded. "Over time," Henry Kissinger said, "trade and investment may leaven the autarkic tendencies of the Soviet system, invite gradual association of the Soviet economy with the world economy, and foster a degree of interdependence that adds an element of stability to the political equation." "There was no thought," Nixon later wrote, "that commercial, technical and scientific relationships could by themselves prevent confrontations or wars, but at least they would have to be counted in a balance sheet of gains and losses whenever the Soviets were tempted to indulge in international adventurism."[14]

Linkage was never as fully formed a policy as containment had been. Relations with the Soviet Union at the beginning of the 1970s evolved in ad hoc fashion. Moscow was anxious for more extensive economic ties. Some parts of the American business community were also interested. Washington went along with the idea. Then the President and other officials made a series of statements holding out the hope that these ties would bring political as well as economic benefits.

In the end they did not. By American standards, Soviet policy outside Europe at the zenith of detente and thereafter was not restrained. To the contrary, it was aggressive, disturbing, and dangerous, and ultimately provoked the collapse of the relationship that the Nixon Administration had tried to construct. The list of Soviet activities to which Americans objected includes assistance to Egypt and Syria in their attack on Israel in October, 1973; aid to the ultimately successful faction in the Angolan civil war in 1974; the continued patronage of the Communist forces in Indochina that conquered their non-Communist opponents in 1975; sponsorship of the radical governments of Ethiopia and Mozambique; publicly proclaimed sympathy for and some aid to the anti-American Sandinista regime in Nicaragua; and the brutal invasion and occupation of Afghanistan in 1979.

Linkage failed in part because the United States was not able to use economic ties as leverage, to expand them to reward appropriate Soviet conduct and restrict them as a way of punishing misbehavior. In the hands of any American government economic relations with other countries are a blunt instrument, if they can be called an instrument at all. The Western economic order is broader than the United States. There are other countries with which the Soviet Union can trade and from which it can seek capital and technology. Britain, France, Italy, Japan and Germany were not disposed to follow the American lead in opening and closing economic channels to the east in response to Moscow's policies outside Europe.[15]

Even if the West could have wielded the "economic instrument" more deftly, it is unlikely that the Soviets could have been prevailed upon to conduct their policies according to the American definition of international propriety. The Soviet Union is not susceptible to economic pressure. It enjoys, if that is the right word, a degree of economic autarky unmatched in the West. Even for countries more dependent on the outside world than is the Soviet Union, the exercise of economic leverage has almost always yielded disappointingly modest results. Sanctions rarely work, as the boycotts of various sorts imposed on Cuba, Rhodesia, South Africa and Poland have demonstrated. None achieved its original aim.[16]

The Arms Race

In addition to the language of physics, one of the central concepts of the discipline of economics is pertinent to an understanding of Western influence on the Soviet Union. Rival states or coalitions are like firms in the same market. Each is affected by the others. Each is in competition with the others; each strives to expand its share of the market at the others' expense. One particular characteristic of commercial rivalry is especially relevant to Western influence on the Soviet Union after 1945. In markets, competitive pressure produces considerable uniformity among the competing units. Firms come to resemble one another in basic ways. There is often an optimal method for manufacturing a product or providing a service. Firms that compete to sell the product or service will be impelled to adopt that method, since not to use it would place them at a severe competitive disadvantage. Important innovations diffuse throughout industries because they are necessary for survival.

So it is with rival states, when they deal with innovations on which *their* survival depends. Military advances tend to spread quickly. States copy the weapons and the organizational changes in the armed forces that their competitors originate. States are not like each other in all ways; the history of relations between Russia and the West testifies to that. But in *military* terms rivals do tend to resemble each other.

The imitation of military advances is a form of cultural transmission but it takes place more rapidly and more deliberately than the spread of ideas, political institutions, or even commercial procedures. And it is a response to the pressures that membership in the competitive system of sovereign states imposes. In the wake of the industrial revolution, the most important military advances have tended to be specific industrial products—weapons that are even more complicated, expensive, and destructive. In the 20th century the diffusion of military innovations has taken the form of the arms race.[17] In the arms race between the two great nuclear powers in the postwar period it is the United States that has generally been the innovator and the Soviet Union the imitator. The United States has therefore exerted influence on the Soviet Union not only through geopolitical opposition but also as a military example.

The military policies of rivals do not necessarily converge in every respect. Military strategies are determined by more than technology. Politics, history, geography, and demography are also important, often more important. At the center of their confrontation, in Europe, the strategies of the two great military coalitions are in fact quite different.

The forces of the Warsaw Pact, which is dominated by the Soviet Union, are poised to attack. Soviet military doctrine was shaped by the traumatic battlefield defeats inflicted in 1941 by the tactics of the German *blitzkrieg*. In the aftermath of the war the Soviet Army itself adopted these tactics. An offensive strategy makes it easier for the Soviets to integrate the troops of the Eastern European satellite nations into a single centralized command. That, in turn, makes it difficult for the Poles, Hungarians, Czechs, and Germans to act independently of the Soviet Union. Soviet authorities may also reckon that in the event of war they must win quick victories lest their coalition, the political underpinnings of which are shaky, collapse as the Eastern Europeans take the opportunity to defect. It is logical for a power confronted with adversaries on two sides, in the Soviet case by the United States and China, to plan to win the war swiftly in order to avoid a long contest of attrition with more populous and industrially productive adversaries.[18] Last, but hardly least, Soviet military doctrine in Europe has been offensive because the aims of Soviet foreign policy there have been offensive. The Soviet Union has aspired to change the *status quo* even if it has never rated the chances of doing so particularly high. It has sought to advance its own political influence; historically Soviet influence has been extended almost exclusively through the use of force.

The Soviet Union did not adopt its military approach in Europe from the West. For NATO, with the United States as its leader, has adopted a defensive strategy. This is in keeping with its political aim. Containment is a defensive policy. NATO's strategy arises, in addition, from political necessity. The Western alliance has felt obliged to defend all of the territory of the Federal Republic of Germany against a Warsaw Pact attack. Establishing defenses all along the inner-German border has left few forces available for offensive operations. Another reason for the absence of forces for such operations is that many of the troops that NATO counts on fielding in case of war are not mobilized and deployed at the front lines in peacetime. The army of the Federal Republic is composed in large part of reserves; the United States plans to bring troops from other parts of the world to the European front if war breaks out. And one reason that the Western forces are not fully mobilized is that governments and public opinion in the West assume that their countries would never start a war; and because their forces are not fully mobilized they *cannot* initiate the fighting and expect to prevail. The United States and its allies therefore plan to fight on the defensive, at least at the outset, in a third great European conflict in the 20th century.

The Soviet Union, however, has followed the pattern of Western innovation in the armaments with which the two sides propose to fight in Europe. Both have retained the basic elements of the combined arms warfare that the belligerents waged in World War II. Both sides have worked to make them more resilient and more powerful. In response to what the other has done each has steadily improved its artillery, tanks and jet planes. In the competition to produce these weapons the West, with its more sophisticated industrial base, has generally held the lead. The Soviet Union has striven to match Western technical advances and sought to compensate for the inferior quality of its weaponry by producing and deploying more of them.[19]

In the 1980s, the cutting edge of military technology is in guidance systems for munitions. These are being made increasingly accurate by advances in sensors and the techniques of processing information. Lasers and computers have brought substantial changes to the battlefield. Here, again, the West has taken the lead and the Soviet Union has struggled to keep pace.[20]

Nuclear weapons are less tied to political and geographical realities than are armaments of other sorts. They are more independent of the traditional determinants of military strategy. Nuclear strategy is more purely the product of technology. Unlike politics and geography, technology is more or less the same for both sides in an arms race. The correspondence between the two great nuclear arsenals and the doctrines governing them, therefore, although not exact, is closer than for non-nuclear weapons.

In the nuclear arms race the United States has generally been the innovator, the Soviet Union the imitator. The United States was usually the first to produce the different types of nuclear explosives and vehicles for delivering them to enemy targets. The Soviet Union has subsequently made its own versions of these bombs and delivery systems. There have been exceptions to this pattern. The Soviet Union has not chosen to follow the United States in every way. The American Air Force emphasized manned bombers of intercontinental range; the Soviet Union has not built a comparable fleet of aircraft.[21] Some innovations occurred more or less simultaneously. The Soviets detonated their first fusion bomb very shortly after the initial American test of this type of explosive. The Soviet Union reached one important milestone before the United States: the launching of the earth-orbiting satellite "Sputnik" in 1957 put the Soviets in space first.

For most of the history of the arms race, however, the United States has exercised unintended (and to Americans, unwelcome) influence on the Soviet Union by serving as a model. American scientists and engineers made the first atomic bomb. Stalin plainly expressed the dynamics of the arms race when he ordered Soviet scientists in 1945 to make an atomic bomb as quickly as possible: "You know that Hiroshima has shaken the whole world. The balance has been destroyed. Provide the bomb—it will remove a great danger from us."[22] The United States led the way in making smaller bombs that could be used as battlefield artillery. Solid-fuel intercontinental ballistic missiles were an American innovation, as was the practice of putting intercontinental-range nuclear-tipped rockets on submarines. It was the United States, again, that first equipped its missiles with multiple independently targeted warheads. In every case the Soviet Union followed the American lead.

In the doctrines governing the manufacture, deployment, and potential use of nuclear weapons, the Soviet Union also for the most part followed in the footsteps of the United States. The case for influence through imitation is more difficult to make for doctrine than for weapons. Doctrine is inherently vague. It is a combination of weapons, which can be used in more than one way, and declarations, which can be misinterpreted or intended to mislead.

As with the weapons, moreover, the match between American and Soviet doctrines is not exact. The Soviets have declared, for example, that they will never be the first to use nuclear weapons; NATO has declined to make that pledge.[23]

Still, during the last forty years a familiar pattern has emerged. The United States has led and the Soviet Union has followed in the development of nuclear doctrine. The United States was quick to proclaim the revolutionary character of the new bombs. They were so powerful, the civilian strategist Bernard Brodie wrote in 1946, that they changed the principal aim of armed forces: "Thus far the chief purpose of our military establishment has been to win wars. From now on its chief purpose must be to avert them. It can have almost no other useful purpose."[24] The Soviet Union was slower to draw this conclusion: Stalin insisted that the discovery of the techniques for making explosives of unprecedented power did not invalidate the historical law that conflict between the Capitalist and the Communist worlds was inevitable. After his death the official position changed. The Soviets allowed that the atomic bomb was not like other weapons and that it did, indeed, affect what had previously been decreed to be immutable principles. "The atomic bomb," as one Soviet statement put it, "does not adhere to the class principle." Deterrence came to be the purpose of the Soviet nuclear arsenal, or so at least official Soviet doctrine proclaimed.[25]

If deterrence was the main aim of nuclear strategy, how was it to be achieved? What sorts of weapons, and of what design, were necessary to keep a nuclear-armed adversary from attacking? The American answer was that at the very least a nuclear arsenal had to be invulnerable to preemptive attack. It had to be resilient enough to retaliate even after absorbing a first strike. If one side had the certain capacity to deliver a devastating salvo in response to the fiercest attack the other could mount, the other would never dare launch such an attack. Accordingly, the American government took care to protect its nuclear forces, putting its landbased missiles in reinforced concrete bunkers underground, keeping a certain number of bomber aircraft airborne at all times, and putting missiles on submarines that could not be tracked and destroyed while at sea. Subsequently the Soviet Union took similar measures.[26]

In the 1950s, a debate took place in the United States over whether a powerful, resilient nuclear striking force by itself would be sufficient to deter the Soviet Union in Europe and elsewhere. The Eisenhower Administration believed that it would be, and relied on nuclear weapons. The American government threatened to retaliate "massively" against aggression by the Soviet Union anywhere in the world. Critics of the Eisenhower defense policies argued that the United States needed a variety of military options, not only the capacity for nuclear punishment, for effective deterrence. Their view was adopted by Eisenhower's successor, John F. Kennedy. His Administration substituted a strategy of what it called flexible response for massive retaliation. The new strategy required a wider range of non-nuclear capabilities.

The Soviet Union went through a similar cycle, a few years after the United States. Khrushchev stressed nuclear weapons at the expense of non-nuclear armaments in Soviet military planning. In the late 1950s he announced that thereafter all wars would be nuclear conflicts. Accordingly, he began to reduce the size of the Soviet Army's non-nuclear forces. His successors adopted different priorities. They presided over a substantial increase in non-nuclear naval, air and ground forces in both Europe and Asia. In the Brezhnev era the Soviet Union, too, acquired the capacity for flexible response. It is plausible to speculate that they learned from the Americans that nuclear weapons alone were not enough to achieve the range of goals to which a great nuclear power aspired.[27]

Soon after Hiroshima the two sides began making proposals for dealing with these new weapons through diplomacy. Here, too, the United States blazed a trail that the Soviet Union followed. The initial American proposal called for bringing all nuclear weapons under the control of an international authority. The Baruch Plan was a scheme for disarmament—for abolishing rather than limiting the nuclear threat. The Soviet Union rejected it, but offered a series of counter-proposals of its own whose common goal was "general and complete disarmament." Disarmament proposals were tabled largely as exercises in propaganda in the early years of the Cold War; their presentations themselves became a form of political combat.[28]

In the 1950s the American side began to set its sights lower. Washington began to seek more limited, and thus more feasible agreements on nuclear weapons. The Soviet Union eventually agreed to this approach; the first of a series of arms control agreements between the two, the Limited Test Ban Treaty, was signed in 1963. By the 1970s, negotiations on arms control had become a permanent feature of Soviet-American relations. The negotiations themselves followed a familiar pattern. Once again, the Americans took the lead. The United States would characteristically make a proposal. The Soviet Union would respond. Based on the Soviet response the American government would draft a new set of suggestions, which would serve as the basis for the next round of discussions.

The most important accord of the 1970s was the 1972 treaty in effect prohibiting defense against missile attack. The treaty implied agreement on the principle that stability rests on unchallenged offensive striking power on both sides, a principle Soviet leaders had emphatically rejected in the 1960s.[29]

Also implicit in the general enterprise of arms control is the idea that nuclear weapons uniquely lend themselves to an equilibrium between the two great powers. Because of the enormous destructive power of the bomb, and the prohibitive difficulty of defending against it, each side can make itself secure with roughly the force levels that the other has. Once mutual vulnerability is accepted, increases in nuclear weaponry lose their utility. There is no way of getting ahead and no point in trying. It becomes sensible, instead, to settle for a draw; to cooperate in establishing limits on armaments rather than striving for meaningless and in any event unattainable advantages.

This line of logic has long been a theme of American writing on nuclear weapons, although it has not always served as the basis of American policy. It has seemed conspicuously absent in Soviet policy. There was little evidence that restraint in the arms competition appealed to the Soviet leaders. As the former Secretary of Defense Harold Brown once put it: "When we build, they build. When we stop, they build." Mikhail Gorbachev, however, has made statements about the nature of security in the nuclear age that seem to endorse the Western idea of equilibrium and embrace the logic of ceasing to pursue advantages in weaponry.[30] His words may therefore represent yet another instance of American influence on the Soviet Union through the process of imitation.

Whatever his words mean, the arms race over which he and his American counterpart presided had reached a stalemate by the 1980s. As with containment in Europe and the rivalry in other parts of the world, it seemed highly unlikely that either side could equip itself with enough nuclear weapons to gain a decisive advantage over the other.[31]

The Russian Pattern of Cultural Transmission

For centuries, Western influence of all kinds seeped into Russia by the slow, uncoordinated, universal process of cultural transmission. Trade, intellectual contacts and travel—the visits of Westerners to Russia and of Russians to the West—brought the fruits of European civilization to the East. They were carried as well by Westerners who came to settle in Russia. Over the centuries, Germans were important bearers of Western culture, particularly around the Baltic but also in the Russian heartland. Germans constituted part of the nobility but also were ordinary farmers, tradesmen and artisans.

Overshadowing this slow, steady diffusion of products and ideas from west to east, however, has been a different, less continuous, more important pattern. From time to time Russia's rulers deliberately imported Western influence. They sponsored efforts to transform the country according to their own designs and on their own schedules. Russia and the Soviet Union have, over the centuries, experienced recurrent episodes of what has been called reform from above.[32]

These periods of intensive reform were inspired by military defeat, or looming foreign threats, or both. Peter the Great launched his campaign to overhaul the backward, isolated peasant society that he ruled partly in response to setbacks on the battlefield. Defeat in the Crimean War served as an impetus for the reforms of the mid-19th century, notably the freeing of the serfs. The Japanese victory over Russia in 1905 triggered a revolution that, although it did not dislodge the Romanov dynasty, did prompt the regime to make a series of political and economic changes that drew heavily on the West.

In each of these episodes Russia's rulers had the same purpose: the strengthening of their state. This meant amassing military might, which in turn required cultivating the economic underpinnings of military power. These invariably had to be imported or copied from the West, where they had been developed. On each occasion, the rulers sought to control the influx of Western influence, welcoming some things but attempting to bar others. Here, too, there was a distinctive pattern. They avidly sought to import the elements of military power and national splendor—the ships, the palaces, the railroads, the steel mills, the automobiles and the atomic energy of the West. But they were equally determined to keep out the political and social foundations of Western material progress. They did not want a free market economy with private property, individual entrepreneurs and joint stock companies, or independent centers of learning and free inquiry, not to mention elected legislatures with real power and working constitutions setting forth individual rights on which the state could not infringe. The autocratic rulers of Russia sought Western "hardware," the fruits of economic advance, without the institutions and beliefs, the "software," that accompanied it in Europe.[33]

This was an understandable set of preferences for them to have. Western hardware reinforced the rulers' positions by strengthening the state of which they were the masters. Western software would weaken them, sowing dissatisfaction with political arrangements in which the few ruled the many in arbitrary fashion.

Russia's rulers were not the only people to try to pick and choose among the cultural wares of the Western "core." Non-Western peoples the world over have had to confront the force of European civilization in the modern era. The Chinese, the Japanese, the Arabs and others have all reacted with the ambivalence of the Russians. They, too, have sought the material achievements of the West, if only to be able to defend themselves against European armies and navies. But they have also often sought to block the spread of Western social and political practices and institutions to their societies. The motto of the Tung-chih restoration, a conservative reform movement in China in the 19th century, expressed a widely shared aspiration: "Western learning with Chinese customs."

The Russian effort to obtain Western hardware while shunning its software differed from similar efforts elsewhere on the periphery of Europe, however, in two ways. First, the Russian version of this global pattern was of longer standing than the others. It was only in the 19th century, with the revolutions in transportation, communication and warfare produced by the industrial age, that Europe intruded on virtually every corner of the world. Russia, situated closer to the European "core" than Japan or China, was directly exposed to the West long before then. The second distinctive feature of Russia's relationship with Europe is that Russia's rulers by and large achieved their aim. They succeeded in importing Western technology and industry while keeping out Western forms of political and economic organization.

However backward in comparison with their Western neighbors, the Russians were always powerful enough to defend themselves and remain independent. Russia was never conquered from the West: France in the 19th century and Germany in the 20th failed in the attempt. The Russian state and its Soviet successor remained generally free of the political, social and economic practices that flourished in Europe and North America. The West has had a profound influence on Russia, but not through deliberate policies and not in a fashion that most Westerners would have preferred.

The cluster of Western values, practices and institutions known as liberalism never took root in Russia. The key to liberalism's failure, in the view of Richard Pipes, is the absence in Russia of the institution of private property, which is in turn the enduring legacy of what he calls the "patrimonial state."[34] Leonard Schapiro has argued that what is crucially missing from the Russian political tradition, and what has set Russia apart from the West for five centuries, is a broad devotion to the idea of the rule of law.[35] To specify private property, or the rule of law, or a combination of them (they are, after all, closely related) or some other institution or belief as the missing ingredient in the evolution of the Russian political system is to raise a further question: Why did the elements of Western culture that are crucial for the development of Western software, whatever they are, never establish themselves in Russia?

There are, no doubt, several reasons. The social composition of the Russian population was never favorable to the growth of liberal norms. In the West these were adopted by the middle classes. For most of its history Russia lacked such a social stratum. It was a huge mass of peasantry ruled in an arbitrary manner by a thin layer of nobles. The world of the peasant was one of hierarchy rather than equality and of distrust instead of cooperation. Preoccupied with his own lot, the peasant generally had little sense of wider civic responsibilities. His was, in short, a world without the attitudes that nurtured and sustained liberal political practices in the West.[36] The indigenous Russian bourgeoisie appeared on the scene late and never became either numerous or influential.

The very success of the policy of acquiring Western hardware while excluding its software also helped to perpetuate the pattern. Russian regimes were strong enough to stamp out or severely restrict the beginnings of political and economic liberalism that did appear during the 19th century. It may be that the prerequisites for an open society can only thrive in a society that is already partly open. And the tsars were strong enough, as other non-Western rulers were not, to keep the West from imposing its laws and customs by force. Capitalism flourished in China's treaty ports because they were controlled by the Western powers. India got its parliamentary traditions from its British rulers. Cultural transmission accelerates when a core state governs a country on the periphery. That never happened in Russia.

There is a final reason for the failure of liberalism in the Soviet Union. One of its basic political tenets—self-government—conflicts with the imperatives of empire. Territorial expansion was a constant feature of Russian history. The tsars brought non-Russians under their control in great numbers. To take the precepts of political liberalism seriously would have meant releasing these peoples, or at least permitting a greater measure of independence than was compatible with Russia's imperial prerogatives. The tsars, and their successors, invariably chose imperial control over liberal practices.[37] In 1863, the Poles revolted against Russian domination. The decision to crush them effectively derailed reform in Russian itself.[38]

The period of Communist rule has followed the traditional Russian pattern of social and political change. Defeat has served as the catalyst. Under the weight of the military disaster of World War I, the Romanov dynasty collapsed. In the chaos that followed, Lenin and the Bolsheviks managed to seize and ultimately to consolidate power. They proceeded over the course of the next two decades to remake Russian society in a fashion brutal even by the standards of the country's past. Sweeping change was engineered from above, spurred in the 1920s and even more powerfully in the 1930s by the looming threat of a hostile capitalist world.

The changes brought Russia the heavy industry of the West without its political practices. Lenin's glib formula that "Communism equals electrification plus Soviets" expresses the familiar Russian aspiration to acquire Western hardware without its political, social, and economic software. Lenin's heirs succeeded on both counts.

The industry they built in the 1930s laid the foundation for world power. After winning the Civil War, the regime defeated Russia's historic rival, Germany, marched its troops through Europe to Berlin and beyond (where they remained 40 years after Hitler's defeat), matched the nuclear weaponry of the United States, and projected its might beyond Europe to places of which the tsars had barely dreamed in Africa, Asia, and Latin America. They did so with an economy that was organized and with a society that was governed in ways quite different from those that prevailed in the West.

The essence of Western economic organization is the market mechanism. Decisions about what to produce, in what quantities, and about the prices at which to sell them, are made by individuals and privately-owned firms acting on their own, without central direction, according to calculations of profit and loss. The Soviet economy is governed by different rules. The state makes all the major decisions. Its criteria are, in Western parlance, "noneconomic." Considerations of price are not central. The main economic assets are owned by the government. In place of the market in the Soviet Union stands the state. The economy works according to the commands of the state, not private calculations.[39]

Similarly, the Soviet political system is, in a sense, the opposite of the kind that exists, in differing variations, in the West. At the heart of the Western political tradition is the separation of state and society. The state's prerogatives are limited. There are areas of conduct on which it cannot encroach. Citizens have rights, which they can exercise without the permission, indeed even against the wishes of the rulers. Among them is the right to choose their own leaders.

In the Soviet Union, especially in Stalin's day, no barrier existed between society and the state. The regime intruded everywhere; it tried to shape all aspects of social life. It crushed every independent center of political and social activity. The name given in the West to the political system that Stalin tried with some success to create was "totalitarianism."

The Stalinist political system was not only the antithesis of the dominant political tradition in the West, it was also a reprise of some features of the Russian past. State ownership of the economy, an all-powerful ruler, an official creed demanding universal allegiance and recurrent violence as a political instrument were part of Soviet life from the 1930s to the 1950s and were elements of tsarist rule from the origins of the kingdom of Muscovy. The often-made comparison between Stalin and Ivan the Terrible has a solid historical basis.

After Stalin's death, the cruelest and most grotesque excesses of his rule abated. Mass terror came to an end. The cult of the leader ebbed and power diffused among a wider group of oligarchs. The strict controls on the everyday life of the Soviet citizen were relaxed.[40] The Soviet political and economic order came to function less like a caricature of a medieval despotism but it did not move appreciably closer to Western forms. The changes that did occur, moreover, were not the result of Western influence. The leaders of the Communist Party abolished mass terror not because they became convinced that violence was an illegitimate political instrument but rather because they feared that they themselves would ultimately fall victim to it. They continued to welcome Western hardware, indeed to get it however they could. Their official ideology exalted science and technology and claimed that the Soviet system was uniquely suited to take advantage of them. But they were no more interested than Stalin had been in promoting popular sovereignty, protecting individual rights and liberties, and cultivating the institution of private property.

Gorbachev and the New Pattern of Change

When he first took office as the supreme leader of the Soviet Union, Mikhail Gorbachev seemed to be cast in the traditional mold of Russian reformers. He brought to power an urgent concern, which was widely shared within the Soviet elite, that his country was falling behind the West. He made clear his determination to catch up.[41] He embarked upon a program of reform that, like similar campaigns in the Russian past, was designed by the rulers to be imposed on the society. Its aim, as before, was to bring Russia the most advanced economic products and processes of the West. Where Peter had sought ships, Nicholas railroads, and Stalin steel mills, Gorbachev and his colleagues want the high-speed computers, commercial and industrial lasers and automated assembly lines of the 1980s.

As his term of office progressed, however, the signs proliferated that Gorbachev differed from his Soviet and tsarist predecessors in an important and potentially revolutionary way. His program of reform, as it unfolded, envisioned importing into Russia not only the hardware, but also what previous Russian rulers had despised and opposed: the software of the West. He began to introduce Western economic forms, or give official sanction to those that already existed illegally. Private and cooperative agriculture received official encouragement. A new law gave citizens the right to organize small private businesses, such as restaurants and repair and catering services. For the first time in over fifty years, enterprises obtained the power, under certain circumstances, to keep what they earned and use it at their own discretion, instead of passing it on to the central authorities. They also got permission to deal with foreign purchasers and suppliers directly rather than, as in the past, only through the offices of a ministry in Moscow. There is, in addition, a new law covering joint enterprises with foreigners. The motherland of socialism is seeking foreign capital.

Perhaps most importantly, the Gorbachev regime has issued directives to reduce dramatically the power of the central planners. Prices and production targets are to be increasingly set by firms themselves, no doubt more and more according to market rules. If carried out on a large scale these changes would establish Western economic ideas, institutions and procedures in Russia much more extensively than ever before.

At the same time, Gorbachev has heralded, and in a few cases actually implemented, startling political innovations. Like his economic reforms, these are borrowed from the West, although the Soviet leader has not publicized their origins.[42]

There is talk of a new legal code to protect the rights of Soviet citizens, for which the Soviet constitution provides but which the regime has never respected. There is talk, as well, of pilot projects for introducing a measure of democracy into the affairs of the ruling Communist Party. More than one candidate is to stand for election—by secret ballot—to lower and middle level Party positions, although the Party is to select the candidates in every case.[43]

Most striking of all is what has come to be known as the policy of *glasnost'*, which is variously translated in English as "openness" or "publicity." Whatever the precise English term for it, *glasnost'* has meant a dramatic widening of the boundaries of permitted public discussion. Subjects that were previously taboo—social problems such as alcoholism for example—have received attention in official journals. The Party-sanctioned history of the Soviet Union is being revised. Proposals for even more radical economic changes than those being officially contemplated regularly receive a public hearing. Party officials, although not Gorbachev himself, have come in for criticism, some of it scathing. Here talk *is* important. Talk is, in fact, policy. Gorbachev has not brought freedom of speech in the Western sense to the Soviet Union but he has sponsored much freer speech than his predecessors permitted.

Gorbachev has encouraged Western economic forms because he and other members of the Soviet establishment have become convinced that they cannot have Western hardware without Western software. Sustained economic growth and the manufacture of the most sophisticated industrial products, they have come to believe, are not possible in the Soviet Union without changes in the existing patterns of economic organization.[44] In Stalin's day this was not so. The regime pursued a strategy of what economists call "extensive growth," in which adding raw materials, capital and labor yields rising production. The Stalinist political system was well suited to this economic strategy. It could mobilize the untapped reserves of Russian society, squeezing it to extract savings while depressing consumption, pouring resources into a few selected industries, and sending people to work in the large plants that were built in the 1930s. By the 1980s the country's reserves were exhausted. Gorbachev and his associates cannot bring peasants from the farms to the factories in large numbers as in the past; there is no pool of underemployed rural workers. Nor, to take another example, can they count on easy-to-obtain oil in large volume, as the Soviet leadership was able to do into the 1970s.

The Soviet Union is faced with the need to shift to an intensive model of growth, which involves making more efficient use of the materials and labor that are available. For this strategy the Stalinist economic system, with enormous power in the hands of the planner and noneconomic criteria for economic decisions, is clumsy and inefficient. Individual initiative, flexibility and innovation are required. These are the strengths of the *Western* economic order. Market rules are much more conducive to intensive growth. Gorbachev seems to be moving—albeit slowly, cautiously, and tentatively—to introduce them.

At the same time, he has proposed changes that are more political than economic in character. It is, to be sure, often difficult to separate the political from the economic. Stalin's political system was in a sense created to oversee the extensive pattern of economic growth. Change in the second will necessarily affect the first. The diffusion of economic initiative would bring about a broader distribution of political power. Moreover, the successful operation of a market system requires human traits such as curiosity, initiative, and a sense of individual responsibility, that are as much political as economic.

Gorbachev is also promoting political change as a tactic in his campaign for economic reform. He has met resistance to the new ways of doing things that he advocates. By permitting broader public discussion, he is undoubtedly hoping to mobilize support for his economic program. He may also have strictly political reasons for the new political ideas that he has endorsed. Just as the Stalinist economic model has become obsolete, so the main instruments of political control forged during the Stalinist era and used extensively by Khrushchev and Brezhnev seem to be losing their effectiveness.[45] Gorbachev may feel the need for new methods of governance apart from the particular program he hopes to carry out.

Gorbachev's Soviet Union is less seriously threatened from abroad than the Russia of the reforming tsars who preceded him. With its huge stockpile of nuclear weapons, the Soviet Union can annihilate any invader from the east or the west or both, no matter how backward the country becomes in all other ways. Nuclear weapons guarantee not just the borders of the Soviet Union but its Central and Eastern European empire as well. They have solved the problem that made the importing of Western hardware so urgent for Russia's rulers in the past.

There is, however, pressure on the Soviet regime from within to improve the performance of the economy. In the post-Stalin period a tacit bargain, a social contract between the rulers and society, has come into being: provision of the rudiments of a welfare state and a slowly rising standard of living in return for political passivity. Such legitimacy as the regime enjoys depends in no small part on its fidelity to its side of this bargain. The exhaustion of the Stalinist economic model has jeopardized the regime's capacity to give the people of the Soviet Union what it has, in effect, promised them.[46]

The country's economic troubles also hobble Soviet efforts to expand its influence outside its own boundaries, especially where it has no troops stationed. Economic failure makes the Soviet Union an unattractive model of social and economic organization. It increasingly appears to the rest of the world to be a state powerful in purely military terms but backward in all others ways. By promoting a global stalemate between east and west, nuclear weapons devalue military might as instruments of influence—although force has by no means been rendered worthless—and put a premium on economic, cultural and social dynamism.

The Soviet Union that Mikhail Gorbachev inherited was dynamic in none of these ways. He and others in the elite plainly find this condition, and the damage that it does to the country's global standing, painful and even alarming. He is willing to risk the pollution of Western political and social norms and to sacrifice a measure of doctrinal purity to try to change it. In this sense Gorbachev is perhaps more a nationalist than a Leninist.

He has presented himself, however, as a wholly orthodox Leninist, someone more faithful to the real, the essential Lenin than were his predecessors. He frequently invokes Lenin's name in support of his proposed changes. This is a predictable tactic. The name of the founder of Bolshevism is hallowed enough in the Soviet tradition, and the master's writings and speeches are broad, diffuse, and ambiguous enough, to serve as a useful sanction for almost anything.

But it would be wrong to take Gorbachev to be wholly cynical. He is certainly not a Western liberal.[47] He plainly has no intention of presiding over the conversion of the Soviet Union to free-market capitalism and pluralist democracy. Insofar as he is consciously importing Western political and economic practices, he undoubtedly believes that he can ration and control them.

The amount of Western software that Gorbachev has thus far proposed to import into the Soviet Union is modest. Despite this, and despite his contention that he is perfecting rather than abandoning socialism, his program has encountered opposition. Party officials see in his proposals a threat to their own powers and privileges. Many of them would surely prefer the continuation of the comfortable stagnation of the Brezhnev years to the uncertain adventure in "restructuring" and *glasnost'* that the current leader is offering. Soviet workers no doubt want more things to buy; but Gorbachev is insisting that they work harder both to make and to afford them. This they will not necessarily be pleased to do. This latest episode of Russian reform may in the end therefore come to very little.

The chances that liberal practices and institutions will at last gain a foothold in Russia are nonetheless probably better now than at any time in the past. Some of the conditions that made the Soviet version of the Russian political and economic system a particularly centralized, autocratic, and generally illiberal one have disappeared.

The Soviet state was founded by genuine ideologues. They fervently believed in a version of socialism that held that it was the task of the state, itself dominated by a self-selected vanguard party, to reshape society. For the Soviet Union's present leaders that ideological impulse is far weaker, to the extent that it exists at all.

The Bolsheviks were, moreover, a small group with limited support and shallow roots in the society they sought to govern. They established a system of dual administration, with loyal Party cadres watching over military commanders, factory managers, and local officials, because they could not trust the people in these positions to carry out their program. They brutally suppressed all independent centers of power and initiative in part because, given their radical plans and their lack of political legitimacy, such centers threatened their rule. The present regime has a far more solid foundation. It has a broad base of support, although it is mainly passive support and probably confined largely to Russians. If it is not legitimate in the Western sense of the term—it does not hold power, after all, as the result of free elections—the Soviet regime 70 years after the revolution is nonetheless an authentically Russian one.

Finally, for the first four decades of its existence the regime felt mortally threatened—by world capitalism, by fascist Germany, and by the Western coalition led by the United States. The fear of foreign threat helps to account for the brutal program of industrialization, including a virtual war against the peasantry in the process of collectivization in the countryside, and the acquiescence in Stalin's cruelties. That program, no matter how bloody, and that leader, no matter how tyrannical, could be justified as necessary bulwarks against the enemy. The nuclear-armed Soviet Union of today is far less vulnerable; indeed, as noted, it is not vulnerable at all in the traditional sense of the term, and Gorbachev and his colleagues appear to be aware of the security that they enjoy as the Brezhnev generation was not.

Thus, the new Soviet leaders may feel confident enough to permit a measure of Western cultural, economic and political influence that their predecessors would have resisted. The sponsorship of the supreme leader, however guarded and limited, is a considerable advantage. And if this leader is better disposed (or at least less resolutely hostile) to Western software than were his predecessors, the society over which he presides is likely to be more receptive to it than the one that the tsars and Lenin, Stalin, Khrushchev and Brezhnev ruled.

The people of the Soviet Union are better educated and far more sophisticated than were their peasant forebears. Most Soviet citizens now live in cities, and it is in cities that the liberal values and attitudes characteristic of the West have flourished. In the cities of the Soviet Union people are now more exposed to the powerful cultural messages of the West than ever before. They have access to Western radio broadcasts, records, tape cassettes, books and periodicals, clothing, and furniture. Although foreign travel is still tightly restricted, more and more people are able to visit other countries. Technology has accelerated the age-old infiltration of Western culture into Russia. One and two generations removed from the traditional Russian village, the average Soviet citizen now lives on the outskirts of Marshall McLuhan's global village.

Soviet citizens are also two generations removed from Stalin's reign of terror, when a mere display of interest in the forbidden fruits of the West was sufficient grounds for banishment to the *gulag* or worse. In Stalin's day, speaking with a foreigner was a crime that was swiftly and severely punished. His successors eased the regime's pressure on the society. They aspired not to transform it but simply to enjoy their own privileges. They demanded only that no one undertake any independent public activity.[48] The Brezhnev generation of Soviet rulers restored to Soviet citizens control over their private lives. In the private sphere there has been room for Western values and ideas. The Brezhnev generation in fact gave more or less official sanction to one feature of Western life: individual consumption. It was enshrined as an unofficial right, and one the regime has felt itself under some compulsion to honor.

Historically the most eager consumers of Western influence were the members of the intelligentsia. That stratum of Soviet society, defined to include those engaged in scientific and technical research as well as journalists and creative artists, has grown considerably in size in the 35 years since Stalin's death. It has obtained a measure of political influence: Brezhnev's ministries made increasing use of expert advice. In comparison with the Russian intelligentsia of the second half of the 19th century their present-day descendants are less closely in touch with the West, but probably more fully integrated into their own society. And the intelligentsia of today are certainly better attuned to Western values than were their predecessors a generation ago.

Most importantly, within this amorphous social stratum Western values have been incubating for two decades. Changes took place under the surface of events during the Brezhnev period. In private conversations, in technical and specialized journals, and in more general publications couched in Aesopian language, controversy, debates, and Western themes began to appear. It is possible to detect, by looking carefully, a shift of emphasis away from the principle that the interest of the Party deserves the highest priority and toward a commitment to universal ethical values: that is, a shift from Lenin to Kant. There has been a comparable movement in the intellectual climate of the Soviet intelligentsia from collectivism toward individualism, from an emphasis on social conformity to an appreciation of diversity, and from the exaltation of the socialist Utopia as the goal of society to a more modest aspiration to the promotion of gradual social improvement.[49] These are the values that have underpinned the liberal tradition in the West.

The Soviet Union is not on the verge of being transformed into a huge, eastern, multinational version of Sweden. But Western political and economic beliefs, practices, and institutions are more welcome there in the latter part of the 1980s than at any time since the decade between the 1905 revolution and the outbreak of World I, perhaps more welcome now than ever before in the long history of the Russian state. While the other two principal types of Western influence on the Soviet Union—containment and the arms race—together have the effect of stabilizing relations between East and West, therefore, the third, the process of cultural transmission, now holds the potential for major changes in world politics.

Conclusion

What Gorbachev has already done, and what he proposes to do, raise two related questions, each of them large, difficult, and momentous. The first is how far the impact of Western software will go. How far will Western influence, whether or not under the sponsorship of the regime, come to shape what the Soviet Union is? The answer to that question, that only time will tell, is no less true for being trite. The second question is what impact whatever internal changes occur will have on Soviet external behavior, that is on what the Soviet Union does.

At some point, it may be that the internal transformation of the Soviet Union will bring about significant changes in its approach to other countries, its aspirations in the international arena, and its preferred policies for achieving them. At that point, the prospects for easing, perhaps even resolving the conflict that has stood at the center for international affairs since the 1940s may dramatically improve.

At some point, that is, cultural transmission may make containment unnecessary and the arms race obsolete by dissolving the political conflict that has given rise to both. The old American conviction that bad regimes cause international conflict may, at least in the case of the Soviet Union, be true. Or it may not be. Or the process of Westernization in the Soviet Union may never approach that sublime point at which a hostile state becomes benign and cooperative.

History provides little guidance on these matters. But historical experience does suggest one final truth: as important as is the process of cultural transmission from west to east for both sides, and indeed for the entire planet, there is little that Western governments can do to accelerate, or direct, or refine it. The West can and undoubtedly will watch, wait, hope, and, where appropriate, applaud what is happening inside the Soviet Union; but it cannot expect to do more. The rest is up to the Russians.

Notes

1. Architects were often actually imported to Russia from the West by the Russian monarchs.

2. The military competition with the West after 1945 is the subject of the section of this chapter on "The Arms Race."

3. This was a staple of the Slavophile movement of the 19th century. See, for example, Edward Crankshaw, *In the Shadow of the Winter Palace: The Drift to Revolution, 1825–1917* (Harmondsworth, England, Penguin Books, 1978 p.b.), p. 279, and Adam Ulam, *Russia's Failed Revolutions: From the Decembrists to the Dissidents* (New York, Basic Books, 1981), pp. 72–3. It finds an echo in some of Solzhenitsyn's statements today.

4. Thus, international politics is often compared to a game, frequently chess, which is by definition a competitive interaction, an exercise in which each player responds to the moves of the other.

5. On this general point see Chapter 9 by John Lewis Gaddis. The policy of containment was originally presented to the American public as a measure of limited duration, which would lead to the "mellowing" of the Soviet Union, at which point the exertions the policy involved would no longer be required (see the next section).

6. The Baruch Plan would have had the same effect on the United States, and so might well not have been adopted by Washington even if Moscow had shown more interest. See Michael Mandelbaum, *The Nuclear Question: The United States and Nuclear Weapons, 1946–1976* (New York, Cambridge University Press, 1979), pp. 23–27.

7. During the 1970s the United States also began to demand that Moscow permit the emigration of Soviet Jews who wished to leave. An unprecedented number—250,000—did leave. Still, the exodus of Soviet Jews is not an unambiguous case of deliberate, well-targeted, successful Western influence on Soviet internal arrangements. In permitting emigration Moscow was no doubt responding to its own internal considerations as well as—indeed probably more than—to American political pressure. The pressure persisted, but when Soviet-American relations soured after the Soviet invasion of Afghanistan and the sharp American response, the number of those allowed to leave fell sharply. Letting some people leave, moreover, although a break with precedent, was not tantamount to altering the procedures by which those who remained were governed. The Soviet government did not grant a general right to emigrate. The case of the Jews (as well as that of the Germans, who left in lesser numbers) was officially portrayed as repatriation: they were being sent where they belonged, to their national homeland, Israel.

8. On the evolution of the Soviet political system since Stalin see Peter Hauslohner, "The De-Stalinization of Soviet Politics," in Seweryn Bialer, ed., *Politics, Society, and Nationality in Gorbachev's Russia* (Boulder, Colo.: Westview Press, forthcoming).

9. The core-periphery distinction fits this pattern less comfortably than it does the other two. The United States and the West were less clearly the leaders, and the Soviet Union the followers, in international politics than in economics and culture. Indeed, the Soviet Union, as a revisionist country, has initiated foreign policies rather than following the American lead. This, at any rate, has been the American view.

10. The United States has not, of course, encouraged the Soviet Union to match its weaponry. To the contrary, it has tried to prevent the Soviets from getting the relevant Western technology.

11. "Conquering Western Europe would not serve Soviet interests, it would merely deprive the U.S.S.R. of a source of advanced technology and present it with headaches analogous to those caused by Solidarity in Poland." Jerry F. Hough, *The Struggle for the Third World: Soviet Debates and American Options* (Washington, D.C., The Brookings Institution, 1986), p. 2.

12. Dean Acheson, *Present at the Creation: My Years at the State Department* (New York, W.W. Norton, 1969), p. 379.

13. The Reagan Administration added a new twist. It tried not simply to prevent Communists from gaining control of countries they aspired to rule, but also to oust those that had already taken power in Afghanistan, Angola, and Nicaragua. The policy of assisting resistance to entrenched Communist governments came to be known as the "Reagan Doctrine." See Michael Mandelbaum and Strobe Talbott, *Reagan and Gorbachev* (New York, Vintage Books, 1987), pp. 55–66.

14. Quoted in John Lewis Gaddis, *Strategies of Containment* (New York, Oxford University Press, 1982), pp. 294, 310.

15. Moreover, the American government cannot readily control the American economy. It is difficult—indeed it is contrary to the spirit of the American tradition and the letter of some American laws—for Washington to conduct a mercantilist international economic policy. There were, in addition, more explicitly political constraints on the use of economic leverage, notably the Jackson-Vanik amendment.

16. The prospects for achieving the goals of the policy of linkage were further reduced by the fact that these goals were extremely ambitious. The American government hoped that the Soviet Union would conduct its relations with the Third World according to Western standards of good behavior. This would have ruled out subverting existing governments and sponsoring Leninist-style regimes, which inevitably scorn democratic liberties. To agree to such restraints, however, would mean, for Moscow, to renounce virtually any influence beyond Europe, since the Soviet Union has no other means to gain it. What the West regards as legitimate instruments of influence—chiefly economic ones—are puny in the Soviet case. Accepting Western norms would therefore mean for the Soviet Union abdicating the role of a global power. Precisely that status, however, has come in the postwar period to be a central aspiration of the Soviet elite.

17. For the argument that arms races are "normal" features of international politics in the industrial era, see Michael Mandelbaum, *The Nuclear Revolution: International Politics Before and After Hiroshima* (New York, Cambridge University Press, 1981), Chapter 4.

18. This thinking lay behind German military plans in both world wars and shaped Israeli military doctrine after 1948. See John Mearsheimer, *Conventional Deterrence* (Ithaca, New York, Cornell University Press, 1983), Chapters 4 and 5, and Barry Posen, *The Sources of Military Doctrine* (Ithaca, New York, Cornell University Press, 1984), Chapter 6.

19. Another instance of Soviet imitation of Western forces is, arguably, the development of the Soviet Navy. At the end of World War II it was little more than a glorified coast guard. By the 1980s it had become a blue-water fleet with aircraft carriers, which previously only the United States had deployed.

20. There is some scattered, circumstantial evidence that the Soviet military is concerned about its capacity to hold its own in this round of the arms race. The Soviets' alarm about the American Strategic Defense Initiative seems to be based in part on the fear that it will enable the West to outstrip the Warsaw Pact in the military application of microelectronics and information-processing. It has been speculated that the former Chief of the Soviet General Staff, Marshal Nikolai Ogarkov, was dismissed from his position by the Politburo in 1984 for complaining that high-tech military innovation was receiving less attention and fewer resources than was warranted. See *The 27th Congress of the Communist Party of the Soviet Union: A Report from the Airlie House Conference* (Rand/UCLA—Harriman Institute, Columbia, December, 1986), p. 49.

21. The Soviet "Backfire" bomber is not, in range and other capabilities, the equal of the American B-52 and B-1.

22. David Holloway, *The Soviet Union and the Arms Race* (New Haven, Yale University Press, 1984), p. 20.

23. The reluctance stems from an asymmetry between the two sides that has its roots in politics. The non-nuclear forces of the Warsaw Pact are larger, and thought to be more powerful than NATO's. Unwilling, for political reasons, to match the Eastern forces, the Western alliance has considered it prudent to retain the nuclear threat in order to deter an attack from the East.

24. Bernard Brodie, *The Absolute Weapon* (New York, Harcourt Brace Jovanovich, 1946), p. 76. On the evolution of nuclear strategy see Michael Mandelbaum, *The Nuclear Question: The United States and Nuclear Weapons, 1946-1976* (New York, Cambridge University Press, 1979), Chapters 3–5.

25. The assertion was controversial in the West, where it was debated whether the Soviet Union was indeed as committed to deterrence as the United States. Some took the view that, while not necessarily trigger-happy, the Soviet leaders were more likely to use their nuclear weapons first in a conflict and more serious about taking measures to emerge less damaged than the West from a nuclear exchange. On the evolution of Soviet nuclear doctrine see Chapter 4 by Robert Legvold in this book.

26. In his memoirs Nikita Khrushchev claimed that he had the idea of putting Soviet missiles underground but that his technical experts rejected it— until they saw that the Americans were doing it. *Khrushchev Remembers: The Last Testament,* translated and edited by Strobe Talbott (Boston, Little Brown, 1974), pp. 48–9.

27. See Chapter 4 by Robert Legvold, and Michael MccGwire, *Military Objectives in Soviet Foreign Policy* (Washington, D.C., The Brookings Institution, 1987).

28. On the evolution of nuclear diplomacy see Mandelbaum, *The Nuclear Question,* Chapters 2, 7.

29. Robert McNamara, *Blundering into Disaster: Surviving the First Century of the Nuclear Age* (New York, Pantheon Books, 1986), p. 57.

30. See Chapter 4 by Robert Legvold.

31. The obvious candidate for breaking the stalemate was the American Strategic Defense Initiative. The Soviet authorities were plainly wary of the program to develop defenses in space. But not even its most ardent supporters actually expected the ongoing programs for research and development to restore American nuclear superiority in the foreseeable future. See Mandelbaum and Talbott, *op. cit.*, Chapter 4.

32. The pattern is described in this book in Chapter 1 by S. Frederick Starr, and in Chapter 2 by Sheila Fitzpatrick. The pattern is part of the conventional wisdom of Western historiography of Russia. Both authors express some reservations about it and add some qualifications and refinements of their own.

33. "Peter the Great . . . was raiding the West for its technical skills, which he then sought to graft on to the ancient Muscovite stock." Crankshaw, *op. cit.*, p. 62.

34. This is the main theme of Pipes, *Russia Under the Old Regime* (New York, Charles Scribner's Sons, 1974). See, for example, pp. xxi–xxii, 24.

35. This is a theme of several of the essays collected posthumously as *Russian Studies*, edited by Ellen Dahrendorf (New York, Viking, 1987). See, for example, pp. 23, 38, 40, 42.

36. Pipes, *op. cit.*, pp. 141, 159. Starr, *op. cit.*

37. This is an important theme of Ulam, *op. cit.* See, for example, pp. 12, 429.

38. Something similar occurred in 1968. The invasion of Czechoslovakia to put an end to the liberal reforms of the "Prague Spring" had the effect of stifling the movement for economic change that some Soviet leaders, notably Prime Minister Aleksei Kosygin, were promoting.

39. The Soviet economic system is described in this book by Robert Campbell in Chapter 3.

40. See Hauslohner, *op. cit.*

41. He was spurred not by military defeat, as in the 1860s and after 1905—although the war in Afghanistan that he inherited was hardly a success—but by a general sense that the Soviet Union was slipping in comparison with other countries in all ways save militarily. See Mandelbaum and Talbott, *op. cit.*, pp. 68–84.

42. On the Gorbachev political reforms see Chapter 6 by Timothy Colton and Chapter 7 by Thane Gustafson in this book.

43. There has been no official talk of making membership in the Politburo open to the choice of a wider constituency than those who are already members.

44. On the crisis of the Stalinist economic model, see Campbell, *op. cit.*

45. This is one of the central arguments of Gustafson, *op. cit.*

46. See Hauslohner, *op. cit.*

47. Colton, *op. cit.*, p. 62.

48. Adam Ulam has put the difference deftly: "Stalin's secret police wanted its customers to confess, Brezhnev's, for the most part, to desist." Ulam, *op. cit.,* p. 424.

49. See Gail W. Lapidus, "Gorbachev and the Reform of the Soviet System," *Daedalus,* Spring, 1987. On the budding of a Western-style "civic culture" in the Soviet Union see Chapter 1.

PART FIVE

Gorbachev and the United States

11

Gorbachev's Russia and U.S. Options

Joseph S. Nye, Jr.

Before Gorbachev

The Soviet Union has been the central problem of American foreign policy for more than forty years. Some causes of the competition have deep roots. De Tocqueville saw more than a century ago that Russia and the United States, as continental-scale nations, were bound to play a significant role in the global balance of power. The Bolshevik Revolution added a layer of severe ideological conflict in 1917, although distance tempered distrust until 1945. A third source of conflict came when World War II reduced the other great powers to secondary roles. In a bipolar world, the United States and the Soviet Union emerged face to face in 1945 and have remained so. The key stakes in the global balance of power are geographically on the rim of the Soviet Union and yet politically aligned with the United States. This is likely to continue. In short, some of the causes of the U.S.-Soviet competition are not susceptible to change simply because of changes in the nature of the domestic society or in the personalities of Soviet or American leaders.

At the same time, there have been striking differences in the intensity of the competition and conflict over the past four decades, varying from alliance in the early 1940s to Cold War to gradual *detente* to renewed hostility. Geopolitical differences may predict competition, but they do not tell us how intense the conflict will be, nor do they explain the cyclical patterns in U.S.-Soviet relations. To understand such variation, we must look at domestic politics and differences in the two societies.

Americans have always found it difficult to agree on the nature of their Soviet opponent. In part, this reflects the open and fragmented way in which Americans formulate foreign policy. Expertise on the Soviet Union is heavily discounted. It also reflects ideological tensions in American domestic politics. Soviet policy is often used as a stick with which one set of Americans beat their opponents in battles that are largely domestic. American disputes reflect the difficulty of dealing with a society as different as the Soviet Union is from the United States. In addition to the obvious ideological differences, there are also characteristics which are Russian, rather than Bolshevik. Absolutism, fear of anarchy, defensive imperialism, shame at backwardness, and—above all—secrecy as a mode of defense have deep Russian roots. In various episodes, such as the bomber and missile gaps of the 1950s, the Soviets have deliberately misled Americans. The results have complicated the overall relationship.

Soviet intentions have been even more difficult to fathom than Soviet capabilities. Unlike societies in which Americans have access to an open press and frequent transnational contact with elites, the Soviet society remains relatively closed. Soviet intentions remain largely opaque. Thus after the Soviet invasion of Afghanistan, some Americans drew ideological analogies between Soviet behavior and Hitler's Germany in the 1930s while others, such as George Kennan, former American Ambassador to the Soviet Union, explained Soviet actions in terms of an historical Russian sense of insecurity.

It is not surprising that such different societies confuse each other and that misperceptions and miscalculations exacerbate the conflict predicted on geopolitical terms alone. So long as the Soviet Union remains largely a "black box," Americans will find it difficult to come to a common agreement on policy. For these reasons, I believe that a more stable U.S.-Soviet relationship with fewer oscillations probably requires domestic change in the Soviet Union. From this point of view, Gorbachev's policy of "*glasnost'*" ("openness" or public airing), "*perestroika*" (restructuring), and "democratization" is particularly interesting and presents both a new challenge and a new opportunity for American foreign policy.

Gorbachev's Changes and Soviet Foreign Policy

Before discussing possible responses to Gorbachev's changes, I should clarify the assumptions I make about those changes. Gorbachev's changes are rooted in domestic economic and social problems. I assume that Gorbachev is not a Western liberal, but a pragmatic Communist who wishes to improve the existing system. He is part of the generation awakened by Khrushchev's partial de-Stalinization and reform, and frustrated by Brezhnev's conservative reaction.[1] He is aware of the depth of the economic and social problems he has inherited, not only the declining economic growth rate, but more importantly, the problems of changing the qualitative nature of economic growth. He also stresses the deep social and political roots of the economic problems. He realizes the importance of moving into an information- and electronics-based economy. It is harder to find harsher assessments of Soviet economic and social stagnation than in Gorbachev's own speeches.

Gorbachev's first efforts at restructuring the economy continued Andropov's initiatives on discipline and modest organizational changes. But this was not enough. The vested interests in the existing political structure were too strong. In the face of such inertia, Gorbachev has added some cultural liberalization and a degree of democratization at lower levels. Economic *perestroika* must be buttressed by a broader program of liberalization including democratization and *glasnost'*. Through the media he is reaching beyond the Party bureaucracy to convince the attentive public that problems are so serious that major change is required. Soviet newspapers have begun to carry open debates about social problems and the need for change. Gorbachev hopes that the intelligentsia and the media will help him transform the parameters of the political-bureaucratic situation and overcome the inertia. Whether Gorbachev is a liberal (in Soviet terms) or merely using liberalization for instrumental purposes matters less than the depth of the changes. If anything, the instrumental value of liberalization should serve to reinforce its significance.

Gorbachev promotes liberalization because of his domestic concerns. His policies are not foreign policy tactics designed either to please or to deceive the West. His liberalization could fall victim to Soviet domestic politics. If Gorbachev is unable to demonstrate benefits from his policies within a few years, he may lose support. This would mean at least the loss of his initiative, or more drastically, his job. Given the depth of Soviet domestic problems and the dilemmas and contradictions in Gorbachev's efforts at reform, the economic success of his policies cannot be taken for granted.[2]

The forces of conservatism in Soviet society are strong. As Stephen Cohen of Princeton notes, the Soviet Union is "one of the most conservative countries in the world." There is the legacy of the tsarist past; the bureaucratization of Soviet life since the early 1930s; the resistance of the *nomenklatura* defenders of privilege; and an ideology that extolls the existing order. Khrushchev's initial de-Stalinization and liberalization was partially reversed by Brezhnev. Gorbachev could suffer a similar fate. But a number of Soviet observers believe this unlikely. In their view, even the conservatives have learned the high cost of the reactionary policies of the 1970s. Moreover, they argue that the new generation is better educated and less tainted by Stalinist connections than were Khrushchev's successors. While some admit the continuation of the role of the KGB and its abusive practices, they point to popular films such as "Repentance" and novels and newspaper debates which condemn such practices more openly and widely than in the earlier period. They argue that even if there is a reaction, it cannot remove all the changes that Gorbachev has made.[3]

Gorbachev's foreign policy, on the other hand, while innovative in tactical terms, is less innovative than his domestic policy. Moreover, it seems closely related to the problems of domestic policy. As Gorbachev said in a *Time* magazine interview in September, 1985, "foreign policy is a continuation of domestic policy. . . . I ask you to ponder one thing. If we in the Soviet Union are setting ourselves such truly grandiose plans in the domestic sphere, then what are the external conditions that we need to be able to fulfill those domestic plans? I leave the answer to that question to you."[4]

Gorbachev's foreign policy is in one way almost the obverse of his domestic policy. Concentration on reform in domestic policy requires a relatively quiet foreign policy. I discern five significant characteristics in Gorbachev's foreign policy. Four of the five represent considerable continuity with the recent past. First is the need for a "breathing spell." In fact, this began before Gorbachev came to office. Cautious Soviet responses to the Reagan Administration's initiatives and a belief that the correlation of forces had shifted predated Gorbachev's coming into office. In addition, a certain breathing spell was imposed by the actuarial tables. A period of permanent transition among elderly leaders in the first half of the 1980s did not lend itself to revolutionary initiatives. Moreover, the military and others seem to have developed an awareness that a reform of the economic base would be necessary for the Soviets to continue their military position. The Soviet response to the Reagan Strategic Defense Initiative (SDI) antedated Gorbachev and probably owed more to general concern about the United States opening a technological Pandora's box with which the Soviets would have difficulty competing than to the particular military characteristics of the hypothesized system. In all of these ways, Gorbachev's overall approach to foreign policy suggests continuity rather than a radical break with the recent past.

A second characteristic of Gorbachev's foreign policy relates to nuclear initiatives and his call for new thinking about arms control. In January, 1986 Gorbachev issued his plan for total denuclearization by the end of the century. He returned to that point at the Reykjavik Summit in October of that year. Once again, Gorbachev's initiatives had clear antecedents in the policies of his predecessors. Soviet views of nuclear weapons have been evolving for some time.[5] There were already suggestions that the Soviet military was beginning to realize that piling up additional nuclear arsenals was not the best investment of their marginal rubles and that there was a law of diminishing military returns in nuclear investment. As for the Gorbachev plan for denuclearization, grandiose plans have a long history in Soviet proposals for general and complete disarmament, and particular proposals related to denuclearization of Europe also continue a long tradition. What is new is the discussion of sufficiency of nuclear weapons and the greater attention to the link between conventional and nuclear arms in what remain broadly-phrased proposals.

The third area of continuity of Gorbachev's foreign policy is his approach to developing countries. Gorbachev's immediate predecessors had already become more cautious about their adventures in the developing world than they were in the 1970s, but neither Gorbachev nor his predecessors seemed willing to write off Soviet interests in areas where they already exist. Gorbachev may wish to disengage in Afghanistan, but there is no evidence that he is giving up the broad range of Soviet interests in the Third World. The fact that the Soviets are not willing to take high levels of risk in areas such as Central America is not particularly new. In the Middle East, Gorbachev's policy does not seem markedly different from that of his predecessors except for some interesting tactical distinctions such as greater flexibility in dealing with Israel.

The most interesting innovation in Soviet foreign policy under Gorbachev is in Asia. While this is not a radical discontinuity with his immediate predecessors, Gorbachev does seem to have pressed farther to improve relations with China and Japan. Gorbachev's speech at Vladivostock in 1986 signalled a heightened awareness of the region's significance and a new priority. To some extent, this may be related to the breathing spell: the reduction of tensions along the Chinese border reduces yet another demand on the Soviet military budget and is a useful device for putting pressure on the Americans. In addition, the Asian initiatives may reflect an awareness of future trends. As one Soviet put it to me, "we have a lot of real estate out there and there is no very good fence around it."[6]

The most striking change in Gorbachev's foreign policy is its tactical sophistication. This may be a result of the presence of Anatoly Dobrynin in Moscow as well as the heightened influence of the Institutes which have greater awareness of the political realities of the United States and Western Europe. One need only compare the heavy-handed Soviet handling of the INF issue that united NATO in 1983 with the subtle dilemmas Gorbachev's agreement to remove nuclear weapons posed for NATO in 1987 to see the significant change that has occurred in tactical sophistication. Instead of ventriloquists' dummies, the Soviets now have a great communicator of their own.

If this cautious characterization of Gorbachev's foreign policy is correct, it suggests that there may be opportunities to strike deals on particular issues because the Soviets wish to buy time and have confidence in their tactical ability to bargain. To some extent, *glasnost'* may help to increase confidence in such agreements. This cautious account may underestimate the change in Soviet foreign policy by focusing on observed behavior rather than declaratory policy. At the level of concepts, the "new thinking" in foreign policy is more dramatic. The Soviets seem to be broadening their concept of security beyond the military dimension; they seem to be serious about the opportunities for economic interdependence; and they talk more about the decline of bipolarity.[7] But this evolution of Soviet thinking has yet to produce major changes in Soviet foreign policy behavior sufficient to reassure those American conservatives who feel that we should make no concessions that strengthen the Soviet system lest the Soviet Union return to the competition with revitalized powers. In their view, the Soviet Union remains a revolutionary power committed to our overthrow; the only hope in the long run is Soviet decline, not Soviet reinvigoration. Even if changes in Soviet foreign policy do occur, it will be difficult for Americans to agree upon their meaning; those who remain suspicious can always discount change as merely tactical.

My own view is that it is not helpful to see the Soviet Union either as a purely revolutionary or as a purely *status quo* power in international politics. Because ideology legitimizes if not always motivates the political elite, there is often a revolutionary and expansive tone to Soviet foreign policy pronouncements and sometimes to its conduct. But it is also worth noting that Soviet behavior has generally been far more cautious and risk averse than its pronouncements. Support for proletarian revolutions has always come second to the safety of the Soviet state. In Europe, which the Soviets still see as the fulcrum of the global balance, the Soviets tend to be *status quo* more than revolutionary in the short term of decades. In a sense, both the United States and the Soviet Union were the great winners of World War II. Neither is eager to reverse the partition which took Germany off the front burner of international politics. Neither wants a nuclearized Germany. Neither has made strenuous efforts to reverse the *de facto* division of Europe into spheres of national interest.

If Hitler's Germany is the example par excellence of a revolutionary world power, it is clear that the Soviet Union is quite some distance from the revolutionary pole in the continuum between revolutionary and *status quo* powers. Caspar Weinberger, formerly President Reagan's Secretary of Defense, does not believe there is "any real change or any real possibility of modification of their basic policies." In my view, this need not prevent cooperation on security issues. Such cooperation can be based on averting risks without requiring agreement on the long term course of history. The critical point is Soviet caution and risk aversion. In the words of Brent Scowcroft, the National Security Advisor in the Ford Administration, "the Soviets, whatever their view of history and the 'inevitable outcome' which 'history' promises—are very cautious and very conservative."[8] On this minimal basis, cooperation on security is possible even if limited by ideology and competition. If this was true even before Gorbachev, then cooperation is possible even if Gorbachev's foreign policy has not changed dramatically from the past. To the extent that the "new thinking" is put into practice, the opportunity for cooperation will increase. Thus far, however, there has not yet been sufficient liberalization to allow Americans to settle their differences of interpretation of Soviet objectives. On the other hand, Gorbachev's policies have made it more difficult for those Americans who argue that the essential totalitarian nature of the Soviet Union renders it as unsuitable as Hitler's Germany for negotiated agreements. In that sense, Gorbachev's liberalization has added a new element through its effects on the American domestic debate.

Reagan's Response

The tale of the Reagan Administration's Soviet policy has been told too often to require more than a brief interpretive summary here. The early policy was marked by harsh rhetoric and rapid increase in the military budget. In addition, actions in Libya and Grenada helped to convince the Soviet Union that Reagan was not merely another Nixon with whom they could easily deal. SDI and the treatment of arms control negotiations as theater for public consumption, rather than as a forum for serious bargaining, added to the diffuse threat the Soviets felt from the Reagan Administration. The problem of generational change and three weak leaders coincided with increased recognition of the economic and social difficulties the Soviet Union faced at home in the early 1980s. In addition, the opportunities that decolonization presented for Soviet advantage in the Third World in the 1970s declined in the early 1980s. In both Moscow and in Washington, there was a belief that the correlation of forces shifted in America's favor from the 1970s to the 1980s. Some sophisticated Soviet observers of international politics have realized that their actions in the Third World in the 1970s were inordinately costly in terms of the U.S.-Soviet relationship.[9] In a sense, history gave Reagan a free ride in the early 1980s.

It is worth noting that the Reagan Administration's policy toward the Soviet Union began to change before Gorbachev became General Secretary in February, 1985. In January, 1984, the President made a conciliatory speech about the prospects for U.S.-Soviet cooperation. While Administration officials later claimed that Reagan had always intended to bargain after rebuilding American strength, the timing suggests more mundane causes. With the onset of an election, the President was drawn back to the center by the fact that the American public prefers a two-track policy towards the Soviet Union. By moving from confrontation to the middle of the road, and by stressing the prospect of cooperation, the President cut off an important avenue of attack for his Democratic opponent. In short, Reagan Administration policy toward the Soviet Union began to change for American domestic political reasons, not because the United States was much stronger or because the Soviet Union had a new General Secretary.

Nonetheless, Gorbachev did make a difference. His tactical skills and ability to appeal to the Western media and public opinion meant that the Reagan Administration no longer had a free ride. Moreover, at the 1985 Summit, Gorbachev's personality and the prolonged conversations between the two leaders seems to have reinforced President Reagan's interest in reaching some sort of agreement as part of his historical legacy. Despite its ultimate outcome, the same desire seems to have been present at Reykjavik a year later.[10]

Notwithstanding these effects of personal summitry, the Reagan Administration remained deeply ambivalent about the prospects for a strategic arms agreement with the Soviet Union. The President seemed torn between his desire to go down in history as a peacemaker who signed a significant arms reduction agreement with the Soviet Union and the man who bequeathed SDI to future generations of Americans. The Soviets indicated a number of times that they might be more flexible about testing parts of the SDI system than their official language suggests, and that therefore a grand compromise relating fifty percent offensive reductions and a ten-year delay in defensive systems might be possible. President Reagan, however, was too committed to SDI to reach such an agreement.

Moreover, the President's own ambivalence was reproduced throughout the higher levels of the Reagan Administration. While some in the Administration believe that a significant arms control deal was desirable, others feared that arms control would be a snare and a delusion lulling the West. Such sharp divisions, including some opposition to any strategic agreement, prevented the Reagan Administration from putting Gorbachev's intentions to a serious test.

This was the situation before the onset of the Iran/Nicaragua imbroglio in late 1986. What is interesting is that in those circumstances, Gorbachev chose to delink the INF portion of an agreement from the larger strategic package. In a sense, he was putting Reagan to the test by accepting an earlier American proposal (which may have been put forward in part for public relations purposes). In any case, the Soviet response suggested both tactical brilliance and a desire on Gorbachev's part for an agreement, even if minor, that would help to legitimize his position at home as well as to legitimize arms control with future American Administrations. The result is an ironic situation in which Reagan has been criticized by Americans such as Nixon and Kissinger (whom he had criticized a decade earlier) for being too eager to reach an arms control agreement with the Soviet Union.[11] The military significance of an INF agreement is far less than its political significance, and any INF agreement is limited compared to the significance of a strategic agreement. But it appears that the clock may be running out for the Reagan Administration to work out the details of a grand compromise in the strategic area or to plan tests or early deployment of the Strategic Defense Initiative that would destroy the ABM Treaty. The major options will likely remain open for Reagan's successor.

Major Options

It has become almost a cliche to say that Gorbachev has presented us with new options in our Soviet policy, but there is far less agreement on what those options are and how we should respond. If Gorbachev's innovations in foreign policy are primarily tactical, why should the United States fall for his tactics? A breathing spell may be in the Soviet interest, but why is it in the American interest? In the words of Republican Congressman Richard Cheney of Wyoming, "I'm not sure it is in our interest that he succeed. We could just end up with a tougher, more impressive adversary." Or in the words of Democratic Congressman Tony Coelho of California, "The good news is that they want a few years off from the arms race. The bad news is that they want to be stronger when they can afford it."[12] According to Dimitri Simes, Fellow of the Carnegie Endowment for International Peace, "Throughout Russian history, the modernizers rather than the conservatives have pursued the most ambitious international strategies. Peter the Great, Catherine the Great, Alexanders I and II proved to be overall more assertive and menacing to Russia's neighbors." In more recent times, Khrushchev's internal liberalization was accompanied by more flexible Soviet foreign policy, "but it also became more vigorous and ambitious."[13] Why then should Americans wish Gorbachev well? Do we really want his reforms to arrest the decline of Soviet power?

One issue over which Americans disagree is the nature of the decline in Soviet power. Most Americans would agree that overall Soviet power seems less impressive today than it did in the 1970s. However, there are differences of view as to whether this is a secular, long-term decline or merely a cyclical dip. Those who argue that what we are seeing is a secular long-term decline argue that the Soviet economic and social problems are too severe to be remedied within the confines of the Marxist-Leninist political system. The fact that Gorbachev's reforms are within that constricting framework guarantees that they will not be able to solve the problems. The central dilemma for the Soviet Union is how to move to the third generation of industrialization which requires an information-based economy. Such an economy requires flexibility and decentralization to reach its full potential. But decentralization poses a critical threat to the existing structure of party power. Since Soviet leaders are unable or unwilling to shed their political strait-jackets, Soviet power is bound to decline in comparison with that of the United States, Japan, or even the People's Republic of China.

Others believe that the decline in Soviet power is cyclical rather than secular. They admit that the Soviet Union is faced with critical dilemmas, but they do not believe the choices are quite as sharp as the first group believes. For example, information technology may be less efficient when applied within a centralized, rather than a decentralized, planning structure, but it nonetheless may be applied to some degree. Moreover, the Soviet Union is endowed with enormous natural resources. There is so much inefficiency in their current use that even small amounts of discipline or small increments of market incentives may bring out a noticeable degree of economic growth. Finally, the Soviet political system insures that there will be political stability and discipline. Party control sets limits on dissent and allows the Soviets to maintain priorities for military expenditures even in a constrained economy. Thus it would be unwise to expect Soviet military power to decline in direct proportion to the economic and social problems of the Soviet Union. Finally, this second view cautions against psychological biases that often infect political leaders' assessments of the "correlation of forces." They note that a mere decade ago, it was fashionable to see the United States in decline and the Soviet Union surging forward in political power. In their view, it is more prudent to assume a cyclical rather than a secular pattern of change in the relative power of the two superpowers.

Not only are there differences in interpretation of what is happening in the Soviet Union, but there are also differences within each school of thought about what would be an appropriate American response. For example, some of those who believe that the Soviet Union is experiencing a long-term decline believe we would be foolish to let them off the hook. Faced with the prospect that our major foreign policy competition may be weakening, why should we try to arrest that process rather than to hasten it along? To paraphrase Maxwell Taylor's comments about Kennedy's actions during the Cuban Missile Crisis, "If you have them over a barrel, why offer them a piece of cake?"

Others who believe that the Soviet Union is in the midst of a long-term decline in power take just the opposite position. In their view, it is important to help the Soviet Union gracefully manage its decline from superpower status. In a world of fifty thousand nuclear weapons, it is critical that we not press the Soviets too hard. After all, it was a declining empire, Austria-Hungary, which initiated World War I. Thus far, the Soviet Union has been expansive in its orientation but generally risk-averse in the way it has pursued its interests. If the Soviet elite loses its optimism about the future, will it begin to accept greater risks in the political competition with the United States and China? Our policy should be a conciliatory one so that Soviet decline from power over time resembles that of Great Britain rather than that of Austria-Hungary. Moreover, the fact that the Soviet Union is unlikely to regain its current level of power, in this view, suggests that we can afford to be self-confident and accommodating in our negotiations. Thus, the appropriate policy for the United States is not to try to squeeze Gorbachev's Soviet Union but to deal with it.

This difference between "squeezers" and "dealers" also exists among those who believe that the Soviet decline is merely cyclical.[14] Those who advocate a more conciliatory policy argue that we should strike a deal while the correlation of forces is in our favor. If Gorbachev needs a breathing spell, he should be prepared to pay for it. Deals struck now will be more advantageous to us than deals struck when the Soviet Union is more confident and assertive. Others who believe that change in Soviet power is cyclical urge a more confrontational American policy. In their view, deals struck now will not hold up when the Soviets regain their sense of relative power. The best hope for the future is serious reform in the Soviet Union. Then, even if the Soviets regain their sense of relative power sometime in the future, it will be an *altered* Soviet Union which will pose less of a threat to us. In this view, the best way to encourage reforms in the Soviet Union is to continue to confront the Soviets with serious external defeats. Without the ability to expand abroad or to import critical resources and technology, Soviet leaders will have to start reforms more serious than those Gorbachev has tried so far.

For those who believe that now is the time to squeeze the Soviet Union, the appropriate policies are: (1) continue trying to roll back Soviet gains in the Third World; (2) organize a coordinated Western policy of economic denial; (3) press ahead with military innovations in which our technology is superior to that of the Soviet Union (in particular, we should continue pressing for early deployment of the Strategic Defense Initiative because of our comparative technological advantage); (4) by and large, arms control agreements should be avoided because they tend to lull public opinion in the West while relieving pressure on the Soviet Union.

For those who believe the appropriate policy is to deal rather than to squeeze, the recommendations are almost the inverse. (1) In regard to developing countries, we should try to arrange talks designed to clarify interests and set limits on conflict rather than try militarily to roll back all Soviet gains; (2) we should not try to organize an economic denial policy but should permit and encourage expanded trade in all but a few strategic goods; (3) early testing or deployment of the SDI should be avoided so as not to jeopardize the Antiballistic Missile Treaty and the prospects for a grand compromise in strategic arms.

These dramatically different options reflect different causal assumptions about change inside the Soviet Union and in Soviet foreign policy. For example, Richard Pipes argues that "such changes for the better that one can expect in the nature of the Soviet government and in its conduct of foreign relations will come about only from failures, instabilities, and fears of collapse and not from a growing confidence and sense of security."[15] Marshall Shulman, on the other hand, argues that "pressures are more likely to be counter-productive if they seek to corner the Soviet leadership, leaving them no exit except humiliation or capitulation, and if they do not offer at the same time a way out, offer room to protect legitimate Soviet interests on acceptable terms."[16]

Charles Gati expresses skepticism about whether we know enough to judge such options. "Unable to reach a firm conclusion about causality, no Western analyst has been able to offer conclusive evidence about the validity of 'whether domestic weakness or strengths leads to foreign policy accommodation or assertiveness.'" Moreover, Gati expresses skepticism about the prospect of external influence:

> There is reason to be skeptical about the possibility of achieving a "lasting adaptation" in Soviet foreign policy as a consequence of external influences. . . . It is not at all clear whether the outside world should

be or should appear to be weak or strong, reassuring or threatening, in order to generate "moderation" in Soviet foreign policy. . . . Accordingly, unless the West has some reasonably accurate assessment of the impact of external "strength" versus external "weakness" on the Soviet foreign policy debates—in other words, unless it knows what combination of external incentives and prohibitions may pave the way to a lasting tendency towards foreign policy moderation—it cannot be confident about the international environment producing such moderation in Moscow. . . . Given the cyclical pattern of the past, it would require excessive optimism, if not naivete, to emphasize aspects of lasting change in Soviet foreign policy since Stalin.[17]

One implication of such radical skepticism about our Sovietological capabilities is to suggest a third option: to take no account of the supposed decline in Soviet power or the domestic changes that Gorbachev is trying to implement in the Soviet Union. Since we do not know what is happening or how that will affect our foreign policy interests or how to make things better or worse, we should have no preference towards squeezing or dealing with the Soviet Union based on any long-term view of the future. On the contrary, our foreign policy would consist of responses to specific Soviet actions or specific opportunities. Like Florence Nightingale's policy for 19th-century hospitals, such an *ad hoc* policy toward Soviet behavior would be guided by the principle "at least do no harm."

What can be said for and against these three major options? The least likely to succeed is confrontation. Even if there were no uncertainties about its effects on the Soviet Union, it is unlikely that it would meet the first critical test of any foreign policy, the ability to sustain support at home. Throughout the postwar period, public opinion polls have showed that the non-attentive public has two major concerns: Soviet expansionism and the avoidance of nuclear war.[18] In principle, the structure of public opinion provides a broad base for a two-track policy toward the Soviet Union. In practice, when the American public feels that its President is not attending to both concerns simultaneously, it leans against the wind. Thus when they feared that Carter was not strong enough against Soviet expansionism, they voted for increasing the defense budget. In the early 1980s, when they feared that Reagan might get them into nuclear war, the majority of the same public supported a nuclear freeze. As the Reagan Administration discovered, and demonstrated by its behavior after January 1984, a purely confrontational approach is unlikely to succeed in domestic American opinion. Arms control is an important part of the process of reassuring the American public (as well as reassuring our allies and dealing with Soviet weaponry). A confrontational strategy downgrading arms control and pursuing SDI to the point of breaking the existing arms control framework is unlikely to gain support in Congress or in the broader public if the Soviets cooperate by undertaking dramatic confirming actions such as pulling out of Afghanistan.

Similarly, it is very unlikely that an administration would be able to pursue a consistent policy of economic denial toward the Soviet Union. In a democracy, too many groups are well placed to demand exception, particularly if the causal relationship between their economic interests and Soviet strategic capabilities is very indirect. It is hard to follow a policy of economic denial or to urge it upon one's allies when domestic politics assures an exception for American agricultural exports to the Soviet Union. If the Reagan Administration could not manage such politics, it is unlikely that its successors can. Even if this were not the case, it has proved extremely difficult to convince other Western nations that they should embargo the export of non-strategic goods to the Soviet Union. The price of maintaining cohesion in the Coordinating Committee is keeping the list of strategic goods narrowly defined.

Finally, the prospects of rolling back Soviet advances in the Third World is problematic as well. It is one thing to support financial and military assistance to guerrilla groups in Afghanistan, but it has proved far more controversial to maintain support for the Contra forces in Nicaragua or resistance groups in Mozambique. Thus the option of confrontation is unlikely to be sustainable in domestic political opinion for prolonged periods of time. Even if we had a better knowledge of its likely effects on the Soviet Union, we would be unwise to pursue a policy we could not sustain at home.

The problem with the third option of merely responding to specific Soviet actions and American opportunities is that it promises to be a rudderless policy. Given the American domestic political process with its legitimate struggle between the Executive and Legislative for control over foreign policy, and with the strengths of various interests groups, purely responsive policy is likely to be blown about not merely by the winds of international change, but also by various domestic political storms.

Moreover, it is not at all clear that we are as devoid of influence (or knowledge of what influence we have) as the third option suggests. It would be very odd if the most important government in Soviet eyes did not have an influence or that we were totally unable to discern any influence. In fact, the United States has probably been able to deter the Soviets from actions when they see unacceptable risks. In short, moderate behavior in areas of the Third World depends to a considerable extent on how the Soviets see their behavior affecting American actions and risking American responses. Similarly, the United States can moderate the Soviet behavior by depriving them of opportunities for expansion at low cost. Maintaining coherent alliances and playing a role in moderating Third World conflicts are important ways of externally influencing Soviet foreign policy behavior. We also believe that agreements can influence Soviet behavior. While arms control agreements in the past have not curtailed many weapons systems which the Soviets were determined to deploy anyway, they do seem to have lived broadly within the limits of the SALT I and II agreements. Although there has been cheating at the margin, it has not been of great military significance. It is more difficult to see how American economic instruments such as trade have influenced Soviet behavior. Theories of linkage prevalent in the early 1970s do not seem to have been borne out, but perhaps the expectations of change were too great for the relatively small scale of the trade.

As for social change, we probably know very little about how to cause reform in the Soviet Union. But we are not quite as ignorant as Gati suggests. Contacts and information have increased considerably in the past decade and a half. We should expect that the sources of reform lie in domestic politics in a large isolated country such as the Soviet Union. It would be odd if this were not the case. Nonetheless, there does seem to be some truth in the view that external hard times tend to reinforce domestic hard lines.[19]

American influence on the Soviet Union is both direct and indirect. There is both governmental influence and non-governmental, or societal, influence. Governmental policies encouraging contact between peoples, which in turn spreads ideas, may be of considerable importance. Similarly, transnational corporations may carry ideas with them. Trade should not be seen only in terms of economic values (which are likely to remain low as long as the climate of distrust is high), but also as a path along which social contacts flow. It would be a mistake to think only of direct governmental actions when considering responses to Gorbachev's policy of *glasnost'*.

The negotiations option also has weaknesses, primarily in depending upon Soviet reciprocity and restraint. For instance, in the effort to reach arms control agreements or to have regional discussions which limit Soviet adventures in the Third World, there is danger that the Soviets will mistake conciliation for weakness. This may have been the case in the 1970s when Soviet responses proved to be particularly inflammatory in American domestic opinion. Although the rightward trend in American public opinion would have occurred anyway, Soviet defense expenditures and actions in the Third World provided excellent ammunition for their right-wing opponents to use in domestic debates. If history repeated itself, the conciliatory negotiations policy would lose domestic political support, and pave the way for a return to a confrontational policy.

It is not clear, however, that the Soviets will behave in the next decade as they did in the 1970s when they believed that the correlation of forces was moving in their favor because of the inward orientation of American policy in the aftermath of Vietnam and Watergate. If the Soviets believe that the correlation of forces is not moving in their favor in the next decade, they may not make the same mistakes. In addition, Soviet leaders may have learned a good deal about the costs of their behavior in the 1970s in terms of its effects on American public opinion and American foreign policy. Even so, the conciliatory policy will run risks of disruption from forces that neither the Soviet Union nor the United States can control. For example, the decline of the Soviet empire in Eastern Europe could lead to bloody interventions which would thoroughly disrupt Soviet-American relations not because of the expansion of the Soviet empire but because of Soviet efforts to arrest its decline.

Obviously, these three major options are highly generalized and specific policies will include elements of all three. Nonetheless, American policy will draw more from the negotiations and *ad hoc* options than from the confrontational. In fact, the Reagan Administration has already tempered the degree of hostility in the U.S.-Soviet relationship. A good case can be made that part of the problem of U.S.-Soviet relations in the 1970s grew out of the gradual realignment of American political parties as the old Roosevelt coalition broke apart in the 1960s over racial issues and Vietnam. As Democrats were pulled to the left and Republicans to the right, policy toward the Soviet Union became an instrument in domestic political battles. Soviet behavior merely interacted with our rightward trend. However, party alignment and dealignment and the rightward trend of the previous decade are unlikely to be repeated in the next decade. On the contrary, public opinion polls show that opinion has not shifted dramatically to the right but remains in the center. In fact, some historians theorize that there may be an idealistic turn in American domestic opinion.[20] If so, the major debates may be between those who urge a positive response to Gorbachev's liberalization and those who argue that we know too little about the internal Soviet situation or how to influence it to take it into consideration in the formulation of our Soviet policy.

Is Gorbachev's Domestic Policy an American Interest?

A number of American conservatives believe that domestic change in the Soviet Union is an essential goal of American foreign policy. For example, Irving Kristol has argued,

We are not going to achieve any stability in this world or reach any level of satisfaction or attainment in American foreign policy until the Soviet Union has been pushed into its ideological reformation—that is to say, until the Soviet Union ceases being a political regime with an established religion called Marxism-Leninism imposed upon the Soviet people.[21]

In principle this should make such conservatives supporters of policies aimed at reinforcing Gorbachev's liberalization. But this is not necessarily the case. For example, if one believes that Gorbachev's prospects are slight, or that these reforms would fall far short of changing the Marxist-Leninist nature of the regime, then Gorbachev's policies are not particularly an American interest. Gorbachev's success is valuable to us only if he wins "big" in American terms (that is, changes the Marxist-Leninist nature of the regime). Otherwise, it might be better that he not win at all. Better a weak Soviet Union than a reformed Marxist-Leninist one. From this viewpoint, the confrontational option may seem more attractive.

I would argue that Gorbachev's domestic policy *is* an important American interest for a variety of reasons. (Whether we know how to advance that interest is a different question.) We do not have to wait for the Soviets to drop their Marxist-Leninist framework before we can see benefits from liberalization and *glasnost'*. One need only go back to the points made at the beginning of this paper, that the competition between the United States and the Soviet Union is likely to continue for solid geopolitical reasons, and that in a world of 50,000 nuclear weapons there will always be the danger of accidents, miscalculations and misinterpretations during crises. I argued earlier that the intensity of the conflict between the two countries has varied greatly in response to domestic politics and societal perceptions. The closed nature of the Soviet society has exacerbated American reactions to Soviet behavior. As Marshall Shulman has argued, "Over-simplified and emotionally colored stereotypes of the other have fostered a 'cycle of reactions' that took on a life of their own, disproportionate to, and only partly related to the real conflict of interest involved."[22] *Glasnost'* can help here. A more open Soviet society will not reduce real conflicts of interest, but it can increase the impact of reality in the conduct of foreign policy of both nations. It is in the American interest that the Soviets follow a realistic foreign policy.

A second American interest in Gorbachev's liberalization is closely related to the first, and that is its effects on U.S. foreign policy. As argued earlier, American foreign policy has often exaggerated Soviet intentions and thus exacerbated the cycles through which our policy tends to run. The opaqueness of Soviet intentions and capabilities has allowed domestic political conflicts greatly to distort American policy toward the Soviet Union. Similarly, the manipulation of the press and the deprivation of human rights in the Soviet Union make it easier to consider it an evil empire with which it is impossible to do business. To the extent that liberalization improves the human rights situation, and *glasnost'* provides better access to the Soviet elite and better information about Soviet capabilities, the reforms will have a good effect on these American political myths. We have a strong interest in a realistic American foreign policy as well as a realistic Soviet foreign policy. Gorbachev's reforms can help that.

A third American interest in *glasnost'* is better information about the Soviet Union. If we are to understand the changes that are occurring, for example those concerning the debate over the decline in Soviet power, we need better statistics as well as access to Soviet interpretations of change in their country. It is important to understand one's adversary. To the extent that *glasnost'* provides us with more information for that task, it is in our interest. Of course, *glasnost'* still has a long way to go. Soviet experts on foreign policy argue privately that "there is less difference between what we say and what we believe than there was in the past," and prominent Soviet writers report that it is increasingly possible "to call things by their real names." But official statements about foreign affairs still lack the mark of *glasnost'*. I remember one conversation with a Soviet who complained about the CIA's reconstruction of the Soviet defense budget which he claimed was exaggerated for American domestic political purposes. I replied that there was an easy cure for that problem—the Soviets should publish accurate defense budget figures. He winced and admitted that I was probably right but confessed that it would require, in his words, "reversing centuries of Russian history."[23] It may be too much to hope that *glasnost'* will encompass defense budgets and military systems, but every step in the right direction helps.

Another American interest in *glasnost'* relates to negotiations and verifying compliance with arms control agreements. Opponents of arms control often make the verification issue a key part of their opposition. Accusations of Soviet cheating are grounds for resisting signing new agreements. Given new military technologies of stealth, concealment, and mobility, future verification procedures will require far more intrusive cooperative measures including on-site inspections. Thus in both a direct and indirect manner, *glasnost'* will be helpful for the arms control process if it makes the Soviet regime less secretive in the eyes of the American public and enhances the prospects for verification of compliance with agreements.

America has a fifth interest in Gorbachev's reforms to the extent that they increase contacts and enhance societal learning in the Soviet Union. Learning is the alteration of beliefs by new information. Individual learning is a necessary but not a sufficient condition for organizational or societal learning. Not everyone learns the same lessons or at the same rate. Social structure and political power determine when learning occurs and whose learning matters. There has been a good deal of learning about foreign affairs among the Soviet elite in the last two decades.[24] Soviet writings about nuclear weapons have become more detailed and sophisticated. Increased contacts generally provide new information which, in turn, can stimulate new learning. For example, Schevchenko reports that Gromyko lobbied to have rising young officers placed on the Soviet arms control delegation because "the more contact they have with the Americans, the easier it will be to turn our soldiers into something more than just martinets."[25] Obviously Soviet learning about foreign affairs well antedates Gorbachev; nonetheless, his reforms are increasing the amount of information and the extent to which that information affects different members of society. This broadened opportunity for learning can help to reinforce or lock in social changes that we regard as desirable. They may help to constrain its reversability.

Most of these American interests relate to openness and liberalization in the treatment of Soviet citizens. There is also an interest in *perestroika,* or economic restructuring, although its net effect is more mixed. While successful economic reforms would strengthen the Soviet Union and make it a more formidable adversary, the expansion of market mechanisms in the Soviet economy could also have beneficial political effects. Greater decentralization and pluralization in the Soviet economy would provide more opportunities for trade and points of access. It is also possible that a somewhat more pluralized society will be more consumer-oriented and less ideological. It might also be less prone to risky actions than a highly centralized society, though such propositions probably depend on many other factors. Though the effects of *perestroika* on American interests are more ambiguous than those of *glasnost',* they may also include positive dimensions.

Finally, the United States has an interest in the third aspect of Gorbachev's reforms, democratization. While democratization is very limited (for example, only a few percent of the June 1987 local elections involved more than one candidate), the United States has long counted the promotion of democracy (and human rights) as an intrinsic symbolic (as well as instrumental) foreign policy interest.[26] While it would be naive to repeat Woodrow Wilson's faith in the democratic nature of the Russian people,[27] even limited steps are in the right direction.

Although I believe that Americans have an interest in Gorbachev's domestic policy, there are limits to what the United States can do in pursuit of that interest. Deliberate efforts to support Gorbachev could have adverse unintended consequences. Open support could hurt Gorbachev's legitimacy in the eyes of internal constituencies. At the same time, making concessions for the sake of helping Gorbachev could be expensive in terms of our other interests. As argued earlier, Gorbachev has thus far pursued a traditional Soviet foreign policy which advances Soviet interests against those of the United States. As Dimitri Simes has warned, "Any Soviet leader might find his credibility among the powerful national security elite badly damaged if change at home were to become coupled with a perceived softness abroad. Nothing about Gorbachev or his career indicates that he is likely to take such chances."[28] Thus it is far from clear that we should or could pay the costs necessary to support Gorbachev. To a large extent, reform will depend upon Soviet domestic conditions.

It helps Gorbachev if he is taken seriously, as Prime Minister Thatcher did on Soviet television. American positions may make a difference at the margin. Summitry may also bolster Gorbachev's position in the eyes of his domestic constituencies. Similarly, the achievement of balanced arms control agreements will enhance his legitimacy and help him to stave off demands for military expenditures. Increased trade and contacts can help to increase the flow of information that broadens social learning and helps to lock in some of the changes that *glasnost'* has begun to bring about. Removal of the 1970s legislative barriers to trade could be a useful step. Admission or observer status in international economic institutions such as the GATT and IMF may help if the terms are not concessional but encourage increased economic liberalization.

Conversely, it is likely that a confrontational option would slow down the development of reform. In a confrontational climate, it would be harder to release dissident prisoners, extend human rights, and allow emigration. Even if the roots of *glasnost'* and democratization lie in Gorbachev's domestic political strategy of lighting a fire under the party bureaucracy, he must respect the limits set by the confines of Soviet patriotism. A confrontational American policy seems more likely to constrain than to encourage the further development of reform.

Conclusions

The Soviet Union has been the dominant problem in American foreign policy over the past four decades. At a high level of abstraction, the United States has sought three broad goals in its Soviet foreign policy: avoiding nuclear war; containing the spread of Soviet power and ideology; and gradually encouraging change in the nature of the behavior of the Soviet Union. Despite the rhetoric, inconsistencies, and oscillation in American policy, the United States has not done that badly. Nuclear war has been avoided and, even more to the point, both sides have learned a great deal about the destructiveness of nuclear weaponry and about the processes involved in managing the nuclear competition. Nuclear learning has occurred. Further, both sides have learned prudent practices of crisis management. The first half of the period with its Berlin and Cuban crises was more dangerous than the second half.

Similarly, the United States has been surprisingly successful at political containment. In terms of George Kennan's original conception of containment, there has been some mellowing of Soviet power. Soviet ideological appeal has greatly diminished, particularly in the areas which matter most in the global balance. While Marxist regimes in Angola, Laos, Vietnam, Cambodia, Mozambique, Yemen, Ethiopia, and Afghanistan represent an extension of Soviet influence, marginal Third World gains are not nearly as significant to the balance of power as the fact that the key areas of Western Europe and Japan, though geographically closer to the Soviet Union, have remained politically closer to the United States. Moreover, the Soviet Union as well as the United States "lost" China. In addition, the Soviet empire in Eastern Europe is far from politically secure. Geopolitically, the Soviets have tended to win the small ones rather than the big ones.

As for the third general objective of the United States, encouraging change in the internal nature of the Soviet Union, it is clear that some change has occurred. Gorbachev's Soviet Union is very different from Stalin's. How much of that, however, is due to deliberate American governmental effort is debatable. In some ways, this third objective may have been affected more by American societal influences than by direct governmental efforts, although one must note governmental efforts can be used to promote societal influences.

Regardless of change, however, it is important to realize that competition with the Soviet Union is endemic to the structure of the bipolar relationship. Hopes to terminate all conflict quickly by accommodation or victory are unlikely to be realized. The American goal should be a more normal relationship between great powers with less ideological definition of interests, and a greater awareness of the potential for cooperation in pursuit of joint interests as the world becomes less bipolar and interdependence increases.[29] The problem is one of long-term management of a balance of power. That, in turn, requires communication and negotiation between the opponents. A successful foreign policy will require indirect means of balancing Soviet power as much as direct means. The United States can best contain Soviet power by constraining its external political opportunities. Maintaining the Western alliance system has been the key to success. It is an area in which the pluralism of the American approach and the American political system has been a help rather than a hindrance. However, maintaining political cohesion in the Western alliance will be more difficult under Gorbachev than under his predecessors.

With all this said, the United States is still interested in change inside the Soviet Union. These changes will be gradual and will respond primarily to internal Soviet needs. At best, the Americans can marginally encourage rather than hope to stimulate or guide domestic change. A managed balance of power requires regular communication and improved information. To the extent that Soviet changes encourage this, they will help the United States pursue such a sensible strategy. Regular meetings and negotiations, including arms control negotiations, should be seen as a means of enhancing transparency and communication. Trade and cultural exchanges should be evaluated not only by the criteria of economic benefits, but also by the effects increased engagement have on enhancing transparency and communication. Finally, the American ability to manage the balance of power depends on balance in American perceptions of the Soviet Union. Increased contacts and openness on the Soviet side which reduce oscillations in American policy and exaggeration in American domestic debates about the Soviet Union will make a more consistent policy possible.

Domestic reform and *glasnost'* in the Soviet Union are American interests, but not ones about which the United States can do much. Reform may be fragile both in terms of the Soviet domestic politics that drive it and susceptibility to disruption from outside the Soviet Union. For example, if liberalization encourages instability in the Soviet inner empire of Eastern Europe, it may be reversed at home or Gorbachev may find his opponents using that fact to constrain or oust him. Moreover, the effects of Soviet intervention, particularly if bloody, could derail negotiations and curtail contacts. Despite these dangers, the Americans would probably be drawn back eventually to a managed balance of power. Over the long run, reform and a greater degree of openness will encourage learning both in the United States and in the Soviet Union and thus make the management of that balance somewhat easier. That is sufficiently important to be considered in all American policy choices. Even if the American government policies can have little more than marginal effects on the direct promotion of domestic reform in the Soviet Union, the United States should remember Florence Nightingale's advice and follow policies that at least do not make things worse.

Notes

1. For an interesting account of the generational changes in the early 1980s, see Dusko Doder, *Shadows and Whispers* (New York: Random House, 1987).
2. See the chapters by Timothy Colton and Thane Gustafson in this volume.
3. Private conversations with literary figures and party members, Moscow, June 1987.
4. *Time,* September 9, 1985.
5. Joseph S. Nye, Jr., "Nuclear Learning and U.S.-Soviet Security Regimes," *International Organization* (Summer 1987).
6. Private conversation with members of international affairs institute, Moscow, June 1986.
7. Robert Legvold, "The New Political Thinking and Gorbachev's Foreign Policy," discussion paper for the Institute for East-West Security Studies, June 1987.
8. Weinberger and Scowcroft quoted in Michael Charlton, *The Star Wars History* (London: BBC, 1986), pp. 97, 106.
9. Francis Fukuyama, "Gorbachev and the Third World," *Foreign Affairs,* Vol. 64 (Spring 1986); and George Breslauer, "Ideology and Learning in Soviet Third World Policy," *World Politics,* XXXIX (April 1987).
10. Michael Mandelbaum and Strobe Talbott, "Reykjavik and Beyond," *Foreign Affairs,* Vol. 65 (Winter 1986/7).
11. *Washington Post,* March 3, 1987.
12. *Washington Post National Weekly Edition,* May 11, 1987, p. 4.
13. Dimitri Simes, "Gorbachev: A New Foreign Policy?" *Foreign Affairs,* Vol. 65, No. 3, 1987, p. 500.
14. The terms come from Arnold L. Horelick and Edward L. Warner III, "U.S.-Soviet Nuclear Arms Control: The Next Phase," in Arnold L. Horelick, ed. *U.S.-Soviet Relations: The Next Phase* (Ithaca: Cornell University Press, 1986), p. 250. For example, see the essays by Richard Pipes and Marshall Shulman in the same volume.
15. Richard Pipes, *Survival Is Not Enough* (New York: Simon and Schuster, 1984), p. 204.
16. Marshall Shulman, *Beyond the Cold War* (New Haven: Yale University Press, 1966), p. 2.
17. Charles Gati, "The Stalinist Legacy in Soviet Foreign Policy," in Erik Hoffman (ed.), *The Soviet Union in the 1980s* (New York: Academy of Political Science, 1984), p. 218 ff.
18. William Schneider, "Public Opinion," in Joseph S. Nye, Jr. (ed.), *The Making of America's Soviet Policy* (New Haven: Yale University Press, 1984).
19. See Strobe Talbott, "Social Issues," in Nye, *ibid.*
20. Arthur Schlesinger, Jr., *The Cycles of American History* (Boston: Houghton Mifflin, 1986).

21. Irving Kristol quoted in the *New York Times,* October 13, 1985.

22. Marshall Shulman, "A Rational Response to the Soviet Challenge," *International Affairs,* Vol. 61 (Summer 1985), p. 381.

23. Personal conversation with institute official, Moscow, May 1981.

24. Joseph S. Nye, Jr., "Nuclear Learning and U.S.-Soviet Security Regimes," cited above.

25. Arkady Shevchenko, *Breaking With Moscow* (New York: Ballantine, 1985), p. 270.

26. Samuel P. Huntington, "Will More Countries Become Democratic?" in Samuel P. Huntington and Joseph S. Nye, Jr. (eds.), *Global Dilemmas* (Lanham, MD: University Press of America, 1985).

27. John Lewis Gaddis, *Russia, The Soviet Union and The United States* (New York: Wiley, 1978), p. 57.

28. Simes, cited above, p. 479.

29. Walt Rostow, "On Ending the Cold War," *Foreign Affairs,* Vol. 65 (Spring 1987).

12

U.S. Policy and Gorbachev's Russia

William H. Luers

The efforts of the Gorbachev leadership to reform the Soviet system and to infuse "new thinking" into Soviet foreign policy offer important opportunities for the United States:

- The most promising opportunities are in nuclear arms reductions and establishing a more solid basis for Soviet-American relations.
- The most challenging and potentially most troublesome area is Europe where the changing political and psychological environment—the result both of Gorbachev's imaginative initiatives and a confused Western leadership—could produce discord. This discord involves regional arms reductions and alliance policies in Western Europe that together with a crisis in Eastern Europe could deflect the course of reforms in the U.S.S.R. and rekindle East-West tensions.
- The most uncertain set of issues has to do with the U.S.-Soviet rivalry in regional conflicts and in the Third World. Even though Gorbachev and his advisors seem disinclined to undertake new adventures in the Third World, the Soviet Union already has large commitments and a global vocation and ideology which we have unwisely underestimated in the past.

Gorbachev seems determined to undertake radical changes in Soviet society. Some of the changes he advocates, particularly improved living conditions for Soviet citizens, release of prisoners of conscience and greater freedom of discussion and debate, are clearly in the interest of the U.S. and of all open societies. Other changes that would strengthen the Soviet economy must be evaluated over time to determine whether the resulting economic growth will be directed toward military power or toward more benign social and economic objectives. Moreover,

Gorbachev is certain to sense frustration and even defeat in the next few years as the Soviet Union shows its penchant to resist change. Nonetheless, what is unfolding is the most interesting and potentially dynamic phase in the relationship of the two superpowers since World War II.

If it continues to evolve according to Gorbachev's present agenda, the Soviet Union is likely to be somewhat easier for Americans to deal with. But Gorbachev's ambitions for himself, and for the Communist Party of the Soviet Union, are surely not benign for U.S. interests. We must equip ourselves to meet a forceful and imaginative leader of an economically and socially troubled Russia.

The Bilateral Relationship

At the center of the U.S.-Soviet bilateral relationship is the danger of nuclear war. There is a presumed determination of both sides to avoid any conflict that might by accident, miscalculation or design ignite the fuse that would lead to the use of nuclear weapons. If it were not for the enormous, ready nuclear arsenals on each side, there would be little compulsion in the U.S. to pursue the type of unproductive, basically antagonistic relationship with Soviet Russia we have had since the end of World War II. Therefore, it is not surprising that at the core of our dialogue is the issue of the management and the control of nuclear weapons.

Yet other issues constantly intrude on the nuclear arms control agenda. The issues of intentions and misconceptions, of ideology and psychology and, ultimately, of closed and open societies distort the agenda and limit the ability of the two superpowers to reach agreements. Managing the political rivalry beyond the nuclear agenda has been the most difficult and potentially incendiary aspect of the superpower relationship.

Bipolarity and Multipolarity

In the most intense postwar effort to manage U.S.-Soviet relations, Richard Nixon and Henry Kissinger designed a global approach and played the China card. The key element in Kissinger's concept of *detente* was to establish a U.S.-Soviet relationship buttressed by a broadly based U.S. effort designed both to entice and entrap the Soviet Union and China into becoming a part of the international community. With all its flaws, the Nixon-Kissinger *detente* still remains the model for a sound American strategy toward the Soviet Union.

The following concepts and elements of the *detente* period are those that need to be retained and strengthened:

- To institutionalize Soviet-American relations through frequent summit meetings, efforts to build cooperative programs, and continuing arms negotiations and agreements.
- To maintain a strong multipolar diplomatic and political effort to sustain close American ties to powers on the periphery of Soviet Russia, particularly China, Japan and Western Europe and to encourage greater Soviet participation on normal terms in international agencies and organizations such as the General Agreement on Tariffs and Trade (GATT), the International Monetary Fund (IMF), the World Bank, and the United Nations itself where Gorbachev has shown new interest.
- To build into the relationship some inducements such as trade and credits, and even some increased transfer of nonmilitary technology as well as continued recognition of the superpower status of the Soviet Union.

There were several elements of the execution of U.S. policy in the period of *detente* that contributed to the collapse of the strategy. The changes that we must incorporate into a new strategy to institutionalize the U.S.-Soviet relationship are:

- We should build a domestic constituency to support a bilateral agenda with the Soviet Union. The inability of the Nixon Administration to keep the American people informed about the process and goals of *detente* is too complex a tale to rehearse here. But any new President who embarks on a policy of relaxation of tensions must persuade the American people that he will remain aware of Soviet reality and past Soviet performance and be determined to keep the Congress well informed.
- We should avoid the appeal of seeking written agreements on the "rules of the game" in dealing with the Soviets, particularly concerning Third World and regional conflicts. Rather than attempting to reach general agreements on "basic principles" we should maintain regular discussions on regional and bilateral issues in order to achieve specific solutions and avoid potential conflicts.
- We should downplay the concept of "linkages" which became the theoretical and rhetorical burden of the era of *detente*. Because American public opinion is volatile and because the President cannot adjust foreign policy toward the Soviet Union in response to every swing of the public's mood or specific legislated policy

of linkage is simply untenable. Linkages will continue to play a role from time to time in applying pressure on the Soviets to do what we favor. But by bringing "linkages" into law, as with the Jackson-Vanik amendment, we tie our own hands and achieve little.

• Finally, we should not underestimate the continuing Soviet readiness to become troublesome in regional conflicts. The United States underestimated the Soviets in this area in the second half of the 1970s, yet Soviet actions in the Third World became the single major cause of the collapse of *detente.*

The problems of developing and sustaining U.S. domestic support for a revised policy of *detente* (under another name) argue for minimizing the bilateral aspects of the relationship and for strengthening efforts and our capacity to build our ties to the increasingly multipolar world. The U.S. political system at its best can restrain Presidents from zealotry and personal political opportunism in periods of relaxation of tensions with the Soviets, and, at its worst, can limit the President's ability to establish agreements and processes to manage the inevitable crises and threats of conflict that will occur. Therefore, the next President should stress the need to institutionalize summitry and negotiations while avoiding the temptation to dramatize and "succeed" or "win" at every encounter. It is almost impossible for a new President to resist the temptation to enter the ring the day after his inauguration ready either to bash or to embrace the current Kremlin leader. He should do neither. Rhetoric and expectation should both be restrained.

The multipolar and multilateral dimension of the political rivalry also deserves more careful examination. Gorbachev and his advisors have set out, in their "new thinking" about Soviet foreign policy, recognition of an "interdependent" world, a refreshing new point of view of the Kremlin leadership under Gorbachev. It is still too early to assess the practical implications of Gorbachev's more open approach to UN peacekeeping efforts and, more broadly, to supporting the UN Security Council and United Nations organizations and other international agencies as channels for Soviet cooperation with the international community. Soviet initiatives toward China, Japan, Israel and the non-radical Arab States, a possible Gorbachev trip to visit non-Soviet clients in Latin America, and the interest being shown in international organizations suggest a new substance as well as a new rhetoric to Soviet foreign policy. Since the peaceful integration of the Soviet Union into the international community and multipolar restraint on Soviet power are precisely our objectives, a policy which seeks to channel part of the bipolar superpower competition into multilateral institutions is long overdue.

Restraining Language and Expectations

While the United States, its elected leaders and its people have had overly ambitious goals for transforming Soviet society, Soviet ideology is still committed to a new world order that the West is unable to accept. Beginning with Franklin D. Roosevelt, each American President, with the single exception of Harry Truman, has believed that through personal high-level contact, or through sincere American efforts, important changes could be brought about in the Soviet vision of the world or at least official Soviet behavior at home and abroad.

The question of whether American policies should seek to change Soviet foreign and domestic behavior will continue to trouble Administrations since that has been an essential element of virtually all American policies toward the U.S.S.R. since 1917. It is clear that the American people have come to expect such ambitious goals from our foreign policy, particularly in relation to Communist Russia. Indeed, many of these objectives have been specifically incorporated into legislation passed by the Congress. It is also evident that American policy objectives that advocate internal change in the Soviet Union can become obstacles to conducting serious relations with a Soviet leadership that is ever suspicious and insecure. Our Presidents must exercise restraint both in language and in expectations regardless of Gorbachev's promises and disappointments.

The language of our relationship with the Soviet Union has been a consistent source of confusion, disappointment, and breakdown in the relationship. From the first time Khrushchev resurrected the phrase "peaceful coexistence," in the late 1950s, Americans have liked it without understanding that the Soviet Union implied by that term an intensified world struggle while avoiding direct conflict with the U.S. The West, try as it may, has never found an ideological counterpart that could capture the flavor of the Western idea of a peaceful world community of independent nations. President Nixon's final acceptance in 1972 of the Soviet ideological formulation of peaceful coexistence in signing the Basic Principles Agreement sent a strong signal to Moscow implying to them that the U.S. had finally agreed to the Soviet rules of the global competition. Some formula is doubtless necessary to serve as a conceptual shorthand for the means of managing the relationship. That formula should probably include the idea of competition and cooperation. Gorbachev and his ideological advisers began in 1987 to reformulate the meaning of peaceful coexistence to downplay the "class struggle" aspects and stress the cooperative aspects.

Detente has also become a source of great befuddlement. In Russia and in Europe this French word has usually been correctly translated as "relaxation of tensions." In America, *detente* has taken on meanings far beyond the precise "relaxation of tensions." *Detente* began to be used to imply a new, more restrained Soviet Union (Salt I and the Basic Principles Agreement), an era of U.S.-Soviet cooperation (the multiple bilateral agreements and exchanges) and a period of freer emigration of Soviet Jews. *Detente* became for many Americans in the late 1970s synonymous with "sell out" to the Soviet Union. *Detente* was largely oversold to and misunderstood by the American public, because we lost track of the original meaning "to relax tensions."

Now Gorbachev has given us *glasnost'* which is invariably incorrectly translated into English as "openness." We also have "democratization." Both of these words, particularly *glasnost'*, are leading the American people into another cycle of potential confusion and disappointment. *Glasnost'* is indeed the most interesting and new aspect of Gorbachev's reforms. Its closest meaning in English is, in fact, "publicity," "public airing," or "open debate" of issues and problems. There is an entirely different Russian word, *otkrovennost,* meaning openness.

The concept of *glasnost'* is a refreshing policy that is gaining support within Soviet society. *Glasnost'* has made possible the discussion, with official sanction, of the sources of weakness and stagnation of the Soviet system, making possible creative responses to them. This is an important and powerful phenomenon in a closed society, but it is *not* "openness" as Westerners or even some Eastern Europeans conceive of the term. Some foreign radio broadcasts to the Soviet Union are still jammed; foreign travel and emigration is still severely restricted; hundreds, if not thousands of prisoners of conscience are still in prisons, labor camps and in internal exile; the KGB is still performing surveillance; the borders are still heavily armed, tourists followed, trade seriously restricted, and data still concealed. An open debate and "airing" is not "openness."

Perhaps one of the greatest sources of disappointment and violation in the bilateral dialogue has been the need of American Presidents to personalize the relationship. All post–World War II American Presidents, except for Truman, to some degree fell into the ego trap. The master of "personal" diplomacy was Nixon. Nixon so distrusted most of his own advisors that he often waived the right for an American interpreter to be present when he spoke "alone" with "Leonid" Brezhnev. Although at first this personalized relationship may have helped warm Brezhnev to *detente,* the Nixon-Brezhnev friendship actually became, after their 1973 bear hug on the South Portico of the White House, a burden to the U.S.-Soviet relationship. This burden grew heavy for the American public who found it increasingly easy to place *detente* in the same category as Watergate and Vietnam as reasons for the decline of the American Presidency. Nixon made *detente* his own catchword and his demise helped give *detente* its pejorative connotation.

Subsequent Presidents have also made the mistake of personalizing the Soviet-American relationship. One of Ford's major political errors in his 1976 Presidential campaign was his failure to receive the recently released Solzhenitsyn in the White House because of Ford's deference to Brezhnev. Carter's ill-advised kiss of Brezhnev at their 1979 Vienna summit meeting and his essential "shock" and "learning experience" on hearing of the Soviet invasion of Afghanistan discredited the seriousness of the President's capacity to understand, much less to manage the relationship. Reagan, after coming around 180 degrees in dealing with the Soviets, won the first round through his unexpected personalized diplomacy in the 1985 fireside summit in Geneva. But Gorbachev turned the tables on Reagan by using his own personal diplomacy to nearly extract far-reaching concessions at Reykjavik that would have been detrimental to the interests of the West, had they been implemented. It was Reagan's apparent naive mishandling of his personal talks with Gorbachev that tended to discredit him and to undermine American public support for the President's effort at arms reductions. Whatever agreements are reached by a Reagan/Gorbachev summit or pair of summits, exaggerated expectations or overly "friendly" gestures in the eyes of the American people could backfire, resulting in either blocking or negating the accords.

The management of the bilateral relationship simply does not allow for euphoria, or for splendid breakthroughs. What is required is determined slogging, carefully studied, tough-minded work on both sides over a long period. The U.S. leadership and the ideologically divided American political elites have not thus far permitted this to happen.

Espionage, National Paranoia, and Human Rights

The Soviet mistreatment of its population, its paranoia over its borders and its national security, and its relentless pursuit of espionage and intelligence activities form the second most important set of obstacles to the management of the Soviet-American relationship.

For decades there have been arrests of spies in both countries. In the 1960s these matters were managed with a minimum of publicity. They were perceived as part of the disagreeable reality of doing business with the Soviets. These arrests and spy dramas are not the central business of the relationship, although the media find them compelling. Administrations should seek to minimize their significance and to press the Soviets to reduce their enormous commitment to intelligence activities against the U.S.

The human rights issues, including the Soviet treatment of dissidents and intellectuals as well as restrictions on Soviet Jews' freedom to practice their religion, to keep alive their culture and to emigrate, have been the most politically troublesome issues with which any U.S. administration has had to deal since the early 1970s. Ironically, it was precisely the "thaw" after Stalinism that made the outside world aware of the diversity and the dissidence within Soviet society. This awareness gave rise to mounting concerns in the West in the late 1960s and 1970s over Soviet violations of human rights. An ironic result of *glasnost'* may be to reveal even more such serious inequities in Soviet society that the American public will turn from fascination to renewed intense criticism of Soviet developments.

The issue of Soviet Jewry and human rights became a focal point of the mid-1970s domestic U.S. debate over the costs and benefits of *detente*. Although the concerns over emigration of Soviet Jews and the harsh treatment of Solzhenitsyn were legitimate, it is fair to say that many members of the Senate and House voted for the Jackson-Vanik amendment primarily because they distrusted the Nixon-Kissinger deals with the Soviets or because they just distrusted the Soviets. The threat of passage of the Jackson-Vanik Amendment helped the emigration of Soviet Jews. In the 1980s, however, following the final collapse of *detente* after the Soviet invasion of Afghanistan, it has produced only negative results. Whereas 51,000 left in 1979, only hundreds had left annually from that time up to 1987.

The attention in the United States to these dramatic human issues has often taken precedence over the geopolitical competition between the two superpowers. For example, in the summer of 1978 there was pressure from the NSC to reduce bilateral contacts with the Soviets because of large-scale Soviet movement of troops and military equipment into Ethiopia to support the Mengistu regime. Some within the U.S. government believed that the unprecedented scale of this Soviet military involvement would have the effect of turning the Mengistu regime into the Cuba of East Africa. Yet others in the government resisted the idea of sanctions or reduced contacts with the Soviet Union. To retaliate for the Soviet decision to send Anatoly Shcharansky to Siberia we reduced contacts with the Soviets in June, 1978. This signal to the Politburo that the imprisonment of Shcharansky was of far greater importance to the U.S. government than the massive Soviet move into Ethiopia reflected the incorrect shape of priorities in Washington and sent confused signals to the Kremlin.

Gorbachev's reforms in Soviet society may be important in helping to manage these volatile elements of the U.S.-Soviet relationship. Because these Soviet domestic affairs affect American attitudes toward the daily management of our principal agenda of avoiding nuclear war, whatever eases the repression in Soviet society probably helps to manage the relationship. The release of prisoners of conscience, the gradual increase of Jewish emigration, *glasnost'* and the beginning of private economic opportunity will all help to improve the atmosphere. As a result American public support for an effort to relax Soviet-American tensions may also grow. It may also result in rising expectations in the U.S. and demands for genuine openness (as distinct from merely *glasnost'*) in Soviet society.

Trade, Credits, and Politics

Soviet-American trade and financial ties, once thought by the Soviets to be the centerpiece of *detente,* have been a source of contention in the relationship for more than a decade. The reasons why the trade relationship did not materialize were the Jackson-Vanik and Stevenson Amendments to the 1974 Trade Act, but many other issues became enmeshed, most particularly, the growing distrust of the Soviet military power under Brezhnev and Soviet willingness to project that power abroad. Another reason was the lack of goods which the Soviets could export to the U.S.

By the late 1970s, four issues became fused around the Jackson-Vanik and Stevenson Amendments:

- emigration of Soviet citizens, particularly Soviet Jews, was the central requirement for the U.S. to grant Most Favored Nation (MFN) treatment and government credits to the Soviet Union.
- human rights violations, although not the specific issue in Jackson-Vanik, became by extension the more generalized reason MFN was not accorded the U.S.S.R.
- transfer of military technology became the major concern over U.S. exports to the Soviet bloc in the late 1970s and 1980s.
- Soviet general economic weakness became also a central issue for many conservative Americans who wonder why the U.S. should assist the troubled Soviet economy through the sale of grain or other U.S. products. Some critics suggested that the Soviet economy and system were in crisis and moving toward collapse. The U.S. should help that process along by holding back trade.

The ideological passions in Washington became more inflamed by these issues than any other on the entire Soviet-American agenda. This debate became so contentious in Washington that it will be difficult for any U.S. administration to change the restricted pattern of U.S.-Soviet trade. Moreover, in the 1970s American companies spent so much time and money and achieved such meager results that corporate America is likely to be slow to reengage even if some trade restrictions are eased after the Reagan administration.

The questions concerning trade and human rights will be the most delicate domestic issues a U.S. administration will discuss with Gorbachev. The United States should seek a sense of Gorbachev's intentions with regard to emigration in general, Jewish emigration in particular, and to the treatment of minorities internally. We should also seek Gorbachev's plans for the 2.5 million Soviet Jews who face not only the increasing cultural and social deprivation of the past decade of rising anti-Semitism, but who are also deeply disturbed by the dark side of *glasnost'*. The more open public discussion under *glasnost'* has permitted the proliferation of more directly anti-Semitic groups such as *Pamyat* which advocates the revival of traditional and orthodox Russian values.

The Soviets would seek from such negotiations a lifting of the ban on credits (the Stevenson Amendment) and, subsequently, the granting of MFN. The Soviets will also seek a relaxation of controls on the sale of technology, U.S. official encouragement to American corporations to enter into joint ventures, and general U.S. support for some Soviet status in the GATT and the IMF.

A principal objective of a U.S. administration should be to seek an agreement with the Congress to decouple the issue of emigration from trade, giving the President a broader authority to urge the Soviets to treat its citizens more humanely. The Jackson-Vanik and Stevenson Amendments have not helped the plight of Soviet Jewry nor general human rights conditions. Gorbachev has, however, taken some first steps that we should recognize.

The first logical step would be for the Executive Branch to reach agreement with the Congress and with American Jewish organizations to suspend the Jackson-Vanik Amendment for five years. If the situation then looks encouraging, the Administration could later seek a suspension of Stevenson. *Our* objective should be to permit the President, closely monitored by Congress, to link credits, trade developments and Soviet desires to enter the GATT and the IMF to Soviet willingness to open up their economy to joint ventures with U.S. business as well as to provide greater knowledge of Soviet gold and financial reserves and Soviet pricing policies. If, indeed, the Gorbachev leadership wishes to enter the international trade and financial community, the U.S. should be equipped to provide both incentives and levers for them to do so without prejudice to the rest of the community.

U.S.-Soviet Relations and Europe

It is in Europe that the two superpowers have their greatest potential for cooperation as well as their greatest danger of a major crisis. It appears unlikely that any crisis outside Europe could so challenge vital U.S. and Soviet interests as to provoke an open conflict. It is still in Europe that the military might of both powers and their allies are concentrated and that their ability to wage war has been enlarged so dramatically in the post war period. Given this concentration of fighting power a mismanaged crisis here could still be catastrophic.

The most vulnerable part of the continent is Central Europe, where the most powerful military forces ever assembled in history are directly facing each other and where the greatest anxieties of the two blocs in the past 40 years have developed. The regimes of the Eastern European members of the Warsaw Pact have not had the support of their populations; they have watched their countries fall behind Western Europe in technological and economic development and historically have been under internal pressure to seek greater independence from Soviet control. Since the East European revolts of the 1950s the West has been aware of, but has not concentrated on, the fact that the Soviet Union's European satellites are a constant source of disagreement and potential conflict between East and West.

Into this volatile environment has come Mikhail Gorbachev. His style and policies are having a powerful impact on Europe. Western Europeans, ever hopeful that Russia will finally change, are finding in Gorbachev a leader of promise and ideas, the likes of which they have not seen for decades. In Eastern Europe, the Gorbachev reform and style are unleashing forces in six countries that may be difficult for the Soviet leaders to comprehend, much less to contain. Simply stated, crises of the type that have taken place in Hungary (1956), Czechoslovakia (1968) and Poland (most recently in 1981) will happen again.

Although less explosive than Khrushchev's 1956 secret speech against Stalin, which reverberated for more than a decade in Eastern Europe, Gorbachev's calls for *glasnost'* (public airing), *perestroika* (restructuring), "democratization" and "new thinking" are shaking the foundations of the Communist old regimes. The leader of the Soviet Union has released political prisoners, declared his proposals open to debate and, most important, suggested new directions for reform of the political-economic system and for changes of military force levels in Central Europe.

In designing reforms for the Soviet Union, Gorbachev has shown confidence that he can channel and control the process despite domestic resistance. When he looks outward to Eastern Europe, his behavior suggests that he has learned a key lesson from Khrushchev and Brezhnev: that failure to control the process of change in the repressed "satellites" would doom his domestic reform program as well as shatter his efforts to charm and divide the West.

The aging leaders of Eastern Europe, however, whose regimes were shaped in the Brezhnev era, have watched with foreboding as that era is swept away in the Soviet Union. They understand that the "new broom" could sweep away much more than a few tired bureaucrats in Central Europe. They seriously doubt that Gorbachev can sustain his reforms. They also recognize what Gorbachev apparently does not: that should the Soviet leader persevere for two to three years, the ensuing change in their countries will be extremely difficult for them to control.

Gorbachev's exhortations and promises to the Soviet people, therefore, become challenges and threats to the ruling elites in Eastern Europe. This comes at a time when age is pushing old leaders toward oblivion, when their economies are struggling to meet multiple demands both from Moscow and their own dissatisfied populations, and when their countries' stagnation in technological and social development is every day increasing the distance between East and West in Europe.

Gorbachev is approaching Eastern Europe with caution and uncertainty. How should the United States approach it?

Promote Gradual Change and Avoid Crises

A comprehensive U.S. policy toward Eastern Europe should take into consideration several fundamental realities of the East European predicament. Such a policy must also be coordinated with the policies of our key European allies, and in particular, of Germany and France.

The first reality is that there is no prospect for fundamental change in the relationship between the Soviet Union and any East European Warsaw Pact member in the near future. By fundamental change I mean, for example, the departure of one or more countries from the Warsaw Pact or Comecon, or a decision by the lenders of one nation no longer to retain the Communist Party as the vehicle for rule. This is true regardless of what Gorbachev says, and for at least the next decade. Soviet security interests will continue to dominate Moscow's thinking, although economic interests and Soviet prestige are likely to be increasingly important factors in Politburo discussions on the satellites. The Brezhnev Doctrine, which arose out of the justifications given for the 1968 Warsaw Pact invasion of Czechoslovakia, suggests that military force is justified to save socialism. The Soviets do believe their "revolutions" are irreversible. More importantly, Soviet leaders believe that Moscow must dominate the territory of Eastern Europe to assure Soviet security. The Final Act of the 1975 Helsinki accords is important in promoting East-West discussion of our differences, but it does not change Soviet interests at all.

The second reality is that political and economic pressures dictate that crises will occur every five to ten years in one or more East European states: the Soviet reaction will naturally be of great importance. But how the West reacts to these crises will also be important. While Western policies should encourage gradual change, they should not promote radical solutions. Each of the major crises in Eastern Europe has distorted the process of change; the Soviet Union's short-term reaction has been to tighten controls and impose stricter limits in the region and within the U.S.S.R. If the impact of Gorbachev's behavior on one or two nations of Eastern Europe is so dramatic that Soviet power is challenged there, a decision to repress reform would affect not only all of Eastern Europe but the entire process of Soviet domestic reform as well. The key question facing Gorbachev and the regimes and peoples in Eastern Europe remains what would provoke another Soviet invasion in Eastern Europe?

Predicting where the next crisis will occur, what form it will take, and what the Soviet response will be in a volatile part of the world is foolhardy. But each nation has the potential for presenting the Soviets with an agonizing set of choices, including whether to take military action:

- Poland is a perennial leading candidate because of its irrepressible anti-Soviet, religious, nationalist population. Jaruzelski sees himself as being at once close to Gorbachev, sympathetic to reform, but knowing that the radical reforms he proposes might not be enough. The Polish population demands more than the party or the Soviets are prepared to concede.
- Romania is in such a deplorable economic condition and the political structure has been so seriously distorted to serve the family interests of Ceaucescu that the Soviets may find dealing with Ceaucescu's succession more like dealing with the passing of a Latin caudillo than the transfer of power in a ruling Communist party. Ceaucescu is constantly worried by a resurgent Soviet leadership. Historically, his compromise with the Soviets has been such that, despite his maverick foreign policy, domestically he runs a country that is almost as closed as the U.S.S.R. How does he

now cope with a Soviet leader who advocates open debate, releases prisoners, and calls for greater "internal democracy"?

- In Hungary, Janos Kadar and his party are publicly delighted that Gorbachev seems to have swallowed a large morsel of Hungary's "goulash communism," including the idea of secret ballots for multiple candidates. Privately, however, they are skeptical of the eventual outcome. The Hungarians are already struggling over whether to press their troubled reform program even further into the political arena, and Gorbachev's still unproven enthusiasms add an unpredictable new factor. The Soviet mistake is most likely to be underestimating the depth to which economic and political reform has taken hold in the society, and trying to change or arrest it. This could occur if the succession creates pressures for reform that threaten the Party leadership's control of the process.
- Bulgaria, under the aging Todor Zhivkov, is attempting slavishly to follow the Kremlin leader. This is one country where the Soviets have been openly critical of the system. Zhivkov, a clever old codger, is the antithesis of Gorbachev.
- In strategically important East Germany the death or departure of Honecker could lead to rapidly changing policies. Honecker, who emerged two years ago as one of the most innovative and "independent" of the Warsaw Pact nations' leaders, appears concerned that while Gorbachev's economic reforms appear consistent with his own, the political implications of glasnost' and perestroika could damage Communist party control of the process in East Germany and even sweep Honecker from power. Yet Honecker's surprising response to glasnost' has been to visit West Germany and use the Gorbachev liberalism to press even further for close inner-German ties.
- Czechoslovakia best illustrates Gorbachev's dilemma. Its regime represents the worst residue of the Brezhnev era and symbolizes all that Gorbachev is attacking at home. Yet any effort to change this stable leadership could open up the dangers of another "Prague Spring," already a subject of Soviet discussions in Eastern Europe. During his April 1987 visit to Prague, where Czechs with no little irony and much curiosity greeted him enthusiastically, Gorbachev cautiously said to Gustav Husak, "We shall be glad if our experience can be useful to fraternal Czechoslovakia." Before Gorbachev's visit, Husak had uttered in public "reform"—a word forbidden in official propaganda since 1969.

It is unlikely that there will be popular disturbances in East Germany or Czechoslovakia of a magnitude to provoke Soviet intervention. But these are the two most important front-line Warsaw Pact allies to which Soviet power is most forcibly committed; thus any change will have great importance.

American policy should incorporate several basic aims. It must promote the yearning for national identity which, after Soviet power, is the second most powerful force in the region. American administrations must plan for the long term and realize that there are no quick "victories." We must be true to our conviction that long-term policies will pay off eventually in a freer, more independent Eastern Europe. We have seen it in Hungary, and indeed throughout the region as Stalinist rigidity has gradually given way to diversity.

Deal With Governments, Technocrats, and Dissidents

The third reality is that each country in Eastern Europe will follow a different path—and each will differ from the Soviet Union in its own way. The Hungarian model, attractive to Westerners since it appears so logical because of its liberalization of domestic political and economic conditions, is not likely to be replicated exactly elsewhere. The economic approach of the German Democratic Republic which has the richer, although not freer society (developing large industrial/ trading combines along with some privatization in key service sectors) may have as much impact on the Soviet Union, and eventually on Czechoslovakia and Bulgaria, as the Hungarian experience has had. Poland, with its religious fervor, its relative intellectual freedom, and its non-collectivized agriculture, presents another unique case. Some form of economic reform is essential in Poland, but the alliance between the military and Communist Party, despite significant new reform efforts, cannot really satisfy the popular Polish yearning for independence. Even Czechoslovaks have evolved their own form of national opposition. They call it "anti-politics." By internalizing their frustrations and energies, the Czechs have evolved a society which is cowed but which enjoys one of the highest standards of living in Eastern Europe. It is, however, ready for political regeneration.

A fourth reality is that despite these differences, change cannot take place in any of these countries without the initiative, or at least the cooperation, of the Communist regimes. The impetus to reform can spring from a variety of sources: leadership changes (G.D.R.), popular pressure from below (Poland), the vision of individual leaders (Hungary), reformist pressure from the party and technocracy (Czechoslovakia), or from Moscow (after Khrushchev's de-Stalinization speech and now in the era of Gorbachev). But in each case the party has been part of the process. If a party elite is not involved, the Soviets would have to intervene.

Czechoslovakia, Bulgaria, Hungary and Romania are likely to lose their supreme leaders within the next five years. Opportunities will arise for new leaders anxious to discredit their predecessors. These heirs will, like Gorbachev, come from the senior party ranks and will have been formed as bureaucrats in the party's stifling environment. Yet the bureaucrats in Eastern Europe are both more sophisticated and more frustrated than their comrades in the Russian party. Thus, new energies in the more European and more open satellites have a chance to erupt, particularly if encouraged to do so from Moscow.

Given the current situation, the United States should expand contacts with senior officials in all these countries and increase contacts with the technocrats and with the scientific and intellectual communities both to learn more about them and to help shape some of the decisions of those who will soon inherit power. The International Research and Exchanges Board (IREX), for example, has been a vital link in maintaining exchange programs with Eastern Europe. Its work should be supported and expanded with U.S. government support.

Contact with the United States, particularly at the level of the party and government, should not necessarily imply U.S. approval. If we can deal with Gorbachev and his colleagues, why should we not deal with the lesser oligarchs in the Soviet colonies? To gain access to them, however, we must have cultural, economic, political and even military relations. We should be selective and not deal with each leadership and bureaucracy in the same way. We have little or nothing to lose: dealing with Communist officials does not diminish the United States. On the contrary, it could enhance our ability to understand and perhaps even affect the future of the region.

The fifth reality is that the activist opposition groups as well as the intellectuals and technocrats are significant forces in defining the main cultural trends and national identities of each country. These groups will not achieve political power, but they keep alive the cultural and linguistic uniqueness of each nation and articulate the anti-party and anti-Soviet sentiments of Eastern Europe. There is now a revival of the concept of "Central Europe" as a cultural and intellectual territory as well as a state of mind distinct from Soviet Russia. The phrase, "Central Europe," as described by the Czechoslovak playwright, Vaclav Havel, refers more accurately to the nations of Poland, the German Democratic Republic, Czechoslovakia and Hungary as nations formerly dominated by the Hapsburg Empire or Germany who experienced the same cultural history and renaissance as the West European nations, and who even today enjoy an intellectual and cultural life distinct from that of Russia.

Representatives of the American government should have regular contacts with intellectuals, technocrats and dissidents as a clear demonstration of our support for human rights, for the 1975 Helsinki Final Act, and for the cultural vitality and independent spirit of these societies. Short-term expediency, such as the process of negotiating or concluding agreements with these governments, should not deter us from this policy. Moreover, these regular contacts should include efforts to expand the flow of information to and from these groups and, most importantly, promote and improve Western radio broadcasts to the region.

Stronger Economies Promote More Independent Nations

My sixth reality of the Eastern European predicament is that the more viable the East European nations become both economically and socially, the more different they become from the Soviet Union and the weaker Communist Party control will be. U.S. policies, it must be emphasized, can neither create nor profoundly affect these economic and social developments in Eastern Europe. West Europeans, particularly Germans and French, can probably have a greater impact on the region than can the United States. By working together the Western nations as a group can be a vital stimulus to change.

Western economic and trade policies are clearly the most useful instruments available to achieve influence over the choices made by the East Europe regimes over the next decade. The Jackson-Vanik Amendment to the 1974 Trade Act and the Stevenson Amendment severely limit our ability to gain influence over decision-making in Eastern Europe. American trade policies should not be tied to emigration policies—since this is not a major U.S. interest, except perhaps in the case of Romania. U.S. trade policies should be related more directly to the trade and economic policies of the East European regimes. We should use our trade and technology to open these societies to Western firms, joint ventures, and nonmilitary technology.

The Reagan Administration has objected to trade with the East not so much because of Jackson-Vanik but out of concern for the loss of American military technology. This is a legitimate concern. Yet, as recent studies of U.S. trade policies and controls over technology transfer have demonstrated, many of the restrictions have been ineffective, misdirected and actually harmful to U.S. exports.

A more active American trade policy in Eastern Europe could, for example, greatly expand the use of personal computers, management information systems, and video cassette recorders. The wide range of new electronic systems for conveying information is having a shattering effect on the restraint of information flow in these closed societies. This phenomenon fed the need for *glasnost'*. Whereas the Czechoslovak government, for example, limits the number of carbon copies of any unofficial document to 12 and restricts the availability of photocopy machines, the proliferation of personal computers and video cassette recorders is rapidly making it impossible to stem the flow of information. It would be advantageous for the United States if American technology were present along with Japanese, Swiss and West German technological products.

We should repeal the Jackson-Vanik and Stevenson amendments, at least as they apply to Eastern Europe, and develop policies to encourage non-strategic trade and economic relations with all East European states. A program of expanded access for American businesses, including joint ventures, as well as a progressively more substantial role for U.S. trade in general, would be more consistent with our commitments under the Helsinki Final Act, and would provide long-term assurances to East European leaders who seek an alternative to total economic dependence on the Soviet Union. It would also bring our policies closer to those of our NATO allies. We should not, however, expand the transfer of military technologies to Eastern Europe or assume a greater share of the existing hard currency debt of Poland or other large debtor nations.

Security Issues and the Growth of National Identity

The seventh reality is that military and security issues in Central Europe will continue to define the limits of political and economic change in the region. The national military and security forces in Eastern Europe, for example, are likely to become increasingly important contenders with the Communist parties for power in some Eastern European countries. It was the security riot police and the military that saved the Polish Communist party from total collapse in the face of the challenge from Solidarity. These forces may not be as loyal to Moscow as the party leadership. Moreover, Gorbachev, looking back on the growth of the Soviet military establishment under Brezhnev would certainly consider military domination of the party as a dangerous trend in the satellites. Such a trend would significantly alter the nature of the Warsaw Pact–Comecon alliance, further weaken Soviet authority in the region, and present a new range of risks and opportunities for Western nations.

General Jaruszelski helped the Soviets avoid a costly invasion of Poland. Yet the Polish military has a long tradition of patriotism that carries the seeds of trouble for the Soviets. In Romania, too, if the Ceaucescu family fails to retain party control after the death or departure of the present supreme leader, the security or military forces would be well placed to take power from a weakened party. And a resurgent military in East Germany, although not now equal in power to the party or the Soviets, would be a disturbing development indeed.

The major Soviet military presence in Eastern Europe is the Soviet Union's ultimate source of control over its satellites. A significant reduction (at least half) of regional conventional forces in Central Europe over the next decade, therefore, would likely promote other types of political dynamics in Europe. Such reductions would certainly contribute to a process of change. Lower levels of military forces in Central Europe might well have the effect of increasing tensions between the United States and the Soviet Union, temporarily destabilizing the region and promoting the evolution of new types of special relations among the states of Europe. One focus of these changing relationships is likely to be the German national question. Should the German question reassert itself as an issue in East-West relations, it is in the interest of the United States to retain strong ties to West Germany, but also to be in a better position with the German Democratic Republic than it is today.

The potential for instability and tension makes it necessary to achieve force reductions carefully: they should be pursued, however, because the eventual benefits would be significant. The evolution of diversity and national identity in Eastern Europe would be greatly encouraged by a policy to manage, over a period of a decade or more, the gradual decline of Soviet and American military forces in the heart of Europe. The United States should work seriously with our NATO allies to create a formula for negotiation with the Gorbachev team on the reduction or elimination of medium-range nuclear weapons (which is already under way), and a significant reduction of conventional forces.

Ethnic Nationalism and Soviet Power

The eighth reality about Eastern Europe is that even though the basic political dynamics within the Warsaw Pact nations cannot be changed by a new Western strategy, our policies must be based on the fact that the internal forces at work in the Warsaw Pact nations make for greater diversity there.

Ethnic nationalism is still a powerful force in Eastern Europe. The ethnic homogeneity of the German Democratic Republic, Poland and Hungary shapes the distinct challenge that each of the three nations present to Soviet authority, whereas the ethnic divisions in Czechoslovakia and Romania give the Soviet Union leverage in Prague and Bucharest. While the ethnic divisions provide the Soviets with leverage to weaken the leadership by playing off ethnic groups against one another, this weakness also breeds uncertainty over whether the diverse groups are capable of producing new types of reform. For example, the Czech and Slovak division could be a powerful factor, as it was in 1968, in producing rapid reform should a Czech replace the Slovak Husak. The Czechs are likely to resume power on a reform platform. On the other hand, the growing strength of Hungarian and Romanian disagreement over the Hungarian minority in Romania erodes the unity of the Warsaw Pact while increasing pressure on the Ceaucescu regime.

At the core of anti-Sovietism is the anti-Russian attitude of these powerful national groups. Thus these countries will continue their struggle to be different from, if not fully independent of, the Soviet Union.

The United States can continue through radio broadcasts, information and exchange programs, and research and scholarship to satisfy the thirst of these ethnic groups for support and greater knowledge about themselves. We cannot and should not, however, seek to exploit ethnic differences per se—through promoting division either within Czechoslovakia or between Romania and Hungary. The recent excesses of Bulgarian repression of the Turkish minorities are all too revealing of the dangers inherent in inflaming age-old animosities.

The Warsaw Pact nations most important to Moscow (and to the West) are Poland, East Germany and Czechoslovakia. They represent the bulk of East Europe's population, industrial might and armed forces. The direction these nations take over the next decade and the type of crises they experience are likely to have a profound effect on East-West relations. Yet Western policies, under the "differentiation policy" have favored Hungary and Romania during the past ten years because of the opportunities and models they present. The American differentiation policy is based on the carrot and stick principal. Give carrots (MFN and political contacts) to countries that adopt reforms or conduct foreign policies somewhat independent of the Soviet Union, or sticks (deprivation of trade and political contacts) to those countries that slavishly follow the Soviets.

We should adopt policies which allow us to turn our attention and energies to these three most important Warsaw Pact members and seek to influence their policies. The United States should compete more creatively and energetically to encourage the different nationalist instincts of the G.D.R., Poland and Czechoslovakia.

There is a prominent notion that America's interest in encouraging Soviet restraint in Eastern Europe can best be served by reassuring Moscow that Western objectives are limited. According to this view, if the West actively promotes the independent behavior of the nations of Eastern Europe, it will increase Soviet insecurity and reduce the chances that Moscow will improve the opportunities for those nations to seek their own national identity. Even if American leaders believed that they could strike a deal with Gorbachev to permit increased flexibility in Eastern Europe in exchange for restrained American activity in the region, such a policy would be completely unacceptable in this democratic society. The American public would view such a strategy as a cynical betrayal.

The United States should maintain its policies of encouraging the national identity and diversity of all the nations of Eastern Europe through periods of U.S.-Soviet tension and *detente*. It is particularly important for the United States not to lose interest in promoting expanded contacts at top and middle levels in Eastern European regimes during periods of *detente*. American policy should not become merely a response to Soviet policy in the region. Our policy toward each nation of Eastern Europe should have its own dynamics, its own energy, and its own consistency.

The Changing Environment in Europe

The American leadership role in NATO has been a cornerstone of U.S. foreign policy since the founding of the Western Alliance. Until a decade ago, the American President was the political, economic, and military leader of the Alliance. Since the Carter and Reagan presidencies, however, this traditional role has been eroded. This has taken place not only because of the weakness of the Carter presidency and the bombast and unilateralism of the Reagan presidency but also because of trade imbalances, currency and financial issues, and decision making on weapons deployment and arms control. Moreover, the close rapport between President Reagan and Prime Minister Thatcher has not made it any easier for the U.S. to deal with Germany and France on Alliance matters.

In the next several years we are likely to see increasing strains in the Alliance because trade and economic issues appear certain to produce further decline in the U.S. dollar, American inflation, expanded U.S. exports and damage to trade relations with Europe and Japan. Moreover, the imaginative proposals of the first attractive Soviet leader in the post war era have produced a new, more confusing psychological environment in Western Europe.

There are several aspects of this changing environment that American policymakers should bear in mind:

- It is likely that during the next few years the German question will reemerge as a central issue for those who yearn for a more unified Europe. The European relationship that is central to a strong Alliance and to the German question is a closer political and even military relationship between France and the Federal Republic of Germany. A role for Germany and France as the European pillar of NATO makes sense for the United States and the Alliance. The United Kingdom cannot be the central player and the United States should encourage a French/German accord to deal with a new dynamic in Central Europe.

- A unilateral reduction of American forces in Europe for economic or political reasons that fails to achieve a comparable Soviet withdrawal would be the worst case, both politically and militarily, for the Alliance.
- We should discuss with our allies a common view of the future of Central Europe. In recent decades there has been a failure of the NATO military doctrine to keep pace with the political realities of a changing Europe. We should develop an understanding with our NATO allies about Central Europe which would take into consideration a lessened role for the military in the two blocs and would look ahead to a much greater political and human interchange across an eroding "iron curtain." We should not only propose the destruction of the Berlin wall but also negotiations— for example which would lead eventually to a neutral Hungary— a neutrality guaranteed by both East and West and achieved over a period of ten or fifteen years, calling for U.S.-Soviet collaboration like that achieved with the Austrian State Treaty.

The United States will need a more energetic, imaginative and focused diplomatic approach to Europe in order to avoid the crises and seize the opportunities that will be the result of this new Soviet leadership. The Soviet Union now appears ready to discuss many of the most sensitive issues of the postwar era. This will confuse and divide both Europes. The United States now has choices: we can turn this opportunity to the West's advantage and achieve some of the dreams of the Helsinki Final Act or we can cling to old patterns, ignore Gorbachev's overtures, underestimate the changing dynamics in Eastern Europe and find American interest in disarray.

U.S.-Soviet Relations and the Third World

The most uncertain factor in Soviet-American relations is the rivalry in the Third World and the potential for confrontation of the superpowers in regional conflicts. It is impossible to predict how the changes of the Gorbachev era will affect that rivalry which has promoted such hostility during the past twenty-five years. If the Soviets and the Americans can establish mutual restraints and even cooperation, the prospects for the bilateral relations are good. The most optimistic forecasts are based on Gorbachev's discussions of "interdependence" and "collective security" in such statements as his September 17, 1987 *Pravda* article in which he suggests that the Kremlin's foreign policy will be seeking to engage the international community, and specifically the United Nations and its peacekeeping efforts, more constructively than ever before.

Since taking office Gorbachev has de-emphasized the Third World; his advisors hint that part of the new thinking will involve a reassessment of costly involvements. Yet there has not been any practical change except for the Soviet important commitment to pay nearly $250 million in arrears to the United Nations. Gorbachev has focused on both domestic reforms and East-West relations and speaks little of the Third World adventures of his predecessors. He inherits, however, a wide range of political, military and economic commitments throughout the world that reflect the global vocation of Soviet power. To Americans Gorbachev is the heir to the distrust from a decade of mounting Soviet efforts to gain advantage through Third World competition.

The Background of the Rivalry

The principal source of tension in Soviet-American relations in the 1970s and 1980s resulted from growing Soviet activity in areas outside Europe. While the tensions of the 1950s and early 1960s were primarily in Europe, especially Berlin and the "iron curtain," by the mid 1960s Cuba and then Vietnam came to dominate the relationship.

The intensifying Soviet-Cuban military partnership in Africa, particularly in Angola and Ethiopia, the Soviet supported Vietnamese occupation of Cambodia, and finally the Soviet invasion of Afghanistan have all resulted in creating in the 1980s the most hostile environment for Soviet-American relations in 20 years. What made the latter part of the Brezhnev era more disturbing than the era of the 1950s and 1960s was the rising tide of Soviet strategic and conventional arms, the growing willingness of the Soviets to use force beyond the periphery of the U.S.S.R. and the military security orientation of the Brezhnev leadership. The Soviets seemed to be seeking to achieve through expanded military presence in the Third World a parity with the United States in political power that would match the parity in the military sphere.

The American reaction in the early 1980s to the Soviets' Third World adventures was to reexamine the assumptions that had led six earlier Presidents to seek a relaxation of tensions with the Soviet Union. In the post Vietnam war era, could the United States continue to seek bilateral agreements with the Soviets to reduce the risk of nuclear war, without appearing implicitly to acquiesce in the Soviet military encroachment in the Third World, including, most disturbingly, the civil wars in Central America? Into this environment came Ronald Reagan with his particularly virulent anti-Communist rhetoric. Americans were ready for his more aggressive tone. Even though many Americans were prepared to acknowledge that their country's foreign policy was part of the Third World problem, few would deny that Brezhnev, with whom Nixon had entered into *detente* in the 1970s, had broken his vows of restraint.

The Reagan Doctrine became the practical application of the Reagan rhetoric. It carried a covert response to the Third World, particularly to Central America, Central Africa, Afghanistan and Southeast Asia. The Carter Administration in its last year began some of the covert activities in Afghanistan. But the Reagan administration returned to a major American commitment to covert or surrogate military efforts against Soviet surrogates—or, as in Afghanistan, against Soviet troops—since the days of containment, which led to the Kennedy "counter-insurgency" programs and ultimately the Vietnam war. That the U.S. support for the "contras," the Muhajadeen, and Savimbi and for the counter-insurgency in Central America helped reverse or "contain" Soviet adventurism is clear. It is also clear that this full-scale commitment to covert actions once again distorted and corrupted the American national security process and establishment. Moreover, once the United States became so openly involved in covert actions in this series of insurgencies, we were unable to phase out our support without risking the lives of thousands of insurgents, without discrediting our country and giving the Soviet Union our encouragement. Clearly, the next administration will have to establish far better oversight over our support for insurgency and the U.S. national security process. It will also have to develop strategies for disengaging our policies from the excesses of the Reagan Doctrine. The attitudes and policies of Gorbachev's new team could have an important impact on the pace and nature of any change in the policies of the Reagan doctrine by the next Administration.

It is unlikely that Gorbachev will significantly reduce Soviet involvement around the world. The Soviets involved themselves in Asia, Africa, and Latin America for several important reasons which Gorbachev has not changed:

• Support for radical and revolutionary regimes (Cuba, Vietnam, Ethiopia, Nicaragua, Angola, et al.) is a vital part of the Soviet world view. Soviet military and economic assistance to Nicaragua, for example, has increased in the past year. While Gorbachev has been in office Mengistu established the single Marxist-Leninist party in Ethiopia, similar to that in Cuba, and Soviet support there continues to grow. There is no diminution of Soviet support for Vietnam or Cuba because both countries are vital allies and military outposts. Gorbachev may press them to moderate and to reform, but it is a question of whether he will use his leverage to do so.

• The Soviet and Cuban ideological debate about the appropriate levels and timing of support for national liberation movements will continue. Historically the Soviets have been cautious about direct support for national liberation except for the period from 1975 to the recent past when Castro encouraged the Brezhnev leadership to be more adventurous in this area. Gorbachev may choose to be more cautious either until another leader emerges, or until another opportunity arises in Africa or in a key nation such as the Philippines. Ideology and opportunism are still a major part of political reality in the Kremlin.

• The security of the Soviet Union and of its borders is an overriding obsession of Soviet leaders. Whether they can disengage from Afghanistan is an important question. The Afghanistan experience has clearly been a sobering one to the Soviet political and military establishments. The Soviets may eventually strike a deal to significantly decrease their forces. Nonetheless, one can never rule out a decision by the Soviet Union to use military force across its border if it perceives either a threat or an opportunity.

The Soviet Union has an empire rather than an alliance. This too may change under Gorbachev. Until now, the Soviets' principal means of relating to other nations outside their bloc has been through military assistance and political and security ties. There are a few important exceptions such as their relations with India, Argentina, and Mexico where distinct historic and geopolitical circumstances have resulted in a more normal range of political, economic, and cultural relations. Gorbachev's more subtle approach and his expressed belief in the "interdependence" of nations may gradually, over several years, change the peculiar military nature of Soviet ties to the other nations and bring about more normal relations with some.

Another factor that may limit the potential for Soviet-American conflict in the Third World is the fact that most of the turbulent areas are now spoken for. Virtually all of the spaces on the global monopoly board are taken by other players. The rise of so many other players and the relative decline of American and Soviet power may inevitably reduce the scope of the combat arena.

Managing The Rivalry

The United States and the Soviet Union should not try to manage the rivalry in the Third World or in regional conflicts through general agreements on "rules of conduct." The future of the rivalry will depend on three developments.

First, mutual self-restraint, which has grown out of the world realities of today and out of such experiences as Vietnam and Afghanistan, should govern the policies of both superpowers more in the future than in the past.

Second, since the Soviet-American rivalry in the Third World will continue to be a source of tension, it should be considered as important an item on the agenda as arms control, and be dealt with through regular negotiations as is arms control. We should seek with Gorbachev and his successors specific agreements to reduce the potential for conflict in areas throughout the world.

Third, we should maintain a continuing commitment to *selective* covert or surrogate insurgency against Soviet-supported national liberation efforts. Our efforts should not be trumpeted, nor carried on as a crusade. Moreover, this commitment must be carefully supervised by an experienced team with the full knowledge of the Congressional Intelligence Committees to assure adequate oversight. Following the excesses of the Reagan Doctrine, it would be a mistake if the next President declared that the United States will no longer be involved in such activity.

It will not be enough for the Administration to conclude that since Gorbachev expresses the view that the Soviet Union has accorded low priority to the Third World that regional conflicts will no longer be of major concern to American foreign policy. Soviet presence around the world, combined with the inertia of Soviet ideology, leadership and policy suggest that a confrontation with the United States in the Third World is likely within the next five years. Therefore, the only reasonable course open to a new President is to establish a priority with the Soviet leadership to work on an agenda for understanding, discussing, and managing the rivalry in the Third World.

Ultimately our success in the rivalry in the Third World and in the peaceful resolution of regional conflicts will depend on the constructive role the United States plays in the world. An America that is an active trading partner, major lender, and a major provider of technology, education, and good will in the Third World is likely to have much greater influence than an America obsessed with its Soviet rival. Therefore, while never underestimating the dangers of Soviet opportunism to U.S. interests, a strong American diplomatic, political and economic presence is the best way for the United States to relate to the Third World—and to the Soviet Union.

13

East-West Relations

William G. Hyland

There has never been much debate about the importance of East-West relations in American foreign policy. The dispute has largely centered on what posture the United States should adopt toward the Soviet Union (e.g., containment, liberation) and how to conduct specific policies (trade, arms control). Periodically, there have also been debates about the interpretation of the domestic situation within the Soviet Union, especially when new leaders have taken power. With the arrival of Mikhail Gorbachev this issue has become the subject of a lively debate.

Before the emergence of Gorbachev in March, 1985, there was extensive speculation about East-West relations in the aftermath of the Soviet invasion of Afghanistan in 1979. Clearly, *détente* was at an end, but there were major uncertainties over what would follow. Many feared that there would be a new series of Soviet-American confrontations, the breakdown of arms control, and an intensification of strategic arms competition. In the early 1980s American policy seemed geared to these concerns.

Contrary to these apprehensions, however, Soviet policy in this period seemed increasingly constrained. Moscow was more or less passive in a series of regional crises: the Falklands, Lebanon, the Iran-Iraq war. Moreover, the Soviets were unable to block the deployment of American missiles in Europe in late 1983. And by late 1984 rather than confronting the Reagan Administration, Moscow was seeking to negotiate with it, and to do so on a traditional agenda with arms control at the top. It is worth noting that this turnabout in 1984–85 preceded Gorbachev.

The Gorbachev Dimension

Soviet policy in 1984–85 was constrained because the leadership crisis had been prolonged. It was almost four years between the final year of Brezhnev's tenure and Gorbachev's accession to office. In addition to the problem of leadership succession, this period was marked by at least two major crises: in Afghanistan the war escalated and in Poland the very essence of communist power—the party's supremacy—was challenged. Moreover, Soviet economic troubles worsened, and Soviet society seemed to be suffering from a growing malaise.

This combination of factors led the West to assume that by the mid-1980s Gorbachev would probably have to pursue a conciliatory foreign policy to buy time to concentrate on his internal problems. After taking office, he suggested as much himself in various public statements and interviews. The reorganization of his foreign policy and national security apparatus suggested that he would conduct a more sophisticated policy than his predecessors. That there was indeed a certain new flexibility in the Kremlin was confirmed by an increased relaxation of several Soviet positions: toward China, Japan, Western Europe, Israel, and, eventually, even toward the United States. Much of the change was only stylistic. But some observers detected in the "new thinking" the seeds of more significant changes, especially about the nature of East-West security, as well as the extent of Soviet involvement in the Third World.

At the beginning of 1988, Gorbachev is pursuing a basically defensive strategy, rather than the aggressive one as feared in 1980, but his tactics include a number of innovations and initiatives. First, he wants to reduce the "encirclement" of the Soviet Union by lessening tensions with the areas on its periphery, especially China and Japan. Unlike his predecessors, he is prepared to make some concessions in dealing with both countries, including a reduction in the military dimensions of the conflict with China. Some withdrawal of Soviet troops along the border is one area of Soviet concessions.

Second, he has apparently concluded that the quest for a genuine strategic superiority over the United States has become fruitless and, consequently, he will settle for a prolonged strategic stalemate with the United States. But in the process Gorbachev must be able to guarantee his comrades that the United States accepts the same assumptions; and this leads him to view arms control agreements as the main vehicle for codifying mutual assumptions about security and the nuclear relationship. In addition, Gorbachev assumes that in the process of working out a new superpower relationship he can cause or encourage the retraction of the American presence in Europe, and perhaps in the Far East as well. Here, too, he will consider many concessions (e.g., the zero option, eliminating all or almost all of the SS-20s from the Soviet force).

Finally, under Gorbachev the Soviet Union is likely to be more prudent in the risks and responsibilities it undertakes in the Third World. This reflects a new and more cold-blooded evaluation of the prospects for the Soviet Union, but it also suggests that Gorbachev does not accept the proposition that the contest with the West can be decided in the Third World, and the effort to gain a clear victory is too burdensome for the potential gains.

Gorbachev seems to recognize that the Soviet Union's global position has weakened. The Soviet state now is forced to play the role more of a conventional world power than of a superpower. It no longer leads a revolution, it can no longer offer ideological inspiration to the world, nor can it any longer pose as the model for economic development.

It is still the master of a European empire, but an empire that is decaying from the corrosive effects of diversity and democracy. The champions of a universalist doctrine have been poor imperialists— precisely because the empire has found the doctrine wanting. The British had the wit to replace the empire with the idea of the commonwealth. The Soviets have created only the threat of intervention. The rise of Solidarity in Poland was a watershed for the Soviet empire; its further decline is only a matter of time. In this sense the lands behind the old iron curtain have become the new sick man of Europe, and the area where the danger of a future war may be greatest.

Of course, it is possible to see in all of this nothing more than shifts in tactics. It can even be argued that the wily old Gromyko would have arrived at similar conclusions about the position of the Soviet Union, but without resorting to Gorbachev's rhetoric. A more persuasive analysis, however, is that Gorbachev views foreign policy in much the same way he sees his domestic situation. That is, he still believes in the underlying system, but he recognizes that radical changes are in order: to achieve the rebuilding of Soviet power, he is willing to pay a price in the near term to achieve longer-term goals. Thus, the innovative elements in Soviet foreign policies will outweigh the elements of continuity.

In sum, the accession of Mikhail Gorbachev to the leadership of the Soviet Party marks the beginning of a new historical period. The transition from Brezhnev to Gorbachev is a genuine change in generations. Gorbachev is the first post-revolutionary leader; he was born fourteen years after the October Revolution. Indeed, he is a postwar leader. He was only ten at the time of Hitler's invasion of Russia. But as both the product and heir of a huge bureaucratic system, Gorbachev's freedom of action is limited. The Soviet system can be changed and reformed, but neither radically, drastically, or quickly. Yet the domestic crisis in the Soviet Union cries out for just that—radical and urgent changes.

This is Gorbachev's dilemma. His only hope of pulling the Soviet Union out of the stagnation of the Brezhnev era is to strike hard at the system and continue the pressures for change. This is producing opposition at all levels, even in the Politburo; thus his strategy means that he is risking his political survival. He has even acknowledged this, but he is likely to persist with his reform program. At some point, probably by the early 1990s, he may well face an internal crisis. If he prevails, he may profoundly change the Soviet Union; if he fails, he may lose power. If he senses that he will fail, a period will follow that could be dangerous for the United States; in either event the temptation to attempt foreign adventures to compensate for domestic failures may prove as irresistible as it has in the past to Soviet leaders. This was the pattern of Khrushchev: when faced with internal opposition he sought a foreign victory in Cuba.

The accumulation of internal and external pressures on Moscow has led many observers to proclaim the "historical decline" of the Soviet Union and to speculate that the present period is not merely a passing phase but the beginning of a long-term trend.

This is surely debatable—and probably wrong. After two hundred years of the growth of Russian power, it is highly unlikely that it has begun to decline because of a decade of adversity. It was only a few years ago that there were equally confident predictions of a new era of Soviet expansion. Even if the Soviet Union has entered what historians will later identify as the beginning of a long-term decline, it will be a matter of many decades, perhaps fifty years, before it is fully evident.

This does not mean that the internal crisis and the crisis of empire are not serious. Indeed, if the Soviet leaders themselves become convinced that they are entering a period of decline, it may be the beginning of a dangerous period for the West.

The Soviet Union will not simply acquiesce in the disintegration of its position of power. Gorbachev was not elected to preside over the dismantling of the Soviet empire. Quite the contrary: many observers already detect a revival of Russian nationalism, one which also poses dangers for the countries on the periphery of the Soviet state; a nationalistic policy might seek greater influence, indeed even physical domination.

Although the position of the Soviet Union has weakened, its revival under Gorbachev is quite possible, though probably not in the near term. In any case, Gorbachev will give priority to domestic policy and his clear preference is simply to buy time in foreign policy. *Thus, the overall combination of circumstances suggests that it is a time of unusual opportunity for American policy to explore a more constructive yet durable relation with the Soviet Union.*

The Reagan Dimension

The beginning of the Gorbachev regime coincided with the high tide of the Reagan Administration. By 1984–85, much of the original Reagan program had been achieved: the Soviets had been brought back to the negotiating table under conditions favorable to the United States. The Administration claimed that it could engage in East-West diplomacy from a position of strength. In this light, the Geneva summit meeting of November, 1985 was considered a Reagan success. Moreover, the Administration had fundamentally altered the arms control debate from bargaining for another SALT agreement to achieving a new balance of offense and defense—a "defensive transition" that would shift the American strategic posture more toward reliance on strategic defense. In addition, the Reagan Doctrine, or its general concept, had finally gained support for the freedom fighters in Afghanistan, the repeal of the Clark Amendment restricting American support to Angolan rebels and—temporarily—the funding for the contras in Nicaragua.

Then, the Administration's fortunes began to turn. The President suffered a foreign policy defeat when the Congress, in a strong vote, overrode his veto of American sanctions against South Africa. The second summit in Reykjavik was a dismal failure that provoked questions about the ability of the President and his team to conduct high-level diplomacy. The midterm elections were also a setback for the Administration; the shift of control of the Senate emphasized the President's lame-duck status and foreshadowed new struggles over foreign and domestic policies. Finally, there was the Iran arms scandal that badly damaged both the President and his Administration. After six years, the Administration faced debates over almost every major aspect of American policy as the political spotlight shifted to the 1988 campaign.

Ironically, East-West relations have emerged as the most likely source of progress. It had seemed, after the Geneva summit, that relations were beginning to return to the norms of the 1970s. But relations did not take a turn for the better. The deadlock that had been implicit in the two sides' arms control positions was made explicit at Reykjavik. What had appeared to be a strategic opportunity for a breakthrough suddenly looked far less promising.

For a time after Reykjavik it was not clear to what extent the earlier assumption about the aims of Gorbachev's policies still held. Before

Reykjavik the conventional analysis was that Gorbachev still needed a pause to consolidate his internal policies; thus Washington anticipated that he would seek an accommodation with the United States. After Reykjavik it was possible that the Kremlin would decide to outwait the Reagan Administration. But then in February Gorbachev took the initiative to revive arms control. And by mid-1987 it appeared that the near-term prospects for Soviet-American relations would be determined by the arms control negotiations, which once again have become the dominant issue between the superpowers.

Whatever the outcome of the third Gorbachev-Reagan round of summitry, it is important to note that the struggle between the two superpowers has been changing—quite significantly so—since the Afghan invasion. The changes have affected the nuclear as well as the political relationship.

The Nuclear Dimension

The danger of war has, in fact, diminished since the early days of the cold war. Never has such a broad and deep struggle lasted so long without a major war, and more than forty years of peace have accustomed most Americans to the idea that a general war is simply unthinkable and, indeed, virtually impossible: the mere existence of nuclear weapons appears to guarantee that they will never be used. Moreover, the global balance of forces works against war between the United States and the Soviet Union. The collapse of the Sino-Soviet alliance has fundamentally altered the strategic position of the Soviet Union. All of the major powers are aligned against the USSR. Moscow is confronted by the probability of a two- if not a three-front war. The Soviet leaders can no longer expect that the outcome of a major war could somehow be advantageous, and this is reflected in adjustments in Soviet doctrine.

Peace is by no means guaranteed, but it seems more likely to endure now than twenty or thirty years ago when there were frequent Soviet-American crises.

Nevertheless, both sides have moved toward making offensive nuclear weapons technologically more usable while vociferously denying any such intention. As a result, technology is outstripping the ability of diplomacy to ensure strategic stability. At the time of the Cuban missile crisis, both sides had a few dozen strategic missiles capable of reaching the other's homeland. The accuracy and reliability of these small systems was far from certain. Ten years later the strategic arsenals had increased at least ten times. After another decade that number of weapons had more than doubled. President Kennedy feared nuclear annihilation in 1962, when Khrushchev clandestinely emplaced 60 missiles in Cuba. Now, six Soviet intercontinental ballistic missiles (ICBMs) carry roughly the same number of warheads.

Numbers of weapons are not in themselves strategically decisive. But the growth in arsenals cannot be summarily dismissed. Large quantities of weapons do affect the psychological and political climate. Both sides tend to see an increase in numbers of weapons not as an effort to reach or maintain a balance, but to gain an advantage. This preoccupation with numbers of weapons—reflected in the near-obsession with reductions in arms control agreements—obscures other, more ominous, developments. For example, nuclear weapons systems are becoming smaller and easier to move and conceal. With the advent of this so-called "stealth" technology, weapons will become more and more difficult to defend against. Innovative technologies, such as lasers, offer new possibilities for both offense and defense.

The ability to control weapons technology through negotiated agreements will probably diminish. Consider one case: the United States is contemplating developing a small, mobile ICBM (the Midgetman); its rationale is that it would be difficult for Soviet forces to locate and attack, and thus would reinforce deterrence. But arms control theory argues that mobile missiles should be banned because their concealable illegal existence, especially in small numbers, probably could not be verified under an arms control agreement, and this would offer a strategic incentive for cheating, even though the cheating might not yield a strategic advantage.

Dilemmas of this kind are bound to multiply. The next generation of nuclear weapons may well be "dual" purpose: they could be armed with either a conventional warhead or a nuclear one. The proliferation of small weapons could mean the practical end to verifiable arms control, at least as it has been conceived over the past decades. To limit, reduce, ban or otherwise control new weapons may well require intrusive inspections and a high degree of cooperation that can only be the product of a significant improvement in political relations.

Most important, strategic defense has returned, after years in the wilderness. Just as it seemed that strategic offensive weapons were invincible, President Reagan began to lay claim to the technological revolution in the name of defending the entire United States. If ever there was a modern genie it is the Strategic Defense Initiative (SDI); it is not likely to be returned to its bottle. With SDI, President Reagan touched the same nerve as the advocates of a nuclear freeze. His rationale was that long-term reliance on nuclear retaliation as the insurance against war was simply not safe enough. In his epigram that it is better to defend than avenge, the President also raised the moral issue of offensive retaliation as a national policy. And he drew instant and strong popular backing for shifting to defense.

Indeed, the morality of nuclear deterrence has come under a broad new assault. The American churches have raised extremely complex philosophical questions: could the use of nuclear weapons in any circumstances ever be considered "just," or is the strategy of threatening the use of nuclear weapons immoral *per se*? In particular, the NATO strategy of threatening to use nuclear weapons first in a European war has also been attacked, not only for its immorality, but for its lack of strategic credibility. Some groups of scientists have added to the growing alarm and resulting confusion, claiming that under certain conditions the entire human race might be extinguished by a "nuclear winter."

In short, an explosive coalition of divergent strategic, moral and political forces has been formed, arrayed against the *status quo*. The old nuclear consensus has been collapsing. And what will replace it no one can say.

Nuclear war, however, is not an abstract exercise. Changes in weaponry or in attitudes toward the weapons will affect strategic and tactical calculations, but even though nuclear weapons have revolutionized warfare, they have not suspended all of the laws of history. Nations still fight for causes, however mistakenly or ill defined. The causes of war are still rooted in conflicts of interests.

The British historian Michael Howard has speculated that if there is a nuclear war, a future historian would explain it by writing that the Soviet Union grew in power and the United States feared it. He had in mind the British analogy: in the late 19th century Britain was confronted by the rise of German sea power; London abandoned its splendid isolation as well as its freedom of action in favor of coalitions to block the Kaiser's ambitions.

In some respects the United States finds itself in the same position. Washington abandoned its hostility toward China in the name of an anti-Soviet coalition. It has adhered to an increasingly unconvincing strategy of threatening nuclear escalation in Europe in the name of preserving its anti-Soviet Atlantic alliance. It has repeatedly intervened in distant regions to thwart Soviet expansion, and, under the Reagan Doctrine, to reverse it. Surrendering one's freedom of action, of course, is a classic recipe for war. Indeed, there is a widespread belief among strategists and statesmen that a Soviet-American war as a consequence of a deliberate choice is a very marginal possibility. But war through "inadvertence" is still possible. The specter of Pearl Harbor has been replaced by that of Sarajevo.

The Political Dimension

The characteristics of the geopolitical conflict have also changed. There is little left of the ideological crusade of the early American policy of containment. The conflict has increasingly taken on the character of a struggle for power and influence along more traditional lines. Ideological conflicts brook no compromises, while power and interests are negotiable commodities: they can be limited in mutually acceptable ways. This is the essence of international politics. The change from an ideological struggle to a conflict of interests explains much about the recent history of Soviet-American relations—why clashes can arise even in sensitive areas, without automatically producing an East-West confrontation.

During the particularly bad period of superpower relations (1980–1985), both sides carefully avoided turning a number of regional conflicts and small wars into a confrontation. The British navy sailed unobstructed to fight in the Falklands; the United States put small American military contingents twice into Lebanon, without a Soviet reaction. Iran and Iraq are engaged in a seemingly endless war, and the United States and the Soviet Union have both supported Iraq. The United States invaded Grenada, overthrew a tinpot Leninist, and shot up Libya, all without so much as a hint of a clash between the United States and the Soviet Union. Some analysts concluded that the superpower rivalry was, in fact, moderating. In the 1970s the limits of *détente* had been defined; in the 1980s the limits of confrontation were defined. Within these boundaries, the two superpowers could coexist. This period thus provides some grounds for reassurance.

Moreover, there is some evidence that the Soviets have become increasingly dissatisfied with the burden of their imperial missions. They seem to be disenchanted with their weaker clients in the Third World, and reluctant to undertake new commitments (e.g., Libya). This attitude could be explained by the unfavorable circumstances of the mid-1980s, and a belief in Moscow that a period of consolidation is required before a new advance.

Some observers, however, believe that more fundamental changes are involved. Thus, Soviet behavior may reflect a basic post-Brezhnev reassessment of policy toward the Third World that has resulted in a more wary approach, and one that is more sensitive to the impact of Soviet behavior on the central relationship with the United States. (See Francis Fukuyama, "Gorbachev and the Third World," *Foreign Affairs,* Spring 1986.)

The nature of the contest in the Third World has also changed. There has always been a tendency to see the various clashes as gains and losses for East or West, and to consider the changes as more or less permanent ones. In the past ten years, however, new issues such as terrorism have arisen that impinge on state relations (e.g., Libya and Syria) but are not clearly East-West conflicts. Countries have adopted positions that defy the old categories: Zimbabwe and Mozambique are neither East nor West, nor truly nonaligned. Iran, a strong point of American influence, has become a new arena of competition between the superpowers; the Gulf remains a critical area for both the United States and the Soviet Union, but the region has become much more volatile. Muslim religious factors are also new, and seem to be as important in the Middle East, if not more important, as East-West factors. Other American strong points—the Philippines and South Korea—could become points of vulnerability. Central America is already a new theater between the Soviet Union and the United States, and South Africa could become one, even though the conflict in South Africa is racial, rather than East versus West.

In sum, the situation in the Third World at the close of the 1980s is much more complex: there is still the potential for sharp and dangerous East-West conflicts; but such clashes seem less likely than in the decades of the 1960s and 1970s.

Another new factor in the Third World is the emergence of the Reagan Doctrine. It postulates a broad resistance to Soviet encroachments. While proclaiming a universal right of intervention, the actual American role varies greatly. Much of the American effort in Angola, Afghanistan, and Cambodia is limited, and seems without much prospect for extending it. In Nicaragua there seems to be a firm commitment by the Reagan Administration but one not supported by the Congress. Even in this case there is no clearly defined United States goal.

The United States seems to have adopted a policy of selective containment, at the very time when the USSR may be adopting a policy of selective commitment. And therein may lie the chance for some moderation of the contest.

No settlements are likely at this stage. But for the first time since *détente,* the two superpowers seem to be carefully testing the possibility of a new relationship in the Third World. It could turn out to be only an interlude before another serious clash, but it could also be the beginning of a process of defining less ambitious objectives, and even setting some ground rules of conduct: the Soviet Union and the United States might agree—tacitly or through negotiations—on the containment of specific Third World conflicts (i.e., Afghanistan or Nicaragua) to prevent them from spreading. And, second, they might agree on a set of more formal procedures for consultations to head off new conflicts.

Prospects

We are now entering the fourth major period in which some progress toward settling our conflict with the Soviet Union is possible. Since the war there have been three moments for such progress: after Stalin died in 1953, after the Cuban missile crisis in 1962–1963, and during the period of *détente*, 1969–1972. Each period has yielded some progress, and consequently the conflict has become less volatile. But each period has ended in failure. It is this inability to stabilize the relationship that is dangerous and that challenges the current American and Soviet leadership.

In retrospect, it is surprising how little has been demanded of the Soviet Union. In 1955, Eisenhower settled for an improvement in the atmosphere and the withdrawal of Soviet troops from Austria. After the Cuban crisis Kennedy and Johnson let Khrushchev escape with only a small penance. Khrushchev feared he would be asked for major concessions in Europe, and he even offered a partial payment by offering to negotiate a non-aggression pact. Rather than recognizing this as a sign of weakness, if not desperation, Washington treated it as propaganda. Thus, Khrushchev was never really tested. Within a year he was gone, along with John Kennedy, and East-West diplomacy ground down to the pedestrian projects of the mid-1960s. The bankruptcy of the West was confirmed in 1968, when once again the Soviet Union was able to invade Eastern Europe with impunity. The heaviest punishment the NATO powers chose to impose was a diplomatic freeze. By April 1969, when NATO celebrated its 20th anniversary in Washington, most of those who attended pleaded with Nixon to resume East-West contacts.

There was one enduring characteristic of this period that has grown in significance: the belief that there could be arms control agreements between East and West. This was Kennedy's major contribution. His speech at the American University in April, 1963 was the first flickering of *détente*. The practical result—a ban on nuclear testing in the atmosphere—was not all that significant. By 1963 public opinion would not have tolerated much more atomic testing in the atmosphere. The major accomplishment was not only stopping tests, but initiating the strategic arms control process: formal negotiations, complex provisions, adequate verification, a solemn treaty duly ratified, and promise of more to come. It was a halting start, but nonetheless a start.

The *détente* of the 1970s extended the relationship much further. In Europe the division of Germany and of the continent, implicitly agreed upon in 1955–56, was formalized in 1970–75; not in the name of the *status quo*, but, in the West, in the name of a new pan-Europeanism. In strategic arms control, the implications of the Kennedy period were codified in the first SALT agreement and the ABM treaty. Both sides accepted vulnerability to a strategic attack, but justified it in the name of an improvement in political relations based on American recognition of the Soviet Union as a strategic equal. In the end these agreements also proved to be only partial settlements, though it was a far more significant period than the brief episodes of 1953 and 1963.

American freedom of action has been rather narrowly contained, given the responsibilities of the United States as a world leader. There have been brief periods when Washington could have been more assertive or more accommodating. And there is no doubt that domestic policies have influenced the attitudes of different administrations toward the Soviet Union. But politics has worked to move policy more toward the center than toward the extremes. On the whole, however, the United States has made the right decisions at the right times. The Marshall Plan, the Truman Doctrine, the creation of NATO, the Cuban confrontation, the opening to China, were assuredly the right choices. So too were the periodic efforts from Truman to Reagan to explore a more constructive relationship with the Soviet Union. By and large it has been the Soviet Union that has thwarted these efforts, and not misguided American policy as is too often charged in revisionist history.

Yet that is no particular comfort in present circumstances. The United States now must deal with current realities, not the record of the past.

American Objectives

Gorbachev is a complicating factor. There is a strong temptation in the United States to "help" him because he presents himself as a liberal reformer—which in fact he may well be. Moreover a good case can be made, as Andrei Sakharov does, that Gorbachev may be the last best hope, lest a far more ruthless regime take over. But this cannot be a basis for Western policy. Gorbachev may be in power for a year, or for decades. He may abandon his reforms and become another Brezhnev or, like Khrushchev, may challenge the West dangerously as his domestic position weakens. What the West needs in order to survive these potential twists and turns is a general strategy that recognizes there are indeed domestic changes underway, but one that tempers that recognition with a hardheaded assertion of Western security requirements. We should help Gorbachev, but only if we thereby help ourselves.

There is a persistent view in the United States that contends that the most effective American strategy is to apply increasing pressure on the Soviet Union. The theory is intriguing. It holds that if faced with external containment and defeats, the Soviet Union will turn inward; the regime will then have to change and it will liberalize internally and become a legitimate partner for negotiations and even an accommodation. This is an enormous gamble for which there is virtually no supporting evidence. Historically, the Soviets, and the Russians as well, have retreated when confronted by adversity abroad; they have compromised, and have even made concessions; occasionally they have reformed, but they have always returned to the fray.

On the other hand, some argue that given the inexorable changes in Soviet society and, therefore, in the nature of Soviet-American relations, the conflict may well begin to wither. If so, perhaps the United States could simply afford to await the inevitable.

There is little historical precedent to suggest that a conflict of the scope and depth of the struggle between the United States and the Soviet Union will fade away. Occasionally such conflicts have been transcended, as new threats have arisen. England and France fought for hundreds of years, only to join in an alliance in two wars against Germany. The only prospect for such a transformation of the Soviet-American rivalry would seem to be the rise of an Asiatic power center arrayed against the occidental world. There has been periodic speculation along this line in the Soviet Union. Both Brezhnev and Solzhenitsyn seemed to have arrived at the same conclusion: that China was the main danger to Russia; some in the United States muse over the dangers of a Sino-Japanese axis. There may be something to this speculation, but it is too fanciful a basis for practical policy.

Moreover, American policy-makers cannot risk waiting for history to transform the conflict with the Soviet Union. In the nuclear era, the United States has to try to make some progress toward a settlement, if only a partial one. This has meant a greater reliance on politics and diplomacy, and diplomacy that goes beyond the prevailing obsession with arms control.

The first objective for American policy, therefore, is to create the circumstances that will make it difficult for the Soviet Union to resume the offensive if and when Gorbachev or his successors have rebuilt Soviet power. In the near term, this approach rests on the assumption that Gorbachev still wants a "breather" in world affairs. But the United States clearly understands his purposes; he wants to gain time to "reconstruct" Soviet power in all its dimensions. It is the task of

Western strategy to make him pay a price for this interlude—a price in strategic stability and in the settlement of regional conflicts.

To deal effectively with the Soviet Union we must realize that much more is involved than developing clever schemes to solve the latest problem of negotiations. The starting point has to be the clear recognition of the source of strength of our international position—our alliance with Europe and Japan. For some reason, we refuse to learn how to live with the undeniable success of American foreign policy since World War II. Despite all the setbacks, the failures and the outright catastrophes, the Western cause has grown in strength. Few alliances have been more successful than NATO; rarely have major powers so quickly put behind them the animosities of a great conflict. And rarely has one of the victorious powers come to dominate the world to the extent the United States has. The United States must continue to support and lead a powerful coalition of forces to contain the Soviet Union, but it will have to do so in an era vastly different from the period of the coalition's creation.

We have won the ideological war; we are close to winning the geopolitical contest in the Third World, except for the Middle East. We long ago won the economic competition. Yet there is a nearly irresistible strain of isolationism in America.

This is reflected in the continuing concern in the United States with altering the Atlantic Alliance and withdrawing from Europe. We must resist the periodic temptation to tinker with a successful alliance, to play with various forms and types of American involvement. There is nothing more encouraging to the Soviet leaders in their time of troubles than the hope that sooner or later the United States will disengage from Western Europe. The struggle for the mastery of Europe, to paraphrase the British historian A.J.P. Taylor, continues and will continue as long as the Soviet Union remains one of Europe's great powers. The balance of world power could still be changed by shifts in this vital area. Preserving the European alliance remains the cornerstone of American policy.

Maintaining an anti-Soviet coalition has become more complicated by our tentative alliance with China; the natural course for Sino-American relations is to move toward a closer military relationship. But while we cannot grant Moscow a veto over American policy, the American connection to China must be handled with extreme care. We have no genuine common interests with China (whether that country "modernizes" or not) beyond the common opposition to Moscow; and the Sino-Soviet relationship will undoubtedly be subject to fluctuations, as both the Soviets and Chinese try to moderate their strategic differences. The new generation of Soviet leaders will seek freedom to maneuver, and sooner or later there will be a new generation in power in Peking that will not have experienced the debates and clashes of the 1960s and 1970s. All of this, in turn, will be unsettling for Washington, unless we accept the limits to our relations with China.

A successful policy of alliance cannot ignore the fact that the industrial democracies will not support a foreign policy that fails to include an effort at *détente* with the Soviet Union. Our western allies and Japan obviously want both containment and coexistence. This is even the crude basis on which the Chinese are prepared to join with the United States. This means in practice that the United States must engage in the process of negotiations with Moscow, including arms control arrangements.

Arms control has had a checkered history. Agreements that seemed important have turned out to be misleading, or ephemeral, and there have been some deep disillusionments. But time and again, arms control negotiations and the idea of limiting or otherwise controlling nuclear weapons has returned to the forefront of East-West relations. This is not accidental; it simply reflects the imperatives of the nuclear era. Some American administrations have made arms control a centerpiece, and others have become engaged more reluctantly. But a pattern seems to have been fixed: East-West relations are in large measure about the control of strategic and nuclear arms. This was dramatically evident in the Reagan-Gorbachev meeting in Reykjavik in October, 1986.

After the Soviet withdrawal from the INF and START talks in 1983, there were no official or formal negotiations about strategic arms control for a full year, the first such breakdown since the negotiations began in November 1969. In retrospect, however, it was more significant that during this interlude both sides maintained some contact and abided by the constraints of the unratified SALT agreements and the threshold test ban. Near the end of the election campaign of 1984, the Soviets ostentatiously resumed discussion with the White House in a meeting between Foreign Minister Gromyko and the President in late September. Shortly after the elections, there was an announcement that the two sides had agreed to enter into new negotiations.

In the negotiations that led to the formal resumption of arms control talks in 1985, however, it was SDI that occupied the attention of the Soviet side. The tortured communique that announced the new talks referred to stopping an arms race on earth and preventing one in outer space. The new talks had three parts: strategic offense, strategic defense, and intermediate-range weapons. For the first time since the SALT I negotiations on the ABM treaty, there was a formal link between offense and defense.

Many observers—including many in the White House—concluded that it was SDI that had brought the Soviets back to the bargaining table. This in turn led to the view that SDI was the ultimate bargaining chip, which could ensure the success of strategic arms control. Gradually there began to emerge what came to be called the "grand compromise": the United States would virtually abandon, or significantly restrict SDI in return for a substantial reduction of Soviet offensive forces.

Shortly before Reykjavik there was widespread speculation that there would be an INF agreement including the complete elimination of intermediate-range missiles in Europe, while leaving some number of Soviet missiles in Asia, and an equivalent number inside the continental United States. The American delegation approached Reykjavik anticipating this outcome.

The debacle at Reykjavik need not be rehearsed. It is obvious that the more utopian elements discussed there will not be pursued. Thus, there will be no agreement to eliminate all nuclear weapons, or to eliminate all ballistic missiles. What remains, however, are the elements of a three-part agreement: (1) a major reduction of strategic offensive weapons (of about 50 percent); (2) an agreement not to withdraw from the ABM treaty or to deploy SDI for some defined period (e.g., ten years), and (3) a separate agreement eliminating American and Soviet intermediate and shorter-range missiles (the so-called double zero).

Even if such a framework is eventually reached the overall significance is that the United States and the Soviet Union would continue for a decade to operate within the mainstream of arms control and strategic policies that have characterized their relationship since the late 1960s. Both sides would retain large strategic offensive forces, even after reductions of 50 percent. Deterrence would still rest on the certainty of retaliation, and there would be no significant defense against strategic attacks. Hence, the populations and military targets of both sides would be vulnerable. Significant imbalances in conventional forces would remain in Europe, but there would be a new debate about the United States' nuclear guarantee to NATO and how to implement it.

Moreover, major policy questions remain, to be addressed by President Reagan's successors. For example, should the United States continue to rely indefinitely on the threat of strategic retaliation to maintain deterrence? What are the risks in such a strategy? Is it credible now, and will it be credible even at severely reduced levels of strategic forces? A more immediate question, in light of possible agreements on INF concerns, is the viability of extended deterrence in Europe: how will it be affected by the elimination of all American missiles from Europe?

Finally, and most critically, have we reached the point that some form of strategic defense is necessary, for strategic, political or psychological reasons? It is difficult to believe that this issue of strategic defenses will be entirely closed, and the technology of space defenses and directed energy weapons will be set aside. It is seems more likely that both sides will eventually seek some stronger defenses. If so, then a new offensive-defensive balance will have to be negotiated in the 1990s. Can such a new and far more complex balance be achieved, and will it be stable? What would be its context?

The Reagan experience demonstrates that the American public will not tolerate a policy of deliberate disdain or benign neglect of arms control. President Reagan found that the public and the Congress insist on a serious and active effort. Moreover, it is also clear that something of the same process is at work on the other side. The Soviet Union has been reluctant to abandon the arms control process. It has been drawn back to it, even under humiliating circumstances.

Nevertheless, arms control has changed since the Nixon agreements of 1972. Agreements must succeed more and more on their own merits. The initial strategic arms control of 1972 could be justified as the catalyst for *détente*. Flawed arms control agreements will no longer be tolerated or be supported in the name of some other distantly related aim or as a step toward broader agreement. This puts an even greater burden on the negotiations. Support for arms control will require a far more meticulous concern for the details of verification to prevent cheating and, above all, a constant concern with broad strategic results; simply limiting or reducing weapons cannot be the basis for a long-term strategic stability (this is the main defect in the zero option). Meeting broad strategic criteria is a formidable task, if only because there is no agreement on what constitutes stability, either in the United States or between the United States and the Soviet Union. It has become far, far more difficult, in light of the revival of strategic defense: creating a durable balance between offense and defense is the very essence of stability.

If the public demands an effort at arms control, American public opinion also insists on an adequate defense and will hold its leaders accountable for failures and defeats that arise from weaknesses in defenses. The paradox is that in order to gain support for the strong defenses that remain the bulwark of the anti-Soviet coalition, every administration must also be seen to be actively pursuing a peaceful relationship with the Soviet Union.

Managing these two parallel tracks has become more and more difficult because of the clashes between the White House and the Congress. Increasingly, the Congress has sought to usurp the conduct of national security policy from the President. This has been particularly true of arms control negotiations and matters involving related agreements: thus the Congress has deliberately tried to make its appropriations for defense dependent on various arms control measures. In effect, the Congress is trying to micro-manage foreign relations at long distance. This assault on the policy prerogatives of the President reached the absurd constitutional point of Congressional insistence on abiding by the unratified SALT II treaty, which had in any case already expired. The situation was scarcely helped, however, by the foolish claim by the White House and State Department that an existing treaty (the ABM treaty of 1972) could be significantly reinterpreted a decade after it was signed, ratified and implemented. This only inflamed the clash between the two branches, raising some constitutional issues in the process.

The struggle between the two branches seems destined to continue, and worsen. The result is to create even greater confusion and to complicate the actual conduct of foreign policy. But Congressional intervention is a permanent new reality: the Congress will persist in trying to limit the operational conduct of foreign policy, compared to the 1950s and 1960s; this is a consequence of Vietnam and Watergate— and now the Iran-contra affair. The ability of the executive branch to conduct truly clandestine activities, e.g., in Nicaragua, has virtually ended. Any use of force, no matter how limited (or indeed, however successful in retrospect) provokes another round of constitutional debate about war powers and leads to new limits on the President's freedom of action. A President's effort to override or circumvent restraints on his actions produces a new clash. Even a highly popular President has had to fight through almost every national security issue. And all of this is further complicated by the fact that the boom and bust cycle of defense spending continues. Thus, as the Reagan Administration reactivated its East-West diplomacy in 1984 through 1986, its defense budget had started to slide drastically. It may take another Presidential election to clear the air, and provide the opportunity for a fresh examination of defense.

Another trend is the weakening of the idea of linkage, of making arms control negotiations or agreements dependent in some degree on political issues. This decline in linkage was probably inevitable: as the size and sophistication of nuclear arsenals has grown, intricate Kissingerian strategies of linkage have carried less and less conviction. Ford did not really practice linkage after Angola. Carter invoked linkage only after the crisis of Afghanistan, and Reagan formally abandoned it, only to try to revive it when confronted by summit meetings.

The decoupling of arms control from the geopolitical issues is bound to limit American policy in a dangerous way. For it remains clear that the chief threats to Soviet-American relations are not only nuclear weapons but regional conflicts as well. Afghanistan should have demonstrated the dangers of de-linking arms control. President Carter had no choice but to withdraw SALT II after the invasion. The current reality, however, is that linkage has become almost impossible. The Reagan Administration gave up even a modest effort at tying issues together. But only an incumbent president has the power and authority to insist on a linkage, and resist the certain pressures to settle for partial agreements. If this trend is not stopped, new and potentially serious disputes in Soviet-American relations are inevitable. For example, would the administration proceed to sign and ratify an INF agreement if Soviet MIGs were sent to Nicaragua?

Whether in arms control or regional negotiations, a serious American diplomacy will finally have to decide, first, how to define and deal with legitimate Soviet interests, and then, how to gain public support for a policy that will inevitably involve some American concessions. Does the Soviet Union have a right to strategic parity, or is this too dangerous a state of affairs for the United States? What is the legitimate security interest of the Soviet Union in the areas on its periphery: in Eastern Europe, in Afghanistan, in China? Does it have an implicit right of intervention in its sphere of influence; if so, does this right include intervention with armed forces? Can the United States tolerate such a permanent threat to peace? What of the link between the internal nature of the Soviet regime, which will never be acceptable to the United States, and the content of Soviet foreign policy? Can the two be separated?

These are not academic questions. They remain at the heart of Soviet-American relations.

To conclude: a viable Soviet-American relationship demands agreements or at least some process to control nuclear arms and resolve regional conflicts. The effort to achieve these two aims is bound to be protracted, and will involve reconciling contradictions almost constantly and finely tuning tactics and strategy. A policy that requires such a consistent and careful management in a democratic society is not doomed to fail, but it is extraordinarily difficult to carry out. Above all, it will have to command the depth of public support necessary to sustain the policy when challenged in the inevitable crisis.

14

The Soviet Union and the West: Security and Foreign Policy

Seweryn Bialer

Seventy years after the establishment of the Soviet state, forty years after its victory in World War II, and more than thirty years after the death of Stalin, the tyrant who believed in Soviet economic and political autarky, the Soviet Union for all its international activism found itself isolated internationally. The universe in which Gorbachev took the reins of the Soviet Union was one in which his country had no major friends, and was strapped with an unruly and economically and politically sick "alliance" of satellites and semi-satellites. America was resurgent and the capitalist countries in Europe and Asia were in the throes of a new technological revolution. The evaluation of the existing situation by the new leadership led to the beginning of major revisions in Soviet thought and action with regard to their security and foreign policies.

Gorbachev's leadership and the internal change in the Soviet Union that he has set in motion are of primary interest to the West because of their potential impact on Soviet international behavior. Gorbachev and his colleagues are well aware that foreign and security policies begin at home, and that their international aspirations depend on the availability of a variety of domestic resources to back them up. The efforts of the new leadership to make the Soviet Union a modern nation are dictated as much by its domestic needs as by its international goals. The situation at home, including the change of leadership, cannot but influence Soviet international behavior and its security policies. Because he believes that domestic vitality is necessary for foreign success, Gorbachev's domestic program is his most important foreign policy statement.

This new leadership understands the decisive influence of domestic strength on foreign policy. Khrushchev was a gambler who tried to achieve success in foreign policy on the cheap. Brezhnev was cautious and conservative: although he presided over the attainment of strategic parity with the United States, he let his country's domestic power deteriorate to the point that it became insufficient to support the Soviet Union's global ambition.

In discussing Soviet security and foreign policies I shall begin with the major underlying domestic and international conditions, move to an analysis of the changes in official rhetoric and conclude with an evaluation of the depth of the changes that have taken place both in Soviet thought and actions.

Soviet Security Policies and "New Thinking" Under Gorbachev

The greatest changes in Soviet international policies under Gorbachev thus far have occurred in the area of national security. The connection between national security and Soviet domestic conditions is particularly strong. Gorbachev and the new leadership group have arrived at three fundamental conclusions:

First, the Soviet Union cannot achieve strategic nuclear superiority over the United States. "Superiority" in this context can be defined as either the ability to strike first and limit the other side's retaliation to acceptable losses or as the ability to achieve strategic preponderance such that the Soviet Union will undermine the credibility of American deterrence in Europe and inhibit American responses in international crises.

Second, the continuation of the arms race with the United States, particularly its expansion into space, where the Western technological advantage over the Soviet Union is considerable, poses the danger of a surge of American technological ingenuity that could endanger the state of strategic parity between the two superpowers.

Third, a continuing and intensified arms race will require greater expenditures than in the past and will focus on high technology forms of systems for delivering nuclear weapons. Such an arms race would require the human and material resources of the Soviet Union that are the most scarce and of the highest quality. The continued arms race might, therefore, sidetrack Gorbachev's economic reforms.

Soviet domestic conditions affect Soviet security policies in three areas: resources; politics and policy making; and ideology and beliefs.

In the area of resources the case for change in Soviet security policies is strong. The apparent proportion of Soviet military expenditures in the economy (Western estimates of which vary from 12 to 20 percent of the Gross National Product) does not even begin to tell the story of the burden that these expenditures place on the Soviet economy. The level of military expenditures deprives the civilian sector of resources, slows economic growth by limiting capital formation, and stunts the growth of the military capabilities of the future by depressing the technological level of the economy as a whole. Emphasizing military projects at the expense of the civilian economy will ultimately exert a negative influence on military preparedness itself.[1]

In politics and policy-making, Gorbachev's leadership has already broken the near monopoly hold of the military on decisions concerning military expenditures. In the Brezhnev era, the military got what it wanted almost automatically. The political profile of the Soviet military during the third year of Gorbachev's rule has been low. Gorbachev's control over the Soviet High Command is strong and the new leadership is imposing its own priorities on Soviet defense policies. Gorbachev is clearly following the advice of Khrushchev, who wrote in his memoirs: "Who in our own country is in a position to intimidate the leadership? It is the military . . . the military is prone to engage in irresponsible day-dreaming and bragging. Given a chance, some elements within the military might try to force a militarist policy on the Government. Therefore the Government must always keep a bit between the teeth of the military."[2] Gorbachev has both the incentive and the ability to push through a policy of stern control of military expenditures and radical arms control measures. Such policies are contrary to Soviet traditions and Leninist sensibilities, but they are now being presented as a creative development of Marxist-Leninst ideas.

The international situation, and particularly the policies of the other superpower, the United States, have an impact on the trends in Soviet arms control policies. Both reinforce the influence of the domestic Soviet factors in favor of reversing the arms race through radical arms control measures. *It is probable that the decade from 1985 to 1995 will mark an end to the cycle of strategic armaments that began after the Second World War and has continued unabated for more than 40 years.* The domestic and international pressures on *both* superpowers are likely to be strong enough to lead them in this direction. It may well be that, at long last, Soviet and American approaches to strategic weapons and national security are converging.

The changes in American national security goals are significant. The second Reagan Administration shifted from its first term position of "arm now, talk later" to a two-track policy that includes serious arms control negotiations with the Soviets. This was made by a President with profoundly conservative instincts and a deep distrust of the Soviets, an important part of whose constituency is ultra-conservative and opposed to *any* arms control agreements with the Soviet Union.

The agreement with the Soviets on the abolition of all medium- and short-range nuclear weapons, while of limited military significance, is politically and psychologically of great importance. Indeed, it may herald a major breakthrough in the future. It demonstrates that radical arms control agreements can be successfully negotiated with the Soviets; that Soviet behavior in the negotiations can be both serious and flexible; and that the complex and sensitive political issue of verification through on-site inspection can be resolved to the satisfaction of both sides. The Intermediate Nuclear Force (INF) agreement provides the impetus for continuing arms control negotiations with the Soviets into the next Administration whether Republican or Democratic.

It is not by chance that two such different leaders as President Reagan and General Secretary Gorbachev, who preside over diametrically different systems, arrived independently at the conclusion that the unending strategic arms race must be ended. Their prescriptions for how to achieve it—Strategic Defense Initiative (SDI) in one case and total nuclear disarmament in the other—are as different as the nations they lead. Yet the impetus underlying the two prescriptions is identical: the recognition of the irrationality of further adding to their bloated nuclear arsenals.

The enormous budget deficits in the United States create increasing pressure for a stabilization of the budget. Reductions in the military budget by the post–Reagan Administration and Congress are virtually inevitable. Moreover, the Strategic Defense Initiative no longer appears to be an insurmountable obstacle to radical strategic offensive arms reductions, as it previously appeared to be. Its costs and technical feasibility are being questioned in the Congress, and it seems probable that the United States will continue to observe the Anti-Ballistic Missile (A.B.M.) Treaty. On the Soviet side, there is a growing recognition that the American Congress is unlikely to forego a radical strategic arms agreement with the Soviet Union to pursue the dubious goal of strategic defense.

American popular interest in the Gorbachev experiment is pronounced. The general impression of the American people, reinforced by the media, is that the Soviet Union has embarked upon a course of great promise. This cannot but have an influence on American attitudes in dealing with the Russians.

Gorbachev's National Security Concepts

What are Gorbachev's new national security policies? The greatest changes in Soviet position are apparent in what Soviet leaders say. Within their "new thinking" on strategic issues two elements stand out: the definition of national security and the Soviet leadership's attitudes toward nuclear deterrence.

The traditional Soviet concept of "national security" has been at the heart of Soviet domestic and international policies from the beginning of the Soviet state. Stalin's forced industrialization, the creation by force of the East European Soviet empire, the concept of the dreaded "capitalist encirclement," the belief in the inevitability of wars between the Soviet Union and the West, Khrushchev's international offensive in the Third World, Brezhnev's military buildup beyond any definition of sufficiency: all were expressions of an understanding of "national security" that was uniquely Soviet. In sum, the Soviets have traditionally carried their preoccupation with security, and their "damage limiting" philosophy, farther than most nations. It is as if they could only be satisfied with a constant quest for "absolute" security. Naturally, other countries have found Soviet measures to attain absolute security inimical to their own interests and have responded with countermeasures that have led to even greater tensions and global instability.

The two main sources of the traditional Soviet concept of "national security" were the Soviet experience of international isolation and clashes with other powers, and the Leninist doctrine of imperialism that defined the 20th century as an era of "wars and revolutions" in which revolutions grow out of wars. Khrushchev's declaration at the 20th Party Congress in 1956 that wars are no longer inevitable did virtually nothing to change the Soviet concept of absolute "national security."

Gorbachev's understanding of Soviet national security in the nuclear age, conditioned as it is on Soviet-American strategic parity, is the first authoritative revision of the traditional concept. Three elements of this revision are of particular note: the introduction of the idea of "nuclear sufficiency"; the creation of the concept of "common security"; and the retreat from evaluating security in purely military terms.

The idea of "nuclear sufficiency" subsumes three related concepts: that a build-up of nuclear strategic weapons beyond the level of Mutual Assured Destruction (M.A.D.) is militarily meaningless; that the security that M.A.D. provides will be as effective at lower force levels as it is now; and that a lower level of strategic deployment increases the security of both superpowers and of the world by making accidental war less likely and by easing psychological tensions.

The concept of "common security" expresses a major departure in Soviet thinking from the practice of traditional Soviet defense policies. For the Soviets, the idea behind it is as simple as it is revolutionary in Soviet terms. The traditional Soviet defense policies may be summed up in a single word: "more." If one hundred missiles were good, then two hundred missiles would be better. Military growth in all branches of the armed forces and in the weapons systems was a constant feature of Soviet defense policies under Stalin and Brezhnev. During Khrushchev's rule, the size of the Soviet land forces actually declined for a time, although this was an exception that was reversed during the years of Brezhnev's leadership.

Each year, the Soviet military budget grew. For a country starting from an inferior position vis-à-vis its enemies and subscribing to a cataclysmic model of international relations, this was not surprising. Yet the Soviets pursued this policy even during the period of recognized strategic parity in the 1970s, and at a time of relaxation of Soviet-American tensions brought about by *detente*. There were no objective reasons for the Soviet leadership to consider their country seriously endangered from abroad. The real motivation for the unending military buildups were subjective: the Soviet leadership's belief that no level of armaments is ever sufficient when the country's security is at stake.

The Soviet understanding of "national security," and the ancillary defense policies, ignored the effects such policies have on the military policies of their adversaries. The Soviet leadership attributed American responses to Soviet military buildups to aggressive American plans and postures, and considered them unrelated to Soviet policies and actions.

Gorbachev's departure from the traditional Soviet understanding of "national security" and his embrace instead of "common security" may at first appear obvious and undramatic. It is, in fact, a major discontinuity in the Soviet way of thinking, a revolutionary departure from the principles on which Soviet defense policies have always been based. If changes of concept become changes in actual Soviet defense policies, the consequences will be enormous.[3]

The third component of Gorbachev's redefinition of national security is his inclusion of non-military factors. The connection between "national security" and "correlation of forces" is becoming increasingly close, with the first emphasizing more Soviet domestic military and non-military influences, and the second referring to events in the international arena.

Gorbachev's concept of national security includes economic power: he considers the modernization of the Soviet economy as a whole to be the foundation of Soviet security. Despite its *historic* significance, the Soviets no longer regard the achievement of strategic parity with the United States as a sufficient guarantor of Soviet security. In Gorbachev's program, strategic parity must be augmented by rough economic parity with the United States. The morale of the Soviet population, the vitality of the country, and the state of its alliances are all part of the General Secretary's understanding of "national security," an understanding he is trying to impose on the military and explain to the political elite. Gorbachev is asserting that a Soviet Union that participates in a strict arms control regime, significantly cuts its nuclear forces, devotes as much or even more attention to its civilian as to its military economy, and is flexible and prepared for difficult compromises in its foreign policy, will be more secure than it is now, or than it would be by deploying thousands of new weapons. It is his task to convince the political elite, and persuade or compel the military elite, to accept this view. Without it, the reordering of national priorities implicit in his thinking about his country's security—part of his program of "renewal"—is likely to lead instead to his political defeat.

The new Soviet thinking on security matters addresses, as well, the question of conventional forces. Gorbachev appears to believe that the elimination of short- and intermediate-range nuclear weapons in Europe and Asia can lead to successful negotiations for a radical reduction of strategic systems only if the imbalance of conventional forces deployed in Central Europe is significantly redressed. He has expressed a willingness to tie the questions of size and deployment of conventional forces to further nuclear arms control negotiations. It may well be that conventional force size, structure and mode of deployment will become the most important items on the agenda of East-West arms control negotiations in the next decade.

Gorbachev's discussion of "new thinking" in Soviet strategic principles does not directly take aim at any policy of his predecessors. In the Soviet Union, it is traditional that when a new leader criticizes the policies of an old leader, he confines himself to domestic policies. Even at the height of Khrushchev's anti-Stalin campaign, the only criticism of Stalin at all related to foreign policy concerned what was referred to as his "error" on the eve of the Nazi invasion, when he was said to have ignored the signals of the approaching danger. Khrushchev did not criticize the Nazi-Soviet pact and even in today's textbooks of Soviet history it is justified without reservation. The patriotism of the Soviet people constitutes the major source of the legitimacy of the Soviet regime. The emphasis on the continuity of Soviet foreign and security policies is, therefore, considered necessary. Questioning past Soviet international policy is deemed dangerous. Yet Gorbachev is implicitly criticizing policies of the Brezhnev era. In closed discussions, and even in meetings with American experts, such criticism is explicit. Soviet experts on international relations and arms control expect that Gorbachev may soon even publicly condemn some of Brezhnev's foreign and defense policies, particularly the deployment in the late 1970s of the SS-20s in Europe and the highly unsuccessful

Soviet campaign against the American deployment of intermediate range nuclear weapons in Europe. Even before then, in the pages of *Kommunist* and *Izvestiia,* Central Committee members Evgeny Primakov and Aleksandr Bovin had already criticized some past Soviet foreign and security policies.[4]

Officially, the Soviet political-military establishment never accepted the American concept of "nuclear deterrence." They called it a policy of blackmail of the Soviet Union and refused to consider the American view that there is a danger of Soviet nuclear attack against the United States or Western Europe. The concept of "deterrence," however, was in fact the fundamental principle on which both the American and Soviet strategic policies were based.

On the surface, therefore, Gorbachev's critique of the concept of "nuclear deterrence" appears to be firmly rooted in Soviet tradition. In fact, however, the current Soviet refutation of the concept of "deterrence" is based on far different logic. Gorbachev does not deny that past deterrence prevented a third world war, nor does he deny the validity of American fears of a Soviet nuclear attack. He argues, however, that the mutual terror of deterrence may not work as well in the future. Most importantly, however, Gorbachev understands the *psychological* nature of deterrence, and he objects to two of its consequences:

First, the internal logic of deterrence leads to the unending spiral of a nuclear arms race between the two superpowers, since neither side can be certain that the level of its own strategic weapons is perceived by the other side as adequate to prevent a nuclear attack.

Secondly, the internal logic of deterrence requires that each side integrate its nuclear forces into the larger structure of its armed forces and its plan for the contingency of a nuclear war. Without each side's belief that in case of an attack by one power the other will use its nuclear forces, "deterrence" will fail to deter.

Gorbachev draws two conclusions from his assessment of deterrence. First, he argues for the total elimination of strategic nuclear forces. Secondly, he argues for a *process* that would gradually reduce the existing nuclear forces, and prevent their modernization. Gorbachev sees this process as the one through which the ultimate elimination of nuclear weapons will be achieved. The first part of Gorbachev's plan is utopian, even if his intent in announcing it was more than propagandistic. The second part, however, is open to serious negotiation. It is consistent with the main conclusions about security matters that the new Soviet leadership has reached.[5]

Soviet Arms Control Positions

It would be wrong to assume that the new Soviet positions are expressed only in terms of hopes. Actual Soviet proposals in the Soviet-American arms control negotiations, and their acceptance of some of the American positions, have gone further. Some examples are:

The Soviet movement in the Strategic Arms Reduction Talks (START) toward a tacit recognition of the Western concept of a counterforce first strike and of the validity of American concerns in this regard;

The Soviet willingness to accept substantial cuts in the number of strategic launchers or warheads in all categories;

The recognition of the validity of the American preoccupation with Soviet domination in super-hardened, powerful and accurate land-based missiles; and an expressed willingness to move the existing mix in the mode of deployment of strategic weapons away from the present asymmetry;

The acceptance of a far-reaching compromise on the rules of modernization of the British and French nuclear forces;

The Soviet agreement to eliminate their Asia-based SS-20 force in return for the American commitment not to deploy intermediate-range missiles in Alaska;

The recognition of the importance of preventing the modernization of nuclear forces once an arms reduction agreement is reached;

The unilateral halt, for many months, of underground nuclear tests and the endorsement of a test ban treaty that could include a limited number of tests approximately every five years for the allegedly necessary quality-control of existing warheads;

The idea of each side permitting the other to inspect *on-site* nuclear underground testing;

The recognition that in the current era of mobile launchers and cruise missiles no comprehensive arms reduction agreement is possible without decisive movements beyond verification by national means to bilateral and/or international inspection on site. Such an agreement must include the principle of random inspection and will be concerned not only with deployment but also with the destruction of weapons and the monitoring of their non-production and storage;

The withdrawal from the untenable insistence on the prohibition of SDI laboratory research and terrestrial testing, in favor of demand for a moratorium of SDI *space* testing and development.

Almost every month since Gorbachev's speech in January, 1986, the statements of the Soviet leaders and their official interpretation in the Soviet press have added new items to the arms control agenda that are acceptable to the Soviets as a part of an overall offensive arms agreement, or at least as legitimate items for negotiation in which compromises and solutions may be found.

The international situation, as well as the public mood and policy trends in the United States, are all conducive to a Soviet reassessment of national security goals and to a new Soviet seriousness in considering radical arms control measures. In addition, a new arms control position by the Soviet Union permits the Soviet leader to take the initiative in the international arena and be recognized as a world statesman. Soviet reassessment of past security policies, the pressures of the domestic economic situation and the improvement in the American political and military position in the international arena compared with the 1970s are sufficient to account for the new Soviet positions on arms control. It helps that in the international arena (and within the Soviet Union itself) arms control initiatives are now also good politics.

Gorbachev's Foreign Policy

The distinction between Soviet security policy and foreign policy is to a large extent artificial. What influences security policy also influences the foreign policy of the Soviet Union. Most of what I discussed above also applies to Soviet foreign policy under Gorbachev. This does not mean that all aspects of Soviet security policy are in harmony with Soviet foreign policy goals, nor that all elements of Soviet foreign policy contribute to Soviet security. As a matter of fact, there was and continues to be a tension between these two dimensions of Soviet international behavior. This tension, unintended by the policy makers, reflects the distinction between these areas of policy and their relative independence of each other.

The primary goal of any country's security policy is to prevent an attack on its own territory or on that of its allies or vassals, and to assure victory in case of war. The primary goals of foreign policies are given to less clear and definitive descriptions because they are more diffuse.[6] Moreover, at different periods in a country's history the relations between its security policy and its foreign policy may be quite different. In the Soviet case, for most of its history foreign policy was subordinated to national security goals—as was the case with the international Communist movement when it was under firm Soviet control. The foremost goal of Soviet foreign policy and the activity of the international Communist movement were intended to prevent the formation of military alliances against the Soviet Union and an attack on the Soviet Union.

Under Stalin, this subordination was absolute. Khrushchev weakened it by seeking power and influence in the Third World. His adventures in the Third World reflected his revolutionary hopes and his zeal in exploiting the dissolution of old empires. They had little to do with Soviet security *per se,* or with the defense of the Soviet homeland. In the Brezhnev era, when strategic parity with the United States was achieved, the largely expansionist aims and practices of Soviet foreign policy, which were clearly unrelated to Soviet security goals, began to grow. They went so far as to become harmful to Soviet security by overextending Soviet resources, contributing to the domestic economic crisis and encouraging the military build-up of Russia's adversaries. One may also look at this process from another perspective and conclude that the Soviet concept of national security had broadened. Under Stalin, it was the security of "socialism in one country" that was assigned the highest priority. During the post–World War II period of Stalin's rule and under Khrushchev it was the security of "socialism in one empire" that became all-important. Under Brezhnev, the concept of national security began to include the growing Soviet position as a global power.

The relation of the goals of Soviet national security policy to those of foreign policy between Stalin's death and the end of Brezhnev's rule had come full circle: from the unquestioned subordination of Soviet foreign policy to the security of the Soviet state to Soviet national security being a base for increasingly ambitious Soviet foreign policy. The Soviet leadership during the Brezhnev era viewed the attainment of strategic parity with the United States as a license to seek expansion by military means in the international arena. Their insistence, which started at the beginning of the 1970s, that they were the "equals" of the United States meant that they had the unquestioned right to expand beyond Europe without a challenge from the United States.[7] At this early stage of Gorbachev's leadership, firm conclusions about the relationship between Soviet security and foreign policy as he sees them would be premature. There is mounting evidence, however, that once again the basic tendency is to subordinate Soviet foreign policy to the security of the Soviet state.

Directions of Gorbachev's Foreign Policy

The changes in Soviet security policy under Gorbachev are more far-reaching and explicit than are the changes in Soviet foreign policy. While the connection between Soviet domestic conditions and Gorbachev's foreign policy is strong, for a number of reasons, it seems to have had a more limited effect on Gorbachev's foreign policy.

In foreign policy, the balance between overlapping superpower concerns on the one hand, and their conflicting interests on the other, is much less favorable to Soviet-American reconciliation than in security matters, where the area of overlapping interests is large. The long-range Soviet-American conflict is real, after all, and not simply the product of misperception. Even if the superpowers were to move away from their status as mortal enemies, they will most certainly remain global rivals even for the long-range foreseeable future.

Realistically, the changes in the Soviet Union and in the United States do not have the potential of doing away with the conflict, but rather of tempering its virulence, of moderating "the rules of the game," of increasing their prudence in international behavior and of moving the two powers away from situations of direct confrontation. If all of these goals can be achieved, we will have arrived at a major turning point in Soviet-American relations. Without the modifications of Soviet and American foreign policies, however, such an achievement will be impossible.

Gorbachev is hampered by the foreign policy blunders and entanglements he inherited from Brezhnev. Starkly described, his dilemma is how to prevent any further decline in Soviet great power status, how to save face and preserve credibility both domestically and internationally, while at the same time bringing to a swift conclusion some of Brezhnev's costly or foolish foreign policies. Afghanistan is a classic example of this problem: the Soviets clearly desire the end of the war but are not yet ready to pay the high price that a workable solution will require.

This limits the changes that Gorbachev can make in Soviet foreign policy. Yet, it would be a mistake to assume that his general program of change has found no expression in Soviet foreign policy on either a conceptual or practical level.[8] The pattern of Soviet international activity and foreign policy plans is discernibly connected with Gorbachev's evaluations of the domestic situation and his plans for reform. Gorbachev alluded to this connection in an interview with the editors of Time magazine: "You know our domestic plans, draw your own conclusions about what kind of a foreign policy this plan requires."[9] Gorbachev's foreign policy is still evolving; the most important and difficult decisions have yet to be made by the Politburo. It is nonetheless fair to say that the present course of Soviet foreign policy is marked by the following characteristics:

- Soviet foreign policy is becoming subordinated, more than at any time in the post-Stalin era, to exigencies at home; Mikhail Gorbachev seems to be turning inward, toward galvanizing a moribund economy and mobilizing an apathetic public.
- The Soviet leadership wants to insulate both the future of the ongoing succession process and the difficult implementation of radical reforms from international challenges, roadblocks and negative interventions.
- The Soviet leadership has decided to substantially cut its commitment of resources abroad. Some of those cuts, (*e.g.,* to the "front-line" black nations in Southern Africa) are politically easy; others, such as those to the East European vassal states, are difficult and may even become dangerous.
- Gorbachev seems determined to integrate Soviet and East European economies more closely—a goal that eluded his post-Stalin predecessors—and to insist that Eastern Europe contribute more to the process of Soviet economic development.
- Soviet policy-makers seem determined to avoid new military adventures abroad even if opportunities present themselves. In such marginal ventures as support for the Sandinistas in Nicaragua, their position is that they will provide enough military and economic support to prevent a victory of the "Contras," but limit their own involvement to avoid a confrontation with the United States, and to stop short of as major a commitment as that to Cuba.
- Gorbachev makes it clear that he wants to cut Soviet losses in the unwinnable war against Afghanistan, the greatest military and political problem he inherited from Brezhnev. He has frequently declared that the war cannot be solved by military means but instead requires a political solution. As of now, however, he is not ready to pay the price necessary to end it. Gorbachev believes that Soviet international credibility will be undermined if the withdrawal of Soviet troops results in a massacre of Soviet collaborators. But the time is probably approaching when a combination of greater Soviet willingness to cut losses, internal efforts at mediation, and U.S. help in making a Soviet withdrawal more palatable will de-escalate conflict and gradually end it.
- To facilitate their program of domestic reconstruction and renewal, the Soviets are increasing their flexibility in dealing with all cap-

italist countries and trying to minimize the existing political points of contention without yet making major concessions, *e.g.,* on the Pacific islands they occupy that are claimed by Japan.

- The Soviet strategy in dealing with capitalist countries is to make radical arms control initiatives the centerpiece of their policies, thus creating public pressure in those countries for better relations with them.
- Gorbachev's policies show no sign that he is willing to give up the Soviets' hard-won international status as a global power and the increased international influence that goes with it. Soviet international activity is directed at preventing any decline in this status. Examples of such policies are the undiminished commitment to Ethiopia, the only genuine Marxist-Leninist government in Africa; the continued commitment to Angola, a strategic country in any future revolutionary war in South Africa; the commitment to participate in Middle Eastern affairs and the increasingly strong desire to be part of Arab-Israeli negotiations.

Neither the domestic Soviet situation nor the international environment is conducive to the forcible expansion of Soviet influence. It is therefore not surprising that Soviet foreign policy under Gorbachev is defensive. At the same time, however, the current international environment does not pose a major threat to Soviet security.

In addition to the growing moderation of American policy in the final years of the Reagan Presidency, there are other aspects of the international situation that limit Soviet security concerns and tend to reinforce the moderating tendencies in Soviet foreign policies. They concern Western Europe, the development of major regional trouble spots, and the modernization and liberalization of China.

The International Situation and Soviet Foreign Policy

Western European attitudes toward the Soviet Union are in many respects at odds with those of the United States. The European tradition of *realpolitik,* so different from the American preoccupation with moral issues, as well as Europe's close proximity to the Soviet Union and exposure to the brunt of Soviet military power, produces in Western Europe a less belligerent, less moralistic and, indeed, a more accommodating attitude.

The Soviet Union has little to fear from Western Europe and much to gain. The successful resistance in Western Europe in 1982 and 1983 to intense Soviet pressures to stop the deployment of I.N.F. was not a sign of increased anti-Soviet sentiments, but rather the result of erroneous Soviet evaluations and clumsy policies. Gorbachev seems to have learned from the I.N.F. experience. He correctly does not share his predecessors' hopes of breaking up the Atlantic alliance and NATO. He has recognized, however, that on almost all important East-West issues, the American and West European positions have drifted further from each other, and that West European, particularly West German, policies within the alliance have become more independent than ever.

In the military field, there is virtually no possibility that West European governments will increase their spending on non-nuclear forces. There is even less chance that Western Europe will become an integrated third military force, drawing on its immense industrial potential and occupying an independent military position between the two superpowers. Whatever Russia has lost by its inability to prevent the deployment of American Pershing IIs and cruise missiles in Europe will be recouped many times over by the Soviet-American agreement to destroy all medium- and short-range nuclear weapons. The I.N.F. agreement will lead to a further decline in the credibility of American extended deterrence among the Europeans. This agreement has also shown that the Russians have less concern for the independent nuclear forces of Great Britain and France, which may make these countries more supportive of radical strategic arms control initiatives directed toward the United States.

Politically, the *detente* of the early 1970s has never been destroyed in Europe. Economically, Western Europe remains an area of Soviet opportunity with prospects for credits, joint ventures and increased trade that far exceed the American potential. Soviet policies aimed at achieving greater accommodation with Western Europe, conducted without any illusion of breaking the Atlantic alliance, are no longer considered a substitute for their central relations with the United States. They simply constitute a separate dimension of Soviet foreign policy, which, in addition to its own merits, may influence American policies toward the Soviet Union in the direction of greater moderation.

The last decade showed that many major military-political problems, not to mention economic problems besetting the world, are beyond the control of the superpowers and sometimes endanger each one in a similar manner. For example, in the Middle East, Islamic fundamentalism is gaining momentum. This force has added a new dimension to the long-standing Arab-Israeli conflict. It endangers the interests of the United States more than Soviet interests in this key area simply because American stakes in the Middle East, particularly its alliance with the conservative Arab states, are higher than those of the Soviet Union. Yet, in the longer run, it threatens the Soviet Union as well.

The Iranians already supply weapons to the Afghan resistance, and their influence on Soviet Central Asia may become considerable.

Most importantly, Islamic fundamentalism is a force that neither the Soviet Union nor the United States can hope to control. Even within the traditional dimensions of the Middle Eastern conflict, the situation of the two superpowers is not stable. The extent, for example, to which Russia actually controls its few allies in the area—Syria and Libya—is debatable. And how can the United States prevent the disaster currently building in Egypt, a friendly linch-pin power, where the major question is not whether the present regime will survive but rather what kind of regime will supplant it?

Terrorism mocks the power of the United States and its Western allies, the major target of its brutal fanaticism. But it is not unrealistic to expect that if the Soviet Union becomes a party to the negotiations in the Middle East and promotes a moderate position, it too will become a target. The Soviet leadership is concerned with international terrorism and is readying plans to respond to it—plans that probably include some degree of cooperation between Western and Soviet intelligence services.

Like the threat of international terrorism, the situation in the Korean peninsula is another example of the limitations of both American and Soviet power. The Soviet Union is not indifferent to the prospect of dangerous destabilization of the military-political situation there. Unrest in the South and a succession of crises in the North may produce tensions in the peninsula that could escalate into military clashes. The Soviet Union does not want such clashes. Yet neither the United States nor the Soviet Union can control these dangers.

Vietnam is clearly an important ally of the Soviet Union, the only power friendly to it in Southeast Asia. The Soviets need the strategic stronghold in this area of the world that only Vietnam can provide through the former American air and naval bases of Cam Ranh Bay and Da Nang. Yet Vietnam, despite its total dependence on the Soviet Union for economic assistance and military supplies, has not granted the Soviets the outright and unrestricted freedom of these bases. Nor does the Soviet Union seem happy with Vietnam's Cambodian adventure, to which China is forcibly opposed and which, therefore, has no end in sight. China's strong military presence on the border with Vietnam prevents, for all practical purposes, a reconstruction of Vietnam's economy, which is now in shambles. The alliance with Vietnam places a heavy material burden on the Soviet Union. This burden, however, does not give the Soviets unrestricted influence over Vietnamese actions. Finally, Vietnam creates a roadblock to Sino-Soviet relations that will persist far into the future and limit the trend of normalization of relations with China.

Closer to home, in Eastern Europe the traditional security and foreign policy clash of Soviet and American interests has become increasingly irrelevant to Soviet problems. It is an understatement to say that the situation in Eastern Europe is both serious and dangerous for the Soviet Union. Gorbachev has thus far been unable to design an East European policy that will both ensure socio-political stability and also maintain the integrity of the Soviet-East European "alliance" without draining Soviet resources. Such a policy is simply impossible. It is not the threat emanating from the United States, much less from Western Europe, that endangers the Soviet empire.

The threat has instead two sources, which are largely independent of the state of East-West relations: the East European striving for independence and for economic growth to which the Soviet Union has nothing to offer; and the Soviets' still unconditional commitment to rule in Eastern Europe. A region that was transformed and controlled by the Soviet Union in order to increase its security has now, ironically, become a major threat to Soviet security, to its foreign policy goals of *detente* with the United States, and to close, profitable relations with Western Europe. Western powers will not incite or supply anti-Soviet rebellions in Eastern Europe. The Soviets have the military capability, and still possess the will, to crush rebellions within its empire. Yet they have few non-military instruments with which to prevent opposition to Soviet political and economic policies in Eastern Europe. Most importantly, their much-vaunted military power is largely irrelevant to the goals of peace and prosperity in Eastern Europe. The potential danger in Eastern Europe has a similar impact on Soviet foreign policy to that of the Soviets' own domestic crisis: it impels them to be concerned with problems close to home, not to overextend themselves, and to seek stability in their relations with the developed capitalist countries.

Even at the apogee of Soviet-American tensions, China remained high on the Soviet agenda. In the long-term, China is probably seen as the major danger by the Soviet political and military elites. In the last decade of Mao's rule, Sino-Soviet tensions reached a high point, including even border clashes. To the Soviets, Mao's China of the late 1960s and 1970s seemed to be a country of fanatics filled with hatred for the Soviet Union, and led by people capable of the most irrational acts imaginable. The rapprochement between China and America in the early 1970s increased Soviet concerns. The Soviet response to concerns about China's intentions was emphatic and expensive. It involved the increased deployment of strategic nuclear weapons, which were targeted against China. It also led to the thoroughgoing modernization and fortification of the Soviet armies stationed on the Chinese borders.

It is unlikely that the radical changes in China after Mao's death reduced the Soviets' long-range concerns about the security threat from the East. Yet from the short- and medium-term perspective, the situation has changed dramatically. Mao's successors replaced the fanaticism of the Cultural Revolution with a program of domestic modernization and liberalization. The modernization of the armed forces came to be of only secondary importance. One-fourth of the Chinese armed forces have since been demobilized. The relations between China and the Soviet Union are moving steadily towards normalization. In a word, the danger from China felt by the Soviet leadership has dramatically declined. In recognition of this, the Soviets agreed to the destruction of their SS-20s deployed in Asia as a part of the INF agreement with the United States, and it is probable that further arms control agreements with the United States will be accompanied by sizable reductions in the strength of Soviet troops stationed in Mongolia and on the Sino-Soviet border.

"New Thinking" in Soviet Foreign Policy

A number of dilemmas face the Soviet leadership. The two most important concern the conflict between Soviet domestic and international goals, and between the importance the Soviets attach to their central relation with the United States and their expansionist policies in the Third World. The Soviet reconstruction program requires the concentration of resources on internal goals. Soviet international ambitions, however, also require a large commitment of resources to support a dynamic foreign policy. Yet such a commitment can only serve to deepen the domestic crisis. The Soviet goal is a stable and beneficial relationship with the other superpower. Experience has shown, however, that the necessary accommodation with the United States is unlikely if the Soviets pursue expansion, particularly by military means, in the Third World.

The "new thinking" propagated by Gorbachev in international relations addresses both of these dilemmas as well as other aspects of the Soviet experience, and some issues placed on the agenda by global developments that the Soviets had never taken seriously. The following elements of the "new thinking" are of particular importance:

1. The dilemma of Soviet domestic *versus* foreign commitment is not one of absolutes. The question is not one of "either/or," but rather one of degree. There can be little doubt that Gorbachev's top priority

is the reconstruction of the Soviet Union's domestic well-being. It shows that the new Soviet leader understands that a dynamic global role for his country cannot be attained on the cheap. The Soviets were in error, as they fully recognize today, when they thought that their solid military would lead to what they describe as "equality" with the United States. Underlying the term, "equality," was the assumption that military power can be used as a substitute for economic, political, and cultural resources. Yet Gorbachev recognizes the inadequacy of military power alone as the basis for a dynamic global role for the Soviet Union. As Brezhnev was willing to pay the expenses necessary to achieve Khrushchev's notion of "parity," Gorbachev appears willing to attain Brezhnev's notion of "equality" by putting a much higher premium on the enterprise with the understanding that it will not be confined to the military sphere, and will take a very long time to achieve.

2. The Soviets' "new thinking" about international relations in general, and their foreign policy and relations with the United States in particular, has begun to address an anomaly that has been self-defeating. Each country's international behavior is shaped above all else by two factors: domestic and historical determinants, and the actions of other nations. The Soviets, however, when trying to explain American actions, or those of their other adversaries, have traditionally placed all the weight on the first determinant and largely ignored the second as an explanatory factor.

At no time did they recognize that their own conduct accounted for much of the behavior of other countries, and in particular the United States. For instance, when the Soviets discussed Afghanistan among themselves, they did not ask whether it was sensible or proper to invade, but rather why America reacted as it did to the Soviet invasion. Before Gorbachev's assumption of power, when the Soviets discussed the reason for the demise of the Soviet-American *detente,* they placed all the blame on the Americans and viewed all Soviet actions not merely as justified but as largely irrelevant to the failure of *detente.* There are indications that this blindness is giving way to a more realistic view. Gorbachev's recognition of the notion of "mutual" or "common" security is probably the most important example of his awareness of the significance of mutual interaction in Soviet-American relations. This is, however, only a beginning. For most Soviets, American foreign and security policies seem not to depend on Soviet behavior. Until Soviet and American policymakers recognize the role of their own decisions in shaping those of the other side, Soviet-American relations will continue to be more troubled than they need be.

3. A steady, if undramatic change is taking place under Gorbachev in the evaluation of potential Soviet gains in the Third World. The post-Stalin history of Soviet policies toward the Third World has been one of both failure and persistence. The Russian aspiration to international greatness and the Soviet revolutionary impulse came to be focused on the Third World, where turmoil created opportunity. This was also a region in which the claims of the other great powers to spheres of influence were questionable. It was an area in which Soviet inroads seemed less likely to lead to confrontations with the United States, or at least to confrontations of a dangerous nature. It was here, therefore, that the deeply ingrained habit of Soviet international behavior of achieving gains at low cost and low risk seemed most promising.

The reality of post-Stalin Soviet experience in the Third World, however, was disappointing. First, the revolutionary potential of these countries proved limited. Khrushchev's optimistic belief that the Soviet Union could create Soviet protectorates on the ruins of former imperial colonies failed to materialize after initial successes. Khrushchev's idea was based on his ignorance of these countries, an application of Leninist formulas that did not fit their situations, a naive belief that the prefix "socialist" makes a country (or its elite) in fact socialist, and on the lack of understanding (shared by many African leaders) that the Soviet economic model of growth is inapplicable to countries where neither nation-building nor system-establishment has been accomplished, and that do not possess even the proverbial "boot straps," the economic means by which they can pull themselves up from utter poverty. (This applies, as well, to all types of black "African Socialism" in the 1960s that later disappeared without a trace; but probably the most expensive Soviet investment that led to a calamity was not in Africa, but was rather in the Indonesia of Sukarno.)

Moreover, experience showed that the leadership of some of the most developed of those Third World countries regarded an alliance with the Soviet Union as a necessary evil, undertaken because of a simple lack of alternatives. Soviet "alliances" in the Third World have often been shaky and short-lived and the Soviets have often gotten little from them. Egypt is the best example; Syria and Libya are not significantly different.

Brezhnev concluded from Khrushchev's failures that instruments of influence—for example, military and economic aid—used to align those countries with the Soviet camp were insufficient and would have to be replaced by instruments of control: contingents of Soviet troops and military specialists, proxy military forces from Cuba, and security forces from East Germany. In Ethiopia, Angola and Yemen, for example, the ties to the Soviets and the weight of the Soviet presence certainly increased significantly. Yet, the Soviets have been unable to transform these dependent regimes into true satellites.

The cost of Soviet expansion in the Third World was high and in some cases, such as in Angola, is still increasing. The Civil War in that country expanded well beyond early estimates, and there is still no end in sight. In addition, the Soviets began to encounter armed opposition, formidable because of its local roots and the fact that it has attracted significant financial and military help from Western powers or China. Today there are probably more national liberation fronts opposing the Soviet Union that receiving Soviet support. The "forces of history" do not necessarily work in the Soviets' favor.

The most important result of Soviet attempts to expand the power and influence of the Soviet Union in the Third World was the effect on Soviet-American relations. By now, the Soviet leadership cannot escape the recognition that its central relationship is endangered by its peripheral adventures. Western intelligence agencies insist that the overall level of Soviet activity and material support in the Third World has not substantially changed under Gorbachev's regime. While a Westerner cannot verify such estimates, it is nonetheless clear that Gorbachev's Soviet Union is unlikely to turn its back on the opportunities for power and influence in the Third World. Nevertheless, discussions within the Soviet foreign policy community and in Soviet-American meetings, which are partly reflected in the professional Soviet journals, indicate that a reevaluation of the Soviet Third World experience is underway, and that this reevaluation follows the logic of the arguments presented above. The extent to which this reevaluation will be reflected in changes in Soviet policies in the Third World depends not only on the Soviet leaders but also on American policy, and its ability to combine support of resistance to Soviet-oriented regimes with efforts to facilitate the liquidation of such adventures as Afghanistan, and to seek accommodation in areas of potential crisis.

4. The final element of the "new thinking" promoted by Gorbachev concerns the question of "interdependence" that is also at the center of discussion of international relations in the West. A central feature of the third industrial revolution is the exponential growth in global interdependence in the economic sphere, and in science and culture, as well. There is growing evidence that this process is beginning to be recognized by the new Soviet leaders. It is becoming clear that they are well aware of the inadequacy of Marxist and Leninist concepts. Marx conceived of an international market; Lenin was concerned with the export of capital and international cartels, that is, with an inter-

national economy; the Soviet Union of today, however, must face a growing interdependence and a global economy.

The idea of a "global economy" is especially troublesome for the Soviets to understand; it is even more difficult for them to grasp its consequences for individual industrial countries. Except for the initial phase of its industrialization, the Soviet Union developed in a state of virtual autarky. While Stalin's successors rejected economic isolation, the Soviet economy of today, despite the nation's immense size, plays a minimal, indeed a marginal role in the global arena. Soviet exports are like that of an underdeveloped country: dominated by raw materials. The Soviet economic weight in the global arena, as expressed by the share of imports and exports of goods, credit and capital in the G.N.P., is so low as to be globally insignificant. To a large extent, it is marginal even for the Soviet Union itself.

Several communist countries, such as Hungary and China, have tried to form links with the global economy to implement their plans of modernization. It is clear that the new Soviet leaders want to expand Soviet international economic contacts through credit, joint ventures and trade. Yet they do not seem to place great emphasis on those expanded relations in their modernization programs. They do not see high-technology capital imports as a substitute for reform, but rather as one of its elements. Nor do they see either capital imports or joint ventures as a substitute for domestically generated technological progress. This attitude indicates that, in at least this respect, their understanding of the patterns of technological progress in the present world is an accurate one.

Technological progress in industrial countries can no longer depend on imports but must be based on self-generated technological growth. This self-generating technological progress, in turn, requires that the theoretical and applied sciences, managerial methods and skills, as well as capital of the advanced nations be accessible to global circulation. Gorbachev's policies and economic reforms are aimed in the right direction insofar as they open more of the Soviet economy and science to global influences. These steps, however, most of which are still on the drawing board, will prove inadequate without additional measures. Soviet participation in the globalization of the economy, science and technology, combined with decisive domestic efforts to create favorable circumstances for managerial interests in technological progress, are not lofty or unrealistic plans to develop the Soviet Union into another Japan. On the contrary, they are the prerequisites to Soviet modernization that are the least that must be done merely to arrest the widening gap separating it from capitalist states. The Soviets are now beginning to understand this, but have thus far made only a few initial steps to transform their understanding into practice.

The Soviet "new thinking" about economic, scientific and cultural "interdependence," if serious, will affect its international relations. Economic and scientific needs would play a much greater role in the formation of Soviet foreign policy, in addition to the traditionally understood "security" requirements. Scientific and cultural interdependence will require an opening of the professional sectors of Soviet society to global interchange, which will modify the penchant for secrecy. In order for the global standards of modernity to influence Soviet development, Soviet enterprise will have to enter into international competition not primarily for the sake of earning hard currency, but in order to expand the isolated islands of modernity within the Soviet economy and use them to spread modernization throughout the domestic scene. Whether the political prerequisites of Soviet power will permit such a transformation remains an open question.

The Soviet understanding of "interdependence" goes beyond strictly economic, scientific or cultural questions. It involves other concerns as well, particularly the environment. The tragedy of Chernobyl, for example, brought home to the Soviets the lesson of interdependence with particular force. Most importantly, the Soviets' growing understanding of the contemporary meaning of "interdependence" is conducive to a new way of thinking that stresses shared interests and no longer views international relations only as a zero-sum game. This type of thinking, alien to the traditional Soviet world view, will require a long period of gestation before it will affect the basic Soviet approach to international relations, and it will need to find strong reinforcement in the West.

The educated strata of Soviet society are increasingly exposed to their leaders' new thinking through the electronic media, the journals and newspapers, and through professional and political discussions. For domestic purposes, in order to secure ratification within the Party apparatus and among Party activists, as well as to provide a legitimizing base for the regime, the new thinking must find justification in traditional ideological terms. While this will not always be an easy job, it is a necessary one. The Marxist-Leninist doctrine, if largely reduced to quotations taken out of context, provides sufficient variety and flexibility to satisfy the requirements of legitimization. This trend constitutes yet another step in a process to which Max Weber referred, the "ritualization" of doctrine, in which the doctrine retains a semblance of consistency and minimizes disagreements about its meaning and consequences by becoming increasingly removed from actual practice. In the Spring of 1987, a high-ranking Party intellectual in Moscow showed me with great satisfaction a quotation from Lenin to justify Soviet moderation in support of the revolutionary process abroad: Lenin wrote that "situations may arise when the interest of humanity at large take precedence over the class interests of the proletariat." The changing Soviet attitude to its revolutionary role in the international arena derives from the evaluation of Soviet experience and a new order of Soviet international priorities. Yet for this Party intellectual, and for thousands of others like him, the ability to justify it in doctrinal terms is important for preserving the consistency and integrity of his thinking. For us it is another sign of the seriousness of the shift in Soviet attitudes reflected in the "new thinking."

The "new thinking" about security and international relations in the Soviet Union that has been initiated under Gorbachev concerns questions of central importance to the contemporary world. Leaders and experts in the Soviet Union are retreating from deeply rooted traditional Soviet approaches and beginning to approach the American way of thinking. Only a small stratum of Soviet officials and specialists has any real understanding of Gorbachev's "new thinking," its implications for re-evaluating Soviet policies of the past, and for the translation of its concepts and analytical framework into realistic policies for the future. But some elements of the "new thinking" have, nonetheless, already found their way into Gorbachev's security and foreign policy. It is as yet too soon to assess their staying power or to know what further practical consequences the "new thinking" will produce. This, in turn, makes it difficult to advocate an appropriate American response to the changes underway in the Soviet Union.

The United States and Gorbachev's Russia

The foregoing analysis gives rise to propositions, principles and questions that pertain to the American policymakers' task of determining policy toward the Soviet Union.

The policies, reforms and "new thinking" promoted by Gorbachev in the Soviet Union are of potentially major significance in changing Soviet domestic and international behavior.

What is especially impressive about these changes is that they concern almost every area of Soviet domestic life and many key questions of Soviet security and international relations. The speed with which these changes have been introduced and continue to be promoted is also impressive. This suggests that major elements of Gorbachev's new course existed in a state of gestation within the political and economic elite and the professional communities for some time during the stagnant years of Brezhnev's leadership and the interregnum that followed.

It suggests that the flaws and failures in Soviet policies of the last fifteen years accumulated to the point at which they created powerful pressure for change. It also suggests that these conditions were waiting, as it were, for a Gorbachev to appear on the scene to galvanize them into significant, even revolutionary change.

At the same time, the speed and breadth of the changes wrought by Gorbachev should give us pause when we evaluate their significance and durability. The changes that have *already* occurred are important. Their chief significance, however, consists in the potential and promise they contain for the future. They are not yet accomplished transformations but rather a process, a trend, only in its early stages. The domestic and international aspects of the "new thinking," much less the new patterns of behavior, have not yet penetrated the Soviet elite, bureaucracy or society. The new and the old in the Soviet Union coexist uneasily and the old still remains stronger than the new.

It is most important that these changes move in the direction in which the West has always wanted the Soviet Union to go: toward greater freedom and openness at home and greater moderation abroad. No one knows where the process of change will eventually lead or what it will accomplish in the longer run. But at this point, in official American statements, we should stress the positive direction of these changes and remember that the best is the enemy of the good.

The changes in the Soviet Union have already gone far beyond mere public relations and tactical maneuvers. In the domestic economy, the changes are at least strategic and if they continue to move in the present direction they will come to modify the normative rules of behavior. In the domestic political and cultural fields the changes inspired from above are for the Soviet leadership primarily instrumental in nature.[10] Whether they will become normative depends primarily on three factors: how long they continue to be instrumental for the Soviet leadership; how broadly and with what intensity of commitment they involve the Russian intelligentsia and workers in the process of *glasnost'* and democratization; and the extent to which they become a part of the Soviet leadership's understanding of the nature of the modern world. In the area of international security, I agree with Robert Legvold that the changes "go beyond tactics and strategy and enter the area of concept and agenda."[11] In the field of Soviet international relations the changes are strategic but, in my opinion, do not yet modify the traditional international aspirations and goals of the Soviet Union.

The sources of the changes in the Soviet Union are not only domestic, but are also to a significant degree international.

The decisive impulse for Gorbachev's program of reconstruction and renewal and for the process of "new thinking" comes from the deepening systemic crisis of effectiveness in the economic, political, cultural and social life of his nation. Yet, a number of international factors also played a major role in promoting the "new thinking" of the Soviet leadership in both the domestic and international spheres: the isolation of the Soviet Union internationally, the fact that it was strapped with a politically sick "alliance" of satellites and semi-satellites, and that the Soviet Union had no real friends abroad. By contrast, America and the European and Asian capitalist nations were all resurgent.

The conclusion that the present cycle of significant change in the Soviet Union was inspired by more than domestic factors is important for the Western assessment of these changes. It suggests that an improvement in the Soviet domestic situation will not, in all probability, signal Soviet abandonment of "new thinking," nor of their positive initiatives in the international arena. Of course, the longer the process of change in the Soviet Union endures and the further it penetrates the elites and society, the greater are its chances of creating normative standards.

The most likely outcome of the Soviet domestic experiment will be neither total success nor total failure. We will not be able to realistically judge the extent of Soviet success or failure for at least 10 years.

Even the most resounding success of Gorbachev's program will not signal the transformation of the Soviet Union into a communist version of Japan, Germany or the United States. Moreover, the most far-reaching failure of Gorbachev's program will not mean the elimination of Soviet military capabilities to the point of inability to compete with the United States. The most probable outcome of the Soviet experiment would also be the best from the point of view of Western interests. While a total failure could create desperation and incite adventurism and a trigger-happy military attitude, a complete success could create arrogance, a belligerent mood, and a heightened desire to translate domestic achievement into international power.

The domestic mess in which the Soviets find themselves defies either easy or quick solution. The timetable of significant progress must be calibrated, as noted, in a framework of no less than a decade. Slowly, the Soviet leadership and the political elite is coming to a sober awareness of how far Russia must still travel to achieve modernity. The pressure for immediate action, and Gorbachev's seeming impatience for change, reflect not so much his expectation of quick success but rather his realistic assessment of the seriousness of current political realities.

Gorbachev has reached a critical point. The honeymoon of his first year in power is over. Since the announcement of practical reform plans, the initially widespread but abstract support for change is giving way to the defense of various vested interests. The opposition to Gorbachev has not receded; his control beyond Moscow is still tenuous; the resistance of the vast bureaucracies is increasing; the social inertia is as strong as ever; and his campaign to seek wider support has just begun. Constant, intense pressure by Gorbachev is necessary at this critical phase in order to break the inertia and generate momentum for change. Timid incremental changes and vast stores of patience would be fatal to the reform program. If the General Secretary cannot visibly improve the standard of living of the working class and the lower managerial strata, his entire long-range program will be endangered and the momentum of the initial years could be lost.

Predictions are always risky. The one thing that can be predicted with certainty, however, is that even if he is firmly in control, the General Secretary's course of action in the coming years will not be one of unrelenting pressure and forward movement, but will involve instead as many tactical zig-zags and feints and retreats as straight-forward advances. If this evaluation of Gorbachev himself after his first three years in office is accurate, if his commitment to radical reforms and determination are genuine, then the retreats will be only temporary. But the changes he has introduced are nonetheless reversible. Marx said that "an idea that takes hold of the masses becomes a material force." This has not yet happened in Gorbachev's Soviet Union. Moreover, Gorbachev has not yet had to face the central dilemma of radical and liberalizing reforms in the Soviet Union: how to promote the devolution of economic power and grant more freedom in order to release the creativity and generate the commitment necessary for modernization, without at the same time endangering the authoritarian base of the Party-State and the privileged interests of the political elite. As a member of the Russian intelligentsia said during the rule of the reforming Tsar Alexander II: "The question for the reforming Russian rulers is how to build a fire that will not produce a flame."

Both in the delicate present stage of Gorbachev's reforms, and in many years to come, it is imperative for the Soviet Union to have stable international relations. It is especially necessary for the Soviets to avoid situations where a danger of confrontation with the United States is present. Both Gorbachev's power needs and the requirements of domestic reforms demand moderation in Soviet foreign and security policy. These requirements in turn will lead to a further evolution of Soviet "new thinking" about foreign affairs and an increased commitment to attitudes contrary to Soviet traditions.

The process of Soviet domestic change and the evolving "new thinking"
on international issues is not taking place in a vacuum: it will be affected
by the evolution of the international situation and by the action or lack
of action of the Western powers.

From the beginning of the Soviet state, the international environment and the actions of other states have exerted a major influence on Soviet domestic development. This influence is even more pronounced in Soviet security and foreign policies. International factors will certainly play a major role in influencing the direction, depth, and durability of Soviet reforms and the process of change in Soviet international behavior.

What would be the best and the worst international circumstances to promote positive change in the Soviet Union? In general, neither a relaxation of international tensions, nor an increase in tensions would constitute an *a priori* negative or positive influence on Soviet domestic transformation. The result depends on the issue in question, particularly in the following areas: the evolution of Soviet "new thinking" in security and foreign policy, such as the process of arms control; the deadlock in Afghanistan; the unity of the Atlantic alliance; the economic health and stability of the key Western countries and of the global capitalist economy; the international communist movement; the Middle East; and Eastern Europe.

- Nuclear arms control is the most promising area for a positive breakthrough in Soviet-American relations and for a partial reconciliation of the two superpowers. The importance of such a development for the benign direction of Soviet domestic evolution and the further consolidation of Gorbachev's power is immense. Agreements with the United States on arms control will be regarded among the Soviet elite and the population as a whole as a major victory for the General Secretary and will increase his popularity and respect.
- The political resolution of the Afghanistan civil war is so much in Gorbachev's interest that we can expect in the near future a greater Soviet willingness to pay the price for this blunder. The United States, however, must be willing to help achieve a compromise, without agreeing to the survival of a communist regime in Kabul.
- The Soviet Union under Gorbachev's leadership is moving away from the unrealistic hopes of breaking up the Atlantic Alliance and NATO; it is imperative, however, to dispel entirely the existing Soviet notion of driving a wedge between America and its allies. This in turn will require an American recognition and acceptance

of the differences between American and European approaches to the Soviet Union, particularly in East-West economic relations. A united Western position on arms control issues, on the deployment of conventional forces in Europe, and in opposition to Soviet expansionism will strengthen the domestic impact of Gorbachev's views that accommodation with the West is necessary and in the Soviet interest; American influence on the Soviet Union requires American domestic economic health and that of the other advanced capitalist societies. The continuation or even acceleration of the global technological revolution in the capitalist world will reinforce the commitment to Soviet domestic initiatives and weaken its aggressive international impulses;

- There have been indications that Gorbachev hopes for a revitalized international communist movement with an increased Soviet influence over its activity. At the same time, he recognizes that it is inevitable that these parties remain independent of Moscow. His hopes of "repaired" relations with foreign communist parties rest on the expectation that the moderate, reformed and innovative image of the Soviet Union that he projects will be attractive to them. Gorbachev's success in reawakening the international communist movement and in increasing Soviet influence over it, of which there are as yet no signs, would probably reinforce the role of ideologues in the Soviet Union. On the other hand, clear indications from key Communist parties such as the Italian one that its past ties with Moscow can never be restored, combined with their encouragement of greater democratization in the Soviet Union, would further curtail the role of the ideologues and strengthen Gorbachev's position.

- The peace process in the traditional Arab-Israeli conflict is at a dead end, and the power positions and credibility of both superpowers in the Middle East have reached a low point. However, the potential for turmoil in the region is increasing and the danger of a Syrian-Israeli war is growing. But if the experience in Lebanon is any indication of Soviet and American behavior in the region, the prudence exercised by both sides will not lead to a dangerous Soviet-American confrontation unless a full-scale Syrian-Israeli war were to break out. The most unpredictable element in the Middle East is Muslim fundamentalism. Neither the Soviet Union nor the United States has devised a policy to neutralize this danger or to harness it for its own purposes. Both American military actions against Iran and Islamic terrorism will evoke strong Soviet protests. But the increased danger of Muslim fundamentalism may well have a positive effect on Soviet-American relations. This heightened

threat of instability serves neither Soviet nor American interests:
it will increase the chances for their cooperation.

• The greatest international influence on Gorbachev's reforms and
his "new thinking" on international relations may come from
Eastern Europe. Major unrest in one of the satellite countries that
provokes a Soviet domestic crackdown or even Soviet military
intervention will undermine Gorbachev's liberalizing domestic reforms and, if it is accompanied by a corresponding change in the
political atmosphere within the Soviet Union, may also lead to a
hard-line foreign policy. Moreover, stability in Eastern Europe
cannot be achieved without Western help, which ought not to be
given except on condition of greater freedom and independence
in these countries. Gorbachev's recognition of this, combined with
Western material assistance, can make East Europe a source of
Western leverage on the Soviet Union and a means of reinforcing
Soviet domestic liberalism and international moderation.

The United States and other advanced industrial democracies have
instruments and capabilities at their disposal to promote positive change
in the Soviet Union.

Michael Mandelbaum in his chapter has convincingly shown that
in the past, the United States and other Western powers have not
succeeded in influencing Soviet internal behavior. In my own writings
I have argued that the United States has no choice but to deal with
the Soviet Union as it is: attempting to influence its international
behavior, but putting no trust in policies that attempt to change the
Soviet Union domestically.[12] I still believe that this was correct for
Brezhnev's rule. Is it still accurate today?

To answer this question, it is necessary to distinguish times of
conservative stagnation from times of dynamic change. Today's Soviet
Union is clearly in the throes of a revolutionary transformation, one
that is being generated internally and impelled by a determined leadership that has formed an alliance with the intelligentsia and is gaining
the support of the educated strata of Soviet society. Under these
conditions, outside forces may influence the process of Soviet domestic
change, although not decisively. Moreover, the direction of domestic
change in the Soviet Union is positive in terms of Western values.
Therefore, any Western efforts to influence Soviet domestic developments will tend to *reinforce an existing internal trend,* rather than
counter a prevailing Soviet orientation, as was the case in the past.

Western efforts to influence the Soviet Union should not be principally directed at domestic issues. Rather, they should be mainly
concerned with the new opportunities to influence Soviet security and

foreign policies. Western success in influencing Soviet international thinking and behavior is likely to have indirect positive repercussions on the domestic Soviet scene, since domestic and international developments are mutually reinforcing in the present cycle of change in Russia.

Western instruments of influencing change in the Soviet Union—as distinct from providing aid to the U.S.S.R.—fall into three categories: economic, political and cultural. The distinction between instruments of influence and instruments of aid is of cardinal importance. The first is conditional, is based on enlightened self-interest, and stresses both incentives and disincentives; while the second is philanthropic, altruistic, unconditional and emphasizes, above all, accommodation.

Economic instruments include trade, credit, most favored nation trade status, joint ventures, Soviet participation in such world bodies as the International Monetary Fund (I.M.F.), the World Bank, the General Agreement on Trade and Tariffs (G.A.T.T.), the licensing of production processes, managerial training and advice. Political instruments include symbolic steps that may strengthen Gorbachev's position of power (*e.g.,* Prime Minister Thatcher's recognition of Gorbachev as a leader of world stature and her description of the changes in Russia as potentially of historic significance); initiatives for systematic and institutionalized cooperation with the United States in areas where our interests overlap (*e.g.,* the fight against certain forms of terrorism, the prevention of the proliferation of nuclear weapons); the conditional acceptance of Soviet participation in mediation of regional conflicts (*e.g.,* the Middle East); the creation of consultative bodies for purposes of the prevention of crises; summit meetings not simply for the purpose of signing major agreements but also for facilitating existing negotiations at lower levels, and the exchange of views on controversial and potentially explosive issues; regular meetings of top military leaders in order for them to learn about each other's doctrines first-hand rather than through the writings of obscure colonels. Cultural instruments include: the continuation and expansion of existing exchanges; an increased presence of each country's representatives on the other's television and radio, as well as in the press; regular exchanges through press conferences by leaders of each country that are fully reported in the other country; fellowships for Soviet students to study the humanities and the social sciences in the United States, and a regular exchange of statistical information and of economic analyses; arrangements of economic consultations; establishment of close and direct ties of American creative associations with similar bodies in the Soviet Union that choose their leaders in authentic elections.

Regardless of the American position, Western Europe, particularly West Germany, will receive with great satisfaction the changes in Soviet domestic, security and foreign policies. They will become increasingly engaged in helping the Soviet Union in its domestic program and will generally support the international initiatives emerging from the "new thinking" of the Soviet leadership.

West European countries in the coming years will be supportive of the Soviets if Gorbachev's domestic reforms and innovative international initiatives continue. The West European governments will be critical of American indifference to what is happening inside the Soviet Union. The possible dissonance between Western Europe and the United States will try the patience of American leaders who are likely to adopt a more cautious approach to Gorbachev's Soviet Union. In one respect the United States must be unbending: the transfer to the Soviet Union of technology with probable military applications cannot be tolerated. But it will be counterproductive to repeat the kind of political blunder committed in the matter of the Soviet-West European gas pipeline, when the United States, in effect, challenged the sovereignty of the West European nations on economic issues.

Can the West be cohesive and mobilize its resources to balance Soviet military power when the traditional enemy is acting in nontraditional and even sympathetic ways? We may be finally dealing with a Soviet leadership on whose harsh dogmatism, blunders and open aggressiveness we can no longer count to enforce the unity of the Western alliance.

The United States should try to influence an entire range of developments in the Soviet Union, and occasionally even risk "help," to promote Soviet evolution in directions consistent with our values and favorable to our long-range interests and to the cause of peace.

It is probable that the changes in the Soviet Union, precisely because they are significant, will eventually make the country stronger than it is now. Should we, therefore, be against those changes? Would it be wise to try to reinforce the current trend in the Soviet Union and even in some cases "help" Gorbachev, who is the symbol and catalyst of these changes?

The central question is not whether the Soviet Union will eventually become stronger, but rather whether it will become an easier country with which to coexist. I believe that if Gorbachev's program of reforms were gradually implemented, the danger from the Soviet Union to the West would decrease rather than increase.

The idea that if the Soviet Union becomes stronger the danger of Soviet expansionism would increase is based on an assumption that need not be true: that the growth of overall Soviet capabilities (e.g., foreign policy resources) will increase the scope of Soviet international ambitions and the range of Soviet expansionist policies. The relationship between Soviet capabilities on the one hand and Soviet expansionism, particularly external military adventures, on the other, is mediated, however, by a number of intervening variables: the perception by the Soviet leadership and political elite of their national interest; the aspirations these people have; the domestic needs and conditions of stability that could result in the use of greater potential foreign policy resources for domestic purposes, among many others. In the context of the Soviet domestic and international situation, if Gorbachev's program of reforms and "new thinking" continue in their present direction, these factors may move Soviet policies in non-expansionistic directions.

No one, including Gorbachev, knows what will finally emerge from the cycle of reforms in the Soviet Union. But we do know the nature of the process that the leadership has begun. We can expect that this process will strongly influence the result. If the present process in the Soviet Union continues for a prolonged period, or becomes permanent, a number of domestic stimuli to Soviet security and foreign policy will come to the fore. Among the most important would be: a greater openness of the political process; the increased influence of an incipient "public opinion"; rising expectations concerning material and religious changes among the population; the declining influence of the military; a greater Soviet involvement in the process of global "interdependence" bringing with it the need for more stable relations with the developed countries; an improvement in the Soviet economic situation and in technological progress that will not narrow the gap significantly between the Soviet Union and the industrial democracies; the further ritualization of the role of Marxist-Leninist doctrine and the continuing decline of the revolutionary impulse; an immense preoccupation with Eastern Europe and the possible emergence of ideas to revise Soviet–East European relations; the reversal of the strategic arms race through radical but gradual arms control agreements, toward which both superpowers are clearly moving; and a visible improvement in Soviet-American relations in the current period of relative Soviet accommodation, such that the Soviet leadership will not want to endanger it.

When a great power is involved in complex and dangerous global politics, there are times when caution is indicated and other times when taking risks is justified. The current cycle of change in Russia may not fulfill American hopes of a breakthrough in Soviet-American relations. They will certainly not eliminate the conflict between Russia and the West, the sources of which have to do with historical experience, divergent ideologies and major differences in international interest. Yet for decades the United States was locked in a conflict with the Soviet Union which seemed impossible to ease in any significant way. There is a great likelihood that conditions for improvement are now finally emerging. The stakes are so immense, the opportunities for change so singular, that they seem to warrant an active American policy toward the Soviet Union that will try to influence the process of change in Russia and even to help Gorbachev.

Haste is not necessary. If what is happening in Russia is not a short-lived new fashion but rather a program of change of long duration, there is ample time for deciding what risks we should take and how we should try to influence the evolution of Russia in the direction of moderation. For America to take bold steps in trying to influence the evolution of Soviet institutions and policies does not at all mean to accept their present limits, intensity and depth. On the contrary, the risks should be taken to broaden the range of Soviet socio-political domestic innovations, to promote greater moderation in Soviet foreign policies, and aggressively to promote changes in Soviet security engagements that are not limited to short, intermediate and strategic nuclear forces but concern also the Soviet deployment mode and size of its conventional forces in Europe and Asia.

The standard of what is possible and probable within the Soviet Union and in Soviet-American relations must be reassessed in light of new circumstances. In the final analysis, for the development of a rational American policy toward the Soviet Union in the new circumstances it will be wise to weigh not only what has already happened and what promises to happen in the Soviet Union, but also the alternatives to Gorbachev and his domestic and foreign policy course. The alternatives do not have to be cataclysmic, as many in the Soviet Union and in the West believe, but the odds are overwhelming that they will not be benign and will offer less hope for liberalizing change.

Brezhnev's *detente* was conceived as an offensive enterprise. Gorbachev's desire for the restoration of *detente* is conceived for defensive purposes. We should resist Soviet encroachments on our vital international interests. But the time has come at least to suspend the idea that we must conduct a crusade in our relations with the Soviet Union. The continuation of such an attitude will leave us standing alone among the developed capitalist societies. But, much more importantly, it will prevent us from exploring opportunities for reversing the military and political trends of the last four decades of our conflict with the Soviet Union; the chances of doing so are now better than ever.

Notes

1. See Nikolai Ogarkov, *Istoriya uchit bditel'nosti* (Moscow: Voyenizdat, 1985).

2. Nikita Khrushchev, *Khrushchev Remembers: The Last Testament* (Boston: Little, Brown, 1974), p. 541.

3. M. S. Gorbachev, *Perestroika: New Thinking for Our Country and the World* (New York: Harper and Row, 1987), p. 142.

4. For example, see Yevgeny Primakov, "New Philosophy of Foreign Policy," *Pravda,* July 10, 1987, p. 4.

5. M. S. Gorbachev, *Izbrannye rechi i stat'i* (Moskva: Izdatel'stvo politicheskoi literatury, 1987) volume 3, pp. 134–36. Also see Seweryn Bialer, "Gorbachev's Move," *Foreign Policy,* no. 68 (Fall 1987), p. 65.

6. For a discussion of Soviet security policy, see Seweryn Bialer, *The Soviet Paradox: External Expansion, Internal Decline* (New York: Alfred A. Knopf, 1986), pp. 295–96.

7. Ibid., pp. 309–15. For another discussion of the impact of Soviet-American strategic parity on Soviet foreign policy in the 1970s, see Raymond L. Garthoff, *Detente and Confrontation: American-Soviet Relations from Nixon to Reagan* (Washington, D.C.: The Brookings Institution, 1985), pp. 55–68.

8. For a more detailed account of the changes in Gorbachev's foreign and security policies, see Chapter 4 by Robert Legvold in this book.

9. M. S. Gorbachev, "Otvety Amerikanskomy zhurnalu *Taim,*" in *Izbrannye rechi i stat'i,* volume 2, p. 366.

10. See Bialer, "Gorbachev's Move," p. 78.

11. See Chapter 4 by Robert Legvold.

12. Bialer, *Soviet Paradox,* pp. 353–55.

Index

ABMs. *See* Antiballistic missiles
ABM Treaty. *See* Antiballistic Missile
   Treaty
Absenteeism, 18
Absolutism, 386
Abuladze, Tengis, 54, 167
Academy of Sciences, 5, 76, 89, 204
   Siberian Division (Novosibirsk), 85,
   95(n32), 239, 294
Acceleration, 157, 187, 254
Administrative organization, 15–16, 29,
   51, 73, 81, 199
Advanced development phase (1955–),
   7–8, 11, 18, 24
"Advanced socialism," 236
Adventurism, 357, 432, 482
Adzhubei, Aleksei, 54, 55
Afanasev, Iurii, 52, 59–60(n20)
Afanas'ev, Viktor G., 216
Afghanistan, 14, 104, 113, 125, 127, 139,
   329, 338, 355, 356, 358, 386, 389,
   398, 416, 432, 433, 437, 438, 441,
   446, 454, 455, 468, 469, 472, 475,
   477, 484
Africa, 125, 355, 368, 431, 432, 469, 470
African Socialism, 476
After Stalin period, 52, 54, 252
Aganbegian, Abel G., 85, 164, 282, 349
Agrarian society transformation, 23
Agriculture, 7, 9, 10, 12, 18, 40, 51, 66,
   211, 252
   market pricing, 15, 163, 208
   output, 72, 78–79, 83, 285
   policy, 66, 73, 78, 83–84, 86–87
   price policy, 66, 73, 77, 86, 87, 90,
   163
   private plot, 84, 86, 90, 165, 269
   recentralization, 164
   See also Collectivization
Agro-industrial complex (APK), 84, 276
Aircraft industry, 88
Aitmatov, Chingiz, 156
Akhmatova, Anna, 168
Aksyonov, Vasily, 137
Alcoholism, 18, 153

Alexander, Arthur J., 88
Alexander I (tsar of Russia), 22, 393
Alexander II (tsar of Russia), 8, 9, 16,
   17, 18, 21, 135, 251, 393, 483
Alexander III (tsar of Russia), 12, 18
Alexeeva, Ludmilla, 137
Alienation, 260, 263, 283, 284
Aliyev, Geidar A., 158
Allende, Salvadore, 336
Allocational choices, 66, 68, 69, 73, 78,
   81, 83, 86, 90, 91
Alma-Ata riots (1986), 162, 203, 287
Amnesty International, 133
Anarchy, 386
Andropov, Yuri V., 136, 137, 138, 147,
   152, 157, 158, 161, 176, 189, 198,
   208, 212, 215, 244, 245–246, 253,
   269, 278, 387
   as leader, 248
And the Day Lasts Longer than a
   Century (Aitmatov), 156
Angola, 125, 126, 354, 356, 357, 431,
   433, 441, 446, 454, 476, 477
Anomie, 153, 191
Anti-alcohol campaign, 199, 261
Antiballistic missiles (ABMs), 115
Antiballistic Missile (ABM) Treaty
   (1972), 363, 393, 396, 448, 451, 452,
   454, 460
Antiformalism, 47
Anti-nuclear groups, 110
Anti-Semitism, 134, 135, 274, 418
Antisocial acts, 29, 144
Anti-Westernism, 47
Antonov, O. K., 76
APK. *See* Agro-industrial complex
Apter, David, 196
Arab States, 412, 471, 485
Argentina, 433
Armenia, 203
Armenians, 138, 139, 179
Arms control, 98, 110, 114–120, 122, 123,
   124, 129, 138, 203, 248, 288, 328–
   329, 331, 335, 338, 363–364, 388,
   392–393, 396, 397, 399, 402, 410,